P9-DME-077

THE HISTORY OF

The American
Sailing Navy

BOOKS BY HOWARD I. CHAPELLE

The History of American Sailing Ships
American Sailing Craft
The Baltimore Clipper
Yacht Designing and Planning
Boatbuilding
The History of the American Sailing Navy

PRESIDENT *and* ENDYMION
January 15, 1815

From a painting by George C. Wales. Reproduced through the
courtesy of the Marine Historical Association, Mystic, Connecticut.

★ ★ ★ ★ ★ ★ ★ ★ ★

THE HISTORY OF

The American

Sailing Navy

THE SHIPS
AND THEIR DEVELOPMENT

By HOWARD I. CHAPELLE

BONANZA BOOKS • NEW YORK

COPYRIGHT 1949 BY

W. W. NORTON & COMPANY, INC.

(F)

This edition published by Bonanza Books,
a division of Crown Publishers, Inc.,
by arrangement with W. W. Norton & Company, Inc.

DEDICATED

TO THE MEMORY OF

GEORGE C. WALES
Marine Artist

PRINTED IN THE UNITED STATES OF AMERICA

★ ★ ★ ★ ★ ★ ★ ★ ★

Contents

★ ★ ★ ★ ★ ★ ★ ★ ★

Illustrations

Plans

Text Figures

★ ★ ★ ★ ★ ★ ★ ★ ★

Introduction

AMERICAN naval history is far more than a running account of naval battles or a panegyric of naval officers. The qualities and characteristics of the ships engaged in noted actions are obviously an important consideration in any naval history. Where steam men-of-war are concerned there is a wealth of material available. In modern times there have been many books giving detailed information on the men-of-war of all the leading powers, which enable the historian and student to estimate the advantages, or disadvantages, under which an action was fought. Modern historians not only take into consideration the power and quality of naval ships, but they also examine the administrative problems of a naval power and its political, economic, and material well-being, to determine the exact national condition of the contending forces. This approach to the subject has widened the field of investigation, in all phases of history, far beyond the bare narrative of naval actions that was once considered to be acceptable naval history.

The period in which sailing men-of-war were employed in the American Navy was an important era, for it saw not only the founding of the United States but also its rise as a naval and maritime power. The traditions of the Navy were established and the foundations of a national maritime policy were laid. However, historians attempting to evaluate important naval actions and the state of national naval power in sailing-ship days find it most difficult to judge the effectiveness of American naval vessels: there are often questions as to the true size of certain ships, the effectiveness of their armament, and their relative speed. An examination of the standard naval histories will show that there has been much confusion in this particular matter; ships are either over-estimated or underestimated in size, power, speed, and effectiveness.

An attempt to establish exact information on various naval ships in the early years of American naval history was found to be difficult; the material was distributed in institutional and private hands or had been buried in government warehouses or storage files. As a result the naval historians were usually forced to fall back on published sources and to attempt with these a new and better analysis. The official records were particularly scanty with regard to the characteristics of naval vessels, and the official lists were commonly contradictory. Even a casual examination of the official records indicated that a great deal of such material had disappeared. It is not surprising, therefore, to find that American naval historians could not give a satisfactory account of naval actions in sailing-ship days, or that they were unable, in many cases, to analyze or evaluate properly the factors that won or lost a naval battle—as indicated by the contradictions in the accounts of actions contained in standard American naval histories.

An account of the development of American naval ships will also open a new approach to the history of ship design and construction. It is often accepted that progress is merely the discovery of new ideas, but experience has shown again and again that until the new ideas are generally accepted there can be no widespread improvement. In the field of shipbuilding, and particularly in governmental shipbuilding, there has usually been some resistance to the introduction of all new ideas. This has invariably been caused by the existence of a vested interest in the status quo, which assumes that the proposed improvements would in some way harm or annoy it. The peculiar position of government with relation to competition often aggravates the resistance to improvement by securing the position of the interests in power. It will be seen that, as a result, the appearance of new ideas, and even widespread acceptance of them, did not insure immediate benefits to the national navy. This makes possible some examination, at least, of the official reasons for neglecting what now appear to have been obvious advantages. Since this involves appraisals of the ability and character of men in authority, it can readily be seen that the history of naval shipbuilding is a matter reaching beyond a mere narrative of technical advance and retrogression if an accurate estimate is to be expected.

There are others besides naval historians and students in this field who have an interest in detailed information on American sailing men-of-war. Perhaps marine artists are the most exacting of these. Here there is a desire for the extremely detailed information on the shape and appearance of noted men-of-war that is required to draw accurate pictures of famous battles. Every artist soon learns that contemporary pictures of naval actions are usually untrustworthy in the delineation of both the ships in the battle and their relative positions. In fact, contemporary pictures of some of the naval actions in the War of 1812 have been found to be wholly imaginary and completely misleading. The knowledge of this has led some marine artists to become extensively interested in that portion of the field of marine research dealing with the design, construction, and rigging of ships of the past. The composition of a picture of a naval action becomes, for such artists, a study of the course of the action in minute detail, with the relative position of the ships plotted in diagrams, together with a careful study of the plans of the ships involved, if these are available. By this method accuracy is insured and often an unusual composition is made possible as well. The work of the late George C. Wales, consisting of water colors of the naval actions of the War of 1812, is a notable example of this search for accuracy in delineation and fact.

Another group having particular interest in shipbuilding history is that composed of ship-model builders, professional and amateur. This group requires the same accurate and well-detailed information on individual ships that is desired by marine artists. However, the ship-model builder often has a much wider interest in types of vessels than is found in marine artists; the modelists often choose some unusual and forgotten type of unimportant small war vessel as a subject, whereas the artist is commonly concerned only with noted ships.

The general reader's interest is more difficult to estimate; yet it is possible that the craftsmanship of the naval constructors in the design of some ships may win appreciation. There are also the curious and often astounding viewpoints of governmental administration in so technical a field as shipbuilding that will warrant attention. In a period when great governmental power is deemed an admirable thing, it would be valuable to give time to an examination of some details of the functioning of a bureaucracy in so vital a matter as progressive shipbuilding, which might readily be assumed to represent any scientific development in governmental hands.

It seems apparent that there is a place for a study of the development of American sailing men-of-war. This should not only include an account of the historical development of the art of designing ships, but should also show, as far as possible, the trends in technical thought and administrative control that in some way affected the American naval ships. The study of purely combat craft would be insufficient, for the supporting service craft (which made the operation of fighting ships effective) need attention if the general efficiency of the national navy at any given period is to be estimated. Such an examination is of course limited in scope. It is apart from the history of naval operations: the stories of gallant naval fights, wily strategy, victory, and defeat. Rather it is an account of the long years of effort, on the part of a few statesmen, naval officers, and constructors, to build a navy capable of upholding the national honor and security should the occasion arise. Perhaps it can be said that naval shipbuilding can be considered a monument to national forethought. Too often, in American history at least, it has been a monument to the neglect of that quality on the part of both the public and its political leaders.

The study to be presented here was outlined, to some extent at least, by an examination of the published naval histories of the wars in which American sailing ships engaged. This enabled some estimate to be made of the questions that particularly troubled naval writers in the past. The limitation of the period of sailing ships in the American Navy could be readily established by accepting the dates of the building of the first and last naval sailing vessels for combat purposes. It seemed particularly desirable to attempt some explanation of the background of American naval ship design and building that began with the Revolution, and this led to research into the naval vessels built in America, in the colonial period, for the British Navy.

It was intended to illustrate the account with reproductions of the contemporary designs of American sailing men-of-war, but these were found to be in such a state that redrawing was necessary. Not only was the physical condition of many plans so poor that they could not be reproduced, but also, final examination of the plans showed that alterations, additions, and revisions were made which were not shown on the original design but which required representation. Redrawing, and in a few cases tracing alone, has been attempted with the greatest care to show the individual ship as faithfully as the writer's knowledge would permit. Many errors existed in the old plans; in correcting these there was always the possibility of erroneous interpretation, but it is hoped that these are not numerous, or serious in nature.

It is apparent that the naval constructors in early days were not required to furnish plans in great detail. Lines and offset tables, a few deck arrangement plans and spar dimensions, or a rough sail plan, were usually considered adequate for building even a large sailing man-of-war. This condition prevents

the presentation of completely detailed plans without a good deal of reconstruction in most cases. There are enough sources of information on such
matters as rigging and masting available in technical books contemporary with
sailing men-of-war to make such reconstructions almost wholly unnecessary
here. There are also many books on shipbuilding in the sailing-ship period
which describe the basic methods of ship construction in practice during various
eras. This makes it unnecessary to enter into a long description of ship construction except where it is desirable to indicate the exact state of American
naval construction at some important period. The deck arrangements, fittings,
and rigging details of naval ships were almost standardized, with relatively few
changes taking place in, say, twenty years. However, it should be observed that
early shipbuilding and rigging books are misleading in one respect: they
do not describe conditions exactly as they were at their dates of publication but
rather are valid for the period ten to twenty years earlier in the majority of
cases. Thus, Chapman's noted book, *Architectura Navalis Mercatoria*, does
not represent the height of shipbuilding progress in the plans it contains, at
its date of publication, 1768. Rather these plans show the height of development
at a period of ten to twenty years earlier.

An attempt has been made to show the interrelation of naval shipbuilding,
authorization, construction funds, design, building, and general naval shipbuilding policy, with national affairs and leadership. It seems necessary to place
much importance on the administrative control of naval construction, for the
official records make it plain that this was often an important factor. Con-
troversial matters of credit for the design of certain ships, the influence of individuals and groups, the soundness of policy, and similar subjects are necessarily examined in detail. Such matters as these are, of necessity, discussed as
matters of personal opinion, but the conclusions are based on an examination
of official records and correspondence, or, where available, upon the private
papers of individuals involved.

It is impractical to list the sources on which this study is based; most of them
are fragmentary, and so the individual reference would become involved and
lengthy. Basically, the account is founded on surviving plans in the National
Archives, which include all those taken from the files of the Navy Department. A few plans which formerly existed in the storage files of the Navy have
disappeared, but copies of some of these had been made before the originals
were lost. Other important sources include the Lenthall Collection in the
Franklin Institute, Philadelphia, Pa.; the Fox Papers in the Peabody Museum,

★ ★ ★ ★ ★ ★ ★ ★ ★

Acknowledgment

THE author is under obligation to acknowledge the assistance of many who have had interest in American naval history or in marine research. These kind friends have given information or helped in the location of plans and papers that have been of inestimable value in this study of American sailing men-of-war. Particular thanks are due to

     The late George C. Wales
     The late George H. Stegmann
     The late Admiralty Curator C. Knight
and to
     Commodore Dudley W. Knox, U.S.N. (Ret.)
     Captain Stephen C. Rowan, U.S.N. (Ret.)
     Lt. Comdr. Marion V. Brewington, U.S.N.R. (Ret.)
     Admiralty Curator H. S. Richardson
     Mr. David Foster Taylor
     Mr. Alfred S. Brownell
     Walter Muir Whitehill
     Vernon D. Tate
     Mr. Bryant K. Rogers
     Mr. Kenneth Roberts
     Mr. R. C. Anderson
     Professor Charles M. Gay
     Mr. Clarkson Cranmer
     Mr. Wayne B. Yarnall

and to the staffs of the National Archives, Office of Naval Records and Library, Library of Congress, Franklin Institute, Pennsylvania Historical Society, Maine Historical Society, Library of the City of New York, Peabody Museum, Salem, Mass.; Newburyport Historical Society; the Naval Museum at Annapolis; the Mariner's Museum, Newport News, Va.; the New York Historical Society; the Boston Public Library; and the National Archives, Ottawa, Ont.

HOWARD I. CHAPELLE

Cambridge, Maryland

Nomenclature Used in Ship Plans

LENGTH between perpendiculars was not consistent in the original draughts of United States Navy ships and seems to have been established at the fancy of the designer. In many cases the after perpendicular was placed at the intersection of the "cross seam," or lower edge of the transom, with the inner rabbet of the sternpost, but in some cases it was at the underside of the lower deck, where it intersected the inner rabbet on the post. In a few cases it was at the "height of breadth" line, where this met the transom. The position of the fore perpendicular also varied; sometimes it was at the intersection of the "height of breadth" line and the inner rabbet of the stem, or at the intersection of the underside of the main deck and the inner rabbet of the stem. In rare cases the perpendicular appears to have been placed without regard to either the deck or "height of breadth." This lack of system made the comparison of length on the basis of "length between perpendiculars" meaningless; so in this book the plans have been drawn with the dimensions and location of perpendiculars brought to a standard system. Except in rare cases the "length between perpendiculars" is the dimension from an after perpendicular placed at the intersection of the cross seam and the inner rabbet of the sternpost to the intersection of the underside of the main deck with the inner rabbet of the stem. In 74's the fore perpendicular would be located at the intersection of the underside of the lower deck with the inner rabbet of the stem and the after perpendicular at the intersection of the same deck line with the inner rabbet of the sternpost.

"Room" and "space" in these plans is the equivalent of the distance between frames, center line to center line. Literally it means space between each pair of frames, in the clear, plus the room required for one complete frame. The sequence of frame numbers or letters in the plans serves to indicate the number of frames between each pair of stations.

Rabbet of the sternpost, stem, and keel is shown by double lines, the inner being the inner rabbet and the outer the outer rabbet. Except in a few cases, the lines of ships shown here are to the inside of the planking. Hence sheer lines are to the underside of rail cap or other mouldings, and deck lines are to the underside of the deck plank at the inside of the ship's side planking.

"Port sill," or "port cill," is a line at the height of the underside of a line of gun ports and shows only, in a ship, when it also represents the top of a belt of thick planking.

Wales are the belt of thick plank on a ship's sides. The wales are shown by horizontal lines in the profile of the ship, more or less paralleling the sheer. In some ships, there was another and slightly thinner belt above the thick wale, the top of which was usually at port-sill height, as in the schooner *Grampus* of 1820–21. The lower edge of the thick wale was dubbed off fair with the bottom plank in United States Navy ships built after 1812, and hence the bottom of the wale did not show on the completed vessel, though often indicated in the plans. The retention of this line was intended to give the builders an idea of the depth of the thick planking forming the wales. After 1824 the top of the wales was also dubbed off and the vessel's sides then became smooth, without step-ups or step-downs being visible in the side planking.

★ ★ ★ ★ ★ ★ ★ ★ ★

CHAPTER ONE

The Colonial Period

THE PROBLEMS of creating a navy in the American colonies at the outbreak of the Revolution were not far different fundamentally from what they would be today in a colonial possession that had revolted against its national government. Then, as would be the case in the present, money had to be raised, a naval organization set up, ships designed and built, arms bought or manufactured, supplies and munitions collected, and the vessels manned. It is obvious that success depended upon all of this being accomplished with the least possible delay. To do this, experienced men were very necessary in all stages.

The importance of trained and experienced men during the Revolution can be illustrated by the general lack of success of the Continental Navy as compared to the Army. The former lacked experienced naval officers and, with few exceptions, had to operate with merchant marine masters and mates whose inexperience in warfare led to many disasters. The Army, however, found some colonial officers who had either seen service in the British Army or were veterans of the colonial wars against the French and Indians. When these officers were in command, operations were usually successful or, at the worst, great disasters were avoided. There were exceptions to this, of course; some of the colonial naval officers who were ex-privateersmen proved highly competent, just as did some of the militia officers in the Army. However, it took time for both to become accustomed to the needs of regular warfare, and this in itself made them less valuable in the early and important phases of the war.

It will be shown that the ships of the Continental Navy were, on the whole, excellent men-of-war. Just as success at sea or in the land campaigns of the Revolution indicated the existence of trained officers and enlisted personnel, the qualities of these ships, combined with their early appearance in the war, indicate the existence of shipwrights trained in naval construction. The trained officers of the armed services could not have come from purely civilian experience; the shipwrights who designed and built the ships of the Continental Navy could not have been developed by the sole experience of merchant-ship construction. There is little in the way of satisfactory record of the men who were responsible for the design of the Continental ships, but examination of the history of colonial shipbuilding in the century prior to the outbreak of the Revolution will show logical reasons for the excellence of the design of American-built men-of-war that made up the bulk of the Continental Navy.

To appreciate fully the state of colonial shipbuilding at the outbreak of the Revolution, it is necessary to know, in general terms at least, the position that had been reached in the art of ship design at the time and the causes of the distinctions between men-of-war and merchant craft. The opinion that ships of the colonial period were designed and built by eye, without plans or model, is apparently a common one. The impression that the ships and small craft of this period were clumsy, slow, ill-formed, and poorly rigged is equally general. Many of these opinions and impressions can be traced to the poor contemporary paintings and illustrations that have survived to recent times. These are very misleading, for the marine art of the period was stylized and highly conventional in detail. As a result, the hulls are shown excessively full and round, with the freeboard made to appear excessive, and the proportion of length to beam and freeboard inadequate for good sailing qualities. The sails are shown as though they were cut to bag excessively, so much so that weatherliness would be impossible to obtain. These contemporary pictures, added to uninformed conclusions reached by some modern historians, have naturally led to the idea that the ships were poorly designed and probably built without the aid of plans. This whole concept of shipbuilding in colonial times is incorrect, as can be readily proved by the building plans that have survived; these are, of course, the most accurate evidence that can be presented.

Shipbuilding began in the American colonies as soon as settlements were firmly established. In most cases shipwrights and boatbuilders were brought over from the homeland so that vessels necessary for colonial transportation could be constructed; these included craft necessary for protection against enemies. At an early date the Spaniards built men-of-war in Mexico, Central America, and Cuba to protect their treasure fleets in American waters. The Dutch and English also built small war vessels at various times. These combat ships were usually constructed in temporary government dockyards by shipwrights brought into the colony for this particular purpose; when their work was done they were usually sent home. This practice prevented the colonies from developing a large shipbuilding industry or naval construction and confined the bulk of their building to small craft to be used in the colonial coasting trade.

American naval shipbuilding, in what is now the United States, may be said to have begun with the building of the fourth-rate *Falkland* for the British Navy at Portsmouth, New Hampshire, in 1690. Not only was she a regular man-of-war and a fairly large ship, but she was contract-built by a privately owned shipyard, employing colonial shipwrights who remained in the colony when their work on this ship was finished. The *Falkland* was followed by the building of a few other vessels before the time of the Revolution, which resulted in the creation of a group of colonial shipwrights experienced in naval construction who could pass on their knowledge through apprentices. It would be easy to overemphasize the importance of this; nevertheless, the matter undoubtedly played some part in the development of American naval construction in the Revolution, and so requires careful investigation and consideration.

The building of these men-of-war in private shipyards in the American colonies is a good indication of the ability and knowledge of their shipwrights. It is difficult to imagine that contracts for large men-of-war would be placed in the American shipyards if their men were incapable of reading plans and ignorant of naval practice. Long before the colonial shipyards began to build warships, naval construction had become a specialized field in ship design and construction and the monopoly of national governments. As a result, all training in this field had likewise become a government monopoly. There were no technical schools then, as there are today, to give a general training in all branches of marine architecture. Therefore knowledge of warship design in colonial times indicated either training in a government dockyard or an apprenticeship to a shipwright or builder who had been a dockyard apprentice. There is little doubt that there were dockyard-trained ship-

builders in the colonies, men who had served an apprenticeship in a government yard and who had emigrated to the colonies; in fact, the existence of
the contract-built men-of-war of colonial construction is in itself sufficient
evidence of this. These men would take apprentices, who would receive the
equivalent of a dockyard training. This insured them of what was then an
education in the latest and most scientific shipbuilding practices, including the
making and use of plans.

The use of plans to design ships was not a new thing in 1690. The practice
had existed in England for about a century or more and had become a standard
requirement in naval work by all the great maritime powers. The British Admiralty had ordered the retention of plans as early as 1650, and plans from
1675 still survive. The methods of projection required to make plans of the
hull form of a ship had developed slowly from the crude drawings of the
late sixteenth century, so that by 1675 reasonable accuracy could be expected.
The advantages of plans were recognized, not only in government dockyards,
but also in many of the merchant shipyards.

The close of the sixteenth century had seen some improvement in the model
of British Navy ships, brought about by the efforts to combat the Spanish
during Elizabeth's reign. In these years the ships had become larger and more
weatherly, though shipbuilders were still generally uneducated and many
ships were dangerous and ill-formed.

The histories of maritime nations show periods when all the factors necessary for improvement in shipbuilding and design come into being and a
nation's naval power and maritime interest reaches a zenith. The seventeenth
century was such a period in English history. Rulers and ministers came to
power whose ambition made naval power necessary; the cultural and economic levels of the nation were raised by foreign adventures and explorations;
interest in science became marked; wars created national danger that turned
public interest to the Navy, and ship designers and builders of genius appeared.
As a result, not only did the English become the leading naval power, but also,
for a short period at least, their warships were superior to those of the rest
of the world.

The opening of the century had found the British Navy insufficient for
national ambitions and requirements. An inquiry was instituted and steps
were taken to improve the naval establishment. Administrative reforms were
made and a particular effort was directed to obtaining better men-of-war. To
improve the design of naval ships, the "Shipwrights' Company," or shipbuild-

ing guild, was given increased responsibilities in the design of new naval vessels. A master of the guild was created, who was made an important member of the civil staff of the naval establishment. This office was filled, by an election in 1606, by Phineas Pett, "gentleman and sometime master of arts at Emmanuel college, Cambridge." Pett was far more than an educated gentleman; he was an experienced shipbuilder and a designer with very advanced ideas for the period. In 1610 he designed the *Prince Royal*, which at the time of her launch was considered to be a model man-of-war in all important respects, including sailing qualities, fighting power, and impressive appearance. In 1612 the Shipwrights' Company was given a new charter and increased prestige. Pett was elected the first master under the new charter. As Commissioner of the Royal Dockyard at Chatham he was also the responsible ship designer of the Royal Navy.

Pett pressed his ideas for improvement vigorously and made plans for a number of large men-of-war. His masterpiece was the *Royal Sovereign*, launched in 1637. This ship was on a greatly improved model and was of great size and power for her time. Because of her good qualities as a man-of-war, the model of this ship influenced the design of Royal Navy vessels for well over a century after her launch. The *Royal Sovereign* had a long career and saw much hard service. She was altered in 1651, when her topworks were reduced, and rebuilt in 1659–60. While awaiting a second rebuilding in 1696 she was accidentally destroyed by fire.

Phineas Pett died in 1647, when in his seventies, and was succeeded by his son Peter Pett. All told, four members of this great English shipbuilding family served as master or assistant master shipwrights in the Royal Navy, between 1612 and 1678. The last master shipwright of the family, also named Phineas, whom Pepys considered a "very knave" and a thorough scoundrel, designed and built the galley-frigate *Charles Galley* in 1675. This vessel and her sisters had a great reputation and will be referred to again. In the design of the *Charles Galley*, Phineas Pett is said to have had the assistance of that noted yachtsman, patron of shipbuilders, and amateur naval architect, Charles II. Charles had a keen personal interest in the technical problems of ship design and construction. He employed, in addition to members of the Pett family, Sir Anthony Deane, who rose to prominence as a designer of naval ships during Charles's reign. Deane designed one of the new galley-frigates, in competition with Phineas Pett, a number of yachts, and a large number of men-of-war. The sailing qualities of all of these were generally

better than had previously been known. Deane also seems to have been responsible for the first "establishment" (standardized dimensions of naval ships),
drawn up in 1675. He acted as instructor to Peter the Great of Russia in
1698, during the latter's visit to England to study shipbuilding. Deane also
devised a method of calculating displacement and prepared a thesis on ship
design.

The period between 1670 and 1695 may be said to have marked the high
water of scientific study in all the fields relating to the improvement in English warship design in the seventeenth century. By 1690 the models of
English men-of-war had reached a high degree of excellence, and the competition of France in ship design and construction had only recently been
felt. The construction of the *Falkland* in America at this time gave the colonial
shipwrights who worked on her an opportunity to see what were then, perhaps, the most advanced ideas in naval ship design and construction, at least
in a moderate-sized ship.

The eighteenth century opened with Great Britain in possession of about
one-third of the whole of Europe's naval power. The French had begun to
improve their ships markedly by the time of Charles II and had adopted the
old Spanish policy of building ships very large for the number of guns they
were intended to carry. In addition they began a study of hull form and
searched for improved construction methods. While well aware of this, the
British tried to find means to economize in the maintenance of their huge
naval organization. The carving and painting that had been so profusely used
on men-of-war were reduced or eliminated, and interior joinerwork in cabins
or on deck was omitted or simplified.

In the sixteenth century some efforts had been made to set up standard
dimensions for each class of war vessel in the Royal Navy. This was to
guide designers in planning new ships to make sure that the vessels of a given
rate had some similarity and approximately the same qualities. Probably it was
hoped that this would lead to the use of spars, sails, and rigging that were
interchangeable in a given rate or class of ship. Obviously such an idea has a
great attraction to a government agency under pressure to economize. Just
as "standardization" has become attractive to modern armed services, so the
"establishment" became popular with the British Admiralty. The idea of one
of the smaller British ships capturing a larger ship of the enemy appealed to
national pride, and this, plus the economy that was supposed to be possible,
led to the fixing of the dimensions of each rate at a minimum that was then

thought practical in peacetime, to be modified as required with the passage of time. With the effort to obtain a cheaper fleet in the early eighteenth century, the "establishment" received much attention and an attempt was made to make all ships conform to the approximate dimensions of their class in the Royal Navy. The results of the peacetime standardization represented in the "establishment" were the same as much of the military and naval standardization of more recent times. Designs for new ships and equipment became obsolete but remained in use until war losses brought home the necessity of change. The stagnation of peacetime standardization was replaced at great cost by the free development forced by wartime competition with an active and enterprising enemy.

The history of the "establishments" between 1706 and 1745 illustrates the effects of peace and war upon the idea of standardization. During this period there were five "establishments": 1706, 1719, 1733, 1741, and 1745. Through these revisions the 60-gun ships, for example, were increased in length of the gun deck but six feet, in beam about four and a half feet, and in depth about three feet. Economy and shortsightedness prevented the English from setting up "establishments" that assured, at the time each new one was instituted, vessels larger than those of any continental power, even though war experience had shown the need time and again.

Actually, the advantages hoped for in the "establishments" were never fully realized. Changes required by war and by the efforts of designers and builders to obtain good qualities in all new ships led to the evasion of the restrictions of the "establishment" as much as could be dared. It was not uncommon for a ship, built in the year a new "establishment" became official, to exceed the standard dimensions by a number of feet. However, the general effects of the "establishment" were still apparent. Ships were small for the number of guns they carried and so were slower and less powerful than the larger vessels used in the continental navies. The sense of power that sprang from the possession of the biggest navy in the world and the satisfaction of victories achieved by a well-manned naval service, combined with the effects of the "establishment," led to a slowing down in the British efforts to improve their naval ship designs, and from 1700 to 1770 there were relatively few improvements. Ships grew in size and the sails and rigging were improved somewhat, but after the bomb ketch had been introduced into the Royal Navy, late in the seventeenth century, no new type of man-of-war appeared until the cutter and schooner were adopted, about 1760. The only changes that took place in this period in the ships of the Royal Navy were the creation of new rates by means of new class designations. From late in the seventeenth century to the American Revolution, the French gradually took the lead in quality of ship design, and their dominance in this field was marked throughout the greater part of the eighteenth century.

The "rating" of ships in the Royal Navy has been referred to so often that some explanation of this system of designation is necessary. The rates, in 1700, were first to sixth: first was 100 guns, second 90 guns, third 70 guns, fourth 54–60 guns, fifth 30–40 guns, and sixth 18–24 guns. The exact number of guns in each rate was never constant; gradually the first rate included all ships from 100 guns upward, the second 90 to 98, the third 64 to 80, the fourth 50 to 60, the fifth 30 to 44, and the sixth 20 to 28. Below the sixth were sloops, bombs, fireships, and other small craft. By 1750 the term "rate" was rarely used, except in some official lists, and was replaced by the gun-number, as "100-gun ship," "44-gun ship" and "20-gun ship," because of the vagueness of the rating designation.

The first half of the eighteenth century, marked by stagnation in British naval ship design, was in the colonies an active period of naval shipbuilding. Not only were a number of naval ships built in the colonies, but also the naval wars brought captured vessels into the colonial ports where shipbuilders and designers might see them. Men whose livelihood depends upon ship design and construction are usually observant and critical. There can be no doubt that such colonials noted any improvements in the design of foreign craft or of the men-of-war built in the colonies.

In judging ship design, the colonial American shipwright had an advantage that relatively few European builders possessed. This was the American's interest in and knowledge of fast-sailing ships and the elements of design necessary to obtain this quality. A combination of international unrest, geographical location, and the oppression of colonial maritime trade by the mother country had forced the American colonials to build fast vessels for practically all trades, even for fishing. The settlements were commonly too small and weak to man heavily armed vessels, even if large armaments were otherwise possible. Fast craft were readily obtained and were both cheaper to build and less expensive to operate. The danger of loss of the colonial craft had a tendency to place a premium on low-cost construction and developed Americans who were unusually competent, or expert, in this matter. All sections of the colonies where the shipbuilding industry existed produced fast, cheap vessels for at least fifty years prior to the Revolution.

The distinction between a man-of-war and a merchant ship in colonial times was less obvious than it is today, but it was just as real. From the time guns had been introduced on shipboard, the design of fighting ships had become more complex. By 1700 the merchant vessel was no longer a success-ful substitute for a man-of-war, no matter how well armed and manned she might be. Only in small craft, in fact, could a merchant vessel be utilized in warfare, and even here, only the special, small, fast ships built for adventure or illegal trade were of any use in war. Merchantmen were employed, of course, when emergency made their use necessary for convoy duty in colonial warfare, but the vessels were rarely successful as fighting ships. They were to some extent counterparts of the heavily armed merchant "cruisers" used in the last war for the same purpose.

Owing to the need of convoy guards, a number of merchant ships were purchased and armed by the Royal Navy during the years of the American Revolution. Since most of these ships were built before 1770, and since some plans survive, it is readily possible to make comparisons between merchant ships and men-of-war of the mid-portion of the eighteenth century. There is no reason to suppose that there were great differences between these pur-chased merchant ships and the colonial vessels, for, in fact, a few of these convoy guards appear to have been American-built.

The technical problems raised by the conflicting requirements of the serv-ice of naval vessels in the days of sail and wooden hulls were serious, and they were much more difficult to solve than in the case of the contemporary mer-chantman. Usually merchantmen were either small, fast-sailing craft of small capacity or slow ships having large holds. The rarest type was one in which ability to carry large cargoes was combined with fast sailing. In fact, it was not until well into the end of the sailing-ship period that such merchant vessels were required and developed. Achieving strength in small wooden ships was not a serious problem, but in long vessels it presented an almost insurmountable difficulty to shipbuilders until well after the Revolution.

The armament and its inherent requirements created the most troublesome problems in the design of sailing men-of-war. Muzzle-loading guns, smooth-bored, often poorly cast of inferior metal and employing shot that did not fit the bore correctly, made rapid fire and accuracy impossible of attainment in colonial times and for long afterward. The only practical way to make the fire of such guns effective, even at very short ranges, was to concentrate them as much as possible in the broadside of a ship. This could be accomplished by placing the guns close together in a row along the side of the ship, leaving space enough between them to permit the gun crews to work. When there were two or more decks, the obvious step was to arm these in a similar manner also, if they were of sufficient height in the ship to be of any use in rough water. However, as the height of guns above water was increased, their weight increasingly affected the ship's stability. It was soon discovered that the arming of a number of decks was limited not only by the size of the ship, but by her stability, and that the most practical approach was to place the larger and heavier guns low in the ship and to arm any available upper deck with lighter and less effective guns. The ends of the ship had to be armed not only to defend the vessel against attacks at the bow or stern but also to permit fire when chasing or being chased. The limitations of space and the interference of rigging would prevent such guns from being very numerous; therefore, effectiveness could be obtained only by employing the guns having the longest range and the greatest accuracy at the ends of the ship. But excesses in this direction were prohibited by the great weight and length of guns of this description.

As the number of guns increased, a greater number of men was necessary to work them. Not only was it necessary to fight the guns; it was also necessary to have enough men in addition to handle the sails and rigging in action, and to do the other work required to maneuver the vessel. By 1700 the number of crew required to work the guns had become so great that it was impractical to place enough men aboard to man both sides of the ship completely in large men-of-war. Huge crews required much space for provisions and water, particularly as men-of-war, to be really effective, had to be capable of remaining at sea for extended periods of time without being supplied from shore or from other ships. The stores had to be located in the hold, for the gun, or upper, decks must be unobstructed enough to fight the guns and to work the gear required to handle the vessel.

The guns, being muzzle-loaders, were run inboard by tackles, or by recoil, to load. Inboard of these guns, when run in, there had to be room to permit movements of large numbers of men and space to pass ammunition. Deck openings were necessary to allow men and ammunition to pass from deck to deck, but these must not interfere with the guns in any way. Thus the armament not only determined the deck arrangements, but also had some control over the amount of beam, or width, of the ships.

Speed was a very desirable feature in men-of-war; a fast vessel could overtake a fleeing enemy ship, or, if necessary, escape from a pursuing one. Speed and weatherliness, or the ability to sail close to the direction of the wind, combined with the ability to turn quickly, gave great advantages in battle maneuvers, permitting choice of position and the use of the broadside batteries to the best advantage. However, speed required sharp, or fine, ends to the hull, which reduced stowage space and weight-carrying ability. It also required a large sail area, with resulting long spars, lofty masts, and a great deal of rigging. The weight of sails and rigging added to that of the guns increased the burden carried in men-of-war.

Strength in hull and spars was essential. The man-of-war had to be strong enough to carry the great weight of guns and stores placed arbitrarily in the hull for fighting efficiency rather than with any regard to the structural requirements. It also had to withstand the tremendous shocks of collision in action, when boarding tactics were employed, and the effects of hits from gunfire upon the ship. The structure and decks had to be strong enough to take the recoil of the guns. The spars had to be stout to carry the large sails even when injured by a hit. Stout bulwarks were very desirable, even on small craft, in order to protect the crew from small-arms fire, to take the shock of recoil of the guns, and to avoid excessive damage in collision.

The necessity of designing ships with the guns well above the water line became obvious in very early times. This position permitted the guns to be fired in heavy weather, or when the ship was pressed with sail. In the days of short-range weapons, the advantage of a high firing position was obvious. But lofty weights soon raised the problem of stability, and the lofty rig required for speed aggravated the difficulty. Throughout the sailing-ship period the problems of stability in men-of-war were a matter of grave concern to all naval designers. Ballast seemed to be the answer to some extent, but this took up space and led to deep draft. The ability of men-of-war to operate in shoal water was an obvious advantage; however, the requirements of weatherliness and stability made this an ideal rarely accomplished.

The seaworthiness of all men-of-war was another important factor, for even the smallest was expected to be able to stay at sea in any weather and to make long voyages. Stability was important in this, as was strength and weatherliness. Hull form played a part in obtaining seaworthiness, but the distribution of weights in relation to that of displacement was also important. The latter determined to a great extent whether a ship would ship water in heavy weather, as well as the length and severity of the roll of the hull in heavy seas and the strains placed upon her structure, affecting her strength. The quickness and length of the roll played a great part in the accuracy of the gunfire, in a day when loading was slow and the mechanics of firing were both slow and uncertain. The ideal man-of-war should therefore roll slowly and easily, without jerk, and without an excessive length of roll that might submerge the gun muzzles, or flood the ports and decks. This too was an ideal rarely accomplished in any sailing man-of-war design.

The effects of these requirements in warship design were conflicting and difficult of satisfactory solution. The greatest problems arose in the effort to obtain speed and gun power. The weights involved in the latter made for heavy displacement hulls, full in shape and wholly unsuited for fast sailing, or even weatherliness. Except in scout and messenger craft of small size, where armament was of minor importance, the naval designer could not aim for speed alone; on the other hand, he could not design solely for fighting power without regard to weatherliness and maneuvering ability, which in themselves were usually elements of speed. After many attempts to combine speed and gun power, naval designers gradually turned to establishing ships of special classification, in which each class or type was designed for a particular purpose. In these classes the most powerful ships were the largest in dimensions, which in colonial times carried 100 guns. Scaling down from this to smaller ships the number of guns was reduced by 10 in each class. Ships of the line, or in modern parlance, battleships, were the 70-, 80-, 90-, and 100-gun ships. The modern heavy cruiser or small battleship was represented in colonial times by the 40-, 50-, and 60-gun ships, while light cruisers were represented by 20- and 30-gun classes. Below the 20-gun ships were brigantines, snows, ketches, and other small craft, with from 4 to 18 guns, as well as special craft such as bomb vessels, galleys, gunboats, and the service craft used for supply ships, transports, and exploration, or for the duties of dockyard service. The rates that were fashionable in European navies changed from time to time, and the 24-, 36-, 44-, 64-, 74-, and 98-gun ships became common in the middle of the eighteenth century. Later the 28-, 32-, and 110-gun ships came into use. The element of speed was expected less in large ships, but as the minimum rates were approached fast sailing became increasingly desirable. The number of guns that classified a ship was the total of those she mounted on carriages;

some small cannon were mounted on upright timbers called "stocks" and were known as "swivels" or "howitzers," or by other names, but were never included among the "guns."

Rowing vessels still played an important part in colonial times, and nearly all small sailing men-of-war were fitted to row. Oar ports located between the gun ports, or on a lower deck if practical, permitted the large crews to move the vessel in a calm by means of long sweeps or oars, each worked by a number of men. Some vessels were particularly designed to be rowed efficiently, such as some of the sailing "galleys" of the late seventeenth and early eighteenth centuries; these ships were usually sharp and light, though otherwise like the regular sailing man-of-war. The true galley type, in which sails were either dispensed with entirely, or made a mere auxiliary to the oar, had gradually been confined to gunboats and to vessels intended to operate in certain geographical areas exclusively—the Mediterranean, for example. Oars were employed in vessels up to 40 guns in many navies as late as 1820, and in all small men-of-war brigs, schooners, and cutters until the end of the sailing-ship period.

The solutions to the problems involved in designing a satisfactory man-of-war differed with each of the great maritime powers. Obviously, the solutions to many of the problems were to build men-of-war as large as possible in all dimensions, or to exaggerate some one dimension. Length gave the greatest advantage in both speed and gun power, but here the designer was blocked by the elastic wooden hull made up of many members that could not be secured tightly enough not to move when the vessel was under strain. Long hulls not only strained and leaked, but they lasted only a short time without repair and were therefore very expensive. Though many attempts were made before the American Revolution to design and build very large or long men-of-war, progress in overcoming the difficulty in their construction was extremely slow. Gradually, however, improved structural design permitted an increase in length.

Another way to obtain the great displacement necessary in men-of-war, and also to obtain strength, was to increase the beam or width of the ship, its depth in the water, or its height out of the water in proportion to its length. These solutions, however, produced slow ships, lacking in weatherliness and maneuverability. Deep draft, if carried to an extreme, was an obvious disadvantage.

By the mid-eighteenth century, England, France, Holland, and Spain had each chosen a particular compromise in dimensions and proportions, which soon became national characteristics of their men-of-war. England generally chose small ships, with rather deep draft, full ends, and slow-sailing qualities. France decided on long, rather narrow ships, fine at the ends and fast-sailing, though usually rather weakly built. Holland selected wide shoal models in which sailing was sacrificed for ability to operate in the shoal waters of her coasts. Spain preferred ships of rather great size, but marked generally by relatively high freeboard. In colonial times, the French and Spanish men-of-war gradually improved, so that by 1740 it was commonly recognized that they were designed on better principles than the British ships. In addition to these elements of size and proportion, each nation gradually developed particular hull forms, so that the hull profile and the shape of the ends and of the midsection also became national characteristics in their naval vessels.

The physical characteristics required in men-of-war were not the only things that made them different from their merchant-ship sisters and made their development entirely independent. The commercial vessels were designed, built, and owned by private individuals. The man-of-war, on the other hand, was the property of the national government in all respects—design, construction, arming, fitting, manning, and operation. The training of men for each of these matters was also conducted by the government. The monopoly in naval construction was under the direct control of a bureaucracy of long standing in colonial times, just as it is today. This monopoly was encroached upon only when private individuals built and owned privateers in time of war, or when a national emergency arose that forced the government to build men-of-war in private shipyards because its own facilities were inadequate to enlarge the navy fast enough. The relation of naval ship design and construction to those of merchant ships in colonial times was not very different from that existing very recently. Designers and builders of commercial vessels rarely knew much about naval vessels unless their early training had been in government work, or they had had experience in wartime naval construction let in some private yard or had worked in a dockyard when war had forced the employment of additional personnel. Then, as in recent years, the government agency responsible for the naval establishment acted independently in developing the design of men-of-war, improving their construction, arming, and fitting without using the nation's civilian facilities to any marked extent.

As a result of this monopoly of the man-of-war, improvement is not constant and, as a general rule, occurs at times quite different from the periods of rapid evolution in merchant craft. The private owner's only concern is to have a ship that is fitted for her trade and that can meet competition, either from her own compatriots or from foreigners. If a ship's design does not permit this, or if she is otherwise unfitted for her trade, she is not repeated in new construction. If her designer, builder, or owner is so conservative or so wedded to an unsuccessful model that he will not keep abreast of the improvements made by competitors, he soon goes bankrupt. As a result, improvements in merchant ships are constantly being made, except in wartime, when merchant shipping and shipbuilding are disrupted. In naval shipbuilding the situation is just the opposite. The reasons for this are easily found in the history of all maritime nations. Peace and economy in government lead to standardization and to neglect in naval construction, and if there is no fear of war the public becomes indifferent to naval matters, particularly to the need for improvement. The bureaucracy that is responsible for naval shipbuilding is left to routine matters, and pressure is brought to bear by political factions to economize, either by complete standardization or at least by elimination of change and improvement. Inefficient or obsolete ships, guns, and equipment remain in use. Designers and technicians lose interest, and the money granted the naval establishment is usually diverted to the maintenance of worn-out ships, repairs to buildings and shore establishments, and unnecessary expenditures in administration. It is not uncommon to find a naval power, after a long period of peaceful stagnation, entering a war with poor ships and equipment, but with huge and largely useless shore establishments and administrative organizations. In a period of prolonged peace the development of the merchant ship has usually been rapid, and so, on the outbreak of war, the naval vessels are in all important respects generally far inferior to their commercial sisters.

When war occurs, however, the picture is commonly reversed. The naval establishment is reorganized and made efficient; poor designers and technicians are removed from responsible offices, standardization or conservatism becomes outmoded, and the design of naval craft rapidly improves in all possible respects and at tremendous cost. If the national danger is great and public interest is, as a result, very high, the naval craft soon outstrip the ships of commerce. If the war is long, it is not uncommon to find that the naval vessels at its end are years ahead of their times, while the design and development of merchant ships are still where they were at the beginning of the war. There are, of course, some craft developed for trade in wartime, such as blockade runners or other vessels suited only to a special requirement. But however great the part played by civilian ship designers, builders, and owners in the wartime development of such types, it is soon found that this class of ship is wholly unsuited for peaceful trade and so must be discarded, though some of the features of design may be adapted to improve the postwar merchantman. The emphasis on emergency requirements in merchant ships built during a war almost invariably makes them expensive to operate in postwar trade. This was almost as true in colonial times as in the more recent years, though of course there have been impressive differences in the scope of modern war.

That the naval ship designers have shown extreme conservatism at times has invariably been due to the causes, just outlined, that are created by a long period of peace. Like the designers of merchant craft, the naval constructor is influenced by education and training. In the long history of naval architecture there have been many periods, both in the past and in recent times, when curious ideas were fashionable and pseudo science ruled much of the education of ship designers. If the colonial ship designer cluttered up his ship with masses of carving that served no useful purpose, he differed but little from his modern counterpart, who decorates his ship with materials shaped in fantastic and useless forms to "streamline" a vessel too slow to require such treatment. If the early ship designer had undue respect for mechanically drawn hull sections, he resembled the modern designer who has too much regard for mathematical formulae and not enough for the practical problems of hull form and actual design.

The chief cause of naval conservatism, however, is the stagnation in the development of combat technique that occurs at times when war is rare, or victory easily achieved. Then the naval ship designer has no new problems to meet and has to consider only the lessons of the past. New ships may be designed in such a time, but they are suited for the "last" war instead of for a future one. Such craft have not only proved to be useless, but have even menaced national security by creating public overconfidence in a "powerful" navy. The young men, officers and naval constructors alike, who rise to prominence by means of ability in time of war, grow old in peace, satisfied with the existing state of things and living in the past glory of the "last" war. Having no competition to cause them alarm, they soon cease to have new ideas; finally they come to resent and fear any innovation that might rouse them to mental activity. The stupidity and pompousness of such men in recent times was as common in the colonial period, and just as dangerous.

Stagnation in a peacetime naval service is usually first apparent in the administrative functions of the bureaucratic establishment. The reason for this is that senior officers are commonly appointed to such posts and are then in a position to make their opinions felt in shipbuilding policies. The administrative function is a powerful one in any naval service, since it not only controls the financial arrangements of the naval shipbuilding establishment but also may affect selection or assignment of technical personnel. Naval shipbuilding has rarely been controlled by trained technicians at the "policy-making level"; rather the higher levels of administrative control have been in the hands of either senior naval officers or political appointees. Under such a system as this it is not surprising to find there has rarely been a steady effort to maintain a really progressive naval shipbuilding program over a long period of peace. In truth, the administrative control of a navy wholly decides the effectiveness of the arm in the long run. This is particularly true with regard to naval ship design. Naval history of the great maritime powers shows time and again that the presence of progressive and capable naval architects in a naval establishment will not alone assure an effective fleet; the administrative control must be equally progressive and competent, and the political interest must be favorable.

Let us now consider the details of colonial naval shipbuilding history and by more specific evidence see the state of ship design and design methods. Unfortunately the lack of definite records leaves many matters to speculation. However, on the face of the existing evidence, it will be apparent that the colonial shipbuilders, who had naval experience, were in all probability as well trained and as competent as the majority of European ship designers and builders of the period. The inferences that may be drawn from the existing evidence might well explain the excellence of the men-of-war of the Continental Navy.

The names of all the ships that were built for the Royal Navy in the colonies are not recorded, or have not yet been discovered. There are conflicting lists and confusion in ship names; however, it is known that the *Bedford* was built in New England not long after the *Falkland*, and also another ship whose name is not recorded with certainty. It is probable that both of these ships were built before 1730. In 1745–49 two vessels were built by contract—the 24-gun

Boston at Boston, Massachusetts, and the 44-gun ship *America* at Portsmouth, New Hampshire. The *Boston* was launched in 1747 or 1748; the *America* in 1749. From 1755 to the outbreak of the Revolution, the Admiralty built a great many small men-of-war on the Great Lakes and on Lake Champlain. The sloops *Oswego* and *Ontario* and the schooners *Vigilant, Lively,* and *George* were built in 1755. In 1756 the brig *London,* the snow *Halifax,* and the sloop *Mohawk* were constructed. In 1759 and 1760 three more snows were built—the *Mohawk, Onandaga,* and *Missisaga.* Between 1763 and 1771 the schooners *Huron, Brunswick, Michigan, Charlotte,* and *Victory,* and the snows *Haldemand* and *Seneca* were built. The largest of these was only 84 feet long. On the seacoast, between 1760 and 1771, at least three schooners were built— the *Sir Edward Hawke, Marble Head,* and *Earl of Egmont*—and about a dozen others purchased, some of them on the stocks.

Except for the large vessels built prior to 1749, the naval vessels built in the colonies were of trifling force and were of no great importance in giving an opportunity for study of the problems of naval construction. The schooners were an American type and were built from American plans or models. The sloops were mere patrol craft and were also built on colonial plans or models. The snows and the brigs were of slightly more importance than the rest; they ranged from 60 to 84 feet length on deck and were of man-of-war design. However, their models appear to have been very shoal, making them suitable for use on the uncharted lakes; in this they differed somewhat from their ocean-going sisters. It will be seen that, however unimportant were the ships built in the colonies after 1749, there was some opportunity for observant colonial shipwrights who were enterprising enough to search for work away from home to obtain experience in construction of naval vessels and, perhaps, a slight knowledge of some of their inherent problems of design. The large men-of-war, however, might logically be assumed to have played a far more important part in the education of the Revolutionary War naval ship designers.

The design of the Royal Navy ships built in colonial America is an interesting field for speculation, for there is little in the way of satisfactory evidence of design responsibility. It is probably safe to assume that these large vessels were built from plans supplied by the Admiralty, but there is difficulty in proving that the ships were actually built in strict conformity with these designs. Since the Admiralty was responsible for preparing the contract, it is apparent that the design and specifications would be prepared by its designers. It would be particularly desirable to illustrate the contract and specifications with plans or a model, in view of the distance between the Admiralty designers and the colonial contractors, in order to obtain satisfactory results. However, the Admiralty practice appears to have been one that has not been entirely unknown in modern American naval construction—the use of a "contract design," which was for guidance only. In recent times the builder has often prepared a detailed and sometimes much-altered design which, though based on the "contract design," was actually an entirely new one when finally approved and completed. The Admiralty seems to have used this system very often in colonial times, furnishing a builder with a plan, or model, based on the "establishment," or plans of an earlier ship. This was not a binding design, however, and the builder was permitted to change the hull form, the appearance, and even the dimensions of the vessel, providing he built a ship equal or superior to the "establishment," as set forth in the contract. The only important difference between the Admiralty practice and that of our modern contracts was that the colonial builder does not appear to have been required to have his revised design approved before construction and so did not make a model or plan for this purpose. The Admiralty agent, or superintendent, was given authority to decide the suitability of the builder's proposed changes or improvements without having to submit them to the Admiralty. This was, of course, the only practical method in a time of very slow communications. Thus, the Admiralty often had no accurate plan of a new ship during construction unless for some reason, such as a controversy between builder and Admiralty superintendent about size, arrangement, or hull form, it was decided that an exact plan should be prepared. However, it was obvious that a plan of all important ships was highly desirable. As a result, when a new ship was completed, the Admiralty often had the ship docked and measured and a correct and well-detailed plan made. This was particularly common when the introduction of copper sheathing, after 1761 in the Royal Navy, made estimates of the cost of this rather expensive metal important. Accurate hull form was required to make such estimates, and drawings were made of nearly all new ships of any importance when built or captured. These plans also show, in many instances, the later alterations in fitting, mast positions, or other details, made after the ship came into the hands of the British Navy.

Usually the "design plan" showed very little detail, and even the stern, or transom, elevation was omitted. The plan made from a ship, however, was usually well detailed, showing much of the carving and outboard detail and, sometimes, very complete deck arrangements superimposed on the outboard elevation. It is usually possible, therefore, to distinguish the contract design from the plan of the ship as built, when both are found. As has been said, the two plans did not exist in all cases. The colonial-built ships are most unsatisfactory in this respect, for with one exception either no plans exist at all or they have not yet been found and identified. It will be seen that the "establishment" cannot be a very satisfactory guide as to shape or appearance of these vessels. The Admiralty practice of the time also made the "establishment" quite ineffective in producing ships sufficiently alike for standardization of fittings while, on the other hand, it prevented a builder from having so free a hand that he would dare to attempt any great innovation in model or proportions, or even in increased dimensions, beyond minor degree, as has been stated earlier.

The question of whether plans or models were used in colonial contracts can be answered only so far as existing records indicate. Plans or "draughts" are occasionally mentioned in the few surviving ship contracts; models are almost never referred to. However, the existence of half-models of Admiralty ships built as early as 1714–19 show that such models were sometimes used. These early half-models were usually made by the use of "moulds"—pieces cut like half a frame, or a cross section, of a hull, mounted at intervals of every three or four frame spaces on a board cut to the profile of the ship and then ribbanded with wooden strips to fair the moulds. Usually in those that have survived to the present time the models were wholly or partly planked in lieu of the ribbands. These early models are, in fact, the same in principle as the American "hawk-nest" half-model, used to design small craft as late as the first part of the present century. In respect to the Admiralty half-models of this description, however, the available evidence suggests that they were not used to design ships, but rather were made from plans to illustrate the effects of changes from the original design. It is possible that some of these models represent "return draughts" from builders, showing the ship they proposed to build and indicating the differences from the hull form and dimensions, or proportions, in the original "establishment." Contrary to a popular conception, half-models were not invented by any American and were not used in America before plans were employed in ship design. Models were often employed in conjunction with plans or "draughts," to show officials who could not read a plan just what the intended ship looked like. At times when plans were in general use, the poorly trained commercial ship designer, who was unable to make a drawing, undoubtedly made a hawk-nest half-model, working by "art and eye" in the same manner as a man making a new design of a ship on paper. This, however, was not considered "scientific" at a time when the hull sections were thought best formed by employing tangent arcs formed to a rule; so it was rarely, if ever, employed in the design of naval vessels. It must also be noted that it was considered easier to transfer the scale dimensions from a plan to the full-size drawing of the ship's frames on the mould-loft floor than it was to do this from a model, even at a far later date than the colonial period.

The use of plans or a model implies the use of a mould loft. The latter is either a platform or the floor of a building smooth enough to draw upon. The shapes of timbers in the ship's structure are drawn full size by transferring scaled dimensions at chosen ordinates in the plan or model to their full-sized counterparts on the mould loft so as to reproduce accurately to full size for the ship the miniature curves of hull shape shown in plan or model. The mould loft in American colonial shipyards will be discussed later. No shipbuilder could use either a half-model or a plan if he was not capable of using a mould loft. If he could work from a model, he could work from a plan. So in either case the existence of a plan or a model indicates that the builder of the ship was competent to understand either. Like many later sailing-ship designers, some early builders found it difficult to make good and attractive plans but could make a model and paint and decorate it like the proposed ship, and so they used these to sell their ideas to owners. Hence the possibility that some of the very old Admiralty half-models were used in lieu of "return draughts" to show a ship as proposed by the builder.

Another type of model much used by the Admiralty was a complete hull model, framed and partly planked, with carvings, deck layout, and exterior details. This type of model was often rigged, all work being done to accurate scale. Today these are known as "Admiralty models" as a class, and they are now, as when they were built, primarily decorative. Originally these models were used to show the statesmen and politicians what fine ships the Navy intended to build and were pictorial in exactly the same way and for the same purpose as the modern ship models which are today seen in many government and naval buildings in this country. They served little or no purpose in either design or construction of new ships beyond insuring, perhaps, that the government officials would be sufficiently impressed by the models to grant the money necessary for the new ships. Solid half-models were also made in early times, though they were less popular than the frame or "hawk-nest" model. The Admiralty block models, dating from about 1732, were made of a solid block of wood. The use of narrow plank the thickness of the spacing of the water lines in the block to permit an easy transfer of the hull shape to the mould loft does not appear until after the Revolution. This may be an American invention, but such a claim will require more support than existing American traditions and the known half-models now offer.

The colonial shipyard differed in no important respect from a contemporary yard in Europe. In the period before the Revolution the shipyards were without machinery; all work was done with hand tools. Even water-power sawmills appear to have been very rarely employed. Sawn timber and plank were got out by "saw gangs" of three or four men. Two of these worked a long ripsaw fitted with handles at each end which were set at right angles to the sides of the saw blade instead of vertically, as in the modern two-man crosscut saw used to fell trees. The logs were rolled over a pit, or onto a crude platform and, with one man below the log and one on it, the saw was worked by hand to get out plank, or curved timbers such as frames. The remaining members of the saw gang moved the timber to the pit or platform, or shifted timber and steadied it as the progress of sawing required. There was much waste of timber; four planks to a log was the rule. Much of the shaping of timbers, both plank and heavy structural members, was done with the broadax, a heavy hewing tool, and with the lipped adz—the latter cutting across the grain and the former in line with it. With these two hand tools a skilled man could do accurate and rapid work; in fact, these two tools are still used today in wooden shipbuilding. Other small hand tools were employed—common handsaws, axes, hatchets, hammers, mauls, mallets, augers, chisels, and gouges which were crude forerunners of the same tools today. Timber was moved about the yard and shipways by gangs of men, teams of oxen, and horses. Wheeled timber carriages were also used in which a large timber could be slung between two high wheels working on an arched axle. The latter was used to aid in lifting a log prior to slinging it by raising and lowering the tongue, which acted as a lever, with the axle at wheel-hubs as the fulcrum. Ships and boats were rarely built under cover, and often there was no building on the shipyard site itself, mould loft and tool shed or stable being on near-by property. The vessels were erected on timber ways, supported by sleepers laid on the ground or by piles. In a few yards the ways were supported by rough stone piers. Some yards had wharves in the yard area for use in finishing a ship after her launch, though until after the Revolution such refinements appear to have been rare in American yards, at least outside the larger towns.

In America the location of shipyards was governed more by the availability

Courtesy Kensington Science Museum

PLATE I. (*Top*) *Model of a British 24-gun ship, 9-pdrs., of 1730–45. She measured 113' on the gun deck, 93' on the keel, 32' beam, 11' depth of hold, and 511 tons. (Center and bottom) Sheer draughts of two British 24-gun ships of 1741–45,* GARLAND *and* MERMAID.

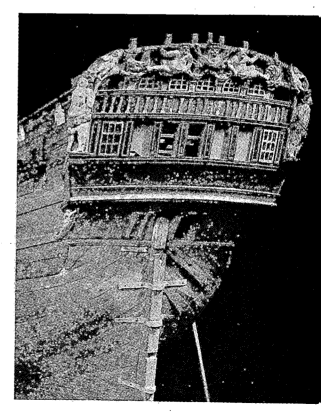

PLATE II. Model of the 44-gun ship AMERICA, 1749, in the Athenaeum, Portsmouth, New Hampshire.
Courtesy Peabody Museum, Salem, Mass.

of timber than by depth of water or by other favorable building conditions. The shipbuilding towns were usually those near a good supply of timber or timber-exporting ports. A good supply of skilled labor was required because transportation was slow, and it was not wholly uncommon for a shipyard to have facilities to house labor, or at least the more skilled portion of it. Large settlements, like Boston, Portsmouth, and New York, depended largely on water transport of timber to supply their shipyards. All of the colonies on the seaboard had shipyards; those yards in the larger settlements usually had the most skillful workers, just as in more recent times, but the country yards were the least expensive.

The art of lofting ships—drawing their shape and structural members in full size, to get out the frames and bent timber to agree with a plan or model— must have developed as soon as plans or models were employed. Little has been written about this part of shipbuilding, even in comparatively recent times. Like the drawing of plans, it has been a "mystery" of the art of shipbuilding, not only in colonial times but long after. The exact date of the introduction of lofting into America is unknown, though probably the mould loft was used by some of the shipwrights brought to America in the early seventeenth century. Lofting practice in America before the Revolution—in fact, before 1800 —was rather crude, and some parts of the ship—the stern, for example—were not laid out full size prior to setting up. The stern was usually built "by eye" except that the rake was taken from plan or model. As a result, the appearance of ships built to the same plan varied a good deal and ships did not always conform closely to the design in shape or dimensions. Accuracy was a matter of training and skill; the government-trained shipwrights were usually far more competent loftsmen than those trained in commercial yards, because the difficulties inherent in naval construction required greater care and accuracy in the preliminary steps of building. By 1700 the methods of lofting the frames, stem, and sternposts and laying off the decorative parts of the ship had been pretty well established. The method now employed of obtaining bevels does not appear to have been known, as the use of the ax and adz and the lack of power saws made it impractical to bevel frames before they were set up in place on the keel. Lofting of the stern and other difficult parts of the hull was developed in England about 1760 and in America about thirty-six years later.

The colonial shipbuilding industry suffered from many troubles. The lack of money in most colonies naturally limited shipbuilding orders and made employment rather uncertain. Metal for fastenings, sailcloth, rope, caulking material, and paint were commonly scarce and expensive. The cost of preparing the timber for ship construction was relatively great, and this usually prevented a builder from keeping on hand a stock of timber that would be seasoned when required. In addition to this, it took a great many years for the colonists to become acquainted with the shipbuilding properties of American timbers, most of which had not been known or used in Europe. In fact, the question of the properties of ship timber remained a matter of violent controversy in America until comparatively recent times, and even now there is not universal agreement. As a result, much timber went into colonial-built ships that rotted very fast, either because it was too green, or because an unsuitable species had been used. However, in spite of the difficulties, the colonial yards were capable of turning out cheap and strong vessels.

Very little metalwork was used in colonial-built vessels; this was also true of most European vessels of the period. All hull fastenings, so far as possible, were wooden pegs, or treenails, driven into holes bored for the purpose and with the ends wedged. Light construction was secured by handmade wrought-iron nails and spikes. Bolts were commonly set up by "upsetting" or riveting, rather than by threaded stock and nuts, and there was very little ironwork used in spars and rigging; chain was rarely seen. The armament of a ship and her anchors employed more metal than her whole structure. Because of the cost of large metal tools, there were few clamps, or jacks, used in building a vessel; her plank was shored, wedged, and pulled into place by tackles and ingenuity.

In spite of having to saw out plank, hew timber to shape, and bore for all fastenings by hand, and also to plank without proper clamps, the colonial shipwrights could turn out sizable vessels in a remarkably short time. This was accomplished not because the vessels were very simple or easy to build, but because a lifetime of use made the colonial adept in the handling of all hand tools and ingenious in overcoming apparent difficulties. Ships were actually built in the woods when necessity arose and drawn to water over the snow by oxen. Improvisation was always a necessity in colonial shipbuilding.

The colonial shipwright was usually a carpenter, caulker, joiner, and painter —in fact, a jack of all the trades necessary to build the hull of a ship. Sailors could rig a ship and make sails, but the shipwright had to make the masts and bowsprit, build spars and tops, and even make blocks. Crude manually operated wooden lathes were used to turn out stanchions and other turned work, and there was usually a wood carver in the community who could fashion figureheads and outside joinerwork or carvings. Many of the men employed in these early American yards could build a boat, a ship, a house, or a barn, make furniture, and repair a wagon. Many of these men were very skillful, and they worked long hours, for a day's work was from sunrise to sunset, six days a week, with few holidays. There were no steady jobs to give security in the colonies. So valuable were shipwrights in colonial times that they were exempt from militia duty or naval impress.

The competence of the colonial American shipbuilder in the construction of fast vessels has been mentioned. This grew out of his need for such craft when his traders were harassed by the national enemies created by numerous wars, by pirates, and, not least, by the laws, regulations, and customs duties at home. Smuggling was common, and there were opportunities for other illegal activities in commerce for which a fast vessel was much better than insurance, or even armament. Hence the American rapidly developed the functions of design that produced both speed and weatherliness in most sizes of vessels. It is probable that many of his ideas were based on the fast ships of the seventeenth century. He apparently took over bodily the model of the early "Jamaica sloop," later called the "Bermuda sloop," as a basis for the fast American schooner. The search for speed in some sailing vessels was almost as acute in pre-Revolutionary years as it was in the early nineteenth century; in both periods the emphasis in America was on small, fast vessels.

Though there were many different rigs used in European sailing vessels in the colonial period, Americans seem to have employed the ship, brigantine, schooner, snow, and sloop rigs almost exclusively after 1700. A few ketches were built, and there were some odd rigs used in small craft—lateen, sprit, and leg-of-mutton. One-masted square-rigged small craft were in use on lakes and rivers. Except for the schooner, however, there is no evidence that these rigs differed in any important respect from their European counterparts. While there has been a traditional claim that an American invented the schooner in 1713, in the light of existing evidence this is no longer worthy of serious consideration. The Americans, however, may justly claim to have developed the rig from that of small boats to that of large vessels in the eighteenth century; by the mid-century they had become almost the sole exponents of this rig in seagoing craft.

Since no plans have been found that represent a colonial-built vessel of earlier than about 1745, a plan of an English man-of-war of 1732 is presented to show the quality of ship design of the time and to illustrate the methods of drawing then in vogue in the Royal Navy. This plan is for a brigantine or snow, classed as a "sloop" and ordered to be built at Deptford, England, May 5, 1732. The drawing shows a long, low vessel well fitted to carry armament such as was then in use, and capable of good speed under sail and oars. It is evident that some sacrifice in weatherliness has been made in her design to obtain shoal draft and ability to row. Two oar ports between each pair of gun ports gave her sixteen sweeps on a side; with two or three men to each sweep she could be swept along at about three knots in a calm. There can be little doubt that this vessel would sail quite well, for her lines, though perhaps full by modern standards of yacht design, are as good as those of many sailing commercial vessels of a century or more later. The name of this sloop of war is believed to be *Cruizer*, for this vessel was built at Deptford in the year shown on the plan, and she was of the dimensions given (Figure 1).

The naval "sloops" had appeared in the Royal Navy as armed small craft in the last half of the seventeenth century. They were probably sloop-rigged with one mast. However, by 1725 "sloops" in the Navy were vessels with the guns on one deck without regard to rig. The vessels thus rated, however, were either one- or two-masted, and carried from 8 to 18 guns. Like the other rates of the period, the sloop classification changed from time to time; by the last quarter of the century a "sloop of war" came to mean a vessel commanded by an officer one grade below a captain in the Navy. Ship-rigged sloops of war did not become common until about the end of the American Revolution.

It will be seen that the *Cruizer* was rather well decorated with carving, though on a much reduced scale as compared with earlier vessels. She appears more modern than one would expect because of her unbroken sheer and low freeboard. The bow, though decorated with an ornate carving, is simple and light in structure. In the completed vessel there would be a light wooden or iron brace from figurehead to the bracket below the cathead on each side, at about the level of the moulding at the underside of the carvings along the bulwarks. The stern is that known as "lute" or "pink," something like that later used in the New England "pinky" fishing schooners. The lute stern, though having the appearance of a pink stern, was different in construction, and its underside was planked in, rather than left open as in the pinky. This type of stern was strong and rather simple in construction and, between 1714 and 1745, was rather popular in the smaller men-of-war of the Royal Navy. The deck arrangement in general was very practical. The deck was flush in the way of the eight gun ports a side, but at bow and stern the deck was raised to make a stern cabin and short forecastle. In neither case does the raised deck reach the rail

Figure 1. Draught of the "sloop" CRUIZER, 1732, showing method of drawing the design of a ship in the colonial period.

top. Not only did these decks give the space below them somewhat more head-room, but they also gave a commanding position from which to steer the vessel and made the deep bulwarks less of a handicap forward in handling the anchor and its gear.

In model and arrangement the *Cruizer* represents nothing very unusual in her time. Some of these "sloops" had raised quarterdecks and low breaks fore and aft in the sheer, as seen in the other examples, but the day of the towering fore and after "castles" was long past. There were hulls that were sharper than *Cruizer*'s, as well as many that were much fuller. The proportion of depth and beam to length shown in the plan was not rigidly adhered to in all "sloops" built in the same period, as will be seen. It is to be noted, too, that the "establishment" appears to have been quite ineffective in standardizing designs in the "sloop" class. Men-of-war in this category in the Royal Navy after 1732 were usually brigantine, snow, or ketch rigged, the snow being apparently the most common rig in this class. By this time the one-masted vessel had become rare among the combat vessels of the Royal Navy, and it did not reappear until the cutter was introduced about 1760.

The method used to project the hull shape of the *Cruizer* shows the progress that had been made in fairing the lines of a ship in a plan by 1732. The principles involved are not entirely dissimilar to the "diagonal" method, which some small-craft designers still use. This is exactly the same principle that was used in the "hawk-nest" half-model. The sections of the hull having been sketched, they were faired, to make certain that plank could be bent over them, by "diagonal" lines in the plan and by battens or ribbands of wood in a model, the latter being very narrow and thin so as to avoid breaking in the rather sharp curves caused by the full ends of the hull. The "diagonals," being so much like battens or ribbands in principle, were discovered to be a simple way of fairing the lines of a ship in the drawing or in the mould loft, and also gave points of measurement for lofting.

In order to understand the process of drawing the hull form, it is necessary to know a little about the principles involved in both the half-model and the drawing of the "lines." The latter term has long been the common shipbuilding term for the drawing that shows the shape of a hull. A half-model and a drawing of the "lines" have much in common. Both represent but one-half of the ship; since both sides of the hull athwartships are alike, there is no need to make more than one-half in a model or a plan. The half-model gets its name from this feature.

The plan and model, then, show one side of the ship; in the model the profile, plan, and cross sections are combined in one block or structure, but this is not practical in a drawing, because of the confusion of lines that would result. Early attempts to delineate a ship's form on paper having shown this to be true, the designers tried to separate the three elevations of the plan. The result was three distinct views of the hull that together represented everything obtained in a half-model—the profile, plan view, and cross sections. On the profile, or side elevation, the outboard appearance could be designed, the carving could be shown, and all the data necessary to locate the masts, gunports, and structural members, and the shape of bow and stern, rudder, and sheer (top of rail) could be included. The plan or elevation below the profile, in the *Cruizer*'s plan, is the "half-breadth" plan, and shows a view from above the half-model as though the latter were so transparent that marks on the bottom of the model could be seen. This elevation shows the shape of the rail and deck as viewed from above, as well as other curved lines necessary to prove that the cross sections are in such relation to one another that planking can be bent around them. The plan that shows the cross sections, placed to one side of the profile elevation as a rule, is known as the "body plan." It shows, first, the shape of the cross sections of the hull located at certain chosen frames; next, the location of the lines used to "fair" the hull (the equivalent of the strips of wood or ribbands on the hawk-nest half-model); and finally the location of measurements (necessary to project most curved lines to be shown in either profile or half-breadth plans) that are plotted on the cross sections in the body plan, even though they may not be represented by lines there as in the example. It may be said here that the location of such measuring lines is usually shown in the body plan and such lines became increasingly numerous in the eighteenth century.

The various curved lines in the plan of a ship's hull form may be best understood by imagining a half-model made of some easily cut material—wax, for instance. This model is a solid block of wax that is shaped exactly like half the ship on either side of the center line and cut vertically along the longitudinal center line so that the back of the model is the exact shape of the hull profile. Perhaps it will be more easily understood if it is assumed that there are to be three identical half-models. One of these half-models, then, is laid on the paper to correspond to the profile or side elevation of the ship as in the plan of the *Cruizer*. This part of the drawing is often called the "sheer plan." By custom, the three elevations in the drawing of a ship's form are known as plans, rather than as elevations, in other types of drawing the "plan" being only that view taken from above the object drawn. On the model that now represents the "sheer plan," the locations of various lines are marked on the model, at the designer's pleasure or best judgment. First he must have the location of the cross sections so that they may be reproduced at exactly the same place in the full-size ship. Since no two sections will be exactly alike, this is important. To save time he will decide to locate the cross sections on various selected frames so that these can be reproduced in the mould loft and act as control sections that will govern the shapes of all the others required. Depending upon the size of the ship, he may take from two to four, or even more, frame spaces as the interval between his control sections.

In the *Cruizer* the designer has chosen to use every third frame, measured from the one that is the largest, or the "midsection." The location of this, in the model, is readily determined, but when the designer is drawing a plan without reference to an existing model he locates this section according to his judgment, experience, and theory of design, just as the man who made a model had to do. Now, from this section, marked 🟠 on the plan, he lays off every third frame, and numbers them accordingly, using numbers for the stations abaft the midsection. Because of the confusion that would otherwise arise, the designer used letters to designate the stations selected in the forebody, the hull forward of the midsection. In later times the stations were numbered, beginning at either end of the hull, but the method shown in the plan of the *Cruizer* was common throughout most of the sailing-ship era. The location of the stations having been laid off, the model is marked with lines vertical to the keel to show these frames. If the stations are widely spaced it will be desirable to have additional control frames at bow and stern, where the curves change shape rapidly, to insure that the mould loft will accurately reproduce the shape of hull intended by the designer. Therefore, at bow and stern, additional frames are shown—in the example, *N* in the forebody and *21* in the afterbody. It will be seen that *N* is one frame space from *M* and *21* is two frame spaces from *19*. This is entirely a matter of judgment, and there was no rule that governed the location of these extra stations or control frames, other than that they fall on a frame and be spaced to insure accuracy in the mould loft.

The model may now be marked with the position of the water line, which theoretically should be determined by the weight of the ship and her displacement. These matters being impossible to determine accurately before the ship was designed, the draftsman located the water line at a draft that was specified in the order for the ship, or according to his judgment. This seems a great difficulty at first glance, but practically this was easy, for in a sailing man-of-war there would have to be ballast, and the amount of this might be adjusted somewhat to give the desired draft. However, unlike the modern racing yacht, the exact draft was of little importance in a sailing man-of-war, for it could vary as much as a number of feet between light draft, when the vessel was not loaded, and the load draft, when the vessel was ready for sea. Obviously the latter would actually change constantly as her stores, water, provisions, and ammunition were consumed. It was only necessary, then, for the designer to conform in general to a draft requirement, if the latter was to be limited. The chosen water line might be parallel to the bottom of the keel or not, as the designer thought best. Usually the sailing water line was located on the completed ship so that the depth from the water line to the bottom of the keel was slightly greater aft than at the bow; this is called "drag." In the *Cruizer* the designer has attempted to approximate the sailing water line and has shown the "drag." This line having been marked on the model, other water lines (or perhaps a more easily understood term would be "level lines") are marked on the model. In the example these are parallel to the keel and arbitrarily spaced at, say, two feet. This is wholly arbitrary, and the spacing is decided on the basis of accuracy in the mould loft, just as the spacing of control frames was. Sometimes the level lines were made parallel to the sailing water line instead of to the keel; here again it was merely a matter of individual preference on the part of the designer.

If the model were now inspected it would be seen that the location of two types of cross sections now exist. The vertical marks will indicate where the vertical and transverse sections may be taken, while the water line and the additional level lines indicate the logical position of some horizontal and longitudinal sections. In order to lay these off a base line has to be located.

In order to simplify his work both the model maker and the draftsman represented the hull form as though the outside planking on the finished ship were not in place. The reason for this is obvious, for they were seeking, primarily, to establish the shape of the frames, which in turn fixed the form of the hull of the completed ship. Now, since the depth of the keel was usually rather great, both for strength and to protect the bottom of the hull in case of running on shore or hitting a rock, and since it was not always straight in profile, greater accuracy by the shipwrights would be insured if the chosen base line were close to the actual frame structure. As a result, the custom was established of placing the base line at the inner "rabbet" along the keel; this was the line of the joint between the inside of the planking and the side of the keel. To make the vessel watertight here, it was thought necessary to groove the sides of the keel in a shallow V to take the edge of the lowest plank of the bottom. This was known as the "rabbet," the innermost edge of the triangular groove being called the "inner rabbet." Actually in most vessels of the period this was usually the top of one of the timbers making up the keel. This line, then, was the base line. The level lines were often spaced from it by measurement, and the stations of the control frames stood perpendicular to it. In a few vessels the bottom of the keel was not parallel to the base line but had greater depth at one end, though this is not the case in the example.

Any other information that would determine the height of any part of the ship's structure could be marked on the "sheer plan" or, as in this case, the model representing it. The varying heights of the deck, for example, could be represented by a line and the position of mouldings to decorate the hull; the gun ports and oar port locations, channels, and any other detail thought desirable could be shown.

Leaving this model for the moment, a duplicate is taken and marked with the vertical cross sections shown in the one used to represent the "sheer plan." The model is now cut along each of these vertical lines. The cut faces of each section can be traced on the paper to represent the "body plan" by using common base and center lines when drawing each face of the sections of the model. The sections forward of the midsection are grouped on one side of the center line; those abaft the midsection are on the opposite side. The midsection is drawn twice, once on each side of the center line.

The model may now be glued together and recut on new lines. These are diagonal to the center line as represented by similar lines on the body plan of the *Cruizer*. These diagonal lines intersect on the center line of the body plan and join the midsection at points that correspond on each side, thus making every diagonal line correspond in angle to the center line on each side. If the glued model is cut along these lines, we would have longitudinal sections whose curved edges each represent the shape of these lines as they pass around the hull.

The third model may now be marked with the water line and the level lines established on the model representing the profile, or sheer, plan. The deck profile may also be established. In colonial days another line was used in addition—the "height of breadth" line used to determine section shape in the mould loft. To obtain this, refer to the body plan and mark on each section the point that appears to have the greatest beam—or, to put it differently, the point that is farthest from the section's center line. These points were transferred to the corresponding frames or stations on the sheer-plan model and a curve struck through them. If there is no one point of greatest beam in a section, the upper and lower limits of the greatest beam in every section are established and transferred. This is the case in the *Cruizer*, and it will be noted that there are two dotted lines on the profile, one a little below the deck line, and one meeting the water line amidships. These represent the "height of breadth." In some drawings the half breadth of the deck is drawn on the "half-breadth plan," but in colonial times this was rare in small craft and the "height of breadth" line was used instead, as in *Cruizer*.

Next, the top of the third model is laid off, from a center line below and parallel to the base line of the sheer-plan model. The new view is the "half-breadth plan" of the top of the rail or sheer. Owing to the profile curve this cannot be traced but must be drawn from measurements at each station or control frame. The model is now cut along the water line and the level lines; each may be traced in outline on the "half-breadth plan" as in the sections—except the water line, which must be laid off by measurements, as in the rail, because it is not parallel to the base and must be foreshortened. The stations must be the lines in the sheer, projected downward. The new lines are represented in the *Cruizer* by solid lines in the "half-breadth plan."

The second model may again be used. It will be recalled that it was cut into diagonal sections longitudinally. The outline of each of these sections may be traced on the "half-breadth plan" so that the plane used is the true or cut face of each and the straight edges correspond with the center line, as in the *Cruizer*'s plan. Next, one of the models may be cut along either of the "height of breadth" lines (both are the same when projected, since their half breadths are identical, and both must be foreshortened in drawing) and lay this off as in the rail or sheer half breadth. The deck might be projected in the same manner, if it were to be shown.

There is one more line in the sheer plan of the *Cruizer* to be explained. This line starts well up at the bow and curves downward under the midsection almost to the base, then passes upward to the stern above the water line. This was called the "cutting down" line and is used in framing the vessel. It represents the tops of the frame timbers, where they cross the keel. This is really an arbitrary line, since it is located by sketching typical frame elevations to scale and laying off the line from these. This line serves no purpose in hull form and is for construction purposes only. Drawings used later on will show other lines, but these will be explained in the references to these plates.

It will be seen from this description that the plan reduces a model to a series of intersecting planes, or cross and longitudinal sections, so that measurements can be more readily taken to reproduce the sections and profile full size on the mould-loft floor. Of course, the skill to determine what would be the best shapes for the profile, sections, water line, level lines, and diagonals, and how to bring them into a predetermined relationship, requires education, experience, and imagination. The methods by which this skill is obtained are described in detail in books on marine design and are outside the scope of this discussion; we are concerned here only with the explanation of the meanings of the various parts of a ship's plan.

The colonial builder was expected to build a ship from this one plan together with instructions or specifications. A deck plan might be furnished to show how the vessel was to be arranged and also the size and position of hatches or any other deck furniture. Sometimes there were plans or sketches of lower decks (or platforms) on which cabins and other below-deck spaces were shown. It was by no means unusual, however, for the builder to have the "draught," like the plan of the *Cruizer*, and nothing else except written or verbal directions as to deck arrangements. No spar or rigging plan was furnished, but merely a set of spar and mast dimensions based on the "establishment," or on a similar vessel, to serve merely as a guide to the sparmaker and builder. Few other plans were made for construction, though there are in existence a number of contemporary drawings that show comparisons between ships, or the parts of certain ships, that were drawn up for discussion by technicians but which were not sent to a builder.

Calculations of the factors in ship design were employed in colonial times. In the late seventeenth century a number of great mathematicians tried to express the elements of ship design in formulae. It was soon learned that it was possible to calculate the weight of a ship from her plan, supposing that she was brought to any water line that could be marked on a correct drawing of the hull form. Estimates of the weight of the structure of a ship, with the weights of everything that was placed aboard, were also made and were used extensively in naval ship design. Efforts were made to explore stability, rolling, resistance, weatherliness, and steering qualities of ships, with particular emphasis on the mathematical approach to these subjects. In addition, a great deal of effort was directed to the mechanical methods of forming the curves

37

Figure 2. Draught of the HAZARD, *sloop of war, 1744, brigantine- or snow-rigged, showing lines used in fairing the hull referred to in the text.*

that make up the lines of ships. Sections formed by tangent arcs and straight lines were proposed and widely accepted. Mathematically constructed diagonals were investigated, and the great Swedish naval architect, Chapman, proposed the use of a predetermined diagonal to which a ship's hull should conform in order to be fast. While none of these theories have survived in modern practice, they initiated the trend toward the use of mathematical expressions of the functions in naval architecture that has existed since. The use of mathematics in design gradually assumed such importance that it was considered essential in the education of naval architects, even to the exclusion of the "art" of making plans and forming hulls. Not only did the use of mathematical terms serve to impress the student and layman with the "science" of naval architecture, the equivalent of the "mysteries of the art" of the seventeenth and eighteenth centuries; these terms also gave a satisfactory feeling of accurate measurement of factors that could otherwise be only vaguely defined. However, by the end of the nineteenth century it was apparent that mathematics would not serve to insure good design without a thorough knowledge of hull-form characteristics. Hence the modern emphasis on model testing. The use of the test model to discover the probable performance of a design prior to building was first attempted in a crude experiment by an Englishman, Beaufoy, in the last decade of the eighteenth century. It might be said with some truth that neither mathematics nor the test model has yet insured good design, for the failure of modern ships to operate satisfactorily is by no means unknown.

The colonial shipbuilder just previous to the Revolution does not appear to have engaged in mathematical investigations extensive enough to have been recorded; he was concerned with what were perhaps the more practical trends of the period. During the seventy years preceding the Revolution, the practical developments of ship design were in a general increase in the dimensions of ships, sharper models, lower freeboard, and fewer encumbrances of unnecessary decoration and topworks than had previously been fashionable. Rigging became less cumbersome and much lighter in these years. The rise in importance of such types of fast seagoing small craft as the English cutter, the French lugger, and the American schooner in this period were perhaps the outstanding accomplishments of ship designers, developed by trial-and-error methods without the aid, apparently, of mathematical investigations.

Except for the fast schooner, the Americans cannot be credited with any original or unusual improvement in ship design prior to the Revolution. Their large privateers in the colonial period were undoubtedly sharp and fast but

were very little different in model from their British sisters. Some of these vessels are referred to as "frigates." Lest this lead to an assumption that such
privateers were the same as men-of-war of this class, it must be explained that
"frigate" was used to distinguish a type of merchant ship in this period, as
well as a special type of man-of-war. The "frigate-built" merchantman had
one flush deck and a raised quarterdeck and forecastle; in this respect the merchant "frigate" had exactly the same deck arrangement that marked her man-
of-war sister. This build, however, did not imply that the merchant "frigate"
or the privateer with this deck arrangement was designed to meet the man-of-
war requirements described earlier. The merchant frigate was still primarily
a carrier; the privateer was a fast ship first and a combat ship second. In colonial
times merchant-ship models were described by many names—"frigate," "hag-
boat," "pink," "bark," "cat," "flyboat," and "galley"—that referred to build
or to the shape of the stern rather than to rig or even to the model of hull. Regardless of the original meaning of these names, they had by 1760 assumed
technical meanings that were employed by shipbuilders to distinguish rather
trifling variations in construction, arrangement, stern design, and general model.
A "bark," "cat," or "frigate" might be small or large and rigged as a ship, snow,
sloop, brigantine, or schooner. This is well shown in *Architecturia Navalis
Mercatoria*, a book of ship plans by the great Swedish naval architect, Frederick
Hennik Af Chapman. This book was published in 1768 but represented vessels
of from twenty to forty years earlier and showed the numerous types of
merchant-ship builds, including "frigates," and also privateers and men-of-war.

To supplement the drawing of the *Cruizer*, the plans of two more sloops of
war of the middle portion of the eighteenth century are shown, the brigantine
or snow *Hazard* (Figure 2), built in 1744, and the ketch *Speedwell* (Figure 3),
built eight years later. The plan of the *Hazard* has been used to identify some
of the lines mentioned when describing the projections in the plan of the
Cruizer. These plans, traced from the original drawings, repeat many of the
projections employed in the drawing of the *Cruizer*, but show important details of the arrangement of the decks. The plan of the *Speedwell* indicates
that the fairing of her lines was done by some method employing tangent arcs
in the sections; the line of radii is shown in her half breadth and indicated on
the sections. Compared to the *Cruizer*, these vessels are fuller and somewhat
more burdensome. Plans similar to these were without doubt prepared by
American shipbuilders for many colonial vessels prior to the Revolution.

The purpose of the plan or model was to permit the design of a hull on a small convenient scale so that the form could be readily seen and judged. However, in order to make the hull design of use, some regard had to be given to the means by which the small-scale hull form was to be reproduced in the full-size ship. For obvious reasons the plan was more convenient in the transfer of measurements from small scale to full size; also the drawing could be readily copied with accuracy equal to that of the original; this was not the case with models. These practical factors, in addition to those of supposedly "scientific" nature, such as mechanical design of sections, gradually brought about the ascendancy of the plan over the half-model in naval design throughout the sailing-ship period. With this emphasis on the art, it is not surprising to find the naval draftsmen of the eighteenth century capable of producing plans of great accuracy and beauty of workmanship. In fact, the marine draftsman of the eighteenth century was capable of producing drawings of greater beauty than have since been seen in this field.

It is fortunate that the state of colonial shipbuilding before the Revolution can be judged by evidence more concrete than mere opinion and a comparison of the known facts of British naval construction with the probabilities of early American naval shipbuilding. The existence of plans of the 24-gun ship *Boston*, built by Ben Hallowell at Boston, Massachusetts, between 1747 and 1748, gives an opportunity to support many of the statements that have been made concerning the quality of colonial shipbuilding. If the plans of the earlier ships were available, more complete evidence would be possible, but no plans of the *Falkland* or the *Bedford* have yet been discovered.

The 24-gun ships were the only men-of-war in the Royal Navy of "frigate build" in the first half of the eighteenth century, there being no class between the two-decked 40- or 44-gun ships and the 24's. The 30-gun ships proposed in the "establishments" were not built in this rate but were completed as small 40-gun ships, armed on two decks, and for this reason they were not in the "frigate" class as armed and built. The "frigate" has already been referred to in regard to merchant ships. By 1745 the term had come to describe not only a build of vessel, but, in the naval service, a ship with one deck fully armed, an armed quarterdeck, and an unarmed forecastle deck. The latter was gradually armed in the last quarter of the century. The early development of the "frigate" is a matter of European shipbuilding history, rather than American. Beginning as a name of a small galley type, the term "frigate" appears to have come to mean a fast ship, and finally a ship of a specified build and armament in naval services. The earlier colonial-built naval ships were two-decked and

PLATE III. Humphreys' model for the projected 74-gun ship of the Revolution, in Independence Hall, Philadelphia.

Figure 3. Draught of the SPEEDWELL, *sloop, 1752, ketch-rigged. Plan shows the use of radii in fairing the lines.*

41

carried 40 or more guns, so the *Boston* appears to have been the first "frigate" built in America for naval service. Whether or not she preceded merchant "frigates" cannot be stated, so the importance of her being the "first" of the type is open to some question.

The plan of the *Boston*, shown in Figure 4, requires little technical explanation. It has been redrawn in the modern manner employing sections, water line, and level lines, as explained in the case of the *Cruizer*. The diagonals are the same in projection, but the deck has been used instead of the "height of breadth" lines. The only other addition is the use of "buttock lines." These are longitudinal sections representing vertical planes through the hull parallel to the longitudinal center line; they were introduced into American plans in the last decade of the eighteenth century. Except for the buttocks and more numerous water or level lines, there has been no important change in the methods of drawing the form of a ship since the middle of the eighteenth century. The plan of the *Boston* shows the lines of the hull and the outboard appearance and also an inboard elevation which shows, in profile, the upper deck arrangements. No deck plan is shown, for none has yet been found.

The plan shows a well-formed hull, of large displacement, which should have sailed quite fast. It will be noted that she has sharp, rather V-shaped sections rather than the round, almost barrel-shaped sections of the *Hazard*. She has twelve ports on each side on the main deck and ports for three guns on each side on the quarterdeck, which would permit her carrying 30 guns if all her ports were filled. She probably actually carried 28 guns, for the *Boston* was almost the same length as a 28-gun frigate built in 1758. There was one port on the lower deck which was probably used as an entry or loading port rather than to mount a gun, though such ports appear to have had guns temporarily mounted in them in some of the 24's when in action. It will be seen here that the guns which a ship actually carried could easily exceed her "rate," a characteristic that marked sailing men-of-war from this time. On the quarterdeck, upright timbers are seen along the rail; these were the "stocks" of the swivel guns, which were small-bore cannon mounted on an oarlock-shaped pivot set in the head of each stock. The top of the stock was banded to prevent the timber from splitting with the force of the recoil. The swivels were never counted as "guns," and often the small carriage guns on the quarterdeck were also excluded. This allowed a satisfactory difference in the statement of the force of a ship when she won or lost a battle—each side quoting the actual number of guns in the enemy ship and the "rate" of their own.

43

Figure 4. Draught of the 24-gun ship BOSTON, 1748. The earliest plan yet found of an American-built ship.

The plan of the *Boston* is a good example of the fact that the sweep of the deck lines, fore and aft, was always much less than in the sheer and outside mouldings. This had existed as far back as Elizabethan times in sailing ships, as contemporary plans of drawings show, but is contrary to many artists' conceptions. The "beakhead bulkhead" is also to be seen in this ship. This was a heavy bulkhead across the bow of the ship, from the gun deck upward. The beakhead deck, or platform, was usually a little above the gun deck in small ships, and in many this part of the vessel's hull looked as if a small piece of the upper portion of her bow had been sawed out of her model, leaving a rectangular notch in her bow profile. The beakhead bulkhead had been an outgrowth of the galley hull. When the forecastle was added to the galley it was a rectangular structure, square across the fore end to allow a number of guns to be mounted there to fire directly ahead. This became a conventional design in later ships, and the platform outside the bulkhead in the bow was then used to handle sail and also for the toilet facilities of the crew. The space was made greater by extending the platform into the cutwater by gratings, placed inside the headrails. By 1740 the beakhead bulkheads were slowly going out of fashion in the small men-of-war. Nearly all sloops, like *Cruizer*, had been given a "round" bow—that is, one without the beakhead bulkhead. In the larger ships the beakhead bulkhead was often masked by being built in a shape like a cupid's bow in plan view, as seen in the *Boston*'s half-breadth plan, where it is shown in dotted lines representing the outside face of this structure. Also, the beakhead bulkheads became increasingly shallow and less prominent.

The arrangement of this ship was probably more or less standard in her class for the period. The hawse holes were on the lower deck, and a deep manger was made by a high bulkhead across the bows directly under the foremost gun port to prevent the lower deck from flooding when she plunged into a head sea (without her hawses being stopped with wooden plugs, as was done at sea in these vessels). Her fireplace, for cooking, was under the forecastle deck, abaft the foremast, and apparently this space was enclosed by a light bulkhead, part of which extended abaft the end of the forecastle deck. Probably the after part of this was permanently fixed, while the rest could be taken down in action. Abaft the mizzenmast, on the gun deck, there appear to have been light bulkheads across the ship to make cabins for the captain and perhaps one for the first lieutenant. The rest of the officers berthed aft on the lower deck, the crew berthing forward. Except for the guns abaft the mizzen and the wheel just forward of it, the quarterdeck was clear of obstructions and was used for handling the ship. The forecastle was also a working deck with two hatches, one for the fireplace chimney and one just forward of the mast.

There are two plans of the *Boston* in the Admiralty files. Both were obviously made after the ship was built. One plan shows a short quarterdeck, the other a long one with an alteration added that apparently carried her gangways forward at the same level as the quarterdeck. The latter plan is used to represent the ship here, for it can safely be assumed that this plan represented her in service.

That the plans of the *Boston* were made after she was built can be established by comparing them with the design plans of ships of her class and period—for example, those of the *Garland*, built in 1748, and the *Mermaid*, built in 1749. The latter design has a long quarterdeck and apparently belongs to the latest establishment, 1745, then in force. It seems reasonable to suppose that the *Boston* was built on the 1741 establishment and altered to fit the 1745 establishment. These design plans show very little detail compared to the *Boston* plans.

The *Boston* was about 5 feet longer than the *Garland*, but looked much like her in profile. She was much sharper in model and had far more deadrise. Compared to the *Mermaid*, the *Boston* is also longer by 3 feet and has an entirely different hull model. From this it would appear that her American builder had redesigned her, while adhering reasonably closely to the contract design. He could not have been more restricted in this matter than were the English contractors in naval ships constructed in private yards. As far as can be judged from the plans, the American builder turned out a vessel equal in appearance and finish to those of the English builders. This is some proof of the competence of a colonial yard in this class of construction and probably in design as well.

The 24-gun ships of the various "establishments" since 1719 had changed little. The earlier ships had their oar ports on the lower deck at the level of the sill of the single port on that deck and carried no carriage guns on the quarterdeck. These ships, in fact, anticipated the "quarterdecked sloops" of the end of the eighteenth century, except that the majority of the latter did not have a raised forecastle deck. The 24-gun ships were armed with long guns, nine- or twelve-pounders, with threes or sixes on the quarterdeck. All of these ships had much the same rig. The photograph (Plate 1) of a model of a 24 in the Science Museum, Kensington, England, illustrates the appearance of a ship of an earlier "establishment" than the *Boston*, but with the same rig.

The ship rig used in the *Boston* was little different from that used at the beginning of the century. She had long lower masts and fairly long topmasts on all three masts. Short topgallant masts were fidded on the fore and main masts only, the mizzen topmast having a long pole instead. The yards on all three masts were shorter than was later the fashion. The mizzen carried a lateen spanker yard; in earlier ships this carried the triangular lateen sail, but about 1748 the four-sided spanker sail came into use in the Royal Navy in the smaller classes. This new sail was set abaft the mizzenmast, the fore part of the lateen yard being barren. Gaff spankers had been introduced much earlier in the sloops and small vessels, but were not common on vessels of more than 20 guns until about the time of the American Revolution. The lateen yard survived, in some large men-of-war, until almost to the end of the century. Above the lateen yard were the mizzen square topsail and the topgallant sail.

In addition to the working sails set on the three yards on fore and main, and on the two above the spanker on the mizzen, naval ships carried a large number of light-weather sails when the occasion demanded. Two square sails could be set, one under the bowsprit and another under the jibboom. Royals could be hoisted above the fore, main, and mizzen topgallant sails; and in addition to four staysails set between the bowsprit and foremast, five could be set between main and fore, and four more between mizzen and main. In addition to all these, a topsail could be set above the spanker yard and studding sails could be rigged out on the spanker. All told, a ship could carry as many as thirty sails in very light winds. Studding sails came into general use in naval vessels shortly before the American Revolution, being employed on the yards of the fore and main masts. The four-sided spanker, when used on a lateen yard, was not secured to the masts with hoops; a hemp "horse" was used, fastened to the mizzen trestletrees and set up on deck, and to this the sail was secured with hanks, as in a staysail. This "horse" was also used in naval snows until about the middle of the eighteenth century. It was finally replaced with the trysail mast, which was stepped abaft and close to the lower mast, with its head secured in the lower trestletrees. This was an innovation apparently taken from merchant ships of this rig. It was desirable, in men-of-war, to have all yards rigged so that they could be quickly brought down on deck. For this reason the foreyard in schooners and the mainyard in cutters also employed a rope "horse," but in these rigs the "horse" was set up from the trestletrees to deck on the fore-side of the masts.

The cut of sails in 1750 differed somewhat from that used in both British and American men-of-war after the Revolution. The sails had great hoist in proportion to spread, in the lower courses and topsails particularly, and were not as "square," and did not have such spread, as they had about 1800. Flax sailcloth was used in the Royal Navy; the weave seems to have been rather loose. Because of the material used, the fore-and-aft sails did not stand very well.

The *Boston* had a rather short life, being broken up in February, 1752. It may be that this was because of the use of green timber in her construction, for the American-built men-of-war are said to have been unsatisfactory for this reason until after the Revolution.

The other ship built about the time of the *Boston* was a 44-gun ship armed on two decks and with a few light guns on the quarterdeck. She was built at Portsmouth, New Hampshire, by a builder whose name cannot be read in the Admiralty records with certainty; it appears to be N. Messervé.[1] Launched in 1749, this ship is listed by Charnock in his *History of Marine Architecture*, published in 1800, as the *Boston*. However, it appears from other lists that this is an error and that the name of the ship was *America*, which bears out the local traditions at Portsmouth. The *America* was 139' 1" on the lower deck and was about six feet longer than called for in the 1745 establishment for 44-gun ships, under which she was built; this again indicates that her American builder was allowed to take liberties with the contract design. No plan has been found of this ship, and it is probable that no "as-built" drawing was made. A model, now in the Portsmouth Athenaeum, is supposed to be of this ship and shows a vessel of this class, as can be seen in the photographs (Plate II). However, the question of how accurate the model is has never been settled.

The *America*, like the *Boston*, had a rather short life. In fact, the only American-built man-of-war in colonial times that appears to have lasted well was the *Falkland*, which was rebuilt in 1719–20. The American-built ships did not stand alone in respect to having short lives; the average life of ships in the Royal Navy during the colonial period was only about ten years. Only a few ships served more than this time without extensive repairs or rebuilding. It appears that insufficient attention was given to seasoning timber and to the ventilation of the ships. This matter became so serious in the Royal Navy

[1] Messervé was a prominent shipbuilder in New Hampshire, Lieutenant Colonel of Colonel Moore's regiment in the first siege of Louisbourg, 1744, and Colonel of a New Hampshire regiment the next year. Went to Crown Point under Abercrombie. Went with Amherst to the second siege of Louisbourg, as Colonel, in charge of 200 ship carpenters. Messervé died there, as did his son, in 1758, of smallpox. Many of the colonial shipbuilders were senior officers in the militia and some held commissions in regular regiments.

that both the causes of rot and the methods of ventilation received extensive study late in the eighteenth century.

No study of colonial shipbuilding in America is complete without reference to the schooners. In this type, the Americans had developed a small seagoing cruiser which was of great usefulness to the naval services, for it was usually weatherly and fast. Unlike the cutter, the schooner when built to large dimensions did not become difficult to handle. In the years immediately preceding the Revolution, schooners had become numerous in American waters, being employed in fishing, in coasting, and particularly in the illegal trades. British naval officers had observed the qualities of these vessels, and a number were built and purchased for naval service just before the Revolution. Most of these schooners were small, carrying four to ten guns, and were intended to be used in the suppression of smuggling on the American coast. The sharp-model schooner had developed in America and was built extensively on the shores of Chesapeake Bay and at New York. In Massachusetts many of the fishermen were on the sharp model. Contemporary newspaper accounts show that during the French and Indian War of 1754–63 a number of fishing schooners captured by the French were operating on the New England coast as cruisers. These schooners were noted as being good sailers, and some were said to be exceptionally fast.

As an example of a schooner of the period built for naval service, the *Marble Head*, built at New York in July, 1767, will serve. This vessel was designed by an American and represents many of the elements of design that later distinguished the noted American "clipper" schooners. This particular schooner was much like the sharp fishing schooners owned in Marblehead, Massachusetts, at the time, if one may judge by the rare descriptions of the latter vessels. The choice of name strengthens such an inference. The drawing of the *Marble Head*, shown in Figure 5, represents a hull capable of sailing well, yet burdensome enough to carry a rather heavy armament for her size. Her model was very closely related to that of the contemporary and noted Bermuda sloop, as may be seen by comparing the *Marble Head*'s drawing with that of the Bermuda sloop from Chapman's book, shown in Figure 6. These sloops are known to have been widely copied in America before the Revolution, and in contemporary advertisements schooners were stated to have been built on their model.

The end of the war with France, in 1763, and the unrest in the years that preceded the beginning of the Revolution, put a stop to the construction of British men-of-war in any of the colonies except for the building of small vessels on the lakes and the schooners for suppression of American smuggling. We are left without definite knowledge of the connection between naval shipbuilding in the colonies in the thirty years preceding the Revolution and that for the

Figure 5. Draught of an American schooner, MARBLE HEAD, *1767, employed as a vessel of the Royal Navy. An early design of a fast-sailing schooner.*

Continental Navy, owing to the lack of records of the names and history of most of the designers of the American ships of the Revolution. However, the inferences that can be drawn, as will be shown later, indicate that the colonial period furnished the experience which developed the ships of the Continental Navy. The Americans had built regular men-of-war, and perhaps had designed some of them; they had developed and built the schooner, both as a fast class of vessel and as modified for a small man-of-war; they had armed and fitted ships for naval service within the colonies; they were abreast of the develop-

Approximate Sail Plan

Bermuda Sloop
from Chapman

Length between perpendiculars 60:9"
Beam Moulded .... 21:2"
Draught of Water .... 12:3"

Ten 4 pdr's (carriage guns) and
12 swivels

Figure 6. Draught of a Bermuda sloop after Chapman, showing the form of vessel
believed to be the parent-type of early American craft built for fast sailing.

50

ments in contemporary ship design in Europe; the colonies where the agitation for rebellion was greatest in the pre-Revolutionary years were those where the last large men-of-war were built. These added up to a background that might explain the American ability to design and build, in certain classes, some of the finest men-of-war in the world immediately after the Revolution began.

★ ★ ★ ★ ★ ★ ★ ★ ★

CHAPTER TWO

The Continental Navy

1775-1785

THE AMERICAN Revolution did not begin with dramatic suddenness; its coming was foretold by some twelve years of political unrest and rioting. This had been sufficient to permit the intelligent to decide that war was a possibility, if not a certainty, long before actual hostilities began. On the American side, however, little could be done to prepare for such an eventuality. There were garrisons in many colonial towns and cities, British men-of-war on the coasts, numerous revenue vessels and customs officers in the ports, as well as many loyalists among the population. Hence any very obvious preparations for rebellion could be readily prevented. Among the Americans there was at first no plan for organized rebellion against the Crown, and public support for this came into being slowly. In spite of warnings and the efforts of some colonial leaders, nothing was done, therefore, to prepare for war beyond arming the militia and collecting some munitions. Except for reinforcing some of the more important garrisons and adding to the revenue vessels, the British government also neglected to prepare for the approaching storm. Had the British ministers shown more competence and less indolence, they could have prevented the colonists from making any effective preparations whatever in the creation of equipment and accumulation of munitions.

Throughout the early part of 1775 open warfare rapidly developed, so that by early fall a colonial army was in the field and American privateers were at sea. Some civil organization had also taken place in the colonies; the delegates to the Continental Congress had been elected and the Congress was in session. Early in October the delegates had appointed a naval committee to buy and fit out vessels for service against the Crown. This committee at once became active and acquired with the funds at hand such vessels as were available and reasonably suited for the purpose. It is plain, however, that the Continental Congress was well aware that merchant vessels could serve for no more than an emergency fleet. While the committee was searching for suitable craft, procuring them, and getting down to work fitting out purchased merchantmen, the Rhode Island delegates began to draft an act to build regular men-of-war. The committee succeeded in obtaining two ships, six brigs or brigantines, three schooners, and five sloops. In addition, the colonial army under Washington obtained four schooners in Massachusetts which were sent to sea to seize munitions needed by the army besieging Boston. Arnold and other Army officers had captured a sloop and two schooners on Lake Champlain. The vessels fitted out by Washington were returned to their owners when their mission was completed, and the Lake Champlain craft could be employed only on the lake. In addition to the vessels procured by the congressional committee for naval services, there were also a number of sloops, schooners, and brigantines of small size bought for packets.

The two ships purchased were quite serviceable craft and were armed with 20 or 24 guns. They were the Philadelphia merchant ship *Black Prince* of about 450 tons, which was renamed the *Alfred*, and the *Sally* (probably also a Philadelphia ship) of about the same size as the *Alfred* and renamed *Columbus*. At first these ships were fitted out with 24 9-pdrs., but the *Alfred*, at least, was soon reduced to 20 guns. Both ships appear to have been rather slow sailers and to have had all the weaknesses of converted merchantmen in naval service.

The brigs, brigantines, and schooners were somewhat more effective craft, for many of them were fast and of fair size, considering their rig and type. The *Andrea Doria* appears to have been a 14-gun brig carrying 4-pdrs., but little is known about her. The *Cabot* was another 14-gun brig and was such a good vessel that she was taken into the Royal Navy after her capture, so her dimensions have survived. She was 74' 9½" long on deck, 53' 7" on the keel, 24' 8" beam, 11' 4" depth of hold, and about 189 tons measurement. While in the Royal Navy she took part in the action on Dogger Bank in 1781; she was condemned and sold out of service June 25, 1783. Another brig of the same type was the *Lexington*, 14 guns, 86' long on deck and 24' 6" beam. Her original

name was *Wild Duck* and she crossed royal yards. There were also the brigantines *Hampden* and *Washington*, the latter obtained at Plymouth, Massachusetts, and also the brig *Reprisal*, 16 guns, about which very little is known. The
schooners were almost entirely sharp-built vessels, some on the model becoming
popular on the Chesapeake, others on the sharp Marblehead fisherman model
used in New England. The *Fly*, sometimes known as the *Cruizer*, was purchased at Baltimore and carried 6 9-pdrs. The *Wasp*, ex *Scorpion*, was also a
Baltimore schooner, while the *Warren* was a fast Marblehead vessel. These
schooners were usually employed as packet and dispatch vessels and did little
or no cruising.

The vessels fitted out by General Washington were probably Marblehead
fishermen and were named *Franklin, Harrison, Hancock*, and *Lynch;* their
original names do not appear. Probably one of these was the *Hannah*, for which
some New Englanders claim the honor of being the first American Navy ship.
This claim is apparently based on mere oral tradition in Marblehead and cannot
be well supported. Probably it is on a par with the Gloucester tradition of the
"invention" of the first schooner and is not to be taken more seriously. The
Harrison was obtained at Plymouth.

The sloops, except the one on Lake Champlain, were seagoing traders, some
of them on the sharp "Bermudas mould" and fast sailers. *Hornet* ex *Falcon* was
of this type, purchased at Baltimore and fitted with 10 guns. The other sloops
were the *Providence* ex *Katy*, bought at Providence and armed with from 6 to
12 guns, the *Sachem* of 10 guns, the *Independence* of 10 guns (lost at Cracoke
Inlet, North Carolina, in 1778), and the 4-gun *Mosquito*, destroyed in the Delaware in 1778.

The packets are difficult to identify; one was the schooner *Georgia Packet*
and another was the *Baltimore*, brigantine. The *Hornsnake* is also mentioned
in this year. Some of these packets may have been chartered vessels.

The Lake Champlain prizes were a schooner, the *Royal Savage*, and a ketch
or schooner, the *Liberty*. There was also a sloop, the *Enterprise*, of 12 4-pdrs.
These vessels were the nucleus of the American squadron on Lake Champlain
in 1776–77. All were shoal-draft hulls of relatively small size.

The purchased Continental vessels, though poorly armed and manned, were
of some service in commerce raiding, for munitions and supplies were much
needed. The greater number of these small craft never saw naval action, but
were utilized to carry dispatches and diplomatic agents, or were engaged in
commerce raiding, or used to carry freight, as circumstances or their size dic-

tated. Nearly all Continental Navy vessels were employed as packets at one time or another.

The *Alfred* was captured by H.B.M. ships *Ariadne*, 20 guns, and *Ceres*, 14 guns, on March 9, 1778, and the *Columbus* was chased ashore and then burned by her crew at Point Judith, Rhode Island, April 1 of the same year. The brig *Andrea Doria* was burned in the Delaware in 1777 to prevent capture. The *Cabot* was driven ashore and captured by H.B.M. frigate *Milford* in March, 1777, and was taken into the Royal Navy as before mentioned. The brig *Lexington* was taken by the British cutter *Alert*, 10 guns, September 20, 1777; *Hampden* was condemned in 1776 at Providence, Rhode Island, after having run ashore; the *Washington* was captured by H.B.M. ship *Fowey* off Cape Ann, Massachusetts, in December, 1775. The *Reprisal* foundered on the Newfoundland Banks in 1778, all hands but the cook being lost. Of the schooners, the *Fly* was burned in the Delaware in 1778, and the *Wasp* was blown up to prevent capture. The *Warren* was captured by the frigate *Milford* in 1776. The sloop *Hornet* was blown up at about the same time as the *Fly* and *Wasp* were destroyed in the Delaware; the sloop *Providence* was blown up by her crew in the Penobscot in 1779, and the *Sachem* is supposed to have been destroyed in the Delaware with the *Hornet*, though this is not certain. The Lake Champlain prizes were either lost in the naval action in the fall of 1776 or were destroyed by their crews to prevent capture in 1777.

While the new Continental Navy was being established by the purchase of ships, the Continental Congress had gone about obtaining some first-class men-of-war of the frigate class. On December 13, 1775, they had passed an act, on the motion of the Rhode Islanders, by which a total of thirteen frigates were to be built: five of 32, five of 28, and three of 24 guns. These were to be ready for sea about the last of March, 1776, or in three months. When it came time to decide which of the colonies were to be selected to build new ships, and how many each was to build, there was a great deal of political interest involved, and perhaps some wishful thinking as well. Working in haste, the Continental Congress delegates assigned the ships to the colonies having the greatest political influence, without regard to their actual ability to produce. At any rate, it was decided that two ships were to be built in Massachusetts, two in Rhode Island, two in New York, four in Pennsylvania, and one each in New Hampshire, Connecticut, and Maryland. Thus Pennsylvania, in spite of having all of her shipbuilding eggs in one basket, Philadelphia, got twice as many ships as any other colony—the justification being an allegation that she had more shipwrights than the other colonies chosen—an absurd claim in the light of both colonial shipbuilding records and actual accomplishment of the program.

To make the act effective, the Congress utilized the previously established "Marine Committee," which was composed of one member from each of the insurgent colonies. Each member had the responsibility of supervising the accumulation of supplies and materials for the naval vessels. The member from each of the colonies fortunate enough to get a ship or two to build began to look about for a builder. In nearly every case the builder selected was of a political complexion satisfactory to the congressional delegate. The results of this shortsighted policy, based on political factors rather than the probabilities of warfare, were soon apparent. While this practice resulted in some cases in the selection of very competent builders and supervisors, nevertheless it led to the unfortunate concentration of a number of building contracts in one town or city, and often in a single shipyard. It may now seem obvious that the selection of large ports, or situations controlled by such ports, was extremely risky, but concentration of war contracts in "target areas" has long been an American practice that, unless corrected, may again bring us to grief. There were, of course, seemingly logical justifications for this concentration. In the large ports there were supposedly ample supplies of labor and the maximum availability of materials. These places were supposedly safe from attack, at least in the early months of the war. But as has often been the case in war, the unexpected happened: in many building locations it was found that both labor and materials were scarce, and the British blockaded or captured the large ports or the entrances to the important waterways. As a result, the program rapidly lost effectiveness.

The credit for the design of the new ships has long been a matter of controversy and cannot be settled beyond any reasonable doubt at this time. The most recent attempt to establish the designer's name was made by Lieutenant Commander M. V. Brewington in an article in *The American Neptune*, Vol. VIII, No. 1 (January, 1948). Brewington has established the correct names of some of the builders and supervisors not previously stated and has given the first comprehensive account of the difficulties that led to the use of more than one design for each of the three classes of frigates. In this article Brewington submitted a strong claim on behalf of Joshua Humphreys. This claim is almost entirely based on the correspondence of William Whipple, delegate to the Continental Congress for New Hampshire. Whipple stated that thirty-one days after the passage of the Act of December 13, 1775, Joshua Humphreys "laid the plans of several men-of-war" before the Marine Committee and that these were approved and copies ordered sent to each of the builders.

The difficulty in fully accepting this claim without more evidence is in the fact that the one official plan that has survived is the one that was used by Humphreys himself to build the frigate allotted to the Humphreys yard, and *this was not drawn by Humphreys.* The argument supporting this assertion is as follows:

The two plans from the Revolutionary War period preserved by the Humphreys family were one of the *Randolph* and one of a 74-gun ship, both of which are now in the National Archives. The plan of the 74 will be taken up later; for the moment it is only of importance to say that it was obviously drawn by the same man that drew the plan of the *Randolph*—the "Wharton and Humphreys Draught," so called. The draftsmanship of a ship designer is as readily recognized as a man's handwriting. The methods used to shape the hull, or to "fair" it, the shape of bow, stern, and cross sections, the neatness of workmanship in the joining of curved lines, and many idiosyncrasies of drawing are invariably sufficient to permit identification of the draftsman, even though his name is not signed to a plan—providing, of course, that there is enough information to permit identification of his workmanship. Now, there is sufficient in the case of Joshua Humphreys, for he was actively employed as a United States Navy constructor during the period 1794–1801; there are two plans in existence that can be definitely identified as his personal handiwork. These are still in the file of Navy plans. They are a draught of a 74-gun ship of 1799 (40–15–6 I) signed by Humphreys and drawn by him, not only by his own statement but also on those of two of his contemporary naval constructors; and an unsigned plan of one of the *Constitution* class of 1794, obviously in the same hand as the 1799 74-gun ship, and named the *Terrible* on the draught (one of the names selected by Humphreys for the frigates) (40–15–6 A). Allowing for the period of from eighteen to twenty-four years that had intervened since the Revolutionary War vessels had been designed, the draftsmanship shown in the plans known to have been made by Humphreys is so different from that of the Revolutionary War frigate and the 74 that it can be said with certainty that the Wharton and Humphreys draught and the Revolutionary War 74-gun ship plan *were not drawn by Joshua Humphreys.* It might also be said, with justice, that Joshua Humphreys was a very poor draftsman; the Revolutionary War

Dimensions

Length bet Perps . . . . . . 132'.9"
Beam, moulded . . . . 34'.0"
  "   extreme . . . . 34'.6"
Depth in Hold . . . . 10'.6"
Draft - Forward 14'.0"; aft 15'.0"
Ⓑ is 51'.6" from F.P.; Ⓑ to Ⓑ is 12'.; Ⓑ to A.P. is 80'.3"
Room and Space 23¼", Water lines space 3'.0",
Buttocks space 3'.0"   Beakhead from F.P. is 3'.9".

an 1. Draught of RANDOLPH *after "Wharton and Humphreys Draught," showing*
.e official designs for the 32-gun frigates.

Dimensions

Length bet. Perps	126'·3¾"
" on Keel for Tonnage	105'·7¼"
Beam moulded	34'·4"
" extreme	34'·10"
Depth in Hold	10'·5½"
Burthen in Tons	681⁵³⁄₉₄

⊕ is 54'·0" from F.P. Stations ⊕ to A space 10'·0"
      " A to B, B to C, C to D, D to E space 6'·0"
      " E to F, F to G, G to F.P. space 4'·0"
O is 72'·3½" from A.P. Stations ⊕ to 1 space 10'·0"
      " 1 to 2, 2 to 3, 3 to 4, 4 to 5, 5 to 6,
       6 to 7, 7 to 8, space 6'·0"
      " 8 to 9 space 3'·0", 9 to A.P. is 2'·3¼"

Waterlines space 3'·7"
Buttocks - 3'·0"
Room & Space 24"

A Draught of the 28-gun frigate Virginia
from the Admiralty Draught

Reconstruction :- Ladders to Quarter
deck and Forecastle, Head Gratings.

Plan 2. Draught of VIRGINIA, 28 guns, after the Admiralty draught made after her
capture.

plans are the work of a good draftsman, revealing a great deal of experience in making plans. It is obvious that, less than a year after going into partnership with Wharton, Humphreys could not have had an apprentice more skilled in drawing than his master.

Joshua Humphreys was a Quaker, born in Haverford, Delaware County, Pennsylvania, on July 17, 1751. About 1765 he was apprenticed to a well-known Philadelphia shipwright and builder, James Penrose, who died in 1771, a short time before Humphreys could complete his apprenticeship. Penrose's widow not only gave him his time, but employed him as master shipwright to complete a ship that had been building at the time of her husband's death. Humphreys was about twenty-one years old at this time.

In 1774, when Humphreys was twenty-three, he went into partnership with his cousin, John Wharton, who was probably a trained shipwright and somewhat older than Humphreys. Wharton was also a politician; he was a close friend of Robert Morris of the Marine Committee and soon became a member of the Pennsylvania Committee of Safety and of the Navy Board, Middle District. He resigned from the latter in January, 1781. Wharton's connections gave the firm an inside track to both Continental and provincial shipbuilding contracts.

There is nothing in the career of this firm that indicates any reason why Humphreys could be considered a "leading" ship designer or builder in Philadelphia as early as 1775. Certainly he was not well known in the colonies at any time during the Revolution. It cannot be denied, however, that the record shows he presented plans to the Marine Committee early in 1776, either in behalf of his firm or of someone employed by Wharton and Humphreys. It is unlikely that he would represent any other builder. Then, if he did not draw the designs, which seems to be a proved fact based on the evidence of the existing plans, who did? Perhaps it was Wharton, or someone not yet identified. It is worthy of mention that, when a question arose about the ships building in Rhode Island, it was not Humphreys who was sent to investigate, but a Nathaniel Falconer of Philadelphia. It is also to be remarked that Humphreys seems to have been omitted from any supervisory capacity in the construction of the Pennsylvania frigates; this would seem to have been a logical duty, were he the designer.

Humphreys' long connection with naval shipbuilding and ship design requires extensive examination to establish the credit actually due him. It is a notable fact that there is little acceptable evidence to fix the names of the designers of many of the early American ships of war.

Designs were prepared, probably in Philadelphia, and approved by the Marine Committee. Copies were ordered which were to be sent to each of the builders or to the sponsors and supervisors. However, the plans were large, being on a scale of three-eighths of an inch to the foot (the surviving plan was originally about five feet long and two feet wide) and there were no suitable means of transmitting these drawings to the distant colonies, since such large plans could not be enclosed in letters. The copies of the ships' plans were completed and ready to be sent out by the second of February, 1776, but it was not until the twelfth that a messenger could be found, a John Bull, who was going from Philadelphia to Cambridge, Massachusetts, with the payroll of the Continental Army at Boston. Bull apparently carried plans for the ships to be built in Massachusetts and New Hampshire. No account seems to exist of how plans were sent to Rhode Island and Connecticut, but one clear-cut fact stands out: plans were not delivered in New England in time to permit any of the frigates to be finished by March, 1776, as required by the authorization. As a result, some of the New England builders seem to have either made their own plans or obtained plans locally. Whoever was responsible for the plans presented at Philadelphia, only the ships built in Pennsylvania and Maryland can be said with certainty to have been built according to the official plans, though there are logical reasons for assuming that those built in New York and Connecticut were also in accordance with the approved drawings. At best, the information on whether or not the official plans were followed exactly is circumstantial, for there is no positive evidence. At least five of the frigates obviously were not built to the official draughts, on the evidence of the archives or of plans made from the ships in question after their capture by the British.

The political considerations that decided which of the colonies were to build the frigates naturally extended to the selection of all individuals concerned in their actual construction, at least in most of the provinces. In New Hampshire, the Marine Committeeman turned the contract over to John Langdon, a Portsmouth merchant-politician and former delegate, who in turn let the work out to three Portsmouth, or Kittery, shipwrights: James K. Hackett, James Hill, and Stephen Paul. Thomas Thompson, master mariner, was made inspector, and a clerk of the yard was appointed. The important function of purchasing was, of course, retained by Langdon.

In Massachusetts, Thomas Cushing handled the matter for the committeeman. Though there were, of course, many yards available, he selected one firm in Newburyport for the construction of both the frigates assigned to the colony.

The builders chosen were Jonathan Greenleaf and Stephen and Ralph Cross; the inspectors were John Avery and John Odin, while Cushing naturally saw to all purchasing matters.

Rhode Island set up a political clambake to handle the business. A board, or committee, of eleven men, with the provincial governor as chairman, was first established. Each member of this board appointed a representative to carry out his assignment. This spread out the gravy very handsomely, but somehow failed to satisfy the citizens. Eventually the whole project was turned over to Daniel Tillinghast. Two builders were selected, Benjamin Talman and Sylvester Bowers, both in Providence. Each was to build a ship.

Connecticut had only one vessel to let out, and the Marine Committeeman took care of the matter neatly by having his brother, Barnabas Deane, handle the contract, which he let to John Cotton of Chatham, Connecticut, where the vessel was laid down.

New York had a board, or commission, in charge of building the two frigates assigned the colony, which was appointed by the committeeman, the latter taking care, of course, to handle some of the very profitable procurement himself. No change in this procedure seems to have taken place. Here again one builder was selected for the two frigates, with an inspector for each ship. The builder was Lancaster Burling of Poughkeepsie; the inspectors were Augustus Lawrence and Samuel Tudor. The vessels, however, were destroyed before they could be completed and prepared for sea.

Pennsylvania's Marine Committeeman set up a board, with himself as chairman. This board, or commission, set up subcommittees, each with certain responsibilities. The matter was well handled in this case, for each subcommittee was made up of local tradesmen, such as master shipwrights, merchant-accountants, ship chandlers, and the like. The contracts were spread out as much as possible by giving one ship to each of four shipyards: one to Wharton and Humphreys, one to Grice and Company, one to Manuel, Jehu, and Benjamin Eyre, and one to Warwick Coats. Brewington states that the builder of one of the frigates was given as "Bruce & Co.," but that no such firm has been found in contemporary tax lists or records; so he logically assumes that the name was misspelled and that Grice was intended. This is also supported by a statement of a member of the Grice family later engaged in naval construction. Only two of the Pennsylvania-built ships were completed, and only one got to sea under the American flag.

Maryland's Marine Committeeman also set up a board or commission to handle the single contract, which was let to George Wells at Fell's Point, with Jesse Hollingsworth as inspector. Wells had to obtain additional shipwrights to speed up construction, and he seems to have employed a good part of those available in the colony. In addition he had the help of groups of Baltimore citizens, and even militia companies were employed on occasion.

The relative importance of the builders and the supervisors, so far as the individual ships were concerned, is not clear. Some of the supervisors were undoubtedly shipwrights (as in Pennsylvania); others were ship captains, or possibly political henchmen of the local committeeman. It is probable that some of the builders merely furnished the yard, tools, and labor while the supervisors actually controlled the construction of the ships. For this reason, perhaps, the Marine Committee correspondence might lead one to believe that the supervisors were actually the shipbuilders. Even at a much later date than the Revolution, it was the custom to write to the superintendents as though they were the builders rather than as though they were mere inspectors.

Many of the places where the congressional delegates had assumed there would be a sufficient supply of labor soon complained of a shortage of skilled shipwrights. These shortages were due to a variety of causes, particularly the increase in privateer construction and the dispersion of skilled men to other localities for economic reasons. It was also the practice in some colonies to turn out the shipwrights for militia duty. The lack of preliminary planning in the allotment of materials, armament, and supplies was another difficulty which caused extensive delays in construction. An attempt to centralize the control of the new ship construction by the Continental Congress was certainly another important factor in causing delays.

Though some of the Continental delegates and Marine Committee members were merchant-shipowners, who must have known that it was practically impossible to complete the new frigates in the time required by the Act of 1775, this did not prevent them from passing the bill without modification of the completion date. It is highly probable that they established the size and the rates of the ships to be built; in any event the Marine Committee appears to have arranged for the designs and to have approved "several" of them when complete. They also attempted to make numerous decisions regarding the specifications and to let the contracts for the armament. There was undoubtedly a natural anxiety to make contracts on some sound basis, and a design and specification for each class of ship was a logical move. So, in spite of the expressed intention to complete the program in about 108 days, it should be noted that 31 days were spent in preparing the designs, prior to approval, and then 20 days more were required to make the necessary copies. Ten days more were needed to find a messenger to transmit the plans of at least five of the ships, with the additional delay of the messenger's time in reaching his destination. As has been remarked upon earlier, this situation not only accounted for much of the delay met with in building the ships, but also was the practical reason for the variations in design of each of the three classes of frigates built under the Act of 1775.

This congressional authorization was intended to produce three distinct classes of ships, graduated in dimensions and armament, so as to obtain 24-, 28-, and 32-gun frigates. Hence it is reasonable to assume that there were to be three official designs or "draughts." This is supported to some extent by existing plans. One of the official draughts of the 32-gun class has survived, and one plan of the 28-gun class was made from the ship after her capture by the British. These seem to indicate that another basic design was used for the latter ships. No plan of the 24-gun class has yet come to light, but the British captured ships of all three classes and made measurements of them. These dimensions can be produced to support the assumption that there were three designs. The 24-gun class measured about 117' 9½" on the berth deck, 32' 10½" beam, and 9' 8½" depth in the hold. The 28-gun class measured approximately 126' 3½" on the berth deck, 34' 10" beam, and 10' 5½" depth in the hold. The 32-gun ships were to measure about 132' 9" on the berth deck, 34' 6" beam, and 10' 6" in the hold. Four plans of ships built under the authorization of December 13, 1775, have survived, three made from measurements taken off the ships captured by the British, showing the vessels as built, and one showing a design that may safely be assumed to be one of the official draughts prepared for the Marine Committee. In addition there are dimensions of three other ships taken into the Royal Navy, of which no draughts have yet been found.

The surviving plans have been carefully redrawn from the original sources to permit clear reproductions. While some "restorations" have been made, these are indicated on the plans so that, in the event additional information comes to light, the material extracted from the original sources can be identified without having to obtain and consult the originals. The reconstructed portions could then be corrected, if it should be possible. In general, all restoration is based on ships similar to the one shown.

Perhaps the most satisfactory way to explore the designs and qualities of these ships will be to begin with the ships' plans that can reasonably be assumed to represent the original designs prepared for the Marine Committee, and then to discuss the ships whose designs appear to have been quite different. In this manner the degree of variation in the designs can be shown and the problems involved in identifying the designers can be more readily presented.

Randolph

Spars

		Masts Whole length	Head	Yards Whole length	Arms
Main	Mast	85'·6"	11'·6"	72'	2'·6"
"	Top	51'	6'·6"	51'	1'·5"
"	Topgall	40'	14'	38'	1'·2"
Fore		78'	10'·6"	69'	2'·2"
"	Top	49'	6'	48'	2'·3"
"	Topgall	38'	13½'	36'	1'·2"
Mizen		75'	9'	54'	1'·4"
"	Top	56'	20'	38'	1'·3"
"	Topgall	—	—	—	—
Bowsprit		51'	—	51'	2'·3"
Jibboom		38'	—	38'	1'·2"
Mizen Yard				69'	

found by M. V. Brewington

Chapelle

Scale in Feet

Spar plan of RANDOLPH *from Humphreys' dimensions.* (See Plan 1.)

Obviously, in view of what has already been said about the delays in the distribution of the plans of the ships, the ships built at Philadelphia, or near by, would with reasonable certainty have followed the official designs. Of the four ships built at Philadelphia, the official building plans of one have been preserved —the *Randolph*, 32 guns, built by Wharton and Humphreys. This plan was in the possession of Joshua Humphreys and later in the hands of his son Samuel, who was also a naval constructor. When Samuel Humphreys died, many of the plans in his possession were left in the office files and so became part of the plan-archive files of the United States Navy. Only two plans belonging to Joshua Humphreys (of the period of the Revolution) have survived; both are of naval ships. In addition there is in existence a half-model, supposed to have been built from one of these drawings, of a 74-gun ship. The Humphreys plans are now in the National Archives with other sailing-ship plans of the Bureau of Construction and Repair, United States Navy Department. The index numbers of all plans hereafter referred to are those of the National Archives index.

The frigates that were intended to be built on the same lines as those of the *Randolph* were as follows: *Raleigh* at Portsmouth, New Hampshire; *Hancock* at Newburyport, Massachusetts; *Warren* at Providence, Rhode Island; and the *Washington*, along with the *Randolph*, at Philadelphia. Actually, none of the ships building under the new program were given names until June 6, 1776, at which time the Continental Congress selected the name for each ship then building.

Plan 1 shows the redrawn plan of the *Randolph*, based upon the original draught (31–4–45) and refaired. Corrections have been made in redrawing to carry out the alterations noted in ink script on the original plan; these alterations also appear in the Humphreys papers. The most important of these were changes in steeve or angle of the bowsprit, location of the masts, and lengths of forecastle and quarterdecks. The original plan shows the general deck arrangement as shown in Plan 1.

The design is of a sharp frigate of the period, following in a general way the British frigates of the period in arrangement of decks and armament. In 1756 the Royal Navy had built four sister 32-gun frigates which proved very satisfactory cruisers. They were the *Southampton*, *Vestal*, *Minerva*, and *Diana*. These were 124′ 4″ on the berth deck, 34′ 0″ beam, and 12′ 0″ depth of hold. Though beakhead bulkheads had by this date almost disappeared in ships below the rate of frigate, the *Southampton* class retained this feature to about the same extent as seen in the *Randolph*'s plan. The next year the British built four more similar 32's, *Alarm*, *Niger*, *Eolas*, and *Stag*. These new ships were slightly sharper-ended than the previous four and measured 125′ 0″ on the berth deck, 35′ 2″ beam, and 12′ 0″ in the hold. In the new ships, the beakhead bulkhead disappeared entirely, the bows being carried up to the forecastle. The British 36-gun frigates were of similar dimensions, so far as beam and depth were concerned, but were about four feet longer than the *Alarm* class. Thus it will be seen that the *Randolph* was a larger ship than the standard frigate of her rate in the British Navy; in fact, she was even longer than the next higher rate, the 36-gun frigate.

The American model used in the *Randolph* differed a good deal from the hull forms found in the majority of contemporary British or French frigates: the American had much more deadrise, or angle of rise, in the bottom, rounder and more regular curves in cross section, far more rake (or slope forward) to the bow, and somewhat less depth and freeboard. Judging by the frame spacing and other evidence, the American ship must have been somewhat more lightly built than her English sisters. There is no evidence of any attempt to copy a foreign model of naval vessel in the American plan—a matter which has been the subject of much careless assumption on the part of some American writers. There is now ample opportunity to explore this matter fully. There are large numbers of plans of naval ships of all maritime nations in the Admiralty Collection of Draughts, National Maritime Museum, Greenwich, England; hence any reasonable comparison can be made. The frigate models used by each of the great maritime powers—England, Spain, Holland, and France—had become well established long before the American frigates were authorized, and, judging by a comparison of plans, it is apparent that the American hull model was not a copy, but was rather the natural development of a previous search for speed under sail in craft smaller than frigates. The lessons taught in these small vessels were applied to the *Boston* of 1748 and to the Revolutionary War frigate designs; certainly by 1775 the Americans must have had very strong opinions on how to design a fast-sailing ship. The Americans took one page out of the French book, for they made each of the new frigate classes larger than the same rates in the British Navy. However, there is no evidence to show whether this was a deliberate copying of French naval policy or whether it was the result of independent observation and theory, as expressed in the earlier *Boston*.

The *Randolph* was one of the two Pennsylvania-built frigates to be completed and the only one to make a cruise under the Continental flag. She was blown up in action with H.B.M. 64-gun ship *Yarmouth* off Barbados, British West Indies, March 17, 1778, all hands but four seamen being lost. Little is known about her sailing qualities beyond what might be concluded from her drawings, which indicate a very fast ship for the time.

The only other plan that can logically be assumed to represent one of the three basic designs approved by the Marine Committee in 1776 is the draught of the *Virginia*, one of the 28-gun class, built at Baltimore, Maryland (Plan 2). In this case the plan is not the original design, but one drawn from measurements made from the ship after her capture by the British. The difficulties that prevented the official plans from getting to New England did not apply to the Maryland frigate; this, with the appearance of the ship as shown in the Admiralty draught, makes it safe to assume the *Virginia* to be representative of the official design of her class. The ships intended to be built as 28's were, in addition to *Virginia*, the *Providence* in Rhode Island, the *Trumbull* in Connecticut, the *Montgomery* in New York, and the *Effingham* in Pennsylvania.

The *Virginia* so resembled the *Randolph* that the writer assumed the ships to have been built on the same lines when he received the draught of the former ship, in 1929, from C. Knight, formerly the Admiralty Curator. On casual inspection it appeared that the *Virginia* had been built by altering the spacings of the water lines and frames from those of the *Randolph*, but when both plans had been redrawn it became plain that this was not probable. It must now be assumed that there was an independent design for the *Virginia*'s class. On the basis of the appearance of the *Virginia* it is also fully apparent that the design of this ship was made by the same man who prepared the draught of the *Randolph*. The dimensions and appearance of the *Virginia* may be safely assumed to represent the official design for the 28-gun class.

A number of comparisons between the plans of the *Virginia* and *Randolph* might be made. The *Virginia* has more deadrise and is deeper, and her bow rake is much less than that of the *Randolph*. Though fully six feet shorter, she is beamier and is actually a more burdensome vessel; for this reason she was rated as a 32-gun frigate by the British after her capture. It is also to be noted that the corrections mentioned as being written on the original draught of the *Randolph* were apparently carried out in the *Virginia*. It is possible that these corrections or alterations were the comments of the Marine Committee, or of their advisers, when the draughts of the three classes of ships were being reviewed prior to approval. The low knightheads shown in both the *Randolph* and *Virginia* are worthy of notice; knightheads were usually very prominent in ships having beakhead bulkheads. The low knightheads shown gave little support to the bowsprit, which depended upon the gammoning and, apparently, a tenon at the stemhead to resist lateral strain. The lack of knightheads of sufficient height to support the bowsprit must have put a heavy strain on the beakhead bulkhead. It seems probable that the low knightheads were an idiosyncracy of the designer. The original plan of the 74-gun ship preserved by Humphreys showed a similar knighthead structure; however, the model built by Humphreys of a ship of this class showed the usual prominent knightheads of the period. Possibly the designer had little experience in large ships and was unaware of the tremendous strains incurred in the head rig of such ships as these frigates and the 74-gun ship.

While the *Virginia* strongly resembles the *Randolph*, it is possible that the official design if available would have shown an even greater likeness, especially since some allowance has to be made for the builder's privilege of making changes. The *Randolph* was certainly the handsomer of the two, but of course this is largely due to the greater length and lower freeboard of the 32-gun ship.

It will be noted that neither of these ships carried guns on their forecastles, which was also true of contemporary British frigates of 28 and 32 guns. About 1780 the British 36-gun frigates were built to carry forecastle guns, but it is not known whether this practice was characteristic of their earlier ships of this class. It will be seen that the Revolutionary War frigate was armed in almost the same manner as the colonial-built *Boston* of 1748 and was, in a general way at least, a very similar ship in all important respects. It should be remarked that none of the surviving plans of the American frigates authorized in 1775 show sweep ports; this is an omission difficult to understand. However, these ships could be swept by using the gun ports, after shifting the guns out of the way, as was sometimes done in European navies. It is possible, of course, that the lack of sweep ports on the Admiralty plans was due to a draftsman's slackness, though this is a doubtful explanation.

George Wells had difficulty in completing the *Virginia*, and the frigate did not get out of the Chesapeake under American colors. In trying to get to sea in 1778, after being blockaded for more than a year, she ran aground in the Bay and was taken by the British ships *Emerald* and *Conqueror*. The *Virginia* was bought for the Royal Navy and remained in that service for about six years before being condemned.

The *Randolph* is the only 32-gun frigate for which we have what was apparently the official draught. The two surviving plans of the other three—the *Raleigh*, the *Hancock*, and the *Warren*—were made from the completed ships after their capture by the British. The *Raleigh* was built by James K. Hackett, James Hill, and Stephen Paul at Portsmouth, New Hampshire. Though the Continental Congress had intended to have the frigates afloat by the end of March, 1776, the delay in getting the designs to the New England builders would surely have prevented the accomplishment of this even if there had been no other causes. The *Raleigh* is a representative case; her plan did not reach Cushing, in Massachusetts, until February 26, and it was then forwarded to Portsmouth through the builders at Newburyport. This would have prevented the *Raleigh* from being started until more than a month after the plan reached her builders, for she would have to be lofted and the moulds or templates made before she could be set up.

The New Hampshire group had apparently been aware of the situation and had taken the initiative to go ahead while the Continental Congress and its Marine Committee were having designs made, approving them, getting copies, and then trying to find a way to get the plans to the builders. It is apparent that soon after the contract was in their hands the Portsmouth builders started their own design and completed it, lofted the lines, and made the moulds, and that they had begun to get the timber out by the time the official plans reached them from Philadelphia. There is no known statement as to who was responsible for the design of the *Raleigh*, although the most likely person was William Hackett.

William Hackett was born at Salisbury, Massachusetts, May 1, 1739. He became an apprentice to his father and uncle about 1751, and eventually took over the yard at Salisbury Point. Sometime prior to 1774 he and his cousin James operated the yard together, and they continued to do so on and off for about thirty years, except for some work done in Portsmouth, New Hampshire. They are said to have used the site of the present Portsmouth Navy Yard there, and it is possible that the *Raleigh* was constructed on this location. James K. Hackett, usually called "Colonel" or "Major" Hackett, seems to have been the senior partner and business head of the firm and William the designer and master builder. As a boy William Hackett saw the British 44-gun ship *America* built at Portsmouth, and it is possible that his elders worked on this ship. By the end of the Revolution William Hackett acquired a great reputation as a ship designer in New England; his cousin James remained the businessman and had many interests besides shipbuilding. The latter had a mental breakdown late in life, caused by financial reverses. There is no doubt that William Hackett was the leading ship designer in the vicinity when the *Raleigh* was building.

There were, of course, others in this part of New England who were able to design ships. None, however, seem to have become as prominent as Hackett, who seems to have been unusually competent both as a builder and as a designer. We know that he was able to draw; one of his plans is in existence. The other designers who were prominent in this part of New England were John Peck of Boston and one member of the Coffin family of Newburyport. The Coffins operated a yard at Newburyport, Massachusetts, and for this reason might have had some connection with the *Hancock* or *Boston* rather than with the *Raleigh*. Peck is known to have been busy with vessels building around Boston at this time.

The plan of the *Raleigh* is shown in Plan 3, redrawn from the Admiralty draught of the vessel, made soon after her capture. Her dimensions follow those of the *Randolph* rather closely, but her hull form is quite different. The similarity of the *Raleigh*'s dimensions to those of the official design, in spite of the fact that the design was well along before the official draught reached the builders, can be readily explained.

The Continental Congress, or its Marine Committee, had obviously specified the dimensions of the ships they wanted prior to the preparation of the official designs. The merchant-shipowners would have felt themselves fully competent to pass on this matter, and it was one that had to be decided before getting out contract drawings and agreements, to obtain uniformity in the latter. Obviously Langdon, who had formerly been a delegate to the Congress and active in the naval debates, must have had complete information on the proposed ships and must have known the approved dimensions. It is also very probable that Hackett, or whoever the designer may have been, made a final comparison when the official draught finally came to hand. It would have been far too late to make a change in hull model or dimensions, but minor alterations and adjustments of arrangement could have been made to comply reasonably well with what the official draught indicated. The *Raleigh*, as built, measured 131′ 5″ long on the berth deck, 34′ 5″ beam, and 11′ 0″ depth in the hold. She was of an entirely different model from that of the *Randolph* and the 28-gun *Virginia*, approaching very closely the hull form of the English 32's of 1758, the *Alarm* class. Like that British class she had a round bow, without any sign of a beakhead bulkhead. The quarterdeck and forecastle were lower and less prominent than in the ships built in Philadelphia and Baltimore. The *Raleigh*'s midsection was marked by a sharp and deep tumble home, in the manner popular in English frigates, and the deadrise of the bottom was similar, somewhat less than in the *Randolph* and much less than in *Virginia*. The model of the hull of the *Raleigh* was, in fact, very similar to that of a contemporary British frigate; the Admiralty drawing shows a well-modeled English-type frigate and nothing more. The round bow exhibited in the *Raleigh* was by no means new, for the British frigates had adopted this construction before the Revolution began. The beakhead bulkhead did not go out of fashion entirely during the period when the American frigates were building; this feature was retained in some foreign frigates and ship sloops as late as the early 1790's, and in ships of the line until after the beginning of the nineteenth century.

The *Raleigh* was launched May 21, 1776, and a contemporary newspaper stated that she was "built" in sixty working days. It should not be necessary to accept this as more than an indication that she was built very rapidly; this was the time from the setting up of her keel to the date of launch, and probably does not imply calendar days. At any rate, the work of lofting the lines, getting out the moulds, and obtaining the timber to start the ship is not included, nor is the time required to finish and rig the ship after her launch. It is evident from correspondence that her building time from lofting to sailing covered the period from late February to midsummer.

The career of this ship in the Continental Navy was rather inglorious and shows that good ships alone are not enough to bring success in naval warfare. On September 4, 1776, the *Raleigh* under Thomas Thompson (her inspector while building) and the *Alfred*, Captain Elisha Hinman, sighted the British West Indian convoy homeward bound, guarded by the 22-gun ship *Camel*, the 14-gun sloop *Druid*, and the 16-gun sloop *Weazel*—the two sloops being ship-rigged. The *Camel* was a converted merchantman like the *Alfred*, but smaller. The convoy was well spread out. The *Raleigh* appeared to windward of the convoy, while the *Alfred* was a few miles to leeward. The British *Druid* engaged the *Raleigh* and, though a much smaller and weaker ship, actually drove her off. The *Raleigh* and *Alfred* then apparently made sail and were followed by the *Camel* and *Weazel* until the Americans had reached a distance where they were no longer a threat to the convoy. The American accounts claimed that a squall broke off the action and that the American ships then waited for the British to engage them. In view of the fact that the two American ships were much larger, faster, and more powerful than the three small English convoy guards, this explanation will hardly stand inspection. It is not surprising that Thompson did not long remain in command of the *Raleigh* after this abortive attack on the West Indian convoy. The *Raleigh* was finally taken by the British on the 25th of September, being driven on shore by the *Experiment*, 50 guns, and the 28-gun frigate *Unicorn*, while trying to escape. John Barry, then her captain, and some of the crew were able to get ashore in the *Raleigh*'s boats. The ship was pulled off undamaged and was taken into the Royal Navy as a 32-gun 12-pdr. frigate. She was condemned and sold out in July, 1783.

It will be seen that the Continental Navy had some very poor officers. Many were political appointees without the qualifications needed for command; others were temperamental and resentful of discipline. Nearly all were without combat experience. The failure of the Continental Navy to accomplish much with the fine frigates built during the Revolution was due almost entirely to a lack of skilled officers, trained and well-disciplined crews, and competent overall command and planning.

One of the two ships built in Massachusetts was the 32-gun frigate *Hancock*, shown in Plan 4 as redrawn from the Admiralty draught made after her capture and purchase by the Royal Navy. This ship was built at Newburyport, with the 24-gun *Boston*, by Greenleaf and Cross. Greenleaf seems to have been in charge of the construction of the *Hancock*, and the Cross brothers were responsible for the *Boston*. Here again there is confusion about the design. The *Hancock* when completed was somewhat different from any of the other ships. For one thing, she was larger, measuring 136′ 7″ long on the lower deck, about 35′ 6″ beam, and 11′ ½″ depth in the hold. Her model was somewhat like the *Raleigh*'s in profile, but her midsection was very much like the *Randolph*'s, though she was both wider and deeper than the Philadelphia ship. She had neither a regular beakhead bulkhead nor a round bow of the usual type. She was round-bowed to the main sheer, but from here up to the forecastle rail line she was suddenly flared out just forward of the catheads, as though she had first been built with a beakhead which later had been finished off round. This is a rather unusual feature, though it is to be seen occasionally in a few other ship plans of the period in the Admiralty Collection of Draughts. There is no apparent advantage of this form of bow except to give some additional room on the forecastle at the catheads; and even this is obtained at the expense of strength. It is evident from the plan of the ship that the builders had departed entirely from the official Marine Committee plan, producing an original design in both model and dimensions. It is highly probable that the same thing had taken place in Massachusetts that had occurred in New Hampshire: the official design not coming to hand, the builders went ahead with a design of their own without waiting for the Philadelphia plans. Like the New Hampshire people, the Massachusetts men knew what the desired dimensions were to be and in the process of working up a new design made each of the ships still larger. Perhaps some local pride went into these matters, and it would not be difficult to imagine that the Massachusetts builders would try to outdo the Philadelphia ships in all possible particulars. In this case they might truthfully be said to have succeeded, for the *Hancock* was described by the British as the "finest and fastest frigate in the world."

Little is known about Jonathan Greenleaf, except that he was a successful shipbuilder who entered a partnership with the Cross brothers of Newburyport sometime prior to the Revolution. The Cross yard had been established by the father of the Cross brothers about 1728–30. Stephen and Ralph Cross, Jr., took over the yard with Greenleaf just before the Revolution; the elder Cross was then alive, and in fact lived until 1788. Ralph Cross, Jr., was born in 1738, his older brother Stephen in 1731. The latter died in 1809, after holding a number of civic offices. Ralph Cross was interested in military affairs and rose through the grades from captain to brigadier in the Massachusetts militia. The designer of the *Hancock* may have been one of the Cross brothers, or he may perhaps have been William Hackett, for the latter is known to have had business relations with the Cross brothers and to have designed at least one ship for their yard at a much later date.

It is quite obvious, at any rate, that the builders produced in the *Hancock* a ship that was different from the official design in all important respects except rate, and by far the handsomest ship of those whose plans have been found. The Massachusetts men, though handicapped by the delay in receiving plans, had made no complaint to Philadelphia, but had gone ahead with designs of their own, regardless of the Marine Committee. It is well, perhaps, to state that the variations from the official plan of the 32-gun frigates could not possibly be charged to improper lofting, for in nearly all cases the ships' lines have no similarity to the approved draught and depart so markedly in dimensions or proportions that the designs are obviously distinct from the Philadelphia drawing. Were there merely slight variations in dimensions or in model, the rather crude and incomplete lofting methods of the period might be held accountable. But where there are such marked differences, as in the case of both the *Raleigh* and the *Hancock*, this seems to be an impossible explanation. The *Virginia* might be said to indicate how the characteristics of the design were retained in a finished ship by the methods of lofting employed at the time, even though she may have departed from the original design in many respects. Since it is reasonable to assume that the designer of each of the frigates built in New England probably revised his plans once the official draught was at hand, the curious combination of similarities and wide departures seen in each ship, as compared with the official draught, is readily understandable.

The *Hancock* and the 24-gun ship *Boston* got to sea early in 1777—the *Hancock* commanded by Captain Joseph Manly, the *Boston* by Captain Hector McNiell. On June 27 they chased the small British 28-gun frigate *Fox*, which the fast *Hancock* soon overtook and captured. On July 6 the three ships were sighted and chased by H.B.M. 44-gun ship *Rainbow* and the brig *Victor*. By daybreak of the 7th the Americans had been joined by a sloop, which was soon burned. At about 6 o'clock in the morning another sail was sighted, which proved to be the British 32-gun frigate *Flora*. The Americans then broke their formation and endeavored to escape. The American ships were foul and out of trim, particularly the *Hancock*. The *Rainbow* chased the *Hancock* and, being clean and well sailed, overtook the American on the morning of July 8, after a long chase in light winds. The *Fox* was retaken by the *Flora*, but the *Boston* escaped. McNiell was cashiered for not having remained in formation and for not supporting Manly. The *Hancock* was taken into the Royal Navy as the *Iris* and became a favorite cruiser by making fortunes for her officers through the capture of prizes. In 1780 she fought an indecisive action against the French frigate *Hermione* and would have taken her had not another French frigate appeared. In 1781 the *Iris* chased and took the American 24-gun ship *Trumbull*. Late in the year the *Iris* was captured by a French squadron in the West Indies and became a cruiser in their naval service. When old, she was dismantled and became a powder hulk at Toulon, where she was found by the British when that port was taken in 1793. When the British evacuated Toulon the old *Iris*, ex *Hancock*, was blown up—the last survivor of the Continental Navy then afloat.

The 32-gun frigate *Warren* was built at Providence, Rhode Island, from a design by Sylvester Bowers. The same thing had happened in Rhode Island that had taken place in New Hampshire and Massachusetts. The official plans did not arrive promptly, so the committee, or board, in charge had the design of the *Warren* prepared by a local master shipwright, Sylvester Bowers, who also was the master shipwright on the 28-gun *Providence*. Benjamin Talman was the master shipwright on the *Warren*. The *Providence* and *Warren* were both completed. The *Warren* was burned to prevent capture August 14, 1779, while part of the Penobscot expedition. No plans of the ship exist, but the following dimensions may be correct: length on the lower deck 132' 1", beam 34' 5½", and depth of hold 11' 0". It is known that Bowers was instructed by the local committee to adjust his design as much as possible to agree with the Marine Committee plan once the latter came to hand. Apparently this change

Draught of the 32 gun frigate "Raleigh"
from Admiralty Draught

Plan 3. Draught of RALEIGH, 32 guns, after the
Admiralty draught made after her capture.

Continental Frigate
"Hancock"

Transom

Plan 4. Draught of HANCOCK, *32 guns*, *after the Admiralty draught made after her capture.*

Principal Dimensions

Length on the Range of the lower deck ---- 136·7"
" " Keel for Tonnage---- 115·10⅝"
Breadth, moulded ---------------- 35·2"
Depth in hold ------------------ 11·0⅜"
Burthen in Tons-- -- ---------- N° 762 ⁸⁄₃₄

As taken off in June, 1779, in the
Plymouth Dockyard, England.

Ø is 54·4" from F.P.
Stations spaced 9·6, 7·6 & 5
L.W.t up 13·3" on F.P, 15·2" on A.P.
WL's spaced 3¾¼"
Buttocks - 48"

from Admiralty Draught.

"Hancock"

was limited to topside appearance, if, indeed, the instructions were ever carried out.

The remaining 32-gun frigate was the *Washington*, built in Philadelphia by Manuel, Jehu, and Benjamin Eyre, and launched August 7, 1776. She was not finished, being scuttled on November 2 of the next year to prevent capture. The hull remaining above water was burned in May, 1778; the bottom was salvaged and sold at Philadelphia. It is reasonable to suppose this ship was a sister of *Randolph*.

The 28-gun frigates, intended to be like *Virginia*, were built on two plans, apparently, for the *Providence* measured 126′ 6½″ on the berth deck, 33′ 8″ beam, and 10′ 5″ depth of hold. Though her dimensions were quite close to the *Virginia*'s, the difference in beam indicates that her builder, Sylvester Bowers, had prepared a new design for her as he had for the 32-gun *Warren*. The *Providence* was launched at Providence, Rhode Island, in May, 1776. Four years later, on May 12, 1780, she was captured by the British when they took Charleston, South Carolina. The *Providence* was taken into the Royal Navy as a 32-gun frigate and sold out in March, 1783, when the Royal Navy was reduced in size by the disposal of old vessels and those needing much repair.

The *Trumbull* was built at Chatham, Connecticut, by John Cotton. Work was started on the lofting of the ship about the end of February, 1776. From what little is known of the vessel it is highly probable that she was built to the official design. This frigate got to sea but was taken by H.B.M. *Iris* off the Capes of the Delaware, as previously mentioned. She was not taken into the Royal Navy, which indicates that the survey found her to be either rotten or a poorly built ship. This vessel has been confused with a large American privateer ship, the *Governor Trumbull*, 20 guns, which was taken by H.B.M. *Venus* in the West Indies. The *Governor Trumbull* was bought into the Royal Navy as the *Tobago*, 20 guns.

The *Montgomery* was one of the two New York frigates never completed; they were built by Lancaster Burling at Poughkeepsie and burned on October 6, 1777, in the Hudson, to prevent capture. The two ships had been launched about the end of October, 1776, but had been slow in completing owing to various causes—the British capture of New York City and the diversion of men and some materials to the squadron on Lake Champlain being perhaps the most important. The closing of the Hudson had made their completion useless in any case by late September, 1776.

The *Effingham* is supposed to have been built by the Grice yard at Phila-delphia. She was launched on the 7th of November, 1776, and was scuttled the next year, with the 32-gun *Washington*. The British capture of Philadelphia and then the seizure of the Delaware by their fleet had effectively ended the building program in Pennsylvania by the last of November, 1777.

The 24-gun frigates accomplished little, yet they appear to have been good ships of their class. Only two of the three ordered were completed. The *Boston*, built by the Crosses of Newburyport, got to sea with the *Hancock*, but was not captured until the fall of Charleston, South Carolina, on May 12, 1780. She was taken into the Royal Navy as the *Charleston*, 20 guns, and was sold out and broken up in 1783. No plans have been found, but her measurements as taken off were 114' 3" on the berth deck, 32' 0" beam, and 10' 3" depth of hold. The *Delaware* of the same class, built at Philadelphia by Warwick Coates, was captured in the Delaware River when the British began operations there in the fall of 1777. This vessel was taken into the Royal Navy under the same name as a 28-gun frigate and her measurements were taken off as 117' 9½" on the berth deck, 32' 10½" beam, and 9' 8½" depth of hold. The *Delaware* was sold out of the Royal Navy in March, 1783. The third 24-gun frigate was the New York-built *Congress*, built by Burling at Poughkeepsie. She was not only launched about the same time as the *Montgomery* but was also destroyed at the same time and place, near Esopus. The *Delaware* and the *Congress* were prob-ably built to the Marine Committee designs, so the dimensions of the *Delaware* may be assumed to be those authorized by the Continental Congress.

It is possible to give a few details of the ships completed under the Act of December 13, 1775, in addition to those shown in the plans. It will be noted that two of the plans, those of the *Hancock* and the *Raleigh*, show extensive orna-mentation at bow and stern, while the Admiralty plan of the *Virginia* (which was also made from a completed ship) shows none. It is probable that few of the ships actually were without much carving; the inventory of the *Virginia* shows she had a "warrior" figurehead, but whether this implied an Indian or some specific individual like John Smith is by no means certain. It was the general practice, apparently, to give these ships a figurehead, an effigy of the person for whom she was named. Hence it is logical to assume that this was the case in the *Randolph*. The ships named for towns or colonies probably had figure-heads having some traditional reference to their namesakes. Since the carvings for the Continental ships could be made while they were under construction, from the draught or by reference to the mould-loft work, there would be no delay in finishing the ship by the use of carving, for only minor alterations were required to fit them properly.

The rig of the Continental frigates varied a good deal because of the variety of dimensions and models. From the little information available it appears that they all carried a spritsail and sprit-topsail under the bowsprit. Most of them do not appear to have crossed royal yards, though all certainly had pole royal

Figure 7. Spar and sail plan of RALEIGH, *1777, from spar dimensions. (See Plan 3.)*

masts. The *Hancock* had royals across on her main and fore masts, set on poles rather than on fidded royal masts, according to a British agent. She also had a lateen yard on her spanker, though its sail did not extend forward of the mizzen-mast. On this was set a square-yard ringtail, apparently. The *Boston*, built in the same yard, had a gaff spanker. Both ships used a light mast, in lieu of a flag-pole on the taffrail, on which was hoisted a lateen yard and sail, the sheet of which was set up on an outrigger over the stern. The *Raleigh* apparently had about the same rig except that she carried no royal yards. Her spar dimensions are somewhat difficult to interpret, but she carried both a mizzen yard and a crossjack, as well as a driver yard and boom, and a long flagpole. The reconstructed sail plan attempts to show the rig (Figure 7). It will be noted that this ship carried studding sails on fore and main. During the Revolution the lateen yard on the mizzen was slowly going out of fashion, so it is found that ships were rigged either way in this period. The rake of the masts in American ships often showed a peculiarity at this time: the foremast was either vertical or had a slight rake forward, while the main and mizzen often raked aft, the mizzenmast more sharply than the main. The bowsprit steeve was being gradually reduced. In the drawing of the *Randolph* the original showed that the heel was to be stepped below the gun deck, but the instructions written on the draught called for the bowsprit to be stepped above the gun deck, which would not only reduce the steeve, or angle, of the bowsprit, but would also give this spar a more secure step.

The painting of the Continental frigates seems to have been done by the builders or the captains to suit their fancy. The materials for painting some of the ships were white lead, yellow ocher, black oil paint, and Spanish brown. Red paint, made from iron oxide, was also used. The carved work was picked off in the colors considered suitable to the subject—white, blue, yellow, brown, and red being used. The sides of the vessels were usually yellow with black mouldings or narrow stripes, or were black with red, white, and yellow stripes in very narrow bands. Some vessels were painted red, but it is believed these were only small craft such as the vessels built on Lake Champlain. The decks were usually oiled, with the bulwarks red or brown. All nettings and weather cloths were black; in a few cases the weather cloths in the head rails at the bow were painted to represent panels or even carving. Netting and weather cloths were used in the waist of the ship, from quarterdeck to forecastle, to mask the heads of the gun crews that would be exposed by the low bulwarks. The quarterdeck rails were often closed in, or raised, in the same manner.

The following descriptions were written by a British agent in Boston:

Hancock, A man's head with yellow breeches, white stockings, blue coat, and yellow buttonholes, small cocked hat with yellow lace, has a mast in lieu of an ensign staff with a lateen sail on it, has a fore-and-aft driver boom with another across, two topgallant royal masts, pole mizzen topmast, whole mizzen yard and mounts 32 guns. Has rattlesnake carved on the stern, netting all around the ship; stern black and yellow quartergalleries, all yellow.

Boston, An Indian head with bow and arrow in the hand, painted white, red and yellow, two topgallant royal masts, pole mizzen on which she hoists a topgallant sail; painted nearly like the *Hancock* with nettings all around, has a gaff, a mast in lieu of an ensign staff with lateen sail on it and mounts 30 guns.

Brig *Lexington,* two topgallant yards and royals, square tuck, painted yellow and a low round(ed) stern painted lead color, black sides and yellow mouldings.

Ship privateer *Reprisal;* Stern painted black and yellow, mouldings on quarters white, black side, no quartergalleries, a figurehead, three topgallant yards and three long mastheads for royals.

The plan of the Continental Congress for the use of the new ships was based on the same optimism that established their estimate of the time required to build the vessels. There were, in fact, no allowances for the tremendous difficulties in completing the ships, getting them to sea, and assembling them to form squadrons. The individual ships that were completed were too weak to break the blockade at any of the ports where they had been building, and so escaped to sea only by stealth. On the other hand, the new ships were far more powerful and expensive than was necessary for commerce raiding or for the packet service. Once any of the ships got to sea, there were no supplies available, except by capture from the enemy, for there were no colonial bases or supply vessels.

The British had effectively cut the Continental Congress's shipbuilding program and canceled the greater part of their naval plans for the future by their capture of New York and the resultant closing of the Hudson, followed by their investing of the lower Delaware and seizure of Philadelphia, and, finally, by the blockade and invasion of the Chesapeake itself. These operations led to the capture of the *Delaware* and the *Virginia,* and to the destruction of the unfinished *Washington, Effingham, Montgomery,* and *Congress*—to say nothing of the loss of a number of the small craft obtained through the Act of October, 1775.

As things turned out, the ships built in the smaller and less important ports were, with the one exception of the *Randolph,* the only vessels that cruised under the Continental flag. Had the British shown any initiative even these ships could have been prevented from escaping to sea, for the British intelligence is known to have been well informed, and it certainly possessed complete and correct information as to the number and location of the ships building for the Continental Navy. However, the Continental Congress made it easy for the British by ordering many American naval ships into the Delaware and to Charleston, South Carolina, so that the capture of the ships was made certain when these localities were attacked. The tactical plans for the Continental Navy seem to have been as vague and ineffective as those of the Continental Congress for military operations. The politicians and demagogues insisted on directing both military and naval operations and movements in spite of continuous disasters.

During the year 1776 the Marine Committee and its agents procured a number of small craft: the cutter *Dolphin* of 10 guns, a schooner named *Enterprise*, the sloops *General Mifflin* and *General Schuyler*, and the galleys *Washington* and *Lady Washington*, the packet *Spy*, and a vessel named *General Arnold*, apparently a small schooner. In addition they bought or built a number of row barges, sloops, gundalows, and radeaux to aid the various state navies in defending the coast, particularly in the vicinity of New York and Philadelphia. One prize was taken into service, the small 10-gun sloop, or schooner, *Racehorse*. She was one of the vessels destroyed in the Delaware in 1777. The records are so incomplete that it is impossible to list the names of all of the small craft owned or manned by the Continental Navy; a great many vessels were private craft chartered to the Continental Congress, and these cannot usually be distinguished from national vessels.

While the ships ordered under the Act of December 13, 1775, were still under construction or fitting out, a new act was passed by the Continental Congress on November 20, 1776, authorizing additional new construction. This directed the building of three 74-gun ships, five 36-gun frigates, an 18-gun brig, and a packet. Three ship sloops appear to have been authorized soon afterward, though the act for building them has not been discovered. Since all the vessels ordered in the Act of 1776, except two 74's and the 18-gun brig, can be accounted for with certainty, it is rather unlikely that the three ship sloops were substitutes for uncompleted vessels previously authorized, though this could possibly be the case.

The three 74's were to be fast, powerful ships. It was intended that one was to be built at Philadelphia, one at Boston, and one at Portsmouth, New Hampshire; probably all were to be built to the same design, as had been the case with the earlier frigate classes. One plan of these American Revolutionary War 74's has happily been preserved by Humphreys and is now in the National Archives (40–15–6, G; 40–15–6, H). This plan of the 74 is in the same hand as that of the *Randolph*, and there can be no question that both were drawn by the same designer. The draftsmanship, the method of presenting the bow and of showing the wales, and also the methods of fairing, are notably alike in the originals. The hull form used in the 74 is very similar to that of the

Randolph in all respects. In addition to this draught of a 74, Joshua Humphreys built a half-model of a 74 for the Navy Board, or Board of Admiralty, and this too has been preserved. The model, a planked decorative half-model in a fairly good state of preservation, is now on exhibit at Independence Hall, Philadelphia.

An assumption that all this is sufficient to indicate that Humphreys was the designer of the 74's faces the same difficulty that raises doubt that he designed the *Randolph*. In addition, close examination of the half-model shows that it is not like the plan in many important respects. Plan 5 shows the design of the 74 redrawn with the restorations noted. The half-model has different quarter galleries, the forecastle rails are not as shown in the plan, and it appears that the model does not have quite the same lines forward as the draught indicates. The writer is of the opinion that the model was made by Humphreys from the draught, to show how he intended to build the 74 to be constructed at Philadelphia, and that he "improved" on the design as a sales argument. Why would he have departed in any detail in making the model if he had made the draught? Further, his papers in regard to the Revolutionary War 74 refer to the "model" and not to the draught. The fact that Humphreys appears to have retained the model indicates that it was not one ordered by the local Navy Board, or by the Continental Admiralty Board, but one he made in an effort to obtain the contract for building the Philadelphia 74. Humphreys prepared a set of spar dimensions for his model which would fit the draught. The sail plan is reconstructed on this basis in Figure 8. There can be no acceptable claim that Humphreys designed either the *Randolph* or the 74 until it can be explained how this was accomplished in drafting work not done in his hand.

Owing to the trend of war which put Philadelphia in the hands of the enemy, no 74 was built there. One 74 had some work done on her at Boston, but this does not indicate that she was ever actually laid down. Only one, in fact, was ever built—the *America*, at Portsmouth, New Hampshire. Colonel James K. Hackett was the builder, with his cousin William the master shipwright or foreman. The ship was laid down in May, 1777, but work proceeded very slowly; only about twenty-four carpenters were employed on her because of a lack of materials and funds. Various orders concerning the ship indicate that instructions were given at one time to depart from the original plan by cutting down the vessel to 56 or 60 guns, but these orders were apparently countermanded. In early June, 1779, the Congress instructed Robert Morris to complete the ship as soon as possible. Later in the month it appointed John Paul

Figure 8. Spar plan for proposed 74-gun ships, from Humphreys' dimensions. (See Plan 5.)

81

Jones her commander, which also made him the resident inspector or super-visor. In spite of the efforts of Morris, the construction of the ship was very slow.

Robert W. Neeser, in an article entitled "The True Story of the *America*" (No. 126 of *The Proceedings of the United States Naval Institute*), quoting an unknown source, gives the following leading dimensions of the Portsmouth-built ship: 182′ 6″ length on upper deck, 50′ 6″ extreme beam, 23′ 0″ depth of hold, 150′ 0″ length on the keel. Thus if the vessel was built on the same plan that Humphreys had, then the Hacketts made the ship 3′ 0″ longer on the keel and 3′ 0″ wider in beam, but without much change in over-all length. The measurement on the upper deck is assumed to be from bow rabbet to rudderpost; if any other assumption is made, then the *America* would be shorter than the draught preserved by Humphreys, and would not then agree with the keel measurement given by Neeser. According to the account given in the reference, Jones found the ship much less complete than he had been led to expect. He also made extensive changes in the ship's design, so far as upper works were concerned. He shifted the mainmast three frames aft, lengthened quarterdeck and forecastle, and raised the waist so that the upper sheer line was flush, which permitted gangways to be used the full length of the waist. He reduced the quarter galleries and lengthened the light poop deck somewhat, on which, Jones reported, the bulwark rail was fitted to fold down. The figure-head was the Goddess of Liberty, with the right arm raised and pointing up-ward and ahead. On the left arm there was a shield with thirteen stars of silver on a blue background.

It is difficult to fit the dimensions and the changes noted to the Humphreys plan, but it must be emphasized that the reference quoted by Neeser was ob-viously written some time after the Revolution and even if authentic is not trustworthy, since it was undoubtedly written from memory.

Jones states that Colonel or Major Hackett was not able to judge the proper scantlings, but that he found the leading shipwright, William Hauscom (Hans-com?) able to work these out. The context of the reference is that the ship's model was on the original draught, while Jones and "Hauscom" made changes in the topsides and were responsible for the scantlings. Contemporary accounts at Portsmouth give the credit for the design of the *America* to William Hackett. The account given by Neeser is subject to suspicion, for it appears obvious that Jones found the ship in frame, yet he seems to claim Hackett could not calculate the scantlings. Either Jones claims too much, or the authority used for the Neeser article is not authentic. At any rate, it is quite impossible to establish at this time the real part that William Hackett had in the design of this ship.

The *America* was launched November 5, 1782. In the meantime, however, on September 3 the Continental Congress had presented her to France to replace the French 74, *Magnifique*, lost in Boston Harbor, in order to show their gratitude to the French king for his help against England. The ship was turned over to her French commander immediately after her launch. Her career in the French navy was short, however, as in 1786 she was found to be rotten and was broken up. The French report indicates that the *America* did not combine all the qualities which a vessel of her class should have, but does not specify what the faults were. In view of the rather sharp lines shown in the draught preserved by Humphreys, it seems probable that the *America* (if built on these lines) lacked the displacement to carry her lower deck guns high enough above the water. The *America* is reported to have been armed with 30 long 18-pdrs., 32 long 12-pdrs., and 14 long 9-pdrs., the latter upon her forecastle and quarter-deck. If this is true, then the *America* had one more port to a side on her lower deck than was called for in the draught in the Humphreys papers; also the ship in the latter was not intended to carry guns on the forecastle. Humphreys' half-model shows the same port arrangement as in the draught. The plan of the Revolutionary War 74 shows a solid rail on the forecastle deck without gun ports or stanchions indicated; the Humphreys half-model shows an open rail, or "drift," also without gun ports or stanchions. Plate III shows the Humphreys half-model: the model and the plan should be compared and both studied with relation to Neeser's statements.

Of the remaining vessels authorized by the Act of November 20, 1776, only the plan of the 36-gun frigate *Confederacy* has been found. It is the Admiralty plan made from measurements of the ship after she was captured and bought into the Royal Navy. The *Confederacy*, launched 1778, was built at Norwich, Connecticut, on the Thames River, by Jedidiah Willets, who may have been either the builder or the supervisor.

There is a possibility that she represents the official design of her class, and there is a plausible argument for such an assumption, based on her lines and those of the ships of the Revolution preserved by Humphreys. A comparison of her lines, shown in Plan 6, with those of the *Randolph* and the Revolutionary War 74-gun ship shows a slight resemblance in hull form and in the appearance of the bow and the beakhead bulkhead, as well as a faint likeness in the ends of the quarter and forecastle rails. The resemblance is sufficiently strong, in the opinion of the writer, to indicate that the *Confederacy* was designed by the same man who designed the *Randolph* and the 74-gun ship.

The *Confederacy* was a remarkable vessel. She was very long for a ship of her rate, almost 160' on deck. Her dimensions were 154' 9" on the berth deck, 37' 0" beam, 12' 3" depth in the hold. Comparing these with the dimensions of a contemporary British 36-gun frigate of about 1780, the *Flora*, we find the latter only measured 137' 0" on her berth deck, 38' beam, and 13' 3" depth of hold. Thus the American was almost 23 feet longer, with a foot less in beam and depth. This was not the only peculiarity of the *Confederacy:* she was almost a "galley-frigate" and had much in common with the British galley-frigate *Charles-Galley* (built at Woolwich in 1676 by Phineas Pett), which measured 131' 1" on her lower deck, 29' 0" beam, and 8' 1½" depth of hold. The *Confederacy* was very like the older *Charles-Galley* in her proportion of depth to length and in the relatively narrow beam. Both vessels were fitted to row on the lower deck, the *Charles-Galley* having more sweeps. Rowing on the lower deck in frigates was not uncommon, however, for both the *Southampton* and *Alarm* classes of 32's built for the Royal Navy in 1756 and 1757 show this feature. This location of the sweep ports was going out of fashion by 1775. What makes the *Confederacy* so much like the older galley-frigates is not merely where she carried her sweep ports, but rather the combination of this with narrow beam and shoal depth. The *Confederacy* was on a fairly sharp model, like the early galley-frigates, and was designed for speed. The ship was armed frigate-fashion, like her earlier compatriots, and had royal poles but no royal yards. Just abaft her wheel, on the quarterdeck, she had a speaking tube leading to the berth deck, which was intended to be used to direct the men who steered the ship there by means of the heavy tiller and its ropes in the event the wheel on the quarterdeck was shot away.

The *Confederacy* was an ornate ship, profusely carved. She was very handsome and comparable to *Hancock* in all respects. She had one oddity in a large vessel of this period: her keel was slightly rockered forward. The *Confederacy* was described at the time of her capture as being a very fast ship and well built.

This ship saw very little service under the Continental flag, for she was captured off the Virginia Capes in 1781 by H.B.M. ships *Orpheus* and *Roebuck*. She was a rather unfortunate vessel. In 1779 she was to carry a French diplomat to Europe, and after many delays she finally got away—only to be heavily damaged in a gale off the Bahamas at the end of the year. She had to put into Martinique to be rerigged. On finally returning to the Delaware it was found she required extensive refitting. After her capture the Royal Navy bought her in and rated her as a 36-gun frigate under the name *Confederate*. She was sold out and broken up about 1783.

The second frigate laid down under the new authorization was the *Alliance*, built at Salisbury Point on the Merrimack River, Massachusetts, in 1777. Wil-

Figure 9. Spar and sail plan of CONFEDERACY *after Admiralty dimensions. (See Plan 6.)*

liam and James Hackett were the builders, and the first is traditionally the designer of the ship. Little is known about the design of this vessel. A contemporary report states that she was 151′ 0″ on the lower deck, 36′ 0″ beam, and 12′ 6″ depth of hold. She would thus be about the same type as the *Confederacy*, if these dimensions are correct, but slightly smaller in size. She was rated variously as a 32- and a 36-gun frigate, the latter being the correct rating. This vessel was given a great reputation for speed and survived the war in the American service; she was sold at Philadelphia June 3, 1785. The ship usually carried 40 guns—28 18-pdrs. and 12 9-pdrs.

The third frigate was the *Bourbon*. Laid down at Middletown, Connecticut, early in 1780, she was launched in July, 1783, after much delay because of lack of funds. In September of 1783 she was recommended to be sold, and nothing further is known about her.

The remaining two frigates authorized were to be built at Gosport, Virginia. These vessels were not completed. The work was first ordered stopped in 1778; then it was decided to complete one of them. But this ship too had her construction discontinued when the British invaded Virginia, and both the unfinished hulls were finally burned during the ensuing campaign. Thus the five frigates authorized by the Act of 1776 had been started, but only two were ever completed and placed in naval service.

The *Ranger* may have been intended for the 18-gun brig authorized under the Act of 1776, but this is very doubtful. It is more probable that she was one of the three ship sloops supposed to have been authorized shortly after the Act of November 20, 1776, came into force. Certainly she was not a frigate cut down during construction. The three ship sloops were the *Ranger, Saratoga,* and *General Gates.* The *Ranger* was captured and taken into the Royal Navy, so her dimensions have survived: 116′ 0″ on the main deck, 34′ 0″ beam, and 13′ 6″ depth of hold. She carried 18 6-pdrs., a small armament for so large a vessel. She was about as large as the 24-gun ships authorized in '75 and was a quarterdecked ship. A contemporary account says that she was oversparred. *Ranger* became a noted name in the American Navy because of this ship sloop. She was a successful cruiser but finally fell into the hands of the British at the fall of Charleston, and was taken into the Royal Navy as the *Halifax.*

The second sloop was probably the *General Gates,* about which little is known. A vessel of this name was apparently building somewhere in New England, as correspondence relating to her was directed to the Boston Navy Board. The vessel seems to have been completed in 1778 and was ordered sold immediately. This causes a doubt as to the identification; the vessel was sold in 1779, long before the war ended. There were also a number of privateers of the same name, though none of them were ships.

The third sloop was the *Saratoga,* built at Philadelphia by Humphreys. Her dimensions have not been found. There are references to her in the Humphreys papers as being a brigantine, but it has been well established that she came out ship-rigged. Perhaps she was the "brig" authorized in the Act of 1776, altered. The *Saratoga* was lost on her maiden cruise in 1780.

Humphreys also built a packet, the *Mercury,* which was probably the one authorized in the Act of 1776. A packet service, to be maintained with three vessels between America and France, was established by the Continental Congress in 1780. This service was under the control of the Board of Admiralty that succeeded the Marine Committee. A number of packets were built during the Revolution, including another *Mercury*, one of three packets ordered in Massachusetts, built from a design by John Peck at Plymouth, Massachusetts, in 1780. She is believed to have been a schooner, while the Philadelphia-built ship may have been a ketch. The British captured a ketch-rigged packet of this name and gave her dimensions as 72′ 5″ long on the main deck, 20′ 5″ beam, and 8′ 8″ depth of hold. This ketch, taken by H.B.M. ships *Fairy* and *Vestal* off the Banks of Newfoundland, September 10, 1780, was reported by her captors to be a new vessel.

Of the vessels authorized by the Act of 1776, two 74's, three frigates, and perhaps the 18-gun brig were never completed. The lack of funds had delayed some, danger of capture had led to the destruction of two of the frigates, and the capture of the chosen site for building one of the 74's had prevented her ever being laid down. The delays were the main factor that prevented the ships from being completed; the colonies had become exhausted, and shipbuilding materials, munitions, and sound money were now lacking. The limits of financing new ships by the Continental Congress had actually been reached by the Act of 1775, and very little money was left for the program established in 1776. It is difficult to trace the new ships because of the very incomplete records on some of them, owing to a loss of the official papers, the chaotic administrative control of the Continental Navy, and the informal methods resulting from the stress and haste of war.

The administrative problems of building new ships and controlling the activities of the Continental ships led to a slow development in organization. The original Marine Committee lasted until the end of 1779. By this time it was fully apparent that the large and cumbersome Marine Committee was not functioning: the members could not assemble often enough, and there were usually too many conflicting ideas when they did meet. Therefore Congress set up a Board of Admiralty of five members, October 28, 1779. This board took over the Navy Boards established by the Marine Committee in 1777. These had been located at three important ports with the apparent aim of decentralizing control and permitting administrative functions to be exercised without the delays caused by the need of communicating with the congressional board. There were three such Navy Boards in existence, one at Boston, the Eastern Department, one at Philadelphia (or elsewhere in Pennsylvania and in New Jersey when Philadelphia was in the hands of the British), and the third at Baltimore, the Southern Department. The Pennsylvania Navy Board was usually referred to as being in the "Middle District." This board was so close to the Continental Congress that the latter's naval committees usually usurped its functions. The Board of Admiralty was not much of an improvement over the old Marine Committee, for the same difficulty existed in getting the five members to meet, and the old habit continued of dealing directly with local contractors and agents, by-passing the local Navy Boards. The Navy Boards were likewise ineffective; the members would rarely be able to assemble, and as a result only one or two of the board members would be active. Gradually the Navy Boards were replaced, in fact if not in theory, by one member who really acted as the Navy Agent for a district.

The next step was to propose a "Marine Department" headed by a Secretary, but this idea finally degenerated into the mere establishment of an "Agent of Marine," without a headquarters staff. Finally, when the appointment of the agent was under consideration, Congress hedged and gave the position to Robert Morris, the Financial Agent, on a temporary basis (September 6, 1781). On November 2 of the same year they made the assignment permanent; thus the duties of the Agent of Marine became part of the function of the Financial Agent. Morris had been perhaps the most active person in naval affairs, so the choice is easily excused. Under Morris, the local Navy Boards gradually declined in activity and the single agent as a substitute seems to have been accepted. It should be remembered that the difficulties of these committees and boards were due to the slow means of travel and communication, rather than to derelictions of the members themselves. The propensity of governments to attempt control of functions by committees, boards, or councils explains the insistence with which the idea of group control of the Continental Navy was retained, in the face of the obvious weaknesses of the system in the colonies.

The armament of all of the new Continental frigates was a grave problem. Prior to the Revolution the manufacture of cannon was unknown in America. Under all the circumstances then existing it was natural, perhaps, that the British government did not allow such activities. While there were numerous colonial foundries and iron mines in New England, New York, Pennsylvania, and the South, there was no one available who was experienced in the business of cannon manufacture. In spite of this, the Continental Congress planned to fit all the new ships with American-made guns. To make this really difficult, they

Figure 10. British naval guns and swivels of the American revolutionary period.

All Deck Lines to underside.

Dimensions

Length bet. Perps. 180'·0"
    " on Keel   147'·0"
Moulded Beam   49'·0"
Extreme "   49'·8"
Depth in Hold   19'·0"

Room & Space 25"; ⊕ is 71'·10" from F.P.
W.L.'s & Buttocks spaced 4'·0."

Draught of an American 74 Gun Ship
of the Revolution. 1777

Reconstruction:
Knightheads; Location of Fore-end of Poop Rail and
Deck; Transom and Beakhead Bulkhead Elevation;
Channels; and parts of the Head.
References: 40-15-6 H; Humphreys' Half-model;
British 74's of approximate date.

Plan 5. Draught of the 74-gun ship, 1777, probably the official design for the American 74's projected by the Continental Congress.

Dimensions

Length bet. Perps.   154'9"
Beam Moulded   36'5"
    „   Extreme   37'0" to 37⅜" Plank
Depth in Hold   12'3"   Draft at Post 16'0"
Length on Keel for tonnage 133'5"
Burthen in Tons   970 86/94
Θ is 69'3" from F.P. Stations Θ to D space 10'0"
                              D to E   „   10'3"
                              E to F   „   8'0"
                              F to G   „   6'3"
                              G to F.P. „ 4'9"
Θ is 85'6" from A.P. Stations Θ to 5 space 10'0"
                              5 to 6   „   9'3"
                              6 to A.P. „ 7'9"
Waterlines spaced 3'2" Buttocks spaced 4'0"
Height of Wing Transom 20'3"
Room & Space was probably 24". (Not measured)

Plan 6. Draught of CONFEDERACY, after the Admiralty draught made after her capture.

decided, at first, to have all the naval cannon made in Pennsylvania and hauled overland to the shipyards where the frigates were building. It is not surprising to find that this plan failed almost completely and that at the last moment other arrangements had to be made, with the results usual in such cases during wartime. The record of the Continental Congress in the management of naval affairs was extraordinarily inept throughout the Revolution.

It was intended, of course, to arm the new ships with standard guns: the 24-gun frigates were to have 24 9-pdrs., the 28-gun frigates, 26 12-pdrs. and 2 6-pdrs.; the 32-gun frigates, 26 12-pdrs. and 6 6-pdrs. All were to have cohorns or swivels in proportion. Because of the failure of the foundries in Pennsylvania to produce the necessary guns, the ships finally came out with a rather mixed and unsatisfactory armament. These armaments changed a good deal in the ships that got to sea, so that there was never any standardization throughout the Revolution. The *Randolph* was fitted out with 26 12-pdrs., 10 6-pdrs., and 12 cohorns. The *Raleigh* had to complete her armament in France and finally had the same number of guns as the *Randolph*, but only two cohorns. The *Virginia* was fitted with 24 12-pdrs., 6 4-pdrs., and 6 swivels. The *Warren* had a very mixed armament—12 18-pdrs., 14 12-pdrs., 8 9-pdrs., and a few swivels. The *Boston* had 5 12-pdrs., 19 9-pdrs., 2 6-pdrs., and 4 4-pdrs., with the addition of 16 swivels. The *Delaware* had 22 12-pdrs. and 6 6-pdrs., with an unrecorded number of swivels. The *Hancock* had 24 12-pdrs. and 10 6-pdrs., besides swivels. All but a few ships had a mixture of American-made guns, cast in foundries in Connecticut, Rhode Island, Massachusetts, Pennsylvania, and Maryland, with guns captured from the British and French guns purchased abroad. There were some few cannon in the colonies when the war began, old fieldpieces and captured French guns of the war of 1756–63; it is probable that some of these also found their way aboard Continental vessels.

When the new program of 1776 came up, the Navy Board of the Eastern District was to arm the *Alliance* and *Confederacy*, frigates, as well as the *Ranger*, sloop of war. It was also to furnish guns for the *Bourbon*, but did not do so, since the frigate was never completed. It must also have been the responsibility of this board to find guns for the 74 *America*. At any rate, they ordered all the guns for the *Alliance* and *Confederacy* from one foundry in Connecticut; when this failed to deliver, they transferred the contract to a Massachusetts foundry, which also failed to deliver in full. The two ships were intended to be armed with 28 12-pdrs. and 8 6-pdrs. each. The *Alliance* carried

28 12-pdrs. and 8 9-pdrs. in service, while *Confederacy* apparently had 28 12-pdrs. and 8 6-pdrs. The *America*'s armament has been described earlier.

The American-made guns were usually copies of the English naval guns in nearly all respects. They were generally of cast iron. Some brass guns were also manufactured, but these were apparently intended for fieldpieces and not for shipboard. The proportions of all parts of a naval gun of the period were based on the diameter of the shot used in it, but each foundry seems to have used its own factors, so that the guns were not standard in length or weight, though maintaining the bore within narrow tolerances. The location of the trunnions often varied; some foundries placed them in line with the bore, while others placed them below the center line of the bore. Naval guns above 9-pdrs. rarely had low trunnions, apparently. The variation in the guns resulted in trouble when gun carriages had to be made before the guns were cast; often the carriages had to be altered when the guns were in hand. Figure 10 shows some of the common British naval guns of the Revolution according to the official designs, but these were not closely followed in casting. Many guns built according to these plans were thicker-walled at the muzzle and so had less taper than shown. Many were longer as well. The guns shown were what were usually termed "short guns," as can be seen by the notes on the variations in length contained in the drawing. Lieutenant Commander Brewington has given an excellent account of the casting of the guns for the Continental Navy in *The American Neptune*, January and April, 1943 (Vol. III, Nos. 1 and 2).

The swivels were far less standardized than cannon. They ranged from what might be termed heavy muskets to small cannon. This class of weapon was supported by an oar-lock type of mount set in the rail of the vessel or on vertical timbers outside the rail called "stocks." Since the mounting of these guns could not be very secure, the size of swivels was limited to the relatively low power that would result in light recoil. The maximum bore of the swivel type of gun was about 2" and the weight of shot was usually less than one pound. Loose shot could be fired, and this made the swivel a very effective gun against personnel in close-range fighting. For this reason many ships carried a few swivels in their tops, as well as in vantage points along the rails, particularly raised above the main rails on the quarterdeck or poop. The gun was extensively used in the early colonial merchantmen for defense purposes and was also popular in small vessels on the American lakes, as it was all that was needed to fight off any Indian (or outlaw) attack on these wilderness seas.

The most common swivels in American hands during the Revolution were guns of the cannon type, from 34″ to 36″ extreme length and from 1½″ to 1¾″ bore, throwing shot of from one-half to three-quarters of a pound. Most of the guns were miniature cannon in appearance. A few had wooden grips secured to their breeches; these were often merely straight sticks, but sometimes they were curved much like a huge pistol grip. There were some smaller swivels of this type (with barrels about 28″ long) that had flintlocks attached, but most of the swivels were fired with a slow match—rope yarn impregnated with gunpowder, pitch, or other material to allow slow combustion. These small swivels fired shot from 1″ up to 1½″ in diameter. There were other swivel-mounted guns of even lighter nature. There were heavy musketlike weapons, with a flintlock firing lead shot somewhat less than 1″ in diameter. These guns were from 60″ to 72″ long and were commonly known as "buccaneering pieces," after the earlier freebooters who had made them popular. Another light weapon of this class was the "blunderbuss," a short, heavy bell-muzzle gun for firing loose shot. Both the buccaneering piece and the blunderbuss had shoulder stocks like muskets. They were never classed as "guns" in rating a ship's armament, nor in fact were swivels as a class so rated.

Some ships carried large swivel cannon of about 2″ bore mounted on heavy wooden brackets inboard the rail; these guns were also used as boat cannon. They were often called "howitzers" but were generally considered to be swivels. "Cohorn," or "coehorn," was a generic name for short light cannon and included light mortars, howitzers, and the smaller swivels—in fact, any cannon-type weapon that could be unshipped and carried by one or two men. Americans seem to have applied the name principally to swivels, with hand-grips at the breech.

In addition to making naval guns longer than standard, the foundries often made them thicker-walled, or "double-fortified." This greatly increased their weight, but also made them capable of handling heavier charges of powder, which increased range. Such cannon were considered equal to the standard gun next above them in weight of shot. Double-fortified guns were usually longer than standard and were used as bow guns, particularly on heavy gunboats. Such guns were apparently rarely above 18-pounders.

With the crude methods employed in manufacturing both guns and shot, it is not surprising to find that the variation between bore and shot diameters was often great. The clearance around the shot in the bore of a gun, termed "windage," was often excessive in both American and British guns. The French guns were more accurately made, and when used with the shot intended for them were much favored for chase guns at bow or stern. The quality of powder also left much to be desired. The American-made powder was particularly poor because of low-quality ingredients and unevenness in their proportions. The cannon sights were usually no more than notches filed in the base ring and muzzle bell; a few guns are said to have had some type of rear sight attached to them, but the design is unknown. It is not surprising to find that the shooting in naval actions of the Revolution was very inaccurate.

Figure 11a. Gun carriage, 1768, as used during the American Revolution.

The "short gun" was the standard British Navy cannon, as opposed to the "long guns," having more length. The American-made guns seem to have been longer than the British standard, though the lack of identified guns makes any general statement regarding American cannon of this period of doubtful value. It appears that some American foundries made guns on the French models, which were somewhat longer than similar British cannon, but it is not known whether many such guns were placed aboard any of the frigates. The "short guns" of the Revolution were not, however, the carronades. These were invented in England in 1779, and by 1781 they were extensively used in the British Navy. They appeared too late in the war, however, to have reached American hands.

The gun carriages were of the type common on shipboard in the eighteenth century, consisting of two heavy side pieces, or frames, mounted on two axles and four wheels; the wheels as well as the axles and side frames were all of timber. The mounts were made to fit the guns, whose measurements were used to determine the size of each part of the gun carriage. The height of the gun ports above the deck was the only factor outside the gun that was used in

Figure 11b. Draught of a gunboat, to carry one gun, of the type employed by the British on Lake Champlain, 1776.

designing a gun carriage. Figure 11 shows the standard British Navy gun carriage of the period. In gunboats having cramped decks, the gun was often mounted on a carriage without wheels, or "trucks": the side frames slid on two heavy timber skids. Some had timber tracks with the carriage trucks retained. British Navy gun carriages were painted red or brown, the guns were black, and the tompions or muzzle plugs were red or yellow, made with a button like the breech of the gun.

In addition to the ships built for the Continental Navy there were a number of vessels of all types purchased or borrowed for naval service from 1777 to the end of the war. In 1777, when the British moved against Philadelphia, the Continental Navy seems to have borrowed or at least manned a number of the Pennsylvania State Navy gunboats. The xebecs or galleys, *Champion* and *Repulse*, carrying 2 long 24-pdrs., 2 18-pdrs., and 4 9-pdrs., were the most important. Both vessels were destroyed to prevent capture. A packet named the *Fame* is mentioned this year, and a 10-gun brigantine, the *Resistance*, was fitted out at New London, Connecticut, for the Continental service. She was captured by Howe's fleet in 1778. A sloop named *Surprise* was also employed in the Continental Navy.

By far the most numerous additions to the American fleet in the year 1777 were the vessels obtained abroad, particularly in France. Benjamin Franklin and Silas Deane had been attempting to get ships from the French for over a year. Deane's instructions from Congress in 1776 were to try to buy or borrow eight ships of the line, an extremely optimistic idea on the part of a particularly hopeful group of politicians. Some small vessels were obtained by devious means early in 1777. Two fast cutters were purchased to act as dispatch vessels, and the *Surprise* of 10 guns was bought by agents at Dover, England, and fitted out at Dunkirk, France. However, the French government seized her and surrendered her to the English. She was said to be a large vessel of her class, and a vessel of this type and name was in the Royal Navy in 1779 which measured 67′ 3″ on deck, 28′ 11″ beam, and 9′ 0″ deep in the hold. Another dispatch cutter was bought at Dunkirk, the *Revenge*, of 14 6-pdrs. and 22 swivels. This vessel reached America and was sold at Philadelphia in 1780 as unserviceable. The *Dolphin*, of 10 guns, another cutter, was also purchased as a dispatch boat in France. These cutters were involved in a number of intrigues by American and British agents, the latter attempting to get possession of the American secret dispatches and the American agents trying to prevent it, and also if possible to involve the French government in the war.

The American agents in France finally did obtain two frigates. The 28-gun *Queen of France* was purchased and sent to America. She was an old ship and was sunk at Charleston, South Carolina, May 11, 1780, to prevent capture by the British on the surrender of that city. By far the most important ship they obtained, however, was *L'Indien*, which passed through their hands in a curious manner. This was a new and very powerful ship built to a French design at Amsterdam, Holland, early in 1777. Soon after the American agents got her they were apparently forced to give her up to the French, who in turn sold her to the Duke of Luxemburg, by whom she was finally loaned to South Carolina. She was renamed *South Carolina*, and after reaching America, she was taken off the Delaware Capes on December 19, 1782, by the *Astrea*, 32, *Diomede*, 44, and *Quebec*, 32, after an eighteeen-hour chase. The importance of the *South Carolina*, ex *L'Indien*, was not in her career, but in the effect her great size and power is said to have had on later American men-of-war. The *South Carolina* was about 154' 0" on the main deck, about 40' 0" beam, and 16' 6" deep in the hold; she carried 24 36-pdrs. and 12 12-pdrs., all French-type guns. The combination of her heavy armament and great length caused her to hog, and she was considered to be a weakly built ship. Because of this she was not purchased for the Royal Navy after her capture. A plan of the ship was published in Vice-Admiral Paris' monumental *Souvenirs de Marine*, Vol. 5; this is reproduced in Plate IV. The drawing shown is not the building plan, of course, but an ornamental draught made after the ship was completed.

The Americans were less successful in 1778, when they acquired only five vessels, most of which were small craft. They obtained the packets *Phoenix* and *Independence*, the latter a brig or brigantine; a prize British transport brig which had been cut down into a galley or block ship of 8 guns—the *Pigot;* a small packet named the *Despatch;* and a merchant ship that was purchased at New Orleans, the *Rebecca*, which was renamed *Morris* and armed with 24 guns. The *Morris* had a very short career, however, as she was lost in a Gulf hurricane, August 18, 1779.

The year 1779 was much more productive; not only did the Continental service obtain ships by purchase and capture in home waters, but they also obtained a number of vessels in France. At home, the ship *Morris* was replaced by a schooner of the same name, presented by some citizens residing in the Spanish colony of Louisiana. The *Providence* frigate had captured a British naval brig, the *Diligent* (or *Diligence*) of 14 guns. This was a regular British Navy brig of war, 88' 5¾" long on deck, 24' 8" beam, and 10' 10" deep in the hold. She was built in 1776 and originally carried 10 guns and 12 swivels. She was burned in the disastrous Penobscot Expedition. A sloop named the

Argo, carrying 12 12-pdrs., was also obtained. Another sloop, the *West Florida*, was captured in the Gulf and taken into service, but was sold at Philadelphia in 1780 as unserviceable. The vessels acquired in France, however, were of far greater importance than any of these. The European squadron commanded by John Paul Jones, which was formed at this time, was made up of such ships as an old French East Indiaman, the *Duc de Duras*, renamed the *Bon Homme Richard*, 42 guns. Little is known about this ship, but the approximate dimensions of her class of Indiamen were as follows: length on the main deck 152′ 0″, beam 40′ 0″, depth of hold 19′ 0″. She seems to have had two decks and a long quarterdeck; there were, however, very few guns on the lower deck. She was sunk in action with H.B.M. ship *Serapis*, 44, on September 23, 1779. The *Pallas*, another old merchantman in Jones' squadron, armed with 30 guns, was finally returned to the French, from whom she had been obtained. A 12-gun brig, the *Vengeance*, a large cutter named *Cerf* (ex *Stag*), of 18 guns, and the 20-gun ship *Ariel* were also borrowed from the French and returned. These ships formed the European squadron and were never brought to America.

The frigate *Deane*, a small 32-gun ship, was obtained on a more permanent basis. She was built at Nantes, France, in 1779, to the order of Franklin and Deane, apparently on a plan obtained from one of the French naval constructors. The draught of this ship seems to have been sent to America, but it has not been found. The dimensions of the *Deane* were given as 96′ 0″ on the straight of keel, 32′ 0″ beam; if these are correct then she was as small as the American 24-gun ships authorized in 1775. She was renamed *Hague* in 1782 and was decommissioned at Boston in 1783. Her armament was given at one time as 24 12-pdrs., 2 6-pdrs., and 8 4-pdrs., with a few swivels.

In the year 1780 only one vessel appears to have been obtained, the *Active*, which was employed as a packet. In 1781 no vessel was added to the Continental Navy, but in the next year two ships were obtained: the ex-Indiaman *Duc de Lauzun*, purchased in France and sold there the next year, and the *General Washington*, a 32-gun ship, formerly a British vessel named *General Monk* which had been taken off Cape May, New Jersey, April 2, 1782, by the Pennsylvania state cruiser *Hyder Alley*. The *General Washington* was sold out of the Continental service in 1784. She carried a battery of 24 9-pdrs. and 8 6-pdrs.; she was 130′ 9″ long and 32′ 8″ beam and had the reputation of being a fast sailer and a good ship.

The very high standard of design exhibited in the American frigates, as evidenced in the plans that have survived, indicates that there was more knowledge of the specialized field of naval ship design in America than has usually been assumed. It seems apparent that this knowledge was not confined to a single locality, but was spread out along the coast. Every large shipbuilding town evidently had men who were acquainted with the technicalities of warship design and construction. It is unfortunate that so little has been found about the education and experience of the men who may have designed the American frigates of the Revolution, even though their connection with the vessels is mere speculation. The most reasonable assumption, for the present at least, is that the designers were men who had served apprenticeships under Admiralty-trained shipwrights. The quality of the design and drafting shown in the plans of the *Randolph* and the Revolutionary War 74-gun ship might support the assumption. Without assuming such training it is difficult to explain their ability to turn out such plans and men-of-war equal or superior to those of Britain and France.

In attempting to establish the methods and theories actually employed in American ship design during the colonial and Revolutionary War periods, we come face to face with an almost insurmountable difficulty, the lack of records. There are no books or manuscripts, apparently, that were written by early American ship designers, and the various collections of papers of naval constructors do not include any before 1792, except Humphreys', and his are far from complete in technical matters. As a result all statements concerning the basic principles of design in this period must be founded on analysis of the relatively few plans that have survived. This is insufficient to permit any real exploration of the probable aims of the designers. Their ideas on the hull-form theories then prevalent in Europe, and the use of calculations and similar technical aids to design, are not available to us. All of the evidence that may be extracted from ship plans of the early periods of American naval development, and the few technical references at the end of the eighteenth century that pertain to Revolutionary War vessels, show that the American designers leaned toward sharp-bottomed ships, of relatively great length in proportion to other dimensions, and with very fine ends for the time. The American designs almost invariably show long, easy runs and moderately full entrances. The excesses in hull form that marked some French experiments in design during the last half of the eighteenth century are not found in contemporary American designs.

It is probable that the variations in the final designs of the Revolutionary frigates were not only due to the various reasons that have already been discussed, but might also have been the result of the old Admiralty practice of allowing deviations from the "contract plans." If the theory of Admiralty-trained shipwrights existing in America prior to the Revolution is correct, it would be quite reasonable to expect that the men they trained would have the same attitude toward the official draughts of the Marine Committee that had existed toward the Admiralty plans of the earlier period—the attitude that they were interesting and informative but by no means a Holy Writ to be followed without "improvements" or other likely interpretations.

The Revolution left many ideas on naval construction that were to affect warship design and building in later years. The desirability of "big" frigates was firmly established in American minds; speed under sail and heavy gun power were deemed the basic specifications of a man-of-war. The failure of small vessels to accomplish much at sea during the Revolution caused such craft to be looked upon as relatively unimportant. The cost and time required to build ships of the line and the expense of maintaining such ships caused the Americans to consider them excessively costly. Their observation of such unusual ships as the *South Carolina*, ex *L'Indien*, and the *Confederacy* had shown them that special consideration would have to be given to longitudinal strength, in long ships, to carry a heavy armament. They had discovered that great length not only permitted a more powerful battery but created a fast-sailing man-of-war, compared to the short ships popular in the British Navy.

There had been little opportunity to show what a squadron of men-of-war could accomplish. Hopkins' squadron attacked Nassau, in the Bahamas, in 1776, but without spectacular results. Arnold's squadron was finally defeated, and the importance of its action against the British was not apparent at all. John Paul Jones' European squadron had failed because of jealousy among the officers, and only the capture of the *Serapis* had attracted attention; but this was looked upon, with some reason, as a single-ship action. The disastrous American expedition to the Penobscot River, in Maine, in the summer of 1779 had cost the colonies many ships and men and had most certainly added nothing to the reputation of squadron actions, so far as Americans were concerned.

Without extensive or particularly successful operations by Continental squadrons, there had been no need for an organized supply-ship system. Since there were no regular dockyards, no service craft were needed. Only the packet ships (not the later passenger vessels but rather small fast-sailing dis-

patch craft) had been required, in addition to the frigates. The colonial privateers, combined with the few Continental frigates that got to sea, had been very
effective and had won fame as commerce raiders. When two frigates or
privateers worked together, on the other hand, there were often failures that
resulted in recriminations and scandal. All of these factors caused great emphasis to be placed upon the employment of single vessels of great power and
speed rather than a fleet or squadrons. Because of this tactical concept the
United States was to develop some of the finest and largest frigate designs
the world had seen. The frigates of the Revolution, built upon superior models
and having both speed and gun power above their rates in other navies, were
the beginning of a trend in naval construction which was to make the United
States a "frigate nation," replacing France as the leading exponent of this
class of naval ship. The American emphasis on large ships of superior design
intended to be capable of extensive operations alone, rather than upon a well-
integrated fleet or squadron, controlled naval shipbuilding in the United States
throughout the remaining years of the sailing man-of-war period and continued, with few exceptions, well into the steamship era. This American idea
was soon to be adopted by many of the great maritime powers when the great
ships of the American Navy had once been seen.

No account of the American Revolution would be complete without reference to the naval activities on Lake Champlain. So far as the Americans were
concerned, the fleet was Army-controlled; it had been built and manned
by Army personnel, and it fought under a brigadier general. Its officers were
either Army officers with sea experience, or privateersmen and merchant officers brought in from the coast. In spite of this, the Lake Champlain squadron
must be considered a part of the Continental Navy, for the Army's part in its
creation and operation was the result of the lack of a formal line of demarca-
tion between the duties and responsibilities of the Continental Navy and Army.
Early in the war, Washington had commissioned four schooners and the Army
had a great many seafaring men in uniform: there was one regiment almost
entirely composed of sailors which served as a marine-transport service as well
as for combat. Army officers served at sea, and at least one commanded a vessel.
Naval officers commanded soldiers. Expediency rather than set responsibilities established the duties of the two services.

The responsibility for furnishing materials, equipment, and supplies was
shared by the Continental Congress, New York, Pennsylvania, Connecticut,
Rhode Island, and Massachusetts. Men were obtained from the maritime colo-

nies and from the regiments in the vicinity of Lake Champlain. It will be seen that the Lake Champlain squadron was neither Continental nor state in character; it was the product of an emergency and the energy and leadership of such men as Arnold, Schuyler, and others of the Army, and of Governor Trumbull of Connecticut.

The Americans had attempted to hold the St. Lawrence after their attack on Quebec in the winter of 1775–76 by the use of a small squadron of armed vessels and the remains of their "Northern Army." The squadron was largely made up of "gundalows" (or praams) which had been built on the St. Lawrence and on the Richelieu River, below the rapids at Chambly. These small craft ranged from about 50 to 64 feet in length and from 16 to 20 feet beam and had been hastily built and fitted. Some were open boats with a forecastle deck on which a heavy gun was mounted, with two to four smaller guns on the broadside. The larger gundalows were decked and had bulwarks (some had a raised quarterdeck) and carried from 6 to 10 guns. All gundalows could be rowed with sweeps when necessary. Some had an outside keel to help them go to windward, but most appear to have been without this appendage. Those having a raised quarterdeck employed the space under it for quarters; the smaller craft had no quarters, and the crews either slept in the open or under a sail rigged as a tent or awning.

The American "gundalow," or, as it is sometimes spelled in contemporary reports, "gundalo" (properly, "gondola"), was double-ended—that is, sharp at bow and stern. Usually she was perfectly flat-bottomed, without either deadrise or fore-and-aft rocker like her European sister the "prame" or "praam." The latter was a Dutch type of hull that had been adopted by many European navies for shoal-water service, carrying rigs most suited for their size and service. Many naval prames were large and were square-rigged, either ship or brig. The American gundalow was occasionally built with from three to five inches of deadrise, giving her a "V-bottom." When deadrise was employed, the gundalow was built with an equal amount of fore-and-aft rocker in her bottom; the chines (the lines formed by the intersection of the sides and bottom on each side of the hull) met the rabbet (line of intersection of the bottom with the outside keel) at the heels of the stem and sternpost. Unlike the bottom, the sides of a gundalow or of a prame usually had curved timbers. The side frames were all on the same curve or mould, except at the extreme bow and stern, where it was necessary to change the shapes of the frames slightly to permit the planking to run fair to the stem and sternposts. The side timbers all flared out heavily from the bottom, except at the ends of the hull; at the bow the flare was great, but at the stern it was commonly less than amidships. The large Dutch prames carried leeboards, but there is no record of these being employed in the American vessels. The gundalow as a rule had a single mast, on which was set a square course and topsail. Some of the gundalows also carried a single jib set flying from the stem, or from a hemp span over it to allow the bow gun to clear the headstay and still fire straight ahead. The jib was probably used to help steering and to aid in swinging the vessel around in action. The larger gundalows had a bowsprit and one or two headsails; the bowsprit was usually fitted to reef in, cutter fashion. The gundalows were heavily sparred and canvased, as they were very stiff. Some vessels of this type were fore-and-aft-rigged, but there is no record of such rigs having been used on either the St. Lawrence or Champlain gundalows.

The American squadron on the St. Lawrence was trapped when the British advanced down the river, and all the vessels were either captured or destroyed when the Americans retreated southward in June, 1776. Among the vessels captured by the British was a large gundalow, which they carefully took apart and moved to St. Johns, on the Richelieu above the rapids. There they reassembled her and employed the vessel against the Americans, in the campaign of the fall of 1776 on Champlain. In the British service she was known as the *Loyal Convert;* her original name was said to have been *Convert*. A rather sketchy plan was made of her when she was reassembled, and this has been found among the Admiralty draughts. A reconstruction of her lines is shown in Figure 12, based on the profile, midsection, and outline of the rail shown in the Admiralty drawing. The body plan is restored on the basis of the hull form of the European prames and other evidence. The vessel had one mast and a bowsprit when she came into British hands, but late in the summer of 1776 a gaff mizzen was added. A rough portrait of this gundalow is included in a sketch of the British squadron made by an officer, C. Randle, just before the naval action of the 11th of October, 1776, and this portrait shows the mizzen; she then carried 7 9-pdrs., though designed to carry 10 guns. There is no evidence that the British changed the vessel, though it is possible that they raised her and added a quarterdeck. In model, below the wales she was very like the later gundalows built on Lake Champlain. Arnold seems to have had a great deal of interest in the St. Lawrence vessels and may have been responsible for their general design, as he was later for the gundalows and galleys on Lake Champlain.

The Americans abandoned St. Johns on June 18, 1776, taking away with them the frame timbers of a small vessel they had found building there when Montgomery captured the place in the fall of 1775. They then had three vessels afloat on Champlain: the large sloop *Enterprise*, armed with 12 4-pdrs.; the

Figure 12. Draught of hull and sail plan of LOYAL CONVERT, *ex American* CONVERT, *a large gundalow on Lake Champlain, 1776.*

schooner *Royal Savage*, armed with 4 6-pdrs., 8 4-pdrs., and some swivels; and the schooner or ketch *Liberty*, of 4 4-pdrs. and 4 2-pdrs. All these vessels had been captured by Montgomery or Arnold in the fall of 1775.

A new schooner was started at Ticonderoga, the *Revenge*, to carry 4 4-pdrs. and 4 2-pdrs., besides some swivels. The Americans hastily set up another shipyard at Skenesboro (Whitehall, New York), and laid down additional craft:

a cutter with the frame timber brought from St. Johns, four large galleys, and eight or nine gundalows. The object of this building was to create a squadron that would defeat or delay the British when they came southward on Champlain. There were neither tools, men, nor supplies immediately available, so desperate efforts had to be made to procure everything necessary from neighboring colonies. Some of the materials intended for the frigates building in New York and Pennsylvania, which could not be completed because their escape was cut off by British captures, were diverted to Champlain.

The British established their base at St. Johns and began to erect several vessels that had been sent in frame from England. A ship sloop (the *Inflexible*) is said to have been put together in twenty-eight days. Two schooners were erected, the *Maria* and the *Carleton,* also the *Loyal Convert,* described earlier, and finally a large "radeau" or block ship, the *Thunderer.* The latter's lines are shown in Figure 13, redrawn from an Admiralty sketch plan in the same manner as was done in the case of the *Loyal Convert.* The *Thunderer,* the most powerful vessel on the lake, was rigged as a bomb ketch, carrying two large howitzers, 6 24-pdrs., and 6 12-pdrs. The British also brought over from the St. Lawrence twenty gunboats each having one gun, four long boats with a field gun each, and twenty-four provision boats or "bateaux."

Both British and Americans employed craft called "bateaux," which were undoubtedly rowing boats much like the gundalows but smaller. They may have been similar to the more recent "lumberman's bateau" or "drive boat," a flat-bottomed double-ended skiff 28' to 32' long, having widely flaring sides something like a dory's. The Americans also used many scows, or flatboats, which also seem to have been called "bateaux." Flat-bottomed scows, skiffs, and punts were in common use in colonial times; they were sometimes called "moses boats" or "pirogues," though the latter name was usually applied to dugout canoes.

"Radeaux" were also employed by the Americans as harbor defense craft, and these were, like gundalows, popular with the state navies set up by some of the colonies. A radeau was nothing more than a rather large sailing scow; the model was probably based on the Thames River barges of the period so far as the English and Americans were concerned. The radeau usually had rounded sides and curved side frames like the gundalows, but had square or scow-shaped bow and stern. Some were flat-bottomed, and some were entirely flat-sided as well; but others, like the *Thunderer,* were quite pretentious in model, having deadrise which also led to some fore-and-aft rocker in the

Figure 13. Draught of the British radeau THUNDERER on Lake Champlain, 1776.

105

bottom. The radeaux usually had an outside keel, and they were rigged as schooners, sloops, brigs, and ketches, or even as ships. It is said that some of the American radeaux sailed very well in smooth water, but most of them could not get to windward except under sweeps. The name "radeau" gradually went out of usage in America, but "gundalow" remained in use as late as the early part of the present century as a name for shoal, flat-bottomed sailing river and harbor craft, though "scow" was more commonly used as a type name.

The Americans had the greatest difficulty in preparing their squadron for action. In fact, it appears that a few of the vessels were not completed in time and that others went into action before they were ready. The cutter was completed and named *Lee*. She was a small shoal vessel and was taken into the British service after her capture, so a plan is in existence. Figure 14 shows a redrawing of the Admiralty draught, with a sail plan reconstructed from various contemporary sketches of the vessel. She was a small cutter, not much larger than a small gundalow, but was finished like a large vessel with a raised quarterdeck, deep bulwarks, and gun ports. She carried 1 12-pdr., 1 9-pdr., 4 4-pdrs., and 2 swivels. Her dimensions were 43′ 9″ long on deck, 16′ 3½″ beam, and 4′ 8″ depth of hold. Though the frames taken from St. Johns were helpful in completing her, she took a good deal more time to build than a large gundalow, and was probably no better a vessel. The *Loyal Convert* measured 62′ 6″ on deck, 20′ 3″ beam, and 3′ 7½″ depth in the hold; it can be seen that she was a far more efficient fighting craft than the cutter-rigged *Lee*.

The four galleys were the *Washington, Congress, Trumbull*, and *Gates*. Only the first three were completed in time to see service in the fall of 1776. The appearance of the galleys can be seen by the plan of one in the Admiralty collection made from the vessel after her capture. Only this galley, the *Washington*, was captured and, like the cutter *Lee*, was employed by the British. Her plan, redrawn from the Admiralty draught, is shown in Figure 15. These galleys were round-bilged, and their model was generally much like that of the *Lee*, but with greater length in proportion to beam and depth. The galleys were rigged with two lateen sails and sparred with masts of about equal length. The *Washington* was rerigged as a brig in the British service, and it is doubtful that the vessel originally had the channels shown in the Admiralty plan of her. A bowsprit was also added when her rig became that of a brig. The *Washington* was 72′ 4″ on deck, 20′ 0″ beam, and 6′ 2″ in the hold; it is probable that the other galleys were similar in all respects. The *Gates* was not com-

pleted in time to take part in the action against the British squadron; she was
destroyed by her crew in 1777 to prevent capture.

The gundalows were probably nearly alike, allowing for the lack of time

Figure 14. Draught of the cutter LEE, in the American squadron on Lake Champlain, 1776, from an Admiralty draught made after her capture.

to prepare plans complete in all details, if indeed any plans were made. One
of the gundalows that were sunk in the action with the British has been found
and raised by T. F. Hagglund, who has made arrangements for the preservation of this interesting marine relic. The gundalow, which was the Philadelphia,
was in a remarkable state of preservation. Her drawing, shown in Figure 16,

Figure 15. Plans of the galley WASHINGTON *in the American squadron on Lake Champlain, 1776, after an Admiralty draught.*

was made from measurements assembled by Mr. Hagglund, Colonel E. P. Hamilton, and the writer, and is reasonably correct, allowing for the distortion caused by age, long submersion, and perhaps hasty building. The workman-ship exhibited in the relic is very good, being obviously that of expert ship-wrights. The *Philadelphia* was an open boat measuring 53′ 4″ over the posts,

15′ 6″ beam, and 3′ 10″ depth amidships. Arnold's specification for gundalows is shown in the same drawing for comparison; his design was 48′ 0″ on the keel, 16′ 0″ beam, and 3′ 6″ depth. A drawing was made in his specification

Figure 16a. Plan of the gundalow PHILADELPHIA as taken off the relic raised from Lake Champlain in 1935, showing her probable appearance in Arnold's action.

that roughly indicated the general form he proposed, and this is the basis of the reconstruction of his design.

In the *Philadelphia* the bottom was planked fore-and-aft on closely spaced floor timbers, apparently twice as numerous as the side timbers, which seem to be spaced 18″ to 20″ on centers. Arnold called for the floor timbers to be spaced 18" on centers. The *Philadelphia* had a heavy keelson, 6" x 8½" on the flat, and was entirely flat-bottomed, but Arnold intended the gundalows to have 4" deadrise and rocker. The *Philadelphia* seems to be spiked throughout, while Arnold expected to "half trunnel and half spike." The decks in the *Philadelphia* seem to have had no crown, though Arnold required 4"; the crown obviously would serve no useful purpose, as no scuppers were cut in the sides of the hull, since the decks or platforms were too close to the load

Figure 16b. A restoration of Arnold's original design for the American gundalows on the St. Lawrence and Lake Champlain.

water line. The bow of the *Philadelphia* has been cut down to clear the muzzle of her 12-pdr. bow gun, whose mount must have been lower than intended to require the rail to be lowered in this manner.

The arrangement of the *Philadelphia* shows evidence of hurried building; it is well designed for the purpose intended, however. The hull just abaft the forecastle, and in the way of the mast, has no flooring or deck, the ceiling is exposed, and there is space to store things in the well thus formed and under the forecastle. Abaft the well there is a low deck or platform about 14' long supported by six 12" x 12" beams laid on the ceiling and notched over the keelson. There are five knees on each side, resting on the deck and the beams, and reaching to the rail to stiffen the sides. They also rest on the side timbers and side ceiling. On this deck are two 9-pdrs., one on each side firing over the rail. They are not opposite one another, to give more room around the guns. There was a roughly built fireplace of brick on the port side against the rail and just abaft the mast position. Abaft the gun platform there was another well about 3' 6" long in which there was a hatch through the ceiling on each side of the keelson for bailing. Abaft this was the quarterdeck platform for helmsman and officers. Two arms chests were located on this platform.

The rail caps were fitted to take tholes for the sweeps and were capped for swivel pivots. The tholes and pivots were not located alike on port and starboard. As a result, the location of cleats and rail bitts was not the same on both sides of the boat. There were sockets in the rail cap for stanchions to support weather cloths which masked the gun crews from enemy sharpshooters. There were not enough weather cloths available, so in the action of October 11 most of the vessels used boughs of evergreens as a substitute. The probable arrangement of weather cloths is shown in the plan.

The rig shown in Figure 16 is wholly a restoration based on very incomplete sketches made by the British officer, C. Randle, who drew the British squadron. The gundalows carried topsails as shown, but it is not certain whether the topmast was a pole or a separate spar fidded as in a large vessel. There are other sketches of the American squadron besides that of the British officer; one found by Mr. S. H. P. Pell is shown in Plate V. This indicates that the gundalows had the weather cloths always rigged around the stern, perhaps to make them look more impressive than they really were.

The gundalows were ballasted with stones, which were stowed under the quarterdeck platform on the *Philadelphia*. These were to trim the boat by the stern and to counteract the weight of the relatively large gun placed in the eyes of the boat. Trim by the stern undoubtedly helped steering under sail, but a boat like a gundalow could not sail on the wind. The American gundalows of the *Philadelphia*'s type must be considered as being of the galley class— rowing rather than sailing boats. Nevertheless, the addition of an outside keel would have made them capable of sailing on the wind, and it is curious that this appendage was omitted in the *Philadelphia*, for it is to be seen in the *Loyal Convert* and was called for in Arnold's specifications for a gundalow.

The gundalows built for the Champlain squadron were *Philadelphia, New York, Connecticut, Providence, Jersey, New Haven, Spitfire,* and *Boston.*

There was apparently another gundalow, the *Success,* but she was not in the action of October 11 and there is no record of what became of her. Either she was one of the vessels not completed in time to join Arnold, or she was re-named and was one of the vessels of the American squadron.

The schooners of the squadron were rather flat-floored craft with cutwaters and, perhaps, figureheads or other carvings. They carried square topsails on fore and main masts. All had short, high quarterdecks. The *Liberty* seems to have been rigged as a fore-and-aft ketch, almost as though she were a sloop with a mizzen added. In one sketch of her she had a single square yard on the foremast and no square topsails. The *Enterprise* was a sloop having square main course and topsail, and she apparently also had a cutwater. The hull models of these craft undoubtedly were somewhat similar to that of the *Lee* or the galley *Washington.* This assumption is supported by the fact that the British schooners had hull models somewhat like these vessels.

The naval action between the American and British squadrons began on October 11 and continued in a running fight until the 15th, during which period the *Royal Savage, Congress, Philadelphia, Connecticut, Jersey, Providence, Spitfire, New Haven,* and *Boston* were either burned or sunk, and the *Washington* and *Lee* were captured. This action ended the campaign, and it was not until 1777 that the British were able to destroy, capture, or force the Americans to burn the last of the Champlain squadron. The *Gates, Trumbull, Revenge, Liberty, New York,* and, perhaps, the questionable *Success* were thus accounted for, with the British in possession of the whole lake.

The Lake Champlain squadrons are particularly interesting in that the various vessels that composed them were built to suit the requirements of use on the lake. They were designed for shoal water and for rapid construction with very limited facilities. Shoal-draft sailing craft were not well known to either the Americans or the British in this period, so when such vessels were required they were usually small and of the rowing or galley class. The disin-clination to employ leeboards in naval craft is not readily explained, for the British at least used them extensively in their river barges. If an outside keel were employed it would increase the draft to an undesirable degree, and the centerboard was as yet unknown. However, one of the British officers on Champlain in 1776, Lieutenant Schank, had begun experiments with the fore-runner of the centerboard, the "drop keel," in 1774 at Boston. His experience in the leewardly lake vessels intensified his interest in the problem, and he is said to have proposed some kind of drop keel in the radeau *Thunderer*, but his ideas were not adopted. It was not until he was a captain and about twenty years had passed since his service on Champlain that he was able to get the British Admiralty to adopt his scheme in shoal-draft naval vessels.

The armament of the American squadron on Lake Champlain was composed of guns obtained from Fort Ticonderoga and other captured posts, along with some that were brought from the coasts. It appears from what has been found that British field guns, as well as naval cannon, were used. There were also some old French guns that were serviceable. The *Washington* had four different calibers of cannon: 2 18-pdrs., 2 12-pdrs., 2 9-pdrs., and 4 4-pdrs. in her broadside, with the addition of 1 2-pdr. gun and 8 swivels on her quarterdeck. Some of the galleys had 1 18-pdr., 1 12-pdr., 2 9-pdrs., and 6 6-pdrs. in addition to from 6 to 8 swivels. Only the gundalows had what might be termed a standard armament: 1 12-pdr. in the bows and 2 9's amidships. Small arms consisted of muskets and a few Pennsylvania-type rifles.

The American vessels appear to have been painted red, or barn color, if the existing sketches are trustworthy. Some of the gundalows were unpainted, however, as paint did not arrive in time and the boats were required at once. It is probable that the bottoms of some, at least, were tarred. Owing to the haste with which the boats were built and the variety of sources from which materials were obtained, it can be assumed that the vessels were not standardized in any respect. For example, on the evidence of the *Philadelphia* and the Admiralty sketches of captured craft some of the vessels had chain plates and deadeyes, some had metal chain plates but no deadeyes, and some had deadeyes without any metal chain plates.

Little is known about the qualities of the American vessels on Champlain, as practically nothing is said in any of the reports, British or American. With their relatively powerful rig, the gundalows were very fast off the wind but could not work to windward. The galleys and the *Lee* were more weatherly than some of the schooners; the *Royal Savage* in particular is said to have been a very poor sailer. The vessels in both squadrons were primarily gun carriers, with ability to row and to work in the comparatively confined areas of the lake, with very little attention given to weatherliness. The prevailing winds and the shape of the lake were deemed to make sailing to windward impractical in the shallow hulls permitted there. The *Thunderer* could not work to windward any better than the American gundalows, and the British ship

Inflexible does not appear to have been much better. The British schooners and the large gundalow *Loyal Convert* were the most useful of the British ships.

The gradual tapering off of hostilities after the fall of Yorktown made it unnecessary to attempt to obtain more vessels. When the war ended, the Continental Navy was disbanded and the few remaining ships were sold to private owners. In spite of the numerous weaknesses that developed from excessive political interference in building, fitting, and manning the ships, as well as the dictation of tactics by congressional delegates, the Continental Navy was able to produce excellent ships and a few very competent fighting officers. While successes against the ships of the Royal Navy had not been numerous, the Americans had done great damage to the British merchant marine by means of their Continental naval force, aided by numerous privateers. The control of naval affairs by committees and boards had shown inherent weakness, and it had become apparent that a single individual supported by a bureau or staff would be required to administer a national fleet. The Continental Congress did not develop the latter organization, but toward the end of the war it did establish a single authority in the "Agent of Marine."

As we have seen, the designing of American ships had not been confined to a government agency during the Revolution, in spite of the efforts of the Marine Committee. Excellent though the designs approved by the Marine Committee had been, circumstances had permitted the builders of many of the naval ships to produce designs of their own; and some of the ships—the *Hancock*, for example—had been superior vessels. Perhaps this was one of the reasons that led to the pre-eminence of the Americans as frigate designers in the years that followed the Revolution.

★ ★ ★ ★ ★ ★ ★ ★ ★

CHAPTER THREE

The Federal Navy

1785-1801

W HEN THE Revolution ended, the Continental Congress could no
longer maintain the Navy. Its personnel was dismissed and the few
ships remaining were sold. The Army was also disbanded; the veteran
regiments of the Continental Line were mustered out. These acts of the Congress were forced upon it by a variety of causes: lack of funds, the war-weari-
ness of the public, and a fear that the troops and the naval personnel might
attempt to seize control of the infant nation. The chief cause, however, was
that the Congress lacked the power to raise funds and did not have the confidence of the individual state governments. The year 1786 found the country
without a national force of any kind and defended only by local militia companies. There was no national currency, and violent internal jealousies were
disturbing the trade relations among the states. The new nation was not respected abroad and was subject to outrages and acts of aggression by even the
most backward and weak of foreign powers.

 In spite of the handicap of internal troubles and a lack of currency and
banking facilities, the Americans built up a large merchant marine as soon as
the Revolution was over. Their ships appeared in the Mediterranean, the
North Sea, the Baltic, and even the Pacific, seeking trade. Laden with raw
materials and such goods of American manufacture as were available, the
American vessels carried on a barter trade to obtain the articles needed at
home. The Americans rapidly became serious competitors of the European

merchants. These merchants, and their governments, began to take steps intended to hamper the American activities—which usually took the form of
instigating the cruisers of some warring nation to seize and condemn American ships and cargoes on any flimsy excuse that could be devised.

The most useful tools for such purposes were the infamous Barbary corsairs of the Mohammedan regencies of Algiers, Tripoli, Tunis, and Morocco—
Algiers being the most important. Long supported by the European maritime
powers, these sea-rovers had looted without real hindrance for generations.
They were small, weak nations—mere ports, in fact—ruled by adventurers
whose tenure of power, and whose personal safety as well, was of short
duration and generally uncertain. Hence negotiations with these rulers were
very unsatisfactory, for the agreements stood only so long as the existing
ruler remained on the throne. Not only were these Barbary rulers subject to
violence from rivals; they were also the vassals of the Turks and were usually
influenced by the turbulent political conditions in Constantinople. Being adventurers and seeking wealth and power, the Beys were readily controlled by
foreign plotters, who used the corsairs to prey upon the shipping of enemies
or competitors even when nominally at peace with such nations. This useful
method of curbing the sea-borne trade of competing nations in the Mediterranean, and even out into the Atlantic, appealed to the maritime powers, and
through treaties and subsidies they had preserved the corsairs from the destruction that would normally have been the lot of a group of pirates, and enabled
them to maintain rather powerful fleets of cruisers whose only business was
to prey upon helpless merchantmen.

With the appearance of American competition in the Mediterranean, the
Barbary corsairs were encouraged to seize American ships, cargoes, and men. It
had long been their practice to enslave all captives taken in their attacks on
shipping, and it was their custom to release these captives only upon payment of
ransom. By treating the captives cruelly it was possible to increase the willingness of the victim nation to pay large sums and pay them promptly. The Bey
of Algiers took particular interest in the newcomers and was active in seizing
American shipping as soon as it lost the protection of the British flag.

At the end of the Revolution the Continental Congress attempted to establish
friendly relations with the Barbary corsairs and sent diplomatic missions to
each. These were only partially successful; with each change in the occupant of
the throne the Americans found themselves virtually at war with one or another
of these troublesome powers. The loss of American shipping and the enslave-

ment of American seamen caused public indignation to mount. This in turn became the motive for establishing the American Navy once the country had a national government.

Until such a government was established there was no possibility of a national navy, in spite of the need made apparent by the activities of the Mediterranean powers. When the federal government came into existence, in 1789, the problem of the corsairs was immediately a matter of its concern. It was widely recognized that the only practical way to deal with these pirates was to employ force, but the country had many internal difficulties to settle before reaching conclusions on its foreign problems. Economics was, of course, the most pressing matter, and the establishment of federal taxation was necessary before anything could be done about a national force to protect American interests abroad. When the new government had solved the most immediate of the problems of internal affairs—or, at least, had settled on a workable procedure for handling matters—it could give attention to the needs of American sea-borne trade.

Public opinion gradually brought the subject of an American naval force to the top of the list of federal government projects. The matter was under consideration as early as 1791, and a congressional committee began investigating the means to be employed in setting up such a force. In this investigation Congress utilized the aid of the Executive Branch, which had been established with a War Office and secretariat, though no provision had been made for the equivalent Admiralty, or Navy, Office. President Washington therefore placed the naval matter in the hands of the Secretary of War, General Henry Knox, who had been a bookseller and a Revolutionary War army officer but had had no experience in naval or maritime affairs. Like so many officeholders since, when faced with responsibility for some problem which they are personally unequipped to solve, he was forced to depend upon the advice of friends and chance acquaintances. Knox turned, naturally, to men who had been naval officers either in the Continental or state navies during the Revolution. He was in the position of a non-musician who was required to buy a piano; it seemed to him that the advice of men who could play the instrument would be the most necessary aid to correct choice.

With Congress demanding detailed estimates, his problem required extensive examination of the requirements in ships, armament, and personnel. These were to be based on what was needed to meet the specific problem of the corsair fleet—which, of course, varied as one or the other of the Barbary Beys agreed to ransom or tribute or declared for peace. Under conditions such as these it was not strange that he became involved, during a period of about two years, in the highly technical problems of the exact dimensions of the ships considered best suited for a given gun power at the time.

Among his advisers were some officers who were acquainted with the *Confederacy*, the *Alliance,* and the French-designed *South Carolina.* There is no doubt that Knox heard much about these ships, particularly the last two, and their performance as compared with the smaller frigates built for the Continental and state navies. Though no detailed record has been found of the conferences held by Knox, the surviving papers and private correspondence show the general trend of thought that developed. It was felt that many of the Continental frigates were too small and too weak. Since the new ships would have to be few in number, it was considered vital that they be as powerful as possible, so that one would be a match for any vessel the corsairs were known to possess—and they were known to have ships carrying up to 44 guns, in service and building. Hence it can be seen why all estimates prepared by Knox for Congress contained references to 44-gun ships as the upward limit of power necessary; the lower limit fluctuated as the economic and diplomatic considerations of the moment indicated. In each estimate, the rates of the proposed vessels having been fixed, it became necessary to decide the probable dimensions of the ships in order to arrive at any reasonable idea of the cost involved. The ratings of the ships were a factor in the estimates for the number of men required to man the fleet. Since the estimates refer to ships between 24 and 44 guns, it is plain that Knox and his advisers had been forced to set up detailed dimensions and costs for all the rates within these limits. As a result, the War Office and Congress seem to have arrived at an agreement on the general dimensions of the ships long before the actual designs were ordered.

Knox's advisers cannot yet be wholly identified, though John Wharton was certainly very influential, as was also a Boston seaman named John Foster Williams. Captain John Barry, too, was relied upon by Knox for marine advice. It has not yet been discovered that any shipwright other than Wharton was consulted, though it is highly probable that Humphreys and others in the vicinity of Philadelphia were questioned informally. The national government was located in Philadelphia at this period, and local men were readily available for consultation. As a result, the influence of the Philadelphians was soon marked in all aspects of the federal Navy.

The Dey of Algiers proved extremely troublesome, and finally on March 27,

1794, Congress passed an act authorizing the construction of six frigates and their equipping and manning. This act founded the Navy of the United States. However, the act was not unconditional, for the ninth section permitted the stoppage of work authorized by the act if Algiers became peacefully inclined. Pains were taken to limit the new naval force so as to prevent the rise of a military or naval interest, which, at the time, was one of the fears of the American political leaders. It was intended that the new naval organization would be one of the responsibilities of the established War Office; the present idea of a consolidated armed-service administration is by no means an innovation in American theory of government organization.

The new act provided for three frigates to carry 44 guns and three to carry 36 guns, and Knox found himself with the responsibility of getting the ships designed, built, and manned. His first step was to procure the services of a shipbuilder and designer. He had become acquainted with the Philadelphia shipbuilder Joshua Humphreys through John Wharton, and he now hired Humphreys to prepare designs for the two classes of frigates. Humphreys apparently did not come into the picture until late in 1793, and by this time the size of the new ships had obviously been settled upon by the conferees at the War Office, as is evident from the various departmental estimates.

We have already examined the problem of Joshua Humphreys' part in the design of the Continental frigates and discussed his early career. Between the Revolution and 1794 Humphreys had become an established shipbuilder in Philadelphia. It is a matter of conjecture and opinion whether or not he can be said to have been a leading Philadelphia shipbuilder even in this period. His contemporaries did not refer to him in this manner, but Humphreys was at least fairly prominent in his community. It has been the fashion in more recent times to say that Humphreys was the leading shipbuilder of the time and that for this reason he was chosen to design the new ships. There is, of course, no real truth in this. He was chosen because he was a shipbuilder and had been available for consultation and also because he had shown great interest in the subject. He had, in addition, the support of his influential cousin, Wharton. His employment by the government was no more proof of prominence or unusual ability in 1794 than government employment today is certain evidence of prominence and extreme competence in a profession. It is evident that the same procedure was followed in selecting Humphreys and his associates that has so often been followed in solving the technical problems of a national government. First, the persons immediately responsible for the solution have neither experience in the particular field nor personal knowledge of the individuals who may be capable of the work; they are wholly dependent on chance and the helpful advice of friends, relatives, and acquaintances for recommendations as to who should be selected for the practical responsibilities. Next, after receiving such "competent" advice, the officeholder makes his appointment, but usually with strings attached; he appoints "assistants" whose advice has equal weight with that of the first appointee. Invariably the solution of the problems encompassed in the original responsibility becomes a matter of conflicting opinions by appointees and finally ends up as an administrative compromise or a group recommendation. This is exactly what finally happened in the design of the frigates. It is a conclusive answer to any claim that Humphreys was appointed because he was such an authority on ship design that his services were indispensable. The appointment had obviously been made simply because Humphreys had been available and was sufficiently interested to work for a time without certain compensation; he also had been recommended by one of Knox's advisers, Wharton. Being a resident of the then capital, Philadelphia, his advice could be obtained without delay, which was an added advantage.

Though Joshua Humphreys was appointed to design the vessel on June 28, 1794, his compensation was to begin May 1. This date did not, however, represent the beginning of his work on the design of the ships. He had apparently made a half-model to the dimensions given him by Knox sometime prior to April, 1794—147' keel, 43' beam, 14' hold, 6' between decks, 7' waist, 30 guns on the main deck. This model he had submitted to the War Office as his design proposal. It is probable that his compensation was arranged to reimburse him for the time he had spent on the model earlier. There is no evidence yet available that Humphreys made a plan, as well as a model, at this stage in the proceedings.

In appointing Humphreys, Knox did not indicate that he was to be considered the chief or principal constructor, even though, as will be seen, it was soon considered necessary to furnish Humphreys with an "assistant," in the classic government manner. The reason why an assistant should be deemed necessary is not clear; perhaps it was soon found that Humphreys was overloaded with work, or it may have been apparent that he was not too well equipped professionally to supervise or plan work to be done at a distance.

Late in the fall of 1793 a young English shipbuilder named Josiah Fox came to the United States. He was then thirty years old, having been born in Falmouth, England, October 9, 1763. He was the seventh child of a wealthy Quaker, and his family had connections, relatives, and friends in Philadelphia.

His oldest brother, Charles, was a miniaturist and the son-in-law of an admiral of the British Navy. Through this particular connection Josiah Fox had been apprenticed to the master shipwright at Plymouth Dockyard. The apprenticeship had been completed October 9, 1786, and being independent of his salary as a shipwright, Fox had spent the intervening years in study at various dockyards and in voyages to study the action of ships of various models at sea. He also visited a number of foreign yards on the Continent, including the famous Arsenal at Venice. He had come to America to study timber and to visit his relatives and family friends, among whom was his cousin Andrew Ellicott, the then Surveyor General. Ellicott took him to members of the Administration, and he was examined by Knox and Captain John Barry. The latter appears to have been a family friend of Fox. As a result of the examination and recommendations, Fox was offered an opportunity to help in the design of the new frigates. While the appointment was still pending, Fox seems to have prepared, with some official sanction, a proposed design for a 44-gun frigate. That some sanction was given is evident from the fact that Knox accepted the plan when it was completed. There being no opening at the moment as a naval constructor, it was agreed that Fox should be temporarily appointed a clerk in the War Office. This does not appear to have been a menial position, for correspondence indicates that the "clerks" were really administrative assistants to the Secretary of War and each had a secretary or clerk of his own. In addition to the administrative duties, Fox was required to help with the design of the new vessels.

While this particular appointment was pending, Fox completed his design and, early in the spring of 1794, turned it over to Knox. The latter had Humphreys' model and, noting the differences in the two designs, turned both over to Humphreys' old partner, John Wharton, for his and others' comments. Humphreys, in the meantime, had shown Fox his model and had asked Fox to make comments and send them to the War Office. It seems obvious that Humphreys and Fox were then on excellent terms and that Humphreys had a high regard for Fox's education and ability.

Humphreys' model was destroyed when the Washington Navy Yard was burned in the War of 1812, so its lines do not exist. However, it is apparent from Fox's comments that the model was not on the lines of the vessels as built. One of Fox's objections to the model was the slight rake of the stem; he also objected to "any hollows in the Body; by no means to have any hollow in either her Waterlines or Timbers in the Fore Body." He objected, too, to the position of the wales (the thick belt of timber along the sides at and above the

Dotted lines show Roundhouse,
Poop, Rail, Drift and upper
Quarter Galleries built on "United
States" only.

L Drift

"43" Aftermost sq frame.

A.P.

Drift
Rail

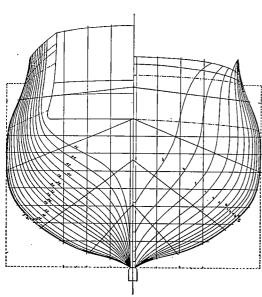

Particular Dimensions
⊙ is 70'9" from F.P.; 104'3" from A.P.
○ is 3'3" – "
* 42 is 14'4" from A.P.
* X is 18'9 – F.P.
Room & Space 26"
Lowest waterline 4'6" above Base :- others spaced 3'0"
Buttocks spaced 4'0"

Draught of 44 Gun Frigates.
'United States', 'Constitution'. 'President.'

Length bet perps.   175:0"
    on gundeck   174:10½"
        keel   145:0½" for tonnage
Moulded Beam   43:6"
Extreme   "   44:2"
Depth in Hold   14:3"

References:- 38·4·2A. Fox and
Humphreys letters, Offsets and
Instructions. Doughtys copy of 1796.

Reconstruction:- Roundhouse for 'United
States' from portrait and Barrys' notes.
Cutwater Profile, per Instructions.

Plan 7. Building draught for the 44-gun frigates CONSTITUTION, UNITED STATES, and PRESIDENT.

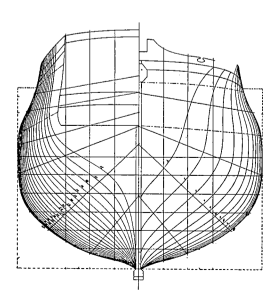

Particular Dimensions
a is 65'·11" from F.P.   b is 5'·1¾" from F.P.
c · 97·4   ·   A.P.   d² · 7'·3¾" · A.P.
e · 3·2½" ·   O.
Room & Space   26½"
Tumble Home   3'·0"
Lowest waterline 3'·3" above Base ; others spaced 3'·0"
Buttocks spaced 4'·0"

Plan 8. Building draught for the 38-gun frigates CON-
STELLATION *and* CONGRESS.

water line) and apparently thought the midsection was placed too far aft. In general, his strongest criticisms were directed to the size of the ships; he thought them so large as to be unwieldy and cumbersome. It is probable that Humphreys had an equal opportunity to comment on Fox's proposal, though his criticisms have not been found, if indeed they were ever committed to writing. It appears that Wharton and others made recommendations that were, in effect, a compromise between the two proposals. These have not turned up, but it is apparent from the correspondence that followed, and the redrawing of plans of the 44-gun ships, that a new basic design was to be prepared incorporating modifications of Fox's and Humphreys' proposals. It is obvious, of course, that the part played by these advisers in the proceedings answers any claim that Humphreys (or Fox either, for that matter) was so prominent that his opinions were authoritative and final. It is seen that Knox was not content with the judgment of either of his technical aides; he wanted a "majority vote" and called in other experts, among them Wharton, to obtain this. It is a curious condition of the historical records that Wharton, who seems to have established such a reputation as a shipbuilding expert, cannot yet be shown to have designed ships; however, it is apparent that he was considered highly competent. At the present time, about all that is known about his shipbuilding career is that he owned the shipyard and was associated with Humphreys in building the *Randolph* during the Revolution.

There is a good deal of mystery concerning the next step. Fox was to have worked as Humphreys' assistant in preparing the draughts and in the mould-loft work that would follow the preparation of the plans. It has never been established that Humphreys prepared the revised draughts (which were the basic designs, or "master draughts"), for the plans that Fox and Doughty made are the only surviving *building* plans of the two classes of ships. Perhaps it should be emphasized that Fox was far better trained than Humphreys in all respects, and was a far superior draftsman. From this it might be inferred that Fox now prepared the design of the 44-gun ships under Humphreys' verbal directions. The surviving correspondence offers conflicting evidence, for Humphreys is found writing letters to Fox, as though he were at a distance, requesting him to hasten the completion of the plans or draughts, which implies that they were not in the close personal contact required for directed designing. It is odd that in making claims that Humphreys was the responsible designer of the two classes of frigates his supporters have never attempted to produce the basic or "master" draught. If such a plan existed it seems reasonable that it would survive, for the naval plan files were, throughout the greater part of the sailing-ship period after the War of 1812, in the hands or under the supervision of Humphreys' son, Chief Constructor Samuel Humphreys. The latter would certainly have been careful to preserve as much of the evidence to support the claim that his father designed these frigates as he could produce, for in his time the controversy as to who was responsible for the design of the frigates had already started and was being given much public attention.

A careful search of the existing plan files in the National Archives has produced one plan that the writer believes to be Humphreys' "master draught" of the 44-gun frigates—the original drawing of their design, as built, and the only drawing that would support any claim that he prepared a basic design for any of the frigates. Plate VI is a photograph of the original draught in question. It will be seen that the draught is unsigned, but the claim that it is Humphreys' work is supported by a comparison of it with a draught that is known to have been made by him. This is his master plan for the proposed 74-gun ships of 1799, which is signed by him and also vouched for in competent contemporary documents still in existence; it is now in the National Archives (40–15–6 I). From this it is possible to identify Humphreys' draftsmanship with reasonable certainty. A careful comparison of the original draught of the 74-gun ship with that of the 44-gun ship shown in Plate VI shows that the workmanship appears to be the same. This is probably the strongest evidence that the plan of the 44 was the work of Humphreys.

The next step necessary is to attempt to establish that the plan was made after the initial designs were completed and therefore after the Wharton recommendations were made. Here the evidence is circumstantial and the supporting arguments become somewhat involved.

The drawing is identified by the name *Terrible* in an oval enclosure above the sheer elevation. This was one of the names for the 44's suggested by Humphreys prior to their building. Though one name he proposed, *Revolution*, was for a time under consideration, none of the names were finally adopted. The name on the plan not only gives some support to the idea that it was Humphreys' work, but it also indicates strongly that the plan was made before the building draughts were prepared by Fox and Doughty; for by the time these plans were made Humphreys' names had been rejected. A more substantial argument, however, rests upon the circumstances surrounding the preparation of the building plans of the ships and the method of their construction.

There is no logical reason for the existence of any plan of the ships in

Humphreys' hand, unless the plan is the basic design. In support of this statement it is argued that the records show that the building plans (and the offsets made from them) were prepared by Fox and Doughty, and that the lofting done in Philadelphia by these two men produced the moulds for all but one of the ships completed under the authorization of the Act of 1794. Humphreys was master builder of the 44-gun ship built at Philadelphia. He used the set of moulds and patterns prepared from the basic mould-loft drawings, which duplicated those sent out to the other yards building the same class of ship. Hence the fact that Humphreys built a ship was no reason for him to make a plan, after the Fox and Doughty drawings were made, since a plan was not required for any loft work in building his frigate. Furthermore, his poor draftsmanship and his very apparent distaste for drawing plans make it reasonably certain that he would not draw a plan of the ship for his own amusement. Since it is reasonable to believe that he did not prepare the plan shown in Plate VI during or after the construction of the Philadelphia 44, it can only be assumed that the plan was made prior to the lofting of the ship. Now certainly he was not required to prepare a draught, in competition with Fox and Doughty, for building. Hence it appears reasonable that the plan must have been made sometime prior to the starting of the building plans. The draught in question does not contain the important features that Fox specifically objected to in Humphreys' original model, but in fact does agree in these matters with the final building drawings for the 44's, so it must have been made after the Wharton recommendations. Thus, by a proceess of elimination, the conclusion is presented that the draught was drawn as the "master draught" for the 44-gun ships and was the basis for the final designs, prepared by Fox and Doughty, that were used for building the ships.

In attempting to show that Humphreys made the master draught, no claim is made that he was, in a strict sense, the sole designer. It has been shown that the size of the ships seems to have been established by the War Office in conjunction with congressional committees between 1792 and 1794. It is also quite apparent that the model of the ships had been subject to much discussion. There is evidence that Humphreys' original conception was altered by Knox as a result of Fox's criticisms of Humphreys' model. By the same token Fox's original plan was also rejected, and hence his part in the design was largely that of a consultant. In short, the designs were what might be considered typical of a government agency's solution of a technical problem of design: the plans incorporated the ideas of everyone available but were the sole technical responsibility of no one person. It is mere speculation to attempt to judge which of the men who worked on the plans actually contributed the most. Both Fox and Humphreys naturally claimed credit, and this led to acrimonious debate which in turn clouded the issue by conflicting statements. Doughty seems to have shifted from first supporting Fox's claims to supporting Humphreys'. Were the papers of either Fox or Humphreys taken alone, it would be easy to conclude that the man whose papers were chosen was the designer; the papers of both, taken together, lead to confusion and a qualified conclusion. For example, the men do not agree as to who made the final draught of the *Constellation;* Fox in one statement says he made it but in another seems to give the credit to Doughty. Humphreys seems to have been under the impression that Fox was making the draught. The facts of the matter cannot be stated with certainty; probably Fox was supervising Doughty in the preparation of the plan. It appears that the men were working very hurriedly in an effort to complete the drawings in time to meet the needs of the various builders. In any case, the existing evidence is that the designs were the sole work of none but were, as has been said, the joint effort of Knox's advisers and the men who made plans or models—Fox, Humphreys, and Doughty.

Both Fox and Humphreys were supposedly members of the Quaker sect; both were subjects of action to expel them from their church as a result of the designing of war vessels. Neither seems to have been permanently separated from the sect, however. Humphreys is believed to have been reinstated, while Fox refused to accept the action of a Philadelphia group on the grounds that they had no jurisdiction over him since he was not a member of that particular group. No reason exists in this matter that would impeach the truthfulness of either. Since both claim credit for the designs of the frigates, the matter must remain for the present, at least, a matter of individual opinion as to which played the more important part. It is quite obvious that contemporary officials were not certain where credit should rest. This is shown by references to Fox and Humphreys in official correspondence and also by the expressions of appreciation and administrative recognition that were given to Humphreys and Fox in letters addressed to them in the same terms of commendation. Perhaps it would be proper, however, to look upon these as administrative acts rather than as technical evidence.

Though Humphreys was undoubtedly the principal constructor at the beginning, it was not long before Fox's superior training evidently permitted him to achieve ascendancy in technical matters. He seems to have introduced to

America the practice of complete lofting of the ship's stern and to have been the first to prepare a complete set of patterns or moulds for this portion of the hull. It is possible that he was also responsible for the introduction of buttock-and-bow lines (vertical planes parallel to the longitudinal center line of the hull) projected in the various elevations contained in the draughts, which appear in American naval ship plans, apparently for the first time, in this period. The trend of events gave Josiah Fox a great opportunity to become prominent in naval construction in the United States, and he eventually had great influence on the design of American men-of-war.

In the past it was the fashion to assume that the Americans copied the French in the design of their fast-sailing vessels. This has already been referred to, in regard to Revolutionary War ships, and the existence of a huge number of ship plans of the sailing-ship period now permits comparisons to be made that completely disprove any claim of French influence. Of course the Americans of the period now under discussion were acquainted with the hull forms used by the French and probably experimented with them, as they did with many other foreign ideas in shipbuilding. A comparison of the surviving plans of the American vessels of the period of 1785–1801 with those of contemporary foreign frigates shows very plainly that the American builders followed British hull models rather than French; only in the proportion of dimensions to gun power was there a similarity to the latter. It can be readily understood why this would be the case, for in the early ships there is reason to suppose that there had been a background of British Admiralty trained men and, in the later period, the Admiralty-trained Fox prepared the building plans of the 44's and of many other ships. He also supervised Doughty in the preparation of the plans of the 36's. His comments on the original Humphreys model of the 44's also had some influence, apparently, on the "master draught" for the 44's. In addition, a few of the War Office advisers had been in the Royal Navy and were acquainted with the British types of men-of-war; such men would naturally prefer similar vessels.

The third person connected with the design of these first frigates, William Doughty, has been mentioned. Little is known about his early years; he was a Philadelphian, and when Fox appeared he was the yard clerk in Humphreys' yard. Doughty was a trained shipwright and draftsman, according to Fox. His position in Humphreys' yard appears to have approximated that of a modern office manager. He was made available to Fox as an assistant and helped draw up the building plans and loft the ships. He is said by Fox to have drawn the building plans for the 36-gun frigates and to have made the necessary copies of these plans, and of the 44's drawn by Fox, to supply the builders. He was eventually to play a very important part in American naval construction, though at the time he first appeared in the work he was by no means a prominent professional. He was a far better draftsman than either Joshua or Samuel Humphreys but not as good as Fox, judging by surviving plans. He proved to be a very capable designer of ships and must have been well trained.

The final drawings of the two classes of frigates represented the joint ideas of many individuals, and as a result the designs combined elements of success and of failure. The ships were very large for their rates; the 44-gun ships were 175' 0" between perpendiculars, 174' 10½" on the gun deck, 43' 6" beam, 44' 2" extreme beam exclusive of wales, and 14' 3" depth of hold. They were 145' 0" on the keel for tonnage, or about 146' 0" straight rabbet. These dimensions were huge for a frigate at the time the ships were designed. These ships were actually 20 feet longer than the improved British 44-gun frigates laid down in 1797, and were also 2 to 3 feet wider. The contemporary French 40-gun frigates were 13 feet shorter and about a foot narrower than the American 44's. The latter had an innovation, also, that increased their power as frigates immeasurably. This was the use of what was practically a flush spar (or upper) deck, above the main deck. Frigates of the Revolution had detached quarter and forecastle decks, only the quarterdeck being armed. As the war drew to a close, foreign frigates were built with guns on the forecastle and light gangways, or bridges, along the sides of the ship, connecting the quarterdeck and forecastle. These gangways were narrow and were for convenience in getting fore and aft on the ships. There were no bulwarks along the gangways; a light rail and netting gave some security and masked the crew from sharpshooters to a limited extent. In the American 44's, the gangways were strengthened and widened to such a degree that the upper deck was practically unbroken, the survival of the open waist amidships being indicated only by a very long and rather narrow hatchway. In addition, the American ships were originally given rather substantial open rails on this deck, running flush and unbroken from the stern to abreast of the foremast. This rail was supported by heavy stanchions which also were arranged to form frames of gun ports. The rail was at first fitted with nettings and waist cloths, but later the rails along the forecastle and quarterdeck were planked up between the gun ports; those amidships were fitted to stow hammocks to form a breastwork proof against small-arms fire in action.

The model of the ships can best be described by plans. Plan 7 shows the final design of the 44's. For their type and period, the American 44's were considered unusually sharp. Compared with the noted California and China clipper ships of the 1850's, the frigates are full-ended indeed; but compared with the down-easters, which were built after the American Civil War, the frigates are at least equally sharp. It must not be supposed that these frigates were ever intended to be extraordinarily sharp; they were an attempt to combine capacity and displacement with fast lines. In this they were very successful. The design of these ships, so far as general arrangement and dimensions were concerned, influenced American frigates to the end of the sailing-ship period.

The design of the 36-gun frigates is shown in Plan 8. No master draught for this class has been found, and it is very probable that none was made prior to the building plan. The reason for this seems plain, for the lines of the 36-gun frigates are practically reduced copies of the 44's. Hence it is probable that Doughty or Fox worked from the plan of the 44's by changing the scale, and that the variations in the rake of the ends of the ships and in other details were the result of compromising the scale conversion, to suit the fixed requirements of space and headroom. The general design for the 36's was similar to that of the 44's, except for the dimensions and the number of gun ports on each deck. The 36's measured 163' 3" between perpendiculars, or 163' 7" from stem rabbet to after face of sternpost on the gun deck. The beam was 40' 0" moulded and 40' 6" over the plank, exclusive of the thick wales. The depth of hold was 13' 0", and the height between decks was 6' 9" on the gun deck and 6' on the berth deck. As in the case of the 44's, the 36's were far larger than ships of similar rates abroad; in fact, the American 36's were so large that they were re-rated as 38's while still under construction.

The plans of all the ships, and the final loft work, were completed in 1795–96, by which time arrangements had been made for building all of the vessels. It had been intended to build the three 44's at Philadelphia, New York, and Boston, and the three 36's at Portsmouth, New Hampshire, Baltimore, Maryland, and Norfolk (or Gosport), Virginia. It was also decided that the vessels were not to be built by contract; rather, yards were to be leased or purchased and the ships built under the supervision of their captains and government-employed naval constructors. The 44 to be built in Philadelphia was set up in Humphreys' yard, and he was retained as naval constructor. A yard was leased in New York, and the well-known New York shipbuilder Forman Cheeseman was appointed naval constructor. At Boston, space in the Hartt shipyard was

leased and one of the three Hartt brothers, Edmund, was retained as yard foreman, but the naval constructor was a Col. George Claghorne or Claighorne.
The arrangements for the 36's were somewhat similar: the Hackett yard at
Portsmouth was taken over, and Col. James Hackett was made the naval
constructor. At Baltimore, David Stodder was made the naval constructor, and
at Gosport a Mr. Morgan was appointed to the post.

The number of each class of frigate to be built seems to have been subject to
much uncertainty. The 36-gun frigate to be built at Gosport was often referred
to as a 44, and even the Secretary of the Navy at a later date appears to have
been uncertain of her rate and class. This was probably due to the fact that she
was much delayed in getting started; Morgan was eventually sent to Georgia
to supervise the cutting of timber. This delay and the lack of materials seem
to have permitted a reconsideration of the size of the ship. In 1795 Fox was
appointed an "assistant naval constructor," with an increase in salary, and was
sent to take Morgan's place. He is known to have been one of the most active
objectors to the idea of very large frigates, and it is possible that his objections,
supported by some naval officers, led to the construction of a smaller ship than
originally intended. It is also possible that a shortage of materials may have been
a contributing factor; the supply of live oak proved to be disappointing. However, the rerating of all the smaller frigates built in this period makes the original rate of academic interest only.

The construction of the ships did not proceed very smoothly; many delays
were caused by lack of materials, or by changes in specifications brought about
as a result of such conditions. Then, in 1795, peace with Algiers was declared
and all work was stopped until Congress passed a supplementary act which
permitted the completion of the three most advanced ships—the 44's at Boston
and Philadelphia and the 38 at Baltimore. The frigates building at New York,
Portsmouth, and Gosport were left unfinished and the yards closed down. After
a good deal of discussion over the names of the ships, it was decided that the
frigate building at Philadelphia would be named the *United States*, the one
at Boston the *Constitution*, the one at New York the *President*, the one at
Portsmouth the *Congress*, and the one at Baltimore the *Constellation*. The
frigate intended to be built at Gosport having been much delayed, no attempt
was made to select a name for her when the others were assigned. This led to
some confusion, but she was eventually named the *Chesapeake*.

The first ship to be launched was the *United States*, at Philadelphia, May 10,
1797. The launching ways were apparently very steep, for she went off too

fast and was damaged. The *Constitution* was launched October 21, 1797, after two unsuccessful attempts brought about by insufficient inclination of the launching ways. The *Constellation* had been launched the month before, September 7, without untoward incidents.

These first ships were rather ornately carved, though little is known about the details of each vessel. The descriptions are largely allegorical and extremely florid, so that little can be judged from them. The *United States* had a figure-head representing the Goddess of Liberty, the *Constitution* a Hercules with club raised to strike, and the *Constellation* a female head representing Nature. The carvings were expensive to maintain and liable to damage, so it is not surprising that they changed rapidly in each ship, gradually becoming more and more simple and light.

The three ships were the subject of some criticism by many of the officers appointed to the new Navy. The great size and draft of the ships caused practical difficulties; many of the ports that had been intended to be used as bases were found too shallow or with too confined an anchorage, and this limited the usefulness of the new ships. One of the frigates, the *Constellation*, while at anchor in the Delaware tailed on to a bank or shoal, and when the tide left her she rolled over, filled, and sank.

The great length of the ships resulted in hogging, for Americans were as yet inexperienced in the construction of vessels of such great size. This, with their deep draft, which not only closed many ports to them but also prevented the use of many repair wharves in the harbors they could use, made repairs expensive. This condition of affairs was undoubtedly influential in the final establishment of navy yards. Another objection to the new ships was that they heeled too much under sail in strong winds, which was thought to be caused by their having too sharp a bottom. The same reason was advanced for the complaint that they lacked stowage space for the provisions and water required by the large crews assigned them. Some of the alleged faults were figments of the captains' imaginations; others were due to poor planning of the establishment rather than to ship design. In fact, the greatest faults of the new ships were not due to any failure of the group who advised Knox, or of the three men who were responsible for the plans of the vessels.

The ships really suffered most in being fitted out, or in finishing, to an extent that the naval constructors could not conceivably have estimated. The *United States*, for example, had a roundhouse added by her captain about as indicated in dotted lines in Plan 7. This added to her displacement and complicated trimming the ship with ballast. Every captain was also permitted to spar and rig the vessel to suit himself and to arm as he saw fit, or at least as available guns permitted. The quantity of ballast and stores placed on board was also a matter of the captain's judgment and opinion, rather than a matter of the constructor's estimates. No records were kept of the changes made in the ships, but it is evident that their appearance must have varied a good deal within the same rate, even if their lines did not. The effects of this condition on the sailing qualities and seaworthiness of the various ships can be imagined.

The relationship between the naval constructors and the ship captains was based upon the earlier idea that the man who played a piano was the best judge of the instrument. Hence the official correspondence, in the period under discussion, is marked by the freedom with which commanders of ships issued orders to the naval constructors and decided how the ships should be armed, fitted, rigged, and even built. From the perspective of the present, some of the American naval officers appear as surprisingly pompous and opinionated amateur ship designers, whose ill-judged decisions spoiled the reputation of many well-modeled ships. Oversparring and overgunning were chargeable to these officers and not to the ship designers.

It can be said, with some truth, that the theory Knox had introduced in selecting his naval advisers—that the best judge of a piano is one who can play the instrument—had now reached a stage where it was accepted that the player was competent to design and build the instrument. As a result, the constructors could produce hulls having all the elements of speed, but the resulting ships could be spoiled by the irresponsible changes of the officers supervising their construction or fitting them out for service. The correspondence of the Secretaries of the Navy in this and the succeeding period is full of complaints and suggestions of officers assigned to various ships. In most cases the officers made costly and unsound proposals for alterations. While no attempt was made to establish the proper relations between the constructors and commissioned officers, the Secretary soon became aware of the propensity of the captains to desire changes, whether necessary or not, and he acted accordingly in many cases—though much damage had been done before he awoke to the situation. The condition described explains why a vessel had a good reputation one year and the next is described as a "slug" or worthless. This makes judgments of the naval vessels at this distance somewhat questionable, if based on archives alone. In justice to the American Navy of the period it ought to be added that other navies had much the same attitude and suffered the same results. It is notable, in maritime history, that governments have the greatest difficulty in maintaining the proper balance between the alleged "practical knowledge" of the operators and the "science" of the designers; the player and the instrument maker are, in turn, in full control.

Overloading with guns aggravated the inherent weakness of the new ships; it increased their tendency to "hog" or become "humpbacked." It was not until nearly twenty-five years later that the American constructors learned how to design and build such long vessels successfully and to allow for any possible overloading. This difficulty led to the ships requiring extensive repairs when less than twelve years old: the *Constellation* was rebuilt and widened 14″, between 1805 and 1812, as she had in only eight years become severely strained by her armament, as well as by having gone aground in the Delaware. The uncontrolled loading of the ships with armament not only increased hogging, but it caused the whole upper portion of the hull to strain as the vessel rolled in the trough of the sea; this caused the structure to become loose and weak.

The armament of the new frigates was to be extraordinarily powerful; the 44's were to carry 30 long 24-pdrs. on the gun deck and from 20 to 22 long 12's on the quarterdeck and forecastle. In addition, they were to have 2 long 24-pdrs. on the forecastle as chase guns. The 38's were to have 28 24-pdrs. on the gun deck and 18 to 20 12-pdrs. on the upper deck. These proposed armaments were not employed, however, because it was decided to use carronades in place of the long 12-pdrs., and also the captains had their own ideas on how their ships ought to be armed. There was in addition the old trouble of getting the proper guns manufactured. The 24-pdrs. of the Federal Navy were not the same in model, weight, and dimensions in all of the ships carrying them. Some of the guns were on the British model, some were fortification cannon, and some were made on what was intended to be the standard model. However, the official establishment for the 44's was 30 long 24's on the gun deck and 20 to 22 carronades, 42-pdrs., on the upper deck. The *Constitution* seems to have carried 32-pdr. carronades instead of 42's in all of her early career. The 38's carried 28 long 18-pdrs. on the gun deck and 20 carronades, 32-pdrs., on the upper deck. The long guns and carronades followed the British pattern rather closely but had less windage and threw a slightly heavier shot. All of the American frigates carried long chase guns on the forecastle, as well as a number of cohorns on the rail. It will be noticed, perhaps, that both classes of frigates had far more ports than guns. The 44-gun ships could have mounted 60 guns, and the 38's 56, by filling all of their ports (exclusive of the bridle ports) on the gun deck. So far as is known, none of the ships ever attempted this, though some of the 44's mounted as many as 56 guns at one time. Such an armament seriously overloaded the ships and hurt their sailing and stability, as well as causing them to strain.

When the new ships were building, it was intended to arm them with long guns entirely, following the American practice in the Revolution. However, the advantages of the relatively new carronade, by now a favorite gun in the British Navy, were slowly becoming apparent, and the new ordnance was soon in demand. The carronade was a British invention, first produced by the Carron Foundry, from which it took its name. The American carronades appear to have been very close copies of the English guns in all respects. The advantage of the carronade over the long gun was in weight, the carronade firing more than twice the weight of shot fired by a long gun of the same weight of gun and mount. The carronade was short, and for this reason it was more quickly loaded than the long gun. Some American naval historians have been inclined to sneer at the effectiveness of the carronade, but the facts were that the carronade was often a more accurate cannon than the long gun, since the designers of the former had reduced the windage to overcome the objections of a very short gun. The long gun had the advantage of greater range, and, if properly bored, was relatively more accurate at extreme ranges of fire. The good features of the carronade resulted in its replacing the small long gun, of 4- to 12-pound shot, on the upper decks of nearly all American and British naval ships. Some ships were fitted out in both navies with an all-carronade armament, but this was found generally undesirable, as the long guns were found generally superior in range. The Americans usually retained the long gun for chase purposes in all ships and also used the long gun as the main armament when practical, employing the carronades as supplementary guns for rapid fire at close range. With the introduction of the carronade, the old swivels and howitzers went slowly out of fashion and were employed only as boat guns, or were relegated to the merchant marine. The Americans often used smooth-bore muskets loaded with buckshot, shotgun fashion, in naval action. They also used rifles extensively. Americans cannot be said to have introduced any innovation in gun design in this period; they were following the best practices abroad in arming their ships, taking the carronade from the Royal Navy, and the idea of employing heavy long guns in the main battery from the French Navy. The latter were using long guns of large caliber at this time and had not adopted the carronade extensively.

Nevertheless, it will be seen that the Americans had introduced one innovation—the two-decked (or, as they came to be called later, "double-banked") frigates capable, at least, of carrying two almost fully armed decks (rather than one and a fraction, as had been the case in the standard frigate of that time). This eventually brought about a change in the large frigates of all the great powers, who finally adopted double-banked ships. Yet when the American vessels first appeared, they were not favorably received by foreign naval officers, and, as has been mentioned, some American officers thought them too large and clumsy to handle well in close action. Relatively great size was an essential feature of the spar-decked ships.

While the Americans were having difficulties with the Barbary corsairs, Europe was becoming disturbed. The French Revolution started while Congress was considering the establishment of a naval force. Soon the great powers were engaged in a destructive war, and the seas were full of privateers and cruisers. The French revolutionists had little respect for international law or relations. The French soon reached the point of seizing American shipping and condemning both vessels and cargoes. By 1798 this matter had reached the stage of an undeclared war, and Congress again found it necessary to consider a naval establishment and to ponder on the need of one far greater than had previously been thought necessary for the country. Congress made appropriations for more ships and for the completion of those started earlier. Doughty was made a naval constructor and sent to New York, and a young shipbuilder named Christian Bergh was made master builder to complete the 44-gun ship that had been started there. Doughty seems to have permitted some slight changes from the original plans, for the ship is known to have been more lightly built than the others of her class and to have had less sheer. It is possible that some liberties were taken with the timbers in the ends of this ship, the "cant frames," or this may have been accidental; at any rate this 44, named the *President*, became noted as the fastest of her class when put into service. She had a figurehead representing President Washington. She was delayed somewhat even after the fresh start and so was not launched until April 1, 1800.

The 38-gun frigate *Congress*, building at Portsmouth, was also completed with the new appropriations and was finally launched April 1, 1800. There is some evidence in existing dimensions of the ship that she was not wholly a sister ship of the *Constellation*, but the mode of measurement employed may account for the apparent difference, about 5 feet in length. The *Congress* had a relatively uneventful career and spent much of her life rotting "in ordinary," or laid up.

The frigate at Gosport was also reinstated. When work stopped on the frigates she was so little advanced that the order in effect canceled her construction. Fox had joined with Truxton and others in objecting to the size of the 44-gun frigates, and their arguments had much effect on the authorities. As a result Fox was permitted to prepare a new design for a 44, of reduced size, that would have the approval of Truxton and other objectors. The authorization for the revised design does not exist (at least it has not been found), but the correspondence shows that the Secretary of the Navy was aware that the new ship was smaller than the previous 44's, for he inquired as to her dimensions and tonnage while she was under construction. Among the Fox Papers there is a drawing, entitled *Congress,* which may be her building plan. The new ship was launched, under the name *Chesapeake,* on June 20, 1799. She was a rather unfortunate ship in the American service, though considered both handsome and fast. This was one of the three American frigates taken by the British in the War of 1812; she will again be referred to in Chapter Five.

While the ships authorized in 1794 were being completed and other vessels were being added to the Navy, a less attractive program of naval shipbuilding was forced on the Americans. The treaty with Algiers had called for the Americans to make a cash payment, which, for various reasons, had been delayed. In order to keep the peace the American diplomats had therefore agreed to present the Dey with a total of four "corsair" vessels, built particularly for the purpose. These ships were to be of naval design and of the best materials. The practice of giving the Barbary corsairs armed ships had long been common with many of the European powers, as part of the continuing conspiracy to employ the Mediterranean pirates against some commercial competitor. In our case, however, the ships were nothing more than a tribute—a sop to keep the peace.

The tribute vessels to be built were to consist of a 32-gun frigate, a brig, and two schooners. A good deal of care was taken to assemble all the information that could be obtained from former captives as to the exact requirements of vessels suited to the use of the corsairs and also their likes and dislikes in regard to ship decoration and arrangement. It was thought that the Dey would be pacified and his friendship purchased if the vessels were superior in every way to those he had received from the European powers. The frigate was, of course, the most important, and the most impressive, of the vessels. After some study the administration selected Josiah Fox to design the ship and James Hackett of Portsmouth, New Hampshire, to build her. She was deliberately made as small as her rate would permit, as can be seen by her dimensions: 122′ 0″ on the gun deck, 32′ 0″ moulded beam, and 10′ 2″ depth of hold. She was launched June 29, 1797, and was a very handsome ship, as was usual with Fox's designs. Though she has no particular bearing on American naval construction, the choice of her designer indicates how rapidly Fox had come to be recognized as a prominent ship designer in the United States. The plan and offsets of the frigate, named temporarily the *Crescent*, are among the Fox Papers in the possession of the Peabody Museum at Salem, Massachusetts.

The smaller vessels are of more interest, however, as they not only show the ideas of American naval constructors of the time, in small man-of-war design, but also because one of them had much influence on later American naval construction. The two schooners and the brig were contracted for at Philadelphia. One schooner, eventually named the *Lelah Eisha*, was designed and built by Samuel Bowers; she was the smallest and was to carry 18 guns, 4-pdrs. The larger of the two schooners was designed by Benjamin Hutton, Jr., and built by Nathaniel Hutton, Jr.; she was to carry 20 4-pdrs. and received the name of *Skjoldebrand* in honor of a Scandinavian diplomat who had been helpful to the Americans in the Mediterranean. The schooner's plan is of value in illustrating the American conception of a small cruiser for the Mediterranean in the period under discussion. Unfortunately there are very few plans of small American naval vessels in this particular period; this adds to the usefulness of the drawing of this "corsair" schooner, shown in Figure 17. Though the *Skjoldebrand* was of the approximate dimensions of some of the American naval schooners, such as *Enterprise*, she does not represent the model of the latter schooner. The "corsair" was an average-sized schooner of the time she was built—77′ 6″ between perpendiculars, 62′ 0″ straight rabbet, 23′ 0″ moulded beam, and 10′ 6″ depth of hold. She had a high raised quarterdeck, which had gone out of fashion in American war schooners at the time she was built. It is probable that this feature was desired by the Algerines, and also that it was intended to make this small ship look more impressive. This schooner is said to have rowed well—a necessity in a Mediterranean cruiser—and to have been a smart sailer.

The brig, or brigantine as she is sometimes called, was the most effective vessel of the lot; she was what was then a large naval brig, designed for speed and for carrying a heavy weight of armament. This vessel was designed and

British squadron on Lake Champlain, 1776, from a drawing made at Valcour Bay by a British officer. (Courtesy Kenneth Roberts.)

ew England vessels at Valcour Bay, 1776, from a contemporary drawing. (Courtesy S. H. P. Pell, Esq.)

PLATE V

PLATE VI. Draught of TERRIBLE, *probably the "master drawing" for the 44-gun frigates* CONSTITUTION, UNITED STATES, *and* PRESIDENT.

Figure 17. Draught of the schooner SKJOLDEBRAND, 1798,
"corsair" for the Dey of Algiers.

Schooner "Skjoldebrand"
Built at Philadelphia, 1797-8 by Nathaniel Hutton Jr. and
Samuel Humphreys. Designed by Benj. Hutton Jr.

Length bet. perpd.   77:6"
         on keel   62:0"
Beam, moulded   23:0"
Depth in Hold   10:6"

137

built by Joshua Humphreys' son Samuel, and was known as the *Hassan Bashaw*. Her plan is shown in Figure 19. She was 93' 2" between perpendiculars, 75' 0" straight rabbet, 27' 0" moulded beam, and 11' 6" depth of hold; she measured 287$\frac{42}{94}$ tons customhouse measurement. This brig represents a good example of an American naval brig of the period; her original plans show evidence that her designer used them as a basis for the designs of two much

Figure 18. Sail plan of the SKJOLDEBRAND *from spar dimensions.*

later American naval vessels. On the body plan of one of the surviving drawings of the *Hassan Bashaw*, the midsections of the sloop of war *Peacock* as "rebuilt" (actually redesigned and an entirely new hull constructed) in 1828 and of the schooner *Enterprise*, built in 1831, have been laid off. This shows that Humphreys used the brig as a basis for the design of the latter vessels—the reason being that the *Hassan Bashaw* had proved unusually fast. She was a moderate "clipper," on the model, somewhat modified, of the famous American "pilot-boat construction" schooners then coming to the attention of the maritime world.

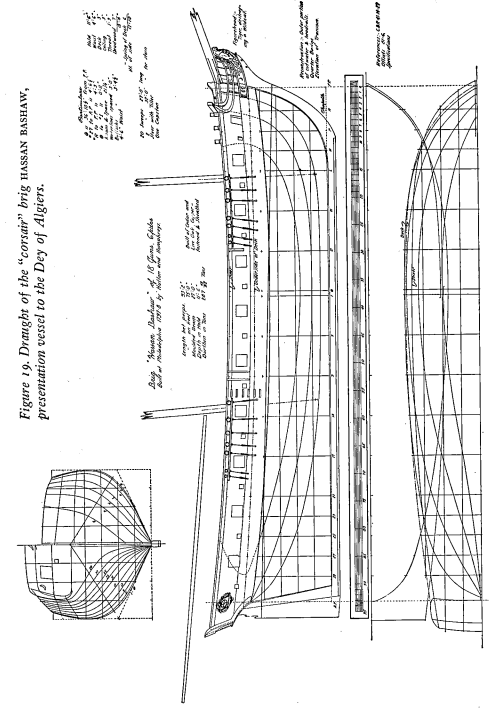

Figure 19. Draught of the "corsair" brig HASSAN BASHAW,
presentation vessel to the Dey of Algiers.

139

The Huttons, Benjamin, Jr., Nathaniel, Jr., and James, were perhaps the most competent naval architects of the period in Philadelphia. Unfortunately little is known about their careers and work, other than a few plans of naval craft that have survived. Benjamin Hutton, Jr., seems to have specialized in designing and lofting; Nathaniel was a designer and builder. James seems to have been a younger member of the family; he too was a very competent drafts-man. The draftsmanship of Benjamin, Jr., and James was superior to that of Fox or Doughty and was, in fact, the equal of the finest work of the European naval architects of the period, judging by the few plans that have been found. Nathaniel Hutton, Jr., and Samuel Humphreys were close friends and were associated in shipbuilding. It appears that the *Skjoldebrand* and the *Hassan Bashaw* were actually built by the two in partnership, though this does not seem to be officially recognized in the contracts. It is apparent, however, that the Huttons had much influence on Samuel Humphreys' later work as a designer. This is evident when Humphreys' plans are examined, for a number of them contain notes in reference to Hutton designs. It is one of the unfor-tunate features of American shipbuilding history that the papers of the Hut-tons, and of a few other early American naval architects, have disappeared. Were this not the case their fame would have been far greater than it is.

The tension with France steadily mounted, and so the new Navy increased rapidly under the new authorizations and appropriations. A number of mer-chant vessels were purchased and converted to cruisers. While a marked effort was made to obtain vessels suitable in every way—fast and able to carry guns—the results proved far from satisfactory in nearly all cases. The purchases began in 1798 and continued on into 1799. They consisted of six ships and two brigs, the latter being new vessels purchased either on the stocks or soon after launch-ing. The need for small, fast cruisers in the West Indies, to suppress French privateers operating against American shipping, placed much emphasis on brigs, schooners, and small, fast ships.

The building program consisted of ships built by contract for the federal government and of "subscription" vessels, built by the merchants of various ports and presented to the government. The government built two 28-gun frigates and three smaller ships of 20 to 24 guns. In addition, two schooners and seven galleys were built. Eight revenue cutters (seven schooners and a sloop) were turned over to the Navy. The merchants built five frigates of rates from 28 to 44 guns, four ships of from 18 to 24 guns, and a brig of 18 guns. A 36-gun frigate and a 14-gun schooner, taken from the French, were also added to the Navy.

The administration of the naval force now passed from the War Office to the newly established Navy Department, which came into existence in the middle of 1798. Benj. Stoddert, a merchant marked by initiative and force of character, was the first Secretary of the Navy. The Navy owed much to his zeal, for he attempted to establish a well-disciplined and superior officers' corps and to bring some order into the management of naval affairs. The old methods set up under the War Office, of utilizing local navy agents as civil officers of the Navy, was continued. The only criticism that might be leveled at Stoddert was his reliance upon certain favorites among the officers for advice and his compliance with political interests in some matters. In justice to Stoddert, however, it must be said that he often brought political favorites and his own advisers to heel when he thought they had imposed upon him. In short, his errors were due to inexperience rather than to any weakness in character or intentions. The navy agents were either prominent merchants or else local men with sea experience and maritime interest.

The position of the naval constructors is, however, of more concern here than the administrative organization of the Navy. As has been stated, at this period the relations between the constructors and the commissioned officers placed the latter in the ascendancy in making technical decisions. There is no evidence that Stoddert was ever conscious of any weakness in this situation. He looked upon the construction organization as a mere convenience in building and fitting out ships. In making inquiries about ships to be purchased he was inclined to consult a captain, rather than the constructors. It was not until some of his purchases were criticized that he finally utilized Humphreys and Fox for this work. Even then the constructors were usually placed in the position of having to receive orders from commissioned officers.

In completing the ships authorized in 1794 the federal government had purchased property, at Gosport, Virginia, and Portsmouth, New Hampshire, either for building shipyards or as storage locations. This led to the eventual establishment of navy yards in these locations, though these facilities came into existence more by the natural trend of events than by a planned development. The deep draft of the new ships played a part in this, as well as the need of fitting out ships, as has been noted previously. When naval hostilities began in mid-June, 1798, the need of localities for repair of ships became a matter of immediate concern. The Gosport Yard (or, as it came to be called, the Norfolk

Navy Yard) and building site became particularly important because it was conveniently situated to service the ships going to or from the West Indies. Fox had been placed here as constructor and was left independent of a commandant. He was engaged in building the *Chesapeake* and in repairs of naval ships until his discharge in the reduction of 1801. The lack of both navy yards and suitable private facilities began to be seriously felt in 1799, and soon the subject of locating a number of navy yards reached the stage of official recognition. Joshua Humphreys was sent along the coast, from New England to Virginia, inspecting possible sites. Throughout the difficulties with France, however, the Gosport site was the only one actually employed as a navy yard.

In addition to Fox, Joshua Humphreys continued to serve as a naval constructor and was utilized also as a navy agent for individual ships. He advised the Secretary occasionally and supervised repairs in the Philadelphia area. His honesty and his capabilities as a practical shipbuilder made him very useful to the Department. In spite of his ability, he was given relatively little design work, compared to Fox. It is probable that his activities in repairing and fitting out ships and in the business of the Department was the main reason for this.

The first two merchant vessels purchased were a Baltimore ship named the *Adriana* and one found at Philadelphia, named the *Ganges;* these were bought May 3, 1798. On the 5th of May another Philadelphia ship was purchased, the *Hamburgh Packet.* On June 15 the merchant ship *Herald* was bought at Boston, the *Montezuma* was obtained June 26 at Baltimore, and the *George Washington* was bought at Providence, Rhode Island, in September, 1798. The two brigs purchased were both obtained at Norfolk, Virginia, and were particularly selected for fast sailing. One was bought in 1798 and the other in June, 1799.

The *Adriana* was renamed *Baltimore;* her customhouse measurements were 103' 9" length, 30' 8" beam, depth not given, $422^{32}\!/\!_{95}$ tons; she had quarter galleries and a "Woman figurehead" and was fitted to carry 20 9-pdrs. She was a new ship launched at Baltimore early in 1798, built by Joseph Caverly. She soon had the reputation of being a slow ship, and in 1801 she was sold.

The *Ganges* retained her old name. She had been built in 1795 at Philadelphia; her customhouse measurements were 116' 4" length, 31' 4" beam, depth 15' 8", 504 tons. She had double quarter galleries (indicating a ship with a high quarterdeck or poop), a stern gallery and a roundhouse, and a figurehead not described; she was fitted with 26 9-pdrs. Her original merchant-ship captain, Richard Dale, who had served with John Paul Jones, took her over as a

Navy captain. This vessel was one of the best of the purchased ships; she too was sold in 1801.

The *Hamburgh Packet* had been built at Philadelphia in 1794; her custom-house dimensions were 94' 9" length, 28' 0" beam, 14' 0" depth, 321^{64}⁄$_{95}$ tons; she had quarter galleries and an Indian figurehead. She was renamed *Delaware* and was armed with 20 guns—16 9-pdrs. and 4 6's. She too proved slow and was sold out in 1801.

The *Montezuma*, which retained her original name, was a 347-ton ship with quarter galleries and a figurehead. She carried 20 guns, apparently 9-pdrs.; her dimensions have not been found. She was a very unsatisfactory cruiser, and was sold at Baltimore in 1799.

The *Herald* also retained her original name. She had been built at Newbury in 1798, and her customhouse dimensions were 92' 8" length, 26' 3½" beam, 13' 1¾" depth, 279^{75}⁄$_{95}$ tons. She had quarter galleries and a "man figurehead." Though commonly referred to as an 18-gun ship, she carried 22 guns—16 6-pdrs. and 6 4's. She was supposed to be a fast ship when offered to the government, but she seems to have suffered from an officious captain; the Secretary of the Navy maintained that she had been spoiled by alterations after purchase. At any rate she proved to be overloaded and an unsatisfactory cruiser; she was sold out in 1801, but had been inactive for some time previous.

The *George Washington* was a 624-ton ship, 108' 0" long on the keel, 32' 6" beam, and 15' 8" depth in hold. She had quarter galleries and a figurehead. Built at Providence, Rhode Island, in 1793 as a merchant ship of the largest class, she was well built but slow. She seems to have been very roomy and was fitted with 32 guns, but was rated as a 24-gun ship. She carried 24 9-pdrs. and 8 6's. She was retained in service for a longer time than the other purchased ships and was not disposed of until 1803. She was sometimes referred to as a frigate because of her size and appearance.

The brig *Norfolk* was purchased at the city she was named after, and was selected because she was thought to be fast. She was built at Gosport by Nash and Herbert, and was new at the time of purchase; she carried 18 6-pdrs. on a flush deck and was a sharp vessel. She was a good sailer and a useful brig, but, said to be rotten, she was sold at Baltimore late in 1800.

The *Augusta* was the second brig purchased at Norfolk. She too was a new vessel, a little smaller than the *Norfolk*, and carried 14 guns—10 6-pdrs. and 4 4-pdrs. She was sold at Norfolk in 1801.

Both brigs were lightly built; the *Norfolk* was about 200 tons, or roughly

88' on deck; the *Augusta* was about 175 tons and around 75' on deck. The *Augusta* caused the Secretary of the Navy some annoyance after her purchase in 1799. He sent her to Boston to be fitted out with stores removed from the *Herald*, which had been laid up as an unsatisfactory cruiser. Upon the *Augusta*'s arrival at Boston, her captain expressed his dislike of taking over a smaller vessel and, together with the local ship carpenters, requested permission to change the vessel—to cut down the spars, which were considered too light for their length, to remove the rudder irons and replace them, and to add to the bulwarks and cabins. By this time the Secretary had learned that the captains were never satisfied with a vessel as she was built and had lost patience. He refused to grant permission to change the vessel in any way; finally becoming disgusted with the Boston clique's insistence that only they were competent to judge a ship, he had the brig sent to Philadelphia and ordered Humphreys to pass on her. Humphreys made a few minor repairs and fitted the brig out; she proved very fast and a good seaboat. She was very stiff, carrying her lee guns two feet above the water in a reefed topsail breeze, and was noted as a weatherly vessel in all conditions, well suited to the West Indies.

In general, the purchased ships were too small to carry the armaments placed aboard them; when they were ready for sea their guns were so close to the water line that they could not be used in heavy seas, or when under sail in a fresh breeze. Some undoubtedly had poor lines for speed, but, judging by the correspondence, a good deal of the difficulty in the ships could be traced to their captains' insistence on changing the ships and on overgunning them. In only rare cases, such as that of the *Augusta*, were the constructors consulted in preference to accepting the captain's verdict. The *Ganges* is another exception. She was taken out as a cruiser by the same captain who had her as a merchantman; therefore there were few changes, and these were partly made under Joshua Humphreys' supervision. As a result, she seems to have been a very useful ship, with a reasonable turn of speed, even when she was under other captains. Once a ship got to sea on her maiden cruise as a Navy ship, the Secretary was usually adamant about making any more alterations.

These purchased vessels were obtained by an authorization of Congress dated April 27, 1798, which was followed by another on May 4. Congress, by the Act of June 30, 1798, also permitted the acceptance of vessels built by the citizens. Nevertheless every effort was made to prevent the construction of unnecessarily expensive ships. The federal government contracted for the construction of two frigates, the *Adams* and *General Greene*. The *Adams*, of 28 guns, was built at New York by Jackson and Sheffield. The latter also designed her; at least he supplied a plan and a model. She was about 113' on the gun deck, 108' straight rabbet, 34' moulded beam, 10' 9" hold, and about 530 tons. She carried 24 12-pdrs. and 4 6-pdrs. This small ship was launched in 1799 and remained in the Navy. At the outbreak of the War of 1812 she was rebuilt as a flush-decked corvette and lengthened about 15'. She was burned in the Penobscot on September 3, 1814, to prevent capture by British boats. The *General Greene*, also a 28, was built by contract at Warren, Rhode Island, by Benjamin Talman and James de Wolf. Measuring 124' 3" on the gun deck, 34' 8" beam, and 17' 4" depth in the hold, she was 654 tons and carried 24 12-pdrs. and 6 6's. Launched January 21, 1799, she remained in service after the reduction of 1801 and in 1805 was converted to a sheer hulk at Washington Navy Yard, where she was burned when the city was captured August 24, 1814. Her plan was indexed in the Navy plan files but cannot now be found. It is not known who designed her, but it was probably Talman.

The smaller ships contracted for were the *Portsmouth*, built at Portsmouth, New Hampshire, by Hackett, 590 tons, 24 guns; the *Connecticut*, built at Middletown, Connecticut, launched June 6, 1799, from the Overton yard; and the 20-gun ship *Warren*, contracted for at Newburyport, Massachusetts, but actually built at Salisbury by an association of builders. The *Warren*, a 385-ton ship, was sold at Boston in 1801. The *Connecticut* leaked after her launch and sank in the river, which caused much delay in getting her commissioned. She rated as a 24-gun ship of 492 tons, carrying 26 12-pdrs., and was one of the fastest ships in the Navy on the West Indian Station.

Two schooners, the *Enterprise* and *Experiment*, were also built by contract, handled entirely by the Baltimore Naval Agent, Henry Yellot. The *Enterprise*, built on the Eastern Shore of Maryland by Henry Spencer, was a square-tuck-stern schooner, 60' on the keel, 84' 7" on deck, 22' 6" beam, 9' 6" depth of hold, 135 tons. She was said to have been 23' beam over the thick wales. No plan of the vessel has ever been found, and the only information on her form, as originally built, is contained in the letters of her commanding officer when she was "repaired" and almost entirely rebuilt at Venice in 1805. He noted that she was almost completely rotten, had a square-tuck stern and a good deal of tumble home in her sides above the water line. It is apparent that she was a typical pilot-boat schooner of the period, fitted with deeper bulwarks than usual. She carried 12 long 6-pdrs. when originally fitted out. This schooner became a noted vessel and was retained in service. She was again rebuilt from the floor timbers up in the fall of 1811 at the Washington Navy Yard, and was then rerigged as a brig with her tonnage increased to 165 tons. About 1806 Fox measured her and found her to be 92' 9" on deck, 80' 6" between perpendiculars, 23' 9" extreme beam, 22' 11" moulded beam, and 10' 10" depth of hold at the mainmast. This was after the first rebuilding, which undoubtedly accounts for the variation in the dimensions.

The *Experiment* was a schooner of the same rate and ordered to the same dimensions: keel 60', moulded beam 22' 6", depth of hold 9' 6", 135 tons. Whether she was built in Baltimore or on the Eastern Shore is uncertain. In an official paper of 1802 William Price of Baltimore was said to have built the *Enterprise*, although this may refer to the *Experiment*. It is possible, of course, that the schooners may have been originally let to Price, who contracted them out to other builders on subcontracts.

Like the *Enterprise*, the *Experiment* was a very successful cruiser, but she was one of the vessels sold in 1801. The swiftness of these schooners, and the fact that their size rated junior officers as commanders, soon made them noted vessels. Commanded by young, bold, and ambitious officers, the two schooners naturally had eventful careers.

The revenue cutters were all new vessels. Not all the existing cutters were to be transferred to the Navy, so it was possible to limit the selection to vessels of recent build. The Revenue Service had been established in 1790, and between 1791 and 1793 nine small schooners and one sloop had been built. These had been found too small, and so larger cutters were laid down in 1797. These were double-topsail schooners, or "jackass brigs," with fore and main square top-sails. Much confusion exists in the records of these vessels, since some of them carried the names of the earlier and smaller cutters. The cutters taken into naval service included all but two of the new schooners. Those chosen were the *Diligence*, built at Philadelphia, the *General Greene*, built by Price at Baltimore, the *Governor Jay*, built at New York, the *Pickering*, built at New-buryport, the *Scammel*, built at Portsmouth, New Hampshire, the *Eagle*, built at Philadelphia, the *South Carolina*, built at Charleston, South Carolina, and the *Virginia*, built at Norfolk. One other, the *Pinckney*, or *General Pinckney*, built at Charleston and taken over on the stocks, was apparently the largest of the cutters. All of the cutters except the *Pinckney*, *General Greene*, and *Virginia* were listed as being 58' 0" straight rabbet, 20' 0" moulded beam, 9' 0" depth of hold, and 187 tons; the last seems to be an error. The *Greene* was 98 tons, and the *Virginia* is noted as being 50' 0" straight rabbet, 18' 10" moulded beam, 8' 6" depth of hold, and fitted with a poop flush with the top of the bulwarks to form a cabin aft. These cutters were armed with 4- and 6-pdrs., usually brass. Fox designed the *Pickering, Eagle,* and *Diligence;* possibly the others were sisters, but this cannot be proved. All the cutters except the *Scammel, Eagle,* and *Pickering* were returned to the Treasury in 1799. The first two were sold out of the Navy in 1801, and the *Pickering* was lost at sea with all hands in the fall of 1800.

No plans that can be identified with certainty as one of these cutters has yet come to light. However, among the plans formerly in the Navy plan files in the Washington Navy Yard, and now missing from the National Archives, were a number of schooner and ship plans without identification—some without an index number. These plans were mostly those from the personal files of some of the constructors and assistants—Humphreys, Doughty, and Rhodes. The writer traced some of these plans before they were removed from the Navy Yard, among them a schooner design that he first supposed to be of the 1797 cutters. This plan, redrawn, is shown in Figure 20. It does not appear that it was the plan used to build the cutters, for the beam is one foot less than that given in the register of the vessels, though the length on the keel, or of the straight rabbet, and the depth in hold can be seen to correspond. The original plan, which has disappeared, was in pencil and seems to have been either a preliminary design or a rather hasty copy of a working drawing. The drawing, though less valuable than it would be if it could be identified, is useful in showing the approximate size of the cutters, as well as the extremes reached, in the period under discussion, in the design of fast schooners. The plan was noted as being of a 14-gun schooner to carry 6-pdrs. but it is doubtful if her displacement was anywhere enough to permit such an armament. It will be seen that she was 77' 0" between perpendiculars, on a length of 58' 0" of straight rabbet; this shows that the cutters must have been approximately the same length—say 70 to 80 feet on deck. The plan also permits a rough idea to be formed of the appearance of the larger schooners, *Enterprise* and *Experiment.* The schooner not only had the square-tuck stern of these vessels, but also had the same tumble-home topsides that seem to have characterized these cruisers. The "round-tuck" stern consisted of what was really two transoms, the lower one square across along the bottom, or "cross seam," with the bottom and lower side planking "tucking" up in a round full curve to the cross seam. The "square-tuck" stern had three distinct transoms, the lower one a V (or heart shape), to which the bottom and lower side transom ran "square," as in the

stern of a modern powerboat. The round-tuck stern can be seen in the drawings of the other ships of this period. The square-tuck stern had pretty well
gone out of fashion in large ships by 1790, but it was retained in many small
craft until the modern counter stern appeared in the first half of the nineteenth
century.

Figure 20. Draught of an unidentified 14-gun schooner showing an extreme design of the period.

It has been the custom to suppose that the designers of the latter part of the
eighteenth century were incapable of designing very sharp-ended sailing vessels, but this is a fallacy. Usually the constructors of the period were limited
in the use of sharp-lined hulls by the necessity of carrying guns and a large
store of provisions. The Secretary of the Navy, for example, usually instructed the navy agents and citizens' associations that the ships they were to
have built were to carry a given number of guns, to be strong, and to sail well,
but that they must carry, say, six months' provisions for a crew of a stated number. This last specification usually prevented a naval vessel from being as
sharp as the privateers or those vessels built for illegal trades. The need of
having fast cutters to stop smuggling often produced revenue vessels that were

very sharp, in both England and the United States, in this period. As has been seen in Fox's criticism of Humphreys' model for a 44-gun frigate, very hollow sharp lines in the bow were usually looked upon with disfavor. However, some of the designers of sharp schooners and pilot boats employed such lines because of the fine ends they desired in their craft. Only rarely did the load water line show any hollow, but the lines below often show a good deal, as in this example. This was an incidental feature of design brought about by a combination of a sharp bow and marked forefoot. The same thing occurred later in the design of the California and China clipper ships of the 1840's and 1850's; most of their designers disliked a hollow load water line, but they were forced to hollow lines below by the very sharp entrance and angular forefoot they employed in the ships. The "long hollow bow" of the clipper ships was a mere figment of journalistic imagination on the part of a newspaperman attempting to describe a ship. Even today, the hollow load water line at the bow is rarely seen in sailing yachts, and few designers place any value on the feature. A sharp entrance can be obtained without hollow water lines only by employing extreme rake in the stem, as in most modern sailing yachts, but this was not always desirable when vessels carried square sails or were very heavily canvased.

The difference between the length on the keel and the length on deck, in American schooners and other vessels of this period, is deserving of attention. The American designers usually employed a good deal of rake in the stem and sternposts, though less in the latter than in the former. The rabbet of the bow in many American vessels was on a large radius, with its axis over the forward end of the straight of the rabbet. In small vessels like schooners this radius was usually about three-quarters of the beam, though it is apparent that this was not a rule or set proportion. In large vessels the radius was usually less—say four-sevenths of the beam. Actually, of course, the rabbet of the stem usually departed somewhat from an arc of a circle, as the designers commonly straightened the curve in profile as it approached the deck line. It is found that, as a result, the American schooners and small craft had a measured bow rake ranging from about three-quarters of the beam to the full beam, and large vessels from about three-sevenths to four-sevenths. The measured stern rake was often small; the post usually raked about one-fourth of the beam in schooners and about one-seventh in large vessels. There were, of course, variations in rake, with a great many vessels falling between the two extremes. Schooners and small craft built in the South and on Chesapeake Bay commonly had more rake than those built at Philadelphia or New York or in New England. It is quite noticeable that small vessels to be fitted with a square rig—brigs, for example—commonly had less fore-rake than schooners with square topsails only. In this matter of rake the Americans were quite consistent, and their design practice differed from that followed in England and France. The English revenue and naval cutter of the period was the British equivalent of the sharp American schooner; this type usually had greater rake to the sternpost than to the stem, or, occasionally, the rakes of stem and sternpost approached equality. The French equivalent of the American schooner of pilot-boat construction was the lugger and some small brigs; these commonly employed less rake to the stem and sternpost than either the American or British fast-sailing craft. The French, however, were less consistent, particularly at the end of the eighteenth century, for they designed some vessels with great rake in the ends and with a variety of midsections whose forms were not employed in either American or British small craft. While the British copied some French ships, they did not use any French features in the design of their very fast cutters, as can be seen by the existing plans in the National Maritime Museum at Greenwich, England. In fact, there is some reason to suppose that the French copied English cutters in some of their fast luggers of the period under discussion.

The schooner in Figure 20 is less extreme in the rake of her stem and approaches the practice of some English constructors. This was probably brought about by the need of gaining displacement without increasing the beam, which could be accomplished by reducing rake. Fox seems to have proposed building an English cutter, and it is probable that he employed its features in some of the schooners he designed. It is possible that the schooner in Figure 20 shows the influence of his ideas in this respect. While there is no evidence to support the idea, the writer believes it is possible that this schooner design was a proposal for a revenue vessel that was not built. It does not appear to have been the work of a Philadelphia designer, judging by an endorsement of the date of receipt on the original drawing.

Schooners of this class were in great demand, particularly in the West Indies. From 1792 to the end of the Napoleonic Wars there was a very active export trade in new American schooners. During the quasi war with France the sale of sharp schooners to French agents was a matter of official concern, and some effort was made to apprehend foreign agents as well as to stop the transfer of such schooners abroad by means of sales of "ships and cargoes" under the guise of regular trade. As early as 1795 the sharp American schooners had achieved enough notoriety abroad to make them much sought after, not only as privateers and illegal traders but also as regular light naval ships. Three-masted schooners appeared, and the average size of the sharp-model schooners increased somewhat. During the years of the French troubles there was much speculative building of schooners, and the model rapidly became more and more extreme, judging by the plans that have been found.

One of the congressional appropriations produced a peculiar class of small craft, the galley. By the Act of May 4, 1798, the Navy Department was authorized to purchase or build up to ten small vessels of the galley type, to be manned by what might be termed naval militia. The personnel was under the control of the War Office, but the boats were to be built and fitted by the Navy. This act produced not only some curious shoal-draft craft but also a confusion in the records. Joshua Humphreys was commissioned to prepare the plan for the first galley; however, the plan seems to have been the work of his son, Samuel. The first design was modified, and finally four designs appear to have been used. Two or three galleys were built by private subscription; these seem to have been designed by their builders. In addition the revenue cutter *Pinckney*, which had been taken over incomplete, was completed by use of the galley funds, the Secretary of the Navy "considering" her a galley for administrative purposes to permit the diversion of funds. Because of this she is usually noted as a "galley," whereas it appears that she was actually a brig or brig-schooner of some size.

One of the designs used to build the galleys has survived, and Figure 21 probably shows the first one built at Pittsburgh. This is for a boat 50' 6" between perpendiculars, 13' 6" moulded beam at the level of the top of the wales, or 14' 4" at plank-sheer, and 6' 8½" total depth. The plan shows that the galley in general model was almost a much-reduced copy of Arnold's galley on Lake Champlain in the Revolution. The armament was an 18-pdr. in the bow and four howitzers or swivels (3-pdrs.) of brass, mounted on stocks along the after rail and on the stern. The crew slept in berths under the side decks and under the center-line gangway; a tarpaulin covered each of the hatchways at night. The officers had a small cabin or cuddy aft. Cooking seems to have been done in a small fireplace on the gun platform forward or ashore if the opportunity arose.

The surviving building instructions by the Humphreys show that a second

Figure 21. Galley of 1799, designed for river and harbor service.

design intended for use on the Mississippi was 45′ 0″ between perpendiculars and 13′ 0″ moulded beam; a third was 51′ 9″ between perpendiculars, 15′ 3½″ moulded beam at rail, or plank-sheer, and 5′ 1″ depth of hold; and the fourth design called for boats 56′ 0″ between perpendiculars, 14′ 6″ moulded beam, and 5′ 8½″ depth of hold. This last design was to be used for three western

Bow gun of a Mediterranean gun vessel.

Admiralty carriage mount for an 18-pdr. carronade, 1808.

Builder's sail plan of the frigate PHILADELPHIA.

PLATE VII

Master sailmaker's plan of the ship of the line INDEPENDENCE.

Master sailmaker's plan of the ship of the line COLUMBUS.

PLATE VIII

river galleys to be built at Pittsburgh, Louisville, and Marietta. The galleys
built on the coast appear to have been usually on the 51′ 6″ design, to carry
one 24-pdr. long gun and six 3-pdr. swivels, manned by twenty-five privates
or seamen and a commander, lieutenant, and boatswain. The larger galleys
had the rail raised above the main sheer line from the bow gun port aft to the
forward end of the rowing hatches; their gun port was much higher above the
water line than in the galley shown in Figure 21. The coastal galleys were
the *Savannah*, built at Savannah, Georgia, the *St. Marys*, built at St. Marys,
Georgia, the *Charleston* and *South Carolina* built at Charleston, South Carolina,
the *Beaufort* built at Beaufort, North Carolina, and the *Governor Williams*
and the *Governor Davie* (or *Governor Davies*), both built at Wilmington,
North Carolina. The known galleys built on the rivers were the *Marietta* and
the *Senator Ross;* the names of the others have not been found. The galleys
Beaufort, *Charleston*, and *South Carolina* may have been the ones built by
subscription; the *Charleston* was first called the *Mars*, and the *South Carolina*
the *Protector*, apparently. The first galley built in the West was one at Pittsburgh, contracted for by John Taylor. Joshua Humphreys received twelve
dollars for the design shown in Figure 21. There was some objection to the
rig of the galleys; some officers wanted to use square sails, but Humphreys very
properly objected. Though the galleys were eminently suited for river service, they were of little value on the coast, except perhaps for harbor defense.

The plan of operation for the galleys proposed in the congressional act did
not work out. The interest of the War Department in the boats was nil, and the
Navy not only built and fitted the boats but eventually manned them as well.
The coastal galleys were disposed of in 1801–2, some going to the Revenue
Service and the others being sold. In 1800 the Secretary of the Navy wrote
that in his opinion one 12-gun schooner on the naval establishment was worth
a thousand galleys under the Act of May 4, 1798. In spite of the uselessness of
the galleys for naval service the boats built in 1798–99 were to mark the beginning of an era of gunboat construction in the American Navy.

One of the modes of increasing the Navy in this period is interesting in
the light of the modern theory that the protection of all groups within the
national sphere is a matter of government responsibility. The popular concept
was quite different in 1798. Since the merchants who owned ships were the
chief sufferers from the seizures of American shipping by the Barbary powers
and other nationals, it seemed reasonable to Congress that they should make
a special contribution to the defense of the merchant marine. As a result, they

provided, in the Act of June 30, 1798, that ships would be accepted by the Navy which were to be built by public subscription. The act authorized the President to accept a limited number to be paid for in bonds of 6 per cent interest and an unlimited number that might be voluntarily presented. In the event the first quota was not filled, the remaining portion of bonds, or "stock," could be paid on the second category. The intention was, of course, to encourage the merchants of the large ports, and the maritime interests in general, to contribute to the naval establishment, with partial repayment, at least, in interest-bearing notes. Of course, the possibility of the outright gift of ships by individuals or groups of citizens was to be encouraged by the government under this particular plan. Great efforts were made to call upon the patriotism and pride of the large maritime towns and cities to accomplish this and to make them outdo one another. Events showed that this procedure of the government seemed reasonable and fair to the general public and to the merchant class. As a result the Navy received a number of fine ships, from frigates down to brigs, some by bond payments and some as gifts.

The only drawback to the plan was that it required much time to raise funds for such a purpose in a community and to get the ships started. As a result, the frigates built by those ports financially able to handle such construction were slow in being completed and few were ready in time to play any part in the trouble with France. The smaller ships, however, got to sea early enough to be of some use.

One of the ports or areas that might have been able to build one large ship chose instead to produce two small ships. Baltimore built two 20-gun ships to carry 20 9-pdrs. on the main deck and 6 6-pdrs. on the quarterdeck. One was to be called the *Maryland* and the other the *Chesapeake*. The latter name, however, had been chosen for the frigate building at Gosport, so the Secretary of the Navy ordered the ship building at Baltimore to be renamed *Patapsco*. The *Maryland* and the *Patapsco* were both launched in June of 1799, and both were sold out of the Navy in 1801. No plans of the vessels exist, but from correspondence of Yellot, the navy agent at Baltimore, it appears that the vessels were 87' 0" on the keel, 29' 0" moulded beam, and 12' 0" or 13' 0" depth of hold, measuring "380 tons" and sharp-built. From a letter written by James Buchanan about the *Maryland* and a letter written to the navy agent by Truxton, it is known that the vessels had a spar deck, or rather forecastle and quarterdeck with gangways, and carried their guns too low. They were, however, good sailers, and the *Maryland* was said to be very fast in light weather.

Figure 22. Draught of an unidentified 20-gun ship with spar deck, 1799.

Among the unidentified plans formerly in the files of the Washington Navy Yard was a rather incomplete drawing of a 20-gun ship much like the Baltimore-built vessels. Figure 22 shows this drawing of a spar-decked sloop of war to carry 20 guns on the lower deck and 4 on the quarterdeck. Such a vessel could have carried the six guns on the quarterdeck noted in the description of the Baltimore ships. The plan shows a miniature frigate, 106′ 4″ between perpendiculars, 29′ 0″ moulded beam, and 13′ 6″ depth of hold. The plan was dated 1799 and so cannot be a design for the Baltimore-built ships. It is possible that the plan was intended for an improved 20-gun ship based on them, with a deeper hold and fewer guns to permit more freeboard. The original plan cannot now be found in the National Archives, so the draftsmanship cannot be identified; the writer, in making a pencil tracing of the original in 1934, made no effort to accomplish this. In view of the fact that the drawing is another that cannot be identified with any degree of certainty, it is of value only in showing the approximate design and appearance of some of the 20-gun ships of the period. The design is of a rather sharp-ended vessel with the midsection placed farther aft than was the practice, at least in the larger ships. The appearance of the vessel would have been very much like that of the frigates of the 32-gun class.

The Baltimore vessels were apparently originally intended to have detached upper decks; Truxton recommended a full spar deck. When the Maryland was criticized it was said that this was one of the causes of objection and that spar decks were not employed in similar vessels abroad. This is an error, for both French and British navies had ship sloops with spar decks, or very wide gangways, as early as 1795. Buchanan wrote the Secretary of State, repeating the earlier criticisms of the spar deck and adding the more just comment that the ship was overgunned for her size. Comparing the ship in the plan and the known dimensions and armament of the Maryland and Patapsco with a British sloop of the period illustrates the mistake made in arming the American vessels. The British sloops of war built on a similar plan between 1795 and 1798, named Termagant, Bittern, Cyane, Plover, and Brazen, will serve to illustrate the point. The Cyane later fell into American hands and was taken into the United States Navy. The British ships were 110′ 0″ between perpendiculars, 29′ 0″ moulded beam, and 13′ 8″ in the hold, using the American system of measurement. They originally carried 16 6-pdrs. on the gun deck, 6 12-pdr. carronades on the quarterdeck, and 2 12-pdr. carronades on the forecastle—24 guns all told against the Americans' 26 guns of heavier weight. Though the

British sloops had sharper bows than the ship in Figure 22, the greater area of the British ship's midsection and her slightly greater length gave her more displacement on slightly less draft.

Overloading with armament became as much a fault in the British Navy as in the American, as can be illustrated in the case of the *Cyane*. This ship carried a total of 32 guns in 1809—22 32-pdr. carronades on her main deck and 8 carronades, 18-pdrs., and 2 long 6's on her quarterdeck and forecastle. The effect of this on the ship was to damage her sailing qualities to a ruinous extent. In both the American and the British Navy the captains were trying to make frigates out of even the smallest ship sloops. If the Baltimore ships were anything like the plan shown here, they were far handsomer ships than the British vessels, and would probably have been faster sailers if they had been properly gunned and rigged. The builders of the two Baltimore ships are not given in government records, but the *Patapsco* is reported in a contemporary newspaper account to have been built in De Rochbrune's yard. She had a Neptune figurehead; the *Maryland* had a figure of the goddess of "commerce and plenty."

Another 20-gun ship, the *Warren*, already mentioned as built by contract at Newburyport, was 385 tons according to the official statements. Taking the dimensions of the ship shown in Figure 22, calculation of the tonnage in accordance with the method then in force shows her to be only a little over 360 tons; it is highly probable, then, that all tonnage in these small naval vessels was grossly overestimated and that the two Baltimore-built ships as well as the *Warren* were only about 350 tons burden. Tonnage statements in this period seem to have been based on varying local practices and are therefore unreliable.

It is apparent from the official correspondence that the Secretary of the Navy sent out dimensions and, in some cases at least, plans of 20- and 24-gun ships for the information of the sponsors of subscriptions. In a letter to Charleston he enclosed a plan of a 24-gun ship, to measure about 538 tons and to carry 24 guns on the main deck and 4 or 6 more on the quarterdeck, the lower-deck guns to be 12-pdrs. His letter indicates that he sent a plan of the ship *Portsmouth*, designed by Josiah Fox, but the plan was not used, as a larger vessel was finally built. In another letter he gives the navy agent at New York an idea of what he considers to be the dimensions of a 20-gun ship: 93' 0" keel, 31' 0" beam, and 13' 6" depth of hold; to carry 20 guns on the main deck, exclusive of the bridle ports, and 2 guns on the quarterdeck. In a letter to Connecticut he asks about the possibility of building an 18-gun ship or brig, and then indicates the desire for a ship of from 300 to 360 tons to carry 18 long 9's. The tenor of his correspondence was to give the sponsors of the subscription vessels an idea of the desired size, leaving it to the local groups to choose a designer and builder and to judge the proper model and proportions.

In this manner he was able to induce the citizens of Newburyport to build the 24-gun ship *Merrimack*, with 20 9-pdrs. on the main deck and 8 6-pdrs. on the quarterdeck. Built by an association of shipwrights, among whom was Cross, this ship was launched October 12, 1798, and was sold at Boston in 1801. He also succeeded in getting the people of the Norwich, Connecticut, area, which included New London, to build the 18-gun ship *Trumbull* of 400 tons, carrying 18 12-pdrs. on one deck. He obtained the 200-ton brig *Richmond* from the citizens of Richmond, Petersburg, Manchester, and Norfolk, Virginia, in 1798. Both the *Trumbull* and the *Richmond* were sold in 1801. A number of other small vessels were projected but failed to be brought forward. The two Baltimore vessels and the *Merrimack, Trumbull, Richmond,* and the frigate *Boston* were the only subscription-built vessels to see active service in the French troubles.

The Secretary's desire to utilize the shipbuilding knowledge of as many communities as possible and the lack of technical supervision by the government's naval architects, or other central authority, that was inherent in the subscription method of obtaining ships (as well as the disorganization of the newly established Navy Department) all created a confusion of records, and it is not surprising to find that few plans of the ships have survived. While it was plainly the intention of the Secretary to obtain plans of each ship built, he was too burdened with duties and responsibilities to be able to follow the matter up and to complete the plan files. The latter, in fact, were at that time of little practical value; because of the newness of the ships, their maintenance had not yet become a serious matter, and so there had been no particular demand for the information that was contained in the plans. About the only purpose they served was to guide the proposals for new vessels.

The Secretary's desire to employ the shipbuilding knowledge of as many areas as possible appears to have arisen from a realization that naval ship design and construction was becoming concentrated, to an undesirable degree, in certain Philadelphia shipyards. The small clique of Philadelphia shipwrights not only dominated the design of new ships to a great extent, but their advice had been accepted to the exclusion of all others. Even Fox could be placed among

Figure 23. Draught of an unidentified 18-gun ship, 1798.

159

the Philadelphia group because of his close personal relations with the merchants of that city.

It is unfortunate that we have found no plan of the small ships built by the government or by subscription that can be identified as the design of any individual vessel. In fact, so far as the Navy plan files are concerned, the only plan of a small armed ship of the period, other than the 20-gun ship last described, is of a vessel whose nature cannot be determined with certainty. The design of this vessel is presented in Figure 23, redrawn from a pencil tracing of the original when it was in the Washington Navy Yard files. Though indexed (40–15–6 E), the plan has not yet been found in the National Archives and appears to be one of the many lost or misplaced in the transfer of the drawings from the Navy Department. This particular drawing, dated 1798, was noted as a copy by Samuel Humphreys. From the appearance of the stem it is concluded that the design was one of Fox's, but as yet no identification can be made. The ship appears at first glance to be a merchantman, but study of the design shows the model to be unusual for a vessel employed in trade. She is too large to have been designed as a fast illegal trader, and too sharp to be a good carrier. It is therefore possible that this plan represents either a ship proposed for naval service, or one intended as a merchant-cruiser. The design might be said to be intermediate between a merchant ship and a sloop of war of the period under discussion. The use of a berth deck in this ship was indicated on the plan, and this would have been needless in a merchant ship. The vessel also was pierced for a rather heavy armament—18 guns, with the possibility of carrying 22—but this did not necessarily indicate a naval vessel; merchantmen carrying up to 22 guns were not uncommon in the American merchant marine at the end of the eighteenth century. A ship of this design would have made a good convoy guard and an effective cruiser. It is possible that the plan may be that of one of the 18-gun ships, but in the absence of the dimensions of these vessels identification is wholly impractical. The design was for a ship 95′ 0″ on the keel for tonnage, 32′ 0″ moulded beam, 13′ 6″ depth of hold, and 116′ 3″ between perpendiculars. The tonnage was not given, but it works out at about 430 tons. She would have been somewhat similar in appearance to some French-built sloops, except for carrying her guns on the upper deck. It is to be observed that the Americans had accepted the basic model and arrangement of the 44-gun ships as the ideal for all classes, from ship sloops upward. This can be seen not only in the 20-gun ship design shown in Figure 22 and in the ship just described, but also in the greater part of the frigate class of the United States Navy.

Though most of the large ships built by subscription were completed too late to be of any real service in the trouble with the French republicans of the Directorate, they were excellent additions to the Navy and were of value in the events that followed the quasi war with France. Five new frigates resulted from the efforts of the merchants of the important ports: the *Philadelphia, New York, Essex, Boston,* and *John Adams;* all were well-built ships on what were then considered very good models.

The merchants of Philadelphia went to Josiah Fox for the design of the frigate they wished to build. The wealth of the port and the pride of the merchants had decided the type of ship to be built; she was to be an "improved" 44-gun ship. Now, Fox was not satisfied with the large 44's, as we have seen, and was convinced that ships of this class somewhat smaller than the *Constitution* type were the most desirable. He was given freedom to design the new frigate as he thought best, and he produced a ship much like the earlier frigates in appearance but differing in dimensions and model. Like the earlier 44's, she was to have what constituted a spar deck. The final dimensions of the *Philadelphia,* or as she was sometimes called, *City of Philadelphia,* were 157' 0" between perpendiculars, 130' 0" on the keel for tonnage, 39' 0" moulded beam, and 13' 6" depth of hold. Samuel Humphreys, Nathaniel Hutton, and John Delavue were selected to build the ship. They completed her in the spring of 1800. This fine frigate is shown in Plan 9; the differences between this drawing and the one in the National Archives (reprinted in *Barbary Wars, Personnel and Ships' Data,* as part of the Naval Documents printed under the supervision of the Office of Naval Records and Library, U.S. Government Printing Office, 1945) require explanation.

The drawing of the ship in the above-mentioned publication is an exact reproduction of the existing draught, with such additions as were necessary to restore a very damaged plan. This drawing of the *Philadelphia* shows a ship with what appears to be a solid spar-deck bulwark, running flush and unbroken from stem to stern. One of the oddities of the plan was that the cutwater and head seemed remarkably modern and more like the frigates built during and after the War of 1812 than like the earlier frigates. Another plan of the ship existed, however; this was a carefully drawn sail plan dated May 16, 1800, which was made by Nathaniel Hutton, Jr., one of the builders. This plan, part

of the papers of John Lenthall, constructor of the U.S. Navy and a former
apprentice of Samuel Humphreys, is in the Franklin Institute, Philadelphia.
It showed a vessel having the apparent lines and dimensions given in the plan in
the National Archives, but with an entirely different cutwater and headrail
arrangement, as well as extensive departures in the rail on the spar deck. In
examining the plan of the *Philadelphia* in the National Archives, it was noticed
that the draftsmanship was not that of Fox, but that it was very much like

Figure 24. Spar plan of the frigate PHILADELPHIA *after spar dimensions. (See Plan 9.)*

that in the plan of the frigate *New York*, also in the National Archives and
reproduced in *Personnel and Ships' Data*. In searching for the plan of the *New
York*, which also showed what appeared to be a solid spar-deck bulwark, the
inboard-works drawing of the *New York* was found. This showed that the
draught of the *New York* was incorrect in the spar-deck rails and other details.
In addition it showed that the *New York*'s draught was not the original, but
rather a plan drawn by an apprentice named Henry Allen. Additional search
brought out the evidence that the plans of both the *Philadelphia* and the *New
York*, as well as a drawing of the brig *Syren*, had been made by Allen from
offsets and building directions in the years 1816–21. This seems to explain the

comparatively modern appearance of the plans now in the National Archives. Accepting the lines shown in Allen's drawing of the *Philadelphia* as correct, since they were made from the offsets, the headrails and spar-deck rails have been taken from Hutton's plan. However, the vessel was intended as a 44, so the draught in Plan 9 shows the probable appearance of the ship as originally designed.

While the ship was building she was referred to as a 44, but before she was commissioned she was rerated as a 36-gun ship. This seems to have been accomplished, in fact, by the omission of the spar-deck rail and gun ports, from just forward of the mainmast to the bow, and the shifting of some of the gun ports on the quarterdeck as well as a reduction in their number. She first carried 28 guns on the main deck, 18-pdrs., and 10 guns on the quarterdeck, type and caliber unknown. In 1803 she carried sixteen 32-pdr. carronades on her quarterdeck and forecastle, which is evidence that her spar-deck rails had undergone another alteration. The sail plan of the ship shown in Figure 24 shows the ports and spar-deck rails arranged approximately as in Hutton's sail plan. Both drawings of the *Philadelphia* presented here have the figurehead shown in Hutton's plan, as well as the same headrail and stem profile. The extensive reconstructions in the plans of the *Philadelphia* are made necessary by the unintentional anachronisms contained in the draught in the National Archives reproduced in *Personnel and Ships' Data*. The quantity of documentary material, and the two plans, relating to this ship, make the reconstructions reasonably accurate, though the figurehead shown is open to question.

The *Philadelphia* was not on the same model as the earlier 44's and 38's, as has been mentioned. She was fuller in the cross sections, near the keel, which gave less deadrise to the bottom. This was apparently typical of Fox's designs for frigates, for it also appears in the plan of the *Crescent*. The design of the *Philadelphia*, by showing radical departures from both the model and the dimensions of the *Constitution* and *Constellation* classes, obviously disposes of any claim that might be made that Fox was solely responsible for the earlier designs.

It might be a matter of surprise that the Philadelphia merchants went to Fox rather than to their fellow townsman, Joshua Humphreys, for the design of the local frigate, but there is no reason to believe that this was a reflection on the ability of the Philadelphian. The fact of the matter appears to be that Humphreys rejected the commission as he was very busy with repairs and the supervision of fitting out vessels for the Navy and was at work on the design of a 74-gun ship while the *Philadelphia* was building. Fox's connections with Philadelphians and his known ability and experience made him a natural choice under the circumstances.

The *Philadelphia* was considered a fast and beautiful frigate. Her end at Tripoli is well known, and the events that surrounded her final destruction produced some of the most inspiring acts in American naval history. In spite of having been considered a very fine frigate, neither her model nor her size and rate had much influence on later design. The Americans were fully committed to ships of great size for their rate.

The next largest frigate built by private subscription was the *New York*, designed by Samuel Humphreys, probably with the help of Nathaniel Hutton, Jr., with whom he was then closely associated. The original plan of the *New York* cannot be found; the drawing made from offsets by Henry Allen, now in the National Archives, and published in *Personnel and Ships' Data*, has been mentioned. While the lines of the ship in Allen's plan are correct, the head and cutwater are not only anachronisms but also are technically incorrect, since they would require the hawseholes to be placed in an impossible position. Plan 10 shows the drawing of this ship, based on the lines preserved in Allen's plan but with the spar-deck rails and other details in accordance with the only original plan that survived, her inboard profile. The headrails and cutwater are conjectural and are based on partial measurements that were given in Samuel Humphreys' memorandum in his offset book (indexed in the National Archives as C & R 81–6), now missing.

The *New York* seems to have been intended as a comparatively small 38; she had ports to permit mounting 50 guns, though of course she could not have borne their weight. She was rerated when placed in commission as a 36. The *New York* was 144' 2" between perpendiculars, 37' 0" moulded beam, and 11' 9" depth in the hold. She was to carry 26 18-pdrs. on her main deck and 14 9-pdrs. on her spar deck, but the 9-pdrs. were apparently replaced by an unknown number of carronades, late in her active service. The ship was built at New York by Peck and Carpenter, in the latter's yard, and was launched in April, 1800. She spent the greater part of her life laid up in the Washington Navy Yard and was burned there when the British took the capital in 1814. She seems to have been a satisfactory sailer as a frigate, but there is little else on record as to her qualities. Her model was somewhat like that of the *Constellation* class, with a rather marked hardness in the bilges and slacker bottom.

Nothing has been found on her carving, but she undoubtedly was heavily orna-
mented.

The third frigate in size was the famous *Essex*. This vessel was built with
funds raised at Salem and in Essex County, Massachusetts, and was built by
Enos Briggs of Salem on a design prepared by William Hackett. She was to
be a 32-gun frigate and large for her rate—140′ 0″ between perpendiculars,

Figure 25. Spar and sail plan of the frigate ESSEX, *typical of the rig in the smaller
American frigates of her period.*

36′ 6″ moulded beam, and 12′ 3″ depth in the hold. Her design is shown in
Plan 11, redrawn from the original plan preserved in the National Archives
(41–9–1 L), with the head and the stern elevation restored. The head is from
the well-known painting of the ship, and the elevation of the stern is wholly
conjectural. The *Essex* was unlike the other American frigates in model; the
sections do not show the rather marked "knuckles" below the water line to be
seen in the other frigates, and they follow approximately the general section
design shown in the unidentified ship plan in Figure 23 and in the unidentified
design of a 20-gun vessel in Figure 22. She was designed with detached fore-

castle and quarterdeck, which were connected by means of the usual gangways along the sides, not quite flush with these two decks. She was somewhat like the Revolutionary War frigates in appearance, but had guns on her forecastle. She was designed with a solid bulwark on her quarterdeck, which seems to have gone out of fashion in the American frigates, but which again became the general practice early in the 1800's. Hackett's drawing of the ship was hurried and very rough; a reproduction of the original plan will be found in *Personnel and Ships' Data*. The *Essex* was a very fast frigate, but by the time the War of 1812 began the changes made by her various commanders and by navy yard commandants had spoiled her sailing. The ships that were easily overweighted, because of sharp lines, were invariably those first spoiled by the "improvements" of their commanders.

The fourth frigate in size was the *Boston*, 32 guns. This ship was designed by Edmund Hartt and built in the Hartt yard, operated by Edmund, Edward, and Joseph Hartt, at Boston, Massachusetts. The ship was launched in May, 1799, and was finished during the summer following. The *Boston*, shown in Plan 12, was a frigate somewhat like the *Essex* in appearance, though different in model, being less sharp. The *Boston* also had her gangways flush with the quarterdeck and forecastle deck and carried 24 guns on her main deck, 12-pdrs., and two 12-pdr. chase guns on the forecastle, with 12 9-pdrs. on the quarterdeck and forecastle. In 1801 12 32-pdr. carronades either were added to 6 9-pdrs. on the upper decks or replaced the 9-pdrs. entirely—which seems more probable. The ship was rerated as a 28-gun frigate when placed on the Navy list. The *Boston* was 134' 0" between perpendiculars, but owing to the way these were established she was actually 136' 6" on the gun deck. Her moulded beam was 34' 6", and her depth of hold 11' 6". She was originally built with an open rail on her quarterdeck, but in her first commission this was planked up to form a bulwark, as in the *Essex*. The *Boston*, as can be seen, was a very handsome frigate, but her plan in the National Archives did not do justice to her beauty—having been drawn, as her designer noted on the plan, without instruments. If the *Boston* and *Essex* are sufficient evidence, the New Englanders employed longer and lighter heads, or cutwaters, on their ships than were popular at Philadelphia. The *Boston* was the only presentation frigate to see action against the French; she captured the small French frigate *Berceau*, which was later returned to France. Captain Little of the *Boston* was not as fortunate as Truxton and did not receive comparable praise and publicity for the capture of the French frigate. The *Boston* was laid up in the Washington

Navy Yard in 1802 and allowed to rot. She was burned when the yard was destroyed in 1814, having by then become unfit for repair.

The rerating of the frigates, to lower rates than designed, was a fashion that seems to have been brought about by a desire to establish a standard relation between rates and dimensions, as existing in the frigates authorized in 1794. Another factor involved was the jealousy of commanding officers regarding the perquisites of seniority; it would have been "disgraceful" for the senior officer to command a 44 that was actually smaller than one commanded by a junior in rank, even though the ships were of the same rate. The squabbles over rank during this period were continuous and violent.

The smallest of the frigates built by subscription was the 28-gun *John Adams*, designed by Josiah Fox and built by the merchants and citizens of Charleston and vicinity, South Carolina. Paul Pritchard was the builder. The frigate's dimensions were variously given in official papers, owing to the fact that her plan was never turned over to the Navy Department. James Marsh, a noted shipbuilder of Charleston, was foreman of Pritchard's yard when the *John Adams* was built, and writing in 1820 to the Navy Department, he stated that the ship was designed to be 86′ 0″ on the keel or straight rabbet, 32′ 0″ beam, 12′ 0″ lower hold, 6′ 0″ berth to gun deck, and 5′ 10″ waist. He said also that the keel timbers were of such length and quality that the committee of the association building her decided to lengthen the ship 5 feet and she was given one more port to the side on the main deck than called for in Fox's draught. Marsh thought she had but 10″ deadrise and said she was a flat-floored ship of light draft that would permit her being taken across the bar at Charleston. Another official set of dimensions shows her to have been 127′ 9″ on the gun deck, 33′ 3″ extreme beam, and total depth from ceiling to gun deck 16′ 10″. Carvings were by William Rush of Philadelphia. She stuck on the ways on the first attempt to launch but got over on the second attempt, June 5, 1799. It was either this ship or the *Adams* whose two sides, according to tradition, were unlike, so that she sailed better on one tack than on the other. From the alleged circumstances supporting this tradition it appears that the ship having this curious feature was the *Adams* after her rebuilding as a corvette, rather than the *John Adams*. The *John Adams* spent much of her life laid up and was permitted to rot; she was finally broken up at the Norfolk Navy Yard in 1829, a new ship of the same name being constructed in the guise of "rebuilding" the old ship.

It can be seen by the ships' plans that have survived that American designers had established what might safely be called a "standard" appearance. The cutwater and its supporting headrails followed a standard practice; the "seat" or "middle" rail (known to shipwrights by a far less polite but more expressive name) was carried up, at the after end, to fair into the knee supporting the cathead; the upper or "hair" rail also turned up at its after end approximately parallel to the "seat" rail, to end outside the bow chock rail, or to form a decorative timberhead. Above the upper rail was a light, straight rail, either of timber or of iron rod, used to support the nettings and weather cloths masking the crews' toilet facilities, which were located on a grating platform contained within the headrails. No troughs or discharge pipes were employed at first, though most frigates were fitted with these improvements by 1810. The lack of these plumbing fixtures often made the ship's bows anything but attractive at close range.

The construction of all the new ships was intended to be very strong, with the hope of producing vessels of a very long life. The problem of finding a species of American shipbuilding timber comparable to English oak was thought to be solved by the use of southern live oak, and this timber was therefore used very extensively in the new ships. However, it did not live up to expectations. In addition, it was found that the available supply was more limited than had been supposed. Other timber was therefore resorted to—white oak, yellow pine, cedar, and various hardwoods. The ships soon showed evidences of rot in spite of the efforts made—but the trouble was probably due more to improper seasoning than to poor timber.

The American preference for a spar deck, or at least for very wide gangways connecting quarterdeck and forecastle, in the frigates and larger ship sloops was based on the desirability of having a clear working space for handling the sails and rigging in action. The spar deck, being at most only partially armed, was very useful for this purpose. However, the administrative system which permitted officers to change the armament almost at will made the temptation great to place additional guns on the spar deck or along the gangways.

The ships were commonly overcanvased and oversparred, as has been mentioned; the desire to obtain speed was at odds with the equally great desire to carry an impressive number of guns, which materially increased displacement and reduced speed. Often, after increasing the number of guns in his ship, the captain felt it necessary to increase sail area by getting longer spars. There are numerous cases where ships were placed in jeopardy by this vicious circle of "improvement." The overcanvasing of American naval ships was eventually to become notorious; it was probably the cause of the loss of a number of small vessels at sea.

In most of the frigates the designers had intended to save weight high in the hull by using open rails on the quarterdeck or along the greater part of the spar deck. Pictures of some of the ships a few years after they were placed in service show that this aim was defeated by the closing in of the quarter-deck rails and the eventual raising and closing in of the forecastle rails to the same height. The original open rails were intended to be covered with netting and painted canvas, or weather cloths, to mask the crew working on this deck from enemy sharpshooters and musketmen; the rails were intended to be strongly built to provide for temporary gun ports along the middle portion of the length of the spar deck, or gangways. With the closing in of the forecastle and quarterdeck rails, the rails amidships on the gangways were replaced by light iron stanchions supporting a light wooden handrail, which was soon made double to support a deep hammock netting. When hammocks were placed in this and covered with a heavy tarpaulin, a light breastwork was created. The low bulwarks of the forecastle and quarterdeck were gradually increased in effective height by adding hammock nettings along their tops, a fashion which had developed gradually in European navies during the previous seventy-five years.

Though the original plans of most of the frigates show the old "rule-joint" rudders, it is evident from the correspondence that some of the ships were built with the "plug-stock" rudders that were gradually becoming common. In the old style of "rule-joint" rudder, the head had to swing in an arc owing to the shape of the stock and the position of the gudgeons and pintles in relation to the vertical center line. In this style the rudder and its head swung after the manner of a door, and so the opening through the transom for the stock had to be very large. This opening was covered by a greased rawhide "boot," or by a heavy canvas "coat," but was nevertheless a source of leakage and weakness. In the "plug-stock" rudder, the stock was offset forward so that its axis was in a vertical line with the center line of the pintles and gudgeons; this permitted the stock to revolve when the rudder was swung and resulted in a small, snug opening in the ship's transom for the rudderstock. The only difficulty with the "plug-stock" rudder was that the offset in the stock could be a source of weakness and many rudderstocks failed because they were improperly built. Though there was some prejudice against the new style of rudders, it

Rail J

Drift J

Fore end of Rail as built,
to Hutton's sail plan.

A.P. 34   32   30   28   26   24   20   16   12   8   4

A   160   155   150   145   140   135   130   125   120   115   110   105   100   95   90   85   80   75

Gundeck J

L. Port Sill

Rail J

L. Sheer

Drift J

Particulars

D. " 66' 3" from F.P.
Room & Space 30½"
Waterlines spaced 2' 4"
Buttocks   "   4' 0"
Gun to Spar Decks 6' 9"
Berth   Gun   "   6' 0"

Frigate "Philadelphia" as a 44.
Designed by Josiah Fox; built by Nath'l Hutton Jr
and Sam'l Humphreys, at Philadelphia.

Length bet perps.	157:0"
" of keel for tonnage	130:0"
Beam, moulded	39:0"
Depth in Hold	13:6"

Rail
Drift
Underside of Spar deck at side
Sheer
Underside of Gundeck at side
Chapelle

65 60 55 50 45 40 35 30 25 20 15 10 9 8 7 6 5 4 3 2 1 0

Sheer
Drift
Rail
Gundeck
Rail

References - Restoration
Lines from Allen's draught, made from Offsets
Headrails, Cutwater, Figurehead Bridle-port,
Sheer mouldings, from Nath'l Hutton's Sail Plan
of 1801 Spar Deck Rail & Gunports forward of
mainmast believed probable for original draught
as a 44 gun frigate

Plan 9. Draught of the 44-gun frigate PHILADELPHIA, after Allen's drawing and builder's sail plan.

Rail

Drift

Sheer

Under

Under

40   38   36   32   28   24   20   16   12   8

145 140 135 130 125 120 115 110 105 100 95 90 85 80 75 70

Gun Deck

Spar Deck   Rail   Drift   Sheer

Particular Dimensions
O is 58·10" from F.P.
O to Sta 4 is 7·2"
Room & Space 24½"
Sta Y is 5·0 from F.P.
Sta 40 139·6 · F.P.
Waterlines spaced 3·10"
Buttocks · 4·0"

Plan 10. Draught of the 36-gun frigate NEW YORK, *after Allen's plan and inboard works plan.*

was not long after the new ships were started that the "plug-stock" rudder became a standard fitting in naval ships. The Americans seem to have replaced the "rule-joint" rudder with the new style by 1801 or thereabouts, changing over the ships already fitted with the older type.

Sketch showing difference between "rule-joint" and "plug-stock" rudders.

The frigates were all fitted with air scuttles on the berth deck. These are shown in the plans of the *Essex* and *Boston*. The scuttles had solid covers hinged at the fore side. The American style was similar to the British; the hinge was horseshoe- or U-shaped, with the open end forward on the cover to give two hinge eyes. These rested on two eyebolts driven into the wale or side of the ship, or else there was another U-shaped hinge plate on the hull, with bolts for pins, one in each eye. The glass was recessed into the hull to permit the cover to close; the glass could be unshipped from the inside.

The scuppers were of the standard type used abroad—lead pipe through the waterways and sides of the ship—and some vessels apparently had leather valves on lower-deck scuppers. These valves were leather strips weighted with lead so that the outside pressure of water closed them; to permit this, the strips were secured at the fore side of the scupper only.

The general design of the frigates and other ships had produced a rather low and long hull. This was considered desirable in windward sailing, since it reduced windage in proportion to size of hull and gave greater sail-carrying power than would be possible in a short, high-sided ship. The gradual changes in the upper rails and bulwarks of the ships had the effect of raising the apparent freeboard, and some of the smaller frigates were undoubtedly harmed by this change in fashion.

It was gradually recognized both by naval officers and by the office of the Secretary of the Navy that frigates and ship sloops, while very useful and highly necessary, were insufficient to create an effective Navy. As early as 1797, Secretary Stoddert suggested to congressional groups the need of 74-gun ships, and late in 1798 he recommended the construction of such vessels. During the preliminary discussions, proposals had been made that 74-gun ships be purchased abroad. The Secretary now pointed out that it was improbable that a foreign power would part with a first-class 74, and that in any event the expenditure of funds abroad would act as an unfavorable balance of trade on the national economy. He consequently recommended that twelve ships of this class be constructed and that the timber for them be acquired at once. He also suggested that, if the ships were not built at once after the timber was procured, the latter could be preserved in storage in wet decks for an indefinite period until needed. In 1799 Congress authorized the purchase of six sets of frames for 74's and authorized funds to "purchase timber for naval purposes." The funds authorized were in excess of those actually required; as a result some islands in the South with live-oak timber on them were bought, and altogether eight sets of ship frames were contracted for by the Secretary of the Navy.

Stoddert had carefully worked out a plan for building up the new Navy. His recommendations in 1799 proposed not only the construction of twelve 74's but also the maintenance of twelve frigates and twenty to thirty smaller vessels as the requirement to protect American interests abroad. The following year he also suggested the purchase of timber for a frigate and for twelve 24-gun ships; in doing so he found it opportune to point out in general terms the increasing need for navy yards or other suitable facilities for the storage of naval materials—though it must be admitted that this was done without much conviction.

In the winter of 1798–99, Joshua Humphreys was employed in assisting the Secretary with advice on the 74's, and in the spring—March 20, 1799—he completed the initial draught of this class. The ships were to be 178' 0" between perpendiculars, 48' 6" moulded beam, and 19' 6" depth of hold, armed with 28 32-pdrs. on the gun deck, 30 24-pdrs. on the upper deck, 12 9-pdrs. on the quarterdeck, and 4 more on the forecastle. Humphreys' plan was rather poorly drawn, but the first design served for discussion purposes. After numerous consultations between the Secretary and his advisers, including naval officers, it was decided to make all the guns 32-pdrs. This required more displacement than Humphreys' draught permitted, and a new drawing was necessary. Samuel Humphreys redrew the design under his father's direction, lengthening the ship 5 feet amidships and altering the position of the gun ports accordingly, but with no change in number. Hutton and Doughty made copies of this plan, all of which survive. The plan by Doughty has the name "Independence" written on its back. The Hutton drawing was dated February 7, 1801, and was the last one made.

The revised design is shown in Plan 13, with the length increased to 183' 0" between perpendiculars. Unfortunately, in the light of later events, the 74's were never built and the timber acquired for them either rotted or was used for small craft and shore construction. The design of the ships is of value, however, as it shows the most advanced ideas in America on what a line-of-battle ship ought to be, at the end of the eighteenth century. Had the 74's been built, they would have been among the most powerful ships of their class in the world, and about the same length as the largest French ships. Having slightly less beam and depth, but with 6 inches greater length, they would have had a tonnage slightly less than that of the French 74's built in the same year that the American ships were designed. The larger of the two ships of the class built for the Royal Navy in 1800 was the *Spencer*, 180' 10" between perpendiculars, 49' 3" extreme beam, and 21' 10" depth of hold; but neither the French nor the British ships were intended to carry the armament proposed for the American design.

The plan prepared by Humphreys, and the lengthened copies by his son and by Doughty and Hutton, show that Joshua Humphreys had an excellent grasp of hull form. The 74's would have been sharp-ended for their class and would undoubtedly have been comparatively fast sailers. They retained the beakhead bulkhead of earlier ships, and in this followed general practice in 74-gun ship design abroad. They were spar-decked in the American fashion, though not intended to carry guns on the wide gangways amidships that were, in reality, the continuations of the forecastle and quarterdeck, which constituted the spar deck in fact, if not in name. Had the ships been built, it would have been found that they were unable to bear the armament proposed for them, but even with a slightly reduced weight of guns they would have been most formidable vessels. If the six proposed ships had been either in commission or ready for fitting out, their existence might have been sufficient to prevent the events that finally led to the War of 1812.

A great deal of preliminary work was done on the 74's; they were lofted and moulds for their timbers were made; rough copies of these were sent to the contractors to get out timber to the required shapes and sizes. Humphreys prepared rather complete specifications for the ships, and it is obvious that the design of the class, and the timber contracts, were seriously considered as a realistic step in establishing a navy of effective force.

The only ships left unaccounted for are those captured from France during the quasi war. Only two of the ships taken were placed on the Navy list, though one small schooner, the *Bon Père*, was taken into the Revenue Service as the *Bee*. She had been captured from the French by the cutter *Eagle* while the latter was in naval hands. The frigate *L'Insurgent*, a good 36-gun frigate, had been captured by Truxton in the *Constellation* after a very hard encounter, February 9, 1799. An almost new ship, *L'Insurgent* was taken into the Navy as *Insurgent*, and the survey of her shows that she measured 148' 0" on the gun deck, 37' 5" beam, and 11' 9" depth of hold. When captured she had 24 12-pdrs., 2 18-pdrs., 8 6-pdrs.—all long guns—and 4 36-pdr. and 2 24-pdr. carronades, or 40 guns all told. Since she was the first capture of a regular man-of-war by a ship of the new Navy, much was made of Truxton and the battle. It was claimed that she was superior in force to the *Constellation*, and both her size and power were reported in exaggerated terms. Actually, she was smaller and was a less effective ship than the big American frigate. The *Insurgent* had a very short career in the American service, being lost at sea with all hands in the fall of 1800. No plan of this ship has yet been found. A small frigate, the *Berceau*, was taken by the *Boston*, as mentioned earlier, but this ship was one of those returned to France at the end of the quasi war. The schooner

Retaliation was a 107-ton, 14-gun schooner carrying 6-pdrs. taken as the French privateer *Le Croyable* by the *Delaware* July 7, 1798. She was pur-chased into the Navy on the 30th of the same month. One account states that she was a Maryland-built schooner. As the *Retaliation* she was taken by the French frigates *L'Insurgent* and *La Volontaire*, November 20, 1798, and taken into the French Navy as *La Magicienne*. Then she was recaptured by the *Merrimack* on June 28, 1799, and was sold as a prize to private owners. She seems to have been either a very unlucky vessel or a poor sailer.

While the various acts had stated the types of vessels to be acquired, in some cases at least, the Secretary of the Navy seems to have enjoyed a good deal of freedom in departing from the exact terms of the authorization. He was, of course, required to stay within the sums authorized. In one case the Secretary writes about six brigs authorized by Congress in 1798–99, but none of these were built. It is not possible to determine under what authority the Secretary acted in specifying the type of ship to be acquired, but reference to some of the acts shows that the understanding as to the exact type of ships must have been an informal one between the Secretary and members of the congressional committees, rather than a decision of Congress to be complied with in full.

The records of the individual naval constructors cannot be accounted for as completely as might be desired. Fox and Doughty could not be hired as naval constructors. As has been mentioned, Fox was officially listed as a "clerk" in the War Office; Doughty was therefore listed as a "clerk" in the Treasury Department while he was employed in drafting and laying down the frigates. Doughty's papers, which are believed to have been burned in a fire at Balti-more while being moved by a descendant, might have shed additional light on some of the questions that have been discussed. Humphreys' and Fox's papers have been preserved; the greater part of Joshua Humphreys' papers are now in the Pennsylvania Historical Society, and a large proportion of Fox's material is now at the Peabody Museum in Salem, Massachusetts. Existing papers of some of the politicians and officeholders of the period add some sup-porting evidence, but all these contain insufficient evidence to permit an un-qualified assignment of credit for the design of all the naval vessels, and particularly to allow final conclusions as to the predominant personalities in the design of the first frigates authorized in 1794. Samuel Humphreys' papers are very incomplete and scattered. The disappearance of many of the plans once in his possession, in the transfer of the plan files from the Navy to the

National Archives, is an irreparable misfortune. The additional loss of many of his notebooks and offset books, which apparently occurred at the same time, is equally unfortunate. Because of these gaps in the technical history of naval shipbuilding, a great many matters of importance must remain in the field of conjecture, at least for the present.

The end of the quasi war with France led to a reduction in the new Navy and its reorganization on a peacetime establishment. This was accomplished by the Congressional Act of March 3, 1803. The wisdom of the act proved somewhat questionable, to say the least. Though the Secretary of the Navy had presented a series of carefully worked-out recommendations for a proper peacetime establishment, his ideas were largely disregarded and Congress decided that the Navy was to be reduced to the thirteen frigates—*United States, Constitution, President, Chesapeake, Philadelphia, Constellation, Congress, New York, Boston, Adams, Essex, John Adams*, and *General Greene*. All the other vessels were to be stripped of naval gear and sold. The ships retained were to be laid up except for six, which were to be manned with crews two-thirds of the war complement. Economy was the watchword, and the sale of the ships was gradually accomplished, except that the schooner *Enterprise* was retained because of the criticism her intended sale had produced in the newspapers and among the maritime population.

Though some of the ships obtained to build up the new Navy had undoubtedly been either unsatisfactory in design or unsuited for naval purposes, there were a few at least that were very fine cruisers. The reduction disposed of these, as well as those not wanted for the service, because of the severity of the slash in ships and personnel. Generally, the small ships had proved very useful, but Congress took the attitude that only the large ships were of sufficient importance to be retained—a position that had unfortunately been taken to some extent by the Secretary's office in making its recommendations. As a result, the Navy not only lost some very fine small vessels, but also lost practically all of its cruisers that had proved so valuable in suppressing the West Indian privateers and marauders. The short-sightedness of this was soon apparent.

The reduction also brought about the discharge of all the naval constructors, as well as a great reduction in the number of commissioned officers and enlisted men. Fox remained at Norfolk and engaged in private business. Joshua Humphreys also returned to his private affairs. Occasionally each was consulted about some minor naval matter. With the new peace establishment, however, all naval construction had ceased and there was little to require obtaining their advice. Humphreys disappears from naval affairs at this time, but Fox and his co-worker Doughty will appear again.

The peace establishment, by the severity of the reduction it entailed, destroyed the greater part of the administrative and operating organization and to an equal extent the progress already made in setting up construction and maintenance facilities of the new Navy. Many capable officers left the service, though an effort was made to retain the most capable and to discharge those that had been inefficient or incompetent. Of the thirteen captains retained under the act, Thomas Truxton (fourth in seniority) was perhaps the most interesting from the shipbuilding point of view. Truxton had been the lieutenant of the Revolutionary War privateer *Congress* at the age of twenty-one, and from 1777 to the end of the war had commanded the *Independence, Mars,* and *St. James* with great success. A Philadelphian, he settled there when the war ended in 1783 and became a merchant, and in 1785 he took over the command of a China trader. With the building of the Federal Navy, he was appointed as one of the first six captains and was supervising officer in the building of the *Constellation.* Made commander of the ship, he fought *L'Insurgent* and took her, and also fought the heavier *Vengeance,* which escaped him. Truxton became involved in many difficulties over seniority, particularly in the case of the appointment of Captain Silas Talbot over his head, as a result of which he threatened to resign. Finally, during the Barbary Wars, he was ordered to command a small squadron in the Mediterranean and finding that he was not to have the perquisites of a flag officer, particularly a captain for his ship, he resigned from the service. He held a few political offices and appointments, and died in 1822.

Truxton was a highly intelligent officer, much interested in the technical side of his career. He had prepared and published a book on navigation, which also contained an appendix (or "annex") giving, in great detail, a rule for the masting of ships. This was illustrated by Josiah Fox with a well-drawn plan of the spars and rigging of the 44's, in accordance with the hull design of the new ships and with the spar proportions as set forth by Truxton. This book was completed shortly after Truxton became captain, and for some time he carried on a friendly correspondence with Fox on matters of naval construction and mutual interest. Truxton was a martinet aboard ship and, like many officers with this characteristic, was often overbearing and officious. The latter characteristic was heightened in Truxton by his friendly relations with Stoddert, who relied upon him for advice on all naval matters, even to the selection of officers and their promotion. However unpleasant Truxton may have been as a commanding officer, his ideas of strict discipline were undoubtedly very desirable in the new Navy. To Truxton, and to one or two other captains, perhaps, the new Navy owed its concept of the high standards of competence expected in its officers' corps. With the capture of *L'Insurgent* and the resulting public praise, Truxton seems to have become overly conceited and very sensitive of his own importance because of which he gradually lost influence. Through attempting to usurp the powers of Fox at Gosport, his friendship with the constructor ceased. This closed his connection with naval shipbuilding. During the time Truxton was supervising the *Constellation*, he was influential in establishing Fox's position and in supporting his views; Fox and Truxton were perhaps the outstanding objectors to the huge American frigates, while Humphreys, Barry, and others supported the new ship concept. The latter, as events were to show, had the best of the dispute.

Though the organization of the new Navy received a serious setback in the Congressional Act "Providing for a naval peace establishment, and for other purposes" of March 3, 1801, the groundwork had been laid for the national Navy, based on the idea of ships superior in size, power, and speed to classmates in foreign navies, and on an officer corps having a high sense of duty and responsibility. The administrative organization was as yet inadequate, though much progress had been made in comparison with the Continental Navy. The events of the period had placed the Secretary of the Navy in firm possession of a recognized authority over the whole naval establishment. As yet there was no conception of a strategic or technical control of the service by a professional staff or a board of officers and technicians. Power rested entirely with the Secretary, not only in the technical field of naval construction and equipment but also in the strategic and tactical control of naval operations. As a result, political considerations often predominated, operations were controlled by clamor at home rather than by war strategy, and construction programs were governed by pressure groups or by the preferences of influential individuals, officers, or politicians.

In the process of building up the new Navy, the design and construction of its ships had not been reserved to a small group of government employees. Private designers had competed, and ships had been built by, or under the supervision of, men who had been trained in merchant yards. The only constructor who can be said to have been fully trained in the exclusively governmental field of naval construction was Fox, and, as has been shown, his influence, though somewhat marked, was nevertheless circumscribed. The Revolution had created a number of men who had some experience in the problems of the design of vessels for naval purposes. These men were civilian constructors when the new Navy was created, and were therefore inclined to compete for superiority. The results can be seen in the individual ships of the Federal Navy, even though they had not been produced in the stress of a serious war, or in a great national emergency.

★　★　★　★　★　★　★　★　★

CHAPTER FOUR

The Gunboat Navy

1801-1812

THE ACT "Providing for a naval peace establishment," passed March
3, 1801, was the first historical illustration of a type of national error
that Americans seem prone to commit—the liquidating of their armed
might before peace is firmly secured. In view of the numerous repetitions of
this mistake, there is no particular use in attempting to account for the men-
talities of a Congress or an administration that would reduce the Navy so
laboriously built up for the quasi war with France while still faced with the
predatory Barbary regencies and the national disgrace of making tribute payments and presents to a group of minor naval powers who made no pretense
of observing their treaty obligations. The same error that was made in 1801
has been made in more recent times. The very recent examples of the flight
of common sense that seems to occur when the state of open warfare is officially declared at an end offer far better opportunities for study of the
excessive optimism of the American people than the relatively minor occur-
rence in Jefferson's administration; then the price paid was small, but it has
steadily risen with each repetition.

At the end of 1801 the new construction facilities were either liquidated or
made inoperative. The property intended for navy yards was utilized entirely
for storage; in some cases portions of the properties were sold. The frames
of the 74's contracted for in 1799 were placed in these storage yards, but in
most localities little was done to preserve the material. The frigates not sent

to the Mediterranean were usually laid up at Washington, under the eye of the Administration, and repairs and upkeep were niggardly attended to. The theory on which Jefferson intended to operate the Navy visualized the frigates laid up "in ordinary" as being in storage and capable of being made serviceable in a very short time. Economy was intended, and by this means the cost of maintaining the ships in cruising service was avoided, since neither crews nor rations were needed in the ships laid up. While it was supposed that the ships could be maintained in ordinary in good condition for a long period with the minimum of expense, this assumption was not fully investigated, and many of the precautions that should have been taken were omitted. The official correspondence shows why this was the case. The administration had to depend upon the advice of naval officers as to the proper means of preserving the vessels, since all of the constructors had been discharged. While many of the officers gave good advice, there was a widespread difference of opinion about preservation methods, and there was now no one in the Navy Department competent to decide which opinions were sound. As a result, most of the vessels laid up deteriorated rapidly; the frigates not placed in service once in four years soon decayed and finally became wholly unserviceable. In this way the Navy lost some fine and valuable vessels.

While the naval peace establishment was being put into operation, in 1801, and the new Navy was being reduced in effectiveness, the relations with the various Barbary regencies, particularly with Tripoli, continued to be most unsatisfactory. By the end of that year the Bey of Tripoli had, in fact, ordered attacks on American merchantmen. In expectation of this the Americans had maintained a squadron of four frigates in the Mediterranean throughout the summer and fall of 1801. Early in the winter of 1801 a relief squadron was organized consisting of two frigates, which were to replace two ordered home from the Mediterranean, and in addition the sole small man-of-war left in the Navy, the schooner *Enterprise*. Tripoli was blockaded by one or two of the American frigates, while another lurked near the Straits of Gibraltar to prevent corsairs from getting into the Atlantic. The Spaniards also made a habit of seizing an occasional American ship, so the frigate at Gibraltar thus served two useful purposes. Congress recognized that a state of war with Tripoli existed and, on February 6, 1802, passed an act authorizing the Navy to attack and seize Tripolitan shipping. Congress also authorized the fitting out of privateers against the Tripolitans. The obvious lack of incentive to fit out privateers against the Barbary regency, which had no real merchant marine, makes this proposal of Congress appear strange. Actually, the explanation is very simple: it was the American naval policy to maintain only the minimum national navy and to depend upon privateers in time of war, paralleling the national military practice of maintaining a very small regular army and placing reliance in an emergency on the state militia regiments and on volunteers. The Tripolitan incident showed the inherent weakness of the policy, but, as will be seen, there was no change in the American attitude toward an effective navy. Jefferson became President in 1801, and the attitude of his administration was violently anti-naval and anti-military. Doctrinaire in judgment, Jefferson was not influenced by the international state in his time and, in spite of the plain warning of future trouble given by the numerous incidents, including outright attacks on American ships by foreign men-of-war, could not bring himself to prepare for war. Rather, he sought some cheap method of defending the country, even at the sacrifice of the merchant marine.

The lack of judgment of his administration in naval affairs was soon apparent. In August, 1802, his Secretary of the Navy, Robert Smith, wrote that a few gunboats were necessary at Gibraltar to protect American shipping from Spanish interference. Just how small vessels were to be maintained on such a station, without a base, was not apparent, and the Secretary was soon forced to give up the idea. Though many suggestions were made for the use of small men-of-war in the Mediterranean, in lieu of the expensive and rather ineffective frigate squadron, the administration did nothing. Only the *Enterprise* (or *Enterprize*, as her name was usually spelled) was available, and a plan for employing small vessels would require new construction or the purchase of suitable craft. This was not an attractive idea to the administration, and some time was wasted before the proposal was finally accepted. Throughout 1802 and well into 1803, a frigate squadron was maintained in the Mediterranean which carried on a desultory blockade of Tripoli. It was not until Captain Edward Preble took command in 1803 that the squadron became efficient, though it was still handicapped for some time by the lack of small cruisers.

By early winter of 1802 the administration had reached the decision that a few small cruisers were needed, and the Secretary of the Navy began to make inquiries among experienced naval officers regarding the most suitable types of vessels for the purpose. On February 28, 1803, the Seventh Congress passed an "Act pertaining to the Navy" which authorized the construction or purchase of four vessels of war, not to exceed 16 guns, and appropriated funds for the purpose. The same act provided for the construction of fifteen gunboats, with funds segregated for this purpose alone.

The Secretary of the Navy, having no constructors available, was forced to utilize the existing establishment in obtaining the new vessels authorized by the act. He examined the recommendations of the naval officers regarding the craft most suitable for service in the Mediterranean, and in the early spring of 1803 he selected three naval officers to supervise the construction of the new vessels—Captains William Bainbridge at Philadelphia, Edward Preble at Portsmouth, New Hampshire, and Samuel Barron at Norfolk, Virginia. At each of these places he intended to construct a vessel. Another vessel was to be built at Baltimore, and Bainbridge was to supervise this also. The navy agents were requested to enter into suitable contracts, and the naval officers were instructed to obtain suitable designs.

It was found that vessels could not be constructed at Norfolk and Portsmouth because both places would require more time to build a vessel than the government intended. It was finally decided to build two brigs, one at Philadelphia and one at Boston, and to build two schooners at Baltimore.

The 16-gun brigs were ordered to meet the definite specifications recommended by the naval officers who had been consulted. They were to be flush-decked brigs, designed to row fast and to have long lower masts and rather short yards; the rig was to be light, high, and narrow to be suited to the sailing conditions met in the Mediterranean. Weight was to be kept out of the ends of the ships; this was to govern the location of the gun ports, which were to permit carrying 16 24-pdr. carronades, one long 18-pdr. gun in the bow, and another in the stern. The bulwarks were to be solid and of suitable height for the guns. It was decided that the vessels were to be 94' on deck, 76' straight rabbet, 25' 6" beam, and 12' 6" depth in the hold. The frames were to be 14" deep at the keel, 8" at the floor heads, 7" at the wale, and 6" at the rail. One of the superintendents, Barron, found fault with the specified beam, and the Secretary agreed to allow it to be increased.

The schooners were to be built to the same dimensions as the *Enterprise*, to carry 14 6-pdr. guns, and to be 84' on the gun deck, 60' on the keel, 22' 6" beam, or 23' to outside of wales, and 9' 6" depth of hold. Bainbridge was particularly instructed to obtain the plan of the *Enterprise* if possible, as the Secretary wished to build to it rather than to a new design. However, the plan was not obtained.

Figure 26. Draught of the brig ARGUS, *full-model hull.*

The brig built at Boston under Preble's supervision was first called the *Merrimack*, then the *Argus*. She was designed by Joseph Hartt and built by Edmund Hartt, master builder of the *Constitution*. A plan of her survives; two copies, in fact, made by Edward Hartt, are in the National Archives. The plan, which is shown, redrawn, in Figure 26, probably represents with reasonable accuracy the ship as built. In the redrawing it was necessary to lower the head and reduce the steeve of the bowsprit, since that shown in Hartt's drawings was much too great, as was indicated in the spar dimensions. Hartt showed so much steeve that the bowsprit would have had to pass through the deck in order to "bury" inboard enough. No deck arrangement has been found. A portrait of the ship exists in the well-known painting of the attack on Tripoli, August 3, 1804, part of which, showing the *Argus*, is reproduced on page 254 of Naval Documents, Vol. V, *Barbary Wars*, U.S. Government Printing Office, Washington, D.C., 1944. The plate is wrongly captioned in the reference as *Nautilus*, which is actually shown as *Argus* on page 72, *ibid*. In this portrait, the vessel is shown to have a figurehead and the quarter badges are omitted. The accuracy of the portrait is open to question, however, by the omission of one gun port on a side; nine are shown in the painting, including a bridle port, whereas it is recorded in both the plan and elsewhere that the vessel as built showed ten ports on a side, with the bridle port. The *Argus* was 94′ 9″ between perpendiculars, 27′ 4″ moulded beam, 80′ on the keel, and 12′ 8″ depth of hold. The plans show her to have been calculated at 298⁶³⁄₉₄ tons. As can be seen, she was a full-bodied vessel, rather full forward and quite fine aft, with an attractive sheer, and rather low in the water. Her design seems to have followed that of a fast merchant brig of her period in order to give the displacement necessary, within the specified dimensions, to permit her to carry her guns and a large quantity of stores. In spite of her rather full lines, the *Argus* was a notable sailer and was a favorite vessel with her officers. She was launched in August, 1803, and went into commission in September. In her early years her armament was 16 24-pdr. carronades and 2 long 12-pdrs.

The second brig was on a different model. Named *Syren*, she was designed at Philadelphia by Benjamin Hutton, Jr., and built by Nathaniel Hutton. The plan of this brig has also survived; a handsome copy of the original design, made by Nathaniel Hutton, Jr., in 1803, is in the National Archives. This plan, redrawn, is shown in Figure 27. The figurehead is as shown on the original, but it is questionable in view of the fact that this brig, when taken by the

Portrait of William Doughty, Naval Constructor 1813 to 1837. (Courtesy Howard N. Doughty.)

Sketch of the SARATOGA, *Lake Champlain. (Study for a painting by George C. Wales.)*

PLATE IX

PLATE X. (Top) Sail plan of schooner LYNX. (Bottom) Sail plan of brig PROMETHEUS.

Figure 27. Draught of the brig SYREN, sharp-model hull.

The United States Fr[igate]
"Essex"

Trim "Ready for Sea"
Best Sailing Trim

Hammock Nettings

Eyebolts

Sidelight

L.W.L

Chapelle

Wale
C P S
Sheer
Deck

Quarterdeck

Gangway
Gangway knee ~
stanchion
Main Deck
E. of Top of Deck
Top of Deck at side
E. of Top of Deck
Berth Deck
Top of Deck at side.

Capstan
Wheel
Main Hatch
Capstan

Inboard edge of Gangway
Gangway of Gratings
Edge of Gangway
Edge of Quarterdeck
Edge of Main Deck

Principal Dimensions

Length on the Gun Deck --------------- 141:0"
" " " Keel -------------- 118:0"
" " between Perpendiculars -------- 140:0"
Beam Moulded ----------------- 36:6"
" " for Tonnage ----------- 37:0"
Depth in Hold --------------- 12-3"
Burthen in Tons ----------- Nº 850 23/95

O is 52'6" from FP   Room & Space 26"
WL's spaced 3:0"
Buttocks " 4:0"

Plan 11. Draught of the 32-gun frigate
ESSEX *based on the original design and
ship portraits.*

Inboard Profile and Plan
"Essex"

Frigate "Boston". 32 Guns
Designed by Edmund Hartt; built by Edmund, Joseph and Edward Hartt.
at Boston.

Length bet. perps.   134·0˝
Length on Gundeck   135·6˝
Beam, moulded   34·6˝
  "   over plank   35·0˝
Depth in Hold   11·6˝

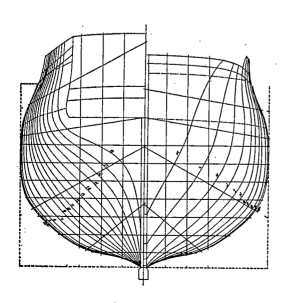

Particular Dimensions
O is 56·6¼˝ from F.P.
1 is 61·7˝   F.P.
Numbered frames spaced 48¼˝ (Room & Space 24¼˝)
Lowest Waterline 2·0˝ from Base, others spaced 2·6˝.
Buttocks spaced 3·0˝

Reconstruction :- Bridle Port,
Netting Rail of Head, Scuttles,
Scuppers, Port Covers, Belfry and
Bitts, from contemporary detail
drawings and frigate plans.
Reference:- 107-11-10.

Plan 12. Draught of the 32-gun frigate BOSTON, *after the builder's plan.*

British during the War of 1812, had a mermaid figurehead (according to a rough plan of the vessel made when fitting her as a lazeretto, or prison vessel, after her capture). The probable head of the vessel in 1812 is shown in a detail in Figure 27. The quarter badges were removed from the *Syren* before 1812, apparently—if indeed they were ever placed on her. She was a slightly smaller ship than the *Argus;* the *Syren* measured 93' 3½" between perpendiculars, 75' on the keel for tonnage, 27' moulded beam, and 12' 6" depth in hold. She carried the same armament as the *Argus*. Her model was sharper than that of her classmates; she had much deadrise and a slack bilge. She was rather full forward, however, and was less fine aft than *Argus*, in order to obtain displacement enough. She was a very handsome brig and an excellent performer in light weather, a condition for which she was particularly designed. Unfortunately her model was one that was readily harmed by overloading, and from this she eventually suffered. The *Syren* was launched August 6, 1803, and went into commission early in September; together with the *Argus* she went to the Mediterranean late in that year.

These two 16-gun brigs were not extraordinary in design or size. There were numerous 16-gun brig classes in the British Navy that were equal in size. The *Diligence* class of eight brigs designed in 1795 measured 95' between perpendiculars, 27' 6" moulded beam, and 12' depth in the hold. The eight brigs built on the plan of the *Dispatch*, designed the same year, were 96' between perpendiculars, 30' moulded beam, and 12' 9" depth in the hold, but these were designed to carry 32-pdr. carronades. Both of these classes approached the *Argus* in model, yet were not exactly like her in midsection. A later class of Royal Navy 16-gun brigs somewhat like *Syren* were the seven brigs designed early in 1805 as the *Challenger* class. This class measured 96' between perpendiculars, 25' 4" moulded beam, and 11' 6" depth of hold, and were to carry 24-pdr. carronades and two long 6's as chase guns. Their model was sharp in section but somewhat full in the ends. In this period the French built many brigs of 14 to 16 guns that were larger than the American vessels. Examples of French brigs taken into the Royal Navy will serve to illustrate the size of some of these: *La Victorieuse* of 12 guns and 12 swivels, captured in 1795, was 103' 1" on deck, 28' 6" moulded beam, and 12' 10" in the hold; *La Jalouse* of 14 guns, taken in 1797, was 102' 10" between perpendiculars, 27' 4" moulded beam, and 12' 11½" depth in the hold; *L'Arrogant* was a 10-gun brig but was 91' 9" on deck, 25' 6⅜" beam, and 11' 2" in the hold. These French brigs were much alike in model, with sections very full

Figure 28. Draught of schooner VIXEN, designed as an improved ENTERPRISE.

187

and round on the bottom and the topsides remarkably wall-sided. Yet these vessels sailed well enough to be purchased for the Royal Navy, in spite of their ugliness in model and appearance.

The two schooners authorized were to have been sisters, but the difficulty in getting them both built led to the decision to build only one and to purchase the other. The vessel built was named *Vixen*. Her plan, redrawn, is shown in Figure 28. Her design was prepared by Benjamin Hutton of Philadelphia, and she was built by William Price of Baltimore. Her launch took place June 25, 1803; she was commissioned in August. *Vixen*'s dimensions were exactly those given officially for the *Enterprise*—84′ 0″ on the gun deck, 83′ 5″ between perpendiculars, 22′ 6″ moulded beam, 60′ on the keel, and 9′ 6″ depth in the hold—yet her tonnage is given as $170^3\!/_{95}$, as against 135 or 165 tons officially given for *Enterprise*. Either there had been an error in the tonnage of the earlier schooner or the official dimensions were in error. After a year as a schooner, the *Vixen* was altered to brig rig, and it was said that this spoiled her speed. In spite of the expressed desire of the Secretary of the Navy that the *Vixen* be on the model of the *Enterprise*, and also the similarity of the dimensions, it seems probable in the light of what is known about the latter vessel that there was very little similarity in model.

The purchased schooner, named the *Nautilus*, was obtained at Baltimore. She was a vessel built on the Eastern Shore of Maryland, apparently by the same man who had built the *Enterprise*, Henry Spencer. No plan of the schooner has been found, but she measured 87′ 6″ on deck, 23′ 8″ beam, and 9′ 10″ depth of hold. Lieutenant Richard Somers was her first commander, and in a letter to his brother, written when he first saw his new command, he gave some description of her. He said that she was very sharp in section, "like a wedge." He thought she was too sharp in the topsides around the bow and, because of her rake, she had too little room in her forecastle. Also her bulwarks were very light, the planking being only ½″ thick. Her run was so sharp that she had to have a cabin trunk aft. Her bowsprit had very little steeve, and Somers wanted this altered. Captain Bainbridge had reported adversely on her, prior to purchase, stating that in his opinion she was too sharp and too low in the water, and had too much rake in the bow and stern. The picture of her in the painting of the attack on Tripoli indicates that she had no head, or knee, in the bow, if the portrait is to be trusted. The *Nautilus* was a very fast schooner, particularly to windward. Her spar dimensions of 1806 indicate that she was rigged as a fore-topsail schooner crossing a fore royal, whereas the painting just mentioned shows a two-topsail schooner. She too was eventually rerigged as a brig, and the change in rig hurt her sailing qualities, as it had done in the case of the other schooners.

By the construction of the two brigs and one schooner and the purchase of another schooner, the very effective small cruisers lost through the naval peace establishment were partly replaced. No sloops of war were yet contemplated, and the new vessels were obtained for a particular service, rather than as a normal development of the Navy list.

The gunboats authorized by the Act of 1803 were intended as harbor defense craft. The steps by which Congress was led to authorize the new gunboats are not wholly clear from available records. It appears that the action was taken independently of the Mediterranean problem, and that the supposed value of this class of naval vessel was enhanced in official quarters by the requirements for such craft in the subsequent operations off Tripoli.

It has been usual to connect the plan for building American gunboat flotillas with the success of this type of craft in Europe. However, there is some doubt as to the validity of this connection. While gunboats were employed by all the navies involved in the War of the French Revolution, they had not been outstandingly successful, and they attracted little attention until 1804, in which year Napoleon had accumulated enough small craft on the French coast opposite the British Isles to arouse the fears of the British government. The French plan for the invasion of Britain had been drawn up by Napoleon as early as 1798 and was based on employing a huge quantity of small craft carrying troops, supported by heavily armed gunboats and a powerful fleet of seagoing vessels. The final plan involved the use of about two thousand small craft, and these were not ready until 1804–5 in enough numbers to cause concern in Great Britain. By this time the Americans were well committed to the gunboat theory. Owing to the relations between France and the United States before 1801, and to the secrecy that surrounded the French plans for the invasion of the British Isles, it is not probable that they were particularly aware of what the French were doing.

The French gunboats and auxiliary craft included a range of types and sizes from large open boats rigged as luggers, about 60' long, to ship-rigged prames 100' long. There were also brigs and ships having round-bottomed hulls but of lighter draft than seagoing vessels. A huge number of large and well-designed shoal-draft luggers were built, armed and fitted with bow ramps, for landing infantry, cavalry, and artillery on beaches in the same manner that landing craft were used in World War II. The German plan for the invasion of England during that war was on exactly the same tactical concept as Napoleon's—employing "invasion barges" in huge numbers with what support was to be available from naval vessels—but with the addition of supporting aircraft. Of course, the Germans would have had another advantage, the use of motor-propelled barges that could operate regardless of the direction and force of the wind. Both the French and the German plans failed to be put into operation because of the final loss of the necessary support. The French "invasion flotilla," often called the "Boulogne Flotilla" after its most important base, was a highly specialized organization employing craft particularly designed for a definite purpose and entirely different from anything visualized in the American ideas for the employment of gunboats.

The Danes also employed gunboats extensively in the Napoleonic wars. They had lost the greatest portion of their naval force in the fall of Copenhagen in 1801 and had replaced the loss as soon as possible with a fleet of powerful gunboats and heavily armed brigs and schooners. However, their gunboats were apparently not ready to accomplish much until after 1804. There is no evidence available to support a theory that the Americans were aware of the Danish plans, or were influenced by foreign gunboats and tactics.

Both the French and the Danes had prepared their gunboat flotillas with a well-defined plan in view, for which gun vessels appeared suitable. The Americans, on the other hand, seem to have had no more than a very general objective in view and prepared no plan of operation for their gunboats. A close search of the correspondence relating to the gunboat flotillas has so far failed to produce any operational justification for the American gunboats except on the western rivers, where row galleys would have been very effective in a day when large craft could be propelled only by sails. As has been seen, the row galley had been introduced on the western rivers in 1799, and similar craft had been built on the coast for harbor and coast defense.

The Jeffersonian plan was at first a repetition of the plan of 1799, to build gunboats for river and harbor service. By chance, events placed emphasis on the type, and this seemingly produced the Jeffersonian theory of employing gun vessels in place of normal naval craft. The trend of events that apparently gave support to the gunboat theory can be readily traced in the archives.

In October, 1803, the Navy suffered a grave disaster in the Mediterranean. The fine frigate *Philadelphia* ran aground at Tripoli, while in chase of a blockade-runner, and was captured by the Tripolitans. This incident led to active operations against Tripoli to destroy the frigate and to avenge the capture of so large a national vessel.

In November and December, 1803, the Secretary of the Navy wrote to

Figure 29. Plan of a Messina gunboat, parancelle rig, employed to guide the design of the first American gunboats.

Captain James Barron and Captain John Rodgers, asking if they were willing to supervise and help design a gunboat. In the fall of 1803 Preble had begun to search for suitable gunboats in the Mediterranean, for use against Tripoli. He had investigated the possibility of getting boats from Naples and had secured a model, or plan, of one of the Neapolitan types of gunboats, which he sent home. This plan (or model) was made available to Barron and Rodgers, but was not to control the design of the new gun vessels. There is no evidence available that any extensive investigation was made as to what was required. The letters of the Secretary indicate only that two experimental gunboats were to be designed and built; they do not outline any of the desired characteristics other than what might be surmised from the data on the Neapolitan boat. In February, 1804, Preble received two plans of proposed gunboats from James L. Cathcart, the American agent at Leghorn, who had been U.S. Consul General successively at Tripoli, Algiers, and Tunis. In one of these plans, Cathcart proposed the use of a schooner rig, the foremast of which was to be a "sliding gunter," which will be seen in the plans later. Cathcart seemingly directed the drawing of the designs he proposed and gave Preble information on the various types of gunboats and bomb vessels that could be purchased, and were suitable, for use against Tripoli. Cathcart visualized the use of mortars in the gunboats, in addition to long guns. He also recommended that bomb ketches like those used in the Royal Navy be employed.

In May, 1804, Preble secured six gunboats, each mounting a long 24-pdr. in the bow, from the Neapolitan government. The boats were actually obtained from Messina. The official dimensions of these boats were 56′ 6″ on the keel, 18′ 0″ beam, and 4′ 6″ depth. The types of gunboats then in use in the Kingdom of the Two Sicilies were what were called "parancelles"—beach boats 40′ to 65′ in length rigged with a single-masted lateen rig, with a jib, and armed with a single gun in the bow, on a slide. The gun could be trained only ahead; though the slide was pivoted at the forward end, its traverse was limited to about 30 degrees. Some of the boats were sharp-sterned, others had square sterns. They were decked and had a small hatch abaft the mast and a small trunk cabin right aft with a hatch and skylight. The boats had bilge keels and were capable of being hauled ashore with a capstan, or "crab," staked out on the beach. The jib was set not on a bowsprit but on a sprit, or temporary spar, having its heel lashed to the mast and its forward end secured with vangs or tackles. It was placed well above the deck to clear the bow gun and could be squared off like a spinnaker pole on a modern yacht. Rowing was usually done by the crew standing on deck; some of the boats had a rowing frame laid on the deck, but this was apparently rather unusual. The deck of the Mediterranean boats usually had a great deal of crown. The Neapolitan boats sailed very fast; their bilge keels acted as leeboards, so they were weatherly in spite of their shoal draft. The six boats obtained by Preble, numbered *1* to *6*, took part in the attacks on Tripoli in August and September, 1804. In October of that year all six boats were returned to the Neapolitan government.

The plan of the Sicilian gunboat sent to the United States has survived. It is shown redrawn, with the rig reconstructed, in Figure 29. The drawing shows the rig of the parancelle and the manner of mounting the gun. This is apparently the hull design sent to the supervisors of the experimental gunboats. Although the letters mention a draught of a Messina gunboat and a draught or model of a Naples gunboat, it seems probable that this single plan is referred to and not two distinct designs.

Preble also borrowed two "bombards" from the Neapolitan government, at about the same time he obtained the Messina gunboats. The bombards were rigged as bomb ketches, square-rigged on the main and with a gaff sail on the mizzen. This Mediterranean type usually had a strong sheer, low raised quarterdeck, and good lines, and was used for convoy guard by the French during the Napoleonic Wars. The bombards were used as bomb ketches at Tripoli and returned to Naples with the gunboats in 1804. They were numbered *1* and *2; No. 1* was damaged in action August 24. No dimensions are on record, but these ketches were probably about 90′ in length.

Three gunboats were taken from the Tripolitans, numbered *7, 8,* and *9* in the American service. Little is known about them, but they seem to have been very small, for *9* was only 31′ 1″ long, 14′ beam, and 5′ in the hold; the length measurement must have been on the keel. The boats were lateen-rigged with one mast and carried a long gun, an 18- or 24-pdr., and two or three swivels. The Americans rerigged them as sloops. *No. 9* blew up August 7, 1804, and the others were sold in Sicily that fall.

Though the records of the gunboats built in the United States are very extensive, there is much confusion in them, and it is almost impossible to establish the various designs used. Of the first two experimental boats, *No. 1* was built under the supervision of Captain John Rodgers at the Washington Navy Yard by master carpenter Peter Gardner. Nothing has yet been found on her design, which is believed to have been made by Captain Rodgers. *No. 1* had one long 32-pdr. and two 6-pdr. swivels. She went into commission in July, 1804. She was considered unfit for ocean work and was placed in the coastal defense flotilla.

No. 2 was built by George Hope of Hampton, Virginia, under Captain James Barron's supervision and was launched in August, 1804. She had a single long 32-pdr. in the bows and seems to have had swivels also. Her dimensions are uncertain, but she was rigged with a single lateen sail and a bowsprit in which a jib was set. Rerigged as a "dandy," or yawl, for crossing the Atlantic, she was sent to the Mediterranean in 1805. Returning home in 1806, she was laid up for a time and finally was lost off St. Marys, Georgia, in 1811.

A plan of a gunboat exists which was apparently sent to the Office of the Secretary of the Navy by Captain Barron. A redrawing of the design is shown in Figure 30. On the original is the following note: "The gunboat to be built under the superintendency of Captain James Barron will be materially different from this draft." This is signed by the initials Ch. W. G., Charles Washington Goldsborough, the Chief Clerk of the Navy Department, who evidently filed the plan. The accompanying letter has not been found. In spite of Goldsborough's note, however, it is possible that the plan represents Barron's gunboat in hull form and dimensions. What the differences were between the plan and the finished boat cannot be established. Correspondence, however, shows that Barron's boat had her gun below the bowsprit somewhat as shown in the plan, for at a later date it was desired to raise the bowsprit to permit the gun to be elevated, but this was found impractical. The gun was so mounted that it could be slid aft and lowered on inclined skids. The design called for a hull 64' 5" between perpendiculars, 16' 10" moulded beam, and about 6' 6" depth in the hold. The vessel was to have an open rail, with the oars working on top of the plank-sheer. The design was for a double-ender and was well planned for sailing and rowing. The plan indicates that she was to have sixteen swivels. The gun apparently could not traverse and could be trained only by lining up the boat on the target. The original sketch shows the bow gun much too low, with the gun platform on the load water line. In redrawing it has been raised to bring the muzzle above the plank-sheer. The correspondence indicates that the finished boat was considered faulty in the mounting and position of the long gun.

In the spring of 1804, William Doughty was appointed naval constructor at the Washington Navy Yard, but on May 4, 1804, he was replaced by Fox, who now received the title of "Head Ship Carpenter and Navy Constructor." In June Fox prepared a gunboat design from which a number of boats were built, but neither the plans nor the dimensions of all the boats can be established with certainty. The design appears to be the one shown in Figure 31, calling for a double-ender, to row and sail in either direction and armed with two long guns, one at each end, on pivots. The boat was shoal-draft and was

Figure 30. Barron's first design for a gunboat.

195

fitted with bilge keels to beach; she was better designed to row than to sail. The rig was to be two lateen sails, and the rudder could be shifted from stern to bow whenever desired. This design was 71′ 0″ between perpendiculars, 18′ 0″ moulded beam, and 4′ 8½″ depth in the hold. The drawing shows the details of the arrangement of the deck and construction. It seems safe to assume that *No. 3* was built on this design by Nathaniel Hutton at Philadelphia and launched in December, 1804. She had two long 24-pdrs. She was never rigged with lateen sails, however, but was fitted with the dandy rig used in *No. 2*, and had leeboards fitted. She went to the Mediterranean in 1805 and returned home in 1806. *No. 4* was built by Fox in the Washington Navy Yard

Figure 31. Fox's first design of a galley gunboat, shoal-draft model.

and may have been on this design; but she had two long 32-pdrs., and it is therefore possible that she was on another plan.

Soon after Fox had completed his first gunboat design he prepared another on the same general model, but deeper than the first. This design is shown in Figure 32, with the lateen rig originally proposed for this class of boat. The new design was on the same dimensions as the first boat, but with more depth—5′ 6″ depth of hold instead of 4′ 8½″. The second design had some deadrise and was better suited for sailing than the first; it also had more displacement because of greater depth and slightly fuller ends, and so could carry heavier guns. On the basis of the larger guns placed on *No. 4* it is very possible that the second design was used for her rather than the first. *No. 4* was launched on March 5, 1804, and was sent to the Mediterranean in 1805.

In September, 1804, Fox proposed a gunboat to carry three pivot guns, but the plan has not been found. He made a plan for Captain Barron in 1805, but it has not been identified. It may be that the following gunboats were built on one of the two designs by Fox shown in Figures 31 and 32: *No. 5* at Baltimore by William Price, launched March 1, 1805; at New York, *No. 6*, launched February 4, 1805, and *No. 7*, launched February 6, 1805; at Boston, *No. 8*,

Figure 32. Fox's second design of a galley gunboat to improve seaworthiness.

launched April 24, 1805; and at Washington Navy Yard, *No. 10*, launched April 30, 1805. All these boats were armed with long 32-pdrs.

No. 9 was built at Fair Bank, Charleston, S.C., by Paul Pritchard and was launched in March, 1805. She seems to have been originally on Fox's double-ender model, 71′ 0″ between perpendiculars, 18′ 0″ moulded beam, and 5′ 6″ depth of hold, but her builder and superintendent were given permission to alter the design, and she was built to the following dimensions: 71′ 0″ between perpendiculars, 21′ 0″ extreme beam, and 6′ 2½″ in the hold, with her deadrise increased from 9″ to 12″. She was rigged as a fore-and-aft ketch and had a square stern and a single rowing hatch along the center line. This boat was therefore on a design distinctly different from that of any of the others; no plan exists other than a rough deck-arrangement layout.

Gunboats 5, 6, 7, 8, 9, and 10 were all sent to the Mediterranean. No. 7 was lost at sea with all hands on the passage out. The boats had to be prepared especially for the crossing: 3 had leeboards fitted as noted; the rest, except 9, had false keels added, 20″ deep (8 had only a 14″ keel added); and all were given the dandy rig. It is probable that 6 was the only one launched with the original lateen rig. None of the new boats saw active service, as Preble had been replaced by Captain Samuel Barron, whose illness, combined with extraordinarily poor advice from a State Department representative, Tobias Lear, had led to stagnation in naval operations in the Mediterranean and finally to a highly unsatisfactory peace settlement.

While Barron was in command of the Mediterranean squadron, he and Master Commandant Thomas Robinson, Jr., purchased four gunboats at Ancona and two trabacolos in the spring of 1805. These vessels were not in combat and were first laid up at Syracuse and then sold in 1807. No dimensions have been found, but a plan of a trabacolo was found in the plan files of the Navy Department (now in the National Archives). This is shown in Figure 33. The trabacolo was an Adriatic lugger, very full and burdensome but excellent in seaworthiness. The Americans probably intended to employ the two trabacolos as bomb vessels, for which they were readily made suitable. While there is no documentary support to the claim that the plan in Figure 33 is one of these vessels, it is of the proper period, and it is probably safe to assume that the plan was sent home to show the boats being purchased.

Early in March, 1804, Preble reported to Secretary Smith at Washington and apparently discussed the need of gunboats and bomb vessels in the Mediterranean, and in April he wrote the Secretary at some length about the matter. Preble put much emphasis on the subject and was ordered by the Secretary to supervise the construction of two gunboats and four bomb vessels; the latter were to be either built or purchased, as found most practical. Preble commissioned Jacob Coffin, a Newburyport, Massachusetts, shipbuilder, to prepare designs. It is apparent that the two gunboats to be built under Preble's supervision were much influenced by Cathcart's earlier recommendations, for in many respects the new boats showed many of the ideas mentioned in Cathcart's letters to Preble. The correspondence indicates that at least four, and perhaps five, designs were prepared.

The first design was for a boat 50′ between perpendiculars, 17′ 0″ moulded beam, and 4′ 6″ depth of hold. The original plans for this boat have not been

Figure 33. Draught of a trabacolo, probably one of those purchased for a bomb vessel by the Americans.

found. The second design was a modification of the first, but particulars are not known. No drawing of this design has yet been identified. The third design was for a boat 55′ between perpendiculars; this is shown in Figure 34. The drawing, made by Coffin, was rather sketchy and was probably a proposal rather than a working drawing. The boat would measure 55′ between perpendiculars, 17′ 6″ beam, and 4′ 6″ depth of hold. The specifications accompanying this plan mistakenly give the moulded beam as 17′ 0″. The design was for a well-shaped boat much like an enlarged ship's launch in model, primarily designed to sail rather than to row fast. The gun mounting was a curious one.

*Figure 34. Drawing of Preble's third design for a gunboat, showing Hawkins'
method of mounting two guns.*

Preble had become acquainted with an inventor named Hawkins, who proposed to mount two cannon, pointing in opposite directions, on a horizontal wheel. When one gun was fired its recoil would turn the wheel, so that the opposite gun would be brought to bear on the target. The advantages claimed for this was that the effect of the recoil on a boat would be much lessened and that two guns could be served very rapidly. Preble had a model made and

PLATE XI. (*Top*) *Sail plan of corvette* GENERAL PIKE. (*Bottom*) *Sail plan of brig* CHIPPEWA.

PLATE XII. (Top) Sail plan of brig SPARK. *(Bottom) Sail plan of schooner* ALLIGATOR.

tested it, as did one of the commanders assigned to the boats, and it was claimed that the arrangement was satisfactory. The complete details of the mount are not described, but it was said that the guns were secured to the platform or wheel with a pin or "hinge" which permitted the gun fired to recoil 4″ before it moved the platform. This was supposed to prevent the circular move-

Figure 35. Preble's fourth design for a gunboat, gunter mast forward.

ment of the gun, when the platform on which it was mounted began to revolve, from affecting the accuracy of the shot. The method by which the guns were trained is not clear; perhaps they could pivot slightly on their individual pins, or possibly the platform had to be moved with handspikes. The brackets of the gun carriage may have rested on rollers or casters attached to them; this is not clear in the references to the mount. The shipbuilders were not responsible for the mount, but constructed only the foundation and the bed on which the platform or wheel was mounted; therefore the specifications go no further. The mount was certainly considered practical by all who

tested it, and at least three gunboats were fitted with guns on revolving platforms. The design in Figure 34 seems to have been used for contract plans in
a number of gunboats; these will be referred to later. The fourth design was
an enlargement of the third, and Figure 35 shows a redrawing of the original
rough plan. The boat was somewhat similar to that of the third design, but,
owing to changes in proportions, she was longer and lower in appearance.
The fourth design was 66′ 0″ between perpendiculars, 18′ 10″ moulded beam,
and 5′ 0″ depth of hold.

Figure 36. Draught of a galley gunboat, probably an improvement on Preble's third
design.

   There is evidence that a fifth design was made, apparently to the same dimensions as the first one. No plan has been identified as the fifth design, but there
is reason to be uncertain as to whether all the designs were made by Coffin,
as will be shown.
   The proposals made by Preble in his first, third, and fourth designs seem to
have been approved by the Secretary of the Navy and were utilized in the contracts for a number of gunboats. However, the Coffin drawings were rather
crude and incomplete. It is stated that copies were made in the Navy Department, probably by Fox. Two drawings survive that may be these "copies"—
which in fact, were independent designs.

Figure 36 is a careful redrawing of a gunboat or "galley" design which may be the adaptation of Preble's third design used by the Department. The original drawing is unsigned but appears to have been the workmanship of Fox. The

Figure 37. The small galley fitted with a sloop rig and two guns.

plan was not wholly complete, as the masts were shown by light pencil lines that had apparently been added later. These indicated that the boat had been rigged in three ways—sloop and two schooner rigs. This plan, though following Preble's third design in a general way, was a wholly distinct one. It called for 55′ 0″ between perpendiculars, 16′ 0″ moulded beam and 4′ 6″ depth in the hold. Whereas Preble's proposals had square-tuck sterns like a rowboat (at least his designs that survive show this), the plan under discussion had a round-tuck like a large vessel and had, in addition, a knee on the bow.

Figure 38. Fox's design for a small galley carrying one gun.

Another design that may perhaps be traced to Preble's proposals is shown in Figures 37 and 38. This is for a boat 50′ 4″ between perpendiculars, 17′ 0″ moulded beam, and 4′ 6″ depth of hold—approximately the dimensions of Preble's first design. The length on the original plan is given as 50′ between perpendiculars in fact, but the frame spacing indicates that the boats on this design would run a few inches over the stated length. This design was also prepared by Fox, and the boat was originally intended to be rigged with a single lateen sail, as shown in Figure 38. However, it appears that most, if not all, the boats supposed to have been built to the design were finally sloop-rigged, about as in Figure 37. The original drawing was marked as having been sent to William Price, at Baltimore. Since he built Gunboat *No. 5*, it may be that the plan is of this boat, though the correspondence indicates a strong possibility that *No. 5* was built to the double-ender design, as previously indicated. In any case, the original design was intended to mount a single gun forward, a long 18- or 24-pdr. This was mounted on skids pivoted at the forward end and traversing in a limited sweep, as in the Messina gunboats. However, the deck arrangement and the heavy displacement of the design permitted the mounting of two guns fully pivoted, and accordingly many of the boats built to the design were fitted with two medium or long 24- or 32-pdrs. on pivots and full circles.

The double-ended designs by Fox were considered a useful type of gunboat, but the commanders and crews seem to have disliked the lateen rig proposed. The boats also were low in the water and were quite wet. It was soon apparent that a modified design was wanted, and so Fox made the design shown in Figures 39 and 40. This was simply a modification of the design shown in Figure 32, with 6″ more depth and the topsides altered. The idea of the boats being capable of working either end foremost, under sail or oars, was given up, and the rudder was permanently located on the stern. The bulwarks were raised fore and aft and more sheer was employed. This design was prepared to utilize the standard rig proposed by Captains Preble and Tingey for the dandy-rigged gunboats that crossed the Atlantic in 1805 and 1806. Some of the boats were sloop-rigged, and in these the mast was placed forward of its location in the dandy rig and a longer bowsprit was employed. The bowsprit in both rigs was fitted to unship, and its heel was secured to the pivot bolt of the bow gun which was locked in fore-and-aft train. Before the gun could be traversed the bowsprit had to be removed. The rigs were modified a number of times with the apparent desire to improve sailing qualities at the expense of rowing ability. This can be seen in the development of the double-ender, where the designs were progressively more seaworthy and better sailers, but became less suitable for operations in shoal and confined waters.

It will be noted that there had been an attempt to produce a number of standard designs. However, there is little evidence that any consideration was

given to establishing the characteristics that would be desirable for any particular field of operation. On the contrary, the designs were made to fit the
personal opinions of a selected group of captains and of Constructor Fox. The
ruling factor otherwise appears to have been economy. Though the original

Figure 39. Galley gunboat with "dandy rig."

intention was to build gunboats suitable for harbor and coast defense, the
Mediterranean adventure had placed emphasis on seaworthiness and sailing
ability because the boats were required to cross the Atlantic. The apparent
importance of sea-keeping qualities had not been modified by experience in
action, as the boats arrived too late to be of service in the attacks on Tripoli.
Hence the original idea was lost sight of completely, and the gunboats were

being designed more as substitutes for regular naval vessels than as craft for
special service.

It is impossible to draw any definite conclusion as to the importance of
Preble in the development of the visionary gunboat theories of the Jeffersonian

Figure 40. Fox's design to improve seagoing qualities of a galley gunboat.

administration. Certainly he contributed something to the idea. In this period
naval officers were fanatical party men, and it was not uncommon for them
to place their professional opinions and acts within the framework of a political
platform. This seems to have been done by many officers in the Mediterranean
and probably accounts for the very uneven performance of the Americans
in the Tripolitan war. It is certainly possible that Preble had permitted his

political partisanship to override his professional judgment, and he may have encouraged the administration to put its faith in gunboat flotillas rather than in a sound naval construction program. However, no real evidence has yet been found to support such a conclusion. Rather, the indications are that Preble put excessive emphasis on gun vessels, which the administration seized upon to develop a political naval policy of its own.

In comparing American designs for gunboats with those in Europe it is apparent that the former gave very little attention to craft required to land on, or to operate from, beaches and that there was no intention of producing boats that would be operated in support of a military movement, as Napoleon had planned. Nor was there any definite plan for gunboats operating in flotillas against enemy naval vessels, for if there had been there would have been more large gun vessels and more types carrying heavy armaments, such as the Danes, Dutch, and French produced during the Napoleonic Wars. On the basis of the correspondence and the gunboat designs that have survived it is very difficult to understand just what was intended to be the operation of the American gunboats in time of war.

It is readily seen that the predominant American designs in the gunboat class were very small craft. The problem of arming such small boats with guns of sufficient size to be effective against enemy shipping was almost insurmountable. While small hulls could be produced that would support the weight of two heavy guns on pivots, it was eventually found that the boats could not use their cannon against targets on their broadsides; the recoil either caused them to capsize or caused such rolling that their fire was highly inaccurate. Various ideas were tried, such as the Hawkins Wheel supported and utilized by Preble, but gradually the idea of gunboats having broadside fire was given up in favor of boats with limited traverse ahead and astern, as will be shown. In the process of development the American gunboats grew first in displacement, and finally in length.

The gunboats that immediately followed the first ten were still to a great degree experimental types. Preble placed two contracts in 1805—one on March 15 with Nathaniel Dyer at Portland, Maine, for *No. 11*, and one on July 1 with Jacob Coffin at Newburyport, Massachusetts, for *No. 12*. It is not clear on what plan *No. 11* was to be built, for she measured, when completed, 73′ 10″ on the rabbet, 18′ 11″ extreme beam, and 5′ 3″ depth in the hold. Preble's correspondence reveals that she had some carving on a knee on the bow and on parts of the stern. It seems probable that Preble's fourth design was the basis for the boat and that it was altered by the builder. The boat was schooner-rigged. *No. 12* was built to the fourth design, shown in Figure 35, for the contract is for the exact dimensions of that design. The finished boat differed slightly, however, for she was 67′ 8″ on deck, 18′ 11″ extreme beam, and 5′ 4″ depth in hold.

Preble employed the sliding-gunter rig on the foremast of the gunboats, as shown in Figures 34 and 35. This rig had been popular in some ship's boats and gave short spars that were easily stored inboard. It is difficult to see what advantages were expected from the gunter rig in these gunboats, however, except that they might lay head to the wind very quietly with sails furled, as the windage on the foremast was much reduced. It may be concluded that the advantage of the rig was slight, for it appears to have been abandoned in the later schooner gunboats. *No. 11* and *No. 12* were sent to the New Orleans station and were condemned about the time the War of 1812 began, by which time their odd gun mounts had been removed.

Gunboats *13* through *16* were built on the western rivers in 1805–6, and all went to New Orleans. *No. 13* and *No. 14* were built by John Smith at Cincinnati, Ohio, and *15* and *16* by Matthew Lyon at Eddyville, Kentucky. Henry Carberry was agent for these. The boats are listed as having been 60′ on the keel, 18′ 6″ beam, and 5′ 0″ in the hold. Apparently all were on Fox's design, shown in Figure 40, according to building directions, but the correspondence seems to imply that Preble's proposals were used, and one of the boats, *13*, had the Hawkins Wheel gun mount. The boats were sloop-rigged and had a 16′ boat, two anchors of 700 lbs., and a kedge of 100 lbs. The armament was two 24-pdrs. It seems highly probable that the cause of confusion in the plans used was that while Preble's proposal, the fourth perhaps, was used in negotiations, the final design used to build the boats was Fox's double-ender.

In addition to the fifteen gunboats authorized February 28, 1802, twenty-five more were authorized March 2, 1805. It appears that only sixteen were built with the funds appropriated by the second authorization, and the balance of the money available under the two Acts was used to obtain the four bomb vessels mentioned earlier. No plans of the bomb vessels have been found other than a few arrangement sketches. One of the vessels, named the *Etna*, was designed by Jacob Coffin and built by William Moulton at Portland, Maine. This bomb ketch was hurriedly run up and was launched in June, 1806. She measured 83′ 6″ on deck, 24′ extreme beam, and 8′ depth of hold. The *Etna*, or *Aetna*, was rigged like the English bomb ketches and crossed a royal on her main, but had only a square topsail above her spanker on the mizzen. The *Vesuvius* was a similar vessel built by Jacob Coffin from his own design and launched in May, 1806. She was probably a sister ship of the *Etna*, though there is a slight variation in their dimensions. These vessels carried a 13″ mortar and ten guns on the broadside—9-pdrs.—and either two 24-pdr. carronades or two howitzers, 8″ bore. The register dimensions of the *Vesuvius* were 82′ 5″ on deck, 25′ 5″ extreme beam, and 8′ 4″ hold; this is close enough to those of the *Etna* to indicate both were on the same design. The rigs were similar in all spar lengths, and both had a cutwater, headrails, and some carving. Neither one was a very good sailer because of faulty balance, and the mounting of the mortars was very unsatisfactory. Both were completed too late to go to the Mediterranean, and they were sent to New Orleans. The two remaining bomb vessels were purchased merchantmen. The *Spitfire* was a Connecticut merchant sloop built in 1803 and purchased by Preble at Boston in April, 1805. She was converted to a bomb ketch and was in the Mediterranean in 1805–6. The *Vengeance* was a Connecticut merchant schooner built in 1804 and purchased at Boston at the same time as the *Spitfire*. She was converted to a bomb ketch at the Boston Navy Yard by Rhodes and Page. Rhodes had built Gunboat *No. 8*. The work on the *Vengeance* was done between April 27 and June 19, 1805. The ketch was then sent to the Mediterranean, and it returned in 1806 to be laid up at New York. Both the *Spitfire* and the *Vengeance* were poorly balanced under the ketch rig, and their mortars were not properly mounted. The *Etna* was struck from the Navy list just before the War of 1812; the *Vengeance* was broken up in 1818, the *Vesuvius* in 1829, and the *Spitfire* in 1820. All appear to have been used as receiving ships for the greater part of their lives.

In following the development of the gunboats, we have omitted mention of two seagoing vessels added to the Navy in 1805–6. By an Act of Congress dated March 26, 1804, two more 16-gun vessels were authorized. Fox was ordered to prepare a design for these on July 6, 1804, and seems to have been given complete freedom in selecting characteristics. According to Fox's own statement, the design was "on the principles of an English cutter," though the design, which has survived, shows very little evidence of this influence unless the statement was intended to indicate that the new design was to have more deadrise than the earlier brigs, and possibly a little more "drag" to the keel. The original design called for brigs to measure 105′ 0″ between perpen-

Figure 41. Draught of the sloop of war WASP with final alterations in the original design incorporated.

211

diculars, 105' 7" on deck, 84' 0" on the keel for tonnage, 30' 0" moulded beam, 30' 11" maximum beam, 13' 9" depth of hold, and 387³⁵⁄₉₅ tons carpenter's measurement. The depth of hold was changed to 14' 1⅝" by raising the deck in construction of the brigs.

Fox began the construction of one brig, the *Wasp*, at the Washington Navy Yard. The other was built by William Price, at Baltimore, Maryland, and was named the *Hornet*. Both vessels were launched as brigs, but the *Wasp* was altered to the ship rig of a sloop of war before being placed in commission. At this stage Fox made additional sketch plans showing the alterations to make her a ship and detailed her spars and new deck arrangement. In addition he made extensive deck measurements of the vessel as built and noted the altera- tions necessary to convert her to the ship rig. The original design had placed the channels just below the port sills, where they would have been in the way of sweeps and would have been endangered in boarding. In revising the *Wasp* the channels were raised. Figure 41 is a redrawing of the original plan incorporating all the changes made during construction and conversion to a sloop of war. The original drawing by Fox has suffered damage and was mounted on linen, which so distorted the plan that it was very difficult to correct the projections. The redrawing has been done with great care in an attempt to obtain as accurate a representation of this noted vessel as is possible with the data available.

The *Hornet* was commissioned as a brig and was not rerigged as a ship until 1811–12. The builder had made some errors in setting up the frames of this ship, and as a result she measured 106' 9" on deck, 29' 7" moulded beam, 31' 5" extreme beam, and 14' 0" hold. Apparently the rake of the stem had been increased slightly and the beam had been reduced 5" either in fairing up the frames or in putting them together. As designed, neither the *Wasp* nor the *Hornet* had quarter galleries, but they were added to the former when she was rerigged as a ship: this may also have been the case with the *Hornet*. The latter was not very satisfactory as a brig, as she lacked stability, and so when her rig was changed her planking was doubled at the bilges and up to the top of the wales, adding 10" to her extreme beam. Both vessels appear to have had billets throughout their careers, but nothing has yet been found about their carvings.

The *Wasp* was launched April 21, 1806; her rig was ordered changed in January, 1807, and she was commissioned late in April of that year. The *Hornet*, which cost a good deal less than the *Wasp*, was launched July 28,

Figure 42. Detail drawing of masts and spars of WASP, *as a ship.*

213

1805, and went into commission in October, 1805, so she was the first completed. The *Hornet* never had her channels as high as the *Wasp*'s, as it was found structurally impractical to raise them. Her builder had placed them higher than the original design called for, however, to clear the rowports, about mid-height of the gun ports. The curved knee under the cathead in *Wasp* was replaced by a vertical one in *Hornet* and the bridle ports were 2′ farther aft in the latter, so that the catheads were forward of the bridle ports, rather than aft as in *Wasp*. The masts were also located differently. The foremast of the *Hornet* was about a foot farther forward, the main two feet farther forward, and the mizzen about eighteen inches farther forward than in the *Wasp*. When the *Hornet* was rebuilt and altered in 1811 she had her gun ports placed closer together and one added on each side, giving her eleven ports, including the bridle port, on each side. This arrangement placed the aftermost port one foot ahead of the foremost end of the quarter-gallery moulding, at the level of the port sill, and must have resulted in a rather crowded gun deck. Both vessels were to be armed with long guns, but only the *Hornet* appears to have been so fitted; she carried 16 long 9-pdr. guns in her first commission. The *Wasp* carried 16 32-pdr. carronades and 2 long 12-pdrs. in 1807. When rebuilt, the *Hornet* carried 18 carronades, 32-pdrs., and 2 long 12's. This was the armament of both sloops in the War of 1812.

The *Wasp* and *Hornet* represented Fox's ideas of what a fast man-of-war should be. He prepared the design with unusual care both in the preparation of the lines and in details. Figures 42 and 43 show his detailed spar drawings for the *Wasp*, which illustrate the attention he gave the matter. It seems probable that the design lacked sufficient stability to carry the brig rig first intended. After being changed to a ship the *Hornet* was considered a very good sailer, and the *Wasp* was deemed a fast vessel throughout her career in the American Navy. The hull form Fox employed in these vessels was somewhat similar to that he had used in the frigate *Philadelphia*, but it was somewhat more extreme in deadrise. The midsection was made rather full at the top of the floor timbers, and then the rise of the bottom was sharply increased. The bilges were rather hard and on a short radius. The advantages of this form were obviously that it made it possible to stow the inside ballast low, that it gave sail-carrying power without spoiling the lines for speed, and that it added to the capacity of the vessels. These two sloops were looked upon as superior vessels of their class, and though their designs were never repeated

Tops, Crosstrees and Caps
"Wasp", as a Ship 1806
After a drawing by Josiah Fox.

Scale in Feet

Fore Top Mast Trestle & Crosstrees

Fore Top

Bow

Fore Trestle & Crosstrees

Fore Cap

Fore Top Mast Cap

Bow

Bowsprit Cap

Main Top Mast Trestle & Crosstrees

Main Top

Bow

Main Trestle & Crosstrees

Main Cap

Main Top Mast Cap

Bow

Mizzen Top Mast Trestle & Crosstrees

Mizzen Top

Bow

Mizzen Trestle & Crosstrees

Mizzen Cap

Mizzen Top Mast Cap

Bow

N.B Drawing shows upper-side of Tops and Crosstrees; Underside or Fore of Caps.

Figure 43. Tops, caps, and crosstrees for WASP.

they influenced the characteristics of the big ship sloops built in the War of 1812.

The two brigs designed by Fox were not greatly dissimilar in size to the favorite design of brigs of similar rate in the Royal Navy. As the American vessels were to fight brigs of the favored Royal Navy design in the War of 1812, it is desirable to make a comparison. In January, 1797, Sir William Rule supervised the preparation of a design for a brig and two ships, to carry 18 guns—16 32-pdr. carronades and 2 guns, 6-pdrs. This design was to be an improvement on earlier attempts to produce a satisfactory 18-gun vessel. That year the new design was used to build the brig *Cruizer* and the ship sloops *Victor* and *Snake*. These vessels proved very successful, particularly the brig *Cruizer*, and the design was made the standard for Royal Navy 18-gun brigs for nearly twenty years. The design called for a vessel 100' 0" between perpendiculars, 30' 0" moulded beam, and 12' 9" depth in the hold. The model was very good, a rather round midsection with slightly hollow floors, moderately fine entrance and run, and rather raking ends. The vessels had a square-tuck stern. This design, with slight modifications in sheer and head, was also used in the 16-gun brigantine class of 1812. The *Epervier*, of this class, was carried as an 18-gun brig in the American Navy after the War of 1812. Her plan will be seen later. One member of the experimental brig squadron tested by the Royal Navy between 1832 and 1845 was built to the lines of the *Cruizer*. The vessels built on this noted design were generally fast sailers and fine sea-boats. They failed in action against the Americans because they were rather ineffectively armed and, to a greater extent, because their crews were not good gunners. There is no evidence that Fox had seen any vessels of the *Cruizer* model, but he was certainly well acquainted with some of the vessels of similar model that had preceded her. It cannot be said that he copied the Royal Navy brigs, however, as the Fox design was for a sharper model. It has been common for American naval historians to describe the British 18-gun brigs of the War of 1812 as greatly inferior to American vessels in design. But the American *Argus*, *Wasp*, and *Hornet* all fought brigs of the *Cruizer* class, which were equal to them in model, as can be seen by comparing the plans of the American vessels with that of *Epervier*.

During the Tripolitan operation the Navy acquired a few unimportant craft by purchase or capture, the most famous of which was the ketch *Intrepid*. This was a Barbary vessel referred to as the *Mastico*, but whether this was the name of the craft or the name of her type is not clear. She was captured by the

Enterprise and *Constitution* on December 23, 1803, and was purchased as a bomb vessel. Her dimensions are given as 60' length and 12' beam; either the beam dimension is an error or she was really a smaller boat than her length indicated. It is probable, from surviving descriptions, that she was a small "bombard," with Tripolitan modifications of the galley type. She was no more than a gunboat, of course. This boat was employed to destroy the frigate *Philadelphia* in Tripoli harbor on the night of February 16, 1804, which was accomplished by boarding the frigate and setting her on fire at her anchorage. Later the *Intrepid* was fitted as a fire ship and sent into Tripoli harbor on the night of September 4, 1804, under the command of Lieut. Richard Somers. She blew up prematurely, killing all of her crew and officers.

A sloop named the *Traveller*, a Massachusetts-built trader, was bought at Malta in the winter of 1804-5. She was a new vessel, having been built only two years before, and was described as being 71 tons, but her dimensions are unknown. She was renamed *Hornet* and remained in the Mediterranean until 1806, when she came home and was sold at Philadelphia in September.

A brig named the *Scourge* was also obtained in the Mediterranean. She was an illegal trader or pirate originally named the *Transfer*, either American or Bermudian built, and was captured by the *Syren* March 18, 1804. She was taken into service as a 16-gun brig and remained in the Mediterranean until well into 1805. She was then brought home to Norfolk and laid up, and was sold as unserviceable in 1812. No dimensions are known, but she was probably a small vessel, since her sixteen guns were only 6-pdrs.

A 10-gun schooner, the *Revenge*, carrying 6-pdrs., was purchased at New Orleans in December, 1806. She was wrecked off Newport, Rhode Island, February 2, 1811. This schooner, about 70' on deck, was said to be so sharp that she could not stow enough provisions to be of use as a seagoing cruiser. Her spar dimensions indicate that she was a fore topsail schooner, very lofty and crossing a fore royal.

Another vessel obtained in this period was the brig *Franklin*, 8 guns, a merchant vessel bought at Trieste in April, 1805. She had been built at Philadelphia in 1795, and measured 72' 4" on deck and 22' 4" beam. She was not intended to be employed as a cruiser, but rather as a supply ship, to transport tribute stores particularly. She came home in November, 1805, and in 1806 made two cruises to New Orleans, where she was sold the next year.

By the Act of April 21, 1806, Congress authorized the construction of fifty additional gunboats, and by another authorization the following year, Decem-

Particular Dimensions
Foreside of M.F. is 73'.6¼" from F.P.
M.F. rises 1'.4"
"41 to "43 is 4'.4"
"43 to A.P. is 3'.5¾"
Knuckle Timber is 5'.0" from F.P.
Room and Space 2'.5¾"
Lowest water-line 4'.0" above Base; others 3'.0½" apart
Buttock 5'.0¾" apart.

Draught of 74 Gun Ships   1799

Length bet. perps   183'0"
  on keel for tonnage 150'1⅜"
Beam . moulded   43'6"
Depth in Hold   19'6"
Burthen in Tons   1858 ½ Tons
  On Lower Deck 28 guns, 32 pdrs
  "   Main "   30   -   :   :   :
  "   Quarter " 12   -   :   :
  "   Forecastle 4   -   :   :
                 ‾74‾

References:-   40-15-6 J - J. Humphreys 1799
               40-15-6 J - J. Humphreys
               41-1-5 A   - W. Doughty
           Benj Hutton's Copy 1800

Plan 13. Draught of the proposed 74-gun ship of the line, 1799.

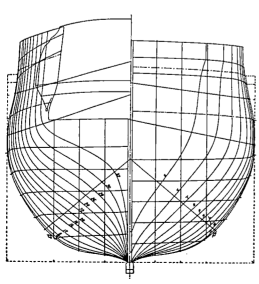

Particulars

O ıı 66'·0" from F.P.
O to Sta l ıı 6'·6"
Stations 5'·1" apart
LWL ıı 16'·0" above Base on F.P.
  "   " 18'·0"   "   "   " A.P.
Other Waterlines parallel and 3'·4" apart.
Buttocks spaced 4'·0" apart.

Macedonian 1812

th bet perps 154'0" (American mode 156'2"
Sided Beam 38'9"
h in Hold 13'6"

N.B. Fitted with Gangways,
open waist.

Underside of Gangway at side (Upper Deck)
E. Sheer

side of Gun Deck at side
Top of Wale

LWL

British Perps.
American Perps

Chapelle F.C.

Gun Deck
Spar Deck
L.W.L.

E. Rail

L.W.L.
Rail
Knuckle
Spar Deck
Sheer

References:
Admiralty Draught of class.
American sketches of ship, 1818

Plan 14. Draught of the prize frigate MACEDONIAN, *a British design for a fast frigate,*
1812.

ber 18, 1807, one hundred and eighty-eight more. The boats built under these appropriations varied in design and size, ranging from small sloops or galleys up to sizable sloops and schooners. The designs employed in most of the contracts cannot be readily identified, and some of the plans that have survived are probably no more than proposals. The records of the boats are generally incomplete, and there is a doubt as to the exact number built, for the number authorized in the two congressional acts were not constructed. Lieutenant Commander M. V. Brewington has made an extensive study of the gunboat records and has compiled a list of all boats which he could find any references to either in contracts or in official lists. This information, with a great deal of material on contracts and specifications of various boats, he very kindly loaned to the writer. This has made it possible to assemble more information on the boats than could have otherwise been done. Nevertheless, the material available is both incomplete and unsatisfactory, so far as establishing the plans used in many contracts is concerned. This is due to the practice that had grown up, with the use of naval officers as building superintendents, of referring to plans in correspondence as "Captain Preble's draught" or "Chauncey's plan." These plans, with few exceptions, can no longer be identified with certainty. The best way to assemble the mass of material available seems to be to trace the boats by number and contract.

Gunboats *Nos. 17* through *27* were built on the western rivers and were on the Fox design used for the earlier boats, *13* through *16*, shown in Figure 40. *Nos. 17, 18,* and *24* were built in Cincinnati, Ohio, the first two by John Smith and the last by Thomas Reagan. *Nos. 19* and *20* were built in Kentucky—it is uncertain whether at Lexington or Louisville—by J. Jordan and James Morrison. *Nos. 21* and *22* were built at Marietta, Ohio, by Edw. W. Tupper and Thomas Vail. *No. 23* was built by John Connell and Peter Mills at Charleston (West Virginia?), and *25, 26,* and *27* were all built by Matthew Lyon at Eddyville, Kentucky. These boats, which seem to have been completed in 1807–8, were armed with two 24-pdrs. and sent to New Orleans. Carberry was the navy agent for these boats, and the contracts were let to western politicians who sublet to the actual builders; of the latter Commander Brewington could establish only Thomas Vail of Marietta. *No. 28* was built at the Washington Navy Yard, where work began early in 1808. The correspondence indicates that she was on "Preble's model."

A new 7 was also built, to replace the one lost at sea. The second 7 was built, on a contract let in November, 1806, at Havre de Grace, Maryland, by Bennett Barnes, who was a subcontractor for Gabriel Christie. According to the contract the boat was to be 60' on deck, 16' 6" beam, and 6' 6" depth, but she actually measured 59' 6" on deck, 16' 6½" beam, and 6' 1½" depth. She was square-sterned and schooner-rigged.

The plans on which these boats were built are in question. In the first place, there were often errors in the contract dimensions, as the length on deck given in some was actually the length on the keel. Errors also exist in the beam measurements, where moulded and extreme beam are confused. The depth was also subject to error, and the final dimensions given when the boat was accepted are not trustworthy. The superintendents often ordered the boats building under their eye to be made deeper than planned. The variation between what was called for in the contracts and what was built is shown in a study Brewington made of the customhouse registers of the gunboats that were later sold as merchant craft. In these it could be seen that boats built under one contract in a yard often varied in depth, length, and beam so much that the design used became doubtful, regardless of the contract stipulations.

In examining the surviving plans and the data in the various contracts it seems possible, at least, that the boats shown in Figures 36, 37, and 38 were among the designs that were called "Preble's," in spite of the fact that they were the work of Fox. The design shown in Figure 36 seems to have been substituted for the third Preble design, shown in Figure 34, while the boat shown in Figures 37 and 38 seems to have been considered Preble's first design. *No. 7* was not on either of these designs, it is certain, and it is probable that she was merely a pilot-schooner model designed by her builders. *No. 28* was probably as shown in Figure 37, since it was said she was on Preble's model.

Nos. 29 through *33* were built at Portland, Maine, by William Moulton, who built three boats, and Eleazer Higgins, who built two. These boats were designed by Coffin and are supposed to have been on Preble's third design (Figure 34). Preble was the agent, and the contracts were let August 25, 1806. Contracts for three other boats on the same design had been let by Preble a few days earlier at Brunswick, Maine, to Ephraim Hunt and Robert Giveen— *34, 35,* and *36. No. 37* may have been built by the same builders, but this cannot be stated with certainty.

Nos. 38 through *41* were built at Middletown, Connecticut, by William Van Deusen, contractor, and James & Thomas Childs, builders. Captain Isaac Hull and Lieut. Thomas Macdonough were the superintendents. The design used is unknown. *Nos. 42* and *43* were built at Newport, Rhode Island, by

Benjamin Marble, with Captains Hull and Stephen Decatur, Jr., as super-intendents. These boats were on "Preble's model"—either his third design or Fox's copy (Figure 36). *Nos. 44* and *45* were built under the supervision of the same officers at Greenwich, Rhode Island, by John Glozier. These were also on "Preble's model." Gunboats *38* through *45* were all let in August and September, 1806.

Contracts were let in New York State in 1806, and a number of young ship-builders who afterward became noted received orders for boats. Captain Charles Stewart acted as supervisor and let contracts to Adam and Noah Brown for four, *46* through *49;* four to Eckford and Beebe, *50* through *53;* and four to Christian Bergh, *54* to *57* inclusive. These boats were all apparently on one design, 47' 4" on the keel, 18' 0" moulded beam, and 5' 6" depth in the hold. They were to carry one long gun on a pivot, a 24- or 32-pdr., and two car-ronades, 12-pdrs., one on each side. Now, Stewart does not seem to have had a plan prepared, but used one that Chauncey had suggested in reply to a query sent him by the Secretary of the Navy in March, 1806. Both Chauncey and Barron had then made new suggestions, and Chauncey had Bergh prepare a plan which he forwarded to the Secretary, accompanied by a set of speci-fications. The plan proposed by Chauncey is in existence; a redrawing of the original is shown in Figure 44.

This design was entirely different from the ones that had preceded it. Bergh produced a boat modeled to sail well, without much regard to rowing qualities. In order to carry a large gun, the boat, though small, was made wide, deep, and burdensome, yet there was a very great effort to obtain as fast a sailer as possible. The design first called for open bulwarks, but it is probable that these were filled in by plank in most of the boats. With the armament as originally planned the trunk cabin shown in the plan could not be used, and this made the boats very cramped for their crews. The two small carronades were looked upon as being of no particular value, so they were omitted in later boats, and in these the trunk cabin was employed. The rig was to be the "Periagua," popularly known about New York as the "perry-auger." This was a type of boat that was a descendant of the early dugout canoes which had developed a distinctive rig—two-masted schooner without a jib. In the "perry-auger" the masts did not have the same rake; the foremast raked sharply forward and the main sharply aft. The rig was a handy one in small craft and was used in the sailing ferryboats and some lighters in New York Harbor. The sail plan was undoubtedly based on the early Dutch two-masters, which also had no

Figure 44. Bergh's design for a gunboat with a Periagua rig, used in building Nos. 50 to 57 and 99 to 104.

bowsprit or jib. The New York boats had short gaffs, and the foresail was loose-footed and "lug-rigged"—that is, without a boom. The New York rig, with its crazily raked masts, may have stemmed from the same source as the old Chesapeake Bay "stick-up" rig, which employed a short foremast raked forward sharply in lieu of a bowsprit; this rig has only recently disappeared from the Bay. The "perry-auger" had some similarity to the "chebacco"

and "dogbody" of Massachusetts Bay, which were also schooners without jibs
or bowsprits and with the foremast placed right in the eyes of the boat. Basically the same rig was used in the later "Block Island boats," but in all the
New England craft the masts raked aft.

The advantages of the "perry-auger" rig were very great, in spite of the
unorthodox appearance of the boats. They were really sloops, with the jib
set on a mast rather than on a stay. By raking the mast forward the same effect
was obtained that would be found in a jib set on a bowsprit; in the "perry-
auger" the bowsprit was not required, and this was an advantage in working
in crowded waters or close quarters, in slips and around wharves. By the use
of the foremast, a straight luff was obtained in the foresail; this was and still
is difficult to maintain on a jib set on a stay. As a result, the "perry-auger" was
considered more weatherly than a sloop. It had still another advantage. The
widely spaced mastheads permitted the use of a huge staysail, after the fashion
of the modern schooner's "fisherman staysail" (which was at one time properly called a "pilot-boat staysail," as the sail was first widely used in American
pilot schooners rather than in fishermen). Though the efficiency of the "perry-
auger" rig was readily proved, the appearance of the sail plan was shocking
to conventional sailors, and the rig finally disappeared in New York waters
about the time of the Civil War. The related Chesapeake Bay "stick-up"
rig became extinct as late as 1936, and one example may have been in use even
more recently. These rigs went out of use because of their unusual appearance
rather than because they were faulty. However, they were best suited for
small craft under 50′ in length; when the work required a larger vessel than this
the schooner rig was easier to work. This is also the explanation of the disappearance of the "chebacco" and "dogbody" boats in the New England
fisheries; like the "perry-auger," they became finally extinct by the time of
the Civil War. Some of the New York "perry-auger" ferryboats were scows,
and many of the rig had leeboards.

Chauncey, Stewart, and Bergh were closely associated in interest, and they
had looked upon the new boats as primarily for the defense of New York
waters. It was natural that they would select a type that was useful around
New York and particularly suited for the local requirements. Bergh's design
and Chauncey's defense of it are the only gunboat proposals that mention
suitability for local use. A few of the commanders assigned to the boats objected
to the rig, and so some of the boats were given the standard schooner rig of
the 55′ gunboats, shown in Figure 45, which has been drawn on Bergh's de-

sign with the bulwarks closed in. When some of the Bergh-designed gunboats
were sold for the merchant service, the customhouse clerks were at a loss to
describe the rig, so they are often listed as "sloops, two masts." Later such
rigs were classed as "cat-schooners."

There appears to have been a similar design prepared, somewhat shoaler

Gunboat Schooner
45' x 16' x 4'-9"
from contracts

20 Sweeps, 20' long

Figure 45. Sail plan of a gunboat, schooner-rigged.

and narrower—45' on the keel, 43' straight rabbet, 16' beam moulded, and
4' 9" deep. These are close to the dimensions given for the modification of
Preble's design in Figure 36. However, it appears evident that another design
existed which has not been found.

Captain James Barron made a number of proposals for gunboats, but only
the design shown in Figure 30 has been found. In 1807 George Hope also made
suggestions through Barron, that river gunboats be 50' on deck, 15' beam, and
5' in the hold, but no plan of such a boat has yet been found. In 1806 Barron

apparently proposed a plan that was widely used. The design called for a boat 60′ between perpendiculars, 56′ on the keel, 48′ straight rabbet, 16′ 6″ beam and 6′ 6″ in the hold. This was a square-stern sloop, though it appears that many were rigged as schooners with their hulls on this design. This is another design that has not been found. The boats must have been much like the Norfolk sloops of the period, which in turn were much like the small schooner pilot boats, but shoaler and flatter on the bottom.

On Barron's plan of 1806 Hope built two boats at Hampton, Virginia—58 and 59. John Pool and Richard Servant of the same town built 60 and 61. Nos. 62 to 65 inclusive were built in Mathews County, Virginia, by John Patterson and Hunley Gayle. Nos. 66 through 69 were built at Portsmouth, Virginia; John and Joseph Forster built 66. It appears that forty-three of the boats built under the foregoing contracts were charged to the appropriation for fifty boats authorized April 21, 1806. From July, 1806, to December, 1807, no new gunboat contracts were let, as it was feared that funds would be inadequate. With the passage of the Act of December 18, 1807, authorizing 188 new boats, gunboat building was resumed.

Nos. 70 through 78 were built by the Washington Navy Yard, work starting in February, 1808. The design appears to have been the one shown in Figure 37, except 73, which was built to an enlarged plan and was given a very lofty rig, as shown by the spar dimensions given for her in the Navy Yard correspondence.

A seagoing vessel appears to have been built with the gunboat appropriations between 1806 and 1809. This was a large English cutter, 73′ on deck, 23′ 8″ beam, and 7′ 6″ depth of hold. The cutter, first named Ferret, was designed by Fox. She was fitted out with funds granted the Navy January 31, 1809, and was ordered to be rerigged as a schooner. Soon after this order was given, her name was changed to Viper and she was rigged as a brig. It is therefore probable that she never went to sea as a schooner. She rated as a 12-gun vessel when commissioned. The depth of hold given seems very shallow for a cutter of her length and beam. No plan of this vessel has been found. A number of cutter hulls were rerigged as schooners and brigs in the Royal Navy between 1778 and 1800. These were cutters which were thought too large for the one-masted rig, or which lacked the stability necessary in a cutter. One such vessel, the Spider, became a well-known cruiser in the West Indies, and many of the other converted cutters were very fast vessels as schooners or brigs.

Gunboats 79 through 88 were built by David Green at Portland, Maine, on a contract made December 30, 1807. These boats had either a single 32- or 24-pdr. on a pivot. They were probably built on the design shown in Figure 37, as it was noted that they were sloop-rigged. The superintendent for the boats, William Bainbridge, wanted to rig them as schooners.

Nos. 89 to 92 inclusive were built at Norwich, Connecticut, and at Westerly, Rhode Island. Amos Cross built two of the boats at Westerly, and Elisha Tracy built two at Norwich. These boats were on the design shown in Figure 37; one of the four had been schooner-rigged by 1815.

Another lot of gunboats was now let in New York, numbered from *93* to *115* inclusive. Six builders were chosen: Eckford and Beebe were to build five, Christian Bergh five, Adam and Noah Brown five, Charles Browne five, Robert Jenkins two, and Thomas Bell one. All were built at New York City except the boats built by Jenkins, whose yard was at Hudson, and the one built by Bell, at Schanks, Long Island. These boats were on two plans: Bergh, Adam and Noah Brown, and Charles Browne used Bergh's design, shown in Figure 44, while the remaining boats were built to the plan mentioned earlier—45′ keel, 16′ beam, and 4′ 6″ or 4′ 9″ depth. Commander Brewington's examination of the customhouse records brought out the fact that one of the boats supposed to have been built to this design actually measured 49′ on deck, 14′ 10″ extreme beam, and 4′ 10″ depth, which indicates how much departure was made from the designs in building.

Gunboats *116* to *135* were built at Philadelphia; seven of these were built outside the Navy Yard. All of these boats were apparently on the design shown in Figure 37. *Nos. 136* to *145* inclusive were built by Price and others at Baltimore on Barron's plan, 60′ on deck, 16′ 6″ beam, and 6′ 6″ depth. According to the tenor of the correspondence they were sloop-rigged, but there is some indication that the plan in Figure 37 may have been used. The designs referred to in the official correspondence are not readily identified, and often, as in this case, the letters indicate that another design, rather than the one mentioned in the contracts or initial reports, was used to build the boats. *No. 143* was certainly on a smaller plan than Barron's, for Brewington discovered her customhouse measurements to be 51′ x 17′ 6″ x 4′ 2″. *Nos. 146* to *155* inclusive were built at Norfolk, Virginia, by Theodore Armistead—dimensions not found. *Nos. 156* through *165* were built by James Marsh and Francis Saltus at Charleston and Beaufort, North Carolina. Marsh built five at his yard in Charleston. Marsh, originally from Philadelphia, had been foreman on the frigate built by the citizens of Charleston. He established a yard after that vessel was launched and for some twenty-five years was the leading builder in that section. All of the gunboats built in North Carolina were on Barron's plan. Another North Carolina builder, Amos Perry, constructed three boats, *166* through *168*, at Wilmington, North Carolina. The boats were supposedly on Barron's plan but were schooner-rigged. *No. 166* was renamed *Alligator* in the War of 1812. The remaining numbered boats were *169* through *176*. No contracts or data have been found on these, but it appears that a total of 177 boats may have been built.

Before leaving these boats, it should be noted that there are other designs that may have been used for some of them, but there is no basis on which to connect them with the known contracts. For example, it is known that the United States Navy possessed some "block sloops" in the War of 1812 which were built before the war started, and which were part of the gunboat flotillas. At least two of these sloops saw action; one, named the *Scorpion*, was part of Barney's flotilla on the Chesapeake, and another was in action on the lower Delaware. No record has been found of the building of the *Scorpion*, and it is highly probable that she was part of one of the many gunboat contracts. The design of a single "block sloop" has survived—apparently a proposal—and a reconstruction of the plan is presented in Figure 46. The boat was to measure 48′ 8″ on deck, 17′ 8″ moulded beam, 18′ 2″ extreme beam, and about 4′ 6″ in the hold. It can be readily seen that this design could be substituted for the one in Figure 37 without its being made apparent by the original contracts. The "block sloops" were no more than self-propelled floating batteries, in which speed under sail or oars was sacrificed to the ability to carry heavy guns. The "block sloops" also had high bulwarks to protect the crews from small-arms fire and to aid in resisting boarders. They were, in fact, a small edition of "block ships" used in many European navies. These were often old ships, too old to go to sea, made into hulks and used for harbor defense. There were, however, a number of "block ships" that were designed and built for the purpose. These were very powerful floating batteries fitted with some sail power. In November, 1806, Captain Stewart and Bergh made a proposal to construct "block ships" for the protection of New York harbor. Bergh's plan, which still exists, called for a three-decked ship, very short and wide, 100′ on the keel, 46′ beam, and 10′ in the hold, to carry 40 guns, 32-pdrs., and 14 carronades, 42-pdrs., on a draft of 10′ aft and 9′ forward (Figure 47). The vessel was never built, but a "block ship" was finally started at New Orleans during the War of 1812, and other proposals for such floating batteries were made during the war.

Another plan of a gunboat is shown in Figure 48. She is a small schooner designed by Bergh as a dispatch boat. This is a pilot-boat schooner 47′ 8½″ between perpendiculars, 49′ 5″ on deck, 12′ 0″ moulded beam, and 4′ 3″

Figure 46. Draught of an American block sloop showing characteristics of this type.

depth in the hold. The schooner was too small to carry a large gun, and it is probable that she was to carry a small carronade on a pivot amidships. The date of the plan is uncertain, but it appears to have been made between 1806 and 1810.

Figure 47. Captain Charles Stewart's and Christian Bergh's proposal for a block ship for the defense of New York.

On the 2nd of July, 1808, the Secretary of the Navy wrote to Captain Rodgers and ordered that a "gunboat be built on Lake Ontario, equal in dimensions to one of the ketches at New York built by Commr. Preble, and two small gunboats be built on Lake Champlain sufficiently large to carry one long 12 pound cannon each." Lieut. M. T. Woolsey was ordered to superintend the construction with Lieut. Haswell and four midshipmen to assist. Captains Rodgers and Chauncey were to furnish the plans and specifications and with Navy Agent John Bullis were to make the building contracts. The large gunboat "must be calculated to carry one large 32 pdr. iron cannon in the bow,

Figure 48. Draught of a dispatch schooner by Christian Bergh.

and 12–18 or 24 pdr. carronades,—or 12 long 9 pdrs.—in the waist. I want her to be made sufficiently large and armed to cope with any vessel of war now in Lake Ontario or with a small sloop of war," wrote Secretary Smith. Contracts with Eckford and Bergh and with John Winans were made by the end of July, 1808. Bergh designed the "large gunboat" to be built on Ontario; her plans are shown in Figures 49 and 50. The design called for a brig 85′ 6″ between perpendiculars, 77′ 6″ on the keel for tonnage, 22′ 6″ moulded beam, 23′ 0″ extreme beam, 8′ 0″ depth in the hold, 262 tons carpenter's measurement. The brig carried the long gun, required by the Secretary, on a pivot mounted on a raised forecastle, 2′ 9″ above the gun deck. Bergh made a mistake in drawing the lines, in that he allowed only 14 carronades on the main deck, but he corrected this in his spar plan, showing the correct number and the spacing as shown in Figures 49 and 50. The brig was very loftily sparred and was very powerful for her tonnage. She was built within five miles of the garrison at Oswego and was launched March 31, 1809. Incidentally, her contract price was $20,505 and 110 gallons of spirits. Her carronades were mounted on carriages, and she had a 32' launch and a 20' boat. The brig was fitted with sweeps and had a sheet anchor of 1,500 lbs. weight, one bower of 1,300, another of 1,200, a stream anchor of 800 and two kedge anchors, one 400 and one 200 lbs. She carried four cables 5", 12", 13", and 11" in circumference. The captain, Woolsey, objected to the raised forecastle and wanted to replace it and the pivot gun with two more carronades, but he was overruled. The brig was named the *Oneida*. She served through the War of 1812 and was sold out of service in May, 1815, but was repurchased. The final fate of the brig has not been discovered. The *Oneida* was a fast brig, according to early reports on her, but at the beginning of the War of 1812 her bottom was in poor shape and her speed was affected. Late in the war she was repaired, and her speed was again favorably reported. Bergh's drawings do not show the head built on her, but by 1812 she had a short cutwater and a billet, with only one headrail, about as shown on the two plates of the vessel here. The position of her bowsprit made the head rather low, and Woolsey said she could not have head netting. The gunboats built by Winans do not appear to have been numbered and were not among the boats already listed. No data on the boats has been found, though there is material on the Lake Champlain gunboats built later.

One gunboat plan that cannot be accounted for is shown in Figure 51. This is an undated plan of a galley 74' 10" between perpendiculars, 15' 0" moulded beam, and 3' 9" in the hold. The boat was to be armed with a long gun forward, an 18- or 24-pdr., and a carronade could be mounted aft. A pencil note on the original plan indicated that the positions of the gun and carronade should have been reversed. The boat shows a strong Mediterranean influence in her bow and stern and was about the size of the gunboats built on the Great Lakes in 1813–14, as will appear later. The spur cutwater and "pink" stern served no useful purpose and did not appear on the War of 1812 galleys. It is possible that this plan is for the boats built on Champlain by Winans, but this is mere guesswork. It is apparent that the boat was unsuited for coastal work and only seaworthy enough for relatively protected waters. The galley was alike in lines at the two ends, like Fox's double-enders, but was a much lighter and faster model than the earlier galleys. Pencil drawing on the original indicated that the forward gun was to be removed from the full pivot and remounted lower on slides pivoted at the forward end with limited traverse. It was found,

Figure 49. Draught of the brig ONEIDA built for use on Lake Ontario.

Spar and Sail Plan
Oneida
c Bergh

Scale in feet

Figure 50. Spar and sail plan of the ONEIDA.

232

perhaps, that the boat could not withstand the recoil of the gun when fired on the broadside.

By the end of 1808 the gunboat program ceased, so far as new contracts were concerned, and no new work was authorized from this time to the beginning of the War of 1812. The only undertaking in this period, aside from the completion of the gunboat contracts, was the rebuilding of some of the seagoing

Figure 51. Plan of a galley gunboat showing Mediterranean influence.

vessels. In 1807 Fox had proposed the cutting down of the frigate *Adams* into a flush-deck corvette. This was approved that year, and the work proceeded in a leisurely manner at the Washington Navy Yard. The *Adams* had been considered too sharp on the bottom for a frigate and drew too much water loaded, but she was reported to be a very fast sailer. Fox apparently thought the change would produce a very useful sloop of war of great size. The rebuilding was not completed until after the beginning of the War of 1812. In the process the vessel was lengthened 15', and so must have been over 132' on deck.

The *Constellation* was also rebuilt, with the result that her beam was increased 14″ and her appearance much changed. It is not known whether the increase in beam was accomplished by doubling her planking or whether her frames were padded out; at any rate the change in the ship appears to have been very extensive. Under the lash of economy, the ornate carvings on naval craft were removed and replaced with simple billets and stern embellishments. The intricate curved headrail arrangement of the cutwater was simplified by replacing the two upper curved rails with one or two straight rails, and the knees under the catheads were now made straight and vertical in many vessels. On the brigs the hawse holes were considered too low, and some of them, *Syren* among the lot, had the hawse raised so that it was above the trail knees. Some of the small vessels also had short topgallant forecastles added, to aid in working the anchor, and the rail in the wake of this was sometimes raised to the level of the top of the hammock nettings.

The schooners *Vixen, Enterprise,* and *Nautilus* and the cutter-schooner *Ferret* were all rerigged as brigs between 1806 and 1811, and some of these craft were extensively rebuilt. The *Enterprise,* which had been rebuilt in the Mediterranean, was again rebuilt, and this time both her model and her dimensions were changed. The schooner was not popular with American naval officers, it seemed.

Fox had become involved in politics and was now in the party in opposition to the administration. He was also at odds with Tingey, the Navy Yard commandant at Washington, who had attempted to dictate to Fox. There was also trouble between the constructor and the workmen in the yard. In July Fox was dismissed by the new Secretary of the Navy of Madison's administration, Paul Hamilton, and no new constructor was appointed. If anything, the handling of naval affairs during Madison's administration was more inept than it had been under Jefferson. Since Madison was a member of the Jeffersonian clique, there was, of course, no change in naval policies in 1809. The Mediterranean became relatively quiet, but relations with England became increasingly disturbed. In spite of this, however, the administration does not appear to have made any preparation for the coming war.

The relation between commanding officers and the naval constructor had not changed. The former were still supreme in technical matters, as evidenced by the power given the captain-superintendents in the gunboat program. Commandants in the various areas had full power to make technical changes at will. Tingey, at the Washington Navy Yard, instigated the changes in rig of the schooners *Enterprise, Nautilus, Vixen,* and *Viper* (ex *Ferret*) to make them brigs, in spite of the objections of Fox. The normal growth of the construction departments of the Navy had been stultified by Jefferson's and Madison's administrations. The navy yards at Norfolk, Washington, Philadelphia, New York, Boston, and Portsmouth had come into real existence, however. Much of the timber purchased for the proposed 74's of 1799 was used in the yards for constructing gunboats and buildings. With his dismissal, Constructor Fox disappears from naval construction history; he eventually settled in Ohio and died there.

While the Navy was declining in effectiveness, commercial shipbuilders in America were making great strides. Ships were gradually becoming larger, and fast brigs and schooners were being built. The sharp vessels increased in average size, so that many two-masted craft exceeded 95′ on deck. Three-masted schooners were coming into use, and the "pilot-boat" model so popular with Americans was being improved and also made more extreme in proportions. Rigs were also in process of development; spars and rigging were becoming stronger and lighter. The period between 1800 and 1812 was one of rapid advances in ship design in both America and Europe.

While the Americans had undoubtedly taken the lead in the design of schooners, and of frigates also, it should not be assumed that they had no competition as ship designers. While there can be no doubt that the Americans did remarkable work in ship design in this period, it is a mistake to assume that they were alone in this or that they had a monopoly on radical designs and new ideas. It does not detract from American accomplishments to find that foreign designers were also progressive and were in fact presenting the Americans with sharp competition for the palm of leadership in design of fast ships. The advances of the French in this period in the design of fast men-of-war and privateers were remarkable. The French were experimenting with hull forms of many types, and some of their large vessels were very sharp both in sections and in water lines. French constructors seem to have been given great freedom and were permitted to try any hull form they believed might have possibilities. The Spanish also experimented with fast-sailing craft, and there was hardly a maritime nation in this period that did not seek increased speed for at least some of its craft.

In spite of the predominance Americans were to take in the development of shoal-draft sailing craft, they were not the inventors of the centerboard, but were rather its developers. The centerboard first appeared as a "drop keel" and, as has been said earlier, was the invention of Captain Schank, while a lieutenant in the Royal Navy, stationed at Boston, Massachusetts, in 1774. Schank was a very ingenious officer. He also developed a method of mounting guns that permitted a single battery to be used on either side of the ship, and he was the leading proponent in the introduction of the "drop keel" into large vessels. It is really doubtful, however, whether he should be called the "inventor" of the drop keel, for a similar fitting seems to have been in use in some Chinese junks and in South American sailing rafts long before his time.

The drop keel introduced by Schank was first a long single plank in a case like that of the modern rectangular centerboard. This was controlled by a tackle at each end and for this reason was not very satisfactory in large craft. This objection Schank overcame by introducing two or more single narrow boards each in an individual case, along the center line of the hull, and each independent of the others. This gave a stronger hull and permitted adjustment of the boards to shift the center of lateral plane that was desirable in a square-rigged vessel. By 1798 he had succeeded in getting the British Admiralty to build a number of drop-keel vessels of some size. These not only included a large cutter, 65′ long, the *Trial*, but also a ship sloop named *Cynthia*, 113′ 2″ on deck, 28′ 7″ beam, and 12′ depth of hold. In addition there were two classes of gun brigs fitted with drop keels: one the *Hasty* class of 16 vessels, 76′ 0″ on deck, 22′ 6″ beam, and 8′ 0″ in the hold; the other, the *Assault* class of 17 brigs, 75′ 0″ on deck, 22′ 0″ beam, and 7′ 11″ depth of hold. One or two small tenders were also fitted with drop keels.

One of the most advanced naval constructors of the period was Samuel Bentham, of the Admiralty staff. This English designer was very radical in his ideas; in 1796 he designed and built two advice (dispatch) schooners for the Admiralty, first called *No. 1* and *No. 2*, but later named *Redbridge* and *Eling*. These were 80′ on deck, 21′ 0″ moulded beam, 11′ 6″ in depth, and 158 tons. They had diagonal bulkheads and very cutaway ends and were, so far as has yet been discovered, the first sailing vessels to employ outside ballast. This outside ballast was cast in short sections, just under 4′ in length, which were placed in line along the bottom of the keel. Each had two lugs at the top which tenoned into the keel and were secured by pins passed through keel and lugs athwartships. The outside ballast was cast so that it was markedly wider on the bottom than at the keel. These schooners also steered with a wheel, geared to a quadrant. They had iron windlasses and mast winches, iron stoves, and other improvements. Both schooners were considered good sailers. Two others, the *Milbrook* and the *Netley*, were built, but on different models. Each was an experiment in hull form. The *Milbrook* was 81′ 8″ on deck, 21′ 0″ moulded beam, and 9′ 8″ depth of hold, and the *Netley* was 86′ 7″ on deck, 21′ 0½″ moulded beam, and 11′ 3″ in the hold. Bentham also designed the strange ship sloops *Dart* and *Arrow*, which had whaleboat sterns, built-in water tanks, diagonal bulkheads, and many innovations in construction, rig, and fittings. They were 128′ 8″ on deck, 33′ 10″ beam, and 7′ 11″ depth of hold; each had three drop keels. Bentham's hull form was cut away at bow and stern and the sections were either V-shaped or U-shaped.

It is a sad turn of fate that Bentham's genius has been forgotten while the reputation of other men, such as Symonds, Humphreys, and others, of less technical accomplishment has been lauded. In addition to his many experiments in construction methods and ship design, Bentham introduced improvements in the Admiralty dockyards—steam sawmills, improved drydocks, and other mechanical aids. His personality appears to have been a somewhat unpleasant one, and there are indications that he was cordially disliked by many of his contemporaries. Henry Peake, a noted Admiralty naval constructor, was impressed by Bentham's ideas in hull design and produced a number of vessels, largely schooners, employing some of Bentham's ideas. The schooner *Rapid*, designed and built in 1808, was one of these; she was 107′ on the range of deck, 22′ 6″ moulded beam, and 12′ 0″ depth of hold. She had raised forecastle and quarterdeck and was to be armed with 14 18-pdr. gun-carronades in the waist, four ordinary 12-pdr. carronades on the quarterdeck, one 12-pdr. gun carronade on the forecastle, and one 24-pdr. gun carronade in the waist as a mortar. She could fight 12 guns on a side.

The pivoted centerboard was apparently first worked out by an English officer named Shuldham, while a prisoner of war of the French at Verdun, in 1809. The American patent for a pivoted centerboard was issued to Joshua, Henry, and Jacocks Swain, April 10, 1811. The Schank drop keel was used in some American schooners and sloops as early as 1806, but the centerboard did not become common until after 1820.

Mention of these matters will serve to bring into proper perspective the state of naval architecture in the United States in the period just preceding the War of 1812. Americans were by no means the most advanced and scientific ship designers and builders; they had as yet produced only their huge, fast schooners and their great frigates. The Navy had no constructor comparable to Bentham, and the most radical American vessels were to be found among the small pilot-schooner types. There was apparently nothing in the American merchant marine approaching the sharp lines used in the British four-masted vessel *Transit*, designed and built by Captain Richard Hall Gower in 1799–1800. The American fast-sailing vessels were not so much radical departures in design as natural developments of the then existing theories of design of fast-sailing vessels. Large, sharp, fast-sailing craft, particularly schooners, undoubtedly made up a greater proportion of the American merchant marine at this time than sharp vessels did in the foreign merchant services. This was due not to American progressiveness so much as to the unprotected state of their trade abroad, which, with the troubled international situation of the period, placed emphasis on speed in many classes of merchant craft.

It has become somewhat common to assume that the controversy over the advantages of a rather full, flat-bottomed midsection, as compared to the sharp midsection of the pilot-boat model, began with the building of the clipper ships in the late '40's and '50's. This was certainly not the case, for there were two schools of thought in the United States as early as 1800. This can be illustrated in the naval vessels built in this period. The *Argus*, by Hartt, and the *Oneida*, by Bergh, combined full, flat-floored midsections with fine ends, while the *Syren* and *Vixen*, by Hutton, and the *Wasp* and *Hornet*, by Fox, had sharp bottoms. The New York and New England builders, in general, seem to have favored the hull form employing very moderate deadrise amidships combined with sharp, well-formed ends, while the builders south of New York preferred the "pilot-boat" section with fine or moderately sharp ends.

The period between 1801 and 1812 produced few changes in naval guns. In America the carronade had become popular, and the long gun on a pivot had now reached its height in professional popularity, which it was to maintain for sixty years or more, until it was replaced by the turret mount. The pivot mounts of long guns were gradually employed in carronades also. The mount most commonly used consisted of a metal ring, or "circle," of from 9' to 12' in diameter, on deck and brought level athwartships by a wooden foundation. This circle was usually of iron, though copper and brass were also employed. The section of the circle was a shallow U shape, hollow side up, about 5½" wide and 1" thick. The inside and outside rims of the top were raised ½" and were about ½" wide. Rollers traveled in the track thus formed. These were on the bottom of two horizontal timbers, 8" to 12" square, called "skids," which were secured together by three or more blocks, or "chocks," and bolted. The skids were parallel and usually a couple of feet apart. On the top inside edge of each there was a rabbet running the full length of the skid. In this the bottom of the gun mount could slide. The skids were pivoted at the middle, or thereabouts, by a heavy pivot bolt, or pin, which passed through the center chock of the skids and thence through deck and a heavy timber below. The pivot bolt was further supported by a cast-metal socket and plate in the deck and was often heavily bushed in the skid-chock, since the strains of recoil were largely concentrated on this structure. The gun mount consisted, as a rule, of the standard broadside carriage without trucks, the bottom of the side brackets of which rested in the rabbets on the upper and inner side of the skids. Sometimes there were rollers on the underside of the brackets, or the trucks were retained and traveled in the grooves in the skids. The gun was trained by prying the skids around by means of handspikes. Recoil was controlled by breechings—heavy rope secured to the breech of the gun and fastened either to ringbolts in the deck about the gun, or on neighboring bulwark stanchions. Small guns had breechings secured to the skids, but this put a greater strain on the pivot bolt than was desirable, so when the gun was brought to bear on a target the breechings were commonly hooked onto ringbolts in deck and rail. Neither gun nor mount was particularly suitable for firing on fast-moving targets.

There were a great many variations in pivot mounts. Some had pivots at one end of the skids and traversed on an arc rather than a circle; some so pivoted could traverse a full 360 degrees. The rollers on the bottom of the skids went out of use gradually, as the guns grew heavier and longer, and the top of the track was then rounded. In such mounts, the casting at the pivot bolt was carried slightly higher than the track, and the skids balanced in the pivot casting. This made it easier to train the skids and gun quickly, as the skids could be lifted off the track to traverse. With the gun brought to "battery" or in the firing position, the weight of the gun and carriage brought one end of the skids to rest on the track, or circle. The details of many mounts can be studied on the plans of the gunboats and other vessels, where their general arrangement can be seen. The need of shallow bulwarks where pivot guns were employed was looked upon as a disadvantage, as the gun crews were thus unprotected from small-arms fire. As in the *Oneida*, the gun on a pivot could be mounted on a raised forecastle or quarterdeck, but the same disadvantage existed. The pivot gun should not be confused with the famous "Long Tom" of the privateers; the latter was a shifting long gun on a broadside carriage and not, as a rule, a pivot gun.

Carronades were mounted on both carriages and pivoted beds; some of these weapons had trunnions, and some were without. Bentham had introduced a non-recoil carronade into the British Navy; it was loaded outside its port and had other disadvantages but was capable of being loaded and fired very rapidly. This carronade did not become very popular in the Royal Navy, where only a few ships were armed with it, and it was never employed in the United States Navy, so far as is known. The Americans did not attempt any innovation in gun design, though, as noted, they did experiment with sights and mounts. Their cannon and carronades were gradually cast without the numerous mouldings and ogees that had marked the earlier guns. In spite of their preference for long guns, it is to be noted, most of the American naval vessels were armed with what was later called a "medium" gun; the length of cannon now ranged from 18.4 to 20.6 times the diameter of the ball. The length was gradually being increased, however, during the period under discussion. Small arms placed aboard the gunboats and other craft were muskets, pikes, boarding axes, cutlasses, and pistols. Dirks and swords, as well as pistols, were regulation for the officers. Rifles were also issued to marines in some cases. The American boarding ax was the same as that issued to the Royal Navy, a tomahawk-shaped ax having a spike at the back.

The gunboats and the brigs laid down in the period under discussion were not important additions to the Navy, with the possible exception of *Wasp* and *Hornet*. Their designs were not unusual, and the governmental construction program added nothing to the advances then being made in the design of American commercial craft. Though conventional in design, the small vessels built for the Navy were usually of good model for their size and limitations. This could be said of most of the gunboats, in fact, though they were wholly inadequate in dimensions for the required armament of this class of naval vessel.

It seems strange today that Americans gave so little thought to building up the Navy in the years preceding 1812, when it must have been obvious to all that war was approaching. The attacks on American shipping by British cruisers, culminating with the *Chesapeake–Leopard* affair in 1809 and the *President–Little Belt* incident in 1811, should have been sufficient warning.

It seems probable that the Jeffersonian policy that looked upon war at sea as primarily an attack on the enemy merchant marine (which could be carried out by privateers) explains the neglect of the national Navy in these years.

As the War of 1812 approached, the gunboat program slowly came to a halt. The discharge of Fox had left the Navy without a constructor, and Madison's Secretary of the Navy made no attempt to replace this technician. Only the gunboats which had been contracted for earlier, but which had not been delivered, were under construction in 1811. Many of the ships in ordinary were decayed and were rapidly becoming entirely useless. The vessels in commission were generally in a poor state, and many were in need of extensive repairs. Though the big schooner had now become almost the national type of fast-sailing vessel and was to be the mainstay of the privateer type, the Navy had now discarded the rig entirely under the influence of a few pompous officers; only a few large schooners in the Revenue Service were in government hands. The navy yards were inactive, and most of them were, in fact, mere storage plants. The abysmal ignorance of both the American politician and the public regarding the function of a navy was about to be corrected in a sharp and highly unpleasant manner.

★ ★ ★ ★ ★ ★ ★ ★ ★

CHAPTER FIVE

The War Navy

1812-1816

IT WAS FULLY apparent by the beginning of 1812 that war with Britain
was fast approaching. The western and southern congressional members
were hot for beginning hostilities, but the New England states and the
larger part of the maritime interests were less enthusiastic. The objections of
the seafaring groups to war with the greatest naval power on earth were
partly a matter of economics and partly political animosity. Seamen and merchants had no feeling of friendliness for the British, for the impressment
of American seamen and the seizure of American ships and cargoes by the
cruisers of the Royal Navy caused strong resentment. However, France had
also been active in arresting American vessels and mistreating their crews,
and public opinion in most maritime communities was almost equally un-
friendly to both of the contending powers. The agrarians of the Jeffersonian
party had never been friendly to sea-borne trade, and the party's "Long Embargo," initiated by Jefferson in his second administration and continued by
Madison, had not only effectively ruined legal sea traders but, by its nature,
had created a vested interest in illegal trade. The merchants ruined by the
embargo, and seamen or officers out of employment because of the embargo,
naturally joined the party in opposition to the administration. On the other
hand, those engaged in the highly profitable illegal trade viewed with the
utmost distaste any act of the administration that would interfere with these
activities. The southern states were politically the partners of the western

states in the Jeffersonian party, and their maritime interests benefited; the embargo was less rigidly enforced in the South, and so seafarers and merchants of the Chesapeake and of the southern ports were sympathetic to the administration and, on the whole, willing to follow party leadership into war.

The shipbuilding trades had been depressed by the "Long Embargo," and this, with the administration's neglect of the Navy and lack of any preparation for war, alarmed those thoughtful enough to appreciate the danger of war with the greatest of naval powers. Lack of business had closed many shipyards and the skilled labor had drifted away, and many good vessels from Philadelphia northward had sadly deteriorated while laid up during the embargo. Only on the Chesapeake and in a few southern ports was there any shipbuilding, and this was confined almost entirely to the construction of fast schooners for the illegal trades and for West Indian adventures. It seemed, therefore, that if war came it would be difficult to get fighting ships to sea with half if not more of the potential shipbuilding facilities of the United States inactive. This seemed particularly important because both the Jeffersonians and the opposition placed reliance on privateers in naval warfare and had little knowledge of the uses of a regular naval force on the high seas.

The difference of opinion regarding the national Navy was quantitative rather than basic. In public opinion it was part of the coast-defense system; to the administration it was a relatively unimportant part to be used only as floating batteries in support of fortification. The opposition, however, wanted the naval ships to function not only as a mobile coast defense but also in defense of sea-borne trade, particularly coastal. Neither party seems to have had a clear concept of naval tactics, and, as in the Revolution, there was widespread doubt that Americans could possibly cope with the British Navy at sea. It was thought that success would be obtained by assault on British maritime trade by means of privateers, combined with land operations against Canada. This suited the diverse groups of the Jeffersonians. The westerners wanted to put a stop to British help to the Indians and to punish both Canadians and British for alleged incitement of Indian warfare. The opportunity to loot Britain's sea-borne trade appealed to southern maritime interests.

The Jeffersonian gunboats had been created in accordance with the party's theory of a coast-defense Navy. The inadequacies of the gunboats were, of course, fully apparent to seafarers and shipbuilders of both the Jeffersonian and Federalist parties. The Jeffersonians deprecated the matter because they felt they would have to rely upon privateers anyway, and the Federalists

complained because the gunboats obviously would not be able to defend even
the coasters, to say nothing of the sea traders. Only a few private citizens
and the naval officers had any idea of sending naval vessels to sea to fight as
well as to destroy commerce. So well fixed was the idea of the uselessness of
the Navy that, as the War of 1812 approached, it was the government's plan
to lay up the frigates in harbors, to strip them, and to use the vessels as floating
batteries and as receiving ships for the recruits being trained for gunboat
service.

The state of the Navy in 1812 was certainly not encouraging to those who
thought the national ships ought to fight at sea and not be kept in port. The
periodical "laying up in ordinary" of the frigates and the economically minded
insistence on putting off repairs had caused practically all of the vessels to
deteriorate, and many were, in fact, wholly unserviceable. The fine frigates
New York and *Boston* in the Washington Navy Yard were now so rotten as
not to be worth repairing. The *John Adams* was in need of extensive repairs,
as were the *Constellation* and *Chesapeake*. The *Congress* was in commission
but also needed extensive repairs. The *Constitution* was fitting, but was without
crew or stores, and only the small vessels—the sloop of war *Wasp* and the
small brigs, *Enterprise, Vixen, Syren*, and *Viper*—were at sea. A squadron
at New York, comprising the *President, United States, Congress, Hornet,* and
Argus, was fully manned and ready for sea. The *Oneida* was at Sackett's Harbor on Lake Ontario, and there were only six gunboats on both the coast and
the lakes that were not either laid up or unmanned. Only the *Adams* was having any work done. She was at Washington being lengthened and cut down
into a flush-decked sloop of war. Only the Washington Navy Yard was
manned; the other yards were in the hands of watchmen and were inactive.
Supplies and munitions were lacking, the Navy was without a naval constructor, and the administrative staff of the Navy Department had been reduced to ineffectiveness. There was no reserve of trained naval seamen, and
naval funds were lacking. One thing alone the Navy possessed, a fine officers'
corps, well disciplined and trained, spirited and aggressive.

It was the officers of the Navy who pressed the reluctant politicians to risk
getting ships to sea when war was declared against Great Britain, June 18,
1812. The successes in single-ship actions that followed raised enough confidence and pride in the general public to force the creation of a wartime Navy.

Two of the naval captains, Stewart and Bainbridge, had gone directly to
President Madison at the moment war appeared inevitable and had pressed

him for authority to permit the naval ships in commission to cruise against the enemy. Immediately on the outbreak of war, one captain, Hull, took his frigate to sea without waiting for orders. The defeat of three fine British frigates by American ships in the first months of the war not only created confidence and tremendous pride on the part of the American public, but also horrified the British public and established American naval prestige in Europe.

Yet, in justice, it must be said that the splendid officers' corps could not, unaided, have been successful. Though most of the American ships were in poor condition, they were better designed and manned than the general run of Royal Navy vessels of the same classes. In addition, the American craft were better armed. Possessed of superior vessels, the American officers had quickly trained the hastily collected crews, and in a few weeks the naval captains had highly efficient fighting machines which proved far superior to the British frigates they met in the early months of the war. It would be inspiring to recount the various frigate and small-ship actions, but this would be outside the scope of this discussion. It was the early victories, however, that led to naval shipbuilding history in this war.

In the period from June to December, 1812, the Navy was slightly increased. It gained one frigate, the *Macedonian*, taken by the *United States* in October, and a 16-gun sloop of war, the *Alert*, taken by the *Essex* in August. Two other British frigates, the *Guerriere* and *Java*, had been captured, but were too much damaged to be preserved and so were destroyed by their captors. One 18-gun brig, the *Frolic*, was also taken, by the sloop of war *Wasp*, but both ships were taken by a British 74 immediately after the action. The *Wasp* was brought into the Royal Navy under the name *Peacock*, to replace a brig of this name that was captured by the Americans, but was lost with all hands off the Virginia Capes in 1813. The Navy lost two of its small brigs this year. The *Nautilus* was taken by the British frigates *Shannon* and *Aeolus* and the 64 *Africa*, July 17, 1812, and the *Vixen* was taken by the frigate *Southampton* November 22, 1812.

Three new vessels were added to the Navy, all of which were apparently bought on the stocks in the builders' yards. The schooner *Carolina* was obtained from the yard of James Marsh, at Charleston, S.C. She was 89' 6" long on deck, 24' 4" beam, and 11' 4" depth of hold, and was armed with 12 carronades, 12-pdrs., and 3 long 9's. The schooner *Nonsuch*, a former Baltimore privateer, was bought at the same port; she was 86' on deck, 21' 0" beam, and 9' 0" depth of hold; she carried 12 12-pdr. carronades and one long 12. A small ship, named *Louisiana*, was bought at New Orleans; she was only 99' 6" on deck, 28' 0" beam and 14' 0" depth in the hold. The *Louisiana* was rated as a 16-gun sloop and seems to have been a rather sharp merchant vessel in model.

Further additions to the Navy were made by taking over some of the larger revenue cutters. They were *Surveyor*, *Active*, *Jefferson*, *Mercury*, *Vigilant*, *Gallatin*, *Madison*, *Eagle*, and *Commodore Hull*. All were schooners; some were large craft and quite new. Except for the *Madison*, little is known about these beyond their names. The *Jefferson* was a schooner purchased for the revenue service a few years before the war, the *Surveyor* was a Baltimore-built schooner bought in 1807, the *Madison* (properly the *James Madison*) was built at Baltimore in 1807–8, the *Mercury* and *Gallatin* were bought the same year, and the *Active* and *Hull* were chartered schooners. The *Vigilant* was built in 1811 by Benjamin Marble at Newport, Rhode Island. The *Eagle* was a purchased vessel bought at New Haven, Connecticut, in 1809.

Another schooner, named *Norwich*, appeared on the Navy list in 1812. No record of her construction or purchase has yet been found, so it is highly probable that the *Norwich* was a hired schooner. A number of small vessels were also purchased in the South; the 8-gun schooner *Ferret* was bought at Charleston, South Carolina, and the 16-gun brig *Troupe* at Savannah. Two small craft were obtained at New Orleans, the 1-gun schooner *Sea Horse* and a dispatch sloop named *Tickler*. A block sloop, the *Scorpion*, was also added to the Navy list, but nothing has been found about her origin; she was probably one of the boats built under the gunboat contracts.

The Great Lakes and Lake Champlain became scenes of naval activity as soon as the war started. In the Great Lakes there were two theaters of operation, Lake Ontario being independent of the others because it was separated from them by Niagara Falls. Except for Lake Erie the remaining lakes were without important settlements, and the few posts on the western lakes could be reached by vessels from Lake Erie. Champlain was independent of the upper lakes and so represented a third theater of operations. These three naval theaters were of immediate importance in the grandiose plans of the Americans for the invasion of Canada. Except for a few galleys, the British forces on the Lakes consisted of three ship sloops and three schooners of the Canadian Provincial Marine, on Lake Ontario. On Lake Champlain the Provincial Marine had a few large galley gunboats and one or two unserviceable vessels. There

Figure 52. Draught of the American revenue cutter
JAMES MADISON *from an Admiralty plan.*

were a ship sloop, a brig, and one or two schooners of the Canadian Provincial Marine on the western lakes. In addition there were some armed fur traders. These vessels made their headquarters in Lake Erie. The Americans had only the *Oneida* on Lake Ontario, two or three small gunboats on Champlain, and no naval craft of any kind on Erie or the western lakes. On all the lakes there were a number of small American trading vessels—sloops, schooners, and a rare brig.

The commander of the *Oneida*, Lieutenant Woolsey, as senior officer on Lake Ontario, was ordered to obtain additional vessels as soon as possible. He had been on the station for some years (in fact he had superintended the building of the *Oneida*) and was well acquainted with the available lake vessels. He went about the purchasing of these with care and seems to have obtained the best craft. The lake was deep, and the schooners were therefore on the clipper model. Since navigation was largely confined to summer months when the winds were moderate, the lake schooners were very heavily sparred and canvased. As a result, they were fast sailers but were not very safe and, when armed, were prone to capsize or to be knocked down and swamped.

Woolsey purchased the following merchant schooners: *Elizabeth*, 2 guns, as a transport; *Fair American*, 2 guns and 82 tons measurement; *Charles and Ann* (renamed *Governor Tomkins* and fitted out with 6 guns); *Experiment*, 53 tons (renamed *Growler* and armed variously with from 2 to 6 guns during her career); *Diana* (renamed *Hamilton* and armed with 9 guns); and the *Collector* (renamed *Pert* and given 3 guns). On the outbreak of the war, the *Oneida* had taken a Canadian schooner named *Lord Nelson*, 12 guns, apparently a Provincial Marine schooner, which was renamed *Scourge*. Another prize, named *Julia*, was armed with 3 long guns. Woolsey also obtained a packet schooner, *Genesee Packet*, 82 tons, which he renamed *Conquest* and armed with 2 or 3 long guns. Many of these schooners had no bulwarks and so carried their guns on pivots.

In November, Captain Isaac Chauncey took command on Lake Ontario and brought with him the New York shipbuilder, Henry Eckford, who immediately laid down a large corvette, the *Madison* of 593 tons, at Sackett's Harbor, New York. Eckford, it will be remembered, had been a gunboat contractor under Chauncey's supervision. He had been born at Kilwinning, a small town near Irving, Scotland, and had come to Quebec when he was sixteen to learn his trade under his uncle, John Black, a noted Canadian shipwright. In 1796, at the age of twenty-one, he came to New York and worked in a boat shop.

Three years later he married, and in 1800 he opened his own yard. This was located in the vicinity of the present Brooklyn Navy Yard. Eckford was an intelligent designer and a man of tremendous energy and industry, as will be seen. In 1808 Eckford joined Lester Beebe in a gunboat contract, and later in the same year he also went into partnership with Christian Bergh to build the *Oneida* on Lake Ontario. When he came to Sackett's Harbor with Chauncey he was not a stranger to the lake. Here he was to show his genius as a designer and builder, as an organizer and manager, and as a master of the art of high-speed production of ships. Eckford and Bergh were close friends, and it is probable that Eckford received much help from the older man, who was a noted shipbuilder as early as 1806. Perhaps the explanation of Eckford's success in shipbuilding can be attributed to a characteristic of his, mentioned by a contemporary: he could and did tell the men how and why the work was to be done.

The British Navy had taken over the Canadian Provincial Marine, and Captain James Yeo, an officer who had an excellent record, was placed in command of all the lakes. He immediately began to bring in ship carpenters and materials and established yards at Kingston and York (now Toronto) to build up his squadron. Late in 1812 he had two ship sloops laid down, one in each of his new yards. His master shipwrights appear to have been Canadians who were eventually displaced by Admiralty men, about 1814. Yeo also strengthened his squadron by enlisting Canadians and by bringing in drafts of men taken from ships of the British Navy at Quebec. He also purchased a few small vessels on Lake Ontario, but it appears that there were fewer commercial craft on the Canadian side than on the American, for Yeo employed few such vessels, even though he was often in great need of small craft.

The building race on Lake Ontario was now begun, each side striving to outbuild the other under the most trying difficulties. The two Canadian bases were poorly equipped and insufficiently manned, and the American base, Sackett's Harbor, was even worse situated. Both sides suffered from the difficulties of getting materials and equipment in from the coast, and there was much sickness among the workmen. The British had so much difficulty that they went to the extreme of having the frames of some new ships prepared in England.

On Lake Erie the British assembled a small squadron of eight craft, schooners, sloops, a brig, and a ship sloop, of the old Provincial Marine or converted trading vessels. One of these was an armed vessel of the Northwest Fur Company, the brig or brigantine *Caledonia*, with three guns on pivots. They soon added another brig, the *Adams* of 14 guns, which had been bought by the American Army at Detroit, Michigan. This brig fell into British hands when Detroit was captured in the first months of the war and was taken into the Provincial Marine as the *Detroit*.

Commodore Chauncey, as commander on the lakes, sent Lieut. Jesse D. Elliott to Lake Erie to establish a squadron to meet the British on the western lakes. He succeeded in capturing the *Caledonia* and *Detroit* by a daring boat attack late in 1812. He also purchased some rather small merchant craft at Buffalo, Erie, and other lake settlements; these were the 1-gun schooner *Amelia* (renamed *Tigress*), the *Catherine* (renamed *Somers*), 2 guns, and the sloop *Contractor* (renamed *Trippe*), 1 gun. Preparations were also started to build more powerful craft at Presque Isle, now Erie, Pennsylvania. Late in 1812 or early in 1813 a small 2-gun schooner was laid down which was launched as the *Scorpion*.

On Lake Champlain American Lieutenant Sidney Smith was ordered to buy suitable vessels, and the best he could find were shoal-draft sloops about 60 feet in length. One of these was named *Growler* and was armed with 10 small guns; another was the *Bull Dog*, renamed *Eagle*, also of 10 guns. The third was the *President*, a 12-gun sloop originally bought by the War Department but turned over to the Navy late in 1812. These, with the gunboats on the lake that had been built before the war, gave the Americans temporary dominance on Champlain. The American base was on Otter Creek, Vergennes, Vermont, where there was a small arsenal. The British base was at Isle aux Noix, where the British had maintained a small shipyard since the days of the American Revolution, though few vessels had been built there in the intervening years.

Returning to seagoing vessels, there are no plans, that can be identified, of the American vessels added to the Navy in 1812, except for a revenue cutter captured by the British. She was the revenue cutter *James Madison*, taken into the Royal Navy after her capture under the name *Alban*. Her lines were taken off after the war, in 1817, by Admiralty draftsmen, and her plans are shown in Figure 52. The *Madison* was a large clipper schooner, 94' 4½" on deck, 24' 2⅝" moulded beam, and 10' 6" depth of hold. In model she was about the same as the privateer schooners of the War of 1812. Like most of her type, this schooner was plainly finished, and no money or time had been wasted on decoration.

The writer has an unidentified plan of another schooner of the same period

Figure 53. An American plan for a schooner with sliding keels.

as the *Madison,* but on an entirely different model. The plan, shown in Figure 53, is of a drop-keel schooner 74′ 0″ between perpendiculars, 24′ 0″ moulded beam, 6′ 6″ depth of hold. The design was prepared by James Hutton, of Philadelphia, sometime before the War of 1812, and was evidently intended as a revenue cutter and survey vessel, judging by the title of the drawing. The plan is of some value, as it shows the details of the employment of drop keels, forerunners of the centerboard.

The two ships of the Royal Navy that were purchased into the American service were the *Alert* and the frigate *Macedonian*. The former had been a merchant vessel—some accounts described her as a collier—that had been bought for the British Navy and rated as a sloop. In the American service she was employed as a supply ship rather than as a cruiser. No plan of the *Alert* has been found. The *Macedonian* was a new vessel at the time of her capture, having been built just before the war. She was built of oak and was one of a class of 38-gun frigates that had become standard in the British Navy. No Admiralty plan of the *Macedonian* appears to exist, but Plan 14 shows the lines of a sister ship, the *Bacchante*, which in turn was on the lines of the frigate *Lively*. The plan shows that the *Macedonian* was a rather sharp-ended frigate, somewhat narrow for her length. American references to the *Macedonian* show her to have been a fast sailer and an excellent vessel in all respects, though she was deemed small for her rate. In view of the numerous comparisons of this frigate with her opponent, the *United States*, by naval historians, the dimensions given on the design may be of interest. The *Macedonian* class is shown to have been 154′ 0″ on the lower deck, or about 156′ 0″ between perpendiculars, American measurement, with a moulded beam of 38′ 9″, and a depth of hold of 13′ 6″. Her figurehead was a bust of Alexander the Great of Macedonia, which was later used on the American-built frigate of the same name. It will be readily seen that the *Macedonian* was a smaller frigate than most of her American counterparts and, in size at least, was comparable to the *Chesapeake*. The *Macedonian* was rather hastily repaired when put into the American service, and this shortened her life.

No plans of the vessels obtained for the American service on the lakes have been found. In view of the circumstances this is not surprising; the lack of any construction organization in the Navy Department in 1812 and the methods employed in getting new vessels built on Lakes Ontario and Erie effectively prevented any plans that may have been used from being retained. On the British side this was not the case, and some few plans of lake vessels have survived. On the British plans alone it is possible to show that the vessels em-

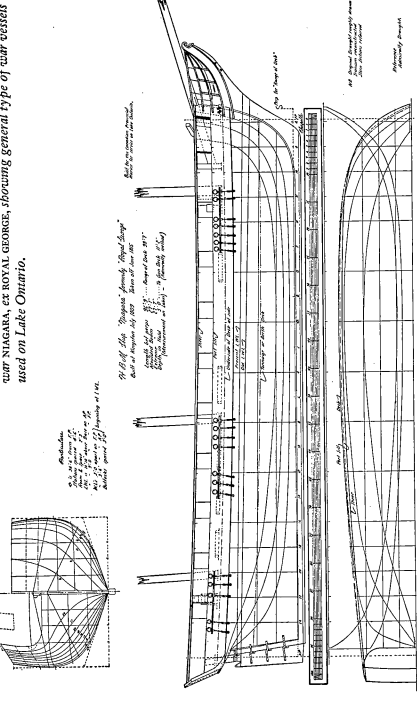

Figure 54. Draught of the Canadian Provincial Marine sloop of war NIAGARA, ex ROYAL GEORGE, showing general type of war vessels used on Lake Ontario.

253

ployed in the three lake theaters of operation were of two basic types, which were in turn the result of geographical conditions. As has been mentioned, the vessels on Lake Ontario were relatively deep and sharp and were of the seagoing type in nearly all respects. The plan of one of the British ships will suffice to illustrate this. Figure 54 shows one of the ships of the original squadron on Lake Ontario—the *Niagara*, formerly the *Royal George*, built at Kingston on the Canadian side of the lake in 1809, for the Canadian Provincial Marine. She was a small ship sloop 96′ 9″ on the lower deck, or about 98′ 6″ on the main deck (American measurement), 27′ 1″ moulded beam, and 27′ 7″ extreme beam. Her depth of hold was given as only 5′ 0″, but the plan shows that this was from the lower deck and that she was 11′ 6″ from ceiling to main deck. Her model was much like that of a seagoing ship sloop of her size and date, though lighter in displacement, and she drew about 11′ 9″ service trim. The *Niagara* was considered a good ship, and she sailed well. She remained in service throughout the war as a cruising vessel. Another ship of the British squadron whose plan has survived is the *Wolfe*, later named *Montreal*. This ship was 101′ 9″ on the lower deck, 30′ 0″ moulded beam, 4′ 6″ hold (but actually nearly 12′ from ceiling to main deck) and on a sharp model that required 12′ 3″ draft. This is sufficient to show that the Lake Ontario ships and small craft were of the seagoing type and that their tonnage was fictitious, being obtained by hold measurement to the lowest deck rather than to the main deck.

On Lake Erie, and on Lake Champlain too, the vessels were rather shoal and very small. Some of the schooners on Erie were of the pilot-boat model, apparently much like that used in the Norfolk pilot boats of the Chesapeake, but the lake was too shoal, particularly on the American side, to permit the use of such deep vessels as were possible on Lake Ontario. The small craft on Champlain were almost flat-bottomed, but in the War of 1812 none of the vessels were as shallow as the Champlain gondolas and the radeau of Arnold's time. The sloops bought by the Americans in 1812 were shallow-keel craft; one was 60′ on deck, 19′ beam, and 5′ 8″ depth.

With the outbreak of the war, American privateers began to get to sea and soon were creating great destruction and loss to British shipping. The first privateers to get to sea were hastily fitted schooners and small craft that operated close to home. Some were pilot boats and fishing schooners having but one gun. Larger schooners, carrying up to 14 guns, began to appear in the fall of 1812, and these were suited for more distant cruising. The effect of these first vessels was to cause the British to bring out a large number of small naval cruisers, schooners, and brigs to protect trade, particularly in the West Indies, and finally to resort to the convoy system almost entirely. The activities of the privateers could be countered only by stopping such vessels from getting to sea, and the British Navy soon began to blockade those ports sending out large numbers of raiders. The strict blockade and the swarm of British light cruising vessels made the American coasts unsafe for small privateers. This soon led the American builders to produce a type of large privateering vessel that had previously been unknown.

The blockade eventually affected naval shipbuilding, but in the early years of the war the danger of national strangulation by the blockade was not realized by either the American public or the incompetent administration. Hence no preparations were made to combat the blockade with suitable naval construction. The victories of the small American Navy at sea actually caused the blockade to become increasingly effective, for, by the end of 1812, British naval prestige had been seriously damaged by the Americans, and the Admiralty tried to make it certain that no more American cruisers got out of port.

As 1812 drew to a close, the American public felt great pride in their Navy, and an aroused public opinion forced a reluctant government to increase naval effectiveness with new construction. The sea victories stood out all the more because of the disgraceful failures on the Canadian border in the early months of the war, when the militia army and incompetently led regulars were unable to carry out the administration's and western politicians' plans for the invasion of Canada and suffered one disaster after another.

When the war began, William Doughty was at Georgetown, in the District of Columbia, operating a small shipyard of his own. He had not been active in politics, like Fox, nor had he influential connections with the opposition party like Joshua Humphreys. The administration therefore found him acceptable and now appointed him naval constructor at the Washington Navy Yard. The Secretary of the Navy, and the administration as a whole, still had no idea of creating an efficient naval establishment. The number of officers and enlisted personnel was rapidly increased to man the newly purchased ships and those employed on the lakes, but the increase was brought about by expediency and not by plan. No administrative organization was set up, and this portion of the naval establishment as well as the construction organization was permitted to grow up aimlessly and without plan, controlled only by the needs of the moment. One by one, the navy yards had been put into use, to repair ships and to act as shore stations. Doughty received his commission February 8, 1813, and his appointment was not as chief constructor but only as the Washington Navy Yard constructor. In January of 1813 Congress authorized the construction of three 44-gun frigates and six 18-gun sloops of war, and Doughty at once began work on the design of these. He prepared one frigate design for the three 44's and two designs for the six sloops.

The three plans were completed, and the necessary copies made, by June, 1813, and contracts were let for some of the vessels. One frigate and one sloop were to be built under Doughty's personal supervision in the Washington Navy Yard, but all others were to be built by contractors. One frigate was given to Joseph and Francis Grice at Philadelphia (*Guerriere*) and the other to Flannigan and Parsons at Baltimore (*Java*). The frigate to be built at Washington was to be named *Columbia*. The ship sloop to be built at Washington was finally named *Argus*, when the brig of that name was captured by the British. Two sloops, later named *Erie* and *Ontario*, were built by Thomas Kemp, at Baltimore. The *Argus*, *Erie*, and *Ontario* were on the same design. The three remaining sloops to be built were on an entirely different model. The *Wasp* was built by Cross and Merrill at Newburyport, Massachusetts, the *Peacock* by Adam and Noah Brown at New York, and the *Frolic* at Boston. The record is conflicting as to whether the last-named sloop was built in the Boston Navy Yard or whether she was built by contract, by Josiah Barker. It is probable, however, that Barker built her under contract, as he was not appointed constructor at the Boston Navy Yard until after the War of 1812. Barker and Edward Hartt were in partnership in 1813–14 and built on the site of the present Navy Yard at Boston.

Doughty was given complete freedom in the designs of the new ships, apparently, as the scanty correspondence indicates that no extensive directions were given him. It is highly probable that the designs of the sloops were intended to be improvements of the earlier *Wasp* and *Hornet*, of increased size and power. As a result, the two sloop designs of 1813 were on the same dimensions—117′ 11″ between perpendiculars, 31′ 6″ moulded beam, and 14′ 6″ depth of hold—but were not of the same model. The *Argus*, *Erie*, and *Ontario* drew 4′ 8″ more water at the sternpost than at the stem, while *Wasp*, *Peacock*, and *Frolic* had a difference of but 1′ 9″. As designed, the two classes had the same appearance above the water, except that the *Argus* class had no quarter galleries or quarter badges. The ships were capable of carrying 22 guns with ease and were to be armed with 20 32-pdr. carronades and 2 long 18's. The *Argus* class, of which two were completed, were on the Baltimore Clipper

Figure 55. Draught of ship sloops ARGUS, ERIE, *and* ONTARIO, *1813, showing pilot-boat schooner influence, in sections and profile.*

model. They were fast ships, but they were said to have steered wildly when first commissioned and so their rigs had to be altered.

Figure 55 shows the design for the *Argus* class. It has been said that the two ships of this design that were finished, *Erie* and *Ontario,* were built closely to the plans. This statement is supported by later plans of *Erie*, made when the ship was lengthened and rebuilt, which show that the contractors had followed the lines very carefully. The *Argus* was burned on the stocks at Washington, August 24, 1814, when the British took the city. The *Erie* and *Ontario* were completed during the war, but the Chesapeake was too closely blockaded for the sloops to get to sea. Thomas Kemp, who was the builder of the ships, was a noted designer in his own right and a builder of privateers and fast schooners. He was responsible for the famous *Chasseur*.

The *Wasp* class were to have been built on the design shown in Figure 56, but there was much variation in the three ships when built. The *Wasp*, constructed by Cross and Merrill at Newburyport, was reported to have been built "quite closely" to the design; the other two ships were not, as is evidenced by plans made from the ships afterward. The *Wasp* was lost at sea in 1814 after making a great name for herself and her commander, Blakeley. Her builders, Cross and Merrill, were noted New England shipbuilders. Cross was the business head of the firm; Merrill was the master builder and boss carpenter of their yard. William Cross was the oldest of the twelve children of Ralph Cross, the builder of the Revolutionary ships and, though trained as a shipbuilder, had held a number of civil appointments and also a commission in the state militia.

Orlando B. Merrill was also a member of a shipbuilding family and had a local reputation as a designer as well as a builder. He was one of the early proponents of the use of the "lift" half-model in designing hulls; indeed, some have claimed that he invented this method, but the credit is open to question. Merrill built privateers and revenue cutters on his own account. One of his half-models has survived which is represented to be the first made on the "lift" system. It has been said that the model is of the *Wasp*, but this is in error.

The builders of the *Peacock*, Adam and Noah Brown, had interesting careers. Noah Brown was born in northern New York, one of a large family, in 1770. His father and three brothers were captured by Indians in 1780, and his father was murdered. One of the brothers escaped, and the other two returned home at the end of the war. Two other brothers served in Washington's army; one was killed. His mother, with five small children, Adam and

Figure 56. Original design for ship sloops WASP, PEACOCK, *and* FROLIC, *1813.*

Noah among them, moved to Stamford, Connecticut, at the end of the Revolu-tion. When Noah was fifteen he left home and learned the house carpenter's trade, at which he worked until 1792. In that year he went to New York as a joiner and was employed there in house building until 1804, when he and his brother Adam went to Newark, near Fort Niagara, on the Canadian border and built a schooner named *Work* for the N. W. Fur Company. Later that year they returned to New York and worked a year as ship carpenters for Cheeseman. In 1805 they went to Sag Harbor, Long Island, and built a whaling ship. Then, until 1807, they worked for George Peck, a shipbuilder, in New York. In 1807, Noah went south to cut oak for the frigate *New York* and returned in the fall. Adam and Noah Brown then worked on this frigate until March, 1808, when the two went into the shipbuilding business for them-selves. They engaged in building and repairing merchant vessels and con-structing gunboats until the outbreak of the War of 1812. By this time they were well established as builders, and with the coming of war they went into the construction of privateers. They built the very noted privateers *General Armstrong*, *Prince de Neufchatel*, and *Paul Jones*. They also cut down a ship named *China* into the privateer *Yorktown*. In 1813 they started work on the *Peacock*, apparently before they had received a contract, for on June 29, 1813, they wrote the Navy Department asking for it. There is no evidence that the Browns ever served a formal apprenticeship as shipwrights. Their performance as ship designers and builders is therefore all the more remarkable, particularly as the ships designed by them were usually noted for speed—*Neufchatel* and *Armstrong*, for example. It is known that one of them made plans, but nothing else has been discovered about their designing methods or how they learned this work.

Figure 57 shows the *Peacock* as built, from lines taken off the ship in 1828 while she was hauled up at New York to be taken to pieces. The *Peacock* was a fast ship in heavy winds and was considered an ideal sloop of war. She had the same armament as the *Argus* class except that long 12's were carried instead of long 18's. The Browns had built two brigs on Lake Erie the winter of 1812–13 and had then returned hurriedly to New York to build *Peacock*, which they seem to have completed in about four months.

The *Frolic* was built by Josiah Barker, a Revolutionary War veteran born at Marshfield, Massachusetts, in 1763. He had learned his trade on the North River, not far from his birthplace, and had set up a yard in Charlestown about 1795. Barker was a successful builder and later a naval constructor. He launched

Figure 57a. Lines of PEACOCK, as built.

Figure 57b. Inboard arrangement of PEACOCK.

the sloop in September, 1813, and on April 20, 1814, she was captured after
a 60-mile chase by H.B.M. frigate *Orpheus*, 36, and the ex-American privateer
schooner *Shelbourne*, 12, off the coast of Cuba. The *Frolic* was taken into
the Royal Navy as the *Florida* and was broken up in 1819. Her lines were
taken off by the Admiralty, and her plan is shown in Figure 58. The dimensions
of the *Frolic*, as taken off, were 119′ 5½″ between perpendiculars, 31′ 5½″
moulded beam, and 14′ 2″ depth of hold, which may be compared with *Peacock*'s 119′ 0″ by 31′ 6″, and 14′ 6″ hold. It will be seen that two of the vessels
were longer than designed, as the builders were not held strictly to the official plans. Probably this was due partly to the lack of supervision given the
contractors. This class of ship sloop was more powerful than the majority
of European classes and was to have a lasting influence on American naval
designing.

Though the new frigates were never to get to sea during the war, their
design is of importance in showing the development of the American frigate
that was now taking place. In the preparation of the new design, Doughty
seems to have been influenced to a moderate degree, at least, by his experience at Georgetown before the war. While a designer and builder of merchant craft, he had become well acquainted with the schooners and brigs built
on the Chesapeake and had become a convert to the very sharp model employed on the Bay. His liking for the type is shown in the ship sloops of the
Argus class, in which he had gone to what was then an extreme design for a
ship-rigged vessel. In the *Wasp* class he had been more moderate, and with the
same restraint he incorporated the sharp model in the new frigate design.
Holding closely to the dimensions of the 44's of 1796, he produced quite a
different model. The new ships were given less tumble home and slightly
more deadrise. The ends of the ships, particularly the bows, were sharpened.
Doughty had to proceed rather cautiously in refining the lines of the new
frigates, as he well knew that the ships would have to carry a very heavy
armament. Too great a loss of displacement due to sharp lines would be disastrous.

The new frigates were given less sheer than the older vessels, following a
change in style that had gradually taken place since 1806. While the ships
were to have a complete spar deck, it was decided that the waist was not to be
armed, as experience with the double-banked 44's and 36's of 1796–99 had
shown that the ships were strained by such an arrangement and, in fact, were
overloaded by the additional guns. The *Columbia*, started on the new design,

was burned with the sloop *Argus* at the capture of the city of Washington, so only two ships of the new design were completed, *Guerriere* and *Java*, named after the British frigates captured and destroyed in the first six months of the war. The design of the new frigates is shown in Plan 15. They were plainly finished as befitted men-of-war built in time of war and in haste. The blockade of the Chesapeake and Delaware was too strict to permit the new frigates to escape to sea during the war, but both ships were good sailers. Flannigan, one of the builders of the *Java*, became a noted designer and builder of fast vessels at Baltimore after the War of 1812. One of the Grice brothers, Francis, who was a builder of the *Guerriere*, was afterward a naval constructor in the United States Navy. The *Guerriere* and *Java* were armed with 33 long 24's on the main deck and 20 carronades, 42-pdrs., on the forecastle and quarter-deck. Their dimensions were 175' 0" between perpendiculars, 44' 6" moulded beam, and 13' 8" depth of lower hold, or 31' 1" height of side, rabbet to plank-sheer.

The new frigates should be compared with the *President*, whose plans are shown in Plan 16, as taken off the ship by the British Admiralty after her capture. It will be seen that the *President* had been altered in appearance since her launch, and the drawing shows the general appearance of her sisters *Constitution* and *United States* during the War of 1812. It can be seen how standardized the appearance of the American frigates had become.

In 1813 a few vessels were obtained for the Navy on the coast. A sloop named *Asp*, of 56 tons, was purchased at Alexandria, Virginia. She was armed with a long 18-pdr. and 2 12-pdrs. The *Helen*, a dispatch schooner carrying four 4-pdrs., was bought at Philadelphia in the fall of 1813. A more effective purchase was the 14-gun brig *Rattlesnake*, built at Medford, Massachusetts, as a privateer. Another brig, the 14-gun *Vixen*, was bought at Savannah, but this vessel was not in the American service very long, as she was captured on her way north, without armament or stores aboard, by H.B.M. frigate *Belvidera*, on December 25, 1813. In this year the frigate *Essex* made her famous cruise into the Pacific and manned three prizes which were temporarily on the Navy list: the *Essex Jr.*, 20 guns, 355 tons; the British letter of marque *Atlantic*; the *Georgiana*, 18-gun ship, a whaler; and the *Greenwich*, 338 tons, 20 guns, also a former British letter of marque. These prizes were employed as tenders to the *Essex* rather than as cruisers; only the *Essex Jr.* ever reached the United States, and she came as a cartel carrying the officers and crew of the *Essex* home on parole. In this year the gunboat *No. 166* was renamed *Alligator* and

Figure 58. Lines of FROLIC, as built.

Particulars

O̅ is 43'11" from F.P.
Timber & Room 2'6"
Stations spaced 8'8" and 4'4"
Waterlines from Base
    1st : 1'9"
    2nd : 3'9"
    3rd : 6'9"
    4th : 9'9"
    5th : 12'9"
    6th : 15'9"
    7th : 18'9"
Buttocks spaced 4'0"

Plan 15. *Draught of the improved 44-gun frigates* COLUMBIA, JAVA, *and* GUER-RIERE, *1813.*

Draught of the Frigates "Guerriere", "Java" and "Columbia"
March 1813   by William Doughty

Length bet perps.   175'·0"
Beam moulded   44'·6"
Depth in Hold   13'·8"

Headrails & Cutwater reconstructed to agree with Hawse locations.

References:-
41-9-12 & other copies
33-4-1A
Offsets
Correspondence

Arrangement Plan of Frigates
Guerriere, Java, Columbia 1813

Spar Deck layout in solid lines
Gun Deck   dot & dash lines

Particulars

O sides 3'-4" and fore O is 69'-0" from F.P.
Stations spaced 8'-8" & 4'-4" Room & Space 26"
W.L. up 16'-6" on F.P.; 18'-0" on A.P.
W.L.'s spaced 3'-4" parrallel to above
Buttocks spaced 5'-6"
    Note:- "W.L." is trim of ship as she came
    into Dock and her sailing trim is more by
    the stern. Full load for sea as marked.

Service Trim

Sheer

Rail

Sheer

Own Deck

Rail

Port Sill

Principal Dimensions

Length on the Lower Deck	173'-3"	
" " " Keel for Tonnage	146'-4¼"	
Breadth, Extreme	44'-4"	
" Moulded	43'-8"	
Depth in Hold	13'-11"	
Burthen in Tons	No 1533 ¾ ths	

As taken off at Portsmouth, England,
in 1815.

The United States Frigate "President"

Deck, at side
Gun Deck, at side
Underside of Berth Deck at side

Rail
Service Trim

Plan 16. Draught of the 44-gun frigate PRESIDENT after the Admiralty plans of the ship, showing general appearance of American 44's in the War of 1812. (Sail plan Figure 59.)

Chapelle
Sheer
Port Sill
Rail
L. W.L.

President

Chapelle
Galley

Gun Deck fittings shown in faked lines

Upper Deck
Gun Deck

so carried on the Navy list. A ketch was bought at New Orleans, the *Etna* or *Aetna*, a vessel listed as being 220 tons, carrying 11 guns. This ketch apparently replaced the earlier bomb ketch of the same name. A schooner of 5 guns was purchased at Georgetown, D.C., as a dispatch boat and named *Hornet*, and a few privateer schooners, bottled up in the Chesapeake by the blockade, were hired as lookout vessels in the lower Bay, to warn of British raids and to aid the gunboats in discouraging small British cruisers from attacking local craft. These were the armed schooners *Revenge, Comet, Patapsco,* and *Wasp.* The *Revenge* was 102' long, 23' beam, and 12' hold, customhouse measurement, built at Baltimore in 1812. The *Comet* was 90' 6" x 23' 3" x 10', built at Baltimore in 1810. The *Patapsco* was 101' x 25' x 11' 5", built at Baltimore in 1812. The *Wasp* was 59' x 17' 3" x 6' 3", built at Baltimore in 1810.

This year the American ship sloop *Hornet* captured and sank the British 18-gun brig *Peacock*, of the standard *Cruizer* design. The American brig *Enterprize* captured the British gun brig *Boxer*, a new vessel built in 1812. The *Boxer* was one of a class of twelve brigs of the *Contest* class, all 84' 0" between perpendiculars, 21' 6" moulded beam, and 11' 0" depth of hold and designed to carry 10 18-pdr. carronades and 2 long 6-pdrs. The prize was not taken into the Navy, as she was considered inferior in size and model to the privateers that might be readily purchased. The former American privateer schooner *Highflyer*, which had been taken into the British Navy as a tender, was also taken but was sold to private owners.

The Americans suffered the loss of three cruisers this year, the most serious being the fine frigate *Chesapeake*, taken by the *Shannon* off Boston. It will be remembered that the *Chesapeake* was not built to the design of the *Constellation* and *Congress*, but to an independent design by Josiah Fox. The original plan of the ship was not retained in the American Navy files, but may be the plan marked "Congress" in the Fox Papers. However, after her capture the lines of the ship were taken off and drawn by Admiralty draftsmen, so a record of her design exists. Plan 17 shows the lines of this beautiful though unfortunate frigate. She was quite different from her sisters in model; in fact, she was somewhat like the *Philadelphia*, which had been lost at Tripoli. The *Chesapeake* was a sharp frigate, compared to the others built before the War of 1812; she had the reputation of being very fast, but her reputation for being unlucky had been firmly established by the *Chesapeake-Leopard* affair. The *Chesapeake* measured 152' 6" between perpendiculars, 40' 4" moulded beam, and 13' 9" depth of hold. Though Fox intended her to be a small 44,

President, 1814

Figure 59. Sail plan of PRESIDENT in War of 1812. (See plan 16.)

she was rated as a 36-gun frigate in the American Navy. Her armament was 28 long 18's on the main deck, 16 32-pdr. carronades on the quarterdeck, and 4 carronades, 32-pdrs., on the forecastle. The *Shannon* was 150′ 1½″ between perpendiculars, 39′ 3″ moulded beam, and 12′ 9″ depth of hold. She was a sister ship of the *Tanais*, on the design of the *Leda*, 38 guns; this class was one of the few frigates having square-tuck sterns at this date.

The brig *Argus* was taken in the Channel by the British brig *Pelican*, another of the numerous *Cruizer* type. The British brig rated as 18 guns, and was 100′ 0″ between perpendiculars, 30′ 0″ moulded beam, and 12′ 9″ depth of hold—altogether a larger and more powerful brig than her American opponent, as may be seen by comparing the dimensions of the *Pelican* with those of the *Argus*, given on her drawing.

The *Viper*, ex *Ferret*, was captured in January of 1813 by the British frigate *Narcissus* after a chase in strong winds. The sloop *Asp* was taken in a boat attack in the Chesapeake and set on fire, but her crew got aboard her again in time to save the sloop. The revenue cutter *Surveyor* was also taken by a boat attack in the Chesapeake. Gunboats had been largely employed in defending coastwise trade in protected waters, such as the Chesapeake and Long Island Sound, or were used for harbor defense, and occasionally one was captured by British boats. Attempts to attack British ships with small gunboat squadrons were wholly unsuccessful, owing partly to the lack of training of the gunboat crews and partly to the small size of the boats employed. Nevertheless, the gunboats were often useful in preventing the boats of the British blockading squadrons from raiding isolated towns and farms for provisions and loot.

The Americans were more successful on the lakes in 1813, owing to the efforts of their builders to produce enough vessels to meet their opponents. Lake Erie was the center of much naval activity in this year. When navigation ended in 1812, the Americans had but one small brig, the *Caledonia*, which, with the brig *Detroit*, ex *Adams*, had been captured by an American boat attack. The *Detroit*, however, had gone ashore after the attack and had been destroyed. Their other vessels were the three small purchased craft, *Somers*, *Tigress*, and *Trippe*, 1 gun each, and the new schooner *Scorpion*, 2 guns. Lieut. Oliver H. Perry had been ordered to Lake Erie, and being senior to Elliott he was now the commodore. In January of 1813, the Navy Department sent Adam and Noah Brown to Lake Erie with instructions to build two large brigs. Noah Brown left New York February 14 with a small gang of carpenters and arrived at Presque Isle on the 24th. Brown went to work at once, but having few men he could make little progress until early March, when more carpenters arrived from New York. Adam had remained at home to procure men and to operate the yard in New York. By this time Noah Brown had most of the timber and framing cut for the two brigs, as well as for three schooners. In April another draft of men from New York reached Brown, and in May some more carpenters came from Philadelphia. In all Brown finally had two hundred men, but he was short of caulking material and iron. A British schooner was found, frozen in the ice in the lake, so Brown and his men went to her, getting provisions, rigging, and cables; they then burned her to get what iron they could. By scouring the near-by posts and settlements, Brown obtained enough iron to complete his task. Finally, late in the spring, he received oakum and iron which the government had been unable to forward earlier because of bad roads. Brown also had great difficulty in getting provisions, which led to strikes that Brown had to settle by convincing the men that he was getting all the food possible. Noah Brown returned to New York in July, leaving his foreman, Sidney Wright, later a noted New York shipbuilder, and sixteen carpenters to finish up. Brown had designed and built two large brigs, the *Lawrence* and *Niagara*, the 75-ton schooner *Ariel*, the gunboat schooner *Ohio*, the *Porcupine*, and probably the *Scorpion*, and had rebuilt the *Tigress*. He was not paid for this work, by the way, until March, 1814.

Brown also built a blockhouse 30' square, a guardhouse 40' x 20', a cook and mess building 100' x 20' (with a loft which was used as a barracks for the carpenters), a blacksmith shop 80' x 16', a barracks for fifty men, an office for Brown and Perry (18' x 18'), four camels or floats to get the brigs over the bar, fourteen boats for the fleet, and all the gun carriages. In building the vessels, Brown was responsible for all woodwork from hull to spars, tops, boats, and gun carriages; the rigging and the sailmaking were done by the crews that were being slowly collected by Perry. The amount of work that Brown accomplished with about 200 men, without power tools, and in a wilderness during the worst winter months, makes some of the modern wartime production feats something less than impressive. The man was tireless and ingenious.

No drawings of the Erie squadron appear to have reached the Navy Department. At the end of the War of 1812 the serviceable vessels were stripped and the hulls sunk to preserve them. The two brigs were thus preserved for many years, but unfortunately no accurate record was made. The hulk of the *Niagara* was raised in 1913, under the supervision of Captain W. L. Morrison of the

Wolverine (ex *Michigan*). The state of the wreckage required extensive re-search in order to make a restoration. With the limited information then available, the brig was rebuilt. In 1939, it was again necessary to rebuild the *Niagara*, and the writer was commissioned to prepare the new plans. With the assistance of Captain Morrison and Captain Stephen C. Rowan, U.S.N., another attempt at restoration was made. The results are shown in Figure 60. It should be observed that this drawing cannot be accepted as wholly accurate, as the topsides of the original brig had rotted so much that little could be preserved when she was raised in 1913. The ends of the ship were particularly difficult to determine; the writer therefore assumes the responsibility for the revised drawing presented here. The reconstructed brig, as built by the Com-monwealth of Pennsylvania (now exhibited at Erie), differs slightly from the plan shown in Figure 60. According to what could be determined from the remains of the original brig, and the dimensions given in contemporary papers, the two brigs were each 110′ 0″ between perpendiculars, 29′ 0″ moulded beam, and 9′ 0″ hold. There is a wide difference of opinion as to whether the brigs had a gammon knee, a plain raking stem, or a cutwater and headrails. In view of the speed with which Brown ran up these vessels, the writer leans toward a belief in a plain stem or a gammon knee. The deck arrangement is wholly conjectural and is based on British war brigs of approximately the same date. Figure 61 shows a design of a British man-of-war brig, designed in 1815 for Lake Champlain, which gives some support to the writer's restoration and is the authority for the greater part of the doubtful details included in the reconstruction drawing of the *Niagara*.

The two brigs were launched in May and by means of the two "camels," or floats, were carried over the sand bar into the lake. The "camels" were two rectangular barges, with one side shaped to fit closely under the hull of the brigs, which could be submerged and secured to each of the brigs in turn, and then pumped out and raised. This would lift the brig and reduce her draft enough to cross the bar that separated the building site from the open lake.

The *Ariel* was a clipper schooner with low bulwarks and had her four long 12-pdr. guns mounted on pivots—one forward of the foremast, two between the masts, and one abaft the main. She was designed for speed, and Brown claimed that nothing on the lake could sail with her. The *Porcupine* had one long 32-pdr. on a pivot and two 12-pdr. carronades. The *Ohio* had one long gun on a pivot, and the *Scorpion* seems to have been a sister ship of the *Porcu-pine*. Some accounts indicate that the *Tigress* was not a purchased vessel but

Figure 60. A reconstruction of the brigs LAWRENCE *and* NIAGARA.

271

was a "gunboat" built by Brown. Brown, as a matter of fact, wrote that he
.built *Porcupine, Scorpion,* and *Tigress,* but this was long after the event,
when his memory may have been at fault. With respect to *Scorpion,* it seems
reasonable that Brown built her and that the record that she was built in the
fall of 1812 is an error, for it is doubtful that there were ship carpenters at
Presque Isle before Brown arrived. It is possible, of course, that the *Tigress*
was also built by Brown and was not the *Amelia,* renamed, as there is much
confusion in the records of the lake vessels, particularly as many had changes
of name. Perry's victory in September liquidated the British squadron on Erie,
and the captured vessels were taken into the American service—the *Detroit,*

*Figure 61. An Admiralty design for brigs to be built on Lake Champlain, 1815,
showing characteristics of brigs used on the American lakes.*

18, and the *Queen Charlotte,* 16, as ship sloops, the *General Hunter* as the
brig *Hunter,* 10 guns, the schooner *Lady Prevost* as a 10-gun schooner, and the
Little Belt as a 3-gun schooner. The *Detroit* and *General Hunter* had been
built at Malden, now Amherstburg, in 1806, and the *Queen Charlotte* had been
built in the same place the following year. The *Lady Prevost* was also built
at Malden, in 1810. These British-Canadian vessels were somewhat deeper
draft than the American brigs built on Lake Erie, as the former's designs
were not controlled by the shallow channel at Presque Isle.

By 1813, the building race on Lake Ontario was well under way. The winter
of 1812–13 was a severe one, and both sides were greatly handicapped by deep
snows and extreme cold, which made the movement of supplies, materials, and
munitions in from the coast a very uncertain matter. Lack of shelter and poor
food, as well as unsanitary living conditions, created much sickness among the
carpenters on both sides of the lake, and this caused unforeseen delays. How-

ever, Henry Eckford was on the same mould as the Browns; he rushed the *Madison* to completion; hurriedly designed and built a small sharp dispatch boat, the schooner *Lady of the Lake*, 89 tons and 5 guns; and started the *General Pike*, a very large 24-gun ship, and a large sharp schooner, the *Sylph*. The *General Pike* was launched 63 days from the day her keel was laid; she was a flush-decked corvette 145′ 0″ between perpendiculars, 37′ 0″ beam, and 15′ 0″ depth, armed with 26 long 24's and 2 pivot guns, probably 24-pdrs. also. The *Sylph* was built in 23 working days, to launching, and was variously armed. At one time she seems to have had 4 long 32-pdrs. on pivots, with 12 long 6-pdrs. on broadside carriages; a year after her launch she was rerigged as a brig and carried 2 long 7's and 16 carronades, 24-pdrs., so apparently her original rig and armament were not considered satisfactory. She must have been a large vessel, as her tonnage is given variously as 300 and 350 tons. Except for a sail plan of the *Pike*, no drawings have been found of these vessels.

On August 24, 1813, the Secretary of the Navy wrote the New York Navy Agent to ask the Browns if they would proceed to Sackett's Harbor and build three sloops exactly like *Peacock*. The Browns agreed, and it was also suggested that they join with Eckford or that he build one sloop. Nothing seems to have come of this, but the incident suggests the possibility that the designs of the 1813 ship sloops and frigates may have been used as the basis of some of the Lake Ontario vessels. However, it is highly probable that Eckford prepared plans for most of the ships built on the lake. The exact relation between the Browns and Eckford is not clear. From official correspondence it would appear that Eckford was in charge of all shipbuilding on the lakes; on the other hand, the contracts with the Browns were independent of Eckford's contracts. For example, the Browns had a contract for building two ships of the line and a frigate at Sackett's Harbor dated December 15, 1814. On this the *New Orleans*, *Chippewa*, and *Plattsburg* were started, and there is no evidence that Eckford had anything to do with them.

In addition to the new vessels built on Ontario, three more schooners were purchased, the *Asp* of 57 tons and 2 guns, the *Ontario*, 2 guns, and the *Mary*, 50 tons. The last was renamed *Raven* and was fitted with a mortar but was usually regarded as a transport and supply vessel. The combination of large vessels of the seagoing type—*General Pike*, *Madison*, *Oneida*, and *Sylph*—with lake schooners created a very unhandy squadron. Effective in smooth water, the squadron was difficult to manage in strong winds, as the small lake vessels were prone to capsize. The *Hamilton* and *Scourge* foundered in a squall in the early morning of August 8. Two days later the schooners *Growler* and *Julia* were captured by the British in the face of the American squadron, through Chauncey's mismanagement and the failure of the two schooners to obey the commodore's signals. The two schooners were recaptured the same season, however, so they were not lost to the Americans.

In the winter of 1812 the British had started the construction of two sloops of war, one at York named *Sir Isaac Brock* and one at Kingston, named *Wolfe*. Yeo had difficulty in getting his building program started, and the two vessels were much delayed. York was weakly defended, and in the spring of 1813 Chauncey attacked the place and captured it with the aid of some troops. He destroyed the *Sir Isaac Brock* on the stocks and carried away a small brig, the *Gloucester*, 10 guns, which he found in the harbor. The *Gloucester* does not appear to have been a serviceable craft, for she was not employed as a cruiser in the American service. The remaining ship sloop, *Wolfe*, was launched at Kingston early in the spring, making the British temporarily superior in force to the Americans. The British fighting squadron now consisted of the *Wolfe* and *Royal George*, ship sloops, the *Earl of Moira, Prince Regent, Sydney Smith*, and *Lord Melville*, brigs, and the schooner transports *Seneca* and *Simcoe*, as well as a few gunboats. When the Americans launched the *Pike* they again became superior in force. Throughout the remaining years of the war Ontario was the scene of very cautious warfare. As either side launched a powerful ship the other retired from the lake, until his builders again made him apparently superior in force. The British ships on the lake in 1813 were relatively small: the *Wolfe* and *Royal George* have been described; the *Prince Regent* was a 71' brig built in 1812, the *Melville* was about 73' long, and the *Moira* 70'. The end of the year saw the British shipwrights at work on two frigates, the *Prince Regent*, carrying 58 guns, and the *Princess Charlotte*, first named *Vittoria*, carrying 42. They also laid down a large ship of the line, the *St. Lawrence*. The Americans, hearing of this, prepared to build additional ships, but they were later in getting started on their program than the British.

Lake Champlain was the scene of some activity. Here Lieut. Thomas Macdonough was now the American commander with a force of two sloops, the *Eagle* and *Growler*, and two one-gun row barges. He also had the sloop *President* awaiting men. Late in June he sent the *Eagle* and *Growler* up to the head of the lake to harass the British. The two sloops chased three British gunboats into the Sorel and were ambushed. The *Eagle* sank in shoal water, and the

Figure 62. Plans of barges and row galleys in the American Navy, 1813–14.

Growler was captured after she ran ashore. The *Eagle* was raised, and the two sloops were taken into the British service. The *Eagle* was first renamed *Broke,* then *Finch* (or *Tench*), and the *Growler* became the *Shannon,* then *Chub* or *Chubb.* The British thus won control of the lake, and Macdonough set about obtaining vessels to regain it. He bought a schooner, or sloop, named *Montgomery*, to carry 7 long 9's and 2 carronades, 18-pdrs., and a sloop named *Preble,* which he armed with 7 long 12's and 2 18-pdr. columbiads. The columbiads were forerunners of the shell guns that appeared after the War of 1812. They were apparently short large-bore cannon, sometimes made by reboring old guns to fire hollow shot and bombshells. They appear to have been much lighter in weight than the regular naval gun and were intended as improvements on the standard naval carronade; most of these guns were classed as 18-pdrs. in the War of 1812. Macdonough also hired a sloop named *Frances* and armed her with 4 12-pdrs. and an 18-pdr. columbiad. As it was obvious that it would soon be necessary to build additional craft, Macdonough applied to the Navy Department for a builder. With the few carpenters available, the barge *Alwyn,* one gun, was built at the American base, Vergennes, Vt. A small sloop was chartered by Macdonough to serve as a dispatch boat on the lake; this was the *Wasp,* 5 guns.

During 1813 Doughty designed a new class of gunboat, the barge. These were double-enders, somewhat like large whaleboats, armed either with a single gun or with one long gun aft and a carronade forward. The barges were sometimes rigged for sailing with one or two lateen sails, but the smaller boats were sometimes fitted for rowing only. The first design was for a 50' barge, made in June, 1813, and building began on the plan in July or August. This design, shown in Figure 62, is probably the one used for the *Alwyn,* built that year on Champlain. The new design called for boats 50' long, 12' moulded beam, and 3' 6" total depth. In September Doughty made another design, this time for a barge 75' over all, 15' beam and 4' 0" depth. This is also shown in Figure 62, and the boats built from it were usually rigged with one or two lateen sails. Late in the year a third barge design was made, for a boat only 40' long, 10' beam, and 3' depth and fitted to row only. This plan is shown in Figure 63. These barges were intended for Lakes Champlain and Ontario, the Chesapeake, and rivers, and were not in any way seagoing coast-defense gunboats. The American barges were, in fact, the counterparts of the large launches carried by some British blockading ships for boat attacks and raids inshore.

Doughty was now acting as the chief naval constructor, with his station in the Washington Navy Yard. Henry Allen was either his apprentice or his assistant. Nearly all of the plans of new ships prepared by Doughty in the war years are preserved only in the working copies made by Allen; the originals cannot now be found. On April 17, 1813, Samuel Humphreys was ap-

Figure 63. Plans of a small row galley by William Doughty.

pointed naval constructor at the Philadelphia Yard. He spent a good part of the year getting the neglected navy yard into working order. Samuel Humphreys, unlike his father, was a competent draftsman and a very able ship designer, rather more conservative than Doughty, but he appears to have designed only one ship during the War of 1812. He had been born in Philadelphia, November 23, 1778, and had worked with his father until the frigate *United States* had been completed, after which he went into business for himself and had a number of associates or partners. Samuel Humphreys, like Doughty, was a strong adherent to sharp-floored small vessels, and Humphreys had designed a number of very sharp schooners before his appointment to the Philadelphia Yard.

Because of the modest building program begun in 1813 the small construction organization was adequate, and the only weakness was the lack of supervision of the contract builders by trained naval inspectors. As before, the building supervisors were usually commissioned officers. The general administration of the Navy was, however, remarkably inefficient; the incompetent secretary and staff were still attempting to manage naval affairs on a political level without regard to the necessities of war. There was no change of importance in the naval administration, and matters proceeded in the same haphazard fashion as before the war. Once again most of the shipbuilding contracts were placed in a relatively confined area, with two vessels building at Washington, three at Baltimore, and one each at Philadelphia, New York, Newburyport, and Boston. Thus five of the vessels could have been kept from getting to sea by merely blockading the mouth of the Chesapeake Bay; the others, with one exception, were in ports of such importance that their blockade was assured when the war began. The placing of the contracts seems to have been hurried, without any regard to the problems of getting the finished vessels to sea. There was still some idea that the government could build ships faster and more cheaply than private contractors. This is indicated by the choice of the Washington Navy Yard to build a frigate and a sloop, though the experience of building the earlier *Wasp* and *Hornet* had shown that the Navy Yard was slower and more costly than the private shipyards. The old tendency to concentrate shipbuilding contracts near the national capital is worthy of notice. There were always "practical" reasons for this. However, the records show that, in view of the huge number of privateers built in 1813, most of which were set up in small towns and villages from Georgia to Maine, there could have been no practical difficulty in spreading out the naval building program, away from the large ports or from those areas whose importance assured an immediate blockade. By the end of 1813 the Chesapeake and the ports of New York, Philadelphia, and Boston were under such strict blockade that even the very fast privateers were having great difficulty in escaping to sea.

The coasting trade was now at a halt, and the privateers and a few fast letters of marque were the only sources of employment; the Navy was still too small to require a large part of the available seamen. The shipyards were busy, however, turning out privateers and letters of marque. By the middle of 1813 the day of the small privateer was practically over. The new type included large schooners, brigantines, and brigs, 90 to 115 feet in length, heavily armed, and worthy antagonists for the smaller British cruisers, and large armed merchant ships.

Of the Navy vessels building under the new program, only the *Frolic* and *Peacock* were launched in 1813, September 11 and September 27 respectively. But neither got to sea until 1814, by which time the *Wasp* was also ready. These three cost almost a third more to build, curiously enough, than each of the two Baltimore-built sloops whose building was much delayed by the shortages of shipwrights caused by the demand for such men to build privateers at Baltimore and on the shores of the Chesapeake. The estimates also indicated that the Navy Yard sloop was going to cost more than any of the others.

At the end of 1813, the need of ships of the line to break the British blockade was fully apparent, and pressure was now being placed on the government to build such ships. It appears that work on the designs for two or three liners was started as early as November of this year. Humphreys probably began designing one to be built at Philadelphia, and Doughty may have made a design for two sisters to be built at Boston and Portsmouth, New Hampshire, but the records are not clear as to either the date the designs were ordered or as to the responsibility for the design of the New England–built 74's.

Early in 1814 the American frigate *Essex* was captured by the British frigate *Phoebe*, 36, and the ship sloop *Cherub*, 18, at Valparaiso, which ended the destructive career of the American cruiser in the Pacific. The first of the new ship sloops to sail was the *Frolic*, in early February. She met a South American "privateer" or pirate and sank her with a single broadside. On April 20, she met H.B.M. frigate *Orpheus*, 36, and an ex-American privateer schooner, now H.B.M. schooner *Shelburne*, 12 guns, and a thirteen-hour chase ensued. The American beat to windward in an effort to escape, but after having thrown overboard her guns, boats, and stores, the sloop was forced to surrender and was taken into the Royal Navy under the name *Florida*. She was finally broken up at Chatham Dockyard in 1819.

The *Peacock* was the next to get to sea, sailing from New York March 12. On the 28th of April she fell in with a small convoy of British merchantmen bound for the Bermudas under the protection of the 18-gun brig *Epervier*, a new brig (or properly "brigantine," since she did not have the spencer mast on her main as in a naval "brig") laid down in 1812 at Rochester, England, by Mrs. Mary Ross, who seems to have been the owner of a well-known yard there. *Epervier* was ordered to carry 16 guns and was on the lines of the 18-gun brig *Cruizer*. The *Peacock* captured the *Epervier* in a short action. The prize, being new and still in serviceable state, was sent home and was purchased into the United States Navy under the same name as an 18-gun brig, armed with 32-pdr. carronades. The brig was considered a fine vessel of her class. Her plan as redrawn from her design draught is shown in Figure 64. In the past, historians have speculated as to the relative size of the British 18-gun brigs and their American opponents, *Argus, Hornet, Wasp*, and *Peacock*. The plan of the *Epervier* will settle the question. This brig was exactly the dimensions of the standard *Cruizer* and on her exact hull lines except for a slightly modified sheer and alterations in her cutwater and above-water appearance. The *Epervier* was one of the *Bacchus* class built in 1811–12.

With the fall of Napoleon, the British were able to give more attention to the American war. The destruction caused by the big American privateers added to the startling defeats of British frigates and man-of-war brigs were matters too important to be left unattended. Not only did the blockade become more strict, but shore attacks were made in an effort to liquidate both American privateers and naval vessels before they could get to sea. The Chesapeake was the scene of many British raids, and as the year drew to a close the Bay was almost completely sealed against the escape of American raiders. In the process, land expeditions were made against the cities of Washington and Baltimore. In the Washington adventure the British were eminently successful, and not only captured the national capital and destroyed many of the public buildings, but they also forced the Americans to burn the navy yard with the two new ships on the stocks, the sloop *Argus* and the frigate *Columbia*. The old frigates *New York* and *Boston* were also destroyed. In the preliminary actions on the Bay, before the capture of Washington, the American gunboats were in combat but had little success. The reports of the American officers indicate the basic trouble with the American boats. With few exceptions they were too small to carry their guns and to withstand the recoil, and owing to their small size they could not carry men enough to resist British boat attacks, to which gunboats were particularly susceptible.

The Medford-built brig *Rattlesnake* was also lost to the American service in this year. She was taken in June, off Cape Sable, by H.B.M. frigate *Leander*, 50, after a long chase in which the brig threw overboard all but two of her guns. The small, fast American cruisers were usually captured in blowing weather by British frigates or liners, when the greater size of the pursuer gave her the advantage.

Figure 64. Plan of prize brig EPERVIER, showing hull form and dimensions of British 18-gun brigs in action against the Americans in the War of 1812.

American perp

Gun Deck

Fore Sill

Rail

Spars

	Masts			Yards		
	Length		Dia.	Length		Dia.
	Yds	In	In	Yds	In	In
Main	30	0	30	27	26	13½
Top	18	9	17½	20	9	12⅞
Galt	9	7	9½	12	13	7½
Fore	27	22	26½	24	7	16¾
Top	16	30	16¾	18	2	11½
Galt	8	3	8	11	0	6½
Mizzen	23	20	22½	14	6	10½
Top	17	27	16¾	13	26	8½
Galt	6	32	6½	9	24	5½
Bowsprit	20	3	28¾	18	2	11½
Jibboom	11	12	12	11	0	6½
Crossjack				20	9	12⅞

Galf

Chesapeake

Length bet. perps   151'-0"   (153'-10" American perps. btd
Beam moulded   40'-4"   153'-0" as designed;
" extreme   40'-11"   Beam moulded intended
Depth in hold   13'-9"   to have been 40'-0"
As taken off in the   and depth of hold 14'-0")
Plymouth Dockyard, Dec. 1814

Particulars
O is 61'-0" from F.P.
Stations spaced 9'-11" and 4'-11½"= Room & Space 2'-5¾"
W.L. N° 1 is 16" above Base.
" 2 - 40" "
Other W.L.'s are 3'-0" apart.
Buttocks " 4'-0" " .

American
Perp.

Chapelle.

References
Admiralty Draught
Fox Papers

Plan 17. Draught of the frigate CHESAPEAKE *as she appeared in the War of 1812, after the Admiralty drawings of the ship.*

Plan 18. Draught of the American
74-gun ship FRANKLIN, showing
alterations made in the original
design.

Building Draught of the "Franklin", 74 guns.
by Sam. Humphreys
Length bet. perps.   187: 10¾"
Beam moulded   50: 0"
Depth in hold   19: 9"

References 40·15·22, 40·15·50
S. Humphreys' correspondence
Lenthall's Papers

Chapelle

Sheer Elevation of the "Franklin"
showing present trim with the additional stores etc. aboard
representing the unsafe condition complained of, 1824

Alterations shown
Handrails & Cutwater altered
Bowsprit lowered
Catheads shortened
Sill Port added
Chanwork & Chains altered
Quarter Deck & Forecastle Rails
lowered and lengthened
Port added, Forecastle Rail
Main Mast shifted
Quarter galleries enlarged
Stern Arch lowered
Rudder enlarged
Ordered since 1815

Chapelle

References Lenthall's plan, Doughty's
report, Yard Commandant's Letters

The *Wasp*, of the new ship-sloop class, got to sea this year, leaving Portsmouth, New Hampshire, on May 1. She fought and captured the British brigs *Reindeer* and *Avon*. The first of these was burned, and the second sank after the *Wasp* had been driven off by other British cruisers. The *Wasp* disappeared in the fall of the year, and it is assumed she foundered with all hands.

The brig *Syren* was captured in strong winds off the West African coast on July 12 by the British 74 *Medway*. As usual, the American brig tried to escape to windward and threw overboard boats, guns, and gear in an effort to get away. The *Syren* was retained in the British service but does not appear to have been employed as a cruiser. In 1815 she was stripped and housed over to be used as a "lazaretto," or hospital ship for contagious diseases.

The *Adams*, now a large flush-deck corvette carrying 26 18-pdr. columbiads and 1 long 12-pdr., had gone to sea, out of the Chesapeake, in January. Her cruise was not very successful so far as captures were concerned, though the numerous times she was chased show that she was as fast as a sloop as she had been as a 28-gun frigate. As a vessel of the latter class she had been considered too sharp; it is a pity that her design cannot be found. The *Adams* finally ran into the Penobscot, in Maine, and in September she was attacked by British boats and her crew destroyed her to prevent capture.

In December the British began operations against New Orleans. Five American gunboats and two tenders were taken in a boat attack on Lake Borgne—*Nos. 5, 23, 156, 162*, and *163*, and the *Alligator* and *Seahorse*. The schooner *Carolina* was subsequently burned, on December 27, during the military operations before New Orleans, while in action against the British.

In addition to the three brigs, *Epervier, Reindeer,* and *Avon,* the British schooners *Pictou* (a former American privateer), *Ballahou,* and *Landrail* were captured and the 22-gun ship sloop *Hermes* was sunk while attacking an American fort. The *Ballahou* and *Landrail* were not impressive captures; they were no more effective vessels than the small American gunboats, being tiny schooners 55' to 56' long on deck and about 18' beam, on a Bermuda design. So far as naval ships were concerned, it can be seen that the British suffered no important losses at sea in this year.

By the end of 1814 it was apparent that the privateers were not effective weapons in a naval war. Though destructive to British commerce and, in combination with the letter of marques, able to bring into the United States many cargoes of great value, they were substitutes neither for naval vessels nor for merchant traders. The privateers could rarely whip any but the smallest and weakest of the British naval cruisers, and indeed, with few exceptions, were not inclined to attack regular naval ships. Thus, they were of no benefit in breaking the strangling blockade. Neither privateer nor letter of marque was effective in cargo carrying; too much capacity had to be sacrificed for speed and gun carrying. Though the privateers often captured very valuable and useful cargoes, too often they did not bring home the items most needed. Of course, a privateer could hardly go about shopping for, say, boots: she had to take what fell in her way. This made prize cargoes of relatively little value in a war economy. The belated realization of this, combined with the effect of naval successes on public opinion, now induced the administration to try to establish an effective navy capable not only of breaking the blockade but also of being far more destructive to the British merchant marine than anything before.

The new plans called for three 74-gun ships to be built, and in addition two squadrons of fast brigs and schooners were to be sent out under Commodores Porter and Perry. The vessels of these two squadrons were to be equal to the best privateers in speed and power but, in the hands of regular naval officers, would be ready to attack British convoy guards or light cruisers and to burn and destroy merchantmen without the necessity of taking prizes for a profit, as was required in privateers. In addition, a number of small craft were to be obtained for use as dispatch vessels, service craft at navy yards, and supply and transport craft, and for other purposes.

The small craft taken into the Navy in this year were schooners and sloops. *Buffalo*, sloop, was bought at Philadelphia for a transport and armed with 4 short 18-pdrs. and 1 long 6. The *Bulldog* was a felucca of 2 guns bought at New Orleans. *Camel* was a sloop tender bought at Philadelphia and armed with 2 long 18's and a long 4 as well as 2 carronades, 24-pdrs. The *Corporation* and *Dispatch* were two schooners of about 50 tons, each armed with two small guns, bought on the coast as packets. Another schooner was the *Ranger*, one gun, bought at Baltimore as a lookout vessel on the Chesapeake. A store ship, the schooner *Tom Bowline*, of 260 tons, was bought at Portsmouth, New Hampshire, in this year and rerigged as a brig or brigantine. This vessel was intended to cruise with one of the two squadrons of light cruisers. Another purchase was a schooner named *Torpedo*, for which no description or intended service has yet been found. A 7-gun schooner, the *Roanoke*, was transferred from the State Department to the Navy.

It was expected that the three 74's could not be completed within a year and that they would not be at sea for at least 18 months after their keels were laid. The 74 *Franklin* was designed by Samuel Humphreys and was built at Philadelphia, apparently under contract, by Humphreys and Penrose; Samuel Humphreys was thus both designer and one of the builders. As originally designed (Plan 18), her appearance was somewhat like the 1799 design of the 74's, except for the round bow and some variations in sheer plan. She was altered both during construction and after launch. Her service appearance is also shown in Plan 18. Her appearance was much admired; she measured 187' 10¾"

32-pdr. carronade mounting, FRANKLIN, *1815*.

between perpendiculars, 50' moulded beam, and 19' 9" depth of hold. Armed with 30 long 32-pdrs., 55 cwt. each, 33 long 32's of 50 cwt. each, and 24 carronades, 32-pdrs., she was found to be overloaded and below her lines to an undesirable degree. She was launched in August, 1815, too late to see action in the war.

The other two 74's were the *Washington*, built at Portsmouth, New Hampshire, by contract with Hartt and Badger, and launched in October, 1814, and the *Independence*, built by Hartt and Barker at Charlestown, Massachusetts, and launched in July, 1814. No design for these two 74's has been found, but both were close to 190' 0" between perpendiculars, 50' moulded beam, and 20' depth of hold; the *Washington* appears to have been 10" longer and 7"

Figure 65. Draught of an American 16-gun brig, 1815.

wider than *Independence*. It is therefore probable that they were on the same plan. Whether Doughty was the designer or whether the vessels were designed by one of the Hartts is uncertain. Apparently no plan for either was ever sent to the Navy Department, for some years later, when the *Independence* was cut down into a huge frigate or "razee," her lines were taken off.

In addition to the 74's, there was to be some building to make up the two raiding squadrons. Three fast brigs were to be built: the *Boxer*, 14 guns, by

Medium and long 32-pdr. gun carriages, FRANKLIN, *1815.*

Beldin and Churchill at Middletown, Connecticut; the *Saranac*, 16 guns, by the same builders; and the *Chippewa* or *Chippeway*, 16, at Warren, Rhode Island. These brigs were to be designed by Doughty, who, it appears, had re-established himself at Washington after the British evacuation. Though the plans of each of the three brigs cannot be identified with certainty, the two brigs shown in Figures 65 and 66 may well represent the two plans used for the three brigs. Figure 65 shows a brig pierced to show 16 guns exclusive of the bridle ports. The design was for a clipper brig 96' 6" between perpen-

Figure 66. Draught of an American 18-gun brig, 1815.

diculars, 27' 0" moulded beam, and 12' 6" depth of hold. The plan was approved by the Navy Commissioners late in 1815, though it was made early in
the year, as there is a reference to the plans of brigs in January. The second
design was for a clipper 18-gun brig, 108' 0" between perpendiculars, 29' 9"
moulded beam, and 13' 9" depth of hold. The three brigs were said to have
been hurriedly built of green timber, for though they sailed well they were
soon rotten. The records of the three brigs are unsatisfactory, as there was
apparently some confusion about their tonnage and armament in the official
correspondence. They were to carry 2 long 18's and 2 long 12's, and the
balance of their armaments was to be made up of 32-pdr. carronades. Each
brig was to carry two more guns than her rating, "as this can be done without
filling the bridle-ports," according to one officer's letter. From this it would
appear that the designs had been prepared for larger vessels than the official
ratings. The three brigs were to be part of one squadron of four under Perry,
the fourth being the purchased hermaphrodite schooner *Prometheus*, which
had been bought in this year at Philadelphia. The *Prometheus* had been built
for a privateer under the name *Escape* by William Sequin at Philadelphia and
was bought there from her owners, Savage and Dryan. She was a typical vessel
of her class, judging by the only drawing of the schooner that has been found,
a carefully detailed sail plan, about 100' on deck, 82' keel, 27' beam and 11' 4"
depth of hold, with raking ends, gammon knee head, and plain, unadorned
stern. She was pierced to carry 14 guns excluding bridle ports, but was now
armed with 2 long 32's, 4 long 9's, and 6 carronades, 32-pdrs.

   The second squadron was to be comprised of five vessels under Porter: the
brigs *Spark*, 14, and *Firefly*, 14, and the schooners *Torch*, 12, *Spitfire*, 10, and
Eagle, 12. A reserve squadron, in effect, was established by the existence of
the *Epervier*, to which were added by purchase the brig *Flambeau*, 14, and
by building, the 6-gun schooner *Lynx*. All of these vessels, except the *Epervier*
and *Lynx*, were built as privateers and then purchased by the government.
The *Spark* was a particularly fine brig built at Sag Harbor, Long Island, New
York, in 1814; she was launched 40 days from the time her keel was laid. She
had been built for Baltimore owners, who had placed the contract at Sag
Harbor because the Chesapeake was so tightly corked by the British that it
was now too risky to attempt to run out, and was probably built to a Maryland
design. Both her model and numerous plans have survived. Her lines are shown
in Figure 67, drawn from a plan owned by Constructor Lenthall, and checked
against her builder's half-model and offsets. Her sail plan has also survived

Figure 67. Draught of brig SPARK, *1815, clipper model.*

289

and is presented here. This brig had a remarkable reputation for sailing qualities and for this reason was recorded, even though she had not been Navy-
designed. She was 100′ between perpendiculars, 26′ moulded beam, and 12′
depth of hold. Some accounts state that she was built in 1813. This brig should
be compared with the two Doughty designs, Figures 65 and 66, to show the
characteristics of the design of clipper brigs in this period. It will be seen
that an almost standard hull model was now in use. Comparison of the sail plans
of the *Chippewa* and *Spark* will also be interesting, in that the two contemporary drawings show the rig of a naval brig in one case and a clipper brig in
the other; the latter (for the *Spark*) shows a lighter rig than the naval brig.
These sail plans show better than words the great spread of sail carried by the
small vessels of this period. The *Spark* was armed with 2 long 18's and 10
carronades, 18-pdrs.

Comparison of the lines of the *Spark* with those of the 16- and 18-gun brigs
shows the effect of naval requirements on vessels of approximately the same
size as the *Spark*. The latter, a successful man-of-war, was much lighter in displacement than her naval sisters because her original privateer owners and her
designer had created no unnecessary requirements. Though the *Spark* could not
carry the rating originally given, 14 guns, and was reduced to 12, she was for
long considered the fastest and finest small cruiser in the Navy. Doughty, in designing the 16- and 18-gun brigs, was forced by naval opinion to allow for
more stores and gun power than was really necessary, judging by the *Spark*.

The *Firefly* was a brig very similar to the *Spark*, but somewhat larger. This
brig was 109′ between perpendiculars, 100′ on the straight of keel, 29′ 4″ beam,
and 11′ 0″ depth of hold. She was armed with 4 long 18's and 10 carronades,
18-pdrs. The *Torch* was another privateer schooner bought at Baltimore, 106′
on deck, 26′ 0″ beam, and 11′ 9″ depth of hold. The *Torch* was rigged like
Prometheus, and her model was somewhat like *Spark*, but with slightly more
rake in the ends and more deadrise, according to one of her officers. The *Spitfire*
had been the Baltimore letter of marque *Grampus*, built at or near Baltimore
in 1812. Her dimensions, according to her register, were 106′ length, 25′ 6″
beam, and 11′ 8″ depth of hold; her naval register said she was 108′ on the
gun deck, 25′ 8″ beam, and 12′ in the hold. She carried two long 9's, one long
18, and 8 carronades, 18-pdrs. The *Eagle* was a 12-gun schooner bought at New
Orleans, said to have been built on the Chesapeake and of 270 tons measurement. The dimensions of this schooner have not been found.

The 6-gun schooner *Lynx* was also of the Baltimore Clipper type, about 80′

16 Gun Brig after the Spark
Length bt perp   22'. 0" or 33'-2"
Beam moulded   25'.0"
Depth in hold   13'.6"

Ⓞ is 44'.3" from I.P
Room & Space, 2'.6" from Base
lowest W.up 1.0" from Base
W.Ls spaced 2'.4"

Traced from original in Lenthall's
Papers

Figure 68. Draught of a 16-gun brig based on the design of the SPARK.

on deck and pierced for 14 guns, but was armed with but 6. She was an extreme clipper schooner without enough displacement to carry the guns she was pierced for; only her sail plan has been found. The details of the rigging of these clipper schooners can be seen in the *Lynx* sail plan. She was built at Washington or Georgetown, District of Columbia, by James Owner. It is not known whether she was built by contract or purchased on the stocks. It is possible that this schooner had been originally intended as one of the reserve vessels to support the two raiding squadrons. However, none of these vessels accomplished anything, as the war ended early in 1815, too soon for the squadrons to be completed.

It is worthy of comment that 1814 saw a complete reversal in the Navy's attitude toward the so-called Baltimore Clipper schooners. Where, in 1804–6, the Navy had eliminated all the very sharp schooners from the Navy List (either by sale or by rebuilding and changing the rig of such vessels as the *Enterprise, Vixen, Nautilus,* and *Ferret*) through the influence of the "practical" officers, such as Tingey, now the trend was toward the clipper schooner, as evidenced by the number of such craft placed on the Navy List in this year. In times of peace the command of a small, sharp schooner was less impressive than the command, say, of a brig, even though the former was by far the more effective ship. In war, however, the most effective vessel was the choice of any competent commander, and under the existing conditions in 1814 the fast-sailing and weatherly schooner was good insurance of both prizes and escape. Pompous dignity was of little value in wartime and impressed few. It had been argued, with some logic, that schooners were unsuitable for naval action, since they were not as easily maneuvered under short sail as a square-rigger; the schooner, unlike the brig, could not be stopped and backed by working her sails alone. This seemed a very sound argument in 1806, but in 1814 it would have been laughed at, for experience had taught that intricate maneuvering of small cruisers was wholly unnecessary, since speed and gun power, properly used, limited the advantages of maneuver, to a very great extent, to the fastest and most weatherly vessel. Speed, the always debatable factor of naval warfare, was now the prime requirement, and particularly so in the small cruisers that had to expose themselves to an overpowering fleet at sea. The hit-and-run privateer schooners had at least taught the Navy that speed in sailing meant survival when the odds were against them, or victory and the choice of position when the odds were favorable or even.

The problem of defending the Mississippi, particularly New Orleans, had been considered as far back as Jefferson's administration and had been "solved" by stationing a few gunboats there. Now there was a strong possibility that the British might attack in this area, and the old "solution" was re-examined. Obviously, the gunboats and tenders were hardly sufficient in the light of experience. It was decided to depend upon the naval ships based at New Orleans and upon the local militia and the few regulars stationed there. The ship sloop *Louisiana* and the schooner *Carolina* were effective vessels, though hardly powerful enough for the purpose. The ketches were of doubtful value. The War Department under Secretary Monroe made no preparations whatever, as was usual with this incompetent politician, but the Navy Department decided to strengthen the naval force there by the construction of a large block ship suitable for the defense of the river and the port of New Orleans.

The vessel was to be a large and powerful corvette, much like the shoal lake vessels built at Presque Isle, capable of sailing and also of entering shoal waters. A contract was let late in 1813 or at the beginning of 1814 to M. Pechon, of New Orleans, to build the vessel, to be rated as a 22-gun ship. It cannot be determined now who was the designer, though the plan of the ship, shown in Figure 69, has survived. The design called for a large vessel that was a cross between a frigate and a ship sloop, in that the vessel had her main armament on a flush deck, like a sloop, but with additional armament on quarter-deck and forecastle, like a frigate. However, unlike a frigate of the period, the ship had a very short quarterdeck and forecastle and no gangways; she was a reversion to the practices in frigate building of an earlier period. Though with some of the structural qualities of a frigate, the new vessel was referred to as a corvette in most official references.

The design in Figure 69 is of the only block ship whose keel was ever laid down for the United States Navy, though there had been numerous proposals for such craft ever since Bergh and Captain Stewart had made their proposal some years before the war. The new ship was named *Tchifonta* while on the stocks and was to measure 152' 9" on deck and 43' moulded beam. She was to draw about 8' 6" ready for service. The ship was to be very plain, without adornment of any kind, and was to be rigged to topgallants only, but very lofty nevertheless. She was to carry a battery of 32-pdr. long guns with 42-pdr. carronades on the quarterdeck and forecastle. Work proceeded rather rapidly on the ship for a few months, but in the spring of the year, or early summer, construction was suspended on orders from Washington, the administration having decided there was no danger of attack in this quarter. As a result the big ship was still on the stocks when the British did attack New Orleans in December and January of 1814–15; thus the Navy Department finally did no more than the War Department to defend the place.

The lakes were the scene of much building activity in 1814. At Sackett's Harbor on Lake Ontario the Americans launched two large brigs, the *Jefferson* on April 7 and *Jones* on April 10. These brigs were to carry 16 carronades, 42-pdrs., and 4 long 24's, rating as 18-gun brigs. Eckford also launched the 44-gun frigate *Superior* on May 2, after she had been on the ways only eighty days. During this time her design had been altered. Originally laid down as a 44, she was lengthened when the Americans heard that the British were building a frigate of greater size. The *Superior* was armed with 30 long 32's, 26 carronades, 42-pdrs., and 2 long 24's—58 guns in all. Eckford also launched the 32-gun frigate *Mohawk* this season. She was on the ways only thirty-four days and was a large ship of her class, to carry 26 long 24's and 16 carronades, 32-pdrs. A small brig was also bought on the lake sometime during the year and named *Ranger*. She appears to have been either a transport or a supply vessel rather than a cruiser. It was Eckford's extraordinary ability to design, lay down, and build ships, ranging in size from a very small schooner to the largest frigates, working in a wilderness and in severe winter weather with sick or dissatisfied labor, and to do all this in extremely short periods of time, that maintained American superiority on Lake Ontario. Certainly Chauncey accomplished little with the fleet Eckford produced for him. The appreciation of Eckford's accomplishments can be judged by the fact that, whereas Chauncey's name has been carried on the American Navy List, no vessel was ever named for Eckford, though Fulton and Ericsson have been honored, as have other civilians—Bancroft, for example. Without Eckford and the Browns, none of the naval officers, Chauncey, Perry, or Macdonough, could have defended the Lakes or prevented the invasion of the northern states.

The British had no Eckford, but their commander Yeo was so crafty that he fooled not only Chauncey but also many naval historians since. Yeo launched two new frigates and, by false rumor, convinced the Americans that they were fully as powerful as the two the Americans were building. So well was this aim accomplished that the *Superior*, laid down as a 44, about 175′ between perpendiculars, was lengthened nearly 20′ on the stocks to permit her to carry 62 guns by filling all her ports. It was found, however, that this overloaded her, so she was reduced to 58. Now, the plan of the *Prince Regent*, the largest of the British frigates, shows her to have been a small double-banked frigate

Figure 69. Draught of the New Orleans block ship, TCHIFONTA, *1815.*

295

about 158′ 0″ between perpendiculars, American measurement, and 42′ 6″ moulded beam, pierced for 56 guns exclusive of bridle ports. By filling all of her ports she could have carried 60 guns. She was smaller than the 36-gun *Constellation*. The other frigate, the *Princess Charlotte*, was of the conventional type—only about 128′ 0″ between perpendiculars, American measurement, and 37′ 2″ moulded beam. This ship was pierced for 40 guns exclusive of the bridle ports. These small frigates could carry their armament only because they did not have to carry large quantities of provisions and, of course, did not carry any water. Hence their displacement was much less than that required for a seagoing frigate of the same length. The lake frigates had their capacity much reduced by means of great deadrise, intended to make them fast and weatherly. The *Princess Charlotte* was extreme in this respect.

The *General Pike*, the American 24-gun corvette, was 145′ between perpendiculars and 37′ beam; she was thus actually a larger ship than the smaller of the British frigates. The *Superior* was nearly 35′ longer than the *Prince Regent* and more heavily armed, yet Yeo's release of "information" convinced Chauncey that the British frigates were equal to his. Actually, Yeo was so well aware of his real inferiority that he began another small frigate and two more liners. The frigate was another double-banked ship, the *Psyche*, whose frame had been built in England and erected at Kingston—about 130′ between perpendiculars, American measurement, and 35′ 11″ moulded beam. She was launched in December, 1814. The two new liners were the *Wolfe* and *Canada*, 191′ 3″ between perpendiculars and 58′ moulded beam. They were slightly larger than the 112-gun *St. Lawrence*, which was 191′ 2″ between perpendiculars and 52′ moulded beam, but the two new vessels were to have a quarterdeck so as to carry 120 guns.

To confuse the Americans, Yeo also changed the names of the ships in the old squadron. All of his schooners had been converted into brigs. The *Wolfe* was now the *Montreal*, the *Royal George* was changed to *Niagara*, the *Melville* to the *Star*, the *Moira* to the *Charwell*, the *Beresford* to the *Netley*, and the *Sydney Smith* to the *Magnet*. The schooner *Prince Regent* had become first the *General Beresford* and now the *Netley*, all in two years.

When the Americans heard about the new British liners, they made plans to build two 130-gun ships and one or two huge frigates during the coming winter. The Browns were now to join with Eckford as soon as they were done at Vergennes, and construction was to begin early in 1815. The Americans made two captures on Ontario in this year, the 1-gun *Blacksnake*, a gunboat, and

Figure 70. Draught of sloop of war SARATOGA, built for Lake Champlain.

the brig *Magnet*, ex *Sydney Smith*. Tension was mounting, as it appeared that the British might have control of the lake as soon as their three liners were ready, one of which, the *St. Lawrence*, was afloat, but not fitted.

Lake Champlain now became an important theater of action. The British had begun construction of a frigate on the lake and had built a large number of gunboats. They also had ready a new brig, the *Niagara*, which they renamed *Linnet*. In March of 1814 Noah Brown was ordered to Vergennes to build a ship and nine gunboats. He designed and built the big corvette *Saratoga*, 26 guns, a flush-decked ship 143' 0" between perpendiculars and 36' 6" moulded beam. She was without adornment, even without a head, and was very loftily sparred. Her lines, in Figure 70, were much like those of the *Niagara* brig, Figure 60, except that the ship had much less rake at the bow. Timber for the vessel began to be cut March 2, and the ship was launched April 11.

The Browns also built the gunboats *Allen, Borer, Burrows, Centipede, Nettle*, and *Viper*, all 75' long, 15' wide, and armed with an 18-pdr. columbiad and a long 24. These were built on the lines shown in Figure 62. It also appears that the Browns either built or repaired the 1-gun *Ballard*. There were at least two old gunboats remaining on the lake when Brown arrived, probably the *Alwyn* and *Ludlow*, and these were repaired. In lieu of the remaining gunboats ordered, it was decided to convert a steamboat hull into an armed schooner. It is not clear whether this steamboat had ever been afloat or was on the stocks when the Browns arrived. At any rate, the vessel was made into a 17-gun schooner and named *Ticonderoga*. She was a long vessel, carrying 8 long 12's, 4 long 18's, and 5 carronades, 32-pdrs., and was nearly flat-bottomed and quite narrow. By early May, the Browns and their gangs were back in New York, but late in June they received word that they were to go back to Vergennes and build a 24-gun brig in all haste. Adam left the day after the order was received, with two hundred men, while Noah stayed in New York to forward material. Fifty-five days after the letter ordering them to build the brig had been written in Washington, Macdonough fought the battle of Plattsburg, with the new brig in his line of battle, for Brown launched the *Surprise* exactly nineteen days after he arrived at Vergennes. The vessel was a large one much like the *Niagara*, to carry 24 long 24-pdrs. She was renamed *Eagle* soon after her launch, and was delivered to the fleet just five days before the battle.

The British squadron came down the lake to aid a British army invading New York along the route Burgoyne had attempted in the Revolution. This

squadron was defeated at Plattsburg, New York, September 11, 1814, and the
ships were all captured except for some gunboats. By this action, the Americans
obtained the *Confiance*, a shallow frigate carrying 36 guns, 147' 5" on the
main deck, 37' 2" beam, and 7' 0" depth of hold. She had been launched
August 25 and had a furnace for heating shot, 27 long 24's, 2 long 18's, and 6
carronades, 24-pdrs. No plan of the ship has yet been found. They also took the
brig *Linnet* and retook the two sloops captured earlier, now the *Chubb* and

*Figure 71. Draught of British lake schooners built at the end of the War of 1812,
probably typical of the smaller lake vessels.*

Finch. The American squadron consisted of the *Saratoga, Eagle, Ticonderoga,*
the sloop *Preble,* and ten gunboats. The sloop *President* was not present, as she
had been captured by the British sometime during the year and was taken into
their service as the *Icicle.* With the defeat of the British squadron, the invaders
retired and the danger on Lake Champlain ended.

By Perry's victory on Lake Erie, the Americans had full control of Erie
and the western lakes. However, in September the schooners *Tigress* and
Scorpion were captured by a British boat attack, as earlier the schooners *Ohio*
and *Somers* had been taken in the same manner. These small schooners were
liable to capture by boat attacks, as they were low-sided and were so small that
their crews were often less numerous than a launch crew. In the fall of the

year the British began building some small schooners for use on the western lakes; Figure 71 shows a typical lake schooner, of the type built on Lake Erie.

The treaty of peace between Great Britain and the United States was signed at Ghent December 24, 1814, but was not ratified at Washington until February 17, 1815. It was still later before privateers and naval vessels were informed of the end of the war, so operations continued through the first two months of the year. In January the frigate *President* was captured by a British squadron off New York while attempting to get to sea. The *President* had gone ashore on her way out and was badly strained and leaky when she met the British. As a result her sailing was far below normal and she was taken after a half-day chase. The frigate was taken into the Royal Navy because she had been so widely admired, but she was too much damaged by her grounding to be of value. She was broken up in 1817, and a ship of the same name was built on somewhat the same lines for the British Navy. This also gained the reputation of being a fast ship.

The additions to the Navy List in 1815 were few. A schooner named *Ghent* was built at Presque Isle by Thomas Eyre. She was 55′ 0″ between perpendiculars, 16′ 0″ moulded beam, and 6′ 0″ depth of hold, and had a long 12-pdr. on a pivot. She was much like the 1-gun revenue cutters built the same year from Doughty's designs. A 12-gun clipper schooner named *Firebrand* was purchased early in the year at New Orleans, and was probably intended as a reserve to the two raiding squadrons then being prepared. The schooner remained at New Orleans for three or four years before being sold. No particulars concerning the vessel have been found, but she was apparently of some size. Another purchase here was the 12-gun ketch *Surprise*. This vessel was purchased as late as March and fitted to carry 12 guns, though finally reduced to 6. She seems to have been intended as a guard ship.

One of the more important ships added to the Navy List this year was the British ship sloop *Cyane*. With a consort, the flush-decked sloop *Levant*, she was taken by the frigate *Constitution* on the night of February 20. The frigate and her prizes anchored in the Cape Verde Islands but soon afterward were driven out by three heavy British frigates. The Americans separated, and the *Levant* was chased back to the Portuguese port, where she was retaken by the British. The *Cyane* was carried to the United States and transferred to the Navy. The ship had been built as far back as 1795 as a member of a class of four quarterdecked ship sloops; in 1798 a fifth sister was built with slight alterations. The *Cyane* was built by a Mr. Wilson by contract. She was a miniature

Figure 72. *Draught of* CYANE *from her Admiralty plan and from drawings of the ship made after her capture by the Americans.*

frigate with detached quarterdeck and a short forecastle, intended to carry 16 medium guns, 6-pdrs., on her main deck, 6 carronades, 12-pdrs., on her quarter-deck, and 2 carronades, 12-pdrs., on her forecastle. Figure 72 shows the design of this ship. She had been captured by the French and recaptured and had gone through many alterations. When she was captured by the Americans she had a spar deck and her waist had been raised, the forecastle had been given bulwarks, and she was, in appearance, a frigate-built ship. However, she was a small vessel for the period of her capture, being only 110′ 0″ between perpen-diculars and 29′ 0″ moulded beam. She had a frigate's midsection but, like many British ship sloops, had very fine ends and had been a good sailer when built. Her sailing qualities had been effectively destroyed, however, by over-gunning. The ship appears to have been in rather poor condition when cap-tured and received rather extensive repairs when taken into the Navy. She was now rated officially as a 24-gun ship and was laid up at the Philadelphia Navy Yard. The *Cyane* was rather more of a trophy than a serviceable cruiser, for she certainly was inferior in all respects to the new American sloops built during the war.

An 18-gun brig, the *Penguin*, was taken and destroyed by the *Hornet*, and the East India Company's cruiser *Nautilus*, a small 14-gun brig, was taken by the *Peacock* in this period, but the latter was returned, as she had been seized after the date established by the Treaty of Ghent as the end of hostilities. One schooner, the *St. Lawrence*, a former American privateer, was captured by the American privateer *Chasseur*. Though a regular naval vessel when captured, she was not purchased for the American Navy, of course, having been a privateer's prize.

During the winter of 1814–15 the building race on Lake Ontario reached its climax. The Americans laid down two 130-gun ships and one large frigate. The Browns went to Sackett's Harbor in February, with twelve hundred car-penters, and joined Eckford. The gangs had been at work six weeks when peace put a stop to the work. Had the Browns and Eckford been allowed to proceed, another six weeks would have seen the completion of two of the large ships and probably the one frigate. One of the 130-gun ships was the *New Orleans*, reported to have been 212′ 0″ on her upper deck, 56′ 0″ moulded beam. The other may have been the *Chippewa*. The frigate was the *Plattsburg*, 58 guns. One or two additional frigates had been intended to be started as soon as these ships were launched. The ships were left on the stocks, the *New Or-*

leans being the most advanced. The British liners on the stocks were housed over, and the unfinished ships afloat were laid up.

On the western lakes the British completed three small schooners of the *Tecumseth* class, shown in Figure 71, and built two classes of lugger-rigged gunboats on Lake Champlain, two of which are shown in Figures 73 and 74. They also began work on the brig shown in Figure 61 for use on this lake, but it does not appear that the vessel was completed. Both sides laid up their vessels, except for a few schooners, and the surplus crews were sent home or discharged.

Figure 73. British lake gunboat, CAUSTIC, *designed for use on Lake Champlain.*

The war ended with the Navy larger and more effective than when it started. Of greater importance, the American public was now convinced of the necessity of a navy and, on the whole, was very proud of what it had accomplished in the war. In spite of an inadequate organization, the Navy Department had become somewhat more effective and the weakness of the establishment had been observed by Congress.

One of the wartime 74's authorized had not yet been laid down. It was intended to build her at Washington, but the Navy Yard there was not yet sufficiently restored to begin work. The navy yards at Norfolk, Philadelphia, New York, Boston, and Portsmouth were manned and in operating condition. Two constructors, Doughty and Samuel Humphreys, were employed. The 74 *Franklin* was nearly ready to launch at Philadelphia, and the other two,

Washington and *Independence*, were fitting out. Though many of the ships of the Navy were hurriedly built of green timber, the bulk of the ships were in good condition. The normal reduction in force that followed the war would permit the disposal of most of the unsatisfactory ships and small vessels.

So far as the construction policy of the Navy was concerned, some progress had been made in the last months of the war. It will be recalled that the senior naval officers had practically dictated the construction policies of the Navy since 1794, with only the veto power of the Secretary of the Navy to check them. The theory supporting the practice was that "practical" men knew what

Figure 74. British lake gunboat, AXEMAN, *designed for Lake Champlain.*

was required better than the technical men, shipwrights and constructors, and were also better fitted to judge such matters than the political head of the Navy. However, the latter could control the officers when they ran contrary to the policy of the administration, particularly in matters of economy. Gradually, the power of the Secretary of the Navy over the commissioned officers in all matters became fully recognized and the Secretary had become the acknowledged commander of the service.

So far as the design of new ships was concerned, there were many advantages in having the officers dictate requirements, since the system insured practical design and construction, with emphasis on combat ability. On the other hand, the conservatism of elderly naval officers often led to the retention of obsolete ship types, or to too much emphasis on a single class of man-of-war. Also, the insistence upon heavy armament, without due regard for the ability of existing ships to carry it, led to grave difficulties. Jealousy in rank led to a pompous disregard of small light cruisers and contempt for sea raiders.

The naval constructors, Joshua Humphreys, Josiah Fox, and William Doughty, had in fact been no more than master shipwrights, primarily concerned with construction and repair and fitting out in the navy yards, with the designing of new vessels requiring but little of their time. The Master Shipwright of the Washington Navy Yard, between 1803 and 1815, really acted as chief constructor to a limited degree; he acted as technical adviser to the Secretary and usually prepared plans of new vessels. However, his recommendations were rarely binding on senior naval officers, who often rigged and altered their commands without regard to his technical opinions. This led to a complete lack of standardization and to expensive confusion, in spite of a stream of directives from the Secretary.

Because of the lack of a central design authority, the shipwrights and officers in the navy yards and contract shipyards felt quite free to depart from the authorized designs and specifications, going so far as to change lines and dimensions. As a result each new ship became a special problem in arming, rigging, and sparring. Sails, spars, rigging, and gun mounts could not be transferred from ship to ship, and it was practically impossible to have a reserve supply of this material made up in advance of needs.

The system of centralized power in the Secretary's hands not only made him carry the burden of attempting to control construction and fitting out; it also made him the strategist, who directed the ship movements and the assignment of officers and commanders. In times of peace, with a very small navy, this had not been a difficult problem, but in war it became a great burden for which a political appointee was little fitted. The quasi war with France had shown this to be beyond the capacity of even a competent Secretary, but the lesson had been overlooked in the change of political control of the country that followed the French troubles.

In an act dated February 7, 1815, Congress attempted to correct the basic difficulty in the Navy Department. This act established a Board of Navy Commissioners, consisting of three officers of rank not less than post captain, to be attached to the Secretary's office to discharge certain duties. These were to prepare rules and regulations necessary for securing uniformity of vessels, equipment, and repairs or refitting; they also were charged with "securing responsibility" in subordinate officers and agents.

The language of the act was somewhat vague, which led to a period of dis-

Types of guns and carronades in the American naval service, 1813–15.

agreement between members of the Board and the Secretary, as to the exact division of power and responsibility. Finally, it was established that the Board's powers were confined to the procurement of stores and supplies, materials and armament, and the design and construction of new vessels. The Board had control over all repairs and refitting and over the constructors, agents, and the navy yards in all matters pertaining to these subjects. The Secretary retained control of vessel movements, naval personnel of all descriptions, and all appointments and assignments. In short, he was still to act as a naval strategist and nominal head of the Navy in time of war, regardless of fitness.

In addition to the three members of the Board there was a secretary. The Board members had the honorary title of Commodore, and one of them was the President of the Board. This office went to the senior officer, of course. Membership in the Board seems to have been at the Secretary's discretion; some officers were members for long periods, while others sat only for a short time. Some officers were assigned to the Board for two tours of duty (one had three) at different periods. The membership of the Board was never changed completely, and there was a fairly constant rotation of members. The first Board consisted of John Rodgers, President, Isaac Hull, and David Porter. Stephen Decatur replaced Hull in the first year. The first secretary appointed was a civilian, James Paulding.

The character of the Board, as a whole, was highly conservative. Since no vessel could be built for the Navy until her plan had been approved and her construction allocated by the Board, it is apparent that the Board's control over the constructors was absolute. Later some constructors were favored by the Board, and as membership in the Board changed, so did the favored constructors. The effect of the Board on the design of naval ships will be seen.

The establishment of the Board resulted in the reorganization of the construction branch. A chief constructor and resident constructors in each navy yard were allowed for, the chief constructor to have authority over the constructors in the yards. All of their reports were to be rendered through the chief constructor, who was to report directly to the Board. The Board quickly brought order into construction, repair, arming, and fitting of vessels of the Navy. It established a working organization of the navy yards and a system in controlling alterations in new ships. It gave an opportunity for more than one constructor to design new ships. A definite responsibility for inspection of new construction and all procurement was assigned. Nevertheless, the control of technical matters remained in the hands of the "practical seaman."

From a naval shipbuilding point of view, the outstanding men of the War of 1812 were Eckford and the Browns, Adam and Noah. Through the efforts of these three the Navy held control of the lakes and prevented the British from invading the North and Northwest, which would have led to their reaching the American shipbuilding centers on the coast through the back door, so to speak. No officer or constructor of the Navy accomplished more. There were no competitors to the Browns and Eckford among the navy yards, or in the contract shipyards on the coasts. A few of the privateer building yards built rapidly, but the vessels they turned out were smaller than those built on the lakes, where building was made infinitely more difficult than on the coast because of climate and geographical conditions, to say nothing of scarcities of labor and some materials. Perhaps the lake builders had one important advantage—no government inspection or red tape to delay them. The moment was too critical to suffer the fumbling delay occasioned on the coast, where government agents lost time trying to make decisions for which they were wholly unequipped in training and knowledge.

The building of the lake vessels required more than setting up a ship, as we have seen in the activities of the Browns at Presque Isle. Eckford not only had to set up a shipyard at Sackett's Harbor; he had to build quarters for his gangs, mess and kitchen buildings, hospital, offices, and blockhouses. Between trips to the lakes, the Browns had found time to build a blockhouse 40′ square at Hell Gate and another at Williamsburg, Long Island. A third was built at Rockaway Beach. The Browns built a steam frigate in their yard, the Fulton-designed *Demologos*, which they launched in the fall of 1814, four months after the keel was laid. She was a vessel 156′ in length, 56′ beam, and 20′ moulded depth, and she had a paddle wheel 16′ in diameter and 14′ wide set in a tunnel between the hulls. This tunnel does not appear to have run the full length of the hull but to have been about 60′ long with sloping ends. The Browns also built another vessel under Fulton's supervision. She was called the *Mute*, according to Noah Brown's statement after the war, and seems to have been a submersible. The Browns also built the noted brig *Warrior*, fitted as a privateer to carry 20 guns. It was sworn that this brig sailed fifteen and a half knots on the return from a cruise.

With the ending of the war Eckford came back to New York and opened a yard. Shortly, however, he was again engaged in naval work. Neither Eckford nor the Browns were asked to deliver the plans of the ships they built until about four years after the war, and the correspondence does not show their answers to the requests. It appears that there was some delay in these builders getting the pay due them under their various contracts. The Browns did no more naval work but became noted builders of packet and other large merchant ships.

The war years had seen some changes in the hull form of fast-sailing craft in America, particularly of naval vessels. The slack, rounded bilges of earlier years had disappeared, and now fast armed small vessels had almost straight

rising floors, hard bilges, and almost wall sides, following a trend that seems
to have begun in England as early as 1803 in the designs of the British constructor Peake. The American vessels apparently were not copies of the British
designs, however; the Americans gave more attention to the ends of their ships
than was common in the Admiralty designs. The change in midsection of the
American brigs and schooners, and ship sloops too, was undoubtedly due to
the need of increased stability to carry heavy guns and more and more sail.
The need of rapid construction in the war years had spelled the doom of
intricate headrails and carvings of earlier naval craft; the reverse curved topsides also went out of fashion, as they required too much curved timber and
narrowed the decks too much. Ships had grown longer, and much experience
had now been gained in building long hulls that would not hog excessively.

   With the war with England over, the Americans turned their attention to the
Barbary pirates again. This time Algiers was the object of American anger.
Decatur was sent out in the new 44 *Guerriere*, with the sloop *Ontario*, the
Constellation, and the ex-British *Macedonian* and *Epervier*. He also had five of
the small cruisers intended for raiding squadrons. The *Epervier* and the *Guerriere* captured the *Mashuda*, 46 (she was eventually returned to the Algerines),
and the small cruisers ran the *Estedio*, 22, ashore and destroyed her. Decatur
had hoped to attack Algiers and the other Barbary piratical powers, but none
of them desired more trouble. The British finally destroyed the power of the
Barbary principalities shortly afterward. The *Epervier* was lost at sea with all
hands late in 1815, on the way home from the Mediterranean.

   With the ending of the War of 1812, the disposal of the war-worn small
craft began. All but a few of the old gunboats were sold, and the greater part
of the schooners that had been purchased on the lakes were also disposed of in
1815–16. The preservation of some of the larger lake vessels was intended; they
were stripped and sunk in water sufficiently deep to avoid damage from ice.
Beginning in 1816, the small purchased seagoing cruisers were surveyed, and
those deemed poorly built or expensive to maintain were ordered to be sold.

   The only addition to the Navy was the ship of the line *Columbus*, authorized
during the war. This vessel was laid down in the reconstructed Washington
Navy Yard in June, 1816, on a design by Doughty, who was also her master
builder. The *Columbus* was 193′ 3″ between perpendiculars, 52′ 0″ moulded
beam, and 21′ 10″ depth in the hold. She had been designed 193′ between
perpendiculars and 21′ 6″ in the hold, but in construction she was raised a few
inches, which made her length increase slightly. Her design, as built, is shown

in Plan 19. She proved to be the most successful of the 74's authorized during the war, though she cannot be said to have been as good as those ships that followed her. The fault of all of the 74's built for the Navy in these years was that they did not have sufficient displacement to carry the armament placed on board.

In April, 1816, Congress set up a plan for the gradual improvement of the Navy. The intent of the new act was to gradually build up the Navy in all classes, as funds could be made available. This permitted a definite plan of expansion which, owing to the lack of money, did not become effective for a couple of years. The official Navy List as of January 2, 1816, was as follows:

Independence	74	at Boston	Ready for service
Washington	74	at Boston	For the Mediterranean
Franklin	74	at Philadelphia	Will be ready in the spring
Guerriere	44	at New York	Ready for service
Java	44	at New York	For the Mediterranean
United States	44	at sea	Mediterranean
Constitution	44	at Boston	Repairing
Constellation	36	at sea	Mediterranean
Congress	36	at Boston	Requires repairs
Macedonian	36	at Boston	Ready for service
John Adams	24	at sea	Mediterranean, as storeship
Cyane	24	at Boston	In ordinary
Block Ship	24.	at New Orleans	On stocks, Tchifonta Lake
Alert	20	at sea	Mediterranean, storeship
Louisiana	20	at New Orleans	To be sold, unfit for service
Hornet	18	at New York	In ordinary
Wasp	18	missing since 1814	
Peacock	18	at New York	In ordinary
Ontario	18	at sea	Mediterranean
Erie	18	at sea	Mediterranean
Epervier	18	missing since July 14, 1815	
Enterprise	14	at New York	In ordinary
Etna	14	at New York	In ordinary, bomb
Flambeau	14	at New York	Recently returned from Mediterranean
Spark	14	at New York	" " " "
Firefly	14.	at New York	" " " "
Chippewa	14	at New York	" . " " "
Saranac	14	at sea	Cruising
Boxer	14	at New York	Recently returned from the Mediterranean
Prometheus	14	at sea	Cruising in revenue service
Spitfire	ketch	at Norfolk	In ordinary
Vesuvius	ketch	at New York	Receiving vessel
Vengeance	ketch	at New York	Sheer hulk
Nonsuch	14	at Norfolk	In ordinary
Spitfire	sch. 12	at New York	In ordinary
Torch	12	at New York	In ordinary
Tom Bowline	12	at sea	Cruising, storeship
Surprise	12	at New Orleans	In ordinary
Firebrand	12	at New Orleans	In ordinary
Roanoke	sch.	at Wilmington, N.C.	Fitting
Hornet	sch.	at sea	Mediterranean
Lynx		at Boston	Fitting

Dispatch	sch.	at Portsmouth	Ready for service
Asp		at Baltimore	Receiving vessel
Corporation		at Philadelphia	Receiving vessel
Ranger		at Philadelphia	Receiving vessel
Buffalo		at Philadelphia	Transport
Camel		at Philadelphia	Transport
Tickler		at New Orleans	Dispatch boat
New Orleans	74	on Lake Ontario	On stocks at Sacketts Harbor
Chippewa	74	" " "	" " " " "
Plattsburg	44	" " "	Frames, not set up
Superior	44	" " "	In state of preservation
Mohawk	32	" " "	" " " "
General Pike	24	" " "	" " " "
Madison	20	" " "	" " " "
Jefferson	18	" " "	" " " "
Jones	18	" " "	" " " "
Sylph	16	" " "	" " " "
Oneida	14	" " "	" " " "
Lady of the Lake		" " "	In service
Niagara	18	On Lake Erie	Ready for service
Lawrence	18	" " "	Laid up
Detroit	18	" " "	Laid up
Queen Charlotte	18	" " "	Laid up
Porcupine		" " "	Ready for service
Ghent		" " "	Ready for service
Confiance	36	on Lake Champlain	Laid up
Saratoga	24	" " "	Laid up
Eagle	18	" " "	Laid up
Linnet	14	" " "	Laid up
Ticonderoga	14	" " "	Laid up
15 barges		at Sackett's Harbor	
6 galleys		at Whitehall, Champlain	
14 barges		at Baltimore	
A few gunboats in addition			
Steam Frigate		at New York	Ready for service
Steam Frigate		at Baltimore	Suspended

★　　★　　★　　★　　★　　★　　★　　★　　★

CHAPTER SIX

The Postwar Navy
1816-1830

THE INTENDED expansion of the Navy could not begin at once, after the war, as funds became available only slowly and there were many problems concerning a new program that had to be settled. Within two years after the war, a program was established that was based on the lessons of the late war, in which the need of ships of the line was recognized. Six improved 74-gun ships and nine new 44-gun frigates were proposed. In addition, consideration was given to the sloop class, which the war had shown to be particularly useful as commerce raiders, and the program was to include ten of this class, larger and more powerful than the 1813 classes. England, and other naval powers, had been impressed with the sloops of 1813 and now had ships that were their equal, so, to keep ahead, the Americans would have to have vessels superior to the early ships of the *Erie* and *Wasp* designs. The question of a very powerful ship of the line was also raised, and there was some agitation for the construction of one or more vessels of 120-130 guns.

The groundwork for the new program was the responsibility of the newly formed Board of Navy Commissioners, and as soon as the immediate problems of standardizing equipment, armament, manning allowances, control of repair, and the other matters relating to the existing Navy were settled, they prepared for the proposed construction. One of the first steps in organization was in the navy yards, which had to be manned and equipped for building the new ships. It was decided to build in the government yards because of the uncertain factor of funds; it was possible that the slow appropriation of funds might keep a ship on the stocks for years, and no private builder would be willing to do this except on a heavy rental basis.

William Doughty remained constructor at the Washington Navy Yard, and Samuel Humphreys was at Philadelphia; the other yards had no resident constructors. Doughty was put to work on the designs of the new 74's and the frigates. The Board then gradually filled the vacant positions of constructor in some of the other yards. Francis Grice, one of the builders of the frigate *Guerriere* at Philadelphia, was appointed to the Norfolk Navy Yard May 7, 1817, and so became third in seniority. In the same year, July 13, Henry Eckford was assigned to the New York Yard. Josiah Barker was placed at the Boston Yard about the same time. Two years later, two more constructors were appointed.

In 1817 the new program got under way with two new 74's being laid down. One was on the design Doughty had been working on; the other was to be designed by and built under the supervision of Henry Eckford. On May 30, 1816, the latter had been requested by John Rodgers, the President of the Board, to make a model and draught of a ship of the line 193' between perpendiculars and 53' moulded beam. In making his request of Eckford, Rodgers had indicated that the members were "desirous of availing themselves of the most approved professional skill of our country." There has been a tradition that the Board imposed conditions on Eckford and opposed his building the new ship. Griffiths seems to have been one of the authorities for this, but both the official correspondence and the plans of the ship indicate that the Board not only approved the original design, but made no alterations and certainly had no objections to Eckford. Furthermore, the fact that after he had begun work on the *Ohio* he was asked to submit designs for other vessels is sufficient evidence of the esteem in which the Board held him and answers Griffith's claim that he was objectionable to the Board. In view of Eckford's excellent commercial prospects, even in the years of depressed business after the war, it seems probable that he looked upon his appointment as a naval constructor as merely temporary employment and an interesting opportunity to design another large man-of-war.

Eckford, having completed his model and draught and obtained the approval of his design by the Board, laid down the new ship of the line in November, 1817, within the New York Navy Yard. Eckford had designed the ship larger than the Board had requested, for the plans called for a length of 197' 2"

Particulars

⊙ is 11.7½' from F.P.
Room & Space 2'5"
W L's spaced 4'0"
Buttocks " 4'0"

umbus, 74-gun ship 1815
th bet. perps 193:3*
n moulded 52:0*
½ in hold 21:10*
Draught shows ship as built.
    Design by Wm Doughty

Plan 19. Draught of the 74-gun ship COLUMBUS, 1815, showing full lines often employed in this class.

Ship-of-the-Line "Ohio"
Designed by Henry Eckford, built at N.Y. 1817-20

Length bet. perps. 197'-2"   Draught at Post 26'-0"
Moulded beam   53'-10"   Cost $547,009 ea.

        Particulars
     O 11 69'-6" from F.P.
     Room & Space 2'-9"
     Lowest WL. 2'-5" above Base Line
     Other WL's spaced 3'-7"
     Buttocks 5'-0" apart

Based on Navy "return plan" made from
Mould Loft offsets and Eckford's building
plan (Webb).

References
40-7-1 . 77-14-10 D, 77-14-9. Eckford's plan
and Offsets (Webb Inst. of Naval Architecture)

Plan 20. Draught of 74-gun ship OHIO, *as built.*

on the lower deck, 53′ 10″ moulded beam, and about 208′ over-all length on the spar deck. A good deal of material on the design of this ship has survived; the original working plan by Eckford has been found among the plans of his apprentice, Isaac Webb, and a complete set of plans made after the ship was built, from offsets picked up off the mould-loft floor and measurements from the ship, have been found in the Navy plan files. From these plans it appears that the only important alterations made in building the ship were in raising her 6″ more than called for in the working draught; the frames were also differently spaced in lofting. None of these alterations were of any technical importance, and it is impossible that they would have caused disagreement between the designer and the Board.

Plan 20 shows the design of this fine ship, the *Ohio*, long considered one of the finest vessels of her rate in the world, if not the finest, and by far the best liner in the American Navy. Not only was she a handsome ship of her type, but she was a remarkably good sailer and a good seaboat, carried her guns high, and stowed her allowances with ease. It was often said that she handled like a frigate. During much of her active career she was employed as a flag vessel, and she was long one of the favorite commands in the Navy.

The armament of the *Ohio* varied from time to time. When she was first built, the liner was armed in what was then considered an effective way: all guns and carronades were of the same caliber, 32-pdrs., but the long guns on the lower deck were somewhat heavier than those on the main. Later, the lower deck was armed with long 42's, the carronades also being 42-pdrs. The total number of guns seems to have varied with each commander—ranging from 86 to 102— yet the ship was always classed as a 74. The *Ohio* was not sold out of the service until 1883, after running for at least forty years of active service— showing how well Eckford built her.

Doughty's design for a 74, laid down in 1817, was the *Delaware*, built at the Norfolk Navy Yard. Soon afterward the other ships ordered built on this design were laid down: the *North Carolina* at the Philadelphia Navy Yard, the *Alabama* at Portsmouth Navy Yard, the *Vermont* and the *Virginia* at the Boston Yard, and the *New York* at the same yard as the *Delaware*. The duplication of ships at Boston and Norfolk represented less of a work load than is suggested by a mere listing of the ships, for only the *Delaware*, *North Carolina*, and *Vermont* were completed as ships of the line. By the end of 1818 all six of the new 74's were on the stocks officially, though actually work was going on in only three or four ships.

Doughty's design for the six 74's is shown in Plan 21, which represents *North Carolina* and *Delaware* as built. These two ships were launched in the fall of 1820, and the third ship, the *Vermont*, did not get overboard until 1848. As originally designed, the ships were to have the curved upper headrails popular at the beginning of the War of 1812, but the straight rails, introduced into the Royal Navy much earlier as a matter of wartime economy, were ordered for all the new ships in 1820. Great care was taken to insure that all the new liners were built to their lines, without the slightest departure. However, the effect of the old custom of changing designs could not be overcome in a few years, and so there were slight variations in the appearance of the *Delaware* and *North Carolina*, particularly in the head and in the position of the foremost ports, which were not brought to uniformity until some five to ten years after their launch. The Doughty design was for ships 196′ 3″ between perpendiculars, and 53′ 0″ moulded beam—slightly smaller than the *Ohio*, as may be seen by a comparison of the two designs. The *Ohio* was a larger ship than even the dimensions indicated, however, as she was quite a lot deeper than the Doughty-designed 74's and carried her guns a good deal higher as a result.

The designs of the *Ohio* and the sisters *Delaware* and *North Carolina* were to be improvements over the four earlier liners, *Franklin, Columbus, Washington*, and *Independence*. The failure of the older ships was in that they were unable to carry their lower deck guns high enough above the water, in service condition, compared to ships of similar rates abroad. Of the older ships, the *Columbus* was the best, next the *Franklin*, then the *Washington*, and last the *Independence*. The last, in fact, was utterly useless as a liner, since she could show but 3′ 10″ of freeboard between the water line and the sill of her lower-deck gun ports amidships, when loaded with war complement and six months' provisions. Even the best of the lot, the *Columbus*, could show only as much as the smaller British 74's, in spite of being a larger and much more powerful ship.

The *Ohio* fully met expectations, but the two Doughty liners were only slight improvements on the *Columbus*. However, the new ships were faster and stronger in construction, so the design was not altered. The *Independence* was now the cause of some recrimination, and a number of surveys were held on the ship in 1816–17. In April of 1817 Doughty recommended that the ship be razeed into a two-decked frigate, or 60-gun ship, by removing her spar deck entirely. However, nothing was done about the proposal for another eighteen years.

As Doughty once pointed out, the unusually heavy armament of the American liners made comparisons with foreign ships of the same nominal rating highly misleading. It was to be accepted that the American ships could either show less freeboard than foreign liners, with the official complement of guns aboard, or could show more by reducing their armament—which even then would leave the American ships superior in force to their European classmates. Actually, the new 74's of 1817–18 were as powerful, in weight of broadside, as many British liners rating 120 guns when the latter were carrying 126 guns and the American liners 102. In justice, it must be said that the new American ships should have been rated as at least 84's, and even then were unusually large for their class when built, and for ten or fifteen years afterward, in fact.

In considering the qualities of the American liners, the policy of arming them should be noted. The War of 1812 had confirmed, it was thought, the early proposition of giving all ships the heaviest armament possible in a given rate. Single-ship actions in the war had shown pretty clearly the advantages of ships so built and armed, and it was decided that all American naval vessels should be superior in size and armament to their European counterparts; hence any American ship not capable of greatly exceeding her rate in gun power was deemed a failure. In the case of the earlier 74's it had been felt that a reduced armament, even though still superior in weight of fire to any European 74, or even 84, was not desirable, because the American ships were of such large dimensions in comparison to the European ships. Though the Columbus and Franklin had met the requirements within reason, they were not considered good enough to be repeated; hence the decision to have new designs.

The three American liners laid down in 1817 were all considered quite fast sailers, particularly the Ohio. As far as the sailing-vessel commander was concerned, 12 knots was 12 knots and there was no particular regard for any relation of length, or size, to speed. Obviously, if a frigate of 165' length could run up to 12 knots under certain conditions and a liner of 190' could go 12½, the latter was fast enough to catch the frigate and so was a good ship, even though the latter's speed in relation to her length was much inferior to the frigate's. Practically, then, there was no real need to become involved in fine-spun argument concerning the efficient design of liners, so far as speed was concerned. Rather, the problem in the design of the liner was to meet the need for carrying the huge weights of armament, stores, and crew, in a strong seaworthy vessel capable of withstanding abuse in combat, rather than in getting the last fraction of a knot out of the model. The liner had to be as manageable as possible, of course, and if she could reach 12 knots or better in strong winds and the accompanying sea conditions, she would meet all practical requirements. Naval designers were perfectly aware that a large ship, of great length and displacement and rigged in proportion, could outsail a smaller ship, of less length and displacement and suitably rigged, under some conditions of wind and sea, while under other conditions the smaller ship might have the advantage in sailing because of her sharper model. Size, particularly length, has always been a factor in actual speed under sail, large vessels having the advantage over smaller vessels under most conditions. By overlooking this, many have become convinced that only the large clipper ships were correctly modeled for high speed, since they often held records for the longer runs under sail. Actually, their greater length would be more of a factor than their model in runs in very strong winds. Furthermore, such is the state of the "science" of sailing-vessel design that throughout the period of the sharp-lined clippers many full-ended vessels competed successfully for the crown of speed. In long runs, where there was likelihood of strong winds over a great period of time, the large ships with full ends usually made better time than smaller ships of sharper models.

The liner, then, really held about the same relation to sharper models of sailing men-of-war that the battleships or large cruisers hold to the fast, small fighting ships of today, so far as speed is concerned. Just as the modern heavy cruiser could overtake a destroyer (of far greater potential speed) in rough water, yet fail to catch her in smooth seas, so the sailing ship of the line might have the advantage in sailing in strong winds over frigate, ship sloop, brig, or schooner, but be inferior to any of them in light or moderate weather, and still be considered an excellent vessel of her class. The competition in design, in liners, was not with the sharp, smaller vessels used in naval warfare, but in the narrower field of her own class. Here again length and size counted, for only by increasing length could the necessary displacement be retained when the ends of the ship were made sharper for speed. Hence, the development of the hull lines of liners was rather slow, and mere possession of sharp lines did not guarantee a successful ship of the line in any respect. There were always limitations on length, for too much length might make the ship unhandy in action, or make her too weak to carry her guns. It took a long time to reach the structural knowledge necessary to build very long wooden ships successfully. The capture of fast frigates, ship sloops, brigs, schooners, and cutters by ships of the line, in the naval wars in the period of sail, is of course the practical answer to any discussion of their relative excellence of design.

There were no sailing vessels that were extremely fast under all the conditions that might be met at sea. It is interesting to note that it was improved armament that finally doomed the ship of the line, rather than her model of hull, for the day of the liner reached into the steamship period.

There is some reason to suspect that Eckford not only employed his own ideas in the design of the *Ohio;* he may also have been acquainted with Doughty's design for the *Delaware* and *North Carolina,* for the latter design seems to have been in existence when Eckford started to design the *Ohio.* It is also probable that Eckford's experience on Lake Ontario had convinced him of the importance of large dimensions for a given rate. The plan of the *Delaware* was among the drawings of Eckford's apprentice, Isaac Webb, and it is possible, at least, that this was a drawing that had been in Eckford's hands. However, the *Ohio* was no mere improvement in lines over the Doughty design; she was a complete departure.

The new liners introduced the practice in the American Navy of naming first-class combat ships after states. A new system of naming naval ships was developing, but it was long before a standard practice evolved for the whole Navy register. In 1817–18 it was intended that liners be named for states, frigates for rivers, and ship sloops for cities or towns. No system for naming small craft seems to have been considered; there was no reason for doing so, of course, since nothing smaller than ship sloops was under consideration at the time.

At the end of the War of 1812, the arming of naval ships with guns of a single weight of shot was popular, since the use of one size of ball simplified supplying the ships, with no danger of part of the ships' batteries being made useless for want of shot. In compliance with the American policy of employing the heaviest broadside fire possible, American ships armed in this manner usually carried 32-pdrs. Liners had long guns on the lower deck, medium guns on the gun deck, and carronades on the spar deck. Frigates carried 32-pdrs. in the same manner unless they were too small; in that case 24's were used. Sloops, it was thought, ought to be able to carry 24-pdrs. when large, and 18's when small. The 42-pdr. was a very large gun, and the drawback to the system was that ships could not carry a full battery of such guns; as a result some liners were shortly rearmed with 42's on their lower deck and also 42-pdr. carronades on the spar deck, retaining medium 32-pdrs. on the gun deck. This of course caused them to revert to the old system of a mixed armament. With the strong desire for guns of great range and power, the uniform armament system was gradually discarded to permit the use of at least a few very heavy guns.

The long, medium, and carronade styles were practically standard in American gun manufacture for naval use. A few short guns were made for special purposes, particularly in sizes under 24-pdrs., but such guns were not used in vessels above a brig. The weight of ball ranged from 6, through 12, 18, 24, 32, and 42 pounds. All naval guns were iron; a few of the smaller guns and carronades, 6- and 12-pdrs., were brass and were used as boat guns or for the revenue cutters.

One shell gun was used to a limited degree in the latter part of the War of 1812—the "columbiad." Little is known about the gun except that it was a short, rather light gun designed as an alternate to the carronade and usually designated as an 18-pdr. It is probable that this gun, like the 8" shell gun that followed it, was a rebored cannon. It was mounted on slides in gunboats and on broadside carriages on ships. The columbiad was apparently a poorly designed gun that had been developed as a result of reports of guns firing "bombshells" being used in Europe.

The war had also produced an improved mount for pivot guns, which would allow this type of gun to be used in vessels having high bulwarks. The improved mount appears to have originated in privateers; it raised the gun and mount to any required height above the deck and made it unnecessary to employ a raised deck of any kind. With the new mount, the pivot bolt was placed on top of an upright wooden post, or column, and the skids were built so that the bolt was at their after ends. At the forward end there were trucks, mounted on brackets, that permitted the skids to be level with the pivot. The gun was mounted on the usual carriage employed in the earlier pivot guns. The height of the pivot post and of the truck brackets was decided by the height required to permit the gun to fire over the bulwarks. This mount was not particularly strong, and for some years it was confined to the use of pivoted carronades. Later it was considered practical to mount long guns up to 18-pdrs., at least, in this manner. This type of pivot mount became popular in all armed schooners, even merchant vessels, and particularly in slavers. The pivot at the after end of the slide, or skids, was advantageous in such craft, as it brought the gun muzzle well outboard in broadside fire, where the gun blast was not likely to cause damage, even when carronades were used. With the latter, slightly higher mounts were required to avoid damaging the bulwarks by the blast. The pivot was now commonly placed about amidships; this limited its fore-and-aft arcs of fire, but this was not considered to outweigh the many advantages of the mount.

The 44-gun frigates were also designed in 1817. The original plans were very similar to the *Guerriere* and *Java* design of 1813, the lines being practically the same, except that the new design was given 6″ more beam and had a fully armed spar deck. The sheer was unbroken, and the spar-deck bulwark had gun ports in the waist. The new design was a double-banked frigate and, in this respect, a return to the earlier 44's of 1794–96. Originally the design showed the square stern seen in *Guerriere* and *Java*, and the frigates were to have the upper headrails curved upward at the after ends. The design also showed about the same amount of sheer as the 1813 frigates.

Doughty completed his plans in 1817, but the lack of funds and the commitment already made for building the new 74's prevented any frigates being laid down immediately. However, contracts were made for the cutting of frame timber for two frigates at the same time that the timbers for the 74's were ordered. Eckford had a contract, dated January 10, 1817, for getting out the frames of two 74's and one frigate. Doughty's son also had a timber contract, but whether for the two remaining ships or for only one is not shown in the correspondence.

At the end of the War of 1812, the Americans not only had to settle with the Barbary regencies but also had to attend to piracy in the West Indies. The long Napoleonic Wars and the American war had allowed this area to go unpoliced, except by the war craft of the contending powers. Each of these powers had encouraged privateering, which had gradually descended to outright piracy. The power of Spain in America was declining, and her venial governors were benefiting by closing their eyes to the use of their harbors and coasts by freebooters of all descriptions. Small piratical settlements in Cuba and in many other Spanish colonies were formed, peopled with the riffraff not only of the Caribbean, but also of Europe. Whites, Negroes, mulattoes, and even Indians manned the piratical vessels from these settlements. In these rendezvous all kinds of craft were fitted out for preying on unprotected merchantmen—rowboats, barges, sloops, schooners, and larger vessels when possible. Many of the schooners were vessels captured by the pirates, but a great many were purchased craft. The greater part of the schooners used by the West Indian pirates were American-built of the pilot-boat model; many were on the shoal-draft Norfolk design. The small size and light draft of the freebooters' craft enabled them to hide, and to retire when chased, in shoal water out of reach of larger deep-draft naval brigs, sloops, and frigates.

While many of the schooners and brigs bought for the raiding squadrons in the War of 1812 were still available, it was felt that the size of these made them rather expensive to operate; furthermore, some of them were in a doubtful state of repair, owing to the haste with which they had been constructed. In lieu of assigning one of these vessels to the West Indian squadron, a new small schooner was bought at Baltimore in 1817, the 130-ton *Fox*, armed with four guns. However, the government did very little, beyond eradicating some of the pirate settlements on the Gulf Coast, until 1820.

During the War of 1812, the need for service craft in some of the navy yards became very apparent. The only way the demand could be met was by the purchase of some local small craft, though this procedure had already been found to be not wholly satisfactory. Service boats were particularly required at the Boston and Norfolk yards, which were engaged in maintenance of naval vessels to a far greater extent than the others. In both ports there were extensive anchorages used by naval shipping. With the coming of peace, the construction of well-designed service craft for these yards began, Boston receiving most of the attention. In 1816 Josiah Barker was ordered to design and build a navy yard lighter, and he produced a schooner 62' 9⅜" between perpendiculars, 18' 0" moulded beam, only 4' 6" depth of hold, and drawing about 6' loaded. Her design is shown in Figure 75. Her model is that of a new England river schooner of the period, which was suitable for a yard lighter that did not have to go to sea.

Doughty was busy with his frigate design, but was also ordered to design an anchor hoy for Boston. The anchor hoy was a boat used to lay down and pick up moorings, and to recover anchors lost when moorings parted. These hoys also were commonly fitted with tanks and supplied water to naval shipping. They were harbor craft and were a standard naval type, used by nearly all the European sailing navies. One had been built at Norfolk in 1804, probably designed by Fox, but no others had been constructed since. Doughty's design, Figure 76, was a sloop-rigged double-ender 40' long and 17' 8" moulded beam. She was capable of sailing either end foremost, so that she was handy in restricted waters and among shipping. The plan was forwarded to Boston October 21, 1818, and the boat was immediately laid down.

The building of these service craft marked the beginning of a slow improvement of the navy yards. Until the end of the War of 1812 the yards had been poorly equipped; now the new building program made it necessary to correct this condition. The probable length of time some of the new ships might be on the ways made it necessary that they have cover, so huge ship houses were built in many of the yards. These were wooden buildings with high arched roofs, covering the entire building slip. The yards were also furnished with mould lofts, offices, masting sheers, and other necessary construction. New heaving-down piers were also built, but no dry dock was constructed in any navy yard until about 1830, though private marine railways

Figure 75. Lighter and water tank schooner.

came into existence in some American ports as early as 1825. The yards were now fenced in, and their waterfronts were improved, so that additional space could be obtained.

The war had taught the importance of the squadron in sea warfare and the accompanying need of suitable maintenance facilities and supply vessels. With the construction of new ships that would make it possible to create squadrons, the facilities and service craft were now being made available. The Board, composed of veterans of the late war, were ready to apply the lessons they had learned and were establishing the foundation for a powerful navy. For the first time in American naval history an effective organization, administrative and service, was coming into existence.

After the War of 1812, no new construction was considered on the lakes, as it was felt that the need was not sufficiently great to warrant the expenditures. The British, however, were disturbed by some American activities and political talk, so they reinforced their lake establishment in 1816–17. On Champlain they built a 32-gun frigate, the *Champlain*, and completed some of the unfin-

Figure 76. Anchor hoy, 1818.

ished small vessels on Lake Ontario, but the big liners were never completed. Some new names appear on the British naval lists for Lake Ontario in these years, but it is probable that these were the wartime vessels renamed, rather than new ships. It is apparent that most of the British lake ships were never in commission, but were laid up as soon as completed. When relations deteriorated on the Canadian border, as happened from time to time, the ships were given overhauls and repaired, but matters of controversy never reached a stage where the manning of the lake squadrons was required. This would have been a breach of agreement that would have been considered a hostile act and would therefore have been done only as a last resort.

In 1819 the only important change in the construction program was the laying down of the first of the new 44's, the *Potomac*, in the Washington Navy Yard under Doughty's supervision. No new vessel was purchased, and the only changes in the Navy Register were the striking off of some of the condemned small vessels taken into service during the late war. The next year, however, was one of great activity: the 74 *North Carolina* was launched at the Philadelphia Yard, and three more 44's were started—the *Raritan* at Philadelphia, the *Santee* at Portsmouth, and the *Savannah* at New York. The design of the 44's had apparently been the subject of much consideration, for in this year a number of changes were made and applied to all the ships under construction. During the year progress was being made on the *Potomac* and *Savannah*, but these ships were delayed a good deal by the alterations. During the year the design was changed in the following respects: the stern was made round, the upper headrails were changed to straight rails, and the sheer was reduced at bow and stern. Work on all the ships did not progress rapidly; in fact, the 74 *New York* proceeded so slowly that she was still on the stocks at Norfolk when the Civil War began and was burned when the Norfolk Yard was destroyed. The *Virginia* was still on the stocks at Boston in 1874, when she was broken up, and the *Vermont* was not launched until September 15, 1845. The *Potomac* was launched in 1822, the *Savannah* in 1842, the *Raritan* in 1843, and the *Santee* in 1855. The sequence in which the frigates were laid down had no effect on the relative date of launch, as will be seen.

The decision of the government to suppress piracy in the West Indies by sending an adequate squadron to this station led to the construction of new schooners in 1820–21. The disposal of the brigs and schooners intended for the raiding squadrons during the late war had now left the Navy without suitable small craft, except the recently purchased *Fox* and one of the clipper brigs that had not been sold, the *Spark*. It was decided to build five small schooners suitable for the service, of a size that would be adequate, yet not so large as to be expensive to maintain or man. The Navy Board decided to have one designed by Eckford and the others by Doughty. The latter prepared a design of a Baltimore Clipper, 86' 0" between perpendiculars, 24' 9" moulded beam, and 10' 3" depth of hold. His design is shown in Figure 77. From these lines the *Alligator* was built at Boston Navy Yard, the *Dolphin* at the Philadelphia Yard, the

Figure 77. Schooners ALLIGATOR, SHARK, DOLPHIN, *and* PORPOISE, *1821.*

Shark at the Washington Yard, and the *Porpoise* at the Portsmouth Yard. There was some difference in the appearance of the four schooners when they were completed, as the manner in which the vessels were to be finished was left to the yards building them. The *Porpoise* and *Shark* were given the regulation head of a man-of-war—billet and headrails. The *Alligator* was given a simple gammon knee with an alligator's head carved on it. The stem of the *Dolphin* is not described and may have been a mere curved cutwater, but it is very possible that she came out with a gammon knee also, as this was a common finish in schooners in this period. There were also differences in mouldings and in the position of channels and deadeyes; the *Dolphin* had her channels below the port sill, the *Alligator* had hers just below the rail cap, and *Shark* and *Porpoise* had theirs about halfway up the gun ports. The *Alligator* and *Dolphin* had mouldings the length of the hull just below the port sills, but this was omitted in the other schooners. The correspondence indicates that the schooner program was in part rather hastily set up, with little time to prepare all the necessary copies of plans and specifications, which may explain the variation in the appearance of these vessels. A great deal of information on the details of these schooners has survived, and the plans were unusually complete for small men-of-war in this period, where lines and possibly a sail plan are usually the most that can be found. In this case the plans included not only lines, but also inboard arrangement, detail of gun mounting, spar plan, and a completely detailed sail and rigging drawing.

In view of the important part the topsail clipper schooner has played in American maritime history, the details of her rig are worth description. The sail plan (Figure 78) shows the sails and rigging in unusual detail and indicates the method used to set the square sails. The fore-and-aft portion of the rig is readily understood and is the standard schooner sail plan of the period. The mainsail, it will be seen, is fitted with what might be termed a "studding sail" boomed out with a boom fitted to the main boom and set to a head yard supported by the gaff, which is longer than the head of the mainsail for this purpose. This is a light-weather sail known as a "ringtail." The mainsail is not laced to its boom but is "loose-footed" and has four lines of reef-points—three parallel to the foot and another diagonally across the upper portion of the sail, the "balance reef." When this last reef was made, the mainsail became in effect a stormsail, or "trysail." The gaff topsail is very lofty, and its head is extended above the topmast by a gunter pole laced to the sail. The gunter pole extends about an equal amount above and below the topmast head. The

Figure 78. Sail plan of 1821 schooners showing arrangement of square sails employed in topsail man-of-war schooners.

foresail has no boom and overlaps the mainsail; this is called a "lug foresail" and was the standard arrangement in American clipper schooners throughout the last quarter of the eighteenth century and the first half of the nineteenth. The foresail has what appear to be four reefs in it, but the lower is really a lacing, which allows the portion of the sail beneath it to be removed. This portion was known as the "bonnet." The purpose of this was to reduce the weight of the sail when it was reefed and, as it often would be in such a case, wet. The foresail was usually carried with one or more reefs in it in gales, when all other sail might be off the vessel. It was therefore desirable to make it as easy to handle as possible. Above the foresail is a main-topmast staysail—a sail very much like the modern schooner's "fisherman staysail," but somewhat smaller in proportion. The headsails are much like those of the more recent fishing schooners, except that the innermost sail, the fore staysail, has no boom and is fitted with a bonnet as well as reef points.

The square sails were all on the foremast and consisted of a large forecourse, a fore topsail and a fore-topgallant sail—all with studding sails. Many modern yachts have been fitted with square sails approximately like those shown in this sail plan, but without the rigging details that made the clipper schooner's rig so practical. It had been found that furling the huge forecourse of a schooner on the foreyard not only made an ungainly bundle of sail, but its weight, particularly when wet, hurt the vessel's stability, and its windage effectively destroyed a schooner's ability in sailing to windward. Also, experience had shown that the yards, if left aloft in strong gales, made the vessel unstable and often unmanageable. The problem was therefore, first, to avoid furling the course on the foreyard and, secondly, to rig all yards so that they could be quickly brought to deck. Safety, in the early days, also required that a schooner be able to make sail rapidly and that she carry a lot of it to obtain the greatest speed the weather conditions permitted.

In order to meet the problems raised, the topsail and topgallant yards were fitted with halyards and held to the topmast with running parrels. By lowering the yards and removing the parrels, halyards, and, of course, the lifts and braces, the spars could be stowed on deck. The foreyard was commonly rigged in the same manner, though some schooners had a heavy jackstay running up the fore side of the foremast, with an eye over the masthead and resting on the fore crosstree, thence to deck and set up with deadeyes and lanyards. A thimble was made fast to the yard to travel on this jackstay, which gave better control when the yard was being lowered in rough weather. As schooners grew larger, their spars became long and rather heavy, so it became the practice to stow the yards across the ship a short distance above the rail, without removing them from the mast entirely. In this position they were lashed to the fore shrouds and were usually high enough above the water to prevent their being dipped when the vessel rolled.

With the yards slung in the manner described, they could be braced up very sharply, since the parrel or truss could be slacked off so that the yards were actually a foot or more from the mast and resting against the lee shrouds. This made the squaresail rig more effective to windward than was the case in later years, when the yards were rigidly secured to the masts with ironwork. Of course, the flexible rig of the clipper schooners had the disadvantage of chafing considerably, and this required watching at sea.

The topsail and the topgallant were bent to their yards in the conventional manner and were furled on their respective yards; being relatively small, they could be neatly furled. The course was a different matter; its great hoist made it a huge sail having more area than even the mainsail. The course was hoisted to the yard by means of a halyard bent to the middle of its head and by outhauls to the yardarms. To make it stand, there was a jackyard laced to the head of the sail which made the sail stand neatly; the length of the jackyard was about half the head of the forecourse. By this means, the sail was lowered and furled on deck when desired, or it could be furled to the yard.

The foot of the forecourse was made as wide as the head, to make the sail as effective as possible. To make this stand properly, a "squaresail boom" was employed. This was a spar of the same length, approximately, as the foreyard, to which the foot of the course was secured by the sheets and fore tacks. The boom was rarely secured to the mast by a truss; it was commonly allowed to rest on the bulwarks, or rail, where it was lashed to convenient ringbolts or cleats. The squaresail boom made the forecourse stand better on all points of sailing and simplified the fitting of the studding-sail booms. A large studding sail was fitted to the course in the usual manner; its boom was on the squaresail boom.

Most of the sail area was on the foremast, and for this reason the mast was usually slightly larger in diameter than the main and had more shrouds. The mainstay was double and ran forward, set up by tackles in the waterways close to the rails at the bow, one stay passing on each side of the foremast. It was necessary to slack off the lee one when the foresail was in use. The clipper schooners did not use the modern springstay between the mastheads;

Section through side of
the 74 "Delaware", 1828

Showing the deadeyes faced fore and
aft, and long iron strap, to allow clear
fire to spar deck carronades. Similar
fitting ordered on all ships 1822 and
continued in force until 1843, when the
deadeyes were again faced athwartships.

Sketch from Grice's
Papers.

Scale

Plan 21. Draught of class of 74-gun ships, 1818, NORTH CAROLINA and DELAWARE.

Particulars
O is 64'0" from F.P.
Room & Space 2'4" Stations 9'4" apart
1st W.L is 1'9" from Base
2nd " " 3'9" "
Other W.L's are 3'0" apart
Buttocks are 4'0" apart
Gun to Spar Deck is 7'4½"

No Reconstruction shown.

Plan 22. Revised building draught for class of 44-gun frigates, 1821, BRANDYWINE, POTOMAC, and class.

this did not come into use in American schooners until sometime around 1840, and it first appeared in coasters.

The clipper-schooner rig, with the overlapping foresail and huge area of square sails, was a highly effective rig on all points of sailing. The seamen of the period believed, very properly, that power makes speed and so, when fast sailing was required, they depended on large areas of sail combined with sharp-model hulls. There can be no doubt that the clipper schooners were faster than even the best of the modern seagoing yachts over a long course, but the clipper rig required a big crew to handle it, which was the reason why this rig was eventually replaced.

The new schooners proved to be fast, but like many of Doughty's small vessels they were a little too full aft to be extraordinarily speedy. Their big rigs and full bows made them somewhat dangerous when driven hard, as they then depressed their bows and had a tendency to dive under. The *Dolphin* was the first laid down. She spent much of her career in the Pacific rather than on the station for which she had been built. She lasted until 1835, when she was found to be rotten and was broken up. The *Alligator* was wrecked on the Florida coast, near what is now Miami, in the fall of 1823. The *Shark* had a long and successful career; she was finally wrecked at the mouth of the Columbia River, on the northwest coast, in September, 1846. The *Porpoise* was wrecked in the West Indies in 1833.

The fifth schooner was designed, as has been mentioned, by Eckford. Late in 1819 the Board of Navy Commissioners had asked him to design a corvette and a "light-draft schooner." Eckford designed the corvette first, and it was not until early 1820 that he finally got to work on the schooner design, which was now the design most wanted. When the schooner design was submitted to the Board, the relatively great size of the intended vessel was the subject of some discussion, particularly in the light of the expressed desire of the Board that the vessel be inexpensive to maintain and fit out. However, Eckford appears to have taken his stand on the stated requirements for armament, combined with light draft, and the matter was finally settled by ordering the schooner built at the Washington Navy Yard. There is no evidence in the discussion over this design of any personal feelings on the part of the Board members or Eckford; it appears merely that the Board raised the question and Eckford made a polite reply.

In 1819 an English shipwright named Henry Steer applied for work in the Washington Navy Yard. Steer was born at, or near, Dartmouth, England, in

Figure 79. Schooner GRAMPUS, *1821, a noted sailer.*

331

1780. He learned his trade under a builder named Newman in New Quay, and after completing his apprenticeship he went to work in the Plymouth Dockyard. In 1815 he went to the island of Guernsey and worked for the French government. He was not only a shipbuilder, but also a competent draftsman and designer. A fellow shipwright in the Plymouth Dockyard, John Thomas, also a competent builder and designer, had gone to America and was working in the Washington Yard. Thomas wrote Steer suggesting that he come to America and, a depression occurring in the trade in Great Britain at this time, Steer and his family—wife and two sons, James R. and Henry T.—arrived in New York and went from there to Washington. A third son, George, was born in Washington in 1820. Henry Steer was employed on the schooners *Shark* and *Grampus*, apparently acting as charge man, and remained in the yard until 1822. His sons Henry and George became distinguished ship designers. The younger, George, designed the yacht *America* and many pilot boats, as well as the clipper ship *Sunny South*. Henry Steers (an "s" having been added to the name by usage) was the designer of the famous Collins steamer *Adriatic* and of many other noted vessels. Doughty had been impressed with the draftsmanship of Henry Steer, and a drawing of a clipper schooner made by the latter is now in the Mariner's Museum, Newport News, Virginia, as part of the Steers Collection. It has sometimes been claimed that Steer designed the *Shark* and *Grampus*, but this can readily be shown to be an error.

The Eckford-designed schooner was named *Grampus;* her plans are shown in Figures 79 and 80. She was 92' 6" between perpendiculars, 97' 0" over all, 24' 6" moulded beam, and 9' 6" depth of hold, according to her offsets. She was designed to draw 11' 0", but was usually ballasted to draw between 11' 6" and 11' 9" in service. She had the characteristic headrails and cutwater of an Eckford design, and her long clean run was an improvement over Doughty's design for her classmates. The Board approved the design September 11, 1820, with the express direction that she be one of the two schooners built in the Washington Yard. Her spar and sail plans have also survived. The *Grampus* was launched in 1821 and proved to be a fast sailer. She was lost with all hands through capsizing in a gale while off Charleston, South Carolina, in 1843. She was considered one of the fastest schooners of her day.

So far as can be discovered, these five were the first seagoing naval schooners to be fitted with the high pivot gun. The Doughty design made no particular provision for the pivot; ports were placed amidships to permit the usual broadside armament. They were to carry 10 6-pdr. short guns and a long 18 on the

Figure 80. Sail plan of GRAMPUS.

pivot. Later the pivot was removed, and two long 18's on carriages were placed aboard. The 6-pdr. guns were soon replaced with 12-pdr. carronades. The *Grampus*, however, was not designed with ports amidships, and so was deliberately drawn for the use of the pivot gun. Her armament seems to have been changed a number of times while she was a new vessel; she had the long 18 pivot gun throughout her career, apparently, and carried 8 to 10 carronades, 12-pdrs.; at one time she had two or more 18-pdr. carronades in place of some of the 12's. The design of the *Grampus* might well have been developed out of the schooner designs that Eckford had produced on Lake Ontario, and it is possible that there were strong similarities.

The launch of the *Ohio* on May 31, 1820, marked the end of Eckford's service as a naval constructor, as he resigned on June 1. His resignation was accepted on the 6th, and he was asked to recommend his successor. He strongly recommended his ex-apprentice, Isaac Webb, who would not accept the appointment. Eckford then recommended his assistant, John Floyd, who was appointed resident naval constructor in the New York Yard. Floyd had been with Eckford for some years and, according to one account, had been with him on Lake Ontario and had helped build the vessels there. Floyd seems to have been a very capable man, but relatively little has yet been found on his career.

Samuel Hartt was appointed naval constructor a year before Eckford resigned, receiving an appointment June 1, 1819. Barker was afterward transferred to Portsmouth. Hartt was then placed at Boston, Floyd was stationed at New York, Humphreys at Philadelphia, Doughty at Washington, and Grice at Norfolk. Hartt belonged to the noted Boston family of shipbuilders, members of which had built the *Constitution, Boston,* and *Argus.* Samuel Humphreys recommended William Easby as a boatbuilder, and Easby was assigned to Washington, becoming master boatbuilder there. Doughty was now acting as chief constructor, for all practical purposes, though he did not have the title, as he was still the senior constructor.

Before resigning, Eckford had made the recommendation that the prize ship sloop *Cyane* be cut down into a flush-decked ship, but as funds were not available, no action was taken on his advice. Eckford now turned to private practice, designing and building merchant ships, as well as men-of-war for foreign governments. By this time the Americans had achieved widespread fame as ship designers and builders and were competing with British and French constructors on equal terms for foreign naval business. In the ten years that immediately followed his resignation from the New York Yard, Eckford built

Figure 81. Sketch of cant timber arrangement in 1821 frigate design to show framing of round stern.

U. S. Frigate Brandywine
copied from Wm Doughty's original draught.

Principal dimensions.   feet — in?
Length between perpendiculars — — — — — — — — 175 — —
— — — Keel for tonnage — — — — — — — — — 145 . 6
— — — Beam moulded — — — — — — — — — 45 — —
Depth of hold — — — — — — — — — — — 14 . 4
From upper side birth deck beam to
upper side gun deck beam at middle line — — — 6 . 10
From upper side gun deck beam to upper
side of Spardeck beam — — — — — — — — 7 . 4½
Carpenters tons — — — — — — — — — 1550 . 69/ths
                                                              /95
Frames spaced 2' 4" apart.

335

two huge frigates, *Amazon* and *South America*, for a foreign power, as well as a few packets, merchant ships, and small craft.

In 1821 the new schooners were launched and another 44, the *Brandywine*, was laid down at the Washington Navy Yard. In starting the new frigate, the design was finally settled, and all the changes incorporated in the others then building were worked into the plans. The new ship, built without any great delays, was launched in 1825 and became a noted sailer and a favorite ship. She was burned at the Norfolk Navy Yard at the outbreak of the Civil War. All the alterations in the original design and in the ships building having been accounted for, the design finally used can be established. Plan 22 is the building plan of the *Brandywine* and of the 44's that followed her. The plan also represents, because of the changes made, the frigates that had been laid down in 1819 and 1820. This was the standard design of the American frigates of this class to the end of the usefulness of sailing men-of-war; only three of the frigates placed on the Navy List afterward were on independent designs. However, the appearance of the sister ships of the *Brandywine*, completed at a much later date, was quite different, since in the meantime the fashion of finishing the cutwater and stern had undergone some changes. In spite of this, the lines were not altered, the original design being considered excellent for this class of vessel.

The sloop *Erie*, built in 1813, had been surveyed in 1820 and was found to be rotten. It was decided to repair her and, in the process, to lengthen her to about 122'. Doughty prepared a new drawing for the ship, making her 121' 11" between perpendiculars, 32' 6" moulded beam, and 14' 9" depth in the hold. While it appears that some of the original ship was saved in the rebuilding, nevertheless the *Erie* was practically a new ship when again launched. The practice of "rebuilding" ships on a new design may be said to have begun with this incident; in this case the redesigning was partial, but it was an easy step to the use of a completely new design, producing an entirely different model and even class of ship in the guise of "rebuilding." The *Erie* as rebuilt is shown in Figure 82. The work was done at the New York Navy Yard, and she was launched late in 1821. She ran for twenty years, first as a cruiser and toward the last as a storeship. She was broken up at Boston in 1841. A storeship of the same name, but smaller, was built to replace her.

The year 1822 was one of activity in the West Indies, and the need of more small vessels on that station became apparent. Consequently eight schooners of about 42 to 65 tons were purchased at Baltimore, and all but one were

Figure 82. Draught of ERIE as rebuilt, 1821.

337

armed with 3 small guns. These schooners were the *Ferret, Beagle, Fox* (the older *Fox* was found too deep for the intended use and so had been sold late in 1821 or early in 1822), *Greyhound, Terrier, Weasel, Jackall,* all 3 guns, and the *Wildcat,* 2 guns. The *Ferret* was lost in the West Indies in 1825, and the others were sold—*Greyhound, Wildcat,* and *Jackall* in 1824, *Beagle, Terrier* and *Weasel* in 1825, and *Fox* in 1838. Little is known about these schooners, except that some of them were on the Norfolk pilot-boat model, while others were of the standard clipper type. The *Beagle* had bulwarks at least; some of the smaller schooners had none. A schooner, the *Revenge,* was also employed in the West Indies with these small vessels; the *Revenge* was formerly the Jeffersonian gunboat *No. 158.*

A storeship, the *Decoy,* was purchased this year at New York. She was a merchant schooner and was intended for the support of the West Indian squadron. The *Decoy* was armed with 6 small guns; she was sold at Norfolk in 1826. The *Sabine,* another 44, was ordered laid down this year at New York; however, work on the ship did not actually begin until February, 1823, and she was not launched until 1855. She was employed in the Civil War and was finally sold out in 1883.

In this year, 1822, the largest sailing man-of-war ever built for the United States Navy was laid down. This was the 120-gun *Pennsylvania,* designed to be the most powerful ship of her class in the world. The design of the ship was prepared by Samuel Humphreys, and the first draught of her lines was completed in 1822. She was intended to be a four-decked ship without a poop, and she showed ports to carry 132 guns exclusive of bow chasers and stern guns. In the early plans she had a small beakhead bulkhead, but as the design developed this was dropped and replaced with a round bow. The whole stern was also changed, and the hull design of this ship developed over a period of at least eight years, if not somewhat longer; she was not launched until 1837. For that reason she will be discussed later, when the design finally employed can be shown in proper sequence. The ship was to be 210′ 0″ between perpendiculars, 56′ 9″ moulded beam, and 24′ 3″ depth of hold; keel to sheer was about 54′ 0″. The ship as completed will be discussed in Chapter Seven. This huge man-of-war occupied the Philadelphia Navy Yard's force of ship carpenters to such an extent that little other work was done there while she was building. This was probably the reason for the delay in building the frigate *Raritan,* even though the Philadelphia Yard was heavily manned, and was then considered next

to the Washington Yard in importance, the two yards being capable of handling the construction of a number of large ships.

The proposal to build such a ship as the *Pennsylvania* indicates how much
the British blockade of the American coast had hurt; now it was fully realized
that the Navy must have vessels of sufficient power to break a blockade, at
some of the important ports, at least, in the event of war. This the huge *Pennsylvania*, accompanied by the smaller but very powerful liners built or building, would be able to accomplish. The combination would be so powerful that
an enemy would not be able to maintain a blockade unless these liners were
captured or destroyed—and no foreign navy had enough huge liners to set up
a blockade that would be certain to overpower such a force. It might therefore be said, with some truth, that the *Pennsylvania* was not built to serve as an
ocean cruiser, but was rather a coast-defense ship designed solely to overcome
or drive off a blockader.

The design of this huge vessel seems to have been based on plans obtained
from Europe. Samuel Humphreys had the plans of the big *Santisima Trinidad*, which had been in the Spanish fleet at Trafalgar, and of the British
100-gun ship *Royal Sovereign*, which had also been in that famous battle. The
plans of these ships do not appear to have been copied in the design of the
Pennsylvania, but they were used, apparently, as a guide in establishing the
general proportions of the huge American vessel. It is probable that the existence of these plans in Humphreys' hands explains the appearance of a beakhead
bulkhead in the original design of the *Pennsylvania*. This type of bow had gone
out of fashion in the British Navy long before the American ship was laid down
but was employed in the *Royal Sovereign* and in the even older *Santisima
Trinidad*. Eckford was probably the only designer in America that could
have dared the design of such a large ship as the *Pennsylvania* without the
aid of foreign information, as he alone had ever designed a ship of such size—if
the tradition that he designed the *New Orleans* on Lake Ontario is accepted.
Eckford, however, was no longer available to the Navy Board.

The requirements of the West Indian station placed four small craft on the
Navy List in 1822–23; these were the "barges" *Galinipper*, *Midge*, *Mosquito*,
and *Sandfly*, commemorating the worst insect pests on the station. These
"barges" appear to have been large open boats fitted to row and sail and may
have been some of the old gunboat barges of the War of 1812 fitted up and
renamed. They carried large crews and one or two guns, and were particularly

useful in attacking pirate craft of similar characteristics among the islands and in shoal water. It is also possible that large ship's launches were utilized; the records are unfortunately insufficient to establish the type of hull and rig employed in these particular boats. They were not carried on the Navy Register after 1824.

For some years the design of a class of ship sloops had been a matter of study and discussion among the members of the Navy Board. Commodore Rodgers, who was President of the Board from 1815 to 1824, had been much interested in this class, and the War of 1812 had shown what the type could accomplish. In 1819, it will be recalled, the Board had requested Eckford to submit a plan of a corvette, and in compliance with this request Eckford prepared the design presented in Figure 83—a 22-gun ship 124' 0" between perpendiculars, 32' 0" moulded beam, and 15' depth of hold. The ship sloop *Madison*, which Eckford had built on Lake Ontario in 1812, had measured about 593 tons; the new design was $510^3\%_{95}$ tons. While the matter is one of pure speculation, it is at least probable that the new design Eckford had prepared followed very closely the design of the earlier ship, for, as we have seen, the Lake Ontario vessels employed much deadrise, judging by what is known about the British ships and by the statements of officers, and others, that certain American vessels were on the sharp model. It is notable that Eckford had become the leading exponent of sharp vessels, with respect to deadrise, sometime between his arrival at New York as a young ship carpenter and the end of the War of 1812. It might be suggested that he became converted to this form of hull through his experience with the lakes but, of course, there is no proof. The Board, having Eckford's design in hand, laid it aside for study.

By 1824, the need for ship sloops, particularly in the Pacific, where American interests in the Oregon Territory and on the South American West Coast needed protection, again occupied the attention of the Board. They now had additional designs prepared. Grice presented a proposal for a ship sloop 119' 0" between perpendiculars, 32' 6" moulded beam, and on a sharp model (Figure 84). Floyd also was ordered to prepare a plan, and his design (Figure 85) was the largest ship of all—136' 0" between perpendiculars, 42' 0" moulded beam, and 19' 0" depth of hold, to carry 24 guns. This design showed much Eckford influence, as was to be expected from a man trained under this ship designer. It is evident that Eckford, Grice, and Floyd were not in agreement as to the proper size or armament for the sloops, but in the main they were agreed in much deadrise and a rather high bilge.

Figure 83. Draught of corvette proposed by Eckford.

Figure 84. Draught of sloop proposed by Grice, 1824.

342

Figure 85. Draught of sloop of war proposed by Floyd, 1824.

343

Samuel Humphreys also prepared a design 126′ 6″ between perpendiculars, 33′ 9″ moulded beam, and 15′ 3″ depth of hold. This design appealed to the Board, and after a few modifications, including the substitution of a round stern for the transom stern first proposed, it was accepted. Figure 86 is the final building plan for the vessels constructed from Humphreys' design; as modified it called for 127′ 0″ between perpendiculars and 34′ 0″ moulded beam. The plan called for 24 gun ports exclusive of the bridle ports and quarter galleries added to the round stern. It was decided to build the ten sloops from this design, the first to be started at the Boston Navy Yard, to be named the *Boston*. It was eventually decided that the ten ships were to be built in the various navy yards, as follows: three at Boston, three at New York, and one each at Portsmouth, Washington, Philadelphia, and Norfolk.

When the preliminary design reached each of the yards, the resident constructors prepared copies, as was the custom. Doughty decided to alter the design, and his plan called for a sloop very like Humphreys' design in model but with 3″ less beam and very full-ended. Barker, who was still at Boston at this time, also made his copy, with variations, calling for a ship 127′ 6″ between perpendiculars but otherwise retaining the original dimensions. Barker's plan omitted the quarter galleries called for by the Board in their modification of Humphreys' original design. The upshot of this situation was that, instead of all the vessels being built to a uniform design, three vessels were built to Doughty's plan and at least one to Barker's, while the remaining sloops were apparently built to Humphreys' plan. This seems to have been done with the consent of the Board, for in Doughty's case at least the official correspondence shows that the Board approved three sloops being built to his plan. Figure 88 is Doughty's design, and Figure 89 Barker's. Thus, the Navy Board had failed to establish uniformity in the design of this class.

It may be said here that the new class of sloops did not add much to the reputation of the constructors involved, for only a few of them proved very fast. They were not particularly handsome ships, and this did not help the designers either. The real source of dissatisfaction with the new class of corvettes can be traced to the Board's insistence upon 24 guns being carried in vessels whose dimensions were better suited to a 20- or 22-gun ship. Eckford had proposed a 22-gun ship slightly smaller than the approved design; Floyd recommended a very large corvette to carry 24. Humphreys' vessel appears to have been a compromise, slightly larger than Eckford's proposal and carrying Floyd's proposal as to armament, 24 medium 24-pdrs. on a flush deck. It was

Figure 86. Draught used for building some of the 24-gun sloops, 1824–29, Humphreys' design.

eventually discovered that the new sloops would not carry their armament, and they were therefore reduced to 20 guns—2 medium 32's and 18 carronades, 32-pdrs.—and were rated as 18-gun ship sloops. Humphreys was well aware of the difficulty in using a relatively small ship to carry a very heavy armament, as is evidenced by the increase in displacement given his design over that proposed by Eckford. As a result the new corvettes were given rather barrel-

Figure 87. Proposed spar plan for 24-gun sloops, 1827.

shaped midsections and full ends. None of these features were helpful to speed under sail. One of the many lessons taught by the War of 1812 was that a corvette should be a fast sailer and ought to carry a battery of long guns, as these were far more effective in her work than carronades, particularly when acting as commerce destroyers, the employment for which sloops and corvettes were primarily designed. Hence the production of a new class of corvette which was not particularly fast and which had to have gun batteries replaced by carronades was bound to invite criticism both in the service and out of it. The class was not a complete failure, but it was not a complete success either, in spite of being larger and more heavily armed than the successful 1813 sloops.

Figure 88. Doughty's draught for 24-gun sloops, 1824.

347

Figure 89. Barker's draught for a 24-gun sloop, 1826.

348

The membership of the Board had been changed a little during the first ten years of its existence. Rodgers was replaced as president by Bainbridge in 1824; Isaac Hull was a member only one year, 1818, David Porter from 1815 to 1822, Stephen Decatur from 1815 to 1820, and Isaac Chauncey from 1822 to 1824. Charles Morris replaced Porter in 1823, and Jacob Jones replaced Chauncey in 1824. Charles W. Goldsborough replaced Paulding as secretary in 1823. Goldsborough was former chief clerk in the Navy Department and a typical bureaucrat of the period. The control of naval shipbuilding and equipment was now firmly placed in the hands of a "service board" comprised of commissioned officers who were "users" or "practical seamen," supported and aided by the constructors, the "technical" advisers. In theory this should have been an ideal arrangement. However, the constructors were completely subordinate to the service board and were also insulated, to a great extent, from civilian developments in ship design and building, since they were no longer forced to compete with outsiders, and their ships were seldom placed in a position where odious comparisons could be made. Since both the Board and the constructors were now jointly responsible for the design of new ships, it can well be imagined how criticism could be suppressed in either the sea service or the navy yards. The long-standing difficulty of the supreme power in design of vessels resting in the hands of non-technical "users" rather than in men trained in shipbuilding and design became apparent. The weakness of the relationship of the constructors to the Board was in the lack of a continuous control of new ship construction, from design to commissioning, on the part of the constructors. The Board could, and did, change its mind after a design was approved and ships built; they might increase the armament, allowances of stores, crew, or the number of boats above the original requirements set forth when the designs were prepared. It will be seen that there was no real improvement in the position of the constructors over the condition that had existed before the Navy Board came into existence; the skilled constructor was still entirely subordinate in the field of his profession to the commissioned officers.

In 1825 the shipbuilding program took a spurt, for five additional 24-gun corvettes were laid down, and two more 44's. The sloops were the *Fairfield*, at New York, launched in 1828; the *Lexington* in the same navy yard, launched the same year she was laid down; the *Vandalia* at the Philadelphia Navy Yard, launched in 1828; the *Vincennes* at New York, launched in 1826; and the *Warren*, built at Boston and launched in 1826. Strangely enough, the *Lexington* and *Warren* are noted as having been built to Doughty's plan, rather than to the resident constructors' drawings. The 44's were the *Columbia*, laid down in the Washington Navy Yard and launched in 1836, and the *Cumberland*, laid down in the Boston Yard and launched in 1842. No new designs were prepared in the year 1825, and all of the constructors were busy with ships building in their yards. The Board was now dealing directly with each of the constructors when any question arose, and this was a burdensome administrative function. The appointment of a chief constructor would relieve the Board members of much of this detail, and so the matter began to receive consideration. In the meantime, the Board was forced to refer technical matters to the constructors located in the vicinity of Washington, Doughty and Humphreys, when the matters were beyond the comprehension of the sea officers.

In the next year, 1826, another 44 and a corvette were laid down—the frigate *St. Lawrence* in the Norfolk Navy Yard, launched in 1847, and the sloop *Falmouth* at Boston, built to Barker's drawing, launched in 1827. The new sloops were being built as rapidly as the yards could turn them out. The older sloops built during the War of 1812, except the rebuilt *Erie*, were in need of extensive repairs, and new vessels were required to take their place. The old *Hornet* had been nearly worn out during the War of 1812 and had received extensive repairs after the war, which changed her appearance a good deal and brought her to look much like the 1813 sloops. The old frigates, *Congress*, *Macedonian*, *United States*, *Constitution*, *Constellation*, and *John Adams*, were either rapidly becoming unserviceable, or were requiring expensive repairs. The problem of retaining old ships in service was becoming acute, for a great deal of the naval appropriations was being spent on them which might better have been applied to new construction, if some way could be found to manage it.

From 1820 to 1826 the New York shipbuilders had been actively engaged in building men-of-war for foreign governments. Eckford, as has been mentioned, had taken the lead in this, but other builders had taken similar contracts, and ships were built for Russia and other European powers as well as for Central and South American governments. Many of these vessels were ordered by revolutionary governments, and there was often a strong element of risk in these contracts for a builder. Among the contracts let in New York were some vessels for the Greek revolutionists. Smith and Dimon had built a huge frigate named *Liberator* for them, but the Greeks were unable to pay for her. By means of political influence the builders were able to dispose of the ship to the American government, and the *Liberator* came into the Navy as the 44-gun frigate *Hudson*, the last privately built sailing frigate in the United States Navy. She was, of course, designed by her builders.

The *Hudson* made but one cruise, on the Brazilian station, and was laid up. In 1844 she was rotten and was broken up at New York. The ship was the subject of much controversy, and it was claimed that she was poorly built. It is now impossible to pass on the truth of this, for it is apparent that there was much prejudice against the frigate in the Navy, chiefly because of the manner in which she was fobbed off on the service, and there is strong evidence that the reports on the ship were sometimes very unjust. Her design was not criticized, for she was actually considered a very good model, but rather her construction and the quality of the timber in her were made the issues.

Plan 23 is a drawing of this frigate. She was 177′ 10″ between perpendiculars, 45′ 0″ moulded beam, and 13′ 8″ depth of hold to berth deck. Her builders had built packets, and the design of the *Hudson* followed these rather than the standard frigate model. The *Hudson* was really a much larger ship than the American 44's and was pierced to carry 66 guns exclusive of her bridle ports. She was a double-banked frigate with an unbroken sheer. Her size and design really made her more like the earlier 64-gun ships than a frigate, but with the coming of the double-banked vessel the true frigate went out of fashion in ships from 36 guns upward. The *Hudson* was plainly finished, but she was a handsome frigate in a strikingly bold manner.

Plan 23 is a redrawing of the original, which was made from the builder's half-model and from measurements made from the ship in 1828, according to a note on the original drawing. It is apparent from this that Smith and Dimon built their ships from half-models rather than from drawings. It cannot be said with any degree of accuracy when the fashion of employing half-models in merchant-ship construction replaced drawings in New York or in the leading yards at other shipbuilding centers. Of course, it is probable that this was a gradual development and not a sudden innovation, but it would be interesting to know the approximate time that models were used by a large majority of the builders. There is reason to suppose that all the shipbuilding centers did not adopt the half-model method of design at the same time. Without going into details of no particular moment to naval design, it can be said that there is evidence that the New York builders did much to introduce the use of the half-model elsewhere.

There are a number of plans of merchant vessels built in New York, Philadelphia, and elsewhere before the War of 1812, and both Christian Bergh and Noah Brown are known to have made drawings of their ships. In 1819, on September 6, the Navy Board wrote Brown for "draughts and plans" of all government vessels he had built; they received one at least, the corvette *Saratoga*. Eckford also made drawings, for much of his work has survived. On the other hand, the half-model was used by Eckford's apprentice, Isaac Webb; Brown's foreman, Sydney Wright; Smith and Dimon; and Noah Brown's adopted son, David Brown, of Brown and Bell. On this scanty evidence it might be assumed that the change from draught to model, as a method of design, took place soon after the War of 1812 in the New York area. From here the practice was spread by the apprentices from the leading New York yards, who went to New England, to the lakes, and southward, as independent builders.

By 1825 the practice had spread throughout New England, at any rate, and was slowly spreading southward. In 1820 it was still not universal on the Chesapeake, however, as the French naval architect Marestier found drawings of schooners in this section and made copies of them for his report on American steam vessels and schooners. At this time the builders at Philadelphia and Baltimore were using half-models to a limited degree, at least, but appear to have depended upon drawings much more than was the case in New York. Conclusions of this nature should be accepted with caution, however, for the evidence is as yet scant and some of it may be misleading. In considering the matter it must be remembered that the use of the half-model did not bar making drawings; the Webbs, for example, made a model first and from this made, in most cases, a drawing of the lines and of some details—deck arrangement and sail or spar plans. Other builders made no drawings whatsoever and took all their measurements directly from the half-models, as is evidenced by offsets that are found recorded on the "lifts" when the models are taken apart. It appears quite certain that the majority of the New York merchant-ship builders had dispensed with all but sail plans and a few deck sketches by 1825 and designed wholly by means of the half-model.

The half-model had the advantage over lines, or a "draught," in that it readily conveyed the shape of the intended hull to anyone, such as a merchant or a captain, who had not been trained in drawing plans of ships. The Navy Board, in fact, usually required a half-model, as well as a draught, of any new design. However, naval practice in designing did not recognize the use of the half-model as a primary design method; the drawing of the lines was first prepared and the calculations made, the important details of arrangement and finish were worked out in plans and, finally, a half-model was usually made to check the plans and to show the non-technical Board just what the ship would look like. The Navy half-model was a cheap substitute for the expensive and handsome built-up model once employed in the British Admiralty, and was not the official design of the ship. However, when the Navy obtained a ship from private builders, they were often forced to accept a half-model in lieu of plans for record, and from the half-model they made a file drawing, as in the case of the *Hudson*. Possibly the reason why the constructors preferred to work with plans is that the weight calculations could be most conveniently made from plans; and weight calculations had now become important in naval ship design. However, all of the constructors had been trained in the use of plans, rather than half-models, and this certainly had much effect on their practices. The merchant builders, however, were not required to make weight calculations, and usually made none of any kind whatsoever, even in large, important vessels such as the North Atlantic packets.

The growing organization needed for the construction of the new ships now required a technical supervisor. Doughty, as senior constructor, would naturally be the person to receive the appointment as chief constructor. However, he had become a man of some wealth, and his son had become active in the lumber business, supplying timber to the Navy. He felt that he did not desire the burden and responsibilities of the appointment, which therefore was tendered to the constructor next in seniority, Samuel Humphreys. Doughty remained as naval constructor in the Washington Yard, but ceased to be active in naval design. In 1837 he resigned and joined his son in the lumber trade. Humphreys was appointed chief constructor November 25, 1826, and accepted December 4, 1826.

With a chief constructor appointed, the resident constructors now made their reports to him rather than directly to the Navy Board as before. If the surviving correspondence of the chief constructor is any indication, the yard constructors made very few written reports, and there was very little technical correspondence of any kind, except where new designs were being allotted for construction. The routine yard reports were made by the commandants, who reported on progress and the state of the yards at regular intervals. It is apparent, however, that the various constructors carried on correspondence among themselves, apart from official letters, and that a good deal of the business was done on an informal basis.

The chief naval constructor was, of course, responsible for all new ship designs; he could either prepare these personally or assign a design to one of his subordinates, as he wished. His attendance on the Board of Navy Commissioners was only occasionally necessary, so he remained for a while at his post in the Philadelphia Navy Yard. Hence no additional constructor was considered necessary to replace him. At this time Humphreys had as his apprentice John Lenthall, who acted as his draftsman and assistant. Lenthall was recommended by Humphreys for appointment as assistant naval constructor at the Philadelphia Yard in 1828. Assistants had been assigned to many of the constructors, who prepared plans and specifications under the supervision of the resident and also helped in supervisory work of construction. Such men as Henry Allen, C. F. Waldo, Richard Powell, and Foster Rhodes were very competent draftsmen, and even designed small vessels in their own right.

In most cases, the characters and personalities of the constructors cannot be accurately estimated by the relatively scant official correspondence that now exists. Much of the official correspondence was formal and of a professional nature, or consisted merely of letters transmitting plans and specifications. In a few cases there is personal correspondence outside the official files, and from this source some opinions might be drawn. Samuel Humphreys appears as an executive of much ability, but somewhat vain and pompous. He was quick to resent slights and stood on his dignity. His relations with the constructors seem to have been very friendly and pleasant, however, though there is little evidence of any close personal relationship, except with those who had been his apprentices. Of the resident constructors, Grice was by far the most progressive and active-minded. He was strongly opinionated and did not agree with Humphreys' ideas on hull design. Floyd was a nonentity as far as design was concerned, and he was interested only in construction problems. Barker seems to have had ability but was not particularly interested in designing. Hartt was as yet untried; he was later to become a noted constructor. Doughty, highly competent and experienced, wished to retire from designing, and in addition there was the delicate question of seniority in his case. As a result of the character of the constructors, it is not surprising to find Humphreys assuming all design work, with the aid of his assistant, Lenthall, and having once done this with the Board's approval, retaining the function as long as the Board existed.

As a result, there was no design work for the resident constructors, who either pottered with the slow-moving construction program, if indolent and unambitious, or branched out into design for commercial interests, as did Grice and, eventually, Hartt and Lenthall. The constructors who maintained outside interests were able to keep abreast of the new developments in merchant-ship design and construction and of the new methods employed in shipbuilding outside of the navy yards. These men came into contact with those interested in steamers and other new types of vessels. The result was that these constructors remained highly progressive and steadily became better informed while the others vegetated. Unfortunately, the outside activities of the more progressive constructors brought them into conflict with the yard commandants on occasion, and this in turn led both the Board and the chief constructor to regard them with doubt and suspicion. Hence, when advice or consultation was desired, the constructors who had applied their whole energies to the naval construction program were usually the most influential. Some of the constructors were growing old with minds shaped in the bureaucratic mould.

In 1827, two more 24-gun corvettes were laid down—the *St. Louis* in the Washington Yard and the *Natchez* in the Norfolk Yard. Both were built rapidly and were launched in 1828. The *Natchez* was the third sloop built to the Doughty modifications, in spite of the fact that it would have seemed rational to employ the Doughty drawings in a single yard, Washington. However, the official designation indicates that *Lexington, Warren,* and *Natchez* were built to the Washington constructor's plans.

The light cruisers of the War of 1812 had gradually disappeared from the Navy Register. Members of the proposed raiding squadrons had been sold or wrecked; the *Boxer* was lost off Honduras in 1817, the *Chippewa* was lost off Caicos, West Indies, in 1816, the *Firefly* and *Flambeau* were sold in 1816. The *Saranac* was sold in 1818, and the fine *Spark* was finally worn out and sold in 1826. The schooners were all sold between 1818 and 1820, except *Lynx*, which was lost at sea in the West Indies in 1820, and the *Nonsuch*, broken up in 1826. The old *Enterprise* was wrecked in the West Indies in 1823. Except for the surviving members of the class of schooners built in 1821, the sharp clipper was rapidly disappearing from the Navy, and no replacements were being made or planned for in the construction program. The old story of neglect of the light, fast cruiser by American naval authorities in time of peace was being repeated—so readily were the lessons of the War of 1812 being forgotten. Again, the small schooner or brig was not a sufficiently dignified command for officers gradually becoming pompous with age and the inactivity of mind developed by peaceful years. Though the ineffectiveness of the privateering system as a substitute for a navy was now recognized, the old habit of expecting to be able to obtain fast raiders from this source had not been conquered.

The old sloop *Peacock* was now worn out with hard service. She had been surveyed a number of times, and it was agreed that she was not worth repair. Still another sloop was urgently needed, so it was decided to "rebuild" her; officially a new ship was not possible, since the congressional appropriation made no provisions for any new ships outside of the existing program of new construction. However, the funds for repair of the old ships were available, and it was decided by the Board that the *Peacock* should be officially "rebuilt." In doing this it was realized that funds budgeted for other old ships would have to be used and that these ships must be allowed to decay still further. However, these vessels too might eventually have the same treatment, in turn, that the *Peacock* was to receive. There was no question in the minds of the Navy Board of preserving the old *Peacock* either in form or in dimensions; the only concern of the Board was to build a satisfactory replacement. By retaining the ship on the register as "rebuilt," the legal question of building a new vessel without proper authorization was avoided. The morality of this method of avoiding compliance with the intent of Congress is of relatively small moment; the Board had the practical problem of maintaining an effective navy with insufficient funds rather than of the examination of moral questions of government administration. However, the "rebuilding" system was eventually to reach extraordinary heights and misled not only Congress but also the public as to the true age of some of the ships of the Navy.

Humphreys prepared a new design for "rebuilding" the *Peacock* in 1827, and the old ship was hauled up in the New York Navy Yard and broken up. In 1828 the "rebuilt" ship was laid down. Her design is shown in Figure 90; she was 118′ 0″ between perpendiculars, 31′ 6″ moulded beam, and 14′ 10″ depth of hold, and had the now fashionable round stern. It will be seen by comparing the "rebuilt" ship with the original that the dimensions had changed but little; however, the lines were much altered. The new sloop was very sharp, with an unusual amount of hollow in her ends for her time. She was too small to carry her armament, however, and both her speed and her stability were adversely affected. It was not until she was reduced for an exploration ship that she showed the speed her model promised. There is no mention in her specifications or in the scanty correspondence relating to the incident, of the retention of any portion of the old ship in the new one; it is possible that some of the

Figure 90. Draught for rebuilding the PEACOCK, *1828, showing a very sharp-ended vessel for a sloop of war.*

357

metalwork could have been used. The new *Peacock* lasted until 1841, when she was part of the Wilkes Exploring Expedition and was lost off the mouth of the Columbia River, Oregon, in July.

The last of the ten 24-gun corvettes, the *Concord*, was laid down in 1827. This ship was built at the Portsmouth Navy Yard, was launched late in 1828, and went into commission in 1830. It should be noted here that the dates officially given for the date of a ship's build are not consistent; sometimes the date of launch was used, sometimes the date the keel was laid, and sometimes the date of first commission. In addition, there was often a lag of time between the date the keel was ordered laid and the day the work on the ship actually began. This makes it very difficult to fix the time the navy yards actually required to build these ships; in the case of the *Concord* it appears to have taken seventeen months to build her hull, ready for launching. It took the same yard four months and seventeen days to build the schooner *Porpoise*. The Portsmouth Yard was much more consistent in time required to build sailing men-of-war than were most of the other navy yards.

The ten sloops authorized were now accounted for; as has been said, they were the subject of much criticism in later years. Their inability to carry the heavy armament assigned them hurt their sailing qualities in most cases, and two were eventually converted to storeships. The *Boston* was wrecked in the Bahamas in 1846, the *Concord* was lost on the African coast in 1843, the *Falmouth* was sold at Panama in 1863, the *Fairfield* was sold in 1852, the *Lexington* was raised and made into a storeship in 1840 and sold in 1860, the *Natchez* was broken up at New York in 1840, the *St. Louis* was sold in 1860, the *Vandalia* was broken up in 1870–72, the *Vincennes* was sold in 1867, and the *Warren* was made a storeship in 1840 and sold in 1863. It will be seen that most of the vessels were carefully built, for they had long lives. Some of them saw many adventures and a great deal of active service; they were, on the whole, a useful class of ship. One or two were noted as being good sailers, at certain times at least, the *Falmouth* and *Vincennes* in particular. This was undoubtedly due to the lighter armament placed aboard these vessels in later years, when they carried but 16 carronades, 32's, and 2 to 4 8″ shell guns. The *Natchez*, *Warren*, and *Lexington* were poor sailers throughout their career. In spite of their lack of grace, the remaining sloops were undoubtedly improvements on the 1813 designs in many respects and should have been equally fast had their runs been sharper. The fact that they did not make equal reputations as fast sailers was due to their full afterbody and to the overloading that always marked the peacetime sailing navy, either in the United States or abroad. Not only were the sloops of the 1820's overgunned, they were also overequipped and carried too many boats and too much spare gear and other unnecessary weights. Had they been treated as were the 1813 sloops in the War of 1812, carrying a normal gun load for their size and stripped of the extra boats and unnecessary gear, it is highly probable that they would have been found better vessels, though rather small for their ratings. Their fault was in the increase of displacement over the 1813 sloops without sufficient increase in length.

The slow rate of construction in building the 74's led to the consideration of changes in design of some of the ships. Humphreys prepared a revised design of this class in 1827 which called for ships 196' 6" between perpendiculars, 53' 0" moulded beam, and 22' 0" depth of hold and fitted with the round stern now popular in the American as well as the British service. The design, Plan 24, shows the improved vessel proposed, but there is no evidence that it was used in any of the ships already laid down. In 1838 it was submitted to the constructors Barker, Hartt, and Lenthall, who approved it, but, again, there is no evidence of its use in construction. It is of value, however, in showing what was, in 1827–30, the American idea of an effective 74, and also the very moderate changes that had taken place in the hull form of the type since 1817.

In 1829 there began an intensive period of "rebuilding." The state of the old ships has been noted previously, and the diversion of funds from the maintenance of all of these ships to rebuild the *Erie* and *Peacock* had hastened the deterioration of the worst ships into an unserviceable state. These were the old *John Adams, Macedonian,* and *Congress.* Orders were now issued for rebuilding the *John Adams.* Survey showed the ship to be so badly decayed that it was no longer worth while to attempt to cobble her up into usable condition as a frigate. Humphreys reported that the funds available made it wholly impossible to "rebuild" her, as was done in the *Peacock,* as a vessel of her original class. The Board, faced with this dilemma, now decided she should be "rebuilt" as a sloop. Humphreys prepared a new design based on his estimate of the probable cost compared to the funds available. The result was a ship sloop only about 100' between perpendiculars; the Board would have none of it. After more study and thought, and a few glances at the budget, it was decided that the frigate *John Adams* should be "rebuilt," or "cut down" into a 24-gun corvette exactly like Humphreys' *Vandalia.* This was ordered done. The old ship was broken up in the Norfolk Navy Yard, and the new sloop of the same name was laid down there and launched in the fall of 1830. Again, there is no evidence that any part of the old ship was used in the new one, though it may have been done. At any rate, "rebuilding" had now reached the state where a ship was not only "rebuilt" on a new design or to new dimensions, but was even in a different class! That such administrative fiction as carrying this sloop on the register as a "rebuilt" frigate could exist is sufficient evidence of the attention Congress was then giving to naval affairs, and also of the bureaucratic evasion of budget requirements that has not been entirely unknown in recent times.

With the *John Adams* taken care of, the old *Macedonian* was now to be taken in hand. The ship had been entirely unserviceable for years but had been carried on the naval registers as a convenient method of obtaining maintenance funds from Congress. By her existence in the register her alleged cost of maintenance could be budgeted and so obtained from Congress; then it was found that the funds could be diverted either to other ships, as in the case of those already "rebuilt," or to the needs of the steadily growing shore establishments and administrative organization. Little or nothing need actually be spent on the ship in question.

Eventually, of course, something would have to be done about this ship, at the expense of some other old crock. Otherwise embarrassing questions might be asked in Congress. The Board felt that the *Macedonian* would have to be rebuilt as a frigate; there were enough sloops, but commands suitable for the senior officers were none too numerous. The old ship, though built of the much-praised English oak, had now become entirely rotten, just as many American-built ships of the equally praised live oak had decayed in a relatively short time when neglected. Humphreys prepared a new design for the ship, a nicely modeled frigate, double-banked, 164' 0" between perpendiculars, 41' 0" moulded beam, and 13' 6½" depth of hold. She was pierced for 58 guns, excluding bridle ports, and was much sharper, both in water lines and in deadrise, than previous American frigates. She was, in fact, a clipper model with a long and well-formed run and was a very fast sailer throughout her career. She was classed as a 36, to rate with the old *Constellation* and *Congress*, and carried 32-pdr. medium guns and a few 8" shell guns in her first commission. She had been intended to carry 32 medium 32-pdrs. and 24 carronades, 32's, but she was unable to carry these armaments, and early in her life most of her spar-deck guns were removed. Her relatively small dimensions and sharp model really made her unsuitable for a full-fledged frigate, and eventually she was

Figure 91. Draught of MACEDONIAN *as rebuilt, a very sharp frigate design,*
1829.

Particulars

O is 65'6" from F P
Room & Space 31½"
W L's spaced 30"
Buttocks - 48"
Height of Main Deck at O. from Base 22'3"
    " Spar   "   "   "   "   30'5"
    " Sheer   "   "   "   "   34'4¼"
    Depth of Rail 8¾"
    Knuckle, 11" above Spar Deck

Plan 23. Draught of the frigate HUDSON, *modeled on packet-ship lines.*

Lower Gun Dk P.S.

Main Dk P.S.

Lower Dk P.S.

L Sheer

Particulars
O is 75'0" from F.P.
Room & space 33"
Waterlines 48" apart.
Buttocks 72" apart.

Plan 24. Humphreys' draught for an improved 74-gun ship, 1827.

reduced to a corvette by the removal of her high spar-deck bulwarks. Work was not begun on this ship for nearly three years after the design had been prepared, as funds had to be accumulated and a yard cleared. The Norfolk Navy Yard was finally selected to build the ship, and work actually began in 1832. The old prize frigate, thus "rebuilt," was not broken up until 1835–36.

The Board personnel had rotated between 1827 and 1830. Bainbridge was relieved as President of the Board in 1827, and Rodgers returned to the assignment, where he was to remain for the next ten years, until 1837. Lewis Warrington was assigned to the Board vice Charles Morris, and Thomas Tingey was assigned for a portion of one year in 1827; then Daniel T. Patterson was placed on the Board in 1828. At times there were vacancies on the Board that were not filled immediately, as the officer having the required seniority might be at sea or otherwise unavailable. However, the length of time vacancies existed was rarely over two months.

Fifteen years after the War of 1812 the war captains were still the senior officers of the Navy. There was no provision for the retirement of aged officers, and promotions were gradually ceasing as the vacancies in the higher grades vanished. The young and progressive officers of the war were now becoming the old and ultra-conservative officers of a peacetime navy. No longer was there the competition of a war to keep the naval officers, responsible for the state of the service, striving for excellence in equipment or tactics. Now the emphasis was on a perfect drill, the "spit and polish" and tasteful deck arrangement, the rendering of the correct ceremonies, the establishment of privileges of rank, and routine peacetime operations. New ideas and new material or methods might make it necessary to change time-honored drills or deck arrangements, or might require study and work; such things were beneath the dignity of the tried veterans of the war. It is not surprising, then, to find the members of the Board increasingly adamant in their opposition to the introduction of anything new, whether a new method or a new type of ship. Instead of the ruthless efficiency of the war Navy, there was a sentimental attachment to traditional things, ships, ceremonies, and drill, that has so often marked the peace navies.

The training of new personnel for naval requirements was now almost wholly a function of the service. No longer were men to be taken from civilian professions or trades and utilized in the Navy. This applied not only to officers but to the construction organization of the Navy as well. Instead of civilian-trained shipwrights or designers, such as Eckford, being accepted, all the construction personnel were now being trained in the navy yards. There the ship carpenters, riggers, caulkers, smiths, and joiners of the Navy were trained in a system of apprenticeship in which they were educated in the naval way of doing things. The constructors had apprentices, who were trained in the naval ship design methods that were in vogue. At last the American Navy was, so far as its constructors and foremen shipwrights were concerned, independent of the merchant yards and was developing a specialized field of shipbuilding from which private ship designers and builders were barred. The naval constructor was no longer exposed to the competition of some talented naval architect outside of the tight little circle of government servants. With a comfortable position assured them by maintaining this state of affairs, it was natural for many of the constructors to look with contempt on the work of the merchant builders and to disregard any improvements in shipbuilding that they might make. When, by some misfortune of politics, the Navy was forced to accept a privately built and designed vessel, it was natural for the constructors to view her with prejudice and to report adversely on her qualities at every opportunity. In this they were given the support of the hierarchy of the navy yards, whose work might suffer by comparison with the privately built man-of-war. In war it is always necessary eventually to come to building men-of-war merchant-ship fashion in one respect at least—that is, "just good enough and no better than needed." In peaceful times, however, naval construction becomes luxurious in the use of costly materials and workmanship—"the best is none too good"—even when the vessel building is nothing more than a garbage scow. By this means the constructors deluded themselves on the excellence of their designs and construction. The system also permitted an easy dismissal of any good features a privately built sailing man-of-war might have, by dwelling on her shortcomings in material and finish.

The matter went beyond mere specifications; the amount of design work that had been done since 1816 had been small, and there had been ample time to dawdle over many of the plans that had been used. This led to the setting up of some imaginary requirements for expensive construction or fittings. It also led to the establishment of a system of design that required unnecessary drawings or calculations in all vessels, whether or not the importance of the ship warranted the care and time expended. Had war come in the late 1820's, the cumbersome designing systems so carefully established would have had to be discarded and a new method hurriedly developed, which by its emergency nature might have been much more faulty than the practices of the civilian profession. This condition has not been unknown in the armed services in recent times and is a characteristic of governmental efforts in the design of naval and military shipping. Instead of the design practices and specification writing being based on a "war view," they are too often founded on "perfection" and on the assumption that labor and materials will be as available when war comes as in peacetime. This was the reason for the frigates and sloops built in navy yards usually costing so much more, and taking so much longer to build, than contract-built ships in time of war.

The same condition existed in the other departments of the navy yards that existed in the drafting room. There was an unnecessary degree of finish given all work, regardless of use, and everything was of the finest, regardless of actual requirements. Cost was high and waste was great in both labor and materials. One apparent advantage was the argument for the system: ships built by navy yard methods usually lasted a long time and were not always requiring repairs. The argument assumed, of course, that the good qualities of the ships in these respects were inherent in a system requiring the "best and most." The fact that some merchant craft had equally long lives, and this with more neglect and harder usage, was conveniently overlooked.

American naval ships had changed their appearance but little in the fifteen years since the end of the War of 1812. They had grown longer in some classes, and now the ornate carvings of earlier years had almost disappeared. The ships were plainer and without the multitude of mouldings and beadings that had decorated the earlier ships. All the external longitudinal mouldings and projections that had been traditional in ships were now gradually being suppressed.

The ends of the ships were changed in more ways than by the omission of florid carvings, however. The stern underwent a change in fashion in the American Navy in 1825 with the building of the first of the 24-gun corvettes. In 1824, when Humphreys made his first drawings for the class, he prepared a number of preliminary designs. His first plan for the new class, like those of Eckford, Floyd, and Grice, called for a square stern in the traditional style, with raking transoms and round tuck below. The final building plans, however, show the round stern that was to be fashionable in American frigates and sloops for many years.

The advantages of the round stern were supposed to be in greater strength as compared to the older stern, and particularly in the possibility of guns being mounted to fire on the quarters. The new stern was introduced in the Royal Navy in 1819–20 by Sir Robert Seppings, the surveyor, or chief constructor; at about the same time a sub-surveyor, Roberts, proposed an elliptical stern.

The round stern and the elliptical were but variants of the same principle; the quarters were rounded off, and the angular meeting of the sides and transom of the old construction was eliminated. This permitted ports to be placed in the quarters, allowing an angle of fire astern, at around 45 degrees to the center line of the ship, long a blind spot in the broadside method of arming naval vessels. By framing up the stern with cant timbers radiating somewhat like the spokes of a wooden wheel, and then bending the planking around these, the stern was made very strong compared to the old transom and round tuck, with its complicated system of framing and many angles and long seams.

However, the practical advantages of the round stern were soon largely imaginary, for the traditional quarter galleries were demanded. In both the Royal Navy and the American service, the old sea officer was dominant; he demanded the retention of the traditional quarter galleries and other conveniences of the older stern. Almost immediately the round stern and the elliptical stern that replaced it were masked by quarter galleries and an arched sternboard, which not only made the quarter gun ports impractical, but also made the stern look very much as it did before the change. The omission of the stern galleries in the first designs of the 24-gun corvettes and their appearance in the building plans illustrate the same influences in the peacetime American Navy that existed in the peacetime British Navy. Perhaps the greatest objection to the early round-stern men-of-war was the very full runs given most of them by the designers, who had not solved the fairing of the new stern sufficiently well to obtain easy buttocks combined with powerful quarters in this style of stern. Of the designers of the 24-gun sloops, only Barker had produced a good afterbody with the new stern.

The years between 1800 and 1830 were marked by a steady improvement in the methods of constructing long ships in the navies of the world. The British had adopted a system, projected by Seppings and others, of using internal bracing. This was a series of diagonally fitted timbers, or "riders," placed on the inside of the frames to stiffen the structure longitudinally. In the American ships, this was accomplished by a complicated system of diagonally set knees and riders and by a trusswork of timber on top of the keelson. This took up much room, and metal knees and diagonal strapping soon took the place of the older timber trusses and bracing. A good deal of attention had been given to the framing of the long wooden hulls that were now becoming common in sailing ships, and in addition to the improved bracing and trussing which gave greater longitudinal strength, transverse strength was also attended to by the introduction of new reinforcing of the knees, used at the ends of the deck beams. These improvements made the ships more rigid and strong, and better able to carry either armament or cargo, for the use of improved bracing was not confined to naval craft alone. The merchant builders were also in need of these improvements, for the merchant ships were rapidly growing in size and length as the needs of expanding sea trades made them desirable.

The bows had changed little except for the surrender of the curved upper headrail. In the Royal Navy, the curved upper rails were gradually replaced with straight rails (seen in the American corvettes and frigates launched in the 1820's) as early as 1812, when the requirements of the long war then engaging her energies caused Great Britain to do everything possible to speed up the construction of her men-of-war and to lower their cost. The American Navy had followed this lead for reasons of economy, and now few ships retained the older curved upper rail and faired-in cathead knees, except for small craft, schooners, and brigs. The cutwaters of American naval ships now became shorter and deeper, giving them a somewhat massive appearance. This, with the straightened sheer and the short, round stern, caused the vessels to look heavy and "blocklike," particularly the 24-gun corvettes. Figureheads were becoming rare except in the liners and in a few frigates; the simple billet was now popular.

There were also many minor improvements or changes. The hammock rails were now projected forward and aft by raising the freeboard at bow and stern by a low monkey rail, which would continue unbroken the line of the top of the hammock rail fore and aft, as in the 24-gun corvettes. Ironwork became more common, and chain was used increasingly on shipboard. The ships were becoming more cluttered with boats and were still overloaded with guns.

The rigs had changed little; the American men-of-war retained their distinctive short lower masts and long topmasts and were, on the whole, grossly overcanvased. Many of the men-of-war could not carry their courses, with topsails and topgallant sails, in winds in which merchant vessels worked under full sail. In strong winds, the huge topsails of the men-of-war often overpressed the ship, particularly in the sloop classes. In the small vessels of the Navy overmasting was extreme and was reaching exceedingly dangerous proportions. The steeve of the bowsprit was slowly decreasing, and the rake of the masts showed less difference between fore, main, and mizzen.

Merchant shipping, which had been limited during the War of 1812 to fast-sailing small craft, was now improving rapidly. American builders were not

only building fine merchant ships; they were turning out vessels that were
the equal of any in the world in speed, size, and strength. The great packets,
looking much like huge frigates, were now appearing and were teaching the
lessons of obtaining speed through ability to carry sail in strong winds. Merchant builders were taking great pains to learn all they could about foreign
ships and to better them. There was great scientific curiosity in the merchant
shipyards, and the term "mechanic" was deemed an honorable one. New York
and the New England ports were replacing Philadelphia as the center of advanced shipbuilding ideas and practice. The Chesapeake area was still producing the fast clipper schooners and brigs, for which it was famous, but the model
of these was slowly changing to give more capacity without appreciable loss
of speed. Already merchant-ship designers were beginning to notice the backwardness of Navy designs and to offer well-meant but, to the majority of the
constructors, highly objectionable suggestions for improvements.

The building of war vessels for foreign powers had been common in American yards through the 1820's. Twelve schooners, designed by Humphreys,
had been built in Philadelphia for the Colombian government in 1824. A ship
sloop named *Kensington*, designed by Eckford, was also built here in 1830;
intended for Russia, she was finally sold to Mexico. In addition to frigates built
by Eckford for Brazil and for the Greeks, a number of corvettes, brigs, and
schooners were built in New York for various foreign powers, and a large
number of schooners and brigs, as well as two corvettes, were built on the
Chesapeake and southward for South American revolutionists and Central
American patriots. Many slavers were built, and the illegal trades were still
attractive. For these the builders turned out small, fast armed craft in large
numbers. So, in spite of the effort to restrict naval ship design to government
employees, the private ship builders and designers were still showing themselves
competent in turning out men-of-war and fast armed vessels, and were still
being given an opportunity to do so.

Steam made little impression on the American Navy in the 1820's. Fulton's
steam battery was employed only as a receiving ship. A small steamer, or
"galiot," named the *Sea Gull* was purchased at Philadelphia and employed in
the West Indies in 1822–23, but she was laid up at the end of this period. None
of the Navy, and least of all the Navy Board, considered that there was any possibility of steam men-of-war; steamers might be useful as tugs and service craft,
or a few might even be armed as coast-defense floating batteries, but obviously
a steamer would not do as a seagoing man-of-war.

The two fields of specialization open to young American naval officers were seamanship and gunnery, in the now American tradition. The first had been well explored, and by 1820 any advances were mere refinements of the art of handling ships and rigging them. Gunnery was a more appealing subject to a curious mind; there were many mysteries of which the practical gunner was well aware but which he could not explain. In this field, too, an officer might expect some slight support from his seniors in view of the American policy of employing the largest and most powerful batteries in their ships. In addition, an interest in the improvement of cannon had appeared in France during the last years of the Napoleonic Wars and had gradually spread over Europe. The English, mortified by their defeats in the naval actions of the War of 1812, had decided that these were due to inferior guns and gunnery and were now seriously trying to improve their position. The study of the science of gunnery now became fashionable, and this finally led to the rapid improvement in naval guns that marked the last days of sailing men-of-war.

The speed of American men-of-war had become an accepted fact both at home and abroad. Where the British were concerned, an exaggerated sense of inferiority in this matter had grown up, both among naval officers and in the Admiralty itself. In fact, it had now become traditional that British-designed ships were slower than those of the United States or France. The fact of the matter was that the tradition was an excellent excuse for an incompetent and bungling captain, or for the popular naval historian explaining why the British were not successful in some particular action or maneuver. It has been pointed out earlier that the British constructors had been experimenting, with great success, in fast-sailing craft as early as 1796, and were doing this in the face of opposition from the conservative sea officers and administrators. After 1800 the experimental work continued, Henry Peake, an Admiralty surveyor (or constructor), being particularly prominent. Peake turned out designs of a number of brigs, schooners, and cutters of narrow beam and sharp lines, some of which were successful and some not. Copies of successful foreign vessels were also built, and on the whole a healthy desire for improvement then existed in the Admiralty.

To further improve British Navy ships the Admiralty had established a "School of Naval Architecture" as early as 1811, to educate "superior shipwright apprentices" in the art and science of ship design. The selected apprentices entered the Royal Naval College at the Portsmouth Dockyard, where they received a sound mathematical foundation in ship design calculations and also were given an opportunity to draw plans and practice lofting. The apprentices were also to have practical experience in the Dockyard, in addition to what they had already had in their earlier training. There was very little sympathy or enthusiasm for this plan among the older shipwrights and administrative officials, and this finally led to the liquidation of the school, as well as to neglect of its graduates, for many years. The school, in fact, lasted little more than a decade.

The school was undoubtedly proficient in teaching the mathematical branch of design and did much to explore the then mystery of stability. Its faculty was headed by Professor Inman, a noted mathematician and divine interested in naval architecture, but not a practical naval architect. The weakness of the school seems to have been the lack of understanding of the application of theory to practice.

The popular criticism of the speed of British men-of-war now led to the establishment of "experimental squadrons," composed of ships and small vessels of various models and rigs, in which competitive sailing was to be the objective, with an intent to establish a method of design that would insure fast and otherwise satisfactory men-of-war. Beginning about 1820, the School of Naval Architecture, the surveyor, Seppings, and a few naval officers, including Hayes and Symonds, designed vessels for these squadrons ranging from brigs to small frigates. Lengthy trials were sailed in 1824–25 and again in 1827–28, but the results were not instructive. Some of the experimental vessels sailed very well under certain conditions, but all-around superiority was not established. Changes and "tuning up" were permitted, and it was very difficult to establish whether the advantages of certain vessels were due to their model or to the "tuning up" they received, so lacking in uniformity were the results of sailing trials. The School of Naval Architecture produced good ships, but these did not show the marked superiority expected from "science" applied to the art of sailing-ship design.

The British experimental squadrons did, however, produce many good designs and gradually raised the level of speed in the various classes of British men-of-war. There was no equivalent squadron in the American service, though the British activities were watched with interest. At every opportunity, American commanders tried out their commands with foreign men-of-war and sent in reports. These had some effect on the Navy Board and the constructors; the criticism implied when an American ship was reported to be outsailed was far more effective than any objections which might be filed on technical grounds by civilian builders and sailors. The effect of foreign designs was thus felt somewhat, and the American constructors took pains that there should be no more slow sailers, such as some of the 24-gun corvettes had shown themselves to be. However, no organized effort was made to insure superior designs, and, in fact, the Americans were now competing with the British rather than leading them in the models of men-of-war.

Since the end of the War of 1812, the old idea of a navy organized as a purely defensive arm had been thoroughly suppressed. Now it was realized that the best defense was attack and that the ships of the Navy had to be designed for sea service, and not for mere coast defense. The only exception to the policy—and that is open to argument—was in the building of the *Pennsylvania*, a fully seagoing liner of great power, whose basic function appears to have been to break a blockade rather than to lead a cruising squadron. Nevertheless, she could have performed either service had it been necessary, so there was actually no real divergence from the naval policy in her construction. In the powerful 74's built or building, the Navy would have had a battle squadron dangerous to any foreign power in the event of war; and these were to be supported by a large number of commerce destroyers, represented by corvettes intended to overmatch similar ships in foreign navies. In addition, the battle squadron had the support of the light or heavy cruisers of the frigate classes, which were capable of also acting as raiders. The American frigates being built were superior to any under construction for European navies, except for a few individual ships at most. Support for the seagoing ships was being established in the existence of navy yards and some service craft. There were still weaknesses—small light craft were lacking, and there was a need for faster corvettes—but on the whole the sailing Navy had at last become an effective instrument of war.

★　　★　　★　　★　　★　　★　　★　　★　　★

CHAPTER SEVEN

The Bureaucratic Navy

1830-1840

THE 1820's had been years of peace, so far as the American Navy was
concerned, with no warlike activities beyond the suppression of piracy
in the West Indies and rather abortive attempts to put down the slave
trade. Stagnation set in, and by 1830 the United States Navy was thoroughly
bureaucratic in organization, controlled, so far as naval construction and design
were concerned, by the Board of Navy Commissioners. The Board members
were still the aging veterans of the War of 1812, and extreme conservatism
was now the rule.

The evolution of the design of the ship of the line *Pennsylvania* reached the
final stages in 1830, and the plans now showed the ship about as she was completed. Minor changes, however, were made after this year, the most important
being a slight alteration in her after cant frames just forward of the sternpost
to ease her run. Her headrails and stern were also altered slightly. Plan 25 is
the final design and represents the ship as she was built. It will be seen that the
Pennsylvania had no pretensions to grace; she was merely a very powerful
gun carrier, of enormous displacement for her length. The designer had apparently recognized her shortcomings and, at the last moment, had revised her
run in an effort to improve her sailing qualities. The *Pennsylvania* was not an
unqualified success after her launch; some officers thought her cumbersome,
leewardly, and crank. To commanders trained in the smart frigates and the
handy 74's—*Columbus, Franklin, Ohio*, and the popular *North Carolina*—the

Plan 25. Building draught for the 120-gun ship PENNSYLVANIA, showing ship as
launched and fitted.

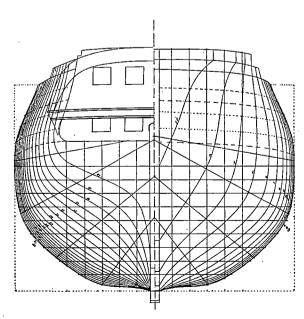

Particulars
O 11 75'- 4' from F.P.
1 11 79' 0' from F.P.   a 11 5'4" from F.P.
Stations spaced 5'0"
1st W.L. 3'0' above Base, others spaced 2'6".
Buttocks 3'3' apart

Razee "Independence"
As taken off to outside of plank in June 1849
at the Gosport Navy Yard (Norfolk).
J.T. Hartt. N.C.

Length bet perps	188'0"
Beam, extreme	51' 6"
Depth in hold	14' 10"

References   28·5·34A   107·17·18 A'
and attached sketches

Plan 26. Plan of INDEPENDENCE *as a razee, made from measurements taken from the ship after her alteration.*

Pennsylvania must have seemed a handful and a poor sailer. However, she occasionally showed surprising speed when in proper trim. Because of the expense of manning her, she saw very little commissioned service, and so her capabilities were never fully explored. Her very high freeboard undoubtedly

Figure 92. Draught of revenue cutters for a northern and a southern station, 1829.

made her less weatherly than the 74's, and her full lines would have prevented her from sailing as fast as the *Ohio*. However, she was no more awkward than most of the foreign liners and was as fast as most ships of her rate. The cost of maintaining this ship was the greatest objection to keeping her in service, and the vessel was, indeed, somewhat of a white elephant to a navy required to be strictly economical. In fact, the whole liner class was very expensive to operate in peacetime, as experience had shown. Hence the slow progress on the liners

Figure 93. Draught of revenue cutter MORRIS *and class.*

then on the stocks. They were kept "under construction" as an economical mode of maintaining ships of the class in some readiness for war, if it should come. From time to time in the early '30's the desirability of creating an improved class of liners was considered, and Humphreys' 1827 design appears to have been extensively studied with this aim in view. However, economy and the experience with the giant *Pennsylvania* prevented anything being done to produce a new class of large liners: frigates and sloops were more useful in a peacetime navy.

Beginning in 1830 the Revenue Service received a number of useful additions to their cruising cutters. As many of the new vessels were to be used later by the Navy, their design becomes a matter of consideration now. As early as 1815, Constructor Doughty had designed three classes of small one-gun cutters. These were followed in 1825 by two classes of more burdensome schooners, one of which was given "drop keels." The relatively small size (60' 0") and force of these cutters, however, made them of little value as naval units. As in the earlier period, when Fox had designed revenue cutters, the function of design for this class was now in the hands of the naval constructors, and in 1829 Humphreys designed two improved cutters, each 62' 0" between perpendiculars and 18' 0" moulded beam. One was for a northern station and the other for a station in the South. The cutter for the North was 10" deeper than the southern schooner, and she was slightly sharper. Figure 92 shows both designs; they were vessels of very heavy displacement. These designs were followed, in 1830, by a much faster one, to be used to build the *Morris* in the New York Navy Yard. The new design was for a very handsome clipper schooner 73' 4" between perpendiculars, 20' 2" moulded beam, and 7' 4" depth of hold. The *Morris* (Figure 94) was pierced to carry 14 guns, brass 6-pdrs. of medium length, or, as an alternate, 12-pdr. carronades. As a cutter, the *Morris* carried but 6 guns.

It was originally intended to build ten cutters in the navy yards, but this was found impractical because of the building program already in effect, so only the *Morris* and three others were built in government yards—the *Alexander Hamilton* and *Albert Gallatin* at the New York Navy Yard, and the *Andrew Jackson* at the Washington Yard. All were built to the *Morris* plan, but with the addition of a naval head; only the *Morris* came out with the simple curved stem and the moulding underneath the gun ports. The rest of the vessels were built by private contract using the *Morris* plan as the "contract design." The builders were not required to hold to the plan, however, and the contrac-

Figure 94. Inboard arrangement of MORRIS and class.

tors prepared new designs. Webb and Allen, of New York, contracted for six cutters—the *Louis McLane*, *Richard Rush*, and *Samuel D. Ingham*, all launched in 1832, and the *Thomas Jefferson* (later renamed *Crawford*), *James Madison*, and *Roger B. Taney*, launched the next year. Isaac Webb, Eckford's able apprentice, made the design for some of these at least, shown in Figure 95. This design called for somewhat larger dimensions than the contract design, 74′ 6″ between perpendiculars, 20′ 8½″ moulded beam, and 7′ 6″ depth of hold. No record has been found to indicate whether all the Webb-built cutters were on this design or whether the others were built to individual plans. The sail plan of the *Jefferson* made in 1843 indicates that this cutter was about ten feet longer than either the *Taney* or the *Morris*. The *McLane* was noted for her beautiful finish and was exhibited at Washington to show Congressmen and influential citizens how the tax money was being spent. The remaining cutters, *Oliver Wolcott*, *Campbell*, *Dexter*, and *Washington*, were all built in New York also, but the names of the builders have not been found.

These cutters appear to have been the first government vessels fitted with geared steering wheels. Joshua Humphreys had proposed this method of steering sometime before the War of 1812, but there is no record of its having been used until the Webb and Allen contracts for the revenue cutters. The steering gear employed in the cutters consisted of a wheel and gear mounted on a shaft, the forward end of which was supported by an A-frame just abaft the steering wheel and the after end by a bearing, swivel-mounted, on top of the rudderpost. The post was fitted with a toothed quadrant, extending forward of the post, which was engaged by the gear on the shaft. This type of gear was found satisfactory for small vessels but was not strong enough for large ships, as the gear teeth sometimes broke, or jumped on the quadrant, when exposed to a heavy strain. The cutters seem to have used this style of gear until about 1850. Humphreys had proposed many other improvements, such as an improved bilge pump, a fire engine, and rudder ironwork, but he was apparently unable to get the government to adopt his ideas when they were presented. Later most of them were employed, but he was not given the credit he deserved, though he had been very active in the support of improved ship fittings and hardware.

Three more revenue cutters were built at Baltimore which were much larger vessels than the *Morris* and the Webb cutters. The *Levi Woodbury* was built by L. H. Duncan, and a second *Washington* and the *Martin Van Buren* by builders whose names are not on record. The *Woodbury* was launched in

377

Figure 95. Draught of revenue cutter ROGER B. TANEY, *a vessel showing some features employed later in the design of the yacht* AMERICA, *1851.*

1836, the *Washington* in '37, and the *Van Buren* in '39. The repetition of the name *Washington* was brought about by replacing the earlier cutter of this name, which was found in 1837 to be infected with dry rot, and so was sold. Of these Baltimore-built cutters, the plans of the *Washington* exist (Figures 96, 97, and 98). This vessel was built as a schooner but was rerigged as a brig in 1838, as she was large for a schooner cutter, 91' 2" between perpendiculars and 22' 1" moulded beam. She was a noted sailer, and her lines show the ideas of the Cheseapeake Bay builders for a fast seagoing vessel at the date of her build. Her deck arrangement was a common one at this period in Chesapeake-built schooners and brigs, the afterhouse extending clear across the ship to form a raised deck, with a sunk poop abaft it. This deck arrangement had been introduced in pilot schooners and remained a characteristic of them as late as 1850. The *Washington* was transferred to the Navy in 1838 and was finally returned to the Revenue Service in 1848. Most of her naval career was spent as a survey vessel.

The lines of another brigantine or schooner are shown in Figure 99. This is an undated plan made by Samuel Humphreys, probably about 1835. The design calls for a vessel on the same general model and dimensions as the *Dolphin* but with an improved run. This plan appears to have been one submitted to the Treasury Department about this time, but there is no indication that it was actually used to build a cutter. The sail plan of the *Jefferson* will serve to show the appearance of cutters of this size and type.

The large cutters formed a useful reserve to the Navy, since they could have been employed either as light cruisers or as dispatch boats in the event of war. Some of them, in fact, were utilized for these purposes in the Seminole War and later in the Mexican War. There was apparently one drawback to the plan of building revenue cutters for the dual purpose (of cutter and naval vessel) that has caused difficulties in more recent times: the cutters grew steadily larger to meet naval requirements, until eventually the point was reached where the vessels were too big and too expensive to operate as revenue cutters. Then the large cutters were surrendered to the Navy and the Revenue Service was forced to build smaller replacements. Proposals for 100' cutters, brigantine- or brig-rigged, were made in the late '30's, but none were built, though two or three designs appear to have been made.

The government held large tracts of timber land in southern states, particularly on the Georgia and Gulf coasts, containing the much-prized live oak. It was found that illegal timber cutting was denuding the government pre-

Figure 96. Draught of the revenue cutter WASHINGTON.

379

serves of live oak. In 1831, two schooners were purchased to act as guards of the timber lands; they were the *Spark* and *Ariel*, each small and carrying but one gun. These two schooners were retained but a short time, however, and both were sold in 1832–33.

The shortage of small vessels in the Navy was now quite marked. This

Figure 97. Deck arrangements of the WASHINGTON.

necessitated the use of large vessels, of the sloop class, in work for which they were unsuited either because of their size, or because of the expense required to maintain them on distant stations. It was finally decided to build three 10-gun schooners, and plans were prepared for the class. Humphreys made a number of preliminary studies of sharp schooners from 100′ downward to 88′ between perpendiculars; the Board, however, decided on the smallest dimensions. The approved design (Figure 100) called for schooners 88′ 0″ between perpendiculars, 23′ 6″ moulded beam, and 10′ 0″ depth of hold. On this plan, the

Boxer was laid down in the Boston Navy Yard, the *Experiment* in the Washington Yard, and the *Enterprise* in the New York establishment. The *Experiment* lived up to her name, as she was to be built on a new construction
apparently employing some light frames and longitudinal stiffeners, which
suggests that she may have been diagonally planked with two or more layers

Figure 98. *Inboard arrangement and spar and sail plan of the* WASHINGTON.

of thin stuff. The intent was, obviously, to develop a way to build vessels with
timber of small scantling. No drawings of the construction, however, have
yet come to light. The schooners were designed to draw but 12′, to fit them
for the West Indian station, and were to carry 8 to 10 carronades, 24-pdrs., and
2 long 9's. These craft were all launched in 1831. They were very useful and
lasted quite well. The *Enterprise* was sold in 1845, and the *Boxer* and *Experiment* in 1848. They were fast sailers for naval schooners, overloaded as they
were with guns and boats. Not only was the *Experiment* different in construction, but there were also minor differences in the appearance of the *Boxer*
and *Enterprise*. The *Boxer* had the old curved upper rail at her head and had

deeper ports with a moulding underneath. She also had slightly greater rake to her upper transom, and her knightheads were narrower than those in *Enterprise*. The model was that of a clipper schooner of the period, but somewhat more full in the bow, perhaps, when compared to the best of the revenue cutters or private-owned clipper schooners and brigs. The *Boxer* was rerigged as a brig in the early '40's. The unpopularity of the schooner in the Navy remained unchanged until the end of the usefulness of the sailing man-of-war,

Figure 99. Sailmaker's sketch of the revenue cutter JEFFERSON.

in spite of the extraordinary popularity of the rig in the merchant marine in the same period and the record of the earlier privateers and naval schooners. The *Enterprise* and her sisters were heavily rigged as schooners and, with their load of guns and boats, were considered tender; the *Boxer* as a brig was by far the worst in this respect.

The exact uses to which the various congressional appropriations were put are now difficult to follow. The authorized construction appears to have exceeded the actual, in some classes of ships, so there should have been some surplus funds to be applied to "rebuilt" vessels. Beginning in 1813, the Act of January 2 had authorized the construction of the last of the wartime-built

383

Figure 100. Proposed schooner or brigantine by Samuel Humphreys.

Figure 101. Draught of 1831 schooner class, BOXER *and sister ships.*

74's and three frigates. One of the latter was burned before she was completed, so there should have been unallotted funds from this source. The Act of April 27, 1816, authorized an additional eight 74's and nine 44's, and also three steam batteries, which were to have frames and engines contracted for, but which were not required to be completed. There is no evidence that the instructions in regard to the three batteries were actually put in force in full, and therefore authorized funds were apparently left from this act. The 1824–25 corvettes appear to have used funds from this source, and it is highly probable that the little remaining went into the "rebuilt" ships and the building of shore stations. It is to be noted that, in 1831, Congress granted some money to permit the rebuilding of the *Macedonian* and *Cyane* and, in 1834, additional sums were granted for the rebuilding of the last-named ship. The art of juggling appropriations in a government agency was then well understood, as was also the exceeding of estimates.

In 1832, the new *Macedonian* was laid down at Norfolk, Virginia. She was launched in 1836 and had as her figurehead the bust of Alexander the Great taken from the old ship. As has been noted earlier, the old British ship was not broken up for some years after the new ship was laid down, and she finally disappeared just before the "rebuilt" ship was launched. It is not possible to explore in full the methods by which this ship and others were accounted for to Congress, and the matter is of relatively little importance now. With the "rebuilt" *John Adams* launched, the *Macedonian* started, the *Cyane* with funds already earmarked for her, there remained the *Congress* to be similarly "rebuilt" and the old *Independence* to be attended to in some manner to make her a useful ship.

In 1833–34 Congress added to the funds available for new construction under the Act of 1816, and it was decided to divert a small portion of these from the ships now on the stocks and to use the money to build a good storeship for the fleet. The various old storeships, purchased from private owners, had become worn out and had been disposed of, and there had been nothing available as a replacement. In peacetime a storeship was used to carry supplies to distant stations and also to act as a packet or dispatch vessel. Humphreys prepared a design of a small ship, on merchant-vessel lines, which was allotted to the Philadelphia yard for construction. The design (Figure 102) was for a ship measuring 109′ 0″ between perpendiculars, 30′ 0″ moulded beam, and 12′ 0″ depth of hold, named *Relief*. The design was nothing unusual; she was pierced to carry 16 small guns, and her usual armament was 4 18-pdrs. and 2 12's,

Figure 102. Draught of the storeship RELIEF, *as built.*

386

Figure 103. Sail and spar plan of the RELIEF, showing spencers on fore and main.

Scale in feet

Store Ships "Relief" Philadelphia 1836

387

medium guns. The ship was launched in 1836 and survived until her sale at the end of the Civil War. Her rig, shown in Figure 103, is notable as the first naval ship to employ spencer masts on both fore and main in any of the sail plans yet found. The spencer mast was nothing more than the snow's trysail mast which was set just abaft the mainmast, and supported at the head by the main cross-

Figure 104. Draught of exploring vessels PIONEER *and* CONSORT.

trees and bolsters. At the foot it either rested on deck or, more commonly, on a table or chock secured to the after side of the main, a little above the deck. On this mast the spanker was hoisted, with its gaff jaws riding on the stick, and the boom either on the stick or on the chock. The purpose of this was to permit the main yard to be lowered to deck without interfering with the spanker. Practically all man-of-war brigs in the American Navy had been actually snow-rigged since about 1806, but the term "snow" had gone out of use. The method of setting the spanker, or trysail, of the snow had also been used for the spanker of frigates and sloops a few years before 1832, but the exact date when this rig was introduced has not yet been determined. The 24-gun corvettes of 1825–26 had spencers on the mainmast but none on the foremast. The innovation in the *Relief* was in the use of the trysail mast, and its attendant gaffsail, on

Figure 105. Draught of a pilot-boat exploring schooner, proposed 1836.

all three masts, instead of employing main and mizzen staysails. In strong winds, a vessel rigged with spencers could be worked to windward under them and would be, in effect, a three-masted schooner. The advantages of this were obvious and the later American sloops and corvettes followed suit. It must not be supposed, however, that the *Relief* or the earlier corvettes introduced the innovation, for merchant ships and some packets were certainly carrying this rig in 1825, if not much earlier; it now seems probable that the rig employed in the *Relief* was first introduced in the packet ships.

In 1829, Edmund Fanning of Stonington, Connecticut, was instrumental in fitting out an expedition to the South Seas. This attracted much public attention. In 1836 the government organized a similar expedition of exploration, known as the Wilkes Expedition. The question of suitable craft for exploration being thus raised, it was decided to build three vessels for the purpose and to purchase one tender. It was considered that these, with a war vessel as flagship, would constitute a useful squadron. Humphreys was ordered to prepare plans to very rigid requirements; the results were far from happy for all concerned. He supplied a design that could be rigged as both a brig and a bark. This design (Figure 104) was used to build the bark *Consort* at the Boston Navy Yard and the brig *Pioneer* at the Norfolk Yard. Measuring 78' 9" between perpendiculars and 25' 4" moulded beam, they were, in short, very deep and tubby craft. The third vessel to be built was a schooner tender. Humphreys, working under the instructions of the Board and Wilkes, prepared a design for a schooner 64' 0" between perpendiculars and 18' 4" moulded beam—a heavy-displacement pilot boat somewhat like the sealing schooners sailing out of New London, Connecticut, at the time. She had a rather good model, as can be seen by Figure 105, but the Navy Board wanted a vessel of greater capacity. Another design was then made by Humphreys, for a schooner 65' between perpendiculars and 21' 6" moulded beam. The model was somewhat similar to that of the first design but much fuller (Figure 106). The schooner was pierced for eight guns and had a large stern cabin about 12' long. The Board accepted this design, and the schooner was built at the New York Navy Yard, as the *Pilot*, in 1836.

The three exploring ships were rigged and tested in 1837; it was found that all three were very slow, the two larger ones particularly so. This was a blow to the planners of the expedition, and after some effort they arranged for the Navy to furnish another man-of-war and, in addition, to buy two New York pilot schooners, the *Independence* and *Seagull*, in 1838, before the expedition was ready to leave. The *Independence*, renamed *Flying Fish*, was 86' 5" long over all and 22' 6" moulded beam; the *Seagull* was slightly larger. The latter went missing off Cape Horn in 1839 while acting as a survey vessel for the expedition, and the *Flying Fish* was condemned at Singapore in 1842 and was sold. She afterward became a notorious opium smuggler, under the name of *Spec*. The substitution of the sharp, light displacement pilot schooners for the Board's schooner and brig illustrates how much the Board of Navy Commissioners really erred in estimating the requirements of the vessels for the expedition. The three useless exploring ships were employed for a time in salvage work and were sold as soon as the matter quieted down. The reputation of the three vessels did not add to the Board's prestige, nor was the "official" designer benefited; in fact the vessels were the laughing stock of the civilian builders and seamen who learned of the fiasco.

In 1834–35 it was decided to build two more small vessels, an "improved"

Figure 106. Draught of PILOT, for survey and exploring service.

edition of the schooners built in 1831. The new vessels were to be brigantines of the same length as the older vessels, 88' 0" between perpendiculars, but the moulded beam was increased to 25' 0" and the depth in the hold to 11' 0". The revised dimensions were intended to create brigantines of greater stability and capacity than the earlier schooners. The lines were very good for a full-ended clipper, as can be seen by Figure 107. The sail plan (Figure 108) will give an idea of the rig of the new vessels. While Humphreys was preparing the new design, Samuel Pook made a proposal for a somewhat larger schooner, 90' 0" between perpendiculars, 26' 6" moulded beam, and 11' 0" depth of hold (Figure 109), but the greater draft caused the Humphreys design to be preferred. About this time Humphreys prepared a design for a sharp, deep brig 88′ 0″ between perpendiculars and 27′ 0″ moulded beam, shown in Figure 109a. This design and Pook's schooner were apparently submitted both to the Navy and to the Treasury, so it may have been intended for cutters and naval service jointly. The idea of large cutters suitable for naval service occupied a good deal of attention throughout the 1830's, and the scanty records make it difficult to determine whether a plan was intended for a cutter or for a naval vessel, or for both.

The two brigantines built from the new design were the *Dolphin* and the *Porpoise*; the former was built at New York and the latter at the Boston Navy Yard. The *Dolphin* was considered one of the fastest sailers in the Navy, after her launch in 1836, and lasted until the outbreak of the Civil War. She was one of the vessels burned in the Norfolk Navy Yard in 1861. The *Dolphin* and the *Porpoise* retained the old upturned upper headrail beneath the cat-heads. The *Porpoise* was rerigged as a full brig a few years before she was lost in the China Seas. The *Dolphin* was altered slightly from her draught during construction; her return offsets show that her aftermost sections were changed to give her easier buttocks than those in the *Porpoise* or in the class draught. The correct body plan of *Dolphin* is shown in Figure 114, showing a proposed design made by lengthening this very fast brigantine. Both vessels were quite successful on the African coast and were among the few American naval vessels that could sail with the best of the British brigs and brigantines met there. The armament of the two brigantines was originally 10 24-pdr. carronades and 2 long 9's. These were the last two-masters under 100′ in length that were built for the Navy.

A schooner yacht, named *Wave*, was purchased for naval service in 1836. The *Wave* had been designed on pilot-boat lines by John C. Stevens and built for him in 1832. She was armed with two small guns and employed as a surveying vessel until 1846. Her model is now in the New York Yacht Club's model room. The revenue brig *Washington*, described earlier, was transferred to the Navy in this year.

Another important undertaking this year was the cutting down of the 74-gun ship *Independence* into a frigate, officially rated at 54 guns. This made her a "razee"—a term applied to liners that had been cut down into frigates or two-decked ships. The practice had been an old one; the British had cut down a number of liners into frigates during the Napoleonic Wars, and the French had

Figure 107. Draught for building the brigantines DOLPHIN *and* POR-
POISE, *1836, altered in building* DOLPHIN.

393

also cut down a few of their ships. The practice had been confined to either old ships of the line whose upper works were weakened by rot and age, or to 74's that had shown a lack of stability or which did not have sufficient displacement to carry their lower deck guns high enough above the load water line to be satisfactory. The cutting down consisted of the removal of the spar, or uppermost, decks, leaving the two lower armed decks intact in most ships, though occasionally the waist guns on the newly formed spar deck might also be re-

Figure 108. Sail plan for DOLPHIN *and* PORPOISE.

moved. The vessel was thus lightened a great deal, and this, with the huge rig of a liner, often made the razee a very fast ship. The *Independence* was the only American liner ever cut down, though it was intended to razee the *Franklin* at one time.

The *Independence*, as a razee, was a very satisfactory ship and proved to be a very smart sailer. No plans were made when the ship was cut down, but later the lines of the ship were taken off in dry dock, and these (Plan 26) show the ship as she appeared after the alteration. The lines were taken off to the outside of her planking, and her measurements were found to be 188' 0" between the corrected perpendiculars (which would be somewhat less than when a 74), 51' 6" extreme beam (about 49' 8" moulded beam), and 14' 10"

395

Figure 109. Schooner proposed by Pook, 1834.

Figure 109a. Draught for a 12-gun brig proposed by Samuel Humphreys.

396

depth of hold. The alterations made the ship the largest frigate in the Navy and, after extensive repairs to her hull, she became a very noted ship. She spent much of her career in the Pacific and was a receiving ship at the Mare Island Navy Yard, California, from 1857 to 1900; she was sold and broken up in 1914. Thus a ship considered a failure and useless for almost twenty-two years became one of the best ships in the Navy.

In 1837 another schooner was purchased, the *Active*, 122 tons, 2 guns, which was intended for a tender for the Wilkes Expedition. Like the *Pilot*, she was found too slow to keep up with the men-of-war in the squadron and so joined the *Pilot* in salvage work, and was sold in 1838. These salvage vessels were really engaged in rescue work. They were sent to sea in the winter months to be on the lookout for vessels in distress. The Navy schooners worked with the revenue cutters for a few years, carrying out this duty. Finally the responsibility for this work was assigned to the Revenue Service alone.

In this year, 1837, two more ship sloops were laid down—the *Cyane*, an administratively "rebuilt" vessel, and the *Levant*, an admittedly new ship. The vessels were sister ships, officially being built from the same design; the *Cyane* was constructed at the Boston Navy Yard and the *Levant* at the New York Yard. The plans for these ships were started in 1836 but underwent some alteration, and when they were issued to the navy yards in the next year they called for a corvette 132′ 3″ between perpendiculars and 34′ 3″ moulded beam. In design the corvettes were improved and enlarged copies of the earlier 24-gun ships of 1825. They had much the same appearance, but they were somewhat easier in the bilges, the run was slightly sharper, and the proportions of length to displacement better suited to speed. Figure 110 represents the building plan of the two ships and contains all of the alterations made in the preliminary design. The extensive changes in the first plans of the ships were obviously an attempt to insure better sailing qualities; Humphreys was probably alarmed by the criticisms leveled at the 1825 corvettes and the exploration vessels and now was insistent that the new ships have a good turn of speed. His improvements and changes were undoubtedly successful; the new corvettes were good sailers and very satisfactory cruisers, though not handsome, carrying their armament and allowances with ease. For a short time the corvettes carried 18 carronades, 32-pdrs., and 4 long 24-pdrs.; the long guns were then replaced with 4 shell guns, 8″. A proposal was made to arm these vessels with an entire battery of long 24-pdrs., but nothing seems to have come of it; perhaps it was decided that this powerful battery was too heavy for the

398

Figure 110. Draught for the CYANE and LEVANT. Dotted lines in the body plan may represent the vessels as built.

sloops. The final design of these two vessels showed Humphreys' progress in achieving better hull forms in the sloop class. Beginning with the 24-gun corvettes, he had improved on them in the rebuilt *Peacock*, by fining the ends, but the small dimensions of that ship had made the experiment unsatisfactory. In the new class he had first resorted to rather full ends to obtain all the displacement the Board apparently required, but on later consideration he again sharpened the ends and in particular greatly improved the run, at the expense

Figure 111. Spar and sail plan for CYANE *and* LEVANT.

of displacement. Even after this reduction in displacement the ships were amply burdensome, as is shown not only by the reports on their sailing and working as cruisers but also by the fact that spar decks were added to the *Cyane* late in her career.

The *Cyane* and *Levant* were the first American corvettes fitted with fore and main spencer masts when launched. The two vessels spent much of their lives on the Pacific stations. The *Cyane* was sold in California in 1887, and the *Levant* went missing with all hands in the Pacific in the fall of 1860. The ships were usually rated as 22-gun corvettes, though sometimes as 18's, and when the fashion of numerical classification came into existence, in the late '30's, these corvettes, with the earlier 1825 sloops, were placed in the "2nd Class" of ship sloops. Their lack of grace and beauty drew the same unfavorable comment that had characterized the earlier sloops.

The next year, 1838, saw the construction of a new class of ship sloops, which were intended to be economical cruisers particularly suited for distant stations, and were to rate as 16-gun sloops, "3rd Class." They were intended to carry a battery of 16 carronades, 32-pdrs., in time of peace, with the addition of two long guns to complete their war armament. The fashion had now become general, both in the United States Navy and in foreign services, of giving ships a light battery in time of peace, and establishing a larger or more effective war armament. The question of the proper size for the new class was a matter of some difference in opinion. Proposals for the new class were made by Grice, who submitted a plan for a sloop 111' 0" between perpendiculars (Figure 112), Barker, who sent in a design for a much heavier displacement ship 114' 6" in length, and Lenthall, who proposed a sloop of the same length but lighter in displacement. It was pointed out to the Board that these small ships would be unable to carry a heavy armament and still be fast, as suited their class. Grudgingly, the Board considered an increase in size and finally seized upon the idea that the new class should be the same length as the 1813 classes, approximately 117' between perpendiculars. Lenthall's design was accepted, but he was ordered to redraw it to greater length. His final design for the new class of sloops called for ships measuring 117' 7" between perpendiculars, 32' 0" moulded beam, and 15' 0" depth of hold. It will be seen that the new sloops were slightly shorter than the old Doughty designs, but were 6" wider and deeper, which increased their official tonnage to 566. The round stern, or rather elliptical stern (since the latter was the type used in the American Navy), was now discarded, and the approved design (Figure 113) reverted to the old transom stern. The new sloops, so far as dimensions and rig were concerned, were practically reproductions of the *Wasp-Peacock-Frolic* class of 1813; only the displacement and model of the new sloops differed from the old. In the new design, the deadrise amidships was straight, rather than slightly hollow, and the greater beam and depth permitted the slight increase in displacement. The design allowed for 18 guns, excluding the bridle ports.

Lenthall produced a handsome class of sloops. It is not known how much of a part the chief constructor had in this design, but in view of the close personal relationship between the two, it seems probable that Lenthall consulted with

Figure 112. Grice's proposal for a 16-gun sloop of war, 1838.

Humphreys while preparing the drawings. There is no evidence, however, to indicate that the chief constructor prepared a preliminary design for Lenthall's guidance. Five ships from this design were ordered—the *Decatur*, to be built at the New York Navy Yard, *Dale* at Philadelphia, *Marion* at Boston, *Preble* at Portsmouth, and *Yorktown* at the Norfolk yard. These small ships, all launched in 1839, were rather popular; they sailed very well and were stiff. The *Dale* lasted until 1906, and was a school ship for many years; the *Decatur* was sold in 1865; the *Marion* was broken up in 1871–72; the *Preble* was accidentally burned in 1863 while acting as a guard ship; and the *Yorktown* was wrecked in the Cape Verde Islands in 1850.

The minutes of the Board meetings are too incomplete to enable an accurate analysis to be made now of the reasons why the "3rd-Class Sloops" were made so small, at a time when the trend in the American Navy was toward greater and greater size in all classes. In Europe, the ship sloops and corvettes were also rapidly increasing in size with each new ship. Had the "3rd-Class Sloops" ever been required to carry out the functions of their type, it is doubtful that they would have had much success, desirable though they might be as station ships in time of peace. In war they would certainly have been no match for large and powerful merchant vessels, suitably armed, such as the North Atlantic packets and the British East Indiamen. The American sloops of the *Dale* class were little more effective, in fact, than many of the large brigs then in the British Navy.

The only vessels purchased in 1838 were the schooners for the Wilkes Expedition, which have been mentioned earlier. When there was a need for small, fast sailing craft, the New York, Boston, Norfolk, Charleston, and New Orleans pilot schooners could be purchased. These swift vessels would meet all needs, whether to carry dispatches or to serve as a tender to a flagship. The pilot boats had become larger and faster with the passing years. Where, in 1812, this type was usually from 50 to 65 feet long, in 1838 many were from 85 to 100 feet in length. In the event of a naval war, these schooners would have been very useful naval auxiliaries.

The frigate *Congress* was the only naval vessel built in 1839. This frigate, as has been mentioned, was another of the administratively "rebuilt" ships. The old frigate, which had been authorized in 1794, was broken up in 1836. She had been unserviceable for years; even during the War of 1812 she was in such poor state that she could be used only for a short period. The *Congress* had been soaking up maintenance funds until it had been discovered that she might

Figure 113. Building draught for the 16-gun ship sloops, 1838.

be used as a budget justification to obtain funds for "rebuilding" old ships into wholly new and useful men-of-war. There need be no attempt to reproduce the old ship in any way; only her official register need be kept intact.

In 1826 Samuel Humphreys had prepared a design for a frigate 179' between perpendiculars, 45' 0" moulded beam, and 14' 10" depth of hold. This design had never been used to build a ship. In 1837 Humphreys prepared a plan for the intended rebuilding of the *Congress;* in this design he followed his 1826 plans, but increased the moulded beam to 46' 6" and the depth to 15' 5". From this revised plan the "rebuilt" frigate was laid down in the Portsmouth Navy Yard that same year.

For reasons which will be dealt with later, there was convened early in 1838 a committee of naval constructors which set up the proper dimensions and characteristics for a "Frigate of the First Class"; these were contained in their report dated July 23, 1838. The report was approved by the Board, which then ordered that a draught be prepared in accordance with the committee's requirements. Humphreys prepared a design which was forwarded to each of the constructors of the original committee—Grice, Hartt, and Barker. The plan was signed by each in token of committee approval. The Board then approved the design in January, 1839.

The approved design of the "Frigate of the First Class" was that of the "rebuilt" *Congress* in dimensions, model, and details. However, the actual building plan of the new frigate was a separate drawing, which was completed in November, 1838, and which had been approved in preliminary form a year earlier. It will be seen (Plan 27) that the new frigate was to be an improved design; in fact, it actually was one that had been officially established by the committee of naval constructors. The peculiar circumstances surrounding the various plans cannot but lead to a suspicion that the report of the committee had been adjusted to fit the ideas of the chief constructor, instead of representing the individual opinions of Messrs. Grice, Hartt, and Barker in full.

The *Congress* was built rapidly; her keel was laid early in 1839, and she was launched in 1841. For years she was considered a very fine frigate, and she was also a fast sailer. She was sunk in action in Hampton Roads on March 8, 1862, by the Confederate steam ram *Virginia,* ex *Merrimac.*

The *Congress* was the last sailing frigate designed for the United States Navy. Though some of the frigates on the stocks were launched after 1841, they were on the design of 1820. The *Congress,* therefore, represented the highest development of the frigate type in the United States. The improvement in frigate design between 1820 and 1838 had actually been slight; the angularity seen in the midsection of the earlier design had now been smoothed out, and in the *Congress* the modern faired midsection appears. This alteration in frame was applied to a limited degree in the 1820 designs still building in 1839, but not to the same degree as in the *Congress*. The old longitudinal mouldings and the projecting wales had now disappeared in American ships; the sides were smooth and fair, without ornamentation. However, the beloved quarter galleries still remained, not only in American naval ships but in merchant ships as well.

Compared to many of the earlier American frigates, the *Congress* had much deadrise. The American constructors of the period were sharply divided regarding the desirability of sharp deadrise in large ships, just as American builders had been long before the War of 1812. Generally speaking, the trend among merchant-ship designers from 1815 to 1840 was toward flat-bottomed ships. This was even true to some degree in the sharp Chesapeake Bay built schooners and brigs in this period. There were, of course, a large group of builders and designers who did not agree with the trend, and these maintained the need and desirability of a marked degree of deadrise. The controversy was to continue into the '50's, and at the end of the sailing-ship period the difference of opinion remained violent. The ruling faction in the Navy—the Board and the chief constructor, supported by the majority of the constructors—was in favor of some deadrise, and it was not until it was necessary to design steamers that the flat-floored model was finally accepted.

In 1832 the sailing trials of the British experimental squadrons had apparently established the superiority of ships formed with very sharp deadrise, as recommended by Captain William Symonds of the Royal Navy. There could be much questioning of the accuracy of the conclusions drawn from the sailing trials, for the tests were far from unbiased and scientific. Nevertheless, they indicated that the ships designed by Symonds were generally faster sailers than those having rounded or flat floors, or with S-shaped midsections, as represented by vessels designed by the School of Naval Architecture, Hayes, or Seppings, or the vessels built to earlier models. This conclusion gave great popular support to Symonds' pretensions, and the surveyor, Seppings, being ready for retirement, Symonds was appointed in his place. With great courage and self-reliance, the new surveyor designed all new ships, without regard to rate and size, with a great deal of deadrise. This, combined with easier and sharper lines fore and aft, created many fast sailing ships in the British Navy, particularly in the smaller classes, from frigate downward. Symonds was not a trained or experienced designer before his appointment; he was primarily a sailor and, like his competitor, Captain Hayes, was no more than an amateur with strong opinions on hull form. As a result it was eventually determined that, while speed of the British ships had been markedly increased by Symonds' principles of design, the improvement had been accomplished at the expense of many of the most desirable qualities in sailing men-of-war, particularly in the larger types of ship. A change in policy then took place, and Symonds was replaced by an officer who made no pretense of being a designer, the design functions going to trained constructors under his supervision. This change enabled a review of the qualities of the various ships designed by Symonds to be made and and, as a result, new British men-of-war ceased to be distinguished by extreme deadrise, particularly in the larger vessels.

The British experiments had been carefully observed by many Americans, and undoubtedly Symonds' appointment as surveyor and the success of some of his vessels may have influenced some American merchant-ship designers and encouraged others in a belief in the desirability of extreme deadrise. During the late '30's a few plans of Symonds' brigs came into Humphreys' hands. Two of these have survived in the Navy plan files. Just as the sailing trials had not convinced all of the British constructors, so all the Americans were not impressed with the results and conclusions. It is interesting to find, in this period and later, that the American constructors were divided into the same factions as the British: Grice was in favor of extreme deadrise, with straight rise of floors; the chief constructor and Lenthall preferred moderate rise of floor, and Pook at first favored hollow garboards. Doughty had employed hollow garboards in the *Wasp* class of 1813, but had used straight floors in the *Erie* class of the same year and in his later designs of small vessels. Hartt and Pook became supporters of flat-floored models in the '30's. Every variation of opinion that divided British naval constructors was apparent among the Americans. Symonds had not originated a new idea, as far as Americans were concerned, but his success in the British Navy had given support to the partisans of extreme deadrise in America, in their contest with the exponents of the packet hull form.

Eckford and Grice might be presented as the leading American exponents of extreme deadrise in large ships, as well as in small craft. Eckford's design for a 24-gun corvette in 1819 and his schooner design of 1820, the *Grampus*, show his ideas regarding sharp deadrise in 1817-20. The frigates he and his former apprentice, Isaac Webb, built for the South American nations Brazil,

Peru, Chile, and Colombia also had rather marked rise of floor. In 1830–31, Eckford designed and built a 26-gun corvette on speculation, which he named *United States;* the lines of this ship show extraordinary rise of floor for a square-rigged vessel. The midsection of this corvette was more like that of an extreme model for a pilot schooner than a ship. The *United States* was. reputed to be very fast and was sold to Turkey for a naval vessel. Eckford went to Turkey in 1831, and that year he became the chief naval constructor for the Turkish Navy. While in Constantinople Eckford designed a very large frigate, the plan of which reached Humphreys' hands in the late '30's and is still in existence. This design indicates that Eckford employed a straight rise of floor as a principle of design of sailing ships, from the smallest schooner to the largest ships. However, he seems to have governed the amount of deadrise to fit the size and type of ship to a far greater extent than his British counterpart, Symonds. Isaac Webb, however, did not have the same high respect for deadrise that his master had, and so the Webb designs were usually rather flat-floored, in the packet style. Eckford died suddenly November 12, 1832, in Constantinople, and David Porter (of *Essex* fame) settled his affairs. It appears from Porter's letters that Eckford designed a large frigate and an advice boat, as well as a ship of the line, for the Turks and that all of these were finished, the liner and frigate after his death.

The design and construction of men-of-war for foreign powers remained a source of income for American builders in the '30's. One of the nations seeking ships was the newly created Republic of Texas. In 1839 Grice was commissioned to design a corvette for the Texas Navy, and the vessel was built at Baltimore by Schott and Whitney. She was a flush-decked ship 130' 2" long, 31' 9" beam, and 15' 10½" depth, customhouse measurement. When Texas joined the Union the remnants of her Navy were taken over by the United States, and the new ship, named *Austin,* was on the American register for a few years, 1846–49, as a ship sloop. A former revenue cutter, the *Ingham,* was carried in the Texas Navy under the name *Independence.* She was taken by the Mexicans and was afterward in their naval service as a cruiser.

The only commercial vessel purchased for the Navy in 1839 was a New York pilot schooner named *Flirt,* of 150 tons. She was bought at New York as a tender and was sold out sometime in the '50's. The need for more small vessels was now apparent to the Board, which had been considering the desirability of a class of fast schooners or brigantines of 10 guns to supplement the earlier *Enterprise* and *Dolphin* classes. The Board thought the new design ought to be slightly larger than either of the two classes just mentioned, but that the length should not exceed 96' between perpendiculars.

There had been a possibility that the Revenue Service might build some large cutters to Navy requirements during 1837–39, but nothing came of the matter. The Board, being made aware of the probability that no such cutters would be built, ordered preliminary designs prepared in 1838. Humphreys had suggested the redesign of the *Dolphin* class, which had proved to be fast sailers. It was proposed to lengthen the model to 96' between perpendiculars, but hold to the same beam and depth as the original design. Lenthall prepared a drawing for Humphreys (Figure 114), which showed that the result would have been a very long, low clipper that would undoubtedly have been very fast but which had insufficient displacement for a naval vessel. Humphreys himself prepared a variant of the same proposal, in which he increased the displacement somewhat. His drawing, while incomplete, shows that the vessels were intended to carry 8 carronades, 24-pdrs., and 2 long 9's on carriages; the vessels were to be schooner-rigged with the foremast 78' and the main 80' long.

Grice was asked by the Board, through Humphreys, to prepare a proposal. He disregarded the length preference of the Board and submitted a plan for a handsome brigantine 100' between perpendiculars, 26' moulded beam, and drawing about 13' 9" (Figure 115), as compared to the lengthened *Dolphin*, which would have drawn about 13' loaded for sea. The Board seems to have studied the matter in a desultory way in 1839–40, before any action was finally taken.

Perhaps the Board's attention was so involved in a controversy over steam men-of-war in this period that it had little time to consider the brigantines or schooners. The matter of steam vessels for the Navy had almost continuously plagued the members since 1834. In that year, an anchor hoy being wanted for one of the navy yards, Hartt had the temerity to submit a proposal for a steam hoy and water tank (water boat). This is shown, in his drawing, to have been a side paddle wheel steamer, with wide guards running the full length of the hull, the dimensions of which were 80' between perpendiculars and 17' 4" moulded beam inside the guards. Hartt submitted the plan and proposal February 28, 1834, but the Board immediately rejected it and ordered Humphreys to prepare plans for sailing hoys; these are shown in Figure 117. The new boats were to carry 14,000 gallons of water and were to measure 65' 0" between perpendiculars, 22' 0" moulded beam, and 7' 0" depth of hold. A num-

A Brigantine

Lines of Dolphin from mould-loft offsets; extended from
86'-0" to 96'-0" bet perps by increasing timber & room to 24"

Length bet. perps. 96'-0"
Beam moulded 25'-0"
Depth in hold 11'-0"

Underside of Deck at inner

Room Particulars
2 spaces 24"
F.P. to 10 : 2'-4"
A.P. to 20 : 2'-4"
W.L's spaced 4'-0"
Buttocks 4'-0"

By Circular of Navy Commissioners
19 Dec. 1838
Phila 2 Jan, 1839 Lenthall

N.B. Body Plan of Dolphin as built

Reference 107.8'-0"
Lenthall Plans

Figure 114. Proposed brigantine on DOLPHIN, showing the correct
body plan of the 1836 vessel as taken from the mould-loft offsets.

409

Particulars
Frame 35 is 17'7" from A.P.
D = 18'5"   F.P.
Room & Space 2'9"
W.L's spaced 4'0"
Buttocks   "   4'0"

Congress, 44 Gun Frigate, 1839
by Samuel Humphreys.
Built at Portsmouth Navy Yard.
Length bet. perps.   179'0"
Beam moulded   46'6"
Depth in Hold   22'5"

Chapelle

References 40·10·9 series
           through K, 40·13·11

Plan 27. Draught of the 44-gun frigate CONGRESS, 1839, the last design to be prepared for a vessel of this class under sail alone.

Plan 28. First-class sloop GERMANTOWN, *showing typical deck fittings of the class.*

Germantown · 1843
Length bet perps   150'0"
Beam moulded   36'0"
Depth in hold   16'8"

Particulars
O is 59'6" from F.P.
Room & Space 2'6"
Base is lower edge of Rabbet.
Waterlines spaced 2'0"
Buttocks   "   4'0"
Keel laid with 7½" camber bet
perps, depth greater aft than
forward, siding 15
Base to Sheer at O is 23'3"

References
109·6·1 A-B
142·4·46
Lenthall plans

Sheer
Portsill
Underside of Deck at side
Scupper
Top of Copper
Chapelle

Deck
Portsill
Sheer
Sentry Platform
Chain Scuttle
Main Hatch
Main Deck
Fore Hatch
Stay Scuttles P.&S.
Forecastle

Side lights
WL # 6

Figure 115. Grice's proposal for a 100-foot brigantine of 10 guns.

410

Figure 116. Sail plan proposed for 100-foot brigantine. This rig was often referred to in the Navy as being a "brig."

Scale of Spars
10 Gun Brigantine, 1839
by Francis Grice

100' bet. perp.
26' moulded beam
11'6" moulded post

Scale in Feet

ber of these were built in 1835 and 1836. These new hoys were able to handle the heaviest anchors and were reasonably seaworthy, so that in good weather they could operate outside protected waters to salvage lost anchors or gear.

Figure 117. Draught of an anchor hoy and water tank, 1834.

In 1836 there were complaints in Congress about the cost of towing naval ships at New York with privately owned tugs; the result was that a small steamer of about 142 tons, named the *Engineer*, was purchased for the purpose in that year. There were over 700 steamers in existence in the United States by this time and, since the destruction of the first steam battery in 1829 by a magazine explosion, the Navy had but two, the *Sea Gull* of 100 tons, laid up at Philadelphia and unserviceable, and the *Engineer*.

The Secretary of the Navy called attention, in 1835, to the authorization for steam batteries contained in the Congressional Act of April 29, 1816, and ordered the Board to have one of these designed and built. The Board disliked the idea intensely and finally suggested to the Secretary that, since they knew nothing about steamers, a competent steam engineer be obtained to advise them. This was done, and Charles H. Haswell of New York became the first naval engineer. The steam battery was built in 1836–37 and on her trials made nearly twelve knots. She was 180′ between perpendiculars and 34′ 8″ extreme beam—a long ship when compared to the sailing frigates—and was named *Fulton*. Three more war steamers were authorized at the President's discretion by Congress, March 3, 1839. Two boards were set up, one composed of senior officers of the Navy and the other of constructors and the one engineer. In spite of strenuous objections from the older officers, the final word rested with Congress, and the Board made its report on the proper size and power for the steamers. As a result the President directed that two huge war steamers be laid down in 1839. These were launched in 1842—the *Mississippi* and *Missouri*. These ships really marked the beginning of the decline of importance of sailing men-of-war, though it was twenty years more before the last die-hards would recognize the supremacy of the steamship. The surrender of the Board, in 1839, to the construction of war steamers was not brought about by a belated realization on the part of its members of the advantages of steamers, but by the pressure from civilians, who were alarmed at the existence of war steamers abroad while the American Navy lagged. In general, the popular concept of the part that war steamers were to play was that they would be effective in calms and would be employed to bring large sailing men-of-war into action by towing, while using their own batteries to protect themselves. They would also be invaluable for coast defense.

During the decade between 1830 and 1840, the improvement of the navy yards continued. The steady requirements of the large program of new construction placed the yards in a favorable situation when making requests for new equipment, additional men, and floating equipment. Lighters, hoys, tugs, and sheer hulks (derrick boats) were now in use in all the yards requiring them. The standard naval lighter was a small scow, 35′ to 45′ in length, that could be moved with sweeps or towed with ships' boats. One of these lighters is shown in Figure 118; according to an inventory in 1838, a boat of this type at the Portsmouth Yard had one or two leeboards and a spritsail and steered with a rudder. The lighters were also decked, and some of them, like the one in Figure 119, served as anchor hoys in protected harbors or close to the navy yards.

The sheer hulks were old craft, ranging from large sloops to ships of various classes, that were worn out and were stripped of masts and gear. They served to float huge sheers, which were necessary to lift out or replace masts. The hulks were often towed, but usually the ship being repaired was brought alongside the hulk, which was tied to some convenient wharf or on a mooring. Masting sheers were also placed on the heads of some wharves in the navy yards, and many yards had both hulk and wharf sheers in service. Tugs were hired steamers, except where the *Engineer* was available from her post at the New York Navy Yard. Steam was employed in sawing timber in all the navy yards by 1840; though it had been introduced in English dockyards as early as 1798, it only appeared in American yards in the 1820's. The exact date when steam saws were first used in American navy yards has yet to be established; saws operated

Figure 118. A Navy lighter, 1836.

by water wheels were used in a few American shipyards as early as 1810, but this source of power was unavailable to the locations of most merchant yards and all the navy yards. The British dockyards were equipped with machinery to a marked extent by 1808, but the Americans were slower, owing to war and economic difficulties. All the American navy yards had been fitted with heaving-down wharves, but only the Norfolk Yard had a dry dock; it went into operation June 17, 1833, with the docking of the 74-gun ship *Delaware*. The pumping machinery in this yard was operated by steam. Ironworking equipment was steadily increasing in the yards, and now far exceeded that formerly required by the old shipsmiths, owing to the maintenance requirements of the yard machinery, as well as the few naval steamers.

The rotation of Board membership was somewhat slower in 1830–40 than before. Rodgers was President of the Board to 1837; Chauncey replaced him and held the assignment until 1840. Charles Stewart was a member from 1830 to 1833, vice Warrington. Charles Morris was again a member from 1832 to 1841, and Chauncey had been made a member in 1833, five years before being appointed president. Alexander Wadsworth was appointed to the Board in 1837, vice Rodgers, and remained a member until 1840. It should be noted that the veteran officers of the War of 1812 were still in control. The steadily growing conservatism of the Navy Board was now widely acknowledged, and this was drawing much criticism. The difficulties of the Board over the construction of the new steamers merely emphasized the backwardness of

Figure 119. A navy yard hoy, 1848.

senior officers of the Navy, and the matter did not enhance public confidence. The chief constructor was now in an unenviable position; his relations with the Board were strained and his public reputation was damaged. Humphreys had obtained two of Eckford's designs for the Turkish Navy, the frigate and the liner, which he offered to have copied for the Board. This had been accepted, but when the plans were done the Board had refused to honor Humphreys' bill. The chief constructor had made an indignant protest which led the Board to reprimand him for discourtesy. So far as the public was concerned, the success of Humphreys' design for the *Dolphin* had not counterbalanced the woeful failure of the exploration ships. The 24-gun corvettes of 1824–25 and the rebuilt *Macedonian* were rumored to be unsatisfactory, and there were the criticisms of the huge *Pennsylvania*. Unfortunately for Humphreys, he was being held responsible, to a great extent at least, for the mistakes of the Board in setting up the required characteristics of the ships he designed. Humphreys had certainly been forced, over his protest in some cases, to comply with the Board's instructions and specifications. Humphreys and his brother constructors attempted to resist the Board's insistence upon excessive basic design requirements, but rarely with much success. Admittedly his ships were becoming marked by a lack of beauty, but this did not make them less effective as men-of-war. Humphreys was in no way involved in the Board's prejudice toward steamships, for he had designed such craft before 1830. In spite of his personal difficulties with the Navy Board and the criticism of his ships by the public, he had obtained a great reputation abroad as a naval constructor. It is said that he was once offered the appointment of chief naval constructor in the Russian service at a handsome salary, but that he refused it on the grounds that he preferred to employ his talents in his country's behalf.

Lenthall was made a naval constructor July 21, 1838, and Pook was made an assistant somewhat earlier. Floyd retired, and Hartt took over his assignment. A number of very able men were now being trained as constructors: Brodie, Rhodes, Hanscom, and Delano, all of whom were to be highly competent in their profession. The apprentice system in the constructors' offices was remarkably successful in spite of the lack of an established system of teaching or a school of naval architecture such as had been attempted in the British service. The reasons for this are easily found. The American constructors were engaged in design work outside of the Navy. Lenthall was designing merchant ships for Philadelphia merchants, including a packet or two for the famous Cope Line; Grice was designing schooners and an occasional ship at Norfolk, and Hartt was active at New York. While it is true that a few of the constructors had fitted comfortably into the bureaucratic mould, most of them had been too ambitious and active to be satisfied with the little that was required of them in the navy yards and had turned their energies to study and the commercial designing that would enable them to keep abreast of progress in their profession. This is a remarkable exception to the rule in a naval bureaucracy in peacetime— all the more so because of the stultifying influence of the Board of Navy Commissioners, which prevented the constructors from utilizing their knowledge for their service. The active constructors increased their knowledge entirely by their own efforts and without official encouragement. Such men were well fitted to teach, for they had a personal interest in their profession and desired scientific knowledge for its own sake. They were well informed in the existing theories of naval architecture, as is evidenced by their designs. Unfortunately little has survived that expresses the state of their knowledge other than this.

It is difficult to arrive at conclusions concerning the design practices of the leading naval constructors in the 1830's by judgments based entirely on surviving plans and papers. However, it can at least be said that Grice, Pook, Lenthall, and Hartt were able to make extensive calculations and were also well informed on the theories of ship design then in existence. The calculations were not particularly difficult or profound; they included displacement and weight calculations, tons-per-inch immersion, center of buoyancy, center of lateral plane, and center of effort—the most common calculations in the design of sailing craft still in use. Stability was not often calculated, as the methods then known were very laborious, and none have been found for American naval ships in the '30's. Little was known about resistance, and the full bow and fine run were still looked upon as necessary to speed, in theory at least, though the sharp bow was gradually becoming popular, particularly as it was proving so successful in the packets.

Construction methods in the navy yards changed very slowly in the 1830's; the most important innovation was the use of some iron strapping in the last years of the decade. The light construction attempted in the *Experiment* attracted little interest and was not repeated. Ironwork was very slowly increasing in the fitting of hulls and in rigging. In this the Navy was very conservative because of the assertion that iron fitting would be shattered by a shot and form dangerous fragments, and that once damaged, the ironwork could not be repaired on shipboard. Chain cables were permitted, and now some vessels had chain gammonings to secure their bowsprits.

It is rather curious that the painting of the ships of the Navy was left to the commander's taste for a very long period; at least no regulations concerning this have been found prior to the '30's. In the War of 1812, the American frigates were usually black, with a bright yellow streak along the gun ports, British fashion. This streak was usually as wide as the ports were high. The 74's had three such streaks if spar-decked, and two if the spar-deck waist was unarmed. Some vessels also had a narrow band on the mouldings, below the upper deck ports. Some frigates had rather wide yellow bands, reaching from a line about the height of the main deck to a couple of inches above the main-deck gun ports. During the War of 1812, the bands were extended forward on the cutwater. The port covers were often the same color as the band, and not checkerboarded in the Nelson style. The guns and port sills were black, tompions white, black, or red. About 1825, the yellow streaks or bands became very light in color and gradually they became white. Small craft, schooners, and brigs, began to use streaks that were only half the depth of the ports; these had their lower edge at port-sill height and ran the whole length of the hull, out onto the cutwater. The inside of the bulwarks, from waterways to rail, was usually red or brown, until the late '30's, when white became common. Decks were left "bright" and holystoned in the Navy throughout the sailing-ship period. Deck furniture and the sills of deck structures were red, but later, when bulwarks became white, they were painted the same color. Mastheads, bowsprit, and royal masts in small vessels were painted black; the lower masts and topmasts of large ships were black until well into the '30's, when white was used. Billetheads were yellow, or green and white. Finally, about 1840, the billets were often painted white without gilding. By 1836 some of the small men-of-war, schooners and brigantines, began to omit the port band entirely, retaining only a yellow or white moulding line in some; in others the side was wholly black. Since nearly all naval vessels were copper-sheathed with "yellow metal," the bottom was a yellow or light green in color, depending upon age. All standing rigging was black. Gun carriages were brown, black, or natural wood, oiled: black was regulation in 1839. Even as late as 1840, American men-of-war were not limited to black and white paint. Boats were often painted to the fancy of the captain, though white hulls were now predominant; the plank-sheer or gunwale might be black, red, or green. Even after regulations fixed the colors to be used in naval vessels, there were many ships that did not conform, well into the '40's. Frigates and liners, in the '30's, generally had the white bands checkerboarded British fashion; sloops and corvettes were less standardized, but the checkerboard seems to have been most common, disappearing in the middle '40's.

The administration of the Navy, in so far as construction was concerned, changed very little in the '30's. The Board's dominance could not successfully be challenged by the constructors in any technical matter, though the character and professional attainments of the chief constructor and his subordinates had by now won the grudging respect of most of the senior naval officers. Suggestions from the constructors were now received with somewhat more attention than had been the case in Fox's and Doughty's times. The chief constructor sometimes took sharp exception to the comments of the Board, and the constructors occasionally differed with their chief. Independence of professional opinion was slowly being accepted and utilized. It was being realized that overriding the constructors in matters pertaining to design and construction, rigging and fittings, or even armament, was a very risky proceeding, for the results were usually most unfortunate. Nevertheless, there was no official recognition of the changing relations, and the '30's saw little improvement in the establishing of detailed requirements for new vessels.

The navy agents had been retained in the establishment of the Board, but with naval construction confined to the navy yards, they no longer placed building contracts but were concerned only with the purchase of materials and supplies. The commandant of a navy yard reported directly to the Board on matters relating to repair and maintenance of vessels, construction and repair of buildings, storage of materials and supplies, and employment of civilian personnel, as well as the estimates and accounts pertaining to such matters. The resident constructor was his adviser in all technical matters and was under his administrative supervision. The constructor was no longer responsible for routine repairs and confined his activities to the new construction in the yards, unless called upon to give advice by the commandant (who was not officially required to accept it, of course) with regard to repairs or some other technical matter relating to ships. The resident constructor was still the master shipwright, it will be seen, and had a force of loftsmen, draftsmen, foremen and ship carpenters, joiners, caulkers, spar-makers, and other tradesmen under him. The relations of the resident constructor to the commandant and the captain of a new ship fitting out in a yard were rather ill-defined, and as a result there were sometimes differences of opinion as to the manner in which a vessel should be rigged, fitted, trimmed, and ballasted.

In attempting to pass judgment on naval ships and the men who designed them, it is necessary to understand the administrative procedure in force during the 1820's and 1830's. From the time of Humphreys' appointment as chief naval constructor to 1838, he prepared the designs for all naval vessels. The Board, in authorizing a design, set down the requirements, size, rate, rig, and desirable characteristics. Sometimes Humphreys was consulted while these were being prepared, but this was rather unusual. Having prepared a plan, Humphreys submitted it to the Board for approval. When this had been obtained (and to get this he sometimes had to alter his drawings) the design was sent to the navy yards in which the vessels were to be built. The resident constructors then prepared "return" plans incorporating any suggestions they might care to make. These were passed on by the Board, with the chief constructor usually present. If the Board could agree that the changes were valid they were incorporated in some or all of the vessels to be built. This was seen in the case of the 24-gun corvettes of 1824–25. By this time, between the resident constructors and the members of the Board, the original design had often been altered a good deal. Generally, the experienced seamen on the Board were more concerned with practical requirements, characteristics that they believed a vessel ought to have, rather than with the technical problem of fitting such characteristics into a given design—as in the case of the exploration vessels of 1836. In the event of failure the fault was, of course, the chief constructor's.

So, in 1838, the criticism of some of the naval vessels led the Board to require that the constructors sit as a committee to approve of all new designs submitted to the Board and also that they set forth their opinions as to the proper dimensions and models of various classes of men-of-war. The basic idea behind this move was to enable the Board to escape responsibility and to obtain the opinions of all the experts available, by vote of the majority. In short, this was to be "design by committee." Various methods were tried to accomplish this end: a number of constructors were requested to send in competitive designs and then by committee action one was to be chosen. The result can be readily imagined. Next the Board attempted to make the final decision but found that they would have to depend entirely upon the recommendations of the chief constructor or assume responsibilities that the Board had already learned to fear. By the end of 1839 there was still no satisfactory procedure for the control of design, nor for the steps to be required before submission to the Board. It had been found that no matter how well a design was prepared and fitted to the Board's requirements, there was always the possibility of irresponsible changes being made either in the process of approval, or before construction actually started. A procedure under which the chief constructor had prepared designs to minute specifications established by a board of officers had failed, and an attempt to make designs by committee had failed; now a new process would have to be found.

The success of the ship sloops in the War of 1812 and the usefulness of the type in a peacetime navy led some officers to support a theory that this class might be made even more effective than most frigates. As guns grew in power and range and became increasingly accurate, a school of thought developed in the Navy which believed that huge corvettes, armed with a few of the most powerful guns these ships might carry, would be more effective than the usual frigate or liner, armed with a large number of smaller guns. The War of 1812 had shown that ships armed with long-range, heavy-hitting guns were generally victorious over ships less heavily armed; furthermore, it was apparent that the heaviest guns in the American ships, usually chase guns, did the greatest damage. With explosive shells coming into use, it was thought possible that corvettes might be armed with a few shell guns, of great size, and a supporting armament of heavy, long-range guns firing solid shot. To carry the armaments proposed by the adherents of such large guns, naval ships would have to be very large for their classes.

The trend in the direction of great size had marked American designs for naval craft since 1794. The gradual increase in dimensions had been prevented, in frigates and liners in the '30's, only by the long-term construction program. Even then, there was an increase in size in the frigate class through the design of the *Congress*. The schooners and brigantines of 1831 and 1834 were already considered too small by 1838. Only in the small ship sloops of 1838–39 had there been a reduction in size; these, however, must be classed as men-of-war built entirely to economic and peacetime requirements, rather than ships designed for existing tactical requirements. Yet even in these small vessels the weight of broadside fire was much heavier than in similar sloops in 1813–15. It was traditional in the American Navy, before 1839, that its ships should be more heavily and efficiently armed than European classmates. From this precept it was but a short step to the acceptance of the principle of arming large ships with a few very heavy guns and omitting the ineffective but numerous small guns that had long been carried in an effort to crowd the greatest possible number of guns into American ships. However, the massive broadside armament was too firmly entrenched in tradition, custom, and administration to be easily displaced, even on the grounds of fighting efficiency.

The possibility of employing an armament made up of a very few guns, of the greatest power and range that the dimensions of a hull could bear, had attracted the attention of both constructors and naval officers for generations. The old Mediterranean galleys had been armed with from two to four heavy guns fitted for bow fire. The famous Swedish naval constructor Chapman had designed, in 1760, galley-type vessels that were armed with a battery of heavy guns along the center line, pivoted so that they could fire over each broadside. Chapman remained the leading exponent of this type of armament until Captain Schank of the Royal Navy armed a merchant ship named *Rattler*, purchased by the Admiralty in 1798, with guns on somewhat similar plan. This vessel, bark-rigged, was renamed the *Wolverine* in the Royal Navy. She could fight her eight main-deck guns on either side, employing thwartship tracks, or skids, and pivot mounts.

The Americans had arrived at the same conclusion as had Chapman and Schank earlier, for in Jefferson's administration they armed their gunboats with a few heavy pivot guns. Eckford and the Browns had followed suit in some of the lake vessels in the War of 1812; the *Sylph*, with her original battery of pivoted long guns, and *Ariel* were examples. The original pivoted battery of Chapman was taken over bodily by the Americans and was used in small vessels, brigs, and schooners—the Americans employing fewer but much heavier guns than Chapman's vessels. So the principle of arming with a few very heavy guns on effective mounts, instead of a full broadside battery of much smaller guns, was no innovation in 1839 and could be accepted even by the veteran officers of the Board—with some misgivings, however. The well-established and long-standing custom of classing naval ships by the number of guns they carried (which in turn had established the rank required of their commanding officers, and rate of pay as well) made an official acceptance of the Chapman-Schank principle of arming very slow indeed. The relation of a ship's rate to a captain's rank and pay was a very real administrative difficulty in the minds of the senior officers of the Board of Navy Commissioners, and it was not until they were faced with the anomaly of the new steamers—huge ships with few guns—that they accepted the idea that the value of a ship was in the effectiveness of armament and that the rank of her captain need not be related to the number of guns in her battery. This, once applied to the steamers, could equally be applied to the sailing men-of-war.

The change from rating a ship's effectiveness by the number of guns she carried to rating by efficiency of the armament was revolutionary in 1840. Custom and tradition are always strong influences on naval affairs, and this was particularly so in the days of the Board of Navy Commissioners, with its membership of aged veterans of a glorious naval war. Such men found it difficult to accept so basic an alteration in the importance of commands, and for many years there were difficulties over the appointment of senior officers to large ships having fewer guns than others in a squadron that were commanded by juniors.

The controversy over deadrise in large ships was not the only one that aroused the tempers of constructors and shipbuilders in the 1830's. Since colonial times, ships had been designed with raking sternposts and bows made to long sweeps or, later, with a strong rake. In the 1820's some American pilot schooners were designed with almost upright stems. These first appeared at Norfolk and later at Charleston, South Carolina, and New Orleans. The boats proving fast and seaworthy, with no loss in steering qualities, the fashion spread to northern pilot boats. In the early '30's the rake of the sternpost was also decreased. About the same time large ships were built in the United States without rake in the ends, reverting to the fashion that had been followed by the French nearly a century earlier. The packets, now growing longer, were among the leaders in having little rake to bow and sternpost; their steadily increasing length made the use of the overhangs created by raking stem and sternpost a serious structural problem. In spite of the theoretical advantages of the raking ends on steering qualities, the success of many ships without rake raised the question of how much importance the time-honored rake of ends really had. As in the matter of deadrise, there was never unanimity on the question of rake, but the extreme rake that had marked the early clipper schooners went slowly out of fashion in the 1820's and 1830's. In full-ended ships, in particular, it was found that an upright stem allowed sharper entrance lines in the bow and that an equally upright sternpost eased the run. The packets were the exponents of this model, and some of them, particularly a few Philadelphia and New York ships, came out with almost vertical stem and sternpost as early as 1835.

The search for speed in packets, in the '30's, attracted the attention of American ship designers and builders to the possibilities of many changes in the hull form of large ships. Gradually the old frigate model which had so long been accepted as the acme for large, fast merchant ships went completely out of fashion. Instead of the bluff bows above the water being formed with S-shaped timbers, they became bell-shaped—thin below and flaring outward above the water line to the deck. The plan of the bow rail may not have grown appreciably sharper, but the shape of the bows below was far finer than it had been in the sharpest of the earlier frigates. The sterns also changed; a few merchant ships adopted the man-of-war's elliptical stern; most retained the old transom stern, but the width of the bottom of the lowest part of the transom, the "cross seam," was made less by rounding the outer ends, which made planking easier. The hollow profile of the lower transom gradually disappeared, and the athwartship camber of both transoms became much less. In keeping with the upright stem, the rake of the upper transom was much reduced, and the ships now began to look straight and heavy, in the naval fashion.

There were many constructors who disapproved of the fashionable packet model. Some believed in deadrise and rake, others in the old frigate model; still others had theories of much sharper bows and finer sterns than had yet been seen. A number of fast river steamers had been built, the models for which, by a combination of requirements for length, beam, and speed, had become long, narrow, and very sharp-ended. There were, therefore, iconoclasts who wanted to apply the same general model to seagoing sailing ships, with the necessary modifications of proportions to permit sail carrying and weatherliness.

One of the obvious experiments that can be seen in plans of American naval vessels in the '30's and earlier was in the shape of the run. Doughty had gradually developed a hull form that carried the body well fore and aft (but made it relatively shallow by use of great deadrise) with a short and rather full run. This "duck" hull form may be seen in his 1821 schooners and in some of his ship sloop designs. The earlier constructors had obviously preferred to employ long, easy runs and rather sharp bows. These features may be seen in the *Constitution* and *Constellation* classes of frigates and in their contemporaries in the smaller rates. Eckford, Bergh, and many of the Chesapeake country builders utilized this method of forming hulls in fast craft, but there was no unanimity on the desirability of such a form. Samuel Humphreys seems to have wavered in adherence to this hull form, for he occasionally resorted to Doughty's short run and long, shallow body; however, his designs were commonly easier in the buttocks than Doughty's had been. All the designers, from at least the time of the Revolution onward to the '40's, had cautiously experimented with hollow in the bow water lines, but not until the '30's does it become apparent that much emphasis was being placed on this feature. Unfortunately, it is almost impossible to explore the theories of the designers in this period, as no statements by them exist regarding the advantages of short or long runs, or of convex or concave water lines, and all that is available on which to base judgments is an occasional plan. These are of limited value in this single respect, since few designers had learned to employ buttock lines in fairing, as had Fox and Joshua Humphreys in the earlier period and Bergh, Eckford, and Webb later. As a result it is highly probable that few designers realized the exact degree of fullness in the runs of their ships. This may well be an explanation of the rapid rise in popularity of the half-model as a mode of design in the 1820's, 1830's, and 1840's.

The time was one of intense curiosity and activity of mind among ship designers and builders in America. With only a few books on naval architecture

ATE XIII. (Top) United States corvette ERIE (rebuilt). (Center) United States sloop of war ONTARIO. (Bottom) United States frigate BRANDYWINE and sloop of war CONCORD.

PLATE XIV. (Top) United States naval schooner, 1843. (Center) United States ship of the line NO·
CAROLINA. (Bottom) United States frigate ST. LAWRENCE.

available, and these European, the average American designer depended upon practical observation to arrive at theories of proper hull form and rig. He was less interested, perhaps, in the mathematical explorations that fascinated the European authorities on naval architecture than in the art of forming hulls to sail fast and to carry well. The first American book on practical ship design appeared in 1839—*The Practical Shipbuilder*, by L. M'Kay, "practical ship-builder and carpenter, of the United States Navy." The book not only gave instructions for "the inexperienced," but also contained plans of various classes of ships as examples referred to in the text. The book had an extensive sale and undoubtedly had much influence on shipbuilders in the United States. M'Kay was not sparing in his criticisms of Navy ships; he refers at some length to their oversparring and mentions the control of the constructors by the Board. His remarks on the latter are worth quoting: "The Navy has suffered from an opposite course [he has said earlier that merchant builders had to depend upon their own judgment for the lack of scientific instruction] and consequently has made no advancement for the last twenty years. I hear of no reason for this other than that the constructors have not been allowed to alter their models according to their own judgment, but have been confined to the improvements of a few individuals who must be united in their plans; whereas, if the constructors had been allowed to put their individual plans into execution, the result would have been the introduction of a course of rapid and advantageous improvements." In short, he had a low opinion of "committee design," even by competent constructors, and he knew that development in design could not be accomplished by a controlling group of any kind, but that it must be left to the individual designer to decide what and how he wants to design. M'Kay had put his finger on the inherent weakness of government control of ship design—the administrative and bureaucratic procedure that invariably leads to attempts to design by majority vote rather than by the knowledge of a single designing authority. The result is always the same; the designs become merely a hash of the opinions of many and the masterpieces of none. The answer to this problem had not been found in 1840—and there is little evidence that it has been found since.

★　★　★　★　★　★　★　★　★

CHAPTER EIGHT

The Last Years of Sail
1840-1855

THE '40's were years of great activity in American shipbuilding. Both sailing vessels and steamships were built in great numbers and on new models. These years saw the first attempts to build iron hulls, sharp-ended packets, and finally the first of the "clipper ships" for the China trade. War steamers were becoming common in Europe and were steadily increasing in size and power. The decade beginning in 1840 was one of the greatest periods of advance in the art and science of marine architecture and engineering that had yet been seen.

The start of this period of progress was a slow one, as far as the Navy was concerned. The weight of the now mentally dormant Board of Navy Commissioners oppressed the progressive younger officers and naval constructors. This, with the lack of public support of naval appropriations, prevented the service from keeping pace with the developments in the merchant marine. No new ships were built by the Navy in 1840; the only addition was the schooner *Otsego*, loaned by the War Department. This small vessel was retained until 1844 and was then returned. The old sloop *Peacock* had been employed on the west coast in exploration and survey work, as part of the Wilkes Expedition, and on July 18, 1841, she was wrecked at the mouth of the Columbia River, Oregon. A small merchant brig was purchased at Vancouver, British Columbia, to bring the officers and men of the sloop home. This brig, under the name of *Oregon*, was carried on the Navy register for a few years; she was placed in ordinary in 1845 and was sold soon afterward. A schooner named *Phoenix*, of 90 tons, was also added to the Navy in 1841; she was a new vessel built at Baltimore, by contract. No plans of the vessel have yet been found, and it is probable that the contractor who built the schooner also made her design. She was retained in the service but a short time and disappeared from the register sometime before 1848. Both the *Phoenix* and the *Oregon* were classed as 2-gun vessels.

The faction among the officers that supported the building of large corvettes with heavy armament had at last convinced Congress and the Board that such ships ought to be built, and Samuel Pook and Humphreys were assigned to the preparation of a sample design. The lines were completed in the summer of 1841 and were for a corvette having a flush deck and a short, heavy, elliptical stern, without quarter galleries. She was a very large vessel for her class and date, measuring 146′ 4″ between perpendiculars, 35′ 3″ moulded beam, and 16′ 3½″ depth of hold, yet she was pierced for only 22 guns, excluding bridle ports. Her armament was to be on the then new battery—18 medium 32-pdrs. and 4 of the 8″ shell guns, 64-pdrs. All guns were mounted on carriages and were of an improved design, with heavy breech and light muzzle. The new style of shell gun was dual-purpose and could fire either shells or solid shot. The new ship, *Saratoga*, was longer than her namesake on Lake Champlain in the War of 1812; she was 13′ 3″ longer than the *Cyane* and *Levant* of 1836–37. Comparing the *Saratoga* with the British 26-gun ship *Alarm*, a Symonds design built in 1843, the American corvette was 15′ 3″ longer between perpendiculars, 4′ 11″ less moulded beam, and 1′ 3″ less depth to the main deck.

The lines of the *Saratoga* (Figure 120) show a moderately sharp ship with a good deal of deadrise, but nowhere as extreme as the Symondite *Alarm*. The model was really an improved *Cyane*, and the *Saratoga* proved to be a very fine vessel in all respects, fast-sailing and very weatherly. In the late '50's she was raised slightly and a grating spar deck was added. The ship was launched in 1842 and lasted until 1907, when she was broken up. For many years she was employed as a cadet school ship. The Portsmouth Navy Yard built the *Saratoga* very rapidly; she was launched eleven months after her keel was laid and went into commission six months later.

The design of the *Saratoga* having been generally approved, the designs of six more large corvettes were authorized, and it was decided to distribute the work among the naval constructors. Each was to be allowed to choose the model and dimensions he thought best without Board or committee consent being first obtained. The requirement to be met in all the new corvettes was that they be superior vessels capable of carrying the same armament as the *Saratoga*. The matter of smaller craft, which had been under consideration by the Board since 1838, was also brought to a head, and four "schooners or brigs" were ordered built. The designs of these were to be prepared by Humphreys and Grice, each to design two.

The new procedure was to allow the designers freedom to shape their vessels as each thought best. However, the change from complete dominance by the Board was difficult to accomplish; thus Humphreys was handicapped by the Board's indecision as to whether the two small vessels he was to design were to be brigs or schooners, and the rig was not actually decided until after he had completed his lines. The schooner was now out of official favor again and so was the brigantine, in spite of *Dolphin*.

The old *Erie*, rebuilt in 1820–21, had now become rotten, so she was hauled out at the Boston Navy Yard and broken up. Some portions of the old ship were then used again to build a new storeship, which was launched in 1842. No plan for this vessel has been found. The explanation may be that the storeship was built to the 1813 lines of the ship; this is indicated by her register dimensions, 117' 11" between perpendiculars, 31' 6" moulded beam, and 14' 6" depth of hold. This storeship carried 4 guns, 9-pdrs., but was considered too small, and so she was sold at New York in 1850; she was afterward run as a bark-rigged merchant vessel and had the reputation of being a fast ship.

The Seminole War had made it desirable to employ some small schooners on the Florida coast to protect settlements and outlying garrisons from Indian raids. The revenue cutters *Jefferson* and *Madison* were obtained by the Navy for this purpose, and another schooner, the *Badger*, was purchased. The two cutters, it will be recalled, were among those built by Webb and Allen in the early '30's; the *Jefferson* was now brigantine-rigged. These vessels were retained only for the duration of the Florida war, and all three were then turned over to the Revenue Service.

Since it had been apparent for some years that the Board of Navy Commissioners was most unprogressive and that it had proved inadequate to administer properly the construction of new ships, public opinion forced Congress to abolish the Board. This was done by an Act of Congress, passed August 31, 1842. In place of the Board, the three officers then members of the defunct group were made the heads of newly formed bureaus; the secretary was made chief of a bureau also. The construction and repair of ships was made

Figure 120. Draught of the first-class sloop of war SARATOGA, 1842, first of a new class.

the function of the "Bureau of Construction, Equipment and Repairs," later called "Bureau of Construction and Repair." Disrespectful officers soon nick-named the bureau the "Bureau of Destruction and Despair." The last three officers to hold membership in the old Board were Warrington, William M. Crane, and David Conner; Warrington was President of the Board, and Golds-borough was the secretary. One officer had been appointed in 1840, John B. Nicolson, but his term had ended in 1841.

The new act established five bureaus—Construction, Equipment, and Re-pairs; Yards and Docks; Ordnance and Hydrography; Provisions and Cloth-ing; and Medicine and Surgery. The act also created the Engineer Corps of the Navy and the office of Engineer in Chief. The Bureau of Construction, Equip-ment, and Repairs was considered as two organizations under one chief. Con-struction and Repairs had control of design, building, and repair of ships; Equipment had the responsibility for all gear, rigging, sails, anchors, cables, fuel, water tanks, stoves, furniture, and other similar items usually supplied to ships. In 1845 the ships in ordinary were placed under the control of Con-struction and Repair; originally they had been under the jurisdiction of Yards and Docks. The records of the Bureau of Construction, Equipment, and Re-pairs are scanty, and there is relatively little in the surviving correspondence of the constructors that gives information on technical or administrative prob-lems.

Humphreys prepared one design for the two brigs assigned to him. His plans (Figures 121, 122, and 123) called for a sharp hull, 100′ 0″ between per-pendiculars, 25′ 0″ moulded beam, and 11′ 0″ depth of hold. The design was obviously based on his successful brigantines of 1834, *Dolphin* and *Porpoise*. The two brigs built from the design were the *Somers*, at the New York Navy Yard, launched in 1842, and *Bainbridge*, in the Boston Yard at the same time. The two brigs were fast and weatherly; they were somewhat oversparred, however, and both were lost at sea. The *Somers* became a notorious vessel; as a cadet school ship she was the scene of an attempted mutiny, and the in-stigator, Midshipman Spencer, son of the then Secretary of War, was hanged with two alleged accomplices. This led to a storm of criticism and the over-hauling of the Navy regulations. The *Somers* capsized and foundered in the Gulf of Mexico, off Vera Cruz, on December 8, 1846, with the loss of forty officers and men. She was commanded by Raphael Semmes, of *Alabama* fame. The *Bainbridge* foundered in the same manner off Hatteras on August 21, 1863, and only one of the crew survived. The brigs were armed with 6 medium

Figure 121. Building draught for the brigs SOMERS and BAINBRIDGE, 1842.

431

"Somers" & "Bainbridge"

Figure 122. Inboard profile of SOMERS *and* BAINBRIDGE.

32-pdrs. and 6 short guns of the same caliber. The latter were soon replaced with 32-pdr. carronades, and eventually the armament was 10 carronades and 2 medium 32's, which were all that the brigs could bear properly.

Grice prepared two designs for the two brigs allotted to him; the first was for the brig *Truxton* (Figure 124), which was built under his supervision at the Norfolk Navy Yard in 1842. The dimensions of the brig were 100' 0" between perpendiculars, 27' 4" moulded beam, and 13' 0" depth of hold. She

Figure 123. Sketch of spar and sail plan for SOMERS.

was somewhat sharper than Humphreys' brigs and was of deeper draft. Grice gave her much deadrise and somewhat slacker bilges than were used in the *Somers* and *Bainbridge*. The armament of the *Truxton* was specified by the constructor, who preferred to use the old 32-pdr. carronades, in preference to the new short guns, because he decided that the small hulls of these sharp brigs could not bear more weight. As we have seen, his conjecture was found to be correct in Humphreys' brigs. The sail plan of the *Truxton* (Figure 125) was typical of her class, and now the foremast of war brigs was fitted with a spencer. The new brig was very heavily sparred and proved to be a very fast sailer. She beat the *Saratoga*, considered a very fast sailer in 1844, and was particularly

Figure 124. Draught of the brig TRUXTON.

Figure 125. Sail and spar draught for TRUXTON, indicating increasing use of chain rigging.

Spar Plan
Brig Truxton
Drawn by Francis Grice

Scale in Feet

435

weatherly in rough water. Her deep draft was the cause of her stranding on Tuxpan Bar, on the coast of Mexico, on August 15, 1846. The wreck was afterward burned to prevent it from falling into the hands of the Mexicans. This fine brig carried 9,790 square feet of sail in her working suit, exclusive of royals and skysails; her launching weight was 168 tons, and her loaded displacement was 355 tons on 13' 0" draft at the sternpost. Her design was the first American naval vessel that has yet been found in which a calculation was made for stability; her metacenter was calculated as being 6.83' above her center of buoyancy, or 3.33' above the load water line.

Another revenue cutter was taken over by the Navy in 1842—the *Van Buren*, mentioned earlier, built in 1839. She was rated as a 4-gun schooner and had apparently been built to the dimensions of the *Morris*, if her registered tonnage is correct. The frigates that had been building slowly since 1820 were gradually being launched; the *Cumberland* and *Savannah* were launched this year. Only one of the frigates had been launched in the '30's; the *Columbia* and five of the nine frigates authorized after the War of 1812 were now completed.

By 1843, the constructors were at work on the designs of the big corvettes. The designs were not all completed at the same time, and so work did not begin on all the vessels in this year in the yards to which they had been assigned. However, it will be easier to describe them together as a class than to take each up in the chronological order of its launch. The first of the designs to be completed were those of the *Portsmouth* and *Plymouth*. The *Portsmouth* was designed by Josiah Barker, and the plans were made by B. F. Delano under the constructors' direction. It was maintained by Barker that this sloop was modeled after a merchant vessel built by him named *Union*, which in turn had been designed on the lines of a French-built privateer. The accuracy of his statement is open to doubt; there is nothing in the design of this handsome ship that indicates an unusual model, as can be seen in Figure 126. Delano once stated that she was drawn as an improvement on the *Saratoga*, built in the same yard a year earlier. The *Portsmouth* had lower bilges and hollow floors, compared to the *Saratoga;* she was also a much larger ship. The *Portsmouth* measured 151' 10" between perpendiculars, 37' 3" moulded beam, and 16' 9" depth of hold; she was armed with 18 medium 32's and 2 Paixhans 8" shell guns, according to her design. Her plans were sent to Washington in May and were approved, and the ship was laid down at the Portsmouth Navy Yard on the 15th of June and launched on the 23rd of October of the same year. She was not ready to commission, however, until November 10, 1844. This sloop was

Figure 126. Building draught for the first-class sloop PORTS-MOUTH.

a very fine ship and had a long career as a cruiser and then as a cadet training ship; she was finally sold and broken up as late as 1915. The *Portsmouth* was a very sleek-appearing vessel, as she had no mouldings and her side was unbroken between the rail cap and the water line. Her stern was almost round, with a very short overhang. After the Civil War she was fitted with a light spar deck, like many of her class; as built she had (like the *Saratoga*) a short, light top-gallant forecastle, and a short poop, made of gratings at the level of the top of the hammock rail, for convenience in handling the anchor and in conning ship. These short decks originally had only light iron stanchions and a life-line, instead of rails or bulwarks, and had first appeared in the 1825 class of 24-gun corvettes.

The Paixhans shell gun, used in these corvettes, was named for Henri Joseph Paixhans, a French general who had developed shell guns and had been in-strumental in introducing them into the French Army and Navy. In 1841 the guns of his design were known as *canons-obusiers* in the French Navy. These were guns of medium length, with a sharp increase in outside diameter begin-ning just forward of the trunnions and extending back toward the breech about two-thirds the length from trunnions to base ring. Here the diameter was reduced sharply to what would have been normal had the taper been con-tinuous from the muzzle end. This design of the breech was permitted by the use of a small-diameter chamber at the breech end of the bore in which the charge was rammed, the shot coming home against the shoulder formed at the forward end of the chamber. The chambering of guns was not new in Paixhans' design; it had been used in carronades for the same purpose, to allow heavy charges to be used by means of the thick walls formed by chambering a large-bore gun. Gradually all shell guns came to be called "Paixhans guns," whether or not they were on the Frenchman's design. The "Paixhans guns" of the *Portsmouth* were actually 64-pdrs. with chambered bore of 8″ and on the bottle-shaped design that had been proposed by Dahlgren of the United States Navy. Later designs of this and larger guns of the same model were known as "Dahlgren guns" and were extensively used in the Federal Navy in the Civil War.

In the design of the *Plymouth* Samuel Pook not only had a second chance to work on a design for a large corvette, but now, unlike the time when the *Saratoga* was designed, he could follow his own ideas in model and in the dimen-sions necessary to carry the required armament. The other constructors de-signing corvettes had the same privileges. As a result, the *Plymouth* was quite

32 pdr

64 pdr. 8 inch, shell gun.

Guns and carriages for the first-class sloops of war, 1840-45.

different in design from the earlier sloop. Pook's new design called for a corvette 147' 0" between perpendiculars, 37' 3" moulded beam, and 16' 3½"
depth of hold. She had much less deadrise than had been given the *Saratoga*,
so that she had lower and somewhat harder bilges. Unlike the *Portsmouth*, the
Plymouth had straight-rising floors and had much less rake to the stem. The
Plymouth was the first of her class to be designed with a full spar deck and, in
this respect, was a reversion to the style of 1798–99. This sloop was built in
the Boston Navy Yard and was launched shortly after the *Portsmouth*, being
finished late in 1844. The new corvette proved to be an exceptional ship, stiff,
dry in rough water, and very fast in both light and heavy winds, and also very
handy. In appearance she was much like a packet ship, but she was sharper-
ended than most of this class. This corvette was much admired abroad and was
considered by many officers to have been the finest vessel of her class in any
navy. The design of this fine ship is shown in Figure 127. Her sail plan is
shown in Figure 128. This ship was like the *Portsmouth* in finish, without
quarter galleries or other gingerbread work.

The sloop *Jamestown* was a vessel very like the *Plymouth* in model and
arrangement; she was designed with a full spar deck and had a straight rising
floor and rather low, hard bilges. She had very little rake in both stem and
sternpost and had sharp ends. She was a longer ship than *Plymouth*, as her
dimensions show: 157' 6" between perpendiculars, 35' 0" moulded beam, and
16' 2" depth of hold. She was also much more ornate, as can be seen by her
building plan, Figure 129. Her design was prepared by Rhodes, one of the least
known of the constructors. Foster Rhodes appears to have been assistant to
Grice and was a very capable designer, judging by the few plans of his ships
that have been found. His sloop was built at the Norfolk Navy Yard and was
launched in 1844. She was somewhat more heavily built than the *Plymouth*.
Like that ship, she was a very good sailer; however, because of her weight, the
Jamestown required careful trimming with ballast. With the *Macedonian*,
she carried food to Ireland in the great famine in 1847, making a very fast passage under hard driving. The ship lasted until recent years, her last days being
spent as a marine hospital in New York Harbor. The model of this corvette,
like that of the *Plymouth*, has a very strong suggestion of a packet ship in it,
though the corvette was relatively sharp-ended compared to most of the
packets built in the early '40's.

The *Germantown* was designed by Lenthall and was built in the Philadelphia Navy Yard from 1843 to 1846. Lenthall's design was for a low-sided

PLATE XV. (Top) First-class sloop of war SARATOGA. (Bottom) First-class sloop of war JAMESTOWN.

PLANS of the BED and CARRIAGE of the COLUMBIADS
AS FITTED ON BOARD THE U.S. BOMB VESSELS
ETNA AND STROMBOLI.

ELEVATION.

PLAN.

FORWARD END.

AFTER END.

Columbiad, mounted for a howitzer on bomb vessels ETNA *and* STROMBOLI.

U.S. Navy gun and carronade, 1827–35.

U.S. Navy 32-pdr. carronade, 1827.

U.S. Navy 24-pdr. medium gun, 1827.

18-pdr. medium gun, War of 1812.

PLATE XVII. No. 1

Figure 127. Building draught for the first-class sloop PLYMOUTH, showing packet-ship influence.

Figure 128. Spar-draught for PLYMOUTH.

442

Figure 129. Draught for the JAMESTOWN.

443

ship, 148′ 6″ between perpendiculars, 36′ 0″ moulded beam, and 16′ 8″ depth of hold. She was lengthened 1′ 6″ in building, and her plans (Plan 28 and Figure 130) show the ship as built, 150′ 0″ between perpendiculars. The *German-town* plans are in far greater detail than most of her class and are therefore of value in showing the deck fittings of the corvettes of her date. She was on a very sharp model and was a handsome ship, as can be seen in her plans. Like her classmates, she was very fast; the *Germantown* was said to have shared a great reputation for speed in light airs with the *Albany*, another of her class. The Lenthall sloop was one of the sailing men-of-war burned in the Norfolk Navy Yard in 1861; her wreckage was raised and sold in 1863.

Plan 28 shows the deck details of this sloop and indicates the gradual increase in ironwork in naval ships that had taken place by 1843. Iron-strap gam-monings had replaced chain or rope, the mooring bitts were now fitted for chain cable, and in other details the ship was brought up to the standards of the best of contemporary merchant craft. The sail plan, though lofty, showed no important difference from others of her class.

The corvette *St. Marys* was designed by Charles D. Brodie and built in the Washington Navy Yard in 1843–44. She was a vessel of much deadrise, like the *Germantown*, though very different in appearance as can be seen by Figure 131. Brodie's sloop was 150′ 0″ between perpendiculars, 36′ 6″ moulded beam, and 16′ 6″ depth of hold. This ship had about the same deck arrangement as the *Germantown*. The *St. Marys* had less rake in her ends than any of the other corvettes except the *Jamestown*. Brodie's sloop lasted until 1908 and was a well-known school ship in her last years. She was a fast and weatherly vessel. Like many of her classmates, built as a single-decked corvette, the *St. Marys* had a spar deck added after the Civil War. Some of the sloops first had a light spar deck of gratings added in the late '50's, but this was converted to a laid spar deck in later years in all cases.

The last corvette to be mentioned was a very beautiful vessel, the *Albany*. This ship was the design of Francis Grice and was built in the New York Navy Yard in 1843–44. The *Albany* was the only one of the new corvettes designed with a square stern, and she also was a reversion to the old Baltimore Clipper model, as will be seen in Figure 132. This corvette was 147′ 11″ between per-pendiculars, 38′ 6″ moulded beam, and 17′ 9″ depth of hold. She had very sharp deadrise and also was very sharp-ended, compared to her classmates. She sat low in the water and looked more like a clipper than any other naval ship. Grice wished to turn out a corvette that would be very weatherly and fast.

Figure 130. Sail plan of GERMAN-TOWN.

Germantown 1844

Scale in Feet

445

446

Figure 131. Draught of the first-class sloop ST. MARYS, *as built.*

Figure 132. Draught of the first-class sloop ALBANY, *an extreme clipper model.*

In this aim he was successful, for the ship gained a remarkable reputation in her short life; she was lost at sea with all hands in the West Indies in 1854. There were some criticisms of the ship, however; she would not stow as much as some of the other corvettes and, like most fast ships, she was very wet when close-hauled in a breeze. Pook wrote that she had far too much deadrise for a large vessel; he was also critical of *Germantown* and *St. Marys*. The difference in opinion regarding the advantages of extreme deadrise had reached a crescendo in the '40's, and, under the literary leadership of John Griffiths, the adherents of the flat-bottomed model were aggressively attacking the sharp-bottomed hull form. Griffiths was an active, if not always accurate, critic of the design of Navy ships.

In the design of the *Albany*, Grice wanted to employ the bark rig; Figure 133 shows the sail plan as recommended by the designer. The bark rig was not common among men-of-war, though it had been used successfully on a few naval ships abroad. In the Napoleonic Wars this rig was used in a few ships, most of which were merchant ships bought and armed for naval service. A few brigs, considered too large for their rig, were fitted as barks. In 1801 the French built a bark-rigged corvette named *Diligente,* which proved very fast, and for years they tried to reproduce the ship without much success. In the 1820's and 1830's the rig became popular in the United States among merchant seamen. This was also true in Britain, and a few British naval vessels were rigged in this fashion. No bark was employed in the sailing Navy in America, except the unsuccessful *Consort,* but Grice believed the rig would be very suitable for his sharp corvette. Unfortunately, the Navy Department thought differently, and she came out as a full-rigged ship, in the conventional manner. The *Albany* could be readily identified by the extreme rake in her masts; this characteristic of the proposed bark rig was employed in her ship rig as well.

There was some similarity between Grice's ideas and those of the British surveyor, Symonds; both believed in sharp deadrise amidships and fine ends. The American, however, usually designed his vessels so that the turn of the bilge, at the intersection of the rising V-bottom and the topsides, was below the load water line. Symonds usually placed the turn of the bilge either at the load water line or slightly above it. Either plan produced a fast hull under sail, particularly in the smaller vessels. The Symonds midsection had been tried out very extensively in America, long before the English constructor appeared on the scene. In the early 1800's a number of pilot-boat schooners were designed and built with exactly the same midsection that Symonds de-

Figure 133. Bark rig proposed for ALBANY.

Scale in Feet.

Albany
as proposed by Francis Grice

449

veloped in the '20's. In these American schooners the bottom amidships was a perfect V with the bilges entirely above the water line; the revenue cutter *James Madison* (Figure 52) is an example of the form. Some of the schooners had very flaring sides instead of the high bilges. Eckford had employed this hull form in *Grampus* while Symonds was as yet unknown as a ship designer. Also, Chief Constructor Humphreys had designed a pilot schooner named *Nimble* about 1806 with the sharp bottom and high bilges that were to mark Symonds' designs in the Royal Navy. These ideas were not new in 1806, of course, for Americans, French, and British had experimented with the hull form as early as 1770. Generally, the very sharp-bottomed hull, with high bilges, had been employed only in small craft—cutters, sloops, schooners, luggers, and brigs; but in the 1790's the French built a ship sloop on this model, the *Bourdelais*, and the English master shipwright on Lake Ontario during the War of 1812, a very able man named Sutherland, had also employed this form in large ships. The Americans had decided that the sharp deadrise combined with flaring sides or bilges above the load water line produced a fast vessel and employed this model in many of their fast schooners. They had found, however, that this same form, when applied to large ships, made a very uneasy roller, one that not only rolled deep but ended each roll with a sharp jerk that might dismast a ship. Hence, when they employed much deadrise in a ship or heavy brig, they usually employed hard bilges below the load water line. The British eventually reached the same conclusion with regard to the "Symondite" hull form that the Americans had with the pilot-boat model. The Americans' extensive experience with this style of model prevented them from taking Symonds very seriously, though the *Albany* was much like a Symondite.

In January, 1843, Grice had completed the design of his second brig, to be named *Perry*. He had intended to employ the round stern in this design, but after making a set of lines he changed his mind, and the final plans were for a brig having a transom stern. The transom in this design had become less angular in shape, for now the cross seam and the lowest part of the transom stern became curved and was developed into the modern counter. The *Perry* (Figure 134) was 105' 0" between perpendiculars, 25' moulded beam, and 11' 6" depth of hold. Her model was that of a Baltimore Clipper, and in many ways it also resembled Humphreys' brigs. The *Perry* was built at the Norfolk Navy Yard during 1843, and upon completion proved to be one of the fastest ships in the Navy. When first tried she was found to be tender, however, and about 1845 her rig was altered slightly, and her boats

Figure 134. Building draught of the brig PERRY, the first American man-of-war to have a counter stern.

451

and armament were reduced. She first carried the armament used in the *Trux-ton*, but two of her carronades were removed by 1850. The *Perry* captured a Confederate privateer in the Civil War; she was finally sold at Philadelphia in 1865, after which she was employed as a merchant vessel.

It was decided to obtain a fifth brig in 1843, and a contract was let to Lang-ley B. Culley, of Baltimore, who was to furnish the design and build the vessel. Culley was a noted builder and had turned out many fast schooners and brigs in the '40's; in 1848 he built a very fast clipper ship named the *Architect*. It is not possible to say why this fifth brig was contract-built, and the records dealing with this contract have not been found. The contract may have been a matter of political manipulation, or it may have been the result of the large amount of work now in the navy yards. At any rate Culley produced the *Law-rence*, a brig of the extreme Baltimore Clipper model, 109' 9" between per-pendiculars, 26' 2" moulded beam, and 13' 3" depth in the hold. Her draft at the post was 16' 6", an extraordinary draft for a naval brig. Her lines (Figure 136) show her interesting model; she was launched at Culley's yard on the south side of the Basin August 1, 1843. She was copper-fastened and -sheathed, and rated as a 10-gun brig carrying the same armament as the *Truxton*. She was an unpopular vessel, and was sold out of the service at Boston in 1846, hav-ing been condemned at New York by a board of officers. Their report was based upon her inability to carry sufficient stores for a vessel of her class and size. There had been various rumors that the vessel was poorly built and that her timber was substandard, but the condemnation proceedings plainly show that this was not the case and that she was an excellent sailer as well. Her draft was certainly excessive for a man-of-war, and the fact that she was contract-built and -designed did not add to her popularity. She was employed as a mer-chant brig for a while, then her rig was altered to a brigantine. Her end has not been discovered.

The *Perry* and *Lawrence* had stern cabins, or "hurricane houses," which were formed by dropping the main deck, close to the stern, low enough to give headroom under a short poop deck built at rail level. This space was closed off by a bulkhead at the break and formed a cabin for the commander. The short, light poop provided a handy place to con the ship and handle the spanker sheets. There were often two hatchways through the forward bulkhead from the main deck into the cabin, but there was no passageway from the cabin below deck, and in the event the cabin was swamped through the hatchways, no water could get below and fill the ship. However, the cabin prevented the

Figure 135. Designer's plan for sails of PERRY.

Scale in Feet

Spar Plan.
Perry Francis Grice 1843

use of the stern ports, and so no guns could be trained dead astern—a dangerous blind spot in a naval sailing ship in wartime.

As far as the captain was concerned, the stern cabin was a most desirable feature when the vessel was in the tropics. This style of cabin had been popular in revenue cutters in 1798, and some of the commanders had tried to have it installed in the 1821 class of schooners, but without success. It had, however, been added to some of the 1825 corvettes and to the storeship *Relief*.

The steering wheel was on the main deck just forward of the stern cabin bulkhead. The *Perry* had no capstan but employed an anchor windlass on the bowsprit bitts. These brigs all carried half-ports; these were port covers divided into two parts horizontally, both being hinged. The upper portion swung upward while the lower part opened downward. Port covers of this style were also used in some of the sloops and corvettes.

There were a number of experiments in the brigs. The *Truxton* had no dead-eyes in her chain plates but had her shrouds brought down through rollers at the top of each chain plate and then the shroud set up on itself with seizings. Chain bobstays and bowsprit shrouds were also used in some of these brigs. For their time they were very advanced vessels and were a credit to their designers, who were now taking advantage of the opportunity to try out new ideas in arrangement, fittings, and rigging. The possibilities of improvement were now much greater than before, since ironwork could be lavishly employed. But the real chance for improvement came from the freedom now granted to the constructors to design as each thought best, without having to meet unreasonable basic specifications or requirements.

A curious schooner was purchased for the Navy in 1843, on the recommendation of Commodore Charles Stewart. This was an experimental yacht named the *On-ka-hy-e*, which had been built by William Capes at Williamsburg, New York, in 1839–40. The schooner was designed by her owner, Robert Livingston Stevens, of Hoboken, New Jersey, in 1837–38 as a result of extensive testing with large sailing models. Stevens and two brothers had been owners of the schooner *Wave*, purchased by the Navy in 1836; a model made to the lines of this schooner was one of those tested. The *On-ka-hy-e*— or *On-ca-hy-e*, as it was sometimes spelled—was on a most peculiar design, as can be seen by her plan, Figure 137, for she had an unorthodox midsection and was a centerboard vessel as well. She was 96′ 0″ over all and about 22′ beam; with her centerboard up she drew nearly 10′. On her trials she proved very fast and extraordinarily stiff, but was slow in stays. Her rig was then altered and

Figure 136. Draught of Baltimore Clipper-model brig LAWRENCE.

455

Figure 137. Plans of the schooner ON-KA-HY-E, *a radical design based on model tests.*

her staying was much improved. She was a good seaboat, but rolled very hard; she once rolled her masts out and had to be towed in. She was sailed against a fast brig named *Exit* and against a pilot boat, the *Jacob Bell,* and beat both. Stevens tried many experiments on this schooner: at one time she had outside ballast and sail tracks; he also put two centerboards in her. The Navy took out her centerboard and added bilge, or sister, keels on either side of her shoe and also gave her square sails on her topmasts. She carried 2 guns. On June 21, 1848, she was wrecked on Caicos Reef in the West Indies, after cruising to Brazil.

The frigate *Raritan* was launched in 1843, which left three of the class still building. The plans of the *Raritan* had been revised by Lenthall from time to time; Plan 29 shows this frigate as she was built. It will be seen that the appearance of the frigates had changed since the plan of the *Brandywine* was drawn, though the dimensions were unaltered. The *Raritan* was found to be a fast-sailing frigate. As built these frigates did vary a few inches in length, owing to minor errors in building; the *Raritan* was actually 174' 10" between perpendiculars when measured by Lenthall for preparing an "as built" plan.

The year 1843 marked the end of the long-drawn-out Seminole War, which had been going on intermittently since 1835. This permitted the disbanding of the mosquito squadron of small schooners that had been operating on the Florida coasts. It was not long, however, before the war with Mexico re-created the need of these small craft.

It is notable that Samuel Hartt is not credited with the design of any sailing vessels in these years. There is no reason for this omission in the records of the Board and of the Bureau that succeeded it, but it seems probable that Hartt was fully occupied in the design of war steamers in the early years of the decade. In 1842 he designed and supervised the construction of the first iron man-of-war in the United States Navy, the steamer *Michigan*. A number of experimental steamers were also built, and constructors Grice, Hartt, Lenthall and Pook were employed in steamship design, but there is evidence to support the assumption that Hartt was the constructor most interested in steamers.

The last spurt in naval sailing-ship construction was over in 1844; though sailing men-of-war were added to the Navy after this year, most of them were small purchased or prize vessels, or were ships placed on the stocks in earlier years and completed after 1844 or 1845. The boom in the years 1842–43 appears to have been at least partly due to the controversy over steamers; the Board and senior naval officers were anxious to utilize any available funds in the construction of sailing vessels at the expense of the steamers, wherever this was possible. However, it was slowly becoming apparent to intelligent and progressive naval officers that the usefulness of sailing men-of-war was being increasingly limited and that steam, as an auxiliary at least, was now highly desirable in naval ships. The constructors appear to have been generally sympathetic to the idea of auxiliary steamers, though many of them disliked to attempt such vessels as long as side paddle wheels were to be used.

In a number of cases steamers had been built both by government agencies

Particulars
O is 63.6 from FP
Room & Space   2.4"
Water lines spaced 2.0"
Bullocks   4.0"

Plan 29. Draught of the 44-gun frigate RARITAN, as built.

St. Lawrence   1847

n the draught of the Brandywine

Sheer

Underside of Spar Deck at side

P.S.

Underside of Gun Deck at side

~ LWL   1849 ~

Alterations in original
draught (Brandywine)
1 Headrails, gripe and cutwater
2. Bridleport shifted
3 Stive of bowsprit
4 Positions and rakes of masts
5 Height of channels
6 Number and position of spar deck
   gunports in waist
7 Counter
8 Rudder
9 Galleries
10 Spar Deck moulding omitted.

F.P.

Chapelle

80 75 70 65 60 55 50 45 40 35 30 25 20 15 10 9 8 7 6 5 4 3 2 1 0

Plan 30. Profile of the 44-gun frigate ST. LAWRENCE.

and by private industry which, for one reason or another, were unsuccessful. In a few cases the private owners failed and could not complete the ships; in others the machinery proved faulty or of insufficient power. A number of ships that had been designed as steamers were completed as sailing ships, as a result of such failures. Eckford had an experience of this kind in the 1820's, and there was an even earlier case on Lake Champlain, in the War of 1812, the *Ticonderoga*. Such a vessel was the storeship *Southampton*, purchased in 1845. She was built at Norfolk, her keel having been laid in October of 1841, as a paddle-wheel vessel. Her machinery was found unsatisfactory, so it was removed and the vessel was rigged as a ship, to carry 2 carronades, 42-pdrs. Her lines (Figure 138) show her to have been a typical seagoing steamer hull of her period, rather narrow for a sailing vessel. She was 152′ 6″ between perpendiculars, but only 27′ 0″ moulded beam, while her depth of hold was 16′ 0″. She was a fast sailer but was considered tender and was sold out of service. The record of this ship is very incomplete; though she is said to have been purchased, there is some indication that she was built for government use. This vessel was used as a merchant ship after her disposal by the Navy. She had the short, heavy cut-water that marked early naval steamers, though her head and bowsprit had been raised when she was converted to a sailing ship.

The 74-gun ship *Vermont* was launched this year, the last ship of the line to be completed as such for the American Navy. Though the *Alabama* was finally launched as the *New Hampshire* in 1864, she was completed as a store-ship. The 74's were now nothing more than a suitable vehicle to "show the flag" on foreign stations, and even here they were gradually being replaced by smaller ships and steamers of greater war potential. The liner was too expensive to maintain by 1845, unless as a flagship. Most of the liners were placed in ordinary in the '40's and allowed to deteriorate.

During 1845 a good deal of consideration was given to the possibility of constructing a large clipper brig and a very long corvette. The matter did not progress very far, as the growing demand for steamers made such craft of doubtful value. However, Humphreys had Richard Powell, an assistant of Lenthall's at Philadelphia, design a proposal for each. The brig, shown in Figure 139, was to be named *Burrows*. She was a very large clipper brig, 126′ 0″ between perpendiculars, 30′ 0″ moulded beam, and 14′ 0″ in the hold. The design called for a peacetime armament of 14 guns and a war armament of 16. The vessel was to be round-sterned and would undoubtedly have been a fast and very powerful brig, had she been built. The plan of the corvette was

Figure 138. Draught of the storeship SOUTHAMPTON after conversion to a sailing
vessel.

459

not finished; it called for a ship 205′ 0″ between perpendiculars, 43′ 6″ moulded beam, and 21′ 0″ depth of hold—a size comparable with the big steam sloops of the Civil War. The corvette was to be a single-decked ship, which would have made her much like the later steamers in hull, though the sailing vessel was to have much deadrise; in fact, her lines were very much like those of the proposed brig. This vessel was to be diagonally strapped with iron and was to carry 26 guns.

The Mexican War, which began in 1846, produced some naval activity. The Mexican fleet at that time was made up almost entirely of ex-merchant brigs and schooners, most of them American-built. A few vessels were purchased by the United States Navy for service in this war, the most important being some steamers and three brigs or schooners fitted for bomb vessels, for the attack on Vera Cruz. These bombs were given the volcanic names that the Navy had employed for bomb vessels ever since the Tripolitan War: *Etna* was a schooner or brig of 182 tons bought at Boston; the *Stromboli* was bought in the same port and was a brig; the *Vesuvius* was another brig bought at New York.

Plans of one of these vessels, the *Etna*, have survived. (Some of the references to this ship spell her name *Etna*, but others properly name her *Aetna*.) The drawings show that the vessel was originally a schooner and that she was either bought under the name *Walcott* or was to be renamed that. *Walcott* was then struck out and the vessel was named *Etna*. She was 80′ 0″ between perpendiculars, 22′ 8″ beam, and about 10′ depth of hold—apparently a coasting schooner. It was first intended to fit her as a topsail schooner, but the mainmast was in the way of the gun, so the rig was made that of a brig, which enabled the mainmast to be moved aft. The armament of these brigs is shown to have been a short 10″ shell gun fitted as a howitzer, rather than the traditional mortar. The gun was mounted on a pivoted slide amidships, with the carriage fitted for high-angle fire. Figure 140 shows the appearance of this vessel and probably represents her sisters. All three were sold out in 1848, as soon as the war was over.

Three storeships were also purchased: *Electra* of 248 tons, *Fredonia* of 800 tons, and the *Supply* of 547 tons—all merchant craft. A pilot schooner named *Reefer* was bought as a dispatch boat, and a small schooner named *Petrel* was built at Baltimore. Another schooner was bought at New York, the 76½ ton *Bonita*, probably a pilot boat also. The revenue cutter *Forward* was obtained from the Revenue Service, and six prize vessels, taken from the Mexicans, were placed on the Navy register. These were the schooner *Nonata*,

Figure 139. Draught for a proposed clipper brig to be named
BURROWS.

461

Figure 140. Bomb brig ETNA, *ex* WALCOTT.

taken in August by the steamer *Mississippi;* the *Mahonese,* schooner, 100 tons, taken off Tampico in November; *Morris,* schooner, ex *Laura Virginia,* taken in the Gulf of Mexico in October; and the fine brig *Malek Adhel,* taken by the *Warren* at Mazatlán, Mexico, in September. The *Malek Adhel* was a vessel built by William Webb for the Pacific trade in 1840; she was 80′ 0″ on deck, 20′ 7″ moulded beam, and 7′ 9″ depth in the hold. The lines of this brig are among those in Webb's book of plans, but the drawings show a flush-decked brig, whereas the customhouse description shows her to have had a quarter-deck to the mainmast at rail level, and she probably had a sunk poop like the revenue cutter *Washington* of 1837. The remaining prizes were the *Tampico*, a schooner originally named *Pueplana*, taken at Tampico in November, and the *Union*, a schooner taken at the same time. The latter vessel was wrecked while in the American service, off Vera Cruz, in December, 1846. All the remaining prizes were sold at the end of the war, in 1848.

In 1847 another prize schooner was added to the Navy, the *Liberdad*, which had been taken by the *Cyane* in Lower California in October of 1846; she was employed as a tender and placed on the register in 1847. She carried a single 9-pdr. and was sold at the end of the Mexican War. A schooner named the *Nautilus* was taken over from the Coast Survey, and the ex-revenue cutter *Taney* was bought at Baltimore. Both schooners went to the Coast Survey at the end of the war. The records of the Navy and the Coast Guard are often at variance on the date of transfer of these early cutters, and the confusion seems impossible to straighten out with existing records.

The frigate *St. Lawrence* was launched in 1848, and her plan (Plan 30) shows another variation in appearance of the 1820 class of frigates. In 1848 and 1849 no ships were added to the Navy, but in the '50's one ship sloop was built, five exploration vessels were purchased, and the remaining frigates of the 1820 class were launched.

Meanwhile Samuel Humphreys had died in office, on August 16, 1846, at the age of 68. He had been inactive, however, since he designed the brigs in 1842, as his health had been poor. Humphreys was succeeded in 1847 by Francis Grice, who went on sick leave in 1859 and died at Philadelphia in 1865. Lenthall was the next chief constructor, succeeding Grice. Samuel M. Pook became a constructor January 1, 1841, and retired in 1866; he died in 1878. He was the father of Samuel Hartt Pook, a noted designer of clipper ships and also a naval constructor. The naval constructors, like the veteran captains of the Navy, had very long careers in those days.

In the '40's a number of modifications had taken place in some of the frigates. The decision to build up a sailing navy of large corvettes soon developed a school of thought that recommended that the serviceable frigates be cut down or razeed into large corvettes. Between 1849 and 1852 the "rebuilt" *Macedonian* was converted from a spar-decked frigate to a spar-decked corvette, stripped of quarter galleries and her head extensively altered. Her spars were lengthened, and a very handsome ship resulted, as can be seen by the draught, Plan 31. This converted her to a 24-gun ship. She remained in service until 1875, when she was sold. Some of the frigates were not cut down, but had their spar decks stripped of guns to make them into huge corvettes; *Constitution*, *Congress*, and some of the 1820 design of frigates were so treated. Part of this was due to the improved armament policy and part to economy; the corvette-armed frigate required smaller crews than a 44-gun frigate of the old classes.

One of the best examples of a cut-down frigate was the *Cumberland*. It will be recalled that this ship was relatively new, having been launched in 1842. She originally carried 40 carriage guns, 32-pdrs., and 10 of the 64-pdr. 8″ shell guns. She was treated in the same manner as the *Macedonian* in 1850–56 and was reduced to a magnificent corvette carrying 26 guns on her main deck, 32-pdrs., and 2 10″ shell guns on pivots, one each at bow and stern, on the spar deck. Plan 32 shows this vessel as altered. The lines of the ship were taken off in 1856; they show the hull drawn to the outside of the planking, as was done in the case of the razee *Independence*. Stripping these ships of the weight of their spar-deck bulwarks and armament, as well as removing the heavy quarter galleries (and the reducing of windage that resulted from the removal of the spar-deck bulwarks and hammock rails) made the ships very fast sailers. Their rig either remained the same as when they were frigates, or their sail area was increased. The *Cumberland* was a corvette when she fought the *Virginia* ex *Merrimac* in the Civil War; she is often referred to mistakenly as a frigate in descriptions of this action.

European navies were somewhat less enthusiastic than the Americans about the razeed frigates, but a few such vessels did appear in the English and French navies. The British had, in fact, cut down a few frigates in the '20's and '30's, but these ships were nowhere as large as the cut-down American frigates. The appearance of these ships, however, indicated how obsolete the improved naval guns, particularly the heavy shell guns, were making the massive broadside armament of the liners and frigates of earlier years. The Americans believed now that shells would be very destructive to large wooden ships and were attempting to maintain supremacy by employing the most powerful guns their ships could float, even though they were forced to cut down their large ships into vessels of lower rates, that would outrange the massed batteries of foreign frigates and ships of the line.

The year 1850 marked the beginning of arctic exploration by American naval

Figure 141. MACEDONIAN *as razeed to a corvette.*

vessels. The Grinnell Expedition in search of Sir John Franklin was organized this year, and special vessels were fitted for the work. These were purchased brigs: the *Rescue*, a 90-ton brig, and the *Advance*, a 140-tonner. The brigs were strengthened and fitted particularly for working in ice. The *Advance* was abandoned in the ice in 1855. Ringgold's expedition to the North Pacific in 1853–56 also required the purchase of vessels. The pilot schooner *Skiddy* of New York was bought in 1852 and renamed *Fenimore Cooper*. She was used as a tender in this expedition and was wrecked on the Pacific coast in 1859. A storeship was also bought, a New York merchant ship named *Sea Nymph*, and named the *John P. Kennedy*, to serve in the same expedition. This vessel was purchased in 1853. The Ringgold Expedition really included two separate squadrons, one commanded by Commander Cadwalader Ringgold and one by Commander John Rodgers. In addition to the purchased ships mentioned, the expedition included *Vincennes*, *Porpoise*, and the steamer *John Hancock*. Another arctic exploring or rescue vessel was purchased and fitted in 1855, the bark *Release*. The work on this vessel was done in the New York Navy Yard under the supervision of constructor B. L. Delano. These exploration vessels were treated as naval vessels though they were not, of course, fighting ships.

The last two of the 1820 frigates, the *Sabine* and *Santee*, were launched in 1855, the *Sabine* at New York, February 12, and the *Santee* at Portsmouth, February 16. Up to the time of their launch there were numerous projects to change them. It was proposed to lengthen them by the bow 20' on the load water line and also to reduce them to corvettes, to be armed with 24 shell guns, 8", on the main deck and 2 pivoted 10" shell guns on the spar deck. However, nothing appears to have been done about these projects, and the ships were completed as lengthened frigates only. In the many years that they had been building their appearance and lines had altered somewhat with the changing fashions. Plan 30 shows the lines of these frigates as reported in 1854. The *Sabine* was sold in 1883, and the *Santee*, after a long stay at the Naval Academy, was finally sold in 1912. These ships were obsolete when launched.

The last sailing man-of-war designed and built for the United States Navy was the first-class corvette *Constellation*, built in the Norfolk Navy Yard in 1853–54. Her design, prepared at Norfolk, called for a large and sharp spar-decked corvette, 176' 0" between perpendiculars, 41' 0" moulded beam, and 21' 0" depth of hold to the gun deck. This ship was, however, administratively "rebuilt," just as the *Macedonian*, *Cyane*, and *John Adams* had been

467

Figure 142. Draught of the spar-decked corvette CONSTELLATION, *now in existence.*

earlier. The old *Constellation*, authorized in 1794, had been repaired again and again; in the years between 1805 and 1812 she had a "great repair" that increased her beam by 14″. She had long been in very poor condition and was broken up in 1852 at Norfolk. A new design had been prepared, and this was laid down in 1853 as the "rebuilt" *Constellation*. The new vessel was a corvette, not a frigate, and she differed in model and dimensions from the original frigate of the name. The differences in the two ships may be readily seen by comparing the design of the corvette (Figure 142) with the design of the original frigate, Plan 8.

Unfortunately some of the semi-official lists of American naval ships have listed this ship as though she had, in fact, been preserved and altered. This has led to many believing the corvette, which is still in existence (1949), to be the oldest ship in the Navy and to have had a continuous identity since 1797. This is as untrue as it would be to accept the "rebuilt" frigate *Macedonian* as the original prize, or the "rebuilt" sloop *Cyane* as another British-built ship. A claim has been made that the *Constellation* now in existence contains material taken from the original and therefore retains her identity. The reply to this claim is that the ship lost her identity by the process of having her model, dimensions, appearance, and rate entirely altered in her "rebuilding" in 1853–54. She was constructed as what was then accepted to be a modern and efficient man-of-war. Therefore, accepting this completely altered ship as the original is as unreal as it would be to accept a cap-and-ball revolver as one of Washington's dueling pistols on the grounds that the gun contained a couple of screws salvaged from the original flintlock.

The "rebuilding" of the *Constellation* in 1853–54 represents a different situation from that of the numerous rebuildings of such naval monuments as the *Constitution* and the British *Victory*. In the case of the corvette, she was rebuilt into what was then a modern ship of war without any attempt to preserve the original, and the only reason her register was maintained, by means of an administrative fiction, was to enable the work to be done without the need of applying to Congress for authority and funds to build an entirely new ship. Yet a new ship was produced, as we have seen by the plans. The *Constitution* and *Victory*, however, in their numerous rebuildings have maintained their form, rate, and dimensions, though it is true that their appearance was slightly altered from time to time. Their present forms are, of course, reconstructions of their appearance at the height of their glory, as near as knowledge would permit when the work was done. The sentimental question of whether or not they have portions of the original ship in them is of small moment; the important thing is that, in rebuilding and reconstruction, they have retained their form, rate, and dimensions and thus their identity. Without attempting to discuss the advisability of retaining the corvette as a national monument, it can be said that the ship neither is the original frigate nor looks like her.

The new corvette *Constellation* was somewhat full-bodied, but she was given sharp ends and compared favorably in her lines with the corvettes built in the '40's. She was intended to be equal in size to the cut-down frigate *Cumberland* and had nearly as powerful an armament. The new ship was to carry 20 shell guns, 8″, on her main deck and, in addition, 2 guns of 10″ bore were to be fitted as shifting guns. She does not appear to have been intended to carry pivot guns on her spar deck, as did the *Cumberland*. In the Civil War it was planned to throw two of her midship ports into one port 10′ long and to mount two heavy guns, one on each side, to fire through this, in place of the four broadside guns thus eliminated. One of the big guns was to be a 100-pdr. and the other an 11″ Dahlgren; both were to be pivot-mounted with a shifting pivot bolt. This plan was never carried out. During the '50's the ship usually carried her 20 shell guns, 8″, but her shifting 10″ guns were omitted. The *Constellation* was considered a very satisfactory corvette of her class and was an excellent sailer, particularly in heavy weather. In her later years her rig was reduced and she was employed as a school ship for a long period of time. Until recently she was stationed at Newport, Rhode Island, at the Naval War College.

While the *Constellation* was being built, another "rebuilding" indicated that the sailing corvette was already obsolete as a first-class man-of-war. The old 74 *Franklin* had been included in the ships to be razeed, but when she was surveyed she was found not worth preservation. She was broken up at the Portsmouth Yard and "rebuilt" as a huge screw frigate, 265′ long. As the amount of money available each year from maintenance funds was small, she was not launched for many years after she was laid down. The Act of Congress of April 6, 1854, authorizing the construction of six first-class screw steam frigates, might be accepted as the official recognition that the day of sailing men-of-war as effective ships was completely over.

Though many sailing men-of-war saw service in the Civil War, they were accepted only as mere substitutes for steamers. Sailing frigates, sloops, and brigs, and a number of purchased armed merchant vessels, were employed, but there was rarely an attempt to use them to oppose steamers, except in the gravest emergencies. A few sailing ships were used in hunting Confederate sea raiders; however, most of them were used to fill out squadrons on stations distant from the scene of war. For many years afterward the more serviceable sailing craft were used as training ships for naval and merchant marine cadet officers, and this permitted some of the corvettes built in the '40's to have exceptionally long lives. It was the superior maneuverability of the steamer, without regard to wind, that created the war steamer, though the early steamers were not fast under power. In fact, a smart corvette or frigate could easily outrun the first clumsy side-wheelers, even when the latter had the help of sails in addition to steam—if there was wind. It was the "if" that finally decided the issue.

Just as the sailing man-of-war lacked certainty of movement, so the sailing craft used in her support were inferior to steamers for the same reason. As a result, the service craft of the '40's and '50's were gradually going over to steam. A few sailing craft were built, however; Figure 143 represents a sailing water boat built at Norfolk in the '40's—a centerboard schooner of a type that had become popular on the Chesapeake and elsewhere. The design was made by Rhodes to produce a fast-sailing tank boat; the water boat in use had by her slowness caused delays to ships waiting to go to sea. The service boats were steadily growing in size, and this schooner was no exception to the trend; she was 80' 0" between perpendiculars.

Sailing craft remained popular for carrying powder, and as late as 1858 sailing schooners and sloops were built for the purpose. These carried powder from magazines located outside the ports, away from danger to the large cities, to the navy yards, where ammunition was placed aboard the ships. They also carried ammunition out to anchorages when necessary. The powder vessels were usually coasting vessels in model and were not very large. Figure 144 is the plan of a powder sloop building in 1857 at New York, a typical centerboard river and harbor vessel of her day. She was only 58' long and had a very long mast in her, but no topmast was carried. A schooner was used at Boston and another at Norfolk, while a sloop about the size of the New York vessel was employed at Philadelphia. Portsmouth apparently shared in the use of the Boston powder boat.

Just as there had been a slow recognition of the virtues of the war steamers by commissioned naval officers, so there had been a gradual acceptance of the need of steamship designs by the naval constructors. It was a rather remarkable coincidence that all of the naval constructors had experimented with steamship

Figure 143. Schooner-rigged water tank and yard lighter.

design long before such craft were desired by the Navy. The rather peculiar circumstances that had allowed the constructors to engage in outside work was undoubtedly the reason for their progressiveness, as compared to the naval officers as a class. There can be little doubt that some of the constructors were far more interested in steamers than others: Hartt seems to have had the greatest personal interest, with Lenthall second. Humphreys had designed steamers as early as 1818, but he apparently was not particularly interested in these craft, or had so little time for design work outside the Navy that he did not continue to experiment with steamship design.

Grice, who had been the most advanced and radical of the sailing-ship designers, cared little about steamer design, yet he produced one of the finest of the early war steamers in the big side-wheeler *Powhatan*. It is regrettable that the personal papers of more of the early naval constructors have not been found, for it would be interesting to learn the viewpoints of such men as Grice and Pook on the same technical questions of ship design and steamers that Griffiths, Bates, and others wrote about in the '50's.

In judging the last sailing men-of-war one is tempted to compare them unfavorably with the clipper ships of the late '40's and early '50's, as Griffiths did. It was assumed in the '50's, and again in recent years, that the California Clippers were the acme in sailing-ship design. This assumption is open to question, for much of the speed of the California Clippers was due to their great length and size, rather than to an improved model alone. This contention is supported by the records of the later down-easters, which, though full-ended compared to the California Clippers of the '50's, were able to establish many sailing records that rate very favorably with those of the much-touted "clippers." However, the gradual increase in length and size accounted for this, to a very great extent, just as the "clippers" had obtained the same advantage over the earlier packets. The model of either type was certainly not the sole reason for the trend toward shorter passages that had been made the criterion of "clipper" category.

The rise of the California Clipper as a type can be traced to a combination of circumstances: a demand for speed in the earlier China traders, the changes in economical cargo-carrying capacity, and the experience already obtained by both builders and seamen, as well as ship owners, with the North Atlantic and coastal packets of the '30's and '40's. By 1825, the packet-ship model was accepted as a desirable one for cargo ships requiring speed, and, as has been said before, the packet was then closely related in model to the frigate. Gradually

Figure 144. Sloop powder boat.

473

Spars

Masts

	Whole Length	Head or Pole
Fore M.	90'.6"	16'.6"
Main M.	103'.9"	18'.0"
Miz. M.	89'.9"	13'.0"
Fore Top M.	51'.6"	9'.0"
Main "	60'.0"	10'.0"
Miz "	45'.6"	7'.6"
Fore t'gall M.	28'.0"	
M "	30'.6"	
Miz "	20'.6"	
Fore royal Pole	19'.6"	6'.0" pole
Main "	21'.0"	6'.0" "
Miz. "	15'.6"	5'.0" "
Bowsprit	57'.0"	
Jibboom	51'.6"	16'.6" bury
Flying "	50'.0"	7'.0 pole 14'.6 "
Spanker gaff	35'.0"	5'.0" 32' "
boom	50'.0"	2'.0"
Main Spencer gaff	30'.6"	2'.0"
Dolphin Striker	16'.0"	

Yards etc.

	Whole Length	Arms
	64'.6"	3'.6"
	74'.6"	4'.0"
	62'.6"	4'.0"
	65'.0"	5'.0"
	77'.0"	5'.4"
	45'.6"	3'.6"
	40'.4"	3'.4"
	44'.6"	2'.6"
	28'.8"	1'.6"
	16'.0"	1'.4"
	20'.6"	1'.4"
	19'.0"	1'.0"
	46'.6"	1'.0"

Particulars

O. " 64'.0" from F.P.
Room & Space 2'.4"
Water lines spaced 2'.0"
Buttocks " 4'.0"
26 32 pdr guns
1 " 10 pivot "
26

References. 40·8·6 Series
.1·2·20 6

Plan 31. Draught of the razeed CUMBERLAND, *made after the reduction of the frigate to a corvette.*

Spars *June 1854*   *Sabine to Santee*

	Masts		Yards etc	
	Whole Length	Head or Pole	Whole Length	Arms
Fore M	97·4	17·	84	4·6
Main M	105·10	19·4	95	4·7
Miz. M	86	13·10	66	7
Fore top M	59·4	9·8	62	4·4
Main " M	63·6	10·3	71·6	5·4
Miz. " M	47·6	7·3	45	3·6
Fore topgalt M	33·3		47	2·3
Main " M	37·3		46	2·8
Miz. " M	73·10		30	1·6
Fore royal Pole	19·3	6	53	1·6
Main	21·7	6	30	1·2
Miz.	21·7	5	19	0·9
Bowsprit	39· out boord			
53' Jibboom	25			
52' Flying Jibboom	23	5·		
Dolphin Striker		16·		
Fore Spencer galf.			36·6	1·3
Main "			31·6	1·3
Spanker			52	2·6
Boom				

Plan 32. Plan of the SANTEE and SABINE, the last sailing frigates launched, bows lengthened 15′ and after frames, cants, and stern altered.

the model was modified, and by 1840 it became flat-bottomed and rather wall-sided, but with increasingly sharp ends. There had been a large number of brigs, brigantines, and ships built during these years on the old Baltimore Clipper model, which had been tested in competition with the new ships of the modified packet design. Popularly the *Ann McKim*, built at Baltimore in 1833 on the Baltimore Clipper model, has been hailed as the "first" clipper ship and the forerunner of the China and California Clippers. While the *McKim* was possibly somewhat more extreme in model than other ship-rigged merchant-men of her time, she was by no means the first Baltimore Clipper built with the ship rig. We have seen that Doughty's ship sloops of the *Erie* class were on this model as early as 1813. As a merchant ship, the Baltimore Clipper was a failure, for it could carry but little cargo in proportion to its size because of its sharp bottom and ends. This same weakness appeared in the naval vessels built on this model—*Lawrence* of 1843, for an example. Neither the *McKim* nor the *Erie* class can be accepted as the first application of the very sharp-bottomed model to square-rigged vessels, for there is ample evidence of earlier attempts in both merchantmen and men-of-war, as has been indicated earlier.

Aware of the disadvantages of the Baltimore Clipper model for a merchant vessel, designers concentrated on improving the nearly flat-floored packet model in order to obtain greater speed. The first outstanding example of the improved packet model was the *Rainbow*, built in 1844–45 by Smith and Dimon of New York, from a design by John W. Griffiths. This vessel has often been claimed as the first "clipper ship"; she could more truthfully be said to have been the acme of the packet model. Her lines, which have been published,[1] show that she was not an extreme departure from previous packet models in any respect, but was merely a refinement. She did not have the "hollow bow" so often accredited to her, nor was she sharper or more extreme than some of the Navy corvettes then building. The *Rainbow* retained a good deal of deadrise and had about the same amount as some of the Navy frigates. Beginning with the *Rainbow*, the sharpening of the ends rapidly increased, but deadrise decreased much more slowly. Some of the clipper ships built for the China trade in the late '40's will serve to show the trend; *Samuel Russell*, built in 1847, and *Sea Witch*, built the year before, retained a good deal of dead-rise. The development of the type was paced by rising freights, which were gradually allowing smaller cargoes to be carried with profit. This condition

---

[1] *The History of American Sailing Ships*, New York, 1936.

reached its peak in the early '50's, and then the extreme California Clipper appeared. When the boom in freight rates subsided the California Clipper became uneconomical and disappeared from the building slips, to be replaced by a model that was an almost complete reversion to the flat-bottomed packet of 1840.

Two points can be made in the comparison of the so-called "clipper ships" and the fast naval sailing ships represented by the corvettes. The first is that the corvettes were designed before the *Rainbow* was laid down, with the sole exception of the *Constellation*. The second is that the lines of some of the corvettes show them actually to have been far more extreme than the *Rainbow*. That the *Constellation* was not as sharp as the extreme clipper ships of her time was due to naval requirements rather than to a failure of the responsible constructor to appreciate sharp lines. The *Constellation* was full, to carry her armament and stores, with her length limited by economy. This was exactly what took place in merchant-ship design when the freight boom was over. The truth of the matter is that the corvettes, particularly the *Germantown* and the *Albany*, were far more extreme models than many of the so-called "extreme clippers" of ten years later. There is no longer room for the grandiose claims that the California, and the earlier China, Clippers were startling departures in design or that they represented a sudden change in ideas. The matter can be put to rest by comparing surviving plans of the older ships with the plans and models of the best of the big clippers of the '40's and '50's, which will show that the slow rise of sharper and longer hulls reached back many decades before *Rainbow* and her sisters appeared, and that the extremely sharp hull was nothing new in 1850, 1840, or even 1800, for that matter.

The corvettes built in the 1840's were excellent examples of the high level of ability of the naval constructors who were responsible for their designs. Each designer was given a free hand to choose the model and dimensions he thought best. As has been seen, the result was a variety of hull forms and dimensions; some of the hulls might be classed as extreme in many respects. It would have been normal, under such circumstances, if some of these ships had been utter and complete failures, owing to overenthusiasm for some particular element of design. That this was not the case in any of the corvettes proves beyond a shadow of a doubt that the naval constructors were unusually competent. The steamers that these men designed later bore out the promise they showed in the '40's.

The changes in appearance that took place in American naval ships in the

years between 1830 and 1855 were of relatively little practical importance
and can be classed as having been due to the slow shift in fashion. Perhaps
the one borderline case was the changes in the head and cutwater. As many of
the drawings show, the head was gradually closed in by planking up the face
of the knees supporting the upper rails of the cutwater with thin plank. The
closing in of the "head" began with the use of painted weather cloths above
the upper headrail, to give some protection to the men using the head. This
was done before the American Revolution. The weather cloths were replaced

Types of hammock rails.

by wood sheathing, vertically staved, in the early '20's. In the middle '30's the
knees supporting the headrails were closed in with plank, and by 1838 the
rails themselves began to disappear. In the '40's the rails had disappeared
entirely, and the whole head above the cheek knees, or trail knees, was planked
in. This was set off by carrying a prominent headrail along the top of the
head to the billet—an extension of the rail cap when practical.

In the '30's the hammock nettings had been replaced by wooden hammock
rails with vertical staving from rail cap to hammock rail on the outboard side
and horizontal panels on the inboard face. In the early '30's the hammock
rails were often carried to just abaft the catheads in small vessels, or to the
knightheads in large ones; but the fashion of running the hammock rails the

full length of the hull by adding monkey rails fore and aft had existed as early as the end of the War of 1812. In the '40's, the hammock rails were extended forward over the head to the bowsprit; the plan of the *Portsmouth* shows this style. This remained the practice in naval ships as long as the wooden vessels were built.

The purpose of the gradual closing in of the head was originally to make this portion of the ship neater and to give added shelter to the men using the toilet facilities there. Privacy was, of course, a factor. These practical considerations were affected by the slowly growing weight of the head, which eventually had to be reduced by removal of the heavy rails and some of the knees. The disadvantages of the closed-in head were that the danger of rot in this portion of the ship was greatly increased and, in action, the head was a dangerous source of splinters and fire when hit by a shell or solid shot. The closing in of the hammock rails and the substitution of staving and wooden rails for netting and rope were peacetime maintenance developments; but wooden hammock rails and staving would also be sources of danger from splinters or fire in action, as was often discovered during the Civil War. The wooden rails, with their staving and panels, were neater than the old nettings, weather cloths, and rope support, but were far less practical. The peacetime urge for neatness and easy maintenance often runs afoul of war requirements.

The alterations in the stern have been described as they appeared, and there were no notable changes in the '50's. The old quarter galleries were going out of fashion very slowly indeed; they were still in existence ten years after the Civil War in American naval steamers of the larger classes, and there were many merchant vessels with these adornments in the '50's. While the cut-waters had grown more pointed in profile, as can be seen in the plans of some of the corvettes, the stern remained short and rather heavy; the rounded finish was retained in the sterns of naval steamers that were built during and after the Civil War, and was one of their ugly features. By 1855 the naval vessels had dropped all adornment except the billet and, occasionally, some carving on the stern and quarter galleries. The channels had become narrower and less prominent, and bar chains to secure the lower deadeyes had come into use.

The stream of investigation into hull form and related problems was now diverted from the sailing ship toward the steamer: as a result of this, and of a steady increase in power that was possible with improving engines and boilers, fast steamers were becoming common in the '50's, and in this the Americans were intensely interested.

The end of the period of the sailing men-of-war was not suddenly apparent, nor was it marked by a dramatic flourish. Slowly but surely steamers replaced the various types of sailing war vessels, until only a few of the latter were in use. Perhaps the sailing warship might have survived longer had she been required to compete only with side-paddle steamers, but the appearance of the screw propeller made the auxiliary steamer practical and hastened the end of the sailing ship. This evolution was completed in the American Navy in the relatively short period of fifteen years; many of the old sailing men-of-war were kept on the register but were laid up in ordinary. As a result, many were wiped out in a single disaster in the first year of the Civil War. The burning of the Norfolk Navy Yard in 1861 created a funeral pyre for the *Pennsylvania, Columbus, Delaware, New York, Columbia, Germantown, Dolphin, Plymouth, Raritan,* and the old *United States.* The Norfolk Yard was to be the agent of the end of two more fine sailing men-of-war: the Confederate steam ram *Virginia,* rebuilt from the steam frigate *Merrimac,* burned in the Navy Yard with the sailing men-of-war, later sank the *Congress* and *Cumberland.* The helplessness of the two ships sunk by the ram left no possible doubt of the passing of the sailing men-of-war: there was no longer a valid reason for their existence other than the sentimental preservation of an era of naval glory.

★ ★ ★ ★ ★ ★ ★ ★ ★

Appendix

SPAR DIMENSIONS

THE SPAR dimensions of American naval vessels were never fully standardized in the days of sailing ships, and each vessel usually had an individual rig. While there were many attempts to set up an "establishment" for the spars allowed each class of ship or vessel, none of these were successful, and it was by no means rare to find sister ships with spars of entirely different lengths. Also the spars employed in a vessel varied from time to time as a refit or her commander caused changes to be made. The following is a list of spar dimensions for naval ships and small craft, dated to indicate that they may or may not be her original set. The methods of measuring varied: masts were sometimes measured from heel to hounds (hounded length) and the length of the head was added to give the total stick length; in other cases the stick length is given and also the length of the head; dimensions of yards and booms are commonly the total length, with the length of the arms also given. With the stick length given, the heads or arms are deducted to find the remaining length of the spars or masts. Some spar dimensions are rarely given—the length of the dolphin striker and the length and diameter of the trysail or spencer masts, when present. Where there are no head lengths of the topgallant masts, this indicates that the topgallent, royal, and pole were in one stick. Spar dimensions, where available, are listed only for those vessels whose plans are in existence. In some cases dimensions will be given even though a sail plan is shown elsewhere in this book, either as a matter of useful data for comparison or because there might be some question of the interpretation used in drawing the sail plans. "Length" is commonly the whole length in the following tables.

ALBANY, 1st-class Ship Sloop, 22 guns, 1843 (Ship rig) (Spars of 1844)

	Length	Diam- eter	Head or Arm		Length	Diam- eter	Head or Arm
Foremast	81' 1"	29"	13' 6"	Fore topmast	50'	16"	8'
Mainmast	89' 7"	30"	13' 6"	Main topmast	50'	16"	8'
Mizzenmast	70' 3"	21"	11'	Mizzen topmast	38' 9"	12"	6' 3"
Bowsprit outboard	33' 4"	30"	—	Fore topgallant mast	25' 3"	9"	—

	Length	Diam-eter	Head or Arm		Length	Diam-eter	Head or Arm
Main topgallant mast	25' 3"	9"	—	Fore topgalt yard	39'	8½"	2'
Mizzen topgallant mast	19' 3"	7"	—	Main topgalt yard	39'	8½"	2'
Fore royal mast	16'	6¾"	—	Mizzen topgallant yard	25'	6"	—
Main royal mast	16'	6¾"		Fore royal yard	28' 10"	6"	1'
Mizzen royal mast	13' 3"	5¼"	—	Main royal yard	28' 10"	6"	1'
Fore skysail pole	8'	5¼"		Mizzen royal yard	17'	4"	—
Main skysail pole	8'	5¼"		Spanker boom	41'	9½"	1'
Mizzen skysail pole	6'	4"		Jibboom outboard	29' 6"	16"	2'
Fore yard	77'	18"	4'	Flying jibboom outboard	19'	8½"	4'
Main yard	77'	18"	4'		(total length 48' 6")		
Mizzen yard	47' 6"	11"	1' 6"				
Fore topsail yard	57' 6"	13"	5'	Spanker gaff	29'	7½"	5'
Main topsail yard	57' 6"	13"	5'	Fore gaff	22'	7"	1'
Mizzen topsail yard	39'	9"	2'	Main gaff	22'	6½"	1'

ARGUS, Brig, 18 guns, 1803

Indent for Articles wanted in the Construction and Equipment of the United States Brig *Argus*, to be built in Boston of the following Dimensions

Length of Keel fayable 77 feet
Breadth of Beam 27 feet
Depth of Hold 12½ feet

Cables

3 Bower cable of 13 inches, 120 fathoms
1 Stream do 13 do , 120 do
1 Cablet do 5 do , 120 do

Spars

Species	Length	Diam-eter	Length head
Main mast	69	20½	10
top mast	30	11¾	5½
topgt mast	32	6¾	12
Fore mast	60	18½	9¾
top mast	30	11¾	5½
topgt mast	32	6¾	12
Bow sprit	40	18½	

Species	Length	Diam-eter	Length arm
Jibboom	33	9¼	
Main yard	50	11¼	2⅓
topsail yard	37	8½	2⅔
Top gt yard	26	5½	1½
Royal yard	17	3½	
Fore yard	50	11	
topsail yard	37	8	
topgt yard	26	5¼	
royal yard	17	3¼	
Main boom	53		
gaff	30		
Sprit sail yard	31½	7	2½
4 Top mast stud sail boom	28	5½	
2 Top galt do do do	18½	4	
1 Ring tail boom	20	5½	

Species	Length	Diam-eter	Length head
2 Lower Stun sail booms	35	5½	
20 Sweeps made of spruce	30	5½	

Rigging

	Inches Circum.	Fathom Long.
Main shrouds	7½	81
Fore shrouds	7½	66
Main stay	9	14
Main spring stay	6	9
Back and topmast stays	6¼	155
Breast back stay and spring stay	5¼	100
Topmast shrouds	4½	120
Top galt back stay	3½	80
Topgalt shrouds	3¼	60
Main and fore lifts	4	60
Topsail sheets	5	66
Topsail lifts	3¼	60
Jack stays and futtock shrouds	3¾	60
Main and fore topgalt sheets	3	60
Main and fore sheets	4	60
Main tacks	5	11
Fore tacks	5	9

Anchors

3 1700 lbs. each Iron stocks
1 640 lbs. do do do
1 Kedge 336 lbs. do do
1 Boat grapnell 60 lbs.
1 do 40 lbs.
1 Creeper 20 lbs.
2 Fire grapnells 30 do each

Boats

1 Cutter with a well and		1 Pinnace	24 feet long
Windlass	25 feet long	1 Jolly boat	18 feet long

Blocks, Hearts, and Dead Eyes, with their Dimensions

N.B. All blocks over 6 inches to be cogged.

Number	Size	Number	Size
40 Deadeyes, 20 iron strapped	9	4 Topsail buntlines	7
16 do , 8 do do	7	4 Reef tackles	7
32 do , 16 do do	6	4 Rolling tackles, 2 double	8
1 Open Heart for the Bowsprit	15	4 Topgallant Halyards	8
1 do	14	4 Fiddle blocks, yard tackles	16
3 Hearts, one Iron Strapped	13	4 do , single	10
1 do , rope do	12	4 Topgallant brace, 2 double	7
4 do , Bobstays	9	4 do Cluelines	7
4 do , Bowsprit shrouds	8	4 Stun sail Halyards	8
4 Hearts for topmast stays	8	4 do do	9
4 do Mⁿ topmast spring stay		4 Boom tackles, 2 double	11
(main)	7	4 Peake and Throat Halyards, 2 double	11
16 do top gallant shrouds	5	1 Throat tye	11
4 Quarter blocks	12	4 Sister blocks	15
4 Fore sheet blocks	11	4 do do	10
4 Fore lifts	10	2 Top leaders	6
1 Main topmast stay block	11	2 Main stay leaders	6
1 do	10	6 Single Blocks	7
1 Fore peake tye, iron strapped	11	12 do	6
2 Top blocks	12	12 do	5
2 For cheeks of the main	11	2 Catt blocks	14
6 main and fore brace	11	7 Snatch blocks from 9–14 inches	
4 Fore sail brace	9	64 Hooks and thimbles	
2 Top sail brace, double	9	70 Thimbles, assorted sizes	
4 For top sail halyard, double	11		
8 Clue garnets	9	1 Messenger, Cablet laid, circum. 7½ inches	
8 Topsail cluelines, 4 double	8	1 Buoy rope do 4½ do	
2 Fore top bowlines	8	1 do do do 2½ do	
2 Sprit sail lifts	7	3 Nun buoys for Bower	
2 Fore bowline	9	1 Wood for stream	
8 Fore lifts, 4 double	7	1 Fish hook	
8 do trusses, 4 double	7	1 Lightning conductor	
8 Fore topgallant back stays, 4 double	7	10 capstan bars	
6 Fore stun sail brace	7		
12 Fore lower buntlines	7	4 Lower stun sail Boom irons	
12 Fore leach lines	6	4 Top mast do do do do	

Note: Channels were first placed below gun ports but were raised to above the ports while the brig was in the Mediterranean.

BOSTON, Frigate, 28 guns, 1799 (Incomplete dimensions, 1804)

Fore Mast 74′ 2″ Dia. 24½″	Mizzen Mast 72′ 0″ Dia. 18″
" Topmast 44′ 7″ " 14¾″	" Topmast 35′ 6″ Dia. 11¾″
" Topgalt Mast 22′ 3½″ Dia. 9″	" Topgalt Mast 19′ 9″ Dia. 8½″
" Royal Mast 16′ 8¾″ Dia. 7½″	" Royal Mast 13′ 4″ Dia. 5″
Main Mast 81′ 8″ Dia. 27¾″	Bowsprit 52′ 6″ Dia. 26¼″
Main Topmast 49′ 0″ Dia. 16½″	Jibboom 44′ 0″
Main Topgalt Mast 24′ 6″ Dia. 9½″	Flying Jibboom 48′ 0″
Main Royal Mast 18′ 4″ Dia. 8¼″	Spanker Boom 56′ 0″

Fore Yard 63′ 6″   Main Topsail Yard 56′ 0″
   " Topsail Yard 48′ 0″   Mizzen Yard 52′ 6″
Main Yard 70′ 0″   "   Topsail Yard 38′ 0″

BOXER, Schooner, 10 guns, 1831

	Whole Length		Heads or Arms
Main Mast	76′ 0″		8′ 6″
Fore Mast	74′ 0″		8′ 6″
" Topmast	35′ 0″		12′ 0″ pole
Main "	33′ 0″		12′ 0″ "
Fore Yard	58′ 0″		2′ 0″
" Topsail Yard	34′ 0″		2′ 0″
" Topgalt "	22′ 0″		1′ 3″
Bowsprit	29′ 0″	outboard 17′ 0″	
Jib Boom	34′ 0″	from cap 17′ 0″	
Flying "	30′ 0″	" " 13′ 0″	
Fore Gaff	26′ 0″		
Main "	24′ 0″		
" Boom	49′ 6″		
Gaff Topsail Yard	32′ 0″		

CHESAPEAKE, Frigate, 36 guns, 1799 (Spars of 1800)

Fore Mast	84′ 6″	Head	11′ 8″	Fore Yard	75′ 9″	Arms	3′ 0″
" Topmast	50′ 6″	"	6′ 9″	" Topsail Yard	54′ 0″	"	4′ 6″
" Topgalt	24′ 3″	Pole	20′ 0″	" Topgalt "	36′ 0″	"	2′ 3″
Main Mast	94′ 0″	Head	13′ 0″	" Royal "	27′ 0″	"	1′ 0″
" Topmast	56′ 6″	"	7′ 7″	Main Yard	84′ 6″	"	3′ 6″
" Topgalt	27′ 3″	Pole	23′ 0″	" Topsail Yard	60′ 3″	"	5′ 0″
Mizzen Mast	80′ 6″	Head	9′ 0″	" Topgalt "	40′ 0″	"	2′ 6″
" Topmast	42′ 0″	"	5′ 9″	" Royal "	30′ 0″	"	1′ 0″
" Togalt	20′ 0″	Pole	16′ 0″	Mizzen Yard	60′ 3″	"	2′ 9″
Bowsprit	60′ 0″	outboard	40′ 0″	" Topsail Yard	40′ 0″	"	2′ 8″
Jibboom	45′ 0″	"	30′ 0″	" Topgalt "	28′ 0″	"	1′ 11″
Flying Jibboom	50′ 0″	"	20′ 0″	" Royal Yard	19′ 6″	"	8″
Martingale	15′ 0″			Spritsail Yard	54′ 0″	"	2′ 6″
Ensign staff	35′ 0″						
Jack staff	15′ 6″	Boom	54′ 0″	Gaff	38′ 0″		

Spars at time of capture by *Shannon* (British report)

	Masts				Yards		
	Length		Dia.		Length		Dia.
	Yds.	In.	In.		Yds.	In.	In.
Main	30	0	30		27	26	19⅛
Top	18	9	17¾		20	9	12⅝
Top Galt	9	7	9⅛		12	13	7⅜
Fore	27	22	26½		24	7	16¾
Top	16	30	16¾		18	2	11½
Top Galt	8	3	8		11	0	6½
Mizzen	23	26	22½	gaff	14	6	10⅛
Top	14	27	13¾		13	26	8¼
Topgalt	6	32	6⅞		9	24	5½
Bowsprit	20	3	28¾		18	2	11½
Jibboom	13	12	12		11	0	6½
Crossjack					20	9	12⅝

CONGRESS, Frigate, 36 guns, 1799 (Dimensions dated 1799)

Fore Mast	84'	Head	12' 6"	Fore Yard	74'	Arms	4' 3"
" Top	52'	"	7'	" top	52' 5"	"	4'
" Topgalt	26' 6"		—	" topgalt	37' 7"	"	2' 2"
" Royal	15' 6"		—	" Royal	28' 3"	"	1' 6"
Bowsprit	60'	Jibboom	45' Flying Jibboom 18' out				
Main Mast	93' 4"	Head	12' 9"	Main Yard	82' 4"	"	4' 3"
" Top	56'	"	7' 6"	" top	58' 4"	"	4' 9"
" Topgalt	29' 8"	*		" topgalt	41' 4"	"	2' 2"
" Royal	16'			" Royal	31'	"	1' 8"
Mizzen Mast	81' 6"	Head	9' 8"	Mizzen Yard	55' 6"	"	2' 3"
" Top	43' 11"	"	5' 8"	" top	41'	"	3' 2"
" Topgalt	23' 10"			" topgalt	31'	"	1' 8"
" Royal	11' 6"			" Royal	23' 3"	"	1' 3"
				Boom	54'		
				Gaff	41'		

CONGRESS, Frigate, 44 guns, 1839 (Dimensions dated 1839)

	Masts			Yards		
	Length	Dia.	Head	Length	Dia.	Arms
Main	105'	34"	18'	95'	22.6"	4' 9"
" top	63'	19⅛"	9' 7"	71' 6"	17.8"	6' 0"
" topgalt	32'	11"	—	44'	10.2"	2' 0"
" royal	21' 8"	—	—	30'	6"	1' 6"
" pole	8' 8"	4"	—	—	—	—
Fore	95'	30.8"	16'	84'	20.2"	4' 6"
" top	56'	19⅛"	9' 6"	62' 6"	15½"	5' 3"
" topgalt	29'	11"	—	41'	9.3"	2' 0"
" royal	19' 4"	—	—	27'	5.4"	1' 3"
" pole	7' 9"	4"	—	—	—	—
Mizzen	87'	24⅕	12' 4"	66'	13.2"	7' 0"
Mizzen top	46' 4"	13.3"	6' 8"	46'	9½"	4' 0"
" topgalt	24' 6"	8"	—	30'	6"	1' 6"
" royal	16' 4"	—	—	19' 6"	3.8"	2' 9"
" pole	6' 6"	3.6"	—	—	—	—

Bowsprit 66'; Jib boom 50' x 14.8"; Flying Jib boom 54' x 10⅓"; pole 8' 8"; Main gaff 28' 6" x 7.1"; Fore gaff 33' 6" x 7.8"; Mizzen gaff 32' x 7.8"; Spanker boom 50' x 10½"; Ringtail 25' x 5"; Jackstaff 14' x 4.2"; Dolphin striker 18' x 7½".

CONSTELLATION, Frigate, 36 guns, 1797 (Spars, 1801)

	Masts			Yards	
	Length	Head		Length	Arms
Fore	86' 6"	12' 6"	Fore	76'	4' 6"
" top	53'	7' 6"	" top	54'	5'
" topgalt	43'	pole 15'	" topgalt	38'	2'
Main	96'	13' 6"	" royal	29'	1' 6"
" top	58'	7' 6"	Main	84'	4' 6"
" topgalt	45'	pole 17'	" top	60'	5'
Mizzen	82'	10'	" topgalt	40'	2'
" top	45'	6'	" royal	30'	1' 6"
" topgalt	34'	pole 12'	Mizzen	57'	3' 6"
Bowsprit	60'		" top	42'	3'
Jibboom	43'		" topgalt	31'	2'
Flying Jibboom	44'		" royal	22'	2'
Martingale	15'		Boom	54'	
			Gaff	40'	

CONSTITUTION, Frigate, 44 guns, 1797 (Dimensions dated 1803)

	Masts Length	Head		Yards Length
Fore	96'	14'		84'
" top	52' 6"	7' 9"		60'
" topgalt	32' 9"			40' 6"
" pole	17'			29'
Main	105' 6"	15' 6"		92'
" top	61' 6"	8' 9"		64'
" topgalt	34' 6"			44'
" pole	18' 6"			31'
Mizzen	90'	10'		64'
" top	50' 10"	7'		46'
" topgalt	26'			30'
" pole	12'			20' 6"
Bowsprit	64'		Spritsail Yard	60'
jibboom	51'		Boom	50'
Flying Jibboom	60'		Gaff	40'
Martingale	21'			

(Set of 1815)

	Masts Length	Masts Dia.	Head	Yards Length	Yards Dia.	Arms
Fore	94'	2' 7"	16'	81'	18"	3' 3"
" top	56'	18½"	10'	62' 2"	12½"	5' 3"
" topgalt	31'	11"	—	45'	9"	3' 6"
" royal	20'	—	—	28'	7"	1' 2"
" skysail pole	36'	—	—	—	—	—
Main	104'	2' 8"	19' 6½"	95'	22½"	4' 0"
" top	62' 10"	18½"	10'	70' 6"	15½"	4' 6"
" topgalt	32' 0"	12"	—	46'	9¾"	4' 0"
" royal	21'	—	—	30'	8"	1' 4"
" skysail pole	39'	—	—	—	—	—
Mizzen	81'	21½"	13' 6"	75'	14"	3' 3"
" top	48'	14½"	7'	49'	9½"	4'
" topgalt	23' 6"	9"	—	32'	7½"	2' 6"
" royal	20'	—	—	20'	6"	3' 0"
" skysail pole	30'	—	—	—	—	—
Bowsprit	65' 4"	2' 8½"		60'	14"	
Jibboom	49'	14"				
Flying Jibboom	52'	12"				

Spanker Gaff 40' x 14"
" Boom 55' x 15"

CYANE, Ship Sloop, 18 guns, 1815, prize (Dimensions of 1818)

	Masts Length	Dia.	Yards Length
Fore	66' 6"	22½"	58'
" top	41' 6"	12⅞"	44'
" topgalt	22' hoist	7½"	33' 6"
" pole	16'	—	22' 4"
Main	77' 6"	23"	64'
" top	46' 9"	13⅛"	48'
" topgalt	23' 6" hoist	8⅛"	38'
" pole	18' 6"	—	22' 6"
Mizzen	52' 0"	16½"	48'
" top	34' 3"	9"	35' 8"

Masts			Yards	
	Length	Dia.		Length
Mizzen topgalt	17' hoist	6½"		25'
" pole	11'	—		14' 6"
Bowsprit	41'	—	Spanker Boom	47' 6" x 9¼"
Jibboom	35' 9"	10"	" Gaff * not given	
Flying Jibboom	38'	6"		

2 large launches

3 anchors 32 cwt and 29 cwt
2 stream 9 " " 6 "

22	32 pdr carronades on gun deck
6	18 pdr " " quarterdeck
2	12 pdr " " gangways
2	9 pdr long guns on forecastle
32	

"Rig to be retained"

124' 9" on spar deck
123' 3" On gun deck
30' 6" beam at spar deck
31' 6" extreme at gun deck
breadth of transom 17' 6"
Height of gundeck 6' 2½"

Height of Berth deck 5' 9"
Depth of hold to gundeck 18' 11"

DELAWARE, Ship of the Line, 74 guns, 1817 (Dimensions dated 1822)

	Masts	Yards		Masts	Yards
Fore	115'	96'	Mizzen	97'	80'
" top	63'	71'	" top	55'	52'
" topgalt	32'	46'	" topgalt	29'	33'
" royal	22'	33'	" royal	20'	23'
" pole	11'	—	" pole	10'	
Main	124' 6"	107' 6"	Bowsprit outboard	56'	
" top	70'	78'	Jibboom from cap	40'	
" topgalt	41'	52'	Flying Jibboom from cap	20' total 60'	
" royal	24'	36'	Spanker Gaff 38'		
" pole	12'	—	Spanker Boom * not given		

FRANKLIN, Ship of the Line, 74 guns, 1815 (Dimensions dated 1817)

	Masts	Yards		Masts	Yards
Fore	106'	90'	Mizzen	98'	80'
" top	63'	67'	" top	53'	49'
" topgalt	37'	45'	" topgalt	29'	33'
" royal	22'	30'	" royal	20'	21' 9"
" pole	6'	—	" pole	5'	—
Main	117'	105'	Bowsprit outboard 48'		
" top	70'	77'	Jibboom from cap 36'		
" topgalt	41'	51'	Flying Jibboom from cap 20'		
" royal	24'	36'	Spanker Boom 60'		
" pole	6'	—	" Gaff 38'		

GRAMPUS, Schooner, 10 guns, 1821 (Eckford's instructions, 1821)

	Masts				Yards & Booms		
	Length	Dia.	Head		Length	Dia.	Arms
Main	78' 8"	18½"	8' 0"	Main Boom	54' 9"	12"	—
Fore	75' 8"	20"	8' 0"	" Gaff	27' 4"	8"	—
Main top	26' 2"	7½"	—	Fore Gaff	27' 4"	8"	—

	Masts Length	Dia.	Head
Fore top	26' 2"	8½"	—
Main topgalt	13' 1"	5"	—
Fore topgalt	13' 1"	5½"	—
Main pole	1' 0"	2½"	—
Fore pole	1' 0"	2½"	—
Bowsprit	29' 1"	18"	
Jibboom	37' 0"	9"	

	Yards & Booms Length	Dia.	Arms
Fore Yard	50' 0"	11½"	2' 6"
" top "	33' 4"	7½"	3' 0"
" topgalt "	22' 0"	5"	1' 0"
Squaresail Yard	13' 11"	4½"	—
" Boom	45' 0"	9"	
Lower stud. Yard	8' 8"	3"	
Fore top stud Yard	12' 0"	3½"	
Gaff tops'l Yard	22' 8"	4½"	
Ringtail	8' 4"	3"	
" Boom	25' 0"	6"	
Lower stud. boom	31' 6"	7"	
Fore top stud. boom	26' 6"	5½"	

N.B. Topmast, topgalt and royal pole are in one stick.

GUERRIERE, Frigate, 44 guns, 1813, built at Phila. (Dimensions dated 1814)

	Masts Length	Head	Yards Length	Dia.	Arms
Fore	93'	16'	81' 8"	22¼"	4' 9"
" top	58'	9' 4"	61' 3"	15¼"	5'
" topgalt	28'	—	40'	10"	2'
" royal	20' 8"	—	27'	6⅛"	1' 1"
" pole	36'		18' 1"	4¼"	0' 8"
Main	104'	18'	94'	23½"	4' 9"
" top	62'	10'	69' 6"	17¼"	5' 10"
" topgalt	31'	—	45'	11¼"	2' 6"
" royal	23'	—	30'	7¼"	1' 7"
" pole	40'	—	20'	5"	0' 10"
Mizzen	83' 3"	14'	72'	18"	4' 6"
" top	48' 6"	7' 9"	46'	11½"	3' 2"
" topgalt	22'	—	30'	7¼"	1' 6"
" royal	17'	—	17' 5"	4¾"	0' 10"
" pole	30'	—	12' 4"	3¼"	0' 5"
Bowsprit	65'		Spritsail Yard 61'	17¼"	5' 0"
Jibboom	43'				
Flying Jibboom	53'				
Spanker Boom	62'				
" Gaff	30'				

HORNET, Brig, 16 guns, 1805

	Masts Length	Head	Yards Length	Arms
Fore	64' 6"	9' 9"	56'	—
" top	39'	4' 11"	43'	
" topgalt	20' 4"	—	26'	
" pole	14'		—	
Main	74'	11'	62'	—
" top	39'	4' 11"	43'	
" topgalt	20' 4"	—	26'	

	Masts Length	Head	Yards Length	Arms
Main pole	14'	—	—	
Bowsprit	45' 9"	Spritsail		
		Yard 43'		
Jibboom	31'			
Spanker Boom	50'			
Spanker Gaff	30'			

INDEPENDENCE, Razee, 54 guns, 1836 (Incomplete list, 1838)

	Length	Masts Head	Dia.	Length	Yards Arms	Dia.
Bowsprit outboard	47.09'	—	38.34"			
Fore	105.8'	17.61'	35.27"	93.40'	3.92'	21.92"
" top	60.72'	9.71'	20.26"			
" topgalt	30.36'	—	10.12"	44.36'	2.43'	9.31"
" royal	20.64'	—	—			
" pole	10.32'	—	—			
Main	115.0'	19.14'	38.34"	101.52'	4.26'	23.86"
" top	66.0'	10.56'	20.26"			
" topgalt	33.05'	—	11.0"	48.22'	2.65'	10.12"
" royal	22.44'	—	—			
" pole	11.22'	—	—			
Mizzen	omitted	14.35	26.84"	66.36'	3.63'	13.86"
" top	49.05'	7.92'	14.35"			
" topgalt	24.75'	—	8.25"	31.34'	1.72'	6.58"
" royal	20.83'	—	—			
" pole	8.42'	—	—			
Jibboom outboard	36.72'	2.20'	19.46"			
Flying " "	29.37'	5.58'	12.62"			

JOHN ADAMS, Ship Sloop, 18 guns, 1830 (Dimensions dated 1835)

	Length	Masts Dia.	Head	Length	Yards Dia.	Arms
Fore	not given			62'	—	2' 8"
" top	42' 6"	14¾"	6' 6"	44'	3'	
" topgalt	36' 6"	8½"	—	29' 6"	6¾"	1' 6"
" pole	16'	—	—	17' 6"	4"	9"
Main	not given			72'	—	4' 6"
" top	47'	15"	7' 0"	52'	—	3' 6"
" topgalt	39' 10"	8½"	—	35'	7"	1'
" pole	18'	—	—	22' 6"	4½"	1'
Mizzen	not given			50'	—	2' 8"
" top	37'	15"	5'	36'	—	2' 9"
" topgalt	28' 9"	6½"	—	22' 6"	6¾"	1'
" pole	12'	—	—	16'	3½"	6"
Bowsprit	not given					
Jibboom	37'	11"	—			
Flying Jibboom	not given					
Spanker gaff	35'					
" boom	45'					

LEXINGTON, Storeship, 1840 (Dimensions dated May 1, 1844)

	Length	Masts Head	Dia.	Length	Yards Arms	Dia.
Fore	71' 6"	12' 6"	26"	66'	4'	16"
" top	43'	7'	14"	50'	4' 3"	11½"
" topgalt	22'	—	8¼"	35'	2'	7½"
" royal	15'	—	6¾"	25'	1' 2"	5"
" pole	6'	—	—			
Main	76' 6"	12' 6"	26"	66'	4'	16"
" top	43'	7'	14"	50'	4' 3"	11½"

| | | Masts | | | Yards | |
	Length	Head	Dia.	Length	Arms	Dia.
Main topgalt	22′	—	8¼″	35′	2′	7½″
" royal	15′ pole	6′	6¾″	25′	1′ 2″	5″
Mizzen	61′ 6″	10′ 3″	18″	51′	2′ 6″	11¼″
" top	34′	5′ 6″	11″	38′	2′ 9″	8½″
" topgalt	18′	—	6¾″	26′	1′ 2″	5¼″
" royal	12′ pole	6′	5½″	20′	0′ 10″	4″

Topgalt, royal and pole in one stick all three masts

Bowsprit outboard	26′	—	26″	
Jibboom "	24′	2′	14″	
Flying " "	15′	6′	8¼″	
Spanker boom	38′ pole	2′	8¼″	⎫
" gaff	29′ "	6′	6½″	⎪
Fore gaff	25′ "	1′ 6″	6½″	⎬ poles are not included in the length
Main "	19′ "	1′	5½″	⎪
Swing booms	40′	—	8¼″	⎭

Breadth of fore and main tops 14′ 4″; mizzen top 11′; Fore and main after topmast crosstrees 8′ 6″;
Mizzen topmast crosstrees 6′ 6″

MACEDONIAN, Frigate, 38 guns, 1812, prize (Spars and sails as taken off, 1818)

Length of the bowsprit outboard	40′	Diameter	2′ 7″		
inboard	16′				
whole length	57′ 6″				
Length of the jibboom	44′	"	1′ 1¼″		
" head	2′ 3″				
Length of flying jibboom	44′ 8″	"	8¼″		
" " head	1′				
Spritsail yard	53′	"	11½″		
" " arms	4′				
Extreme length of foremast	87′ 8″	Diameter	2′ 4″		
head	14′ 6″				
" " " foretopmast	53′ 10″	"	1′ 5½′		
head	10′ 4″				
Length of fore topgallant mast to hounds	25′ 6″	"	9½″	⎫	
Length of fore royal mast	17′ 6″	"	7″	⎬	in one, total
skysail to truck	5′ 3″	"	4¾″	⎭	length 48′ 3″
Extreme length of mainmast	94′ 6″	Diameter	2′ 8″		
head	15′ 8″				
" " of maintopmast	59′ 0″	"	1′ 6¼″		
head	11′ 11″				
Length of main topgaltmast to hounds	27′ 8″	"	9¾″	⎫	
Length of main royal mast	19′ 0″	"	8″	⎬	in one, total
Skysail mast to truck	7′ 6″	"	5¾″	⎭	length 54′ 2″
Extreme length of mizzenmast	69′ 6″	Diameter	1′ 9″		
head	12′				
" " mizzen topmast	46′	"	1′ 2″		
head	7′				
Length of mizzen topgaltmast to hounds	28′ 9″	"	7″	⎫	
Length of mizzen royal mast	14′	"	5½″	⎬	in one, total
Skysail mast to truck	4′ 2″	"	4″	⎭	length 38′ 11″

Extreme length of main yard	84'	arms	3' 8"	diameter	1' 7½"
topsail "	63' 3"	"	6' 0"	"	1' 2"
topgalt "	43' 8"	"	2' 9"	"	0' 9"
royal "	30'	"	2'	"	0' 6"
Extreme length of fore yard	74'	"	3' 6"	"	1' 6"
topsail "	56'	"	5' 6"	"	1' 0¾"
topgalt "	39'	"	2' 9"	"	0' 8"
royal "	27'	"	2'	"	0' 5½"
Extreme length of mizzen yard	68'	"	9' 0"	"	1' 1"
topsail "	43'	"	3' 9"	"	10"
topgalt "	28' 6"	"	1'	"	5¾"
royal "	19'	"	0' 7"	"	4½"

Lower stud yards	20' long	5" diameter	"
fore top ditto	19' "	5"	"
" topgalt ditto	15' "	3¾"	"
" royal ditto	10' "	3"	"
Main topmast ditto	20' "	5"	"
" topgalt ditto	15' "	3¾"	"
" royal ditto	11' "	3¼"	"
Gaff	43' "	9"	"
Boom	58' "	11¼"	"

Length of the lower studdingsail booms each 49', diameter 9½"

" " " fore topmast " " "	39'	"	7½"
" " " " topgalt " " "	29' 6"	"	6"
" " " " royal " " "	21'	"	4"
" " " main topmast " " "	44' 8"	"	7½"
" " " " topgalt " " "	33'	"	6"
" " " " royal " " "	23'	"	4"

Fore top is 18' 6" wide and 12' fore and aft
Main " " 20' " " 13' 9" " " "
Mizzen " " 15' 6" " " 8' 10" " " "

Sails

Item	Head	Foot	Hoist	Inner Leach	Tack	Outer Leach
Fore course	62'	62'	37' 6"			
Fore topsail	41' 6"	62'	45' 6"			
" topgalt	33'	41' 6"	25'			
" royal	23' 6"	33'	17' 6"			
" skysail	17'	23' 6"	13'			
Mainsail	73'	80'	38' 6"			
" topsail	49'	73'	53'			
" topgalt	37' 6"	49'	27' 6"			
" royal	26'	37' 6"	19' 6"			
" skysail	18'	26'	14'			
Mizzen tops'l	32'	43' 6"	41' 6"			
" topgalt	25'	32' 6"	16'			
" royal	16'	25' 6"	14' 6"			
Jib of jib		29' 6"	69'	65'		
Flying jib		29' 6"	73'	62'		
Main jib long		42'	73'	78'		
" " short		38'	88'	72'		
Main staysail		60'	72'	45'		
Middle "		39'	37' 6"	38' 6"	19'	
" topgalt "		34' 6"	38' 6"	38' 6"	15' 6"	
Main royal "		30'	30'	22' 6"	11'	

Item	Head	Foot	Hoist	Inner Leach	Tack	Outer Leach
Fore topmast "		26'	54'	47'		
Mizzen staysail		36'	41'	37'	18'	
Spanker	38'	54'	30'	54'		
Gaff topsail		39'	63'	53'		
Upper topgalt staysail		32' 6"	35'	28' 6"	15'	
Foretopmast stud sail	19' 6"	35' 6"	—	46'	—	54'
"topgalt"	14'	26'	—	25'		31' 6"
Main topmast stud sail	22'	26'	—	54'	—	63' 6"
" topgalt " "	15'	27' 6"	—	27' 6"	—	35'
Fore royal stud sail	8' 6"	15'	—	17'	—	21'
Main royal "	9'	17'	—	19' 6"	—	23'
Lower stud sail	43'	43'	38' 6"			
" " " No. 5	38'	38'	38' 6"			
Storm mizzen	24'	27'	30'	47'		
Mizzen skysail	12'	16' 6"	9'			
Fore storm staysail }						
Mizzen " " } dimensions not taken						

NEW YORK, Frigate, 36 guns, 1800 (Dimensions dated 1800)

	Masts			Yards	
	Length	Head		Length	Arms
Fore	80' 4"	12' 6"		70'	3' 10"
" top	50' 2"	7' 3"		50'	4' 3"
" topgalt	40'			35'	1' 8"
" pole	13' 4"			26'	1'
Main	87' 4"	13' 2"		76'	4'
" top	52' 9"	7' 6"		55'	4' 6"
" topgalt	42'			30'	1' 10"
" pole	14'			27'	1'
Mizzen	80' 4"	9' 9"		55'	3'
" top	39'	5' 8"		38'	3'
" topgalt	42'			27'	1' 6"
" pole	14'			omitted	
Bowsprit outboard	37'		spritsail yard	50'	4' 3"
Jibboom	53'		" topsail "	35'	1' 8"
Ensign staff	26' 5"		Spanker Boom	51'	
Jack "	13' 2"		" Gaff	37' 4"	

PENNSYLVANIA, Ship of the Line, 120 guns, 1837 (Dimensions dated 1837)

	whole length Masts	whole length Yards		whole length Masts	whole length Yards
Fore	121'	100'	Mizzen steps on orlop	99'	80'
" top	63'	75'	" top	55'	52'
" topgalt	37' 6"	48'	" topgalt	33'	33'
" royal	22'	23'	" royal	20'	23'
" skysail	17'	—	" skysail	10'	—
Main	132'	110'	Bowsprit outboard	54'	
" top	70'	82'	Jibboom from cap	43'	
" topgalt	41'	52'	Flying jibboom from cap	24'	
" royal	24'	36'		Spanker boom	61' 6"
" skysail	18'	—		" gaff	38' 10"

PHILADELPHIA, Frigate, 36 guns, 1799 (See dates given within)

Dr.—The Committee of Merchants for Masting Frigate *Philadelphia*, 1800. To

1 Main mast 92' 6" (Whole length, head 13)		
Cheeks and paunch	57'	each
Hounds and Bracketts	6' 6"	each
Main Tressel trees	16¾"	
Bolsters	3"	
Cross trees	54' 6"	
Main top	19' 6"	
Swivel stocks	7' 2"	
Top rail	18'	
Main cap	16¾"	
1 Fore mast	83' 3"	
Hounds and Bracketts	6' 6"	
Tressel trees	15½"	
Bolsters	3"	
Cross trees	51'	
Fore top	18'	
Swivel stocks	7'	
Top rail	17'	
Fore cap	15½"	
1 Mizen mast	82' 3"	
Hounds and Bracketts	4' 6"	each
Tressel trees	12½"	
Bolster	2"	
Cross trees	25'	
Mizen top	13' 6"	
Toprails	12'	
Mizen cap	12½"	
1 *Main topmast*	55' 6"	
Tressel trees	9"	
3 Cross trees	10'	long
Cap	9"	
1 *Fore topmast*	50'	
Tressel trees	8¼"	
3 Cross trees	9'	
Cap	8¼"	
1 *Mizen topmast*	41'	
Tressel trees	6¾"	
2 Cross trees	7'	
Cap	6¾"	
1 Main topgalltmast	44'	
Fidd	7"	
1 Fore topgalltmast	40'	
Fidd	7"	
1 Mizen topgalltmast	33'	
Fidd	5"	
1 Bow sprit	55' 6"	
2 Bees ford	7'	
Chocks under	5'	
Cap	12½"	
Saddle and 6 cleats		
1 Jib boom	55' 6"	
Martingale	14'	

1 Fore Yard		72' 6"
Battens		36' 3"
2 Cleats		
Cross jack yard		58'
Battens		29'
2 Cleats		
1 Sprit sail yard		52'
Battens		13'
2 Cleats		
1 Main topsail yard		58'
Battens		29'
2 Cleats		
1 Fore topsail yard		52'
Battens		26'
2 Cleats		
1 Mizen topsail yard		41' 6"
Battens		20' 9"
2 Cleats		
1 Spritsail topsail yard		34' 9"
Battens		
2 Cleats		
1 Main topgalt yard		38' 8"
Battens		
2 Cleats		
1 Fore topgalt yard		34' 9"
Battens		8' 6"
2 Cleats		
1 Mizen topgalt yard		27' 8"
Batten		7' 6"
2 Cleats		
1 Main royal yard		29'
2 Cleats		
1 Fore royal yard		26'
2 Cleats		
1 Mizen royal yard		20' 9"
2 Cleats		
1 Spanker boom		58'
Jaws		18"
1 Hollow cleat		
1 Saddle		
1 Mizen boom		36'
1 Hollow cleat		
1 Mizen gaft		36'
1 ditto		41'
Jaws for ditto		18"
1 driver yard		34' 9"
2 Lower Sterring sail booms		45'
2 do yards		26'
2 Main top mast do booms		43'
2 Yards		24'
2 Fore do do booms		38'
2 do do do yards		21' 6"
2 Main topgalt do booms		29'
2 do do yards		16' 6"

2 Fore topgalt steering sail booms	26'	
2 do	16'	
1 Ensign staff	28'	
2 Jack staffs	14'	
2 Fire booms	30'	
1 David	39'	
	Cost	$1993.39

Philadelphia, April 26th, 1800

Dr The Committee of Merchants for Spare Spars, &c.

1 Main topmast		55' 6"
1 Mizen topmast		41'
1 Main topgalt mast		44'
1 Fore topgalt mast		40'
1 Main topsail yard		58'
1 Fore topsail yard		52'
1 Main topgalt yard		38' 8"
1 Fore topgalt yard		34' 9"
2 Lower steering sail booms		45'
2 ditto	yards	26'
2 Main topmast ditto	booms	43'
2 ditto	yards	24'
2 Fore top mast do	booms	38'
2 ditto	yards	21' 6"
2 Main topgalt ditto	booms	29'
2 ditto	yards	16' 6"
2 Fore topgalt ditto	booms	26'
2 ditto	yards	16'
1 Fore topmast		50'
18 Rough spars		
2 Buoys 10" each		
39' 6 x 8 scantling		
6 spars		

April 26, 1800			Cost of spare spars		$ 551.96
For Launch					
1 Main mast	32'		1 Main boom	19'	
1 Main topmast	6'		1 Foremast	30'	
1 Main gaft	5'		1 Fore gaft	6'	
Jaws		6"	Jaws		6"
For barge					
1 Main mast	29' 6"		1 Fore mast	28' 6"	
Pinnace					
1 Fore mast	19'		1 jigger mast	12'	
1 Fore yard	12'		1 Sprit	12'	
Jolly boat					
1 Main mast	12' 6"		2 Sprits	12' 6"	
1 Fore mast	11' 6"		8 Boat hook staffs		
			Coast of spars		$ 41.67

May 8th cash	$1000.00	
June 7th cash	1632.60	
	$2632.60	$2587.02

A Bill of Top Stuff for Frigate *City of Philadelphia*

4 Pieces Main trussle trees	14 feet	18 in. by	9 in.	
4 pieces Fore trussle trees	13½ "	17	8½	
4 pieces Mizen trussle trees	10	16	6½	

	Whole Length	Diameter	Head, or Arm
3 pieces Cross trees	20	5	9
3 pieces Cross trees	19	5	9
3 pieces Cross trees	15	4	7
4 pieces Caps	6½	14	14
4 pieces Caps	6	13	13
4 pieces Caps	5	11	11
2 pieces Caps	6½	13	13

Three planks 10 feet long 4 inches thick to be cut through and through and to have 9 inch spring from end to end one way. 20 white oak 1½ plank 20 feet long and not less than 12 in. wide.

Bill to Jacob Lamb. June 20, 1799.
Dimensions of Masts and Yards for Frigate *City of Philadelphia*
(From Humphreys' Letter Book, Pennsylvania Historical Society)

Spar	Whole Length	Diameter	Head, or Arm
Main mast	92.6	28	13.
Foremast	83.3	25	12.
Mizen mast	82.3	19¼	9.
Main topmast	55.6	16⅜	7.
Fore topmast	50.	15½	6.3
Mizen topmast	41.	12½	5.
Main topgalt mast	44.	9	17.6
Fore topgalt mast	40.	8¼	16.
Mizen topgalt mast	33.	6¾	13.
Bowsprit. Outboard 39'.	55.6	28	
Jibboom	55.6	12½	15.
Main yard	81.6	19	4.
Fore yard	72.6	16¾	3.9
Cross jack yard	58.	12½	3.
Main topsail yard	58.	13½	4.9
Fore topsail yard	52.	12½	4.4
Mizen topsail yard	41.6	9¼	3.
Main topgalt yard	38.8	8¾	2.
Fore topgalt yard	34.9	8	2.
Mizen topgalt yard	27.8	6¼	1.6
Main royal yard	29.	6¾	1.6
Fore royal yard	26.	6¼	1.6
Mizen royal yard	20.9	5	1.
Spanker boom	58.	13	
Driver yard	34.9	8	
Lower stunsail booms	45.	9	
ditto yard	26.	5¼	
Main topmast stun sail boom	43.	8½	
ditto yard	24.	5	
Fore topmast stun sail boom	38.	8	
ditto yard	21.6	4¾	
Main topgalt ditto boom	29.	6	
ditto yard	16.6	3½	
Fore topgalt ditto boom	26.	5¼	
Mizen gaff	36.	10	
Ensign staff	28.	6	
Jack staff	14.	3	
Dolphin striker	9.6		
Fire booms	30.	9	

Main top 19.6 feet wide; Fore top 18. feet; Mizen top 13.6 feet.
Received above dimensions from Captn William Jones, one of the Committee of Merchants.

GERMANTOWN, Corvette, 1844 (Approved establishment)

	Masts & Booms			Yards		
	Length	Dia.	Head	Length	Dia.	Arms
Fore	76' 3"	26"	13' 6"	73' 2"	17¼"	3' 1"
" top	45' 9"	16"	8'	56' 4"	14¼"	5' 2"
" topgalt	22' 10"	9"	—	34' 8"	7¼"	2'
" royal	15' 6"	—	—	22' 10"	4⅝"	1'
" pole	5' 6"	—	—	—	—	—
Main	83'	28"	14' 6"	79' 6"	18¾"	3' 4"
" top	49' 9"	15¼"	8'	61'	15¼"	5' 6"
" topgalt	24' 10"	9"	—	37' 8"	7⅞"	2' 1"
" royal	16' 10"	—	—	24' 10"	5"	1' 2"
" pole	6'	—	—	—	—	—
Mizzen	72' 4"	20½"	10' 10"	56' 4"	11⅞"	4' 6"
" top	37' 4"	11"	6'	39' 9"	10"	3' 8"
" topgalt	18' 8"	6¾"	—	24' 6"	5⅛"	1' 4"
" royal	12' 8"	—	—	16' 2"	3¼"	9"
" pole	4' 6"	—	—	—	—	—
Bowsprit outboard	32'	28"				
Jibboom from cap	26'	14⅛"	9"			
Flying Jibboom whole length	46' 9"	8½"	4'			
Spanker Gaff	33'	7"	5' 0"			
" Boom	44'	10⅛"	2'			
Fore Gaff	none	—	—			
Main "	none	—	—			

JAMESTOWN, Corvette, 1844 (Approved establishment)

	Length	Dia.	Head	Length	Dia.	Arms
Fore	77'	26"	14' 5"	75'	18½"	3' 6"
" top	46'	15¼"	8'	56'	15"	4' 6"
" topgalt	25'	9¼"	—	35'	8½"	2'
" royal	17'	—	—	26'	5½"	1' 6"
" pole	7' 9"	—	—	—	—	—
Main	84'	28"	14' 5"	80'	18½"	3' 6"
" top	50'	15¼"	8'	60'	15¾"	5'
" topgalt	25'	9¼"	—	38'	8¾"	1' 6"
" royal	17'	—	—	28'	5¾"	1' 6"
" pole	7' 9"	—	—	—	—	—
Mizzen	73'	21"	10' 9"	55'	11½"	3' 1"
" top	37' 4"	11¼"	6'	38'	10"	3'
" topgalt	18' 9"	7"	—	23'	5½"	1' 6"
" royal	18' 8"	—	—	13'	3½"	9"
" pole	5' 9"	—	—	—	—	—
Bowsprit outboard	32' 5"	26"	—			
Jibboom from cap	39'	14¾"	2' 4"			
Flying jibboom whole length	46' 8"	8¾"	5'			
Spanker gaff	36'	8"	5'			
" boom	48'	10"	1'			
Fore gaff	36'	8"	5'			
Main gaff	23'	6½"	1'			

PLYMOUTH, Corvette, 1844 (Approved establishment)

	Length	Dia.	Head	Length	Dia.	Arms
Fore	77' 3"	25½"	14' 3"	76' 3"	18"	3' 3"
" top	47' 6"	15¼"	7' 6"	59' 6"	14"	6'
" topgalt	23' 4"	9"	—	36' 2"	7½"	2'
" royal	16' 3"	—	—	25' 3"	5"	1' 2"

Fore pole	8'	—	—	—	—	—
Main	82' 10"	27½"	14' 3"	76' 3"	18"	3' 3"
" top	47' 6"	15¼"	7' 6"	59' 6"	14"	6'
" topgalt	23' 9"	9"	—	36' 2"	7½"	2' 0"
" royal	16' 3"	—	—	25' 3"	5"	1' 2"
" pole	8'	—	—	—	—	—
Mizzen	66'	19"	10' 10"	51' 9"	10¾"	2' 10"
" top	37' 3"	10¾"	5' 11"	41'	10¼"	4' 9"
" topgalt	18' 6"	6½"	—	24' 1"	5¼"	1' 3"
" royal	12' 9"	—	—	17'	4"	9"
" pole	6'	—	—	—	—	—
Bowsprit outboard	32'	27"	—			
Jibboom from cap	25' 11"	13¾"	1' 6"			
Flying Jibboom whole length	46' 8"	8"	3' 11"			
Spanker Gaff	33'	7"	4' 3"			
" Boom	44'	10"	1'			
Fore Gaff	26'	6"	3'			
Main "	23'	6½"	1'			

PORTSMOUTH, Corvette, 1844 (Approved establishment)

Fore	76'	26"	15'	74'	18½"	3' 6"
" top	48' 6"	16"	8'	55'	13¾"	—
" topgalt	25'	9"	—	36' 2"	8½"	2' 1"
" royal	17'	—	—	26'	6"	1'
" pole	6'	—	—	—	—	—
Main	84'	27"	15'	74'	18½"	3' 6"
" top	48' 6"	16"	8'	55'	13¾"	—
" topgalt	25'	9"	—	36' 2"	8½"	2' 1"
" royal	17'	—	—	26'	6"	1'
" pole	7'	—	—	—	—	—
Mizzen	*	19"	11'	55'	13¾"	—
" top	37' 6"	13"	6'	39'	9"	3' 6"
" topgalt	18'	6½"	—	26'	6¼"	1' 4"
" royal	12' 6"	—	pole 5'	18'	4¼"	—
Bowsprit outboard	31'	27"	—			
Jibboom from cap	25'	14"	—			
Flying jibboom whole length	40'	8¼"	—			
Spanker Boom	44'	10¼"	—			
" Gaff	33'	7½"	—			
Fore Gaff	— none	—	—			
Main Gaff	— none	—	—			

* head of mizzen mast is 2' above main top

ST. MARYS, Corvette, 1844 (Approved establishment)

Fore	77' 3"	25⅜"	12' 10½"	74'	18"	3' 6"
" top	47' 7"	15"	7' 7"	56' 3"	14½"	5'
" topgalt	25' 4"	9½"	—	36' 7"	7"	2'
" royal	16' 10"	7½"	8' 6"	24' 7"	5"	1'
" pole	5'	3¼"	—	—	—	—
Main	85'	27¾"	14' 2"	77' 6"	18⅝"	3' 6"
" top	52' 4"	15"	8' 1"	58' 4"	14½"	5' 0"
" topgalt	25' 4"	9½"	—	37' 1"	8¼"	2'
" royal	16' 10"	7½"	8' 6"	24' 3"	5"	1'
" pole	6'	4"	—	—	—	—

	Masts & Booms			Yards		
	Length	Dia.	Head	Length	Dia.	Arms
Mizzen	65' 5"	19"	11' 10"	57'	12¼"	4'
" top	40' 1"	13⅛"	6' 1"	40' 3"	9½"	3' 3"
" topgalt	20'	7½"	—	26' 2"	5½"	1'
" royal	15' 3"	5' 6"	7'	19' 2"	4"	9'
" pole	4'	2¾"	—	—	—	—
Bowsprit outboard	42' 9"	27¾"	—			
Jibboom from cap	26'	—	—			
Flying Jibboom whole length	44'	—	—			
Spanker Boom	48' 2"	9½"	3'			
" Gaff	37' 6"	8"	4' 5"			
Fore Gaff	25'	7½"	1' 5"			
Main Gaff	22' 3"	7¼"	1'			

SARATOGA, Corvette, 1844 (Approved establishment)

	Length	Dia.	Head	Length	Dia.	Arms
Fore	76'	24"	13' 2"	68'	16¼"	3' 6"
" top	45'	16"	7' 9"	52'	11½"	4' 9"
" topgalt	23'	9¼"	—	34'	7½"	1' 9"
" royal	15' 9"	5⅞"	—	25'	4¾"	10"
" pole	6'	5"	—	—	—	—
Main	83'	27"	14' 2"	76'	17¼"	3' 6"
" top	49'	16"	8'	57'	12½"	5'
" topgalt	25'	9½"	—	38'	8"	2'
" royal	17'	6"	—	28'	5¼"	1'
" pole	6'	5½"	—	—	—	—
Mizzen	66' 6"	19¼"	11'	49' 6"	11½"	2' 9"
" top	39'	12¾"	6' 4"	36' 6"	8½"	3' 6"
" topgalt	20'	7¼"	—	23' 6"	5¼"	1' 4"
" royal	13' 8"	4½"	—	16'	3½"	6"
" pole	6'	5½"	—	—	—	—
Bowsprit outboard	32'	27"	—			
Jibboom from cap	23'	12"	—			
Flying Jibboom whole length	44'	8"	8'			
Spanker Boom	39'	9"	—			
" Gaff	30'	7"	9'			
Fore Gaff	26' 6"	6¼"	—			
Main Gaff	19' 6"	5¾"	—			

POTOMAC, Frigate, 44 guns, 1822 (Dimensions dated 1839)

	Masts			Yards		
	Length	Dia.	Head	Length	Dia.	Arms
Main	105'	34.6"	18'	95'	20"	4' 9"
" top	63'	19.3"	9' 7"	71' 6"	16"	6'
" topgalt	32'	11"	—	45'	9.5"	2' 6"
" royal	22'	8.8"	—	30'	6.5"	1' 6"
" pole	10'	—	—	—	—	—
" skysail gunter mast	37'	6.3"	—	20'	4.5"	1'
Fore	95'	31.5"	16'	84'	18.5"	4' 6"
" top	56'	19.3"	9' 6"	62'	14.7"	5' 3"
" topgalt	29'	11"	—	41'	9"	2' 3"
" royal	20'	7.5"	—	27'	6"	1' 4"
" pole	9'	—	—	—	—	—
" skysail gunter mast	34'	5.5"	—	18'	4"	9"
Mizzen	84'	24"	12' 4"	66'	14"	7'
" top	46' 4"	13.5"	6' 8"	45'	10"	3' 6"

	Masts Length	Dia.	Head	Yards Length	Dia.	Arms
Mizzen topgalt	24'	8.5"	—	30'	6"	1' 6"
" royal	17'	6"	—	19'	4"	9"
" pole	7' 6"	—	—	—	—	—
" skysail gunter mast	28'	4.6"	—	13'	3"	6"
Bowsprit	66'	—	—	Spritsail 62'	14.7"	5' 3"
Jibboom	50'	14.3" at cap	—			
Flying Jibboom	54'	9.5"	4'			
Jib of Jibboom	40'	—	—			
Spanker Boom	50'	11"	—			
" Gaff	35' 8"	8.5"	4'			
Main "	30'	8"	—			
Fore "	30'	8"	—			
Dolphin Striker	17'	7½"	2' pole			

Fore topmast stunsail	boom		49'	10"
do.	yard		28'	5.5"
" topgalt "	boom		36' 6"	7"
do.	yard		21'	4"
" royal "	boom		24' 6"	4.5"
do.	yard		14'	3"
Main swing boom			51' 3"	10.5"
do. yard			31'	5.5"
" topmast stunsail	boom		42' 6"	9"
do.	yard		24'	5"
" topgalt "	boom		32'	6.5"
do.	yard		18'	4"
" royal "	boom		21'	4"
do.	yard		12'	3"
Mizzen topgalt "	boom		22' 5"	4"
do.	yard		12'	2.8"
" royal "	boom		15'	3"
do.	yard		8'	2.3"
Forecastle awning yard			20'	
Smoke sail yard			16'	
jack staff above cap			16'	
Main trysail mast		11" dia.		
" " "		11" "		
Mizzen " "		9" "		

PRESIDENT, Frigate, 44 guns, 1800 (Dimensions dated 1801)

	Masts Length	Head	Yards Length	Arms
Fore	90'	14' 8"	81'	4' 3"
" top	58'	7' 9"	60'	5'
" topgalt	47'	—	41'	2'
" royal pole	17'	—	30'	1'
Main	100'	15' 5"	90' 6"	4' 6"
" top	61' 7"	7' 9"	66'	5'
" topgalt	50'	—	44'	2'
" royal pole	18'	—	32'	1'
Mizzen	87'	11' 3"	66'	3' 6"
" top	45'	5' 8"	45'	3' 6"
" topgalt	37'	—	32'	1' 6"
" royal pole	13' 3"	—	24'	1'

| | Masts | | | | Yards | |
	Length	Head			Length	Arms
Bowsprit	67'	outboard 42'	Spritsail		60'	3' 6"
Jibboom	64'		" topsail		41'	
Flying jibboom	29'		Spanker Boom		67'	
Ensign staff	30'		" gaff		46'	
Jack staff	16'					

Dimensions of Spars of U.S. Frigate PRESIDENT (From Humphreys' Notebook)

Spar	Whole Length	Size	Heads Arms
Main mast	100.	2.7¾	16.11
Fore mast	91.4	2.4½	15.3
Mizen mast (this must have stepped on orlop)	86.	1.10	13.6
Main topmast (exclusive of heel block)	62.	1.7	9.6
Fore topmast ditto	58.	1.7	8.6
Mizen topmast ditto	50.	1.3	7.7½
Main topgaltmast (exclusive of pole)	33.	.11	
Fore topgaltmast ditto	30.6	.11	
Mizen topgaltmast ditto	26.	.8½	
Main royal mast	22.	.7¼	
Fore royal mast	20.4	.7¼	
Mizen royal mast	17.4	.6	
Main sky scraper mast	16.6	.5¾	
Fore sky scraper mast	15.3	.5¾	
Mizen sky scraper mast	13.	.4¾	
Main yard	92.	1.9	3.10
Fore yard	80.	1.6¾	3.4
Cross jack	72.	1.1¼	6.
Main topsail yard	69.	1.3	5.9
Fore topsail yard	60.	1.1¼	5.
Mizen topsail yard	45.	.10	3.9
Main topgalt yard	44.6	.9½	2.7
Fore topgalt yard	40.	.8½	2.4
Mizen topgalt yard	30.	.6¼	1.3
Main royal yard	30.	.6¼	1.3
Fore royal yard	26.6	.5⅛	1.1
Mizen royal yard	20.	.4¼	.10½
Main skysail yard	20.	.4¼	.9
Fore skysail yard	18.	.4	.8
Mizen skysail yard	13.4	.3½	.7
Spritsail yard	60.	1.1¼	.5
Bowsprit	65.3	2.7¾	
Jibboom	48.	1.2	
Flying jibboom	53.	.9½	
Spanker boom	69.	.13¼	
Gaff	45.	.10	
Ringtail boom	30.	.6¾	
Ring tail yard	15.	.4	
Lower steering sail swinging boom	50.2	.10	
ditto yard	26.3	.5¼	
Maintop mast steeringsail boom	47.6	.9¾	
ditto yard	26.3	.5¼	
Fore ditto boom	41.6	.8¼	
Fore ditto yard	22.10	.7	

Spar	Whole Length	Size	Heads Arms
Main topgalt steering sail booms	35.6	.7	
Ditto yards	19.8	.4	
Fore ditto booms	31.	.6¼	
Ditto yards	17.1	.3¾	
Mizen topgalt ss boom	23.	.4¾	
Ditto yards	13.	.2¾	
Main royal ss booms	23.	.4¾	
Ditto yards	13.	.2¾	
Fore royal ss booms	20.9	.4	
Ditto yards	12.	.2	
Mizen royal ss booms	15.6	.2	
Ditto yards	8.10	.2	

Dimensions of hermaphrodite schooner built by Wm. Sequin 1814, bought by Savage and Dryan and sold to the U.S. called the PROMETHEUS

Spar	Length	Head (Pole, or Arm)	Spar	Length	Head (Pole, or Arm)
Fore mast	62.	9.	Fore topgallant yard	26.	1. arms
Fore topmast	34.	5.	Fore royal	18.	.9 inchs
Topgallantmast	28.	12. pole	Main yard	48.	2.
Main mast	83.	8.	Main topsail yard	36.	.18 inchs
Main topmast	36.	12. pole	Main topgallant yard	22.	.12 inchs
			Main boom	58.	
Fore yard	50.	2. arms	Jibboom	38.	10. pole
Fore topsail yard	38.	2. "	Fore and main gaff	30.	

82 feet straight rabbet. 27 foot beam. 11′ 4″ hold.

Dimensions of schooner REVENGE spars, 1807

Spar	Length		Spar	Length	
Main mast	79.	8.	Fore topmast	40.	14. pole
Fore mast	77.	8.	Gunter mast	37.	
Fore yard	61.	2.	Main topmast	36.	14. pole
Topsail yard (fore)	36.	2.	Jibboom	49. outboard 24 feet	
Topgallant yard "	26.	1.	Flying jibboom	38. " 14	
Royal yard "	18.	.9 inchs	Fore gaft	28.	
Main yard	56.	2.	Main gaft	26.	
Topsail yard	32.	2.	Ringtail boom	26.	
Topgallant yard	24.	1.	Ringtail gaft	14.	
Royal yard	16.	.9 inchs			

RALEIGH, Frigate, 32 guns, 1776.

	Dia.	Length	Dia. Head
Mainmast	3′ 3″	86′	1′
Topmast	1′ 4″	50′	6″
Topgallant mast	8″	28′	2″
Foremast	2′ 1″	79′	11″
Foretopmast	1′ 3″	46′	5½″
Fore-topgallant mast	7″	26′	2″
Mizzen mast	1′ 6″	74′	8″
Mizzen topmast	11″	37′	4½″
Mizzen top-gallant mast	5″	18′	2″
Bowsprit	2′ 2″	51′	
Jib boom	1′	36′	
Main yard	1′ 6″	70′	
Main topsail yard	1′ 1″	54′	
Main topgallant yard	7″	36′	
Fore yard	1′ 4″	64′	

	Dia.	Length	Dia. Head
Fore topsail yard	1' 1"	50'	
Fore topgallant yard	6"	30'	
Spritsail yard	9"	45'	
Spritsail topsail yard	7"	35'	
Mizzen yard	10"	66'	
Crossjack yard	10"	50'	
Mizzen topsail yard	8"	36'	
Mizzen topgallant yard	4½"	22'	
Main studdingsail booms	9"	38'	
Fore studdingsail booms	9"	38'	
Topgallant studdingsail booms	5"	25'	
Ensign staff	6"	30'	
Jack staff	3"	15'	
Lower studdingsail booms	8"	40'	
Driver yard	5"	22'	
Driver boom	—	35'	

(Signed)—Thomas Thompson

SYREN, Brig, 16 guns, 1803 (1807)

	Masts		Yards	
	Length	Head	Length	Arms
Fore	59' 4"	10' 5"	53' 8"	2' 6"
" top	37'	6'	38' 8"	2' 9"
" topgalt	31' 6"	—	26' 10"	1' 5"
" pole	16'	—	20'	8"
Main	64'	10' 5"	53' 8"	2' 6"
" top	37'	6'	38' 8"	2' 9"
" topgalt	31' 6"	—	26' 10"	1' 5"
" pole	16'	—	20'	8"
Bowsprit	39'	Spritsail Yard	38' 8"	
Jibboom	32' 10"	Main Boom	57'	
Flying jibboom	31'	" gaff	31'	
Martingale double	9' 2"			

UNITED STATES, Frigate, 44 guns, 1797 (Dimensions by Fox, 1807)

	Masts		Yards	
	Length	Head	Length	Arms
Fore	90'	14' 7"	81' 2"	3' 5"
" topmast	54' 10"	8'	58'	4' 10"
" topgalt	27' 5"	4'	41'	2' 1"
" royal	19' 5"	—	29'	1'
Main	100'	16' 3"	91' 4"	3' 10"
" top	60' 11"	8' 11"	65' 3"	5' 5"
" topgalt	30' 6"	4' 6"	43' 6"	2' 4"
" royal	21' 7"	—	32' 7"	1' 2"
Mizzen	86'	12' 8"	65' 3"	2' 9"
" top	45' 8"	6' 8"	43' 6"	2' 9"
" topgalt	22' 10"	3' 4"	29'	1' 8"
" royal	16' 2"	—	21' 9"	9"
Bowsprit	64'	outboard 43' 6"	58'	2' 5" spritsail
Jibboom	46' 7"	" 30' 8"		
Flying jibboom	51' 8"	" 20' 6"		
Martingale	15' 6"			
Jack staff	17'			
Ensign staff	33' 10"		Spanker Boom 65' 3"	
			" Gaff 45' 8"	

Later set (Dimensions as of 1815)

	Masts Whole Length	Masts Dia.	Head	Yards Whole Length	Yards Dia.	Arms
Fore	89' 9½"	2' 6½"	11' 6"	81' 6"	1' 4"	4'
" top	59'	1' 6¾"	8' 9"	65' 6"	1' 2"	5' 6"
" topgalt	32' 11"	10½"	5' 1½"	41' 6"	8¾"	2'
" royal	19' 11"	7½"	—	29' 2"	6¼"	1'
" pole	17' 1"	6"	—	24'	4"	—
Main	101' 6½"	3'	17'	92' 2"	1' 11¾"	4'
" top	63' 2"	1' 6¾"	9'	69' 9"	1' 2½"	5' 6"
" topgalt	35' 10"	11"	5'	48' 6"	9"	2'
" royal	22'	7½"	—	33'	6¾"	1' 2"
" pole	18'	6"	—	24'	4¼"	—
Mizzen	78'	1' 10"	12' 10"	69' 6"	1' ¾"	4' 6"
" top	45' 9"	1' 2¼"	6' 7"	52'	9"	3'
" topgalt	26' 8½"	7¼"	3' 5"	30' 6"	8"	1' 6"
" royal	16' 2"	4½"	—	22'	5"	9½"
" pole	13'	4"	—	16' 4"	3"	—
Bowsprit	65' out 43' 6"	2' 8"	—	60'		4' 6" sprit
Jibboom	48' 6"	1' 1½"				
Flying jibboom	58'	9"				
Jib o' jibboom	42' 8½"	8¼" to 4"				
Martingale	15'					

Spanker Boom 66' x 1'
" Gaff 46' 9" x 10"

VINCENNES, Ship Sloop 2nd Class, 18 guns, 1826 (Dimensions dated 1826)

	Masts Whole Length	Head	Yards Whole Length	Arms
Fore deck to cap	57' 6"	12' 6"	64'	3'
Main " " "	64' 6"	13' 6"	70'	3' 3"
Mizzen " " "	56'	10' 3"	49'	2' 9"
Fore top	43' 6"	6' 10"	50' 6"	4' 9"
Main "	47' 3"	7' 6"	53' 6"	5'
Mizzen "	35' 3"	6'	39'	3'
Fore topgalt	22' 3"	—	31'	2'
Main "	24'	—	32'	2'
Mizzen "	19'	—	23'	1'
Fore royal pole	15'	—	21'	1'
Main " "	16'	—	23' 6"	1'
Mizzen " "	12'	—	15'	9"
Fore skysail pole	7'	—	—	—
Main " "	7' 3"	—	—	—
Mizzen " "	6'	—	—	—
Bowsprit out, from rabbet to cap	31'			
Jibboom from cap	23' 6"			
Flying jibboom from cap	17' 6"	5'		
Dolphin striker	12' 6"	1' 9"		

Spanker Boom 37' 6" | 2' 3"
" Gaff 30' | 5'
Main Gaff 20' | 1'

VIXEN, Brig, 12 guns, 1804 (Dimensions dated 1806)

| | Masts | | Yards | |
	Length	Head	Length	Arms
Fore	49' 7"	8' 5"	46'	2' 2"
" top	30' 9"	4' 11"	32'	3' 4"
" topgalt	26' 4"	—	21'	1' 4"
" pole	12' 5"	—	15'	5"
Main	55' 7"	9'	46'	2' 2"
" top	30' 9"	4' 11"	32'	3' 4"
" topgalt	26' 4"	—	21'	1' 4"
" pole	12' 5"	—	15'	5"
Bowsprit	29' 4"	Spritsail	32'	3' 4"
Jibboom	28'	Spanker Boom	47'	
Flying jibboom	29' 3"	" Gaff	30'	

WASP, Ship Sloop, 16 guns, 1806 (Dimensions dated 1807)

| | Masts | | Yards | |
	Length	Head	Length	Arms
Fore	63'	9' 10"	56'	2' 4"
" top	37' 9"	5' 6"	41'	3' 5"
" topgalt	18'	—	27'	2' 3"
" pole	15'	—	20'	9"
Main	70'	11'	62'	2' 7"
" top	42'	6' 1"	45'	3' 9"
" topgalt	20'	—	30'	2' 6"
" pole	16'	—	22'	10"
Mizzen	60'	8' 6"	41'	1' 8"
" top	31' 6"	4' 7"	30'	1' 10"
" topgalt	15'	—	20' 8"	1' 8"
" pole	12'	—	15' 6"	7"
Bowsprit	43' 6" outboard 29' 6"	Spritsail	41'	1' 8"
Jibboom	34'	Main Boom	41'	
Flying jibboom	38' 4"	" Gaff	27'	
Martingale	11' 6"			

YORKTOWN, Ship Sloop 3rd Class, 16 guns, 1838 (Dimensions dated 1838)

	Masts Whole Length	Yards Whole Length		Masts Whole Length	Yards Whole Length
Fore	65' 6"	60' 9"	Mizzen	54' 6"	52'
" top	42'	45'	" top	32'	34'
" topgalt	21'	30' 6"	" topgalt	16'	21'
" royal	13'	20' 6"	" pole	5'	—
" pole	6'	—	Bowsprit outboard 30'		
Main	72'	67' 6"	Jibboom from cap 22' 9"		
" top	45'	50' 6"	Flying Jibboom from cap 13' 3"		
" topgalt	22'	34'	Spanker Boom 34'		
" royal	14'	22' 9"	Spanker Gaff 28'		
" pole	7'	—			

HASSAN BASHAW, Brig, 1798

| | Masts | | | Yards |
	Length	Head	Dia.	Length
Fore	56' 8"	8' 3"	23"	48'
" top	36'	5'	20"	36'
" topgalt	29'	—	12"	25'

	Length	Masts Head	Dia.	Yards Length
Fore pole	10'	—	—	20'
Main	73'	8'	28"	42'
" top	33'	4' 9"	20"	33'
" topgalt	27'	—	12"	22'
" pole	9'	—	—	17'

Boom	52' 6"
Gaff	30'

Bowsprit 40' outboard 27'
Jibboom 29' outboard from cap
Fore top 13' 6" width
Main top 12' "
Martingale not given

Spritsail yard 32'
Jibboom and flying jibboom in one
Mainsail to peak well
6 shrouds aside lower
4 topmast shrouds aside
1 standing backstay and 1 breast stay

1 long boat with well & windlass
1 yawl to nest
1 yawl on stern

PEACOCK, Ship Sloop, 18 guns, 1828 (Dimensions dated 1828)

	Length	Masts Dia.	Head		Length	Masts Dia.	Head
Main	70'	1' 11"	12' 2"	Fore pole	9' 9"	—	—
" top	42'	13.2"	7'	Mizzen	52' 7"	1' 3.3"	9' 9"
" topgalt	21'	7.9"	—	" top	33' 7"	9.2"	5' 7"
" royal	16' 2"	5.1"	—	" topgalt	16' 10"	5.1"	—
" pole	10' 10"	—	—	" royal	12' 11"	4.1"	—
Fore	63'	1' 8.7"	10' 10"	" pole	8' 8"	—	—
" top	37' 9"	11.9"	6' 3"	Rake of masts 3/8" 4/8" 7/8" Bowsprit 3/4			
" topgalt	18' 10"	7.1"	—				
" royal	14' 5"	5.3"		Yards not given			

WASHINGTON, Revenue Brig, 1846 (Dimensions dated 1846)

	Length	Masts Head	Dia.	Length	Yards Arms	Dia.
Main cap to deck	43' 6"	8'	19"	48' 10"	2' 10"	10½"
" whole	52' 10"					
Fore cap to deck	41' 9"	8'	19"	48' 10"	2' 10"	10½"
" whole	50' 9"					
Fore & main top	29'	4' 10"	9½"	37' 6"	3' 2"	8½"
Fore & Main topgalt	16'	—	6½"	24' 2"	1' 6"	5"
Fore & Main Royal	10' 8"	3'	—	17' 3"	10"	3¾"
Bowsprit outboard	16' 4"	—	19"			
Jibbom "	16'	—	9½"			
Flying "	12' 6"	—	5½"			
Main boom	42' 10"	—	9"			
" gaff	27' 9"	4'	7"			
Fore "	21'	2' 4"	6"			
Martingale	8'	1' 4"	4½"			
1 stern boat 20'						
2 quarter boats 20'						

SHIPS' BOATS

BARGE: This class of boat in the American Navy, 1830–1860, was a sharp-ended whaleboat sometimes used in lieu of a gig in rough water. Some vessels also carried a surfboat in addition to their allowance. The surfboat, or lifeboat, was invariably carried in quarter davits.

SURVEY SHIPS were fitted with special boats; these were a launch 32' x 10' x 4' 4", carvel-planked and square-sterned. Two cutters were also fitted: these were clench-built with full, sharp sterns; the first cutter was 29' 6" x 7' 8" x 2' 10"; the second cutter was 26' 10" x 6' 10" x 2' 8". The cutters were fitted with bilge keels. Survey boats were first built for the *Peacock* in 1828, and their designs were used thereafter.

BEACH BOATS: Many ships on the Mexican coast during the war with Mexico were fitted with a special class of boat—square-sterned surfboats about 40' x 11' x 5'. Beach boats were employed in landing troops on shore and were fitted with a bow gun (a boat howitzer).

NAVAL BOATS: The American Navy gave a great deal of attention to the design of ships' boats in the years between 1820 and 1840. As a result, naval boats used aboard sailing men-of-war in this period were on excellent models and far superior to craft of the same type built since the Civil War.

William Easby at the Washington Navy Yard, John Wade at Boston, and Peter Herbert at the Norfolk Yard were noted for their boats. It was rare for a design of a boat to be prepared by a constructor; such plans were usually the work of the master, or acting master, boatbuilder in the navy yards. Easby usually acted for the Board in standard boat designs 1820–30.

PRESIDENT in 1806 had

1 launch, sloop rigged
1st cutter, lug rigged, 2 masts
2nd cutter, settee rigged, 2 masts
3rd cutter, sliding gunter rigged, 2 masts
4th cutter, sprit sails, 2 masts

Jolly boat, lateen rig
1st gig, lateen rig, one mast
2nd gig,　do.

Ship sloops in War of 1812 usually carried 4 to 6 boats, Brigs, 3 to 4 boats

1821 schooners carried launch 23' x 7' x 2' 10".

1st cutter 20' 4" x 5' 3" x 2' 3"　　　　　　　stern boat 18' x 4' 7" x 2' 0½"

Boats for a 44-gun ship in 1820

Launch	34' x 9' 7" x 3' 9"		
1st cutter	32' x 8' x 3' 7"	3rd cutter	26' x 6' 6" x 2' 11" (stern boat)
2nd cutter	28' x 7' x 3' 2"	Two quarterboats	25' x 6' 3" 2' 9"
		Gig	28' x 5' x 2'

Boats of a 74 in 1820

Launch	38' x 10' 6" x 4'	5th cutter	25'
1st cutter	36' x 8' 8" x 3' 8"	1st gig	30'
2nd cutter	27' x 6' 8" x 2' 10" quarter	2nd gig	28'
3rd cutter	25' 6" x 6' 8" x 2' 7"	Life boat	27' x 7' x 3' quarter
4th cutter	27'	Jolly boat	20'

JOHN ADAMS, 1832, boats

Launch	29' 6"	16 oars 16'	
1st cutter	27' x 6' 9" x 2' 7"	12 oars 14'	
Quarterboat	25' x 5' 6" x 2' 3"	12 oars 14'	
Quarterboat	24' x 5' 10" x 2' 3"	10 oars 14'	

Quarterboat	24' x 5' 10" x 2' 3"	10 oars 14'
Jolly boat	20' x 5' 2" x 2' 1½"	8 oars 17'
Gig	26' x 4' 6" x 2' 1½"	5 oars 17'

GRAMPUS, Schooner, 1830, boats

1 Cutter	9 oars 13'	1 Launch	12 oars 15'
1 Quarterboat	5 oars 15'	2 Quarterboats	4 oars 14'

Figure 145. First cutter and launch for POTOMAC.

Figure 146. Gig and second cutter for POTOMAC.

Figure 147. Quarter boat and third cutter for POTOMAC.

Figure 148. Stern boat for schooner GRAMPUS.

Figure 149. First cutter and launch for GRAMPUS.

BAINBRIDGE, Brig, 1843, boats

Launch	24' x 7' x 2' 10"	14 oars 15'
Cutter	21' 6" x 5' 10½" x 2' 4"	10 oars 13'
Two quarterboats	22' x 5' 2" x 23"	5 oars 15'
Sternboat	17' x 4' 8" x 20"	4 oars 14'

CUMBERLAND, class 1847, boats

Launch	34' x 9' 6"	Two quarterboats	28' x 7' x 2' 6"
Three cutters	32' x 9'	Stern boat	28'
	30'	Gig	28'
	26'		

PLYMOUTH, 1845, boats

Launch	Two quarterboats
Two cutters	Stern boat

(No dimensions exist. See establishment for Corvette 1st Class below.)

ALBANY, 1844, boats

Launch	36' x 8' 6" x 3' 6"	18 oars 15'	Quarterboat	27' x 6' 6"	12 oars 13'
Cutter	32' x 7' 6" x —	16 oars 14'	Quarterboat	26' x 6' 6"	12 oars 13'
Cutter	26' x 6'	12 oars 13'	Stern boat	25' 6" x 5' 6"	5 oars 16'

DECATUR and class, 1838

Launch	30' x 8' 6" x 3' 8"	16 oars 15'
Cutter	27' 6" x 7' 2" x 2' 10"	14 oars 14'
Quarterboat	25' x 5' 10" x 2' 6"	12 oars 13'
Quarterboat	25' x 5' 10" x 2' 4"	12 oars 13'
Stern boat	21' 6" x 4' 8" x 2' 2"	5 oars 16'
Dinghy	16' 6" x 5' x 1' 8"	4 oars 14'

Allowances of boats, U.S.N., 1835–1848

From Notebook of Master Boatbuilder John Wade of the Boston Navy Yard

RAZEE—*Independence*

	length	depth	beam		length	depth	beam
Launch	36'	x 4' 4"	x 10' 1"	Cutter	27'	x 2' 6"	x 6' 9"
"	33'	x 4'	x 9'	Whaleboat	28'	x 2' 5"	x 7' 2"
Cutter	30'	x 3'	x 7' 11"	Barge	34'	x 2' 6"	x 6' 6"
"	27'	x 2' 9"	x 7' 2"	Gig	34'	x 1' 10"	x 5' 2"

74-gun ships to be allowed one additional gig and two cutters, or one cutter and a second launch

FRIGATE—(*Potomac* and class)

	length	depth	beam		length	depth	beam
Launch	34'	x 4' 2"	x 9' 6"	Cutter	27'	x 2' 6"	x 6' 9"
"	31'	x 3' 10"	x 8' 5"	Whaleboat	28'	x 2' 5"	x 7' 2"
Cutter	28'	x 2' 10"	x 7' 5"	Barge	28'	x 2' 4"	x 6'
"	25' 6"	x 2' 7"	x 6' 8"	Gig	28'	x 1' 8"	x 5'

CORVETTE 1st Class (*Portsmouth* and class) (*Cumberland* and *Macedonian*)

	length	beam	depth		length	beam	depth
Launch	30'	x 8' 5"	x 3' 10"	Cutter	26'	x 6' 6"	x 2' 4"
Cutter	27' 6"	x 7' 5"	x 2' 10"	"	26'	x 6' 6"	x 2' 4"
"	25'	x 6' 8"	x 2' 6"	"	25'	x 6'	x 2' 3"

SLOOP 2nd Class (*Vandalia*, *Cyane*, and class)

	length	depth	beam		length	depth	beam
Launch	29'	x 3' 8"	x 8' 3"	Cutter	26'	x 2' 4"	x 6' 6"
Cutter	26' 6"	x 2' 9"	x 7' 2"	"	25'	x 2' 2"	x 6'
"	26' 2"	x 2' 4"	x 6' 6"				

SLOOP 3rd Class (*Decatur* and class)

	length	depth	beam		length	depth	beam
Launch	26'	x 3' 4"	x 7' 4"	Cutter	25'	x 2' 3"	x 6'
Cutter	24'	x 2' 8"	x 6' 6"	"	24'	x 2' 2"	x 5' 10"
"	25'	x 2' 3"	x 6'				

BRIG (*Bainbridge* and class)

	length	depth	beam		length	depth	beam
Launch	24'	x 3' 0"	x 6' 10"	Cutter	22'	x 2' 2"	x 5' 6"
Cutter	22'	x 2' 6"	x 6'	"	22'	x 2' 2"	x 5' 6"

1st Cutter for Frigates 1854
for Santee & Sabine

Scale

Plank ⅞″ side 1⅛″
Frames mould 1⅜″ side 1¼″
spaced 12″

2nd & 3rd Cutters same model
but measuring:
2nd Cutter 25′6″ × 6′9″ × 1′
3rd ″ 27′0″ × 6′9″ × 1′6″

Frames mould 1¼″ side 1¼″

Figure 150. Plan of cutters for frigates, 1854.

Barge for Frigates 1854
for Santee & Sabine

Plank ⅞″
Frames mould 1⅜″ side 12″ spaced 18″

Scale

Figure 151. Barge for frigates, 1854.

Gig for Frigates 1854
for Santee & Sabine

Scale

Planking ¾"
Frames mould 1¼" side ⅞"
space 12"

Figure 152. Gig for frigates, 1854.

2ⁿᵈ Launch for Frigates 1854
for Santee & Sabine

Scale

Plank 1¼"
Frames mould 2½" side 1¾"
spaced 12"

Figure 153. Second launch for frigates, 1854.

510

Figure 154. First launch for frigates, 1854.

BRIGANTINE (*Dolphin* and class)

	length	depth	beam			length	depth	beam
Launch	24′	x 3′	x 6′ 10″	Cutter		22′	x 2′ 1″	x 5′ 6″
Cutter	22′	x 2′ 6″	x 6′	"		22′	x 2′ 1″	x 5′ 6″

SCHOONERS (*Boxer* and class)

	length	depth	beam
Cutter	22′	x 2′ 6″	x 6′
"	22′	x 1′ 1″	x 5′ 3″
"	22′	x 1′ 1″	x 5′ 3″

N.B. Most captains exceed their allowances by carrying their own gig.

Rough Copy of Directions for Building a Revenue Cutter, 1829. (From Samuel Humphreys' Offset Book.)

Keel of white oak sided 9″
Deadwood amidships to be sided 9″
Deadwood fore & aft of live oak to be sided 9″
Sternpost knee of live oak fayed on keel and to the foreside of inner sternpost and over this knee the deadwood is to be built keeping the shortest pieces below.
4 bolts to be driven the knee viz. 2 through the knee and keel before the deadwood bolts are driven. Care must be taken that the deadwood bolts and sternpost knee bolts do not come into contact. The bolts of knee and deadwood to be rivetted on the underside of keel and aft side of sternpost. Bolts through the knee to be of diameter ¾″; bolts through the deadwood to be diameter ⅞″.
Inner sternpost live oak, main sternpost live oak sided 9″
Stem of live oak sided 9″
Apron of live oak sided 1′ 3″
The deadwood and apron bolts to one foot above the floating line of copper, dia. ¾″
Floor timbers, futtocks, toptimbers of live oak sided 6″
To be moulded at floor heads 6½″
To be moulded at port sill or planksheer 4″
To be moulded at rail 3¾″
To be completely framed, frame bolts dia. ¾″
Every other floor timber to be bolted with one copper bolt dia. ¾″
The alternate floor timbers to be bolted after the keelson is fitted with copper bolts, dia. ¾″ with a drift added.
Keelson live oak sided 9″
Main transom live oak to be bolted with 2 iron bolts dia. ⅞″
The remaining transoms of live oak sided 7″ and bolted with ⅞″ dia. copper bolts
Knightheads and hawsepieces of live oak sided 9″
Outside plank: the running plank of white oak 2¼″ thick. The outside plank abreast the deck 3″ thick; from thence the plank will

gradually and fairly diminish to the thickness of the running plank of bottom. The upper edge of the plank next below the planksheer 2½″ thick.
Planksheer of white oak or yellow pine 2½″ thick. From Planksheer to Rail the space will be boarded outside only with narrow 1″ white oak or yellow pine boards fastened to stanchions 27″ asunder. To have five ports on each side and two in the stern with shutters.
No strake or plank outside from the light waterline upwards amidships to be in width more than 8″
The fastenings of outside plank from keel to one foot above load water line to be of copper; spike may be composition, bolts copper. There will be no treenails.
Each strake to be fastened to one frame, comprising two timbers, with 3 composition spikes of 6″ length where plank is 2¼″ in thickness and one copper bolt ⅝″ dia. to be drove through and rivetted inside. Butt bolts and woodends bolts of copper ⅝″ dia.
Ceiling Plank of yellow pine 2″ thick
Breast Hooks of live oak two below deck hook to be fayed and fastened before ceiling is put on and fastened with copper bolts ¾″ dia.
Clamps white oak or yellow pine 3″ thick at upper edge and 2½″ at lower edge.
A list or air strake 6″ wide to be formed next below the strake under the ceiling
Beams of yellow pine sided 9″ moulded 7½″ to be kneed at each end with one lap and one lodge knee sided 5″ excepting mast beams which are to have a dagger knee in lieu of lap knee, to be bolted with ¾″ dia. bolts.
Deck plank yellow pine 2½″ thick width not to exceed 8″. To be fastened with iron spikes and plugged. Partners of masts of live oak to be kneed.
To be fitted with a trunk cabin as per draught
To be coppered to the waterline 8′ aft and

7' forward with 24 oz. copper

To have a complete set of masts and spars. The principal ones to be of the following names and dimensions:—

Mainmast 58' 2" whole length, 7' head
Foremast 56' 6" " " 7' "
Fore Yard 36' " "
Fore tops'l yard 24' whole length
Foretopgalt " 16' " "
Fore topmast 31' and 12' pole
Fore gaff 17'
Main Gaff 16'
Main Boom 32'
Bowsprit outboard 12'

Lowermasts and bowsprit of yellow pine, remaining spars of spruce and to be in proportion.

To have one foresail, one mainsail, one jib, one foretopsail, No. 1 canvas

One squaresail, one topgalt sail, one lower studdingsail, one gaff topsail, one flying jib of light canvas. An awning fore and aft with No. 2 canvas, with stanchions complete.

To have three shrouds to the foremast on each side and two to each side on the mainmast of 5½" rope.

The forestay 7" with remaining standing and running rigging to be in one proportion of the best russia hemp, to be patent laid and of equal fineness and strength with that used in the Navy. The blocks for the sheet, halyards, braces to be patent bushed. To have one hempen cable 9" and one prog chain cable 1" dia. 60 fathoms. Two anchors each weighing 500 lbs. clear of stock. The anchor for chain cable to have an iron stock. To have all fixtures necessary for working a chain cable. One hawser 6", 75 fathoms. One kedge anchor with anchor stock weighing 300 lbs. clear of stock. To have a capstan, camboose, hammock stanchions, waist clothes, ring and eye bolts for relieving tackles, two iron davits on each quarter for boats.

All the outside planking including the deck planking to be planed. Forecastle floor in lengths about 14'. To have 16 berths. Trunk cabin to have a skylight and two sliding lights on each side and is fitted with four berths and lockers. To have store rooms between the stern frame and after bulkhead of cabin in length about — feet; to have magazine beneath cabin floor. To have two store rooms, one on each side, before the cabin in length 6 feet. The length of the cabin floor including storerooms 19'. To have two scuttles near the storerooms leading to the hold. The scuttle leading to the magazine to have raised coamings and a cap of lead. To have the necessary bars and locks. To have two boats of suitable size. To have two coats of paint. To have casks sufficient to carry 1500 gals. of water.

Dimensions of a Revenue Cutter for the North as drawn for the Treasury Dept. May 1829

Length between perpendiculars 62'
Beam moulded 18'
Depth in hold 8'
    Deadwood 2½'
    Throats 9"
    Ceiling 2"
    Hold 8' 0"
          9' 1½"

9' 1½"
deduct spring of beam 4"

9' 1½"
4"
8' 9½"

deck plank 2½"
port sill above deck
Height to top of planksheer
Planksheer to rail
rail cap
Whole Height

2½"
8"
9' 8"
2' 1"
3"
12' 0".

No 3 Dimensions of a Gun Boat & Materials

Length between perpendiculars 55'
Breadth moulded 17' — (6"?)
Depth from the ceiling to upper part of the deck beams 4' 6"
  Nine inches dead rising to half floor
Keel sided 9 inches & moulded 12 inches deep

Floor timbers. Sided 6 inches & moulded on the keel 7 inches, at the head 5 inches
Futtocks moulded at the foot 5 inches, at the wale 3½ inches
Keelson sided 10 inches & moulded 10 inches, and bolted through every other floor tim-

ber with bolts ⅞th of an inch diameter

Stem sided 9 inches and as deep fore & aft as possible

Two wales 7 inches wide & 3½ inches thick of good oak

Running plank 2 inches thick of oak or yellow pine

Ceiling plank 2 inches thick of yellow pine

An air streak 4 inches wide under the clamp for the free admission of air

Three beams in midships to support the guns. Sided 12 inches, moulded 9 inches in the middle & 6 at the end. Two carlines let in fore & aft sided 12 inches and 9 inches thick, four cross carlines sided 8 inches & 4½ inches thick with double lodging knees & one hanging knee under each beam, to run down as far as the form of the sides will admit.

The bed for the gun carriage to traverse upon; to be 15 feet in diameter & to be raised in the middle 3 inches & at each side to be level, to be laid on the deck plank of good sound white oak. To have a groove 8 inches wide & 3 deep, to be 3(?) feet in diameter for the wheel of the gun carriages to traverse in.

Note on back of drawing:

Drawn at the Request of Edward Preble Esq and forwarded by your Humble Servant
Jacob Coffin

Stancheons—under the beams 5 inches square

Combings for the hatches fore & aft 14 inches deep, & 4½ inches thick yellow pine fitted with close hatches or gratings.

Fore & aft beams. Sided 8 inches & moulded 6 inches in the middle & 4 inches at the ends, of yellow pine.

Thowells to be iron let into a bolster nailed on the plank shear

Oars to be rowed in grummets

Schooner rigged with the masts stept into the keelson.

Rudder 3 feet 4 inches at the bottom—back to be diminished to form a handsome rudder.

To have a bilge piece on each side of the bottom to run parallel with the keel, 3 feet 6 inches therefrom 28 feet long sided 7 inches & 10 inches deep, bolted on the floor timbers

Cable bitts placed before the mast with cross pieces for the cable

Deck plank 2½ inches thick, perfectly clear from sap & defects

Comm^re Preble's Ideas
Adopted

Letter attached to C & R plan #80-7-19

Capstans, 1806

Dimensions of parts on each ship

Part	gun deck United States	spar deck United States	gun deck President	spar deck President	gun deck Essex	spar deck Essex	Syren
Dia. of drum head	4' 7"	3' 11"	4' 6"	3' 9" ⸜	3' 11"	3' 5"	2' 10½"
Large hoop dia.	1' 1"	9½"	11"	9½"	10½"	9"	8½"
Next in dia.	4' 1¼"	3' 6"	3' 9¾"	3' 2¼"	3' 6"	3' 0"	2' 5½"
Length of bar holes	2' 8¼"	2' 1½"	2' 6"	2' 0¼"	1' 11¼"	2' 1"	—
Holes athwartships	1' 0"	10½"	1'	10½"	1'	8"	7½"
Hole in drumhead for head of barrel, square	4½"	4¾"	4½"	4½"	5"	5¼"	3¾"
*Length of whelps	1' 3"	1' 2½"	1' 3"	1' 0½"	1' 2"	1' 2½"	10½"
*Whelps fore and aft at heel	3' 5"	3' 4"	3' 8"	3' 5"	3' 8"	3' 4"	3' 1"
Do. just below moulding	11½"	7"	10½"	7"	7¼"	6"	5"
Do. athwartships at heel	7½"	5"	8"	4¾"	5¼"	4½"	3¼"
Barrel in dia.	9"	7½"	7¼"	6¼"	6½"	5½"	5"
Spindles in dia. between upper and lower capstans	2'	1' 7⅛"	2'	1' 9"	1' 4"	1' 8"	1' 1¼"
Do. at head	—	7"	6"	—	5¾"	—	3½"
Do. at heel	—	5"	4½"	—	4"	—	3"

* There appear to be errors in these dimensions, probably due to the transposing of some dimensions by the clerk who prepared the original copy.

Figure 155. A United States Navy capstan of the period 1803–1820. Capstans were not standard designs.

Gun Mounts 1806

	President	United States	Essex
Length of carriage	5′ 6″	5′ 11½″	4′ 5¾″
Breadth of fore part of bracket	1′ 10½″	2′ 1″	1′ 9″
Ditto after part	11⅜″	1′ 0″	10½″
Bracket sided	5⅜″	5½″	4⅜″
Breadth of transom	1′ 0″	1′ 2¾″	11″
Transom sided	5¼″	5¾″	4⅜″
Breadth fore part of carriage	2′ 4½″	2′ 3″	1′ 9¾″
Do. after part	3′ 2½″	3′ 0″	2′ 3¼″
Fore Axle tree fore and aft	6½″	7¼″	5″
Do. deep	8½″	7¼″	7½″
Dia. fore truck	1′ 5½″	10″	1′ 4″
Fore truck thick	5½″	6″	—
Aft Axle fore and aft	1′ 0½″	11⅜″	12″
Do. deep	6¾″	6¾″	4¾″
After Truck dia.	1′ 3½″	1′ 4″	1′ 2″
" " thick	5½″	—	—
Bed bolt dia.	1½″	1¼″	⅞″
Breeching in clear	5″	4⅞″	4″
Bolts through bracket dia.	1⅛″	1¼″	¾″
Gunbolt in aft end bracket in clear	2″	2⅜″	1⅞″
Gunbolt in aft part of aft axletree in clear	1¾″	—	—
Bolt in transom Dia.	1½″	—	¾″
Trunion hole dia.	6″	—	5″

Carronade mount of the UNITED STATES, 1796

Length of skid	7′ 0″	Aft " "	6″
Breadth	2′ 4″	Eyebolts dia	⅞″
Thick	7″	Dia of eyes in bolts	3⅝″
Length of beds	4′ 0″	Dia in clear	1⅞″
Breadth fore end	1′ 8″	Breechings in clear	5″
" aft "	1′ 10″	Bolts in skids and beds	¾″
Fore end thick	7″		

NORTH CAROLINA, 74-gun Ship

Her hammock stanchions were ordered placed 4′ 9″ apart and were to be approximately 24″ high.

Ironwork on 42-pdr. carronade mount, Nov. 11, 1818

2 nose plates 4¾″ x 1″	36 lbs.	Eyebolts 1¼″ dia.	23
Ring train and truck plates 3″ x 1″	75	Slide Plates 2″ x ½″	20
Filler plate 3½″ x ⅝″	14	7⅞″ bolts	18
Straight bolts 1⅛″ dia	30	Train, fighting and naval bolts 3″	60
Traverse plates 4″ x ⅞″	12	Tiller 1½″ x 1½″	18
" bolts 3¾″ dia.	35	Screw 2½″ dia	24

Rigging for gunboats building on the Ohio 1805

Rigging item	Circum.	Rigging item	Circum.
Bowsprit shrouds	4″	Runners tackles	3½″
" horses	3″	Deck tackles	3″
Forestay	7″	Jackstay	4″
Collar	5″	Square sail halyards	2½″
Leg to forestay	7″	Yard ropes sq. sail	2″
Shrouds	6½″	Horses " "	3″
Lanyards	2½″	Truss " "	3″
Topmast lift double	4½″	Topmast stay	3″
" tackles	1¾″	" shrouds	3½″
Jib stay	4″	" Halyards	3″
" halyards	2″	Sq. sail braces	2½″
Fore halyards	2½″	" " lifts	2½″
Main sheet	3″	Topsail lifts	2″
Main throat halyards	2½″	" horses	2¼″
Peak halyards	2¾″	" braces	1¾″
Throat downhauls	1½″	" buntline	1″
Peak "	1½″	" clewlines	1″
Boom pendants	4½″	" bowlines	1″
" tackles	2½″	" sheets	2½″
Fore sheet	3″	Foot rope for boom	2½″
" downhauler	1¼″	Gaff topsail halyards	1″
Jib sheet	2″	Tackle for do.	1″
" downhauler	1½″	Stay for gaff topsail	1½″
" pendants	7½″	Pendants halyards	¾″
Runners	5¾″	Ensign halyards	¾″

(WARREN & FALMOUTH)
General Instructions for building a Sloop of War
of 626⅖₉₅ tons Carpenters Measurement

Keel

Of white oak, to be a number of pieces not more than 3 Scarphs to be in length not more than 10' nor less than 9'. Each scarph to be fastened with 5 copper bolts of dia. 1" taking care that they are driven in the space between the floors and rivetted with copper rings. There will be driven in the lips of each scarph 2 copper bolts each ¾" diameter. The scarphs to be plain without jogs and 2 coaks let in at 2' apart in each scarph, 2' in length, 2½" in thickness and 8" in breadth.

The keel when finished will be sided 1' 2½" and moulded clear of rabbet (which will be cut close to the upper edge of the keel and form the base line) 1' 6½".

To be finished with a shoe or false keel in lengths of 12' to be put on after the keelson and floor bolts are driven and rivetted as hereafter described; to be in thickness 7½", making the whole depth of the keel below the rabbet when finished 2' 2". To be bolted athwartships at about 6' asunder with copper bolts ¾" in diameter.

False Keel

To be fastened to keel with copper bolts ⅝" in diameter and 1' 3" in length. The false keel as well as the bottom of the keel to be coppered before they are fastened together.

Dead wood

Amidships and abaft sided same as the keel from sternpost to Frame P, (from foreside of Frame P); 1' 8" in depth amidships; and Forward and aft by the rising staff; to be scarphed together with scarphs in length [*missing*] and so divided as to come between the scarphs of the keel. Let the lower piece of after deadwood be shortest in the form of a wedge, the point forward, and let a knee be fayed on the front of the heel of inner post and along the keel with arm length of 4' 6"; body 6'.

Taking care that one bolt thro the throat goes through the post close to its heel & one thro the after end of the keel.

Let the front of the arm of this knee be square so that the ends of the pieces composing the deadwood may fay well against it, tennoning each piece into the arm.

The deadwood amidships will be fastened with copper bolts in length 2 and ⅓rd the thickness of the deadwood where it is less than 10" deep; diameter of bolts ⅝".

Let these bolts be no closer than simply to make the deadwood fay well to the keel inasmuch as the floor and keelson bolts will make it perfectly secure. To be fastened abaft with 1⅛" dia. copper bolts well driven at about 2' 2" apart in a fore and aft direction & so as to clear the rabbet on each side. The forward piece of the deadwood to be live oak trimmed to the mould-depth & length of the mould. The bolts to be rivetted under the keel, on back of post & front of stem upon copper rings.

Stern Post Knee

of live oak faying on top of deadwood, the arm running to the berth deck— this knee to be sided the same as the deadwood Body to be in length about 11' fastened with copper bolts to be driven thro the posts & rivetted upon copper rings upon the after side. Bolts 1⅛" in diameter.

The knee will be coaked into the deadwood in the same manner as the scarphs of the keel

Stern Post	of live oak sided the same as the keel and moulded at the height of the cross-seam clear of the rabbet 1' 0" and moulded at the heel clear of the rabbet 2' 6". Bearded at the keel aft side to say 8' 6". To keep its full siding on aft side of cross-seam. If the piece will not work its full moulding size all the way, let it do so as far down as light waterline; from thence to the heel the back may be of white oak, jogging it at the butt 2½" or 3" into the front piece. The heel of the front piece will have two tennons in the keel—the after piece one.
Inner Post	of live oak fayed upon the sternpost from one foot above the cross-seam down to the keel sided at head 1' 10" the sides parallel down to the aft side of the after cant timber where it will be snaped so as to fay well with it & below it will be regulated by the bearding line as per moulds. Moulded at head 8"—at heel 1' 2" and to be bolted into the post below the loadline down to the head of the stern post knee with copper bolts 1⅛" diameter nett. The bolts thro the knee will be sufficient for it fastening below & above the loadline the bolts will be iron of the same size
Stem	of live oak sided the same as the keel; the length, shape etc. determined by the moulds. The scarph to be 4' 6" in length excepting the one upon the forefoot of keel which will be made as long as possible but not less than 4' 6". The scarphs to be jogged about 2¼" & a space left for a well-seasoned live oak or locust key to be driven in so as to set the lips well home.
Apron	of live oak to be sided 1' 8"; the length to be determined by the moulded. Moulded at head 10" at heel 2' 6". Fastened to the stem with copper bolts below the loadline and iron above it—in diameter 1⅛" nett. To be driven at 2' 2" apart and rivetted upon rings on the front of the stem. Scarphs to be in length 2' 9".

Floors
1st Futtock
2nd do.
3rd do.
Top &
Half-top
	of live oak sided 10½"
	   do. do. 10½"
	   do. do. 10½"
	   do. do. 10½"

Timbers Moulded	of live oak sided 10" at throat of floors amidships 1' 3" at floor ribbands 10½" at 1st futtock heads 9⅜" at 2nd futtock heads 8¼" at 3rd futtock heads 7¼" at top timber heads 6" These are the mouldings the timbers are to hold when dubbed off inside and out ready for the planking. The throat of the floors forward and aft will be regulated by the cutting-down line as marked on the rising staff. The floors had better be first fayed to their stations; then the floor ribband run keeping them in place by cleats nailed on their sides and up and down the sides of the keel & a ribband nail thro the ribband driven within an inch of the head. Then let the frame be put together keeping them 2" apart by furrings in the wake of the bolts which will be square iron with edges chamfered—in diameter 1". Three bolts in each scarph. In planking let the furrings be taken out so as to admit the salt which must rest on the fillings between the frames. In raising the frames let the heels of the 1st futtocks be hoisted upon the ribband until the sirmark comes nearly to its place then the head of the frame be raised having previously lifted up the floor

timber forward of the frame about to be raised so as to give room for bolting it into the sides of its appropriate floor.

The throats of the floors to be bolted as the frames are raised with a copper bolt in each 1⅛" in diameter.

The cutting-down having previously been dubbed off.

Cant Timbers

to be fayed closely together without furrings and ¾" taken off the side of each timber between the bolts leaving in their wake about 4" as stops, thus a more free circulation will be given the air.

Take care that the pitching spots on the heels of cant moulds be correctly transferred to the heels of the timbers and deadwood so that when raised the timbers may be kept at their proper heights. The heels of the cants to have 2" left on their insides so that they may be let that much into the deadwood with a jog 1 foot from their heels & when fairly dubbed off for planking let their heels be secured with one copper bolt in each; 1⅛" diameter.

Cant timbers to be sided the same as the square timbers.

Snapings

of 2 futtocks & lower half-cants as follows

Q commences 6" below 3rd beveling line and snapes to 8½" at bearding line or heel.

R commences 3" above 5th bevelling line & snapes to 8½" at bearding line or heel.

S commences 7" above 5th bevelling line & snapes to 2½" at bearding line or heel.

T commences 8" below 5th bevelling line and snapes to 2½" at bearding line or heel.

U commences 9" below 4th bevelling line & snapes to 5" bearding line or heel.

38 commences at 11" above 6th bevelling line & snapes to 0" at bearding line or heel, or "off to nothing."

37 commences 9" above 7th bevelling line & snapes to 0" at bearding line or heel; this snape commences on top timber.

36 commences 11" above 6th bevelling line & snapes off to nothing at bearding line or heel.

35 commences at 10" below the 7th bevelling line & snapes off to nothing at bearding line or heel.

34 commences 2" above 6th bevelling line & snapes off to nothing at bearding line or heel.

33 commences 11" above 6th bevelling line & snapes off to nothing at bearding line or heel.

32 commences 4" above 6th bevelling line and snapes off to nothing at bearding line or heel.

Snapings of Cants 1st Futtock

38 commences 5" above 2nd bevelling line and snapes to 9½" at bearding line or heel.

37 commences 6" above 2nd bevelling line & snapes to 9½" at bearding line or heel.

36 commences 5" below 2nd bevelling line & snapes to 9½" at bearding line or heel.

35 commences 32" below 2nd bevelling line & snapes to 9½" at bearding line or heel.

34 commences at 10" below 2nd bevelling line & snapes to 9½" at bearding line or heel.

33 commences 32" below 2nd bevelling line & snapes to 9½" at bearding line or heel.

32 commences 26" above 3rd bevelling line & snapes to 7½" at bearding line or heel.

Keelson

of white oak in two depths, or in three, so that the whole depth shall be the same—each depth sided 1' 2½"; moulded 11".

The scarphs not to come over the scarphs of the keel so as to make a good shift, 6' in length. Fayed without hook or jog & two coaks in each—coaks 8" wide and 2½" thick, 1' long.

The upper piece will be fayed fairly on the lower one & coaks let into them all fore and aft—coaks to be in length 1' 4" and in width & thickness as above. The after end of the keelson will be jogged over the after floor timber and will be continued to the sternpost knee against which it will be fayed & the space if any under the keelson at the jog be filled by a chock faying between the deadwood & keelson.

Stemson

of live oak sided same as the keelson & be fayed with a scarph upon the fore end of the keelson which will be jogged down like the after end of the dead-wood. Scarphs will be not less than 4' long. Fayed with a jog of 2" leaving room for a key with which to set it home & along the apron up to the birth deck—moulded at head 10".

There will be driven thro the keelson & each floor timber one copper bolt 1¼" in diameter: rivetted upon rings on the underside of the keel and to be driven on one side thro one floor and on the opposite side thro the other floor taking care that they go clear of the rabbet of the keel & on the opposite side to the floor bolts. Those driven thro the keelson and stemson to be of the same size and rivetted upon rings upon the front of the stem. After the bolts are all driven down and the corners of the keelson chamfered off let there be a capping of 3½" oak plank 12" wide filling the space between the chamfers fayed all fore and aft & well nailed with iron upon the top of the keelson. This cap will prevent the keelson being wounded by the mortices for the heels of the after deck stanchions—let it be finished with a 1" chamfer on each corner.

Knightheads & Hawse Pieces

sided 1' 2"; moulded at head and heels as per mouldes. To be bolted into the apron and each other with iron at about 2' 2" apart. Iron 1" in diameter. They will have their heels snaped off so as to fay well against the fore side of the fore-most cant timber. They had better be fitted & put together on the ground before being raised; then taken apart and hoisted to their places & fastened piece by piece as the easiest method. Let there be an iron bolt driven thro the foremost cant timber into each of the heels of the knightheads & hawse pieces 1" in diameter.

Hawse Holes

when leaded to be in the clear 1' 1" diameter.

In running the ribbands let the frames be set in & out as may be required in consequence of their having sprung in raising—strong wrainstaves & chains will accomplish this point and prevent a great deal of unnecessary dubbing & weakening of the timber. In bevelling the timber let the stock of the bevel be kept square with the back of the timber.

Running Plank of the Bottom

to be of white oak 3½" thick. Bilge Strakes at floor heads to be 5 in number on each side; the middle strake 5" in thickness the strake above & below it 4½"; & above and below these two 4".

To be dubbed flush with the running plank of the bottom. No plank to be more than 12" wide at amidships.

Wales

to be 6 in number on each side—the two middle ones to be 6" thick and those above & below diminishing gradually until they work fair or flush with the running plank of the bottom below & with the strake between the ports under the rail which will be 3" thick leaving the ship's side free of any projection below the rail. The planks will all be put on with fair edges without hooks or jogs & the fastenings will be of copper from the lower edge of the wales amidships down to the keel. The running plank with 9" spikes or small bolts are to be preferred & the thickstuff with bolts ⅝" diameter nett: in length twice and one-third the thickness of the plank thro which it is to be driven. There will be so many of these fastenings as will draw the plank well to the timbers and the residue to be locust treenails after a 1¼" auger. The treenails will be in number a proportion to the metal fastenings as three to one—that is to say there will be three treenails to one metal fastening. The points of the treenails will be dipped in tar previously to being driven & they will go well thro the ceiling & finally be cut off on the outer and inner sides of the ship; the heads to be caulked in a triangular manner & the points to be wedged with heart pine wedges. In addition to the above fastenings the thick stuff on the bilges will be bolted with ¾" copper; the bolts to be about 10' apart in each strake and so driven that those in one strake may come between those in the strake above & below & not in the same timber. *Note.* Instead of treenails from light waterline say from about 9' below the port cills amidships let bolts be substituted to go thro and be rivetted upon rings. To be of copper as high as within 4' of the port cills and all above of iron. Let two bolts in each strake go thro each frame & rivet on the ceiling & two short fastenings. The plank will thus be square-fastened from the keel up to the ports but in the topsides it will be cross fastened with short fastenings—that is to say there will be one spike and one short bolt in each strake and every timber.

Butt bolts   will be driven into the bottom as high as the wales and copper bolts nett ⅞" diameter for each butt. To be driven thru the frame next on each side the one on which the strake butts & to be rivetted on the ceiling on copper or composition rings. These bolts will not be driven until after the strake above and below the one where the butts are to go, are to be caulked.

In shifting butts in the planking let there be at least 6' between each & let there be three strakes at least between every two butts on the same timber. Let all the plank be so bevelled that the seams shall be outgauged about, or rather more than, 1/16" for every inch the plank is in thickness; so as to prevent it from caulking off etc. Let the butts be well opened so as to receive the oakum—a butt of 5/16" is little enough for a 3" plank.

In planking let the sap be avoided as much as possible and in all cases where a plank may have any sap on its edge let the heart side be put on the timbers. Let the hooding ends of the running plank be ¼" less in the rabbet of post & stem than its thickness amidships.

Bilge Strakes   at floor heads there will be 4 in number on each side; the two middle ones 5" thick and the strakes on each side of these 4½". To be chamfered off to 4" at floor heads if not covered by the clamps—thick strake 3 in number—in thickness 5" and 4½". Fasten the clamps and thick stuff with bolt twice & one third the thickness of the plank thro which they are driven; to be nett ¾" diameter. The plank to be well drawn down on the timbers and all the seams bevelled so as to make square work. The same shift of butts to be observed as on the outside of the ship. There will be no hooking or jogging except on the clamps. The forward and after ends of the strakes to be as narrow as to shew the same number of strakes below the clamps of the birth deck as there are amidships.

Berth Deck Clamps   to be 3 strakes in number; in thickness 6", 5" & 4", jogged down into each other 1½" and the jogs 8' in length; the lower edge to be chamfered to 4".

Berth Deck Beams   of heart pine free from sap sided 13" and moulded by gundeck mould 11". To be kneed at each end with one lodge knee sided 6½"; arms to be in length—

and more if to be had, 4′. There will be 1″ trimmed off from the upper edge of the clamps under the lodge knees to admit air leaving a jog of about 6″ next each beam for the knees to rest on. After the beams are cut off to their proper lengths let there be holes bored about 4′ 6″ in length into the ends of the beams by a pump boring bitt 2″ inside dia. to be filled with coarse salt & plugged up. Let their ends be grooved across from corner to corner with a 1″ gouge & from the plug down to the end and along the underside to about 2″ within the clamp.

The knees to be fastened through the sides of the ship with 1″ dia. copper bolts. Three bolts through the body of each knee of iron, of the same size thro the beams—three bolts through the arms. Let the point of each knee be nailed into the beam with two 5″ spikes to prevent its splitting. The bolts to be rivetted on substantial rings. Let the knees be kept in the middle of the beams between their upper and lower edges so as to divide the wood equally above and below for bolting. The knees will be jogged 1½″ into the side of the beams at about 2′ from their ends taking nothing off the beams at the end of the knee nor anything between the jog and the side of the ship—nor will any wood be taken from the beam below the knee from its point to the jog it being chined in & the knee faying down closely upon it. There will be a space left at the jog running quite to the lower edge of the beam for a seasoned key of locust to be driven in after the knees are bolted. *Note.* By letting the arms of the knees lay upon the clamps & their bodies along the beams greater length may be had if required.

Ledges — of heart pine free from sap to square 5″. One between each beam except where the rooms may be too large so that in no case must the space between beam and ledge be more than 2′.

Carlins — or fore-and-aft pieces of heart pine free from sap to square 7″ in three ranges—one in the middle of the deck & one on each side dividing the ledges into 4 lengths.

Plank — of heart pine free from sap shakes or large knots & not more than 10″ in width: 2½″ thickness. Average length to be 40′. To be fastened into the beams with 6″ spikes, into the ledges with 5″ spikes which are to be punched down so as to admit above the heads a heart pine plug to be put in dipped in white lead, ¾″ in thickness.

Partners — of fore and main masts of heart pine square 8″—to be kneed with four lap knees each, sided 6″ and bolted with ¾″ dia. iron. Those of mizzen mast same size; knees sided 5½″ and bolted with iron a full ⅝″ diameter.

There will be a half-beam in the wake of the main hatch with a ledge on each side of it; the half-beam sided 2″ less than, and moulded the same at the side of the ship as the whole beams—to continue the same moulding size 4′ 6″ from the side and taper thence to the coamings of the hatch into which it will be let down, to 8″ secured to the coamings by two lap knees sided 5″ & kept 1″ from the top of the beam. Kneed at side of ship like the whole beams. Neither knees beams ledges or plank of the deck will be planed except the coamings, side of hatches, edges of beams etc. to be rounded.

Mast steps Fore & Main — to be of white oak formed as those of the frigates. The side base pieces to outer sides from keelson 2′; sided 10″ and 5′ in length. Secured to floors by iron bolts 1″ diameter—cross pieces sided 10″, moulded 1′ 6″, in clear apart 1′ 10″. Fore and aft pieces sided 10″ and in the clear apart 11″.

Mizzen step — of live oak to be placed on the birth deck.

Pumps — will step on the floor timber running down to within 2½″ of it & be supported on one side by a jog upon the keelson and on the other by a jog upon the step.

Stanchions	of white oak reaching from top of keelson to under side of each beam to square 6½″. Chamfered an inch on each corner to within 5″ of the head and heel which will remain square; tennoned into oak cap, under the beams.
Breasthook	of the birth deck live oak in length 14′ and sided 11″. The deck plank will be nailed into the hook which will be fayed well against the timbers and bows of the ship. Two hooks below this, same length & size as deck hook and moulded in the throat clear of the stemson 11″; all to be fayed against the timbers & be fastened with 9 bolts, copper, 1⅛″ diameter. The throat bolts to be driven from the inside and rivetted upon the front of stem on a ring; the others driven from the outside & rivetted upon rings. If there should not be depth enough from the throat of the breasthooks to admit their jogging over the stemson and faying along the bow leaving the moulding size, here called for, the deficiency will be made up by chocks fayed on the back of breasthooks against the bows & sides of stemson.
Waterways	of white oak finished 11″ in depth and 12″ breadth; averaging in length 40′ as near as possible. The edge next the deck trimmed to 4″ and next to side of ship 4½″. The edge next to deck to be chined in 2″, the wood taken off thence by a straight line across as per margin. There will be two strakes of pine 4″ thick and 10″ broad next the waterways—the waterway and the strake next to it will be let nicely down 1½″, dovetailed over the beams and ledges. The inside strake will be let down the same depth by taking the wood out of the top of the beams thus giving a jog against the edge of the plank quite across. These strakes will be bolted thro the waterways & side of the ship with two bolts between every two beams, of copper ¾″ diameter (one bolt may serve). The inner lower edge of the inner plank to be chamfered to the thickness of the deck plank.
Stanchions	in one row stepped on birth deck of white oak—one under every gun deck beam, squared 5½″ and chamfered as in the hold.
Coamings & Ledges	of hatches to be in height above the deck plank 4½″—sided 6″.
Spirketting	of white oak to be 3½″ thick and 11″ wide. Having a list of 3″ above it—at the upper edge of the list as also of the list below there will be primings cut for salting. Let them be kept clear of the list so as to contain the salt in order to get which into the rooms under the ports it will be necessary to bore 1¼″ auger holes thro cills over each room which can be afterwards plugged up.
Gun deck Clamps	of white oak 6″ thick and of a width sufficient to fill the space down to the upper edge of the list which they will form jogged into each other as those on the deck below.
Gun deck Beams	of heart yellow pine free from sap sided 14″ or 15″. moulded 12½″ or 13″ managed as those below & springing by 4½″ in 31′.
Knees	of live oak or white oak limbs or roots, lodge & dagger, lodge side 7½″ and dagger 8″. Arms to be 4′ 6″ long. Bodies of daggers long enough to butt on berth deck waterways. To have one lodge & one dagger at each side of the beam. Fastening 1″ dia. iron.
Ledges	of heart yellow pine free from sap—number same as below & square 6½″.
Carlins	Do. square 8½″.

Coamings   of fore & main hatch 1′ 10″ in width, 6½″ thick, to be let down upon oak fore and afters squaring 8½″ so that the whole depth when finished will be 2′ 6½″. The height above deck plank to be 1′ 6½″. Those of the after hatch to be the same depth but ½″ less siding. The head ledges will have a bolt driven thro them and the coamings at each corner of the hatch and two bolts in each ledge between the coamings and the beam, of 1⅛″ dia. iron. The fore and aft pieces on which the coamings are to rest will be chined down 1″ on their upper sides & about ½ the thickness of the coamings, into which the coamings will be fitted by a corresponding chine upon their lower edges, for the purpose of resisting the pressure of the caulking. They will be secured at each end by a knee siding 5½″.

Plank   of this deck to be heart pine free of sap 3½″ thick and not more than 10″ wide; average length 40′. To be fastened to the beams with 8″ iron spikes, 7″ spikes in ledges. To be managed as those on the birth deck and the plank to be planed on both sides. Thick strake next the waterway jogged down as on birth deck, 5″ thick.

Waterways   of white oak, average in length as near as possible to 40′; edge next the deck to be 5″ thick, next the side 5″; whole depth finishing with port cill 1′ 10″, 12″ wide.

Spirketting   Gundeck spirketting 5″ thick.

Waist Plank   of heart pine 4″ to 3″ thick.

Rail Cap   of white oak 6″ thick, scarphs hooked into each other & in length 3′ 6″. Projecting without outside the planking 3″ and inboard inside planking 1¼″.

Ring & Eye Bolts   Omitted from instructions.

Partners   of fore and main masts of live oak 9″ depth & 1′ 3″ breadth framed so much as to admit wedges all around in thickness 4″. Knees as on the berth deck with lap knees sided 6″ bolted with same size iron as those on deck below.
of mizzen mast live oak depth 7″ and breadth 10″; knees as above sided 5″, bolted as on deck below.

Breasthook   of live oak sided 1′ and 15′ in length. Moulded at throat not less than 1′ 2″ and the deck plank to be nailed onto this hook which will fay well against the timbers as on deck below. A hook between decks same size—all fastened with 1⅛″ dia. iron.

Catheads   of tough white oak sided 1′ 2″ and moulded 1′ 1″. They will rest upon the rail mould so as to cut it half off and fay against the inside of the waist & be secured by iron bolts through the side of a diameter of 1⅛″.

Poop Clamps   of roundhouse will be heart pine 3½″ thick. *Note.* It is possible that this may be altered to a hurricane house. (stern cabin)

Poop Beams   of heart pine one half to be sided 9″ and the other 7″—moulded 6½″. The larger ones to be kneed with a lodge knee at each end to be kept close to the lower edge of the beam and the small beams let down into the knees like ledges—to be bolted with ¾″ dia. iron. The beams of this deck will spring so much by a regular curve that there shall be more height amidships than at the sides by 4″ and the height of sides between gun deck plank and round house beams will be 6′.

Forecastle Beams	will be same size as those of poop, managed in the same manner but springing by the gundeck mould.
Planking	of poop and forecastle decks will be 2″ thick of heart pine free from sap and fastened with 5″ iron spikes plugged and planed on both sides.
Waterways	of poop & forecastle, or planksheer white oak 3″ thick. Chines down about 3″ within the timbers to be the thickness of the deck plank so as to lead the water to the gun deck.
Bowsprit	must fay close upon the apron & stem head; there will be a chock over the bowsprit between the knightheads and let into them 1″ on its lower side at each end which will make the chocks 2″ longer than the space between the knightheads along the lower edge of the chock.
Breasthook	over bowsprit to be up & down 9″ and fore and aft 10′
Port Cills	of live oak 6″ thick. Take care that these cills make a fair sheer & the decks kept at their proper distance from them.
Rudder	will be of the common straight necked kind; the back of the post had better be bearded somewhat so as to take less bearding from the rudder. The back of the post will be trimmed the moulding way per draught.
Iron Tiller	to be in length clear of rudder head per draught 9′, 4½″ square at rudder head and 2½″ square at inner end, with the edges chamfered.
Deck Hooks abaft	one for each deck fayed against the timbers same size as breasthooks & one beneath the berth deck, all live oak and bolted as the breasthooks.
Outside of Ship	to be planed from about 6′ below the port cills up to the rail and the waist inside as also the poop and forecastle decks and all spike heads plugged same as decks.
Caulking	Let the oakum be made from the best junk, not more than ⅓rd wont be driven quite home to the timber—the seams payed with pitch taking care to cover the oakum well so as to leave no part bare & that the work be not caught by rain unpayed.
Watering	When the ship is caulked as high as the gun deck let her be watered by pumping or otherwise until the water reaches the fore end of the keel and then let there be several buckets full thrown down each space between the timbers through the list under the gun deck & the leaks that may appear marked by two or three careful men under the bottom. Let this be done twice all around the ship and then let the water be let out by an auger hole or two abaft in the wake of the sternpost knee or deadwood; the pitch having been scraped away from the seams previous to watering. The bottom will then be payed with pitch boiled so hard as not to fly off in driving the coppering nails.
Coppering	After the bottom is thus payed the copper will be put on, having previously been punched with a countersink punch and nailed directly on the pitch without any doubling—unless otherwise directed to use felt—so as to avoid its being quilted as much as possible. Previously to putting on the copper & while the work is progressing the seams are to be fitted flush with spun yarn. Let the sheets of copper be nailed first in their middle, then diverging towards their outer edges so as to prevent puckering.

Channels — of white oak of a width sufficient to permit the lanyards to clear the ridge rope of the hammock stanchions—thickness at ship side 4½″ and 3¼″ at outer edge—to be bolted with 1″ dia iron.

Chains — in three links—the one around the deadeye to be in length below the deadeye to its diameter—toe link in length 1′ 4″. The middle link to fill up between the two as per draught.
The deadeyes to strap so as to stand athwartships instead of fore and aft

Chains — Fore and main of iron—to be 1⅜″ full—mizzen 1⅛″ nett. Chain bolts fore and main 1½″ diameter, mizzen 1¼″. Ringbolts, size of ring only 1¼″. Preventer plates made from square iron 1¼″ x 1¼″—mizzen 1⅛″ square. To be semicircular & swaged & when finished they will be in breast

Preventer Plates — for the fore and main breadth 1¾″, thickness 1″
mizzen, breadth 1½″, thickness ⅞″; in length about 2′.
The chain bolts will be driven thro the sides above and below the deck so as to be drifted out when necessary & in order to give them additional strength let them be upset about 5″ in from the head so as for that distance they shall be ⅛th larger than where they go through the timbers; by this means the timbers will not be so much wounded as though they held their full size and the bolts will have the strength which is required.

Channel Stays — Four on the main and fore channels each, on each side, and three on each of the mizzen channels. Secured by an arm, and underneath and across the channel forming a knee; the stays to be all in breadth 2¼″; at the top the thickness is 1⅜″ and at the bottom ¾″. The arm will be of the same size. There will be an eye at the upper end 3″ in the clear and a ring bolt through the lower end of the same size as those of the preventer plates and in range with the bolts at the lower ends of the two links. There will be a ring in every other chain bolt 5″ in the clear 1¼″ dia. iron.

Swinging Stun'sail Boom Irons — one on each end of fore channel 2½″ square at neck and 1½″ at outer ends. Arm to be 3′ in length from heel to eye at the outer end.

Channel Cranes — for supporting the spare spars & yards—to embrace the channel above and below—one on the main and one on the mizzen on each side—neck to be 2¼″ square; saddle round in dia 2¼″ and to fit yard 1′ 1″ diameter.

Cable bitts — of white oak, one pair, square 1′ 1½″ and to step into the birth deck tapering from full size at lower edge of gun deck beam to heel 9″ square.
Crosspiece is 10′ in length, 1′ 1″ up and down, 1′ 5″ fore and aft and 1′ 4″ from deck to under side. Rounded on aft side. May be made in two pieces; the piece next to bitts may be of oak ¾ of the whole breadth and the after piece of heart pine treenailed into the other. The crosspiece is held in place by a

hook and eye bolt—the eye bolt to be driven into the fore side of it near the upper edge so as to keep the arms of it close alongside the inside of the bitt and the hook is fastened into the bitt.

There will be a ringbolt about half way along the body of the bitt rider the size of the deck stopper bolt and an eye bolt thro the end of the knee 1¼" in diameter. The eyes of all bolts whether for rings or eyes must be close with throat pieces welded in them so as to make them strong.

Bowsprit Bitts square 1' tapered to 9" at berth deck.
Deck stopper ring bolts—4 on each side—the aftermost bolt to be at the after part of main hatchway 1¼" diameter, ring 5" in the clear.

Hammock Stanchions To be in length so that the ridge rope shall be as high as the forecastle and poop decks and in breadth, in the clear 1' 1". The stanchions will be let down onto, not into, the rail to avoid wounding it. The outside legs of the stanchion will mortice thro the moulding of the rail leaving a full inch of wood outside of them; the rail on the inside is scored in for the leg to ship into & then a staple will be driven across it in the rail.

Note The rooms in the frame must be filled in with live oak or well seasoned white oak from keel to birth deck. The filling is driven from the outside except where it may be necessary to drive it from both sides to make close work. To be well caulked and payed on both sides. The ship must be secured by her wales, breast and deck hooks before filling in to prevent the frames from spreading. This will render a ceiling in the hull unnecessary with the exception of the thick strakes directed for the floor & futtock heads. These thick strakes should be bolted thro and thro at proper distances and well rivetted on rings. Let all spike heads above load line be well plugged.

Galleries to be so placed as to embrace the after port for the entrance into the gallery. The tiller to ship under gun deck.
Circular 14 Dec. 1825

Chains not to be secured until masts are in & then so as to give the greatest room to the ports & the best spread to the rigging so as not to obstruct the ports. Deadeyes to stand athwartships instead of fore and aft
Circular 31 Dec. 1825

Armament the port fixtures to be calculated for long 24 pound medium guns port cills 22" from the deck
Circular of 9 Feb. 1826

Note. Of the points & particulars which in building must remain as directed by the building instructions prepared by Mr. Doughty for the sloops to be built to his draught or as corrected from the directions of the Board viz.

Sloops built by Mr. Doughty's draught must comport with the first building instructions issued by the Board in
The sidings of the keel and deadwood fore and aft
"   "   of stem and stern posts
"   " apron
"   "   " all the square frame timbers
"   "   "   " cants
& the snapings of all cants which by Mr. Doughty have not been furnished

March 4 1826 to Captain Crane
March 15 1826 to Comm'r's Barron & Biddle

Warren commenced building June 1826
Falmouth   "   " December 1826
Reference 142-8-20

Comment:—

This is typical of the building instructions issued by the Board of Navy Commissioners and shows the attention given to detail specification as well as the method of making alterations through the transmission of circulars or form letters to all yards. Usually these circulars were made endorsements on the original building instructions if made prior to the start of actual construction of a vessel. The building instructions were often issued in a printed booklet or a broadside sheet, a practice which was followed in the United States Navy when private yards were to bid, at least as early as the War of 1812.

The copper used in naval ships in 1826 was in sheets about 14 inches wide and from 36 to 48 inches long. Following British practice, the copper was in various weights—32, 28, 18 and 16 oz. per square foot. The heaviest was used in three or four strakes around the water line and down on the bows to the fore gripe. Twenty-eight-ounce copper was used to cover the remaining portion of the bottom with the thin stuff, 18 and 16 oz., used between the main and false keels, on the shoe of the rudder and in other close places. To punch the copper, it was first marked with two straight lines from corner to corner and then lines were drawn parallel to these about 3 or 4 inches apart. Where these lines crossed, punched holes were made for nailing. The plates lapped at all edges; those forming butts lapped toward the stern and those forming seams lapped downward. The lapping seems to have been in reverse order to that employed in the British service.

Some of the terms used in the instructions are now obsolete. "Chining" meant cutting a square rabbet; "faying" fitted with a tight joint; the "rising-staff" was a marked staff made in the mould loft for establishing the height of the throat of each floor timber. "Coaks" were blocks fitted in the seam between two timbers to lock them against longitudinal movement. "Jogging" is now usually called notching.

Dimensions of Gunboats and Materials

Length between perpendiculars   71'-0"
Breadth moulded   18'-0"
Depth from ceiling to upper side
   of deck beams at O on middle line   5'-1"
Trunk in length   37'-0"
Floor timbers sided   7"
Moulded on keel   7"
Moulded at Floor heads   6"
Lower futtocks sided   6"

Toptimbers sided 6" moulded at topside 4"

Keel sided 10" and 9" deep and reduced at the ends to 7" siding.

Keelson to be 9" sided and 10" deep, and to be bolted to the keel through every other floor timber with one bolt ¾" diameter

Stem to be sided 8" at head and of the siding of keel below

Stern post sided 8" and of the siding of the keel below—reduced to 5" at the back of the heel and to be moulded at the rabbet the same as the stem.

Wales to be 3 strakes on each side and 3" thick.

Running plank of the bottom to be 2" thick

Ceiling to be 2" thick and a strake left out under the clamps 6" wide for the admission of air to the frames—and the frame timbers to be kept 2" apart, for the same purpose

Clamp to be 2½" or 3" thick and the beams to let down 1" into them.

Beams to be 10 in number sided as per draught and moulded 7".

Knees two to each beam and one hanging ditto to each of the 2nd beams from bow and stern, all of which to be sided 5"

Stanchions—one stanchion to be placed underneath each of the 3 foremost and 3 aftermost beams

Coamings—4 pieces sided 5" and 14" above the deck to run from the 3rd to 8th beam from forward, the two amidships ones to be in the clear 3'-3", to admit the gun to be housed between them; between the coamings on each side to have gratings fitted for admission of air below, and 15 thwarts fitted under the gratings on each side to ship at pleasure for rowers. Tholes of iron placed between each and 17 in number on each side to enable the boat to be rowed either end foremost as occasion may suggest.

Netting cranes—to have 15 double netting cranes on each side spaced clear of the tholes; the lower part to ly 9″ above the bolster on the gunwales to admit the oars to play freely under it and the breadth of the crane to project from the gunwale; the upper part of the eye for the ridge rope to be no higher than 4′ from the deck and the spread of the crane in the clear 11″, which space just admits a hammock.

Bitts—a pair of bitts situated afore the mast 5″ square with a crosspiece stretching from one to the other for pins and the ends to project 8 or 10″ to belay topsail sheets.

Deck plank to be 2″ thick free from all sap shakes and other defects and to be quartered.

Oars; the longest to be 25′ and made light as strength will permit; the shortest 23′ and made of good ash if it is to be had.

Pumps, one on each side the mast close to the foremost bulkhead of wardroom 6″ in the bore, to be placed as clear of the masts and oars as possible.

Rudder, broad at the heel 2′ 9″ fitted with two braces and to have an iron strap over the head securely bolted athwartships.

Hawse holes, to have two hawse holes forward and the like number aft; the holes to be in the clear 6″.

Ringbolts—through the sides—12 forward and 12 aft, of 1⅛″ iron for working the guns—other ring and eye bolts fitted as per draught.

Timber heads—4 on each side forward and 4 aft sided 6″ and 10″ above gunwale.

Catheads 4 in number to project 18″ beyond the bows and quarter sided 6″ and fitted so that the skid can traverse clear and the guns work freely over them.

Breasthooks—2 in the holds.

Guns—to have 2 circles of iron fitted on deck forward and aft for the gun skids to traverse on; the inner one to be 3″ broad; the outer one same breadth and ⅝″ thick. The outer part of small one to be distant from the center of the pin 6′ 2″; it is necessary that the circles be fitted exact that in case the carriages and skids may be ordered from this place that they shall fit to exactness—and it is more over proper that the upper surface of the circles should lie level with each other that the skids may traverse freely over them and all the trucks have equal bearing. The wardroom to be situated abaft the foremost mast beam and to extend 6′ 4″ aft, to be fitted with 2 berths on each side. Abaft the after bulkhead the magazine and officers storeroom is to be placed, to be fore and aft 4′; the magazine to be on the starboard side and 4′ wide with a passage adjoining; the officers storeroom to occupy the opposite side.

The cabin to commence from the magazine bulkhead and to extend aft 12′ 8″ and to be fitted with 2 berths on each side. A platform to be laid on the keelson from the foremost bulkhead of wardroom to the aftermost bulkhead of cabin and a board on each side to be left loose to deposit shot on the ceiling.

Dimensions of Masts and Spars for the Gunboats Building at Ohio Sloop Rigged

Main mast whole length	57′	
" head	7′	
" diameter at partners	1′ 4″	
Main Boom	50′	
" Gaff	25′	
Bowsprit without board	18′	

and length inboard to run to the centerpin of skids where the heel is secured by running the end into a strap fitted to a temporary pin which fits into the center pin of skid and to go with an iron clasp fitted to the stemhead. When ever the gun is run on the skids the bowsprit unships.

Topmast whole length	24′		
" head	4′		
Crossjack Yard	32′	whole length	
Topsail Yard	23′	"	"

Josiah Fox, Navy Constructor
Navy Yard, Washington, 10 Sept., 1805

Index

and List of Naval Vessels

1775–1855

Governor Tomkins, 1812: 248
  Schooner, 6 guns; dimensions and builder unknown; 96 tons; the *Charles and Ann*, a merchant schooner purchased on Lake Ontario Oct. 4, 1812; sold May 15, 1814.
Governor Trumbull, privateer: 74
Governor Williams, 1799: 153
  Galley; built at Wilmington, N.C.
Grampus, 1821: 332, 334, 406, 485, 486, 504
  Schooner, 10 guns; dimensions, length 92' 6" b.p., beam 24' 6", depth in hold 9' 6"; 171½ tons; builder, Washington Navy Yard, 1821; capsized off Charleston, S.C., 1843, all hands lost.
Grampus, letter of marque: See *Spitfire*
Granite State: See *Alabama*, 1818
Green, David: 224
Greenleaf, Jonathan: 60, 71, 72
Greenleaf and Cross: 71
Greenwich, 1813: 264
  Armed ship; dimensions and builder unknown; 338 tons; British whaler taken by *Essex* May 29, 1813, in South Pacific; disposal uncertain.
Greyhound, 1822: 338
  Schooner, 3 guns; dimensions and builder unknown; 65 tons; 31 men; purchased at Baltimore, Md., 1822; sold there, 1824.
Grice, Francis: 256, 313, 334, 340, 354, 364, 400, 406, 407, 408, 417, 433, 440, 444, 448, 450, 457, 463, 472
Grice and Company: 60, 75
Griffiths, John: 313, 448, 472
Grinnell expedition: 466
Growler (1st), 1812: 248
  Schooner, 2 guns; dimensions and builder unknown; 53 tons; 40 men; merchant schooner named *Experiment* purchased on Lake Ontario, 1812; captured by British Aug. 11, 1813; retaken by Americans Oct. 5, 1813; again taken by British May 5, 1814; renamed *Hamilton* in British service.
Growler (2nd), 1812: 274, 276, 299
  Sloop, 10 guns; dimensions, length 60' b.p., beam 19', depth in hold 5' 8"; builder unknown; purchased on Lake Champlain, 1812; captured by British July 3, 1813; renamed *Shannon*, later *Chubb*; retaken by Americans Sept. 11, 1813; sold July, 1815.
Guerriere, 1813: 256, 264, 309, 313, 320, 486
  Frigate, 44 guns; dimensions, same as *Columbia*, 1813; builder, Joseph and Francis Grice, Philadelphia; launched June 20, 1814; broken up at Norfolk, Va., 1841; battery (1817), 33 long 24's and 20 42-pdr. carronades.
Gunboats: 94, 153, 189-209, 218-33, 241, 243-44, 513-14, 516, 528-29

Gundalow: 101, 102, 106, 108-13
Gun mount: 93, 94, 200, 201, 202, 319, 418, 515, 516
Guns: 11, 12, 42, 88-95, 113, 132, 133, 163, 166, 319, 320, 368, 420-22, 438
Gun, shell: 438, 464
Gunter rig: 192, 209

Hackett, James K.: 59, 67, 68, 80, 82, 129, 136, 145
Hackett, William: 68, 69, 72, 80, 82, 164
Hagglund, T. F.: 107, 108
Hague, 1777: See *Deane*, 1777
Haldemand, R.N. snow, 1763-71: 20
Halifax, R.N. snow, 1756: 20
Halifax, R.N. ship: See *Ranger*, 1777
Hamilton, 1812: 248, 274
  Schooner, 9 guns; dimensions and builder unknown; merchant schooner named *Diana*, purchased 1812, Lake Ontario; capsized Aug. 10, 1813, all hands lost.
Hamilton, British schooner: See *Growler* (1st)
Hamilton, Col. E. P.: 108
Hammock rails: 366, 476, 477
Hampden, 1775: 54, 55
  Brigantine, 14 guns; dimensions and builder unknown; purchased 1775; sold at Providence, R.I., 1776
Hancock (1st), 1775: 54
  Schooner, 6 guns; dimensions and builder unknown; fishing schooner fitted out in Massachusetts, 1775; returned to owner 1776.
Hancock (2nd), 1776: 64, 67, 69, 71, 72, 73, 74, 76, 77, 84, 90
  Frigate, 32 guns; dimensions (English measurement), length on gun deck 136' 7", beam 35' 6", depth of hold 11' ½"; 750 tons; builder, Jonathan Greenleaf and Stephen and Ralph Cross, Newburyport, Mass., 1776; captured by H.B.M. ships *Rainbow*, 44, *Flora*, 36, *Victor*, 18, July 7, 1777; renamed *Iris;* captured by French, 1781; blown up at Toulon, France, 1793.
Hannah, 1775: 54
  Schooner; dimensions and builder unknown; reputedly fitted out at Beverly, Mass., 1775, for Continental service; probably renamed, as no record of *Hannah* has been found.
Hanscom, naval constructor: 416
Hanscom, William: 82
Harrison, 1775: 54
  Schooner, 6 guns; dimensions and builder unknown; fishing schooner fitted out in Mass., 1775, by order of Gen. Washington.

P9-DOF-164

STONEWALL

BOOKS BY MARTIN DUBERMAN

Cures: A Gay Man's Odyssey (1991)
Mother Earth: An Epic Drama of Emma Goldman's Life (1991)
Hidden from History: Reclaiming the Gay and Lesbian Past, co-editor (1989)
Paul Robeson (1989)
About Time: Exploring the Gay Past (first edition, 1986; second edition, 1991)
Visions of Kerouac (1977)
Male Armor: Selected Plays, 1968–1974 (1976)
Black Mountain: An Exploration in Community (first edition, 1972; second edition, 1993)
The Memory Bank (1970)
The Uncompleted Past (1969)
James Russell Lowell (1966)
The Antislavery Vanguard, editor (1965)
In White America (1964)
Charles Francis Adams, 1807–1886 (1963)

MARTIN DUBERMAN

STONEWALL

A DUTTON BOOK

DUTTON

Published by the Penguin Group
Penguin Books USA Inc., 375 Hudson Street, New York, New York 10014, U.S.A.
Penguin Books Ltd, 27 Wrights Lane, London W8 5TZ, England
Penguin Books Australia Ltd, Ringwood, Victoria, Australia
Penguin Books Canada Ltd, 10 Alcorn Avenue, Toronto, Ontario, Canada M4V 3B2
Penguin Books (N.Z.) Ltd, 182–190 Wairau Road, Auckland 10, New Zealand

Penguin Books Ltd, Registered Offices:
Harmondsworth, Middlesex, England

First published by Dutton, an imprint of New American Library,
a division of Penguin Books USA Inc.
Distributed in Canada by McClelland & Stewart Inc.

First Printing, May, 1993
1 3 5 7 9 10 8 6 4 2

Copyright © Martin Duberman, 1993
All rights reserved

REGISTERED TRADEMARK—MARCA REGISTRADA

LIBRARY OF CONGRESS CATALOGING-IN-PUBLICATION DATA:
Duberman, Martin B.
Stonewall / Martin Duberman.
p.   cm.
Includes bibliographical references and index.
ISBN 0-525-93602-5
1. Stonewall Riot, New York, N.Y., 1969.   2. Gay liberation
movement—United States—History.   3. Gay men—United States—
History.   4. Lesbians—United States—History.   I. Title.
HQ76.8.U5D85   1993
306.9'0664'0973—dc20   92-36694
                                                            CIP

Printed in the United States of America
Set in Janson and Gill Sans

Designed by Steven N. Stathakis

Without limiting the rights under copyright reserved above, no part of this publication may be reproduced, stored in or introduced into a retrieval system, or transmitted, in any form, or by any means
(electronic, mechanical, photocopying, recording, or otherwise), without the prior written permission
of both the copyright owner and the above publisher of this book.

AGAIN AND ALWAYS—
FOR ELI

Becoming human is becoming individual, and we become individual under the guidance of cultural patterns . . . which give form, order, point, and direction to our lives. . . . [But] we must . . . descend into detail, past the misleading tags, past the metaphysical types, past the empty similarities, to grasp firmly the essential character of not only the various cultures but the various sorts of individuals within each culture, if we wish to encounter humanity face to face.

—CLIFFORD GEERTZ
The Interpretation of Culture

C O N T E N T S

ACKNOWLEDGMENTS

My greatest debt is to the six people who trusted me to tell their stories and endured the multiple taping sessions needed to make that possible: Yvonne (Maua) Flowers, Jim Fouratt, Foster Gunnison, Jr., Karla Jay, Sylvia Ray Rivera, and Craig Rodwell. I sent the completed manuscript to all six to check for factual inaccuracies, and listened carefully to their occasional disagreement with this or that emphasis —but all understood that finally I could not surrender to them the authorial responsibility to interpret the evidence. Unless otherwise noted (which happens with some frequency), all the quotations in this book are from the transcripts of those taped interviews with my six subjects, together totaling several hundred hours; I'm alerting the reader here to the source of most of the quotations in order to avoid having to make repetitive citations throughout the book itself.

I have also been fortunate in being allowed to use several major archival collections still in private hands. In this regard, I am especially indebted to Foster Gunnison, Jr., and William B. Kelley. My ability to tell the story of the pre-Stonewall political movement in some detail has largely hinged on having access to those two extraordinary collections. In addition, the rich International Gay Information Center (IGIC) Papers—formerly known as the Hammond-Eves Collection— in the New York Public Library Manuscript Division has recently been processed and contains invaluable records and correspondence.

All of this material has proven to be so fresh and informative that

I have paused at certain points in the book to convey it. But not, I hope, paused too long; wherever I felt the documentary details threatened to overwhelm the narrative and convert the book into a traditional monograph, I have relegated them to the (sometimes lengthy) footnotes—which I have in turn relegated to the back of the book.

I am grateful to a number of people (other than the six subjects themselves) who allowed me to tape-record their recollections and thereby flesh out a number of critical points in the narrative: Martin Boyce, Nick Browne, Ryder Fitzgerald, Robert Heide, Robert Kohler, Sascha L., Thomas Lanigan-Schmidt, Chuck Shaheen, Jim Slaven, Gregory Terry, Joe Tish, and Ivan Valentin. I am also indebted to Steven Watson for providing me with tapes and transcripts of interviews he did in the late seventies with Marsha P. Johnson, Minette, Sylvia Ray Rivera, and Holly Woodlawn.

For assorted other favors, source materials, encouragement and leads, I'm grateful to Mariette Pathy Allen, Desmond Bishop, Mimi Bowling, Renée Cafiero, Barry Davidson, Richard Dworkin, Dan Evans, Barbara Gittings, Eric Gordon, Erica Gottfried, Liddell Jackson, Marty Jezer, Kay "Tobin" Lahusen, Tom McGovern, Joan Nestle, Duncan Osborne, Jim Owles, Gabriel Rotello, Vito Russo, Bebe Scarpi, Bree Scott-Hartland, La Vaughan Slaven, Mark Thompson, Jack Topchik, Jeffrey Van Dyke, Paul Varnell, Bruni Vega, Rich Wandel, Fred Wasserman, and Thomas Waugh. For the Stonewall chapter, I am indebted to Dolly and Leo Scherker for permission to consult materials that their son, Michael, had gathered for a planned oral history of the Stonewall riots that was tragically aborted by his premature death. I have included only a few brief remarks from Scherker's interviews (so cited in each instance in the accompanying footnote), but hearing in full his twenty or so tapes has broadly informed my own work.

Finally, my manuscript has greatly benefited from the careful readings Jolanta Benal, Matthew Carnicelli, John D'Emilio, Frances Goldin, Arnie Kantrowitz, William B. Kelley, and Eli Zal gave it; their cogent responses caused me to rethink any number of sections in the narrative. The pioneer activist Jim Kepner—whose encyclopedic knowledge of the gay movement is unrivaled—provided me with a detailed, incisive commentary that saved me from error and deepened my understanding at many points. I have also been extremely fortunate to have had Arnold Dolin of NAL/Dutton as the

book's editor and Frances Goldin as its agent. Both have guided *Stonewall* through its various incarnations with the dedication and skill for which they are already well known.

Finally, to my partner, Eli Zal—to whom this book is dedicated—I owe the priceless gift of sustained, loving support.

P R E F A C E

"Stonewall" is *the* emblematic event in modern lesbian and gay history. The site of a series of riots in late June–early July 1969 that resulted from a police raid on a Greenwich Village gay bar, "Stonewall" has become synonymous over the years with gay resistance to oppression. Today, the word resonates with images of insurgency and self-realization and occupies a central place in the iconography of lesbian and gay awareness. The 1969 riots are now generally taken to mark the birth of the modern gay and lesbian political movement —that moment in time when gays and lesbians recognized all at once their mistreatment and their solidarity. As such, "Stonewall" has become an empowering symbol of global proportions.

Yet remarkably—since 1994 marks the twenty-fifth anniversary of the Stonewall riots—the actual story of the upheaval has never been told completely, or been well understood. We have, since 1969, been trading the same few tales about the riots from the same few accounts—trading them for so long that they have transmogrified into simplistic myth. The decades preceding Stonewall, moreover, continue to be regarded by most gays and lesbians as some vast neolithic wasteland—and this, despite the efforts of pioneering historians like Allan Bérubé, John D'Emilio and Lillian Faderman to fill in the landscape of those years with vivid, politically astute personalities.

The time is overdue for grounding the symbolic Stonewall in empirical reality and placing the events of 1969 in historical context. In attempting to do this, I felt it was important *not* to homogenize

experience to the point where individual voices are lost sight of. My intention was to embrace precisely what most contemporary historians have discarded: the ancient, essential enterprise of *telling human stories*. Too often, in my view, professional historians have yielded to a "sociologizing" tendency that reduces three-dimensional lives to statistical cardboard—and then further distances the reader with a specialized jargon that *claims* to provide greater cognitive precision but serves more often to seal off and silence familiar human sounds.

I have therefore adopted an unconventional narrative strategy in the opening sections of this book: the recreation of half a dozen lives with a particularity that conforms to no interpretative category but only to their own idiosyncratic rhythms. To focus on particular stories does not foreclose speculation about patterns of behavior but does, I believe, help to ensure that the speculation will reflect the actual disparities of individual experience. My belief in the irreducible specialness of each life combines with a paradoxical belief in the possibility that lives, however special, can be shared. It is, if you like, a belief in democracy: the importance of the individual, the commonality of life.

For the six portraits in the book, I have deliberately chosen people whose stories were in themselves absorbing odysseys, and yet could at the same time speak to other gay men and lesbians. Jim Fouratt's struggles to remain within the Catholic Church, for example, or to gain entrance into the world of the New York theater, do not *duplicate* anyone else's religious or artistic experiences, yet should prove sufficiently similar to illustrate them broadly. Yvonne Flowers's ambivalence, as a black woman, about white lesbian bars, is not *precisely* anyone else's reaction to the bar scene, yet will be familiar enough to many to call out comparable feelings in them.

The six people I ultimately decided to profile seemed to "fit" well together. Their stories were different enough to suggest the diversity of gay and lesbian lives, yet interconnected enough to allow me to interweave their stories when, in the second half of the book, the historical canvas broadens out into the Stonewall riots, gay politics, and the first Christopher Street Liberation Day March.

This is not to say that these six lives represent all possible variations on gay and lesbian experience in the Stonewall period. To only *begin* to enumerate the many absent possibilities, these stories say nothing about rural or village, Chicano- or Italian- or Asian-American gay lives—nor anything about what it was or is like to be a gay postman, a lesbian pharmacist, a bisexual pop star. No group of six

could possibly represent the many pathways of gay and lesbian existence. But they can suggest some of the significant childhood experiences, adult coping strategies, social and political activities, values,
perceptions and concerns that centrally characterized the Stonewall
generation.

If the first sections of this book, with their focus on individual
lives, are designed to make past experience more directly accessible
than is common in a work of history, they are decidedly not designed
as "popularized" history—by which is usually meant the slighting of
historical research or the compromising of historical accuracy. My
emphasis on personality might legitimately be called novelistic but,
in contrast to the novelist, I have tried to restrict invention and remain
faithful to known historical fact. As in my previous books, I have
searched diligently for previously unknown or unused primary source
materials (and have been lucky enough to have found them in abundance), and have scrupulously adhered to scholarly criteria for eval-
uating evidence. Just as dull, abstract prose is no guarantee of
reliability, so lively human representation is no indicator of slovenly
scholarship.

My hope is that the focus on individuals and on narrative will
increase the ability of readers to identify—some with one story, some
with another—with experiences different from, but comparable to,
their own. I know of no other way to make the past *really* speak to
the present. And gay men and lesbians—so long denied any history
—have a special need and claim on historical writing that is at once
accurate *and* accessible.

MARTIN DUBERMAN
October 1992

T H E   C A S T

CRAIG RODWELL: Raised in a Chicago school for troubled boys, he arrived in New York as a teenager, emerged as a radical figure in the Mattachine Society, opened the Oscar Wilde Memorial Bookstore and spearheaded the first Christopher Street Liberation Day March.

YVONNE FLOWERS: The only African-American child attending an all-white grade school in New Rochelle in 1942, she grew up to become a jazz fanatic, a devotee of nightlife, an occupational therapist and teacher, and one of the founders of Salsa Soul Sisters.

KARLA JAY: Born in Flatbush and a graduate of Barnard, she joined the feminist collective the Redstockings, as well as the Gay Liberation Front, subsequently completed a doctorate in comparative literature, authored a number of books and earned a full professorship.

SYLVIA (RAY) RIVERA: Hustling on Times Square at age 11, she became a street transvestite, a fixture in the Times Square area, a fearless defender of her sisters, and the founder of STAR—Street Transvestite Action Revolutionaries.

JIM FOURATT: Brought up in Rhode Island, a teenager of precocious intelligence, he joined and left the priesthood, became a New York actor, hipster, antiwar protestor, and a major spokesperson for the countercultural Yippie movement.

FOSTER GUNNISON, JR.: The privileged scion of a wealthy yet emotionally distant family, he forsook business and academic careers, plunged into the pre-Stonewall homophile movement, became its archivist, and helped plan the first Christopher Street Liberation Day March.

GROWING UP

CRAIG

Marion Rodwell had been reluctantly boarding out her young son, Craig, during the week. Divorced and working in Chicago as a low-paid secretary, Marion hadn't known what else to do; she couldn't afford to stay home and she didn't have enough money to hire a competent baby-sitter. For several years, Craig lived during the week—Marion reclaiming him on weekends—with Mrs. Ryberg, a kindly woman who took in a number of neighborhood children. As soon as he was old enough, Mrs. Ryberg gave him chores to do, including the job of kneading yellow coloring into the margarine to make it look more like butter (this was wartime, with butter unavailable). Craig liked Mrs. Ryberg so much that he hadn't minded the work, though it was strenuous and he was little more than a toddler.

But when Craig was five, Marion decided he should be in a more stimulating environment, and she turned to an inexpensive day-care center on Chicago's North Side. But it quickly became apparent that the low rates reflected the minimal individual attention given. Marion felt at her wit's end when a Mrs. Merkle, who sometimes worked at the day care center and had taken a shine to Craig, told her that she would board the boy full-time if Marion would pay her a small sum each week. Marion agreed, hoping Mrs. Merkle would be able to give Craig the daily affection and attention he needed.

Attention he got, but very little affection. Mrs. Merkle also took in laundry to piece out an income, and she put Craig to work running sheets and towels through a mangle, watching hawk-eyed to make

sure the five-year-old didn't slack off. Craig worked in constant terror of getting his fingers caught in the mangle, and he soon grew to hate Mrs. Merkle. But she found the arrangement profitable and began to play with the idea of adopting Craig as her own son (or indentured servant). Word of Mrs. Merkle's intention reached Marion and threw her into a panic. Mrs. Merkle had a husband, and Marion feared the courts might equate that with "having a stable home." Desperate, she confided in her boss. A devout Christian Scientist, he had connections with the church-affiliated Chicago Junior School for "problem" boys, and before long he had arranged for Craig to be admitted there free of charge.

Craig never forgot that fall day in 1947 when his mother drove him out to Chicago Junior. At age six, he didn't entirely understand what was happening to him, but his fright was palpable. The school was located some fifty miles outside of Chicago, set deep in the country between the towns of Dundee and Elgin. A complex of old, marginally maintained buildings, Chicago Junior was surrounded by woods and sealed off by a chain-link fence. Before leaving Craig off, Marion did her best to comfort him, assuring her son that with some forty other boys as playmates, he would be happy at the school. She promised that she would unfailingly come to see him on the third Sunday of every month, the only day visitors were allowed on the grounds.

But Craig had not been reassured. During his first month at the school, he cried himself to sleep every night. And every morning at breakfast, he threw up the unfamiliar hot cereal. A housemother cured him of the crying by sternly lecturing him about how unhappy his mother would be should she learn of his "bad" behavior. Another housemother cured him of the vomiting by picking him up by the neck from the breakfast table, marching him into the bathroom and forcing him to stand over the toilet and *eat* the vomit.

The housemothers came in two basic varieties: the stern ones who mechanically kept to the rules (and kept the boys at arms' length), and the warm surrogate mothers. Mrs. Wilkins, the music teacher, who doubled as a substitute housemother, quickly became Craig's favorite. The students lived in three dormitories, twelve to fifteen boys in each, and a housemother slept in a small room adjoining each dorm. Whenever Mrs. Wilkins was in charge, she let the boys do pretty much as they liked—make noise, and stay up past their bedtime—and usually refrained from checking up on them in the middle of the night.

She would also read them stories. Craig had two favorites. One

was about a pair of boys who wanted to be brothers so badly, they pricked each other's fingers and formed a "blood bond." The other was "The Happy Prince." As Craig retells that story, it took place in a poor middle-European city that had a richly jeweled statue of Prince Somebody or Other in its main square. One day, a pigeon sitting on the Prince's shoulder noticed that a tear had formed in his eye. When the bird asked the Prince why he was unhappy, the Prince explained that the people in the city were starving because of poor crops, and he urged the pigeon to take the emerald embedded in his eye and sell it to buy the people food.

On and on the story went: The Prince would cry, would encourage the pigeon to sell the diamonds on his sword handle, the rubies on his breastplate—and so on—to provide coal for the people's stoves, warm clothing to put on their backs—and so on. At the story's close, all the jewels are gone, but the Prince is happy in the knowledge that the people no longer suffer. Craig adored the story and contended in later years that it had taught him important lessons about the need to share worldly goods with those less fortunate. (He also learned in later years that the story was written by Oscar Wilde.)

There were only two men on staff at the Chicago Junior School. One was Mr. Lazarus, who had himself been a student there and who in summer months would take some of the boys out for a midnight swim in the ancient concrete pool on the grounds and then astonish them by diving underwater, pulling off his bathing suit, and letting his ass shine naked in the moonlight. No one, so far as Craig knew, was ever invited to touch it.

The only other man at the school was its superintendent, the hated Mr. Kilburn. He enjoyed pitting the boys against each other in competition for his favor and each night would award the most "deserving" student the supreme honor of carrying a huge dinner tray to him and his wife in their apartment on the top of the classroom building; the bearer's reward was a Baby Ruth candy bar. Craig never once got to carry the tray. For after getting over his initial fright and settling into the school's routines, he had quickly become something of a rebel—the boy who challenged authority and "sassed" back.

That would alone have earned Kilburn's dislike. What intensified it was his conviction that Craig was a sissy. Two hours of sports were mandated at Chicago Junior for every student every day of the year. Craig, as the tallest boy in his group, was good at basketball, but inept in baseball—scandalously so, in Kilburn's view. Deciding he would teach Craig how to throw the baseball "like a real boy," Kilburn

made him trudge a mile to the baseball field after dinner each night to get the appropriate coaching.

What convinced Kilburn that Craig's prospects in life were dim was his discovery that Craig had been sending away for autographed pictures of movie stars, had managed to collect several dozen, and—scandalously, again—had been sharing them with the other boys. Kilburn promptly confiscated the collection and thereafter opened all of Craig's incoming mail to make sure it contained no offending material. To underscore the horrendous nature of Craig's crime, Kilburn meted out his favorite punishment: Craig was given "one hundred burdock"—that is, assigned to dig up a hundred of the burdock plants that dotted the grounds; the burdock had long, deep roots, and to kill it one had to laboriously dig out every last piece.

This was but one of several Dickensian features of the school. Corporal punishment, including paddling, was commonplace; one teacher's favorite method was to beat offending students with an electric cord. The boys themselves did almost all the work on the place, keeping up the grounds, helping in the kitchen, serving the food. They marched in formation to meals in the dining hall, had to sit on the front part of their chairs to keep their backs stiff, and during breakfast were forbidden to speak. Strictly enforced prayer sessions began with Bible study at five A.M. and were reinforced periodically throughout the day, even during football huddles. When Craig didn't understand something in the Bible, or in the writings of Mary Baker Eddy, which the boys were also made to study, he would raise his hand and say so. Most of the teachers treated this as a form of defiance. They sternly warned Craig that he was being "difficult," and his reputation as a rebellious child spread.

The draconian spirit at Chicago Junior produced a variety of bans. No incoming phone calls were permitted; the one phone on the place was locked up in the laundry room. Entertainment consisted of an occasional bonfire in fall and an occasional swim in summer, plus carefully monitored television once a week (the boys were allowed to watch only *I Remember Mama* and Sid Caesar's *Your Show of Shows*, and the set was turned off during commercials for fear the cigarette and beer ads might prove too appealing). And any boy being punished for any reason was automatically denied his monthly visiting day—which meant Craig sometimes didn't get to see Marion for months at a time.

Among the boys' few diversions were occasional square dances, which they would perform for the Evanston Women's Club and other

local groups as a fund-raising device. Half the boys would dress in regular clothes, and the other half would don little skirts and halters, which the housemothers had sewn for them. As a reward for the performance, each boy would be given a stocking filled with candy, fruit, and pennies.

There was also a Halloween party every year in the gym. The housemothers would again make costumes for the boys; one year Craig went as a fat lady, with a pillow stuck under his dress and lipstick smeared on his face. (When the boys lined up to have Craig give them kiss marks on the cheek, Mr. Kilburn ordered a halt.) The thirteen-year-old seniors were taken into the town of Elgin once a month to learn the fox-trot and the waltz—though the boys viewed this as punishment, not entertainment.

Despite these rigors, Craig was happier than not during his seven years at the Chicago Junior School and retains "wonderful, vivid memories" of the place. They center, not surprisingly, on the intensely emotional, sometimes erotic friendships that developed among the boys themselves.

Craig's first crush, when he was seven, was on an older boy (aged eight) named Bob Palmer. Bob's talented piano playing made him something of a school star and Craig "just worshiped" him. Epiphany came on a cold winter night. In the freezing, drafty dorms each boy kept an extra blanket at the foot of his bed, and Craig awoke one morning to discover that his blanket had been pulled up over him. He "just knew" Bob Palmer had done it, had gotten up in the middle of the night to make sure his little friend was warm.

Craig was the first boy in his age group to reach puberty, and in the showers the others never tired of staring in amazement at his emerging pubic hair. Harry, a slightly older boy, moved matters to the next logical stage. He took Craig out to one of the gigantic oak trees in the woods that the boys (disobeying the rules) loved to climb, and when they were standing at the top of the tree, he unzipped Craig's pants and said he was going to show him something. Craig immediately got a roaring hard-on and Harry masturbated him. To Craig's astonishment, "white stuff" flew out of his penis, great gobs of it covering his jeans—followed by panic over how to explain the stains to his housemother. Craig and Harry finally concocted a tale about "finding a can of white paint while playing in the woods."

Not all the boys were as winning as Harry. Chicago Junior, was, after all, a school for "disturbed" youth, and a few of the boys really did have problems beyond being overweight or having rejecting par-

ents. When Ted invited Craig for a romp in the woods, the scenario moved quickly beyond white paint: Ted wanted to stick a pin up the opening in Craig's penis. Craig had the good sense to jump up and run. Ted tried to give chase, but he was a large, clumsy boy and Craig easily outdistanced him. Eventually Ted was sent to St. Charles, the nearby state reformatory. "We're going to send you to St. Charles" was a standard threat at Chicago Junior, though one infrequently carried out.

Most of the sex play among the boys involved kissing and masturbation, though "cornholing" was known to happen, and oral sex was frequent enough for rumors of it to reach Mr. Kilburn. He at once convened an assembly—always a weighty event at the school— to express his indignation over rumors that boys were "inserting their penises into other boys' mouths." He demanded that each boy submit a statement to him, declaring whether he had or had not ever committed that mortal sin.

Craig had deeply internalized the Christian Science notion that "truth is power and that truth is the greatest good," and he forthrightly declared in his statement that he had indeed engaged in the forbidden behavior. Worse, his tone was not defensive and he made no apology. Yet to his surprise, Kilburn did not punish him, even though some of the boys who confessed *were* put to pulling burdock or breaking up rocks. Craig supposes that Kilburn had already written him off as hopeless—after all, he had been the only person in the school to favor Stevenson over Eisenhower in the 1952 election—and was probably afraid Craig would make even more trouble if punished. The episode confirmed Craig's belief—which was to be central in his life—that "telling the truth" was in the end always the best policy.

The boys, of course, went right on having sex with each other. Not everybody participated, but none of them looked askance at the activity. Intense friendships and frequent touching were so integral to the special environment they inhabited as to seem utterly natural; even the nonsexual boys would walk back and forth to the dining hall unself-consciously holding hands. Occasionally a housemother would tell them they "shouldn't" do that, which made Craig aware for the first time that some people regarded his feelings as wrong—infuriating him, even at that early age.

The boys generally ignored "spinsterish" injunctions, and as soon as the lights under the housemother's door went out at night, they would jump into each other's beds. According to Craig, there was "no sense of shame about it and we always knew and talked about

who was going with whom." Craig had sex with nearly half the boys in his own class of ten; several of them, in later years, did self-identify as gay.

In seventh grade, when he was eleven, Craig got himself a "steady." He and Tony were passionately in love, but only incidentally sexual—kisses, massages, and hand-holding were about the sum of it. But they spent as much time together as possible; if Craig had dishwashing duty after dinner, Tony would wait for him outside the hall so they could walk back to their dorm together.

One day, daringly, the two boys decided to play hooky. Both were avid baseball fans—Craig adored the Chicago Cubs, Tony the Milwaukee Braves. When they learned that the Cubs and Braves were due to play a doubleheader against each other at Chicago's Wrigley Field, they decided they *had* to go, and Tony somehow got hold of enough money to buy them train tickets to Chicago. They planned to stay for only the first game so that they could get back to the school before dark and not be missed. But once the excitement got hold of them in Wrigley Field, they forgot about their resolution and stayed till the doubleheader was over. That meant catching a late train that stopped a full three miles from the school. They walked the distance in the dark along the scary railroad tracks and, to keep up their courage and to avoid falling between the trestles, held hands the whole way.

When they arrived at the dorm at eleven that night, Mr. Kilburn was waiting for them, "just livid." The boys tried to prove how responsible they'd been by telling Kilburn they had carefully held hands during the entire three-mile walk. Mrs. Kilburn, who was present for the interrogation, said something snide about "faggots," and Craig and Tony were not only punished but split up into different dorms. That might have been bearable, except that Tony, soon after, abruptly stopped speaking to Craig and acted as if he no longer existed. Tony never did explain why, but Craig surmised it had something to do with having been frightened by the accusation of "faggot." The rejection deeply upset—and puzzled—Craig for many years thereafter.

Y V O N N E

Yvonne's mother set her jaw, and the family knew that one more immovable decision had been reached: the youngest of two daughters, Yvonne (generally called "Chickie") would *not* go to the segregated Lincoln Elementary School, but rather to the all-white Daniel Webster Grammar School. In 1942, blacks were not expected, not in New Rochelle, New York, any more than in the South, to make militant demands. But Theo Flowers had never let herself be guided by timid counsels. She had joined the Communist party nearly a decade earlier, impressed by the role it had played in defending the Scottsboro Boys—those nine hapless black youths falsely accused of raping two white women in 1931—and convinced that no other political group gave a damn about black people. She was far too independent ever to become a dutiful party functionary, yet she was never shy about acknowledging her political sympathies. When New Rochelle passed an ordinance requiring Communists to register, Theo, not about to deny her affiliation, marched down to the town hall and registered.

So when Theo said no to the segregated Lincoln School, her ten-year-old daughter, Yvonne, though "a nervous wreck" at the likely amount of high-volume public anger that lay ahead, felt certain that the New Rochelle authorities had already lost the battle. After all, her very birth had been successfully contested; because Theo had refused to deliver in a hospital that practiced overt discrimination, Yvonne had been born in the nearby Mount Vernon Hospital rather than in New Rochelle.

The school board tried to thwart Theo by redrawing district lines so that the street on which the Flowers family lived would fall outside the Daniel Webster School zone. But Theo brought formal charges of gerrymandering and won her case in court. And so, just as Yvonne had anxiously predicted, she took her place in the fifth grade class at Daniel Webster in the fall of 1942. (Nearly twenty years later, in 1961, the New Rochelle school system became the site of the North's first court-ordered desegregation, at which time a Federal judge ordered the closing of Lincoln Elementary, with its 94 percent black student population. That order was resisted for two more years, but

in 1963 a new school board ordered Lincoln razed and its students bused elsewhere.)

Yvonne was the only black child attending Daniel Webster in 1942, but she already knew many of her classmates from the neighborhood and never felt harassed or even isolated while at Webster. Yet despite her friends and her obvious intelligence, Yvonne never became an A student. Later in life she would recall the teacher who told her that she was "a C student and would always be so," and that she should never think of anything so out of her league as a college education. "On some level, I believed her," Yvonne says, and describes herself as an "underachiever" throughout her life.

Yet she ascribes that, overall, less to racism than to the intimidating effect of growing up with a high-powered mother she felt unable to measure up to. For Theo Flowers not only was politically aware, but also spoke five languages, read voraciously, had had a promising concert career as a singer of German lieder (a bout with tuberculosis forced her to give up singing), and was something of a local "griot" —a wise woman—consulted for political advice and courted for support throughout the city of New Rochelle.

Many of the black people in town were related, being descended from two large families that had settled there generations ago. And in the thirties and forties, a village atmosphere still prevailed. The goat man and his herd came down Yvonne's block twice a week, and the vegetable sellers and fish peddlers even more frequently. Almost all the blacks in New Rochelle knew one another, so when Theo went to the store on Saturday morning, the family knew not to expect her back until late in the day; everybody had to talk to her about something, and a cup of coffee or a drink could go on for hours.

Theo also loved to party. Indeed, it wasn't illness alone that had ended her singing career, but also an unwillingness to make the necessary sacrifices or endure the needed discipline. She had been attracted to her first husband, Yvonne's father, in part because, as a boxer (his brother was Bruce Flowers, a well-known fighter in the twenties and thirties), he lived a fast-lane life—so fast-lane that he died of alcoholism when Yvonne was four.

Theo's second husband, with whom Yvonne grew up, managed bars and always had a bottle of scotch nearby. He was an easygoing man, a life-of-the-party type who knew how to keep everybody laughing. He did sympathize with Theo's political views, and especially her blunt pro-black stance, and at dinner the family conversation often revolved around what President Roosevelt had said that day and what

the impact was likely to be on black people. But he lacked Theo's dynamism and felt awed, sometimes overwhelmed, by her energy. Theo was unquestionably the dominant figure in the house and her husband knew better than to try to curtail her. When her love of gambling sometimes kept her out at the neighbors all night playing poker (or "pokino," the local favorite), he might pace the floor and fret—but he refrained from walking the two blocks to tell her to come home.

Theo's own parents were scandalized at their daughter's independent views on religion. They had both come from devout homes in the border states, and together ran a restaurant in Yonkers. (Cooking had long been a family specialty: Yvonne's great-grandfather and great-granduncle had been cooks in the U.S. Navy at the turn of the century.) Theo's mother was an ardent Catholic who practiced African spiritualism on the side, and her father was a devout Baptist. They had compromised by bringing Theo up Episcopalian, but could never compromise over her secularist bent as an adult; they refused to accept the Sunday morning habit in the Flowers home of listening to the famed Wings Over Jordan Choir on the radio as a legitimate equivalent for going to church.

At their insistence, Theo agreed to send Yvonne to Sunday school, but her own secularism rubbed off on the child. When it came time, at age twelve, for her baptism, Yvonne—who had also inherited her mother's independent spirit—refused to go through with it because she "didn't believe." But unlike Theo, confirmed in her secularism by her radical-minded friends, Yvonne felt deeply troubled at her lack of belief and the way it isolated her from her dutifully baptized peers. She talked with her minister, who showed annoyance at her stubborn insistence on *understanding* the Creation and at her confessed discomfort at going on her knees to Jesus, a white man. It wasn't until her mid-twenties that Yvonne would finally find the compatible God she had long sought.

She was equally stubborn about her sexuality. Entering high school in 1946 at age fourteen, she quickly acquired a steady boyfriend. They loved each other and stayed together throughout the four years of high school, but when Yvonne was fifteen and he sixteen and they attempted to have sex, she said he was "too big" and the act went unconsummated. Since he was also her best friend, she confided to him that she had felt erotically attracted to other girls from an early age—could remember standing in front of a mirror at age six or seven

and defiantly shouting that "when I get grown, I am going to have all the girlfriends I want to have."

She didn't have to wait that long. While still in her early teens, she started to "mess around" with a friend of her mother's, a beautiful woman who looked like Lena Horne. Though Theo had a number of gay friends in her sophisticated circle, and though Yvonne had always felt able to confide in her mother, she kept the affair a secret. Yet in a more general way, she did try to tell her family about her attraction to women. Indeed, she was no more than twelve or thirteen when she abruptly announced it one night at the dinner table.

Her family's reaction was the equivalent of "pass me the peas" —as if she hadn't said anything at all. She next tried putting the news in a letter, which she read aloud at the dinner table. Again, nobody said a word, as if they hadn't heard her. It was only years later, after Yvonne had left home, that she and her mother finally talked openly about her sexuality. Theo accepted her daughter's insistence that she was lesbian once she understood that it wasn't going to keep her from getting an education or having a career, wasn't going to stop her from having "plans and dreams." In Yvonne's view, much of the homophobia that exists in the black community is a function of middle-class aspirations, and the taking on of the narrow values of that class. Theo had a radical's disdain for mere assimilation and scorned white bourgeois provincialism. Her politics of inclusion made it necessary for her to accept and applaud differences of all kinds—though in regard to her own daughter's lesbianism, the best she could manage was tolerance.

Yvonne was no less precocious in her early obsession with jazz. She had grown up around music, but by age twelve had (abetted by Frank, a clerk in the New Rochelle record store who shared her zeal and fed it with weekly releases) developed her own special taste for bebop—for Dizzy Gillespie, Charlie Parker, Tadd Dameron and, above all, for Thelonious Monk. She tortured her family by playing her 78s over and over at top volume, until everyone knew every line on every Thelonious Monk record. By the time Yvonne was fifteen she had become so immersed in bebop and progressive jazz that she researched and wrote a ten-page "history of jazz." It was for her own edification, not to fulfill a school assignment.

It was also at fifteen that she persuaded "Aunt" Janet, one of her mother's hell-raising friends, to take her to the New York City jazz clubs—the Royal Roost, Birdland, and the other hangouts that dotted

Fifty-second Street, then the jazz mecca of the world. Yvonne had had her first drink at twelve, and had quickly taken to it, but she never viewed the jazz clubs as places to party. She was one of those dead-serious fans who listen to music with such intensity that they become nearly oblivious to the drinking and seduction scenes taking place on the periphery. Nobody dared mess with her; she was there to *listen*. Later, when her particular favorite, Thelonious Monk, played at the Five Spot for two years, Yvonne became a fixture at the club. One night she went straight up to Monk and told him he was the only man she would ever marry. He gave her a silly, spaced-out smile.

K   A   R   L   A

Karla's parents told her that Jews were "the Chosen People" and the *goyim* were not to be trusted ("the minute something goes wrong, they'll turn around and call you a kike"). Such cultural assumptions aside, Abraham and Rhoda Jay saw themselves as, if anything, *anti*-religious. Abraham's grandfather, a tyrannical, ultra-orthodox rabbi, used to drag his grandson out of bed at four o'clock in the morning to help make a *minyan*. It turned Abraham off religion for the rest of his life, and Karla never remembers setting foot in a synagogue (the one time Abraham took his children to temple to experience a *seder*, the presiding Reform rabbi—to Abraham's chagrin—skipped the service). Karla knew she was Jewish, but had no real idea what that meant—"except that other kids had Christmas trees and we didn't."

When his two children were born, Abraham was so determined to avoid giving them traditional Old Testament names—indeed, he disliked his own name, preferring to be called Eddie—that he simply looked at the shipping schedule in the newspaper and chose from the list of ships arriving or departing. Fortunately for his daughter, a Danish freighter, the *Karla Dane*, was docking on the day she was born, so she was spared being called Lusitania for the rest of her life—or, God forbid, Queen Mary.

Abraham's mother, Becky, was the only grandparent Karla got to know at all well. Becky had come to the United States with her parents in the late nineteenth century to escape the pogroms in Russia. On their way across the Atlantic, their boat had sunk and they had

had to spend several days in a rowboat. The experience left Becky frightened of water for the rest of her life—and caused her to forget where precisely in Russia she had come from. Or so she claimed. For whatever reasons of her own, she refused to talk about the old country. She spent her life raising children and cooking food in the back of the saloon her husband owned.

Not that Karla ever learned much more about her mother's family. "It was like a wall of silence," Karla later said; "my parents never spoke about the past. They were very closemouthed." The sum of what she was told about her maternal grandmother was that she had been born in the United States; and about her grandfather, that he had been born in Austria and had run a fruit stand in Brooklyn before retiring.

And it was only as an adult that Karla discovered that her own exceedingly beautiful mother had had, as a teenager, a first marriage. Rhoda had fallen deeply in love with a fellow student at Erasmus Hall High School in Brooklyn; though told he had a "rheumatic heart" and only a short time to live, she had insisted on marrying him. In a desperate effort to save her young husband, Rhoda took him to Florida, where he soon died. To compound the tragedy, his family blamed her for his premature death.

For the rest of her life, Rhoda would be a deeply unhappy woman: frequently ill and barricaded in her room; known as quarrelsome and difficult. She waited until she was thirty to remarry and then chose Abraham, whom she did not love, because it seemed as if he would be a good provider. Abraham, at five feet two and nearly two hundred pounds ("He had been brought up on sour cream," Karla later quipped), wasn't physically attractive and, though forty, had never married. But he was a bright, jovial, good-tempered man, if inclined to be stubborn. (Stubbornness, Karla says, "is almost like a disease in my father's family.") Abraham was apparently in love with Rhoda but later, perhaps to cover his pain at the unhappy union, would joke that he had married her because she was thin and he had wanted to give his kids a fighting chance.

Abraham was a hard worker. He had dropped out of school at age twelve to help out in his father's saloon, had thereafter been a truck driver, and had then—at the time Rhoda met him—gone to work at his uncle's dunnage company on the docks. In those years, dunnage firms handled the bins and containers in which all overseas freight was shipped; Abraham's job was to count and haul lumber.

It was backbreaking work, and life on the docks could be dangerous —he was shot at least once—but his salary was enough to support his mother and two sisters.

He and Rhoda were married in 1942. Their son, Paul (Karla thinks maybe her father was reading a list of Christian saints on the day he chose her brother's name), was born in 1943. Karla was born four years later—during a blizzard that trapped her father and brother in a Long Island railroad car for twelve hours while her mother was in labor in a hospital (an ordeal that they all frequently reminded Karla of in later life). Neither parents nor siblings got along well. Karla insists that throughout their childhood her brother had precisely three expressions: "Shut up," "Drop dead," and "Get out of my room."

Abraham and Rhoda were more talkative—or rather, argumentative—with each other, but not much more friendly. They dealt with each other primarily through evasion (a childhood friend of Karla's reports that all she can remember of Rhoda is a closed door). With Rhoda taking to her bed for long stretches and Abraham working seven days a week on the docks (though he was decidedly interested in his children when he *was* present), Karla might well have suffered severe emotional deprivation had it not been for the timely appearance of Nene.

Nene (a nickname her brothers and sisters had settled on when they couldn't pronounce "Lulubelle") was a black woman in her late twenties hired by the Jays as a live-in maid when Karla was four. Nene was married, but her husband was older, liked to drink, and could be abusive, so Nene (who had no children of her own) welcomed the live-in job. When she arrived, Karla was still sleeping in a crib, and she had a lot of trouble adjusting to the bed that Nene now insisted on. But Karla had no trouble at all getting used to Nene herself. She was a warm-hearted, loving human being of immense goodwill, with a wonderful sense of humor, a great smile, and a happy laugh. Nene, unlike Rhoda, was never depressed—indeed, she was the only person who could get along with Rhoda, which she accomplished by simply shrugging at her angry outbursts. Small and slim, Nene was agile and energetic, but always slowed her quick pace so that young Karla could keep up without effort. Nene became, in essence, Karla's primary parent.

Nene's passion was baseball. At every possible opportunity, she would take Karla to Ebbets Field to watch the Dodgers play (Paul rarely came along; he was a sickly child, afflicted with asthma). The first thing Karla remembers reading is baseball scorecards, which she

and Nene (who couldn't read well) would pore over. Karla loved
Ebbets Field more for the peanuts than for the baseball, but she was
a good-natured, uncomplaining child who felt absolutely content as
long as she could be with Nene. "It never occurred to me as a small
child," Karla would later say, "that I was not going to grow up black
like Nene. It never occurred to me that we were different. I did get
some strange looks, though, after I started elementary school. I
sounded like the only black kid in an all-white school."

Karla was also lucky in having a wonderful aunt (by marriage)
living two houses away from the Jays in Flatbush. Aunt Betty, nick-
named Queenie, had been a vaudeville singer, had married several
times, cursed like a truck driver, told dirty jokes, had a raucous sense
of humor, and sang at all the family gatherings—usually accompanied
by her dachshund, Judy. Queenie had no patience with the notion of
a woman learning her proper, antiseptically limited, place. Not only
did she drive a car—which was then highly unorthodox for a
woman—but she played touch football with the boys in the street,
and thought nothing of jumping in to rescue Paul when, as happened
often, he fell prey to the other kids in the neighborhood. Betty was,
like Nene, a rescuer by nature—and Paul and Karla needed all the
help they could get.

If Karla took her optimistic good nature from Nene, she showed,
like Queenie, an early impatience with traditional female roles. As
far back as she can remember, Karla was called a tomboy. Queenie
told her that she had been a tomboy, too, and to pay the label no
mind. But everybody else kept nervously reassuring Karla that she
would "outgrow it." Many years would pass before she would be able
to define fully what "it" was, but what Karla knew early on was that
she would rather be playing punchball with the boys in the street
than jumping rope or playing house with the little girls.

Karla's mother was decidedly disappointed in her. Though ill
and withdrawn during much of Karla's childhood, Rhoda would rouse
herself to clean the house (obsessively, over and over: "Jewish
women," Queenie would sardonically say, "cleaned as a substitute for
sex"); to prepare an occasional gourmet meal (Nene usually did the
cooking); to play an occasional game of canasta; and, above all, to
shop. Rhoda liked dressing well almost as much as she liked a good
bargain, and with a true shopper's fanaticism would return over and
over again to Loehmann's famed bargain store to watch hawk-eyed
until the price fell to the lowest possible level. She later admitted that
she spent money to get back at her husband, whose earnings had

begun to slip. Along with buying herself clothes, Rhoda would periodically bring home pretty little Ginny or Barbie dolls for Karla, and a proper doll carriage to carry them around in.

Karla wouldn't go near the dolls. But nothing could discourage Rhoda from continually adding to the collection, not even the insistent way Karla would unceremoniously dump the dolls from the carriage and install her beloved, battered teddy bear in their stead. Her best (and lifelong) friend, Jessica, on the other hand, adored the dolls and good-natured, generous Karla let her play with them to her heart's content. That annoyed Rhoda still more. "She simply couldn't see from behind her own eyes," Karla later said. "She saw this child she wanted to have. This child was not me."

If Karla's tomboyishness alienated her mother, it did not isolate Karla in the neighborhood; the role, she later recalled, "wasn't all that unacceptable"—in Flatbush, anyway. Her cheerful nature helped make her popular. Though she was given to playing practical jokes and pranks, there was nothing malicious or mean-spirited about her. She would never hurt anyone intentionally, and she disliked physical fights; but if she never started one, Karla, who was strong and knew it, usually finished it. Her Flatbush neighborhood was essentially middle-class Irish, Italian, and Jewish, but it grew rougher as she grew older, and by the time she was ten she had joined one of the proliferating gangs as its sole female member. They used an abandoned shed behind a bakery as a clubhouse, and periodically fought other gangs in the neighborhood—but nobody then had guns, and serious injury was rare.

Though Karla preferred to run rather than fight, she did get into a fair number of brawls. She was once attacked by a group of girls and burned with cigarettes, and another time a girl ripped open the back of her leg with a compass. When one of the neighborhood boys hit her in the face, Karla smacked him back—and broke his jaw. When another little boy came after her, she got him in a leg lock and cracked several of his ribs. Her disposition was friendly, but from an early age, Karla proved a tough, stoic little kid, a determined survivor.

Karla's athletic ability also contributed to her acceptance, especially since her skill was marred by clumsiness. She was good enough at running and at punchball to join the boys in the street, yet a puzzling lack of depth perception made her terrible at touch football and stickball; all this made her an accomplished, likeable klutz rather than an awesome superwoman. She fell down so often and got so many

scratches and cuts that her father at one point started good-naturedly calling her Stitch.

Most of her awkwardness was due to extreme nearsightedness that for a long time went undiagnosed; if she bumped into a wall, her parents simply ascribed it to her being "the worst clod who ever walked the earth." When she started public school in Brooklyn, she was given an eye test, but when the technician pointed to the chart and Karla said she couldn't see anything, it was thought that she was "clowning around again." That, combined with poor reading skills, got her put in a class for slow learners—a nightmare experience which lasted some four years and from which she barely escaped in time to make up for lost skills.

Her class of mostly delinquent, emotionally disturbed children (as adults, a number of them ended up in Dannemora prison) was considered unteachable. At the beginning of every day, the reluctant teacher assigned to them would put lists on the blackboard which the children were told to memorize; in one column were the characteristics of a "good citizen," such as cleanliness; in the other were those of a "bad citizen," with special emphasis on "communism."

The children were thought too stupid to learn their own names, so each was assigned a number. Karla's was 36. She became so used to responding to it that at home Nene could sometimes get her attention only by calling out "Thirty-six!" When it finally was discovered that Karla's vision was 12,000/300, and she won a transfer to a regular class, she found herself way behind the other kids. But once she did begin to read—as a fourth-grader—she turned to books avidly: Because of her nearsightedness, she had never developed any alternative interest in television.

Starting at age five, Karla was sent away summers to Camp Swatonah in the Catskills; Abraham thought it wise to give her a break from family squabbling. Rhoda was usually too ill to visit, but Nene and Abraham came up periodically to check on how Karla was doing. They needn't have worried. She took to camp immediately, never felt a twinge of homesickness, and went back happily every summer until she was twelve. She was mystified at the kids who would cry for their parents and mope miserably around the bunk. The only time Karla cried was at the end of the summer—when she had to go home.

She had terrible crushes on the female counselors. "It was my first awareness," she later said, "that I was gay," though at the time, of course, she lacked that descriptive vocabulary. The counselors were

mostly Southern teenagers with stark "duck" haircuts, and in retrospect Karla has little doubt that most of them were lesbian. All she knew at the time was that when she first saw these women, she said to herself, "I am more like them than I am like my mother or even Nene." "I knew I was different as a little kid, but when I saw these counselors I knew I was like them in some fundamental way. I had no words for it. I don't know whether I defined it as being athletic or what, but I felt an immediate identification with them."

But when—aggressive little kid that she was—Karla tried to crawl into their beds, she scared them half to death; they'd respond, at most, with an affectionate wrestle/cuddle before quickly kicking her out. Karla had better luck with her fellow campers. They were in and out of each other's beds constantly, and Karla was able to expand considerably on her growing knowledge of the female body and sex organs—knowledge she had begun to accrue at home by enticing the neighborhood girls to let her play doctor with her brother's toy medical kit.

But her happy summers at camp came to an end when her parents decided the money would be put to better use by enrolling Karla in private school. Her parents put a high value on the education they themselves had never had. After an older boy on the block got stabbed in the back at Walt Whitman Junior High School (where Karla was due to go), Abraham and Rhoda immediately enrolled her instead, as an eighth-grader, in the all-girl "Bromley Institute."* Bromley was as close to an upper-class finishing school as Brooklyn had to offer, and there were only twenty-eight students in Karla's class. Always quick to adjust, she took to the school from the start—and not simply because she now found herself in an all-female atmosphere.

R A Y

Ray was only three when it happened, but he remembers what was playing on the television set in the background (*Have Gun, Will Travel*), what his mother was wearing (a strapless turquoise dress) and

---

* Wherever names have been changed, quotation marks are used at first reference in order to indicate a pseudonym.

the brand of rat poison (JR). She mixed the poison into two glasses of milk, drank one herself, then put the other down in front of him and told him to swallow it. He tried to, but the taste was so bad he stopped after a few sips. His mother got angry; she poured sugar into the glass and again ordered him to drink. When he gagged, she impatiently took the glass out of his hand and drank it down herself. Then she went into the bathroom, came out a few minutes later with her makeup on, started to cry—and then suddenly ran out of the apartment to the neighbors'.

The next thing Ray remembers is the hospital: orderlies rushing to pump his stomach, his mother vomiting uncontrollably. She lingered for two days and then—aged twenty-two—died. When Ray saw her laid out at the funeral parlor, he figured she was sleeping, and Grandma Viejita told him that that was right. Later, at the cemetery, Viejita tried to throw herself into the open grave and had to be restrained.

For years afterward, she denied that her daughter had killed herself—until Ray finally confronted her with a truth he had long since accepted: "She killed herself and I know that!" Ray screamed at his grandmother. "I remember the look on her face when she was doing it! I remember everything. . . ." By then, ten-year-old Ray even had a theory as to why she had tried to take him with her: "Moms knew I would have to suffer a long life, and I would be completely different than anybody else."

Viejita took Ray and Sonia, his two-month-old sister, from their apartment in Spanish Harlem to live with her in Jersey City. Ray's natural father, José Rivera, had disappeared years ago; his mother's second husband, a drug dealer who had fathered Sonia, showed no interest in the children. José reappeared only once, when Ray was four. Viejita called him into the room one day, pointed to a stranger sitting there, and said, "This is your father." When José tried to kiss him, Ray yelled, "I don't have a father!" kicked him in the shins, and ran out of the apartment. José never came by again.

Nor did he ever send child support. Viejita (an affectionate term for "Old Lady") had to bring them up on her own. Born in Venezuela, she had raised her own daughter alone in New York—her Mexican husband having deserted her when she got pregnant. Now in her mid-forties and employed as a pieceworker at the Pickwick Mills factory, Viejita was lucky if she could bring home fifty dollars a week. Yet she did her determined best to keep the refrigerator full and clothes

on the children's backs—that is, until Sonia's father reappeared one day and took her off to live with a couple he knew who, like himself, were Puerto Rican.

Viejita was never the same. Sonia had reminded her of her own daughter, and that made the loss doubly devastating. After years of trying, she finally tracked down Sonia and her adopted family in Brooklyn. But when Viejita and Ray went there for dinner, the evening proved a disaster; annoyed that Sonia kept calling her adopted mother Mommy, Ray finally blurted out, "That's not your mother! You're my sister and you don't even know that! Your moms is dead!" Sonia's "mommy" politely ushered Viejita and Ray out the door. It was years before they were invited back again, and Viejita threatened Ray with death if he so much as mentioned the past. Ray managed to hold his tongue, and the day went off well. Thereafter, Viejita was occasionally allowed to visit, and she periodically sent Sonia gifts and money; but Ray never saw his sister again.

Viejita seemed to blame him for the separation. She told him he was a "troublemaker," that she had only wanted Sonia, not him. When he left a spot of dirt after cleaning the apartment, or when he failed to iron her blouse just so, she would beat him. Ray didn't doubt that Viejita loved him in her own way, but he turned increasingly to Sarah, an upstairs neighbor who had known his mother and was herself childless. Sarah would buy him little things that his grandmother couldn't afford, and she would listen to him talk about his unhappiness.

In 1958, when Ray was seven, Viejita fell ill and sent him off to St. Agnes, a Catholic home for boys. She felt well again within six months, but delayed bringing Ray back home until the nuns strongly recommended that she do so. But she didn't seem to want him around anymore and started to board him out on weekdays. She at first sent him to people she knew in the neighborhood and then, for a long stretch when he was nine, to Elisa, a Colombian friend whom Viejita had sponsored as an immigrant. Elisa and her husband lived in a nice house in Sea Cliff, Long Island—they were the only Hispanic family in the town—and they sent him to the local Catholic school. Elisa was good to Ray most of the time—as long as he meticulously completed the many chores she gave him—but when she got in "one of her moods," she would beat him for the slightest infraction, or for no reason at all, and not just with a belt but with a two-by-four plank. She also beat him on the day she invited him, aged ten, into her bed and he refused to go.

On weekends, holidays and during the summers, Ray would return to Viejita, who had moved to Manhattan's Lower East Side. She was never too happy about his return. The neighbors had begun to tease her about Ray's effeminacy, predicting he would soon be a full-fledged *maricón*. What they didn't know was that he had already, at age seven, had sex with his fourteen-year-old cousin—and by age ten was having sex regularly with a married man down the block.

Returning from the man's apartment one evening with hickeys on his neck, Ray couldn't understand why Viejita was staring at him so fixedly. At first he thought it must be his eyebrows again. He had taken to trying on Viejita's clothes when she wasn't home, sashaying around the house in padded bras and panties. Then one day he had gotten the idea to shave his eyebrows, but he had botched the job and had to paint them over with Viejita's eyebrow pencil. That night, completely forgetting, he had washed his face thoroughly and gone into the living room to say good night to his grandmother. "Where are your eyebrows?" Viejita had asked evenly. Faced with disaster, Ray had mumbled something about having lost them down the sink and had said he would go look for them. Viejita had held him fast, but to his surprise had not beaten him. She had quietly gotten out her eyebrow pencil and had repainted Ray's face.

But this time, seeing the hickeys on his neck, she was not so benign. Where did he get them? she demanded. Thinking fast but not exactly well, Ray said he got them from Millie, the girl down the hall. "She tried to attack me downstairs!" Sure, sure, said Viejita, try telling me another—and she hauled off and whacked him. "Next thing I know," she screamed, "you'll be hanging out with the rest of the *maricónes* on Forty-second Street!" It was not the first time Ray had heard Forty-second Street mentioned. When he, Viejita, and a group of neighbors from the block had passed the Times Square area on their way to Coney Island for the day, he had heard them make snide comments about the "fags" who hung out there. He had stored the information away, not yet fully understanding it, not quite ready to have a firsthand look.

But then more trouble developed at school. Ray had started wearing face makeup in the fourth grade, but for a couple of years nobody had seemed to notice, or care. (Nobody, that is, except for his fifth-grade teacher, a married man with eight children who had taken to driving Ray home from school and then one day had seduced him in the backseat.) Perhaps Ray's athletic abilities in track and gymnastics had given him some protective covering, for if he was effeminate, he

was also wiry and tough, widely known as someone you didn't mess with.

But in the sixth grade somebody did. He was skipping rope one day with the girls, and wearing what was then called "full face" makeup (eyeliner and mascara), when a classmate named Glen called him a faggot. Ray whirled on him—"You don't call *me* no faggot!"—and although Glen was two heads taller, beat him up right then and there in the playground. Called into the principal's office, Ray explained what Glen had said. "Now do I look like a faggot, Mr. Sloan?" Ray demanded—which took some bravado, since he was dressed in skintight pants and was still wearing makeup. Mr. Sloan, for whatever reasons of his own, agreed that Ray did not. He suspended Ray for a week—and Glen for a month.

But that marked the end of Ray's formal education. In 1962, at age eleven, tired of Viejita's beatings and the neighborhood mockery, he left home for good. He headed straight for Forty-second Street.

J I M

Jim's family life shifted so often before he was five years old that he ended up feeling he had no family at all. And he would later let stand some of the rumors that surrounded him about being the son of the chairman of the board of Pepsi-Cola (thus conveniently making Joan Crawford his stepmother), or about his father having been a circus performer. "Circus" is in fact an apt invention and metaphor for the emotional acrobatics that surrounded Jim's childhood.

His mother, Connie, ran away from a convent school in New Jersey when she was fifteen to live with thirty-five-year-old James. Fouratt, Jim's father. Connie and James never married: she refused to wed outside the Catholic Church, and he refused to wed in it. She left him after giving birth within a three-year period in the mid-forties to three boys (one of whom died in infancy); ever after, she deflected all questions about that period of her life.

When Connie, not yet eighteen, decided to leave James Fouratt and start over, she went to the state of Washington to live with her own mother, Florence. Descended from an upper-class French family, Florence, too, had early realized that her first marriage was a mistake, had divorced Connie's father (a butcher whom she accused of being

a drunk) and had quickly remarried. When Connie went to live with Florence, she left young Jim in New Jersey with James, telling the boy that she would be sending for him shortly.

But she and Florence soon concluded that leaving Jim with his father had been a mistake, that James might not later be willing to give the boy up. Deciding to take no chances, they concocted a kidnaping. Florence and her husband simply appeared one day when Jim was on his way home from school, and told him to get in the car. Since he knew his grandmother, he obliged; but later, safely resettled in Washington, he cried bitterly over the new puppy he had been forced to leave behind. It was only some thirty years later, in the seventies, that Jim reconnected with his father—briefly, since the hoped-for knight in shining armor turned out to be a bookie and an alcoholic, an ill, bigoted old man who lectured Jim about his "sick" values.

Connie's new life in Washington started well. Still young, and very attractive, she entered a state beauty contest—and won. Then it was discovered that she had two sons and had been "divorced" (to conceal Connie's nonmarriage, Florence had somehow arranged bogus divorce papers). Stripped of her crown, Connie nonetheless had a millionaire suitor to fall back on. That is, a conditional suitor: He wanted to marry her but refused to raise her children. Florence urged Connie to accept the proposal and offered to adopt the two boys herself—a solution that would not have sat well with Jim, who had developed considerable antipathy for his grandmother.

Just as Connie was agonizing over her options, her own father, whose second wife had recently died and left him with a daughter younger than Jim—is it any wonder that the confusions of Fouratt family history fed the need for plausible invention?—invited her to live with him in Rhode Island. Connie decided that was her way out, and, leaving the younger boy with her mother, she took Jim, now aged five, and understandably bewildered at yet another shift in the family configuration, to her father's house in East Providence.

He lived in a neighborhood that was basically working-class Irish-Portuguese-Italian, and strongly Catholic. (Connie herself, though a believer, only became devout later in life.) Within two years of moving in with her father, Connie married Bill Malone, a short-order cook, the son of an Irish cop and a telephone operator. In adulthood, Jim would come to think of his immediate family as having been dysfunctional—his mother doting on him more than on her husband.

But Connie and Bill tried to do well by him, pinching pennies to send him to a good (and as it turned out, liberal) parochial school. Clever, bright, eager to learn, Jim took to his new school immediately and, encouraged by some of his more freethinking teachers, was soon reading the progressive Catholic publication *America*, as well as materials put out by Dorothy Day's radical Catholic Worker movement. Precociously articulate, Jim could stand on his feet and talk rings around his contemporaries, and he also had highly developed social skills that quickly thrust him into leadership positions. Yet, puzzlingly, he was behind his peers in spelling and writing and had trouble committing anything to paper. Only years later, in his twenties, did he finally discover that he was dyslexic.

That was not the only way he was different. His family, perhaps as awed as his contemporaries by his perky verbalness, tended to treat him like an adult—his mother, after all, was only fifteen years older, and her husband was a year younger than she. Jim was also an unusually beautiful boy, somewhat undersized and slight, but perfectly featured, an angelic blue-eyed blond so pretty that as a three-year-old he had been chosen to be a "Whitcomb baby" in the famous series of ads that illustrator John Whitcomb designed for Gerber baby foods.

Jim's prettiness would often be mistaken, especially as he got older, for blandness or passivity, the surface stereotype belying the complex inner reality. He was, in fact, an intricate mix of sweetness and dynamism, and his cherubic mask misrepresented an assertive temperament. "My sensibility was much more female than male," he later said, "but my Gestalt was male." Often called "girl" or "faggot," he identified with neither, though his "gay spirit" (as he later liked to call it), his sense from an early age of being different, did make him compassionate toward other outsiders. Since most people need to hang on to the illusion that others are one-dimensional—that makes them *seemingly* more comprehensible and manageable—the complex Jim would all his life be puzzled by the way people reacted to him as if he were *either* (and only) a passive boy or a warrior male.

He was further set apart by illness. As a youngster he had rheumatic fever twice, and then leukemia, and didn't go to school for two years. Given massive doses of cortisone—the drug had just come on the market and not much was known about its properties—he blew up to three hundred pounds (and never did develop an Adam's apple). Bedridden for more than a year, he lived in a world apart, putting on little shows in his room with stick figures, endlessly watching television and listening to soap operas on the radio.

He became so adept at performing that after he recovered, and while still a teenager, he was chosen to emcee *The World Around Us*, a local television show devoted to current affairs. And his fluency in public speaking led to his election as president of the Rhode Island chapter of Junior Achievement, a national organization founded to teach teenagers about the wondrous workings of capitalism by encouraging them to set up their own little businesses (Jim ended up winning the National Junior Achievement sales award for a French dressing he created).

He was even pro-McCarthy. At the tender age of seven, Jim was signing people up for membership in the Committee of One Million, founded to support Senator McCarthy. He dutifully carried petitions from door to door soliciting members, and when the door sometimes got slammed in his face, he would complain to his mother—he describes himself as a "self-righteous priss" in those years—that such people were refusing to be "good Americans." She finally put an end to his canvassing by ripping up the petitions—not out of political progressivism (she really had no politics) but out of some powerful fear of "making trouble." "My whole subsequent political life," Jim later said, "has been a form of atonement for my McCarthy petition."

By the time Jim was in high school, his numerous activities had him crisscrossing Providence. To save money, he would hitchhike and before long discovered that blow jobs were one of the side benefits. Men would pick him up in their cars and, in exchange for sex, drive him anywhere he wanted to go. He soon found out that certain street corners were favored, and thereafter confined his hitching to those. He never feared getting into a car; as a survivor in his own family, he felt he had developed extrasensory instincts about potential danger.

But once, in his late teens, those instincts failed him. A truck driver, perhaps attracted to his long blond hair and delicate features, picked him up and drove him to a place where other truckers gathered. Together five of them raped him, brutally ripping open his rectum; then they left him, bleeding, on the side of the road. A cop car finally came along but, instead of being helpful, the cops ridiculed him as a "faggot" and told him that he had asked for it. He ended up in a hospital for several days.

In 1960, when still a junior in high school, Jim won early admission to Harvard. It seemed a dream come true; he had already vowed *never* to go to a local school, like Providence College or Rhode Island College, never to become "the working-class kid stuck in a trap." But then reality hit: His family simply couldn't afford the

Harvard tuition, and somehow nobody, neither his teachers nor his parents, suggested that he apply for scholarship money. Crushed, Jim, aged sixteen, decided to quit high school and become a priest.

As a moralistic, at times self-righteous young man, he was attracted to the do-gooding part of a priest's life, but had never been a fully convinced believer or felt certitude about the validity of Catholic dogma. The particular order he chose had been founded in the nineteenth century by Isaac Hecker (a baker at the transcendentalist community Brook Farm, who had later become a priest), and among its glamorous celebrants were the two "show-business priests," Father Norman O'Connor ("the jazz priest") and Father Elwood Kaiser (who produced movies for television and Hollywood). Given the order's showy tolerance for nonconformity, it seemed to Jim—in his own words, "a precocious, smart-assed" young man—just the right place for him. But as it turned out, only certain kinds of nonconformity were tolerated, which Jim—in some ways deeply innocent—was slow to discover.

Though he had gotten his fair share of blow jobs while hitchhiking across Providence, Jim only kissed a man for the first time when visiting New York City during the summer following his first year in seminary. Soon after that momentous occasion came another. At a poetry reading, he fell in love on the spot with the poet himself and went to bed with him—only to discover, when back in the seminary the next day, that he had caught crabs. Not that he had any idea what the squiggly little moving dots on his body were, or where they had come from; in his naïveté, he went to the head of the seminary to ask him about the strange visitation. The head, who had been a marine chaplain, sternly told Jim to shave every hair off his body—and would say no more.

But Jim's English teacher, with whom he had gotten friendly (and who was himself homosexual and would later leave the order), took Jim aside and tried to warn him that he was on dangerous ground. He explained that two members of the order had recently petitioned to be ordained as openly homosexual priests—and had not only been turned down, but had been thrown out. Something like a homosexual panic had ensued in the order, he warned Jim, and the issue had become extremely sensitive. Just how sensitive, Jim soon found out.

Another seminarian, angry at Jim for having made fun of his tiny penis in the showers, reported to the authorities that Jim had pictures of nude men in his desk. As indeed he did. Called in by the ex–marine chaplain to explain, Jim said he found the pictures "aesthetically pleas-

ing." Was he a homosexual? the chaplain demanded. Yes, Jim said, he thought he was—but added that he saw no conflict between that and becoming a priest. Like Craig Rodwell, Jim had been brought up to believe that if you were honest, all would turn out well. He now learned otherwise. The chaplain told him he would have to leave the seminary at once, and gave him fifteen dollars for bus fare back home.

Jim was stunned and humiliated; he had become used to being treated like a winner. And as a winner, he refused to believe that his feelings were "sinful" or that his relationship with God had in any way been compromised. He was very clear about that, indeed had always been clear about that: He *knew* when he had done wrong and he had never felt that way about his sexuality. Telling his parents, however, was quite another matter. Sex was not something discussed openly in his house (though years later, when Jim did tell his mother that he was gay, she was supportive, only asking that he not inform his stepfather, whose uncle Freddy, a transvestite, was already more than the family could handle). So Jim said something vague to his mother about having decided that seminary was "not right" for him after all. And then he did what he had wanted to do all along: He went to Harvard.

Not as a matriculating student, but to live with two friends of his from East Providence whose families *had* been wealthy enough to pay their tuition. Jim simply moved into their room in Adams House and started sitting in on classes. It was a poignant time: He got close to becoming part of something he had long aspired to, yet he remained at a distance from it—an auditor, not a full participant. What made it all bearable was falling in love. He met a man who did promotional work for the Phoenix Theater (in the early sixties, among the most innovative and prestigious of theatrical companies) and, at the man's urging, decided to move to New York to be with him.

Jim arrived in the Big Apple in 1961—the same year Ray Rivera, aged eleven, left his grandmother's apartment and headed up to Times Square. Jim's excitement about starting a new life soon dissipated: The man he had followed to New York, it turned out, already had a live-in lover. He did at least make good on his promise to get Jim a job with the Phoenix, placing him in the subscription department; from there Jim quickly earned a promotion to stage manager and bit player with the Phoenix Traveling Theater, a troupe that performed in high schools. It may not have been the new life Jim had anticipated, but the world of the theater would in fact become exactly that for him. He soon moved in with two gay men connected with the Phoenix

who were eager to share expenses on a West Eighty-seventh Street apartment, found that he could live on his fifty-dollar-a-week salary by restricting his diet to pizza and Coca-Cola, and resolved, true to the "show-business" Catholic order that had kicked him out, that he would become a Broadway star.

F O S T E R

The Gunnison home on Hampshire Circle, in the wealthy New York suburb of Bronxville, was notable for its grand staircase, its squash court, its sunken garden (which could be filled with water during winter for ice skating), and its butlers' rooms—complete with a Filipino butler named Dabby. Foster Gunnison, Sr., had built the house during the Great Depression. He had inherited some money, and on his own had made a good deal more in his double career as lighting designer and builder. The lighting career had come first. A pioneer in the use of glass brick and carved structural glass—indeed, in the whole concept of what is today known as "architectural lighting"— he had started the firm of Cox, Nostrand and Gunnison when he was twenty-three. It specialized in Art Deco design and handled many of the largest installations of the 1920s and early 1930s, including the President's office and Cabinet Room in the White House, the Empire State Building, the Center Theater (now demolished) in Rockefeller Center, the Chrysler Building, the Waldorf-Astoria, Radio City Music Hall, the RCA Building, and the Daily News Building.[1]

In the following decade, Gunnison launched a second career. Impressed with Henry Ford's mass-production techniques, he decided to apply them to building prefab houses in modular parts that could be shipped anywhere and reassembled. He bought an old furniture factory in New Albany, Indiana, used his designer skills to turn out inexpensive, assembly-line homes, and applied his sales skills to set up a national dealership system. Before long he had sold enough Gunnison Homes to build a modern plant; he eventually became known as the founder of the prefabricated-housing industry in America.

Handsome, driven, gifted, he married a woman whose beauty and surface charms were a match for his own, though her more modest lineage was not. Whereas Caroline McAllaster's family had been in

the United States a mere three generations, the first Gunnison, Hugh, had arrived in Boston in 1631, and had ultimately become a judge and a deputy to the Massachusetts General Court. The succeeding four generations of Gunnisons were shipwrights, carpenters (one served in the revolution, under John Paul Jones) and farmers, giving way in the fifth generation to ministers and army officers, and in the sixth to Herbert Foster Gunnison, who became publisher in the late nineteenth century of the *Brooklyn Eagle*, the distinguished newspaper that had earlier been edited by Walt Whitman.

Though Foster Sr. had little regard for Caroline's family (twenty years later he characterized her father, with derisive exaggeration, as a man who "never did a tap of work until he was thirty years old because he spent all of his time gambling"), he and Caroline do seem to have been in love when they married in 1918. But by the time Foster Jr. was born, in 1925, the ardor had decidedly cooled. Intensely preoccupied with his work, Foster Sr. had never had a deep investment in family life, and from the early years of the marriage had gotten involved in a series of side affairs—not all of them, apparently, with women. Both his wife and son eventually came to suspect that Foster Sr. was a bisexual and that his live-in "assistant" down at New Albany was in actuality a male lover.

At any rate, Foster Sr. was neither a devoted husband nor a consistently caring father. He spent an increasing amount of time living apart from his family, absorbed in supervising his new business in Indiana. By the early thirties, Caroline and Foster Jr. were, except for occasional visits, essentially living alone in Bronxville during the winters and at Gypsy Trail Club, an exclusive residential community outside Carmel, New York, during the summers.

Foster Jr. did, in the 1940s, spend several long vacation periods with his father at New Albany, where he was proudly exhibited to Senior's friends and business associates as the forceful, super-achieving chip off the old block that the inhibited, troubled youngster was decidedly not. Moreover, the father's overemphatic doting on his son in public contrasted sharply with the stern lectures he gave Junior in private about the boy's assorted shortcomings—lectures that alternated with constant admonitions to those "moderate habits of living" Foster Sr. had trouble incorporating into his own life.

Foster Jr. was, in his phrase, "a victim of well-intended overmanagement"—a charitable interpretation of what seems on his father's side to have been essentially a driven determination to shape his offspring into an acceptable image. Foster Jr. would later ruefully

claim that "my father put me on a pedestal way beyond anything that I merited." But that assessment, too, seems dubious, seems to reflect a combination of wish fulfillment (the pedestal) and a habit of self-deprecation ("beyond anything that I merited") that his father's hec-toring reproofs had helped to engender. Much closer to the mark is Junior's suggestion later in life that his abilities had "always been underestimated"—the negative appraisal of his gifts having been early internalized, and thereafter communicated to others.

His mother was far worse at nurturance. Like her husband, Car-oline was a charming, popular companion to her peers, but a cold, endlessly critical, domineering parent. She was obsessed with being liked and with being socially correct, and was far too self-centered to give a child sustained affection. When alone with Foster Jr. she would, far more than her husband, castigate the boy for his imperfections. She was not above recounting the "terrible time" she had had giving birth to him (two other pregnancies had ended in miscarriages), or repeating how much she had hoped for a nice little girl. Caroline always kept her word, paid her debts like clockwork, and was generally admired for her honesty and reliability. But she was also a volcano of buried resentment: She menaced Foster Jr. with a knife several times; suggested (when he was six) a double suicide pact; and period-ically threatened to call the police and have him taken away.

Not surprisingly, Foster Jr. had frequent illnesses that confined him to bed, and when he was four or five, he developed a severe case of asthma. The family first tried sending him to Bermuda, where he got worse, and then to Richmond, Massachusetts, where he got no better. Finally, when he was nine and so underweight that serious doubts about his survival arose, the doctor suggested he be sent to board at the recently opened Thomas School in Arizona, a place that catered to children from well-to-do families. Most of the children at Thomas suffered from psychological or physical problems—it was an upper-class version of the combined school-and-orphanage that Craig Rodwell was to attend near Chicago a decade later.

The school was set in a beautiful, barren stretch of desert on the eastern outskirts of Tucson, surrounded by the distant Santa Catalina hills, with the nearest structure, the picturesque adobe ruins of old Fort Lowell, nearly two miles away. Foster Jr. was accompanied out West by his parents, but when school started in late September 1934, they left. Foster was assailed by homesickness throughout much of his first year. But he soon fell in love with the desert, and gradually became acclimated to being away from home.

The Thomas School had only forty students, divided between day students and boarders, and its young male teaching staff had been recruited almost entirely from Ivy League colleges. The school also kept a stable of horses (and a stablemaster). Foster quickly learned how to ride, and went out nearly every afternoon after classes to explore the desert terrain, chasing jackrabbits and rattlesnakes (he threw up the first time he watched the stablemaster skin one of the snakes to make a belt). The woman who operated the school, perhaps predisposed in Foster's favor by his father's gift of a library, turned him into something of a pet, letting him come into her room early each morning to snuggle in her bed with a puppy she owned while she got ready for the day. She was not a particularly warm person—indeed, she could be something of a disciplinarian—but Foster thrived on the special attention. Well before the end of his five-year stay in Arizona, his asthma had entirely disappeared.

After he returned home in 1939, his father decided to build the largest model Gunnison Home for his own family in the Gypsy Trail compound, and for the next three years Foster Jr. and his mother were nearly year-round residents there. He attended the local Carmel high school and then spent two years at Culver Military Academy in northern Indiana, where his father had once been a summer cadet. Unpredictably, Foster Jr. enjoyed Culver: He was able to continue his riding there and, although he never achieved any substantial military rank at the school, he felt, "as a person dependent upon authority," that the structured, disciplined, subordinate life suited him well.

After graduating from Culver, he entered Haverford College in the fall of 1944. Foster Senior had handpicked the Pennsylvania school as suitably small and prestigious. But Foster Jr. never took to it, and in his first term very nearly flunked out. He got a 42 in physics and a 54 in government (with 60 as a passing grade)—and his *highest* grade was a 68 (in English). His father, for once, handled the situation with some tact. While pontificating in his usual way about "the need to complete whatever one starts," and while managing parenthetically to deplore Junior's sloppy handwriting in his letters, Foster Sr. was nonetheless able to emphasize the positive: It was now clear, he wrote his son, that Junior's bent lay in liberal arts, not in engineering or scientific subjects—however much father and son might have hoped otherwise—and he urged Junior to be grateful that he had learned in the nick of time what his strengths were, and could therefore play to them in planning his future professional life.[2]

But Junior's unhappiness in fact encompassed more than a few uncongenial courses. He confessed to his father that he had been in "a constant state of depression" since arriving at the school. He found "every phase" of life at Haverford disagreeable: The food wasn't to his taste; the boys—mostly Quakers—had a set of ideals he did not share and could not fathom; there was no high-powered sports program; and, perhaps worst of all, he had discovered that his roommate "exhibited several glaring tendencies toward Communism." Foster felt wretched, lost fifteen pounds, and had "a constant tired feeling." Realizing that his father might ascribe those ailments to malingering, to a lack of "stick-to-it-iveness," he shrewdly played to a set of complaints Foster Sr. might find more congenial: He needed a school, he wrote his father, that was closer to home and that placed more emphasis on "college spirit" and on fraternities; and he confessed to a special hankering to be on a campus that had a chapter of Beta Theta Pi (the family fraternity for several generations).

Foster Sr. took the bait. Misreading his son as usual, he announced that he had hit upon exactly what was needed to pull Junior out of the doldrums: a coeducational college. It would give Junior "a brighter life," and that in turn would stimulate success in his studies. But Senior refused to consider a transfer until his son had satisfactorily demonstrated that he could "conquer all your problems at Haverford—even though you are unhappy." With the promise of release in the wind, Junior studied around the clock and in the second term of his freshman year achieved "a very creditable average." Fulfilling his side of the bargain, Foster Sr. allowed his son to transfer to Columbia, which accepted him on condition that he repeat his freshman year.

In the late forties, Columbia had one of the best football teams in its history, and Foster Jr. became a rabid fan, experiencing near delirium when Columbia pulled "the upset of upsets" in breaking Army's long undefeated string of victories. With a new lease on life, and trying his best to fit the collegiate mold, he did join his father's old fraternity, Beta Theta Pi, and in fact enjoyed the camaraderie—including the repeated trips he and a group of brothers took to Union City, New Jersey, or to the Globe in Boston to catch the burlesque shows. It was the comedy Foster liked, not the sex.

Indeed by now, aged twenty, Foster was well aware—though he had done only a little adolescent experimenting with friends—that his orientation was homosexual. At Columbia he sometimes dated to keep up with his peers, but fled in alarm at the occasional discreet

signal from a fraternity brother that some kind of sexual advance might be welcome. When one of them (a man later well known in publishing) directly propositioned Foster, he was so shocked and self-protectively "incensed," that he grabbed a dry mop and chased him out of the room. Indeed, Foster's uncertain footing in matters of sex was to result in a pattern of lifelong celibacy. Once, in his mid-forties, he got an "expertly administered, absolutely delightful" blow job; that would be the sole sexual experience of his adult life. Which helps to account, perhaps, for the special zeal with which he embraced every opportunity to bury himself in organizational work, to toil, with vast enjoyment, and semi-anonymity, on behalf of a cause he believed in.

He discovered his penchant for organizational work even before he graduated from Columbia. On one of his visits to New Albany in the mid-forties, his father had taken him to visit the local chapter, in nearby Louisville, Kentucky, of a recently founded national men's singing organization designed to preserve what was viewed as the disappearing folk art of barbershop quartets and choruses. The Louisville chapter was made up largely of local businessmen, and it was the networking, not the music, that had drawn Foster Sr. But the barbershop bug immediately bit Junior and became a lifelong passion with him. For a few years he sang in a male chorus, but later found that he enjoyed the business end even more; he helped to organize local, then district, then national programs, and took special satisfaction, one spring day in 1961, at being present for the formal ceremony in the office of Governor John Dempsey of Connecticut that proclaimed April 8–15 a week for officially celebrating the venerable institution of barbershop quartet singing.

In 1949, the year Foster graduated from Columbia, his father and mother, already long separated, finally decided on a formal divorce. But the settlement proved protracted and acrimonious, with each parent trying to enlist Foster Jr. as an ally. For a time, his father would have the advantage. Foster Sr. saw that his son, after graduation, was floundering, uncertain what kind of work to take up and where his aptitudes might lie, and so offered to set him up with a Gunnison Homes dealership in St. Petersburg, Florida. He assured Junior that he would accumulate considerable capital in short order. That alone had appeal, but what appealed still more was the possibility that his father might finally, after years of doubt about his son's commonsense abilities, find in him something like a worthy business associate.

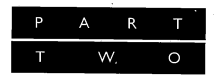

P A R T

T W O

YOUNG
ADULTHOOD

YVONNE

Yvonne's sister had gone to college in Georgia, but Yvonne was having
no part of it. There was no way, she told her mother, that *she* was
going to go south to college. *No* way. Theo couldn't argue with her
too much; having brought her daughter up in her own outspoken
image, and having imbued her with proud, pro-black attitudes, she
realized Yvonne might be right in predicting that she would end up
dead in a Southland still rigidly insistent on segregation.

But why in heaven's name, Theo wanted to know, had Yvonne
settled on Seattle University? Was the Far West the only possible
alternative to the Deep South? Yvonne said something sly about how
pleased Grandma would be because Seattle was run by the Jesuits,
and then, more seriously, insisted on how well suited the school was
to her own burgeoning interest in philosophy; what could be better
than the chance to read scholastic philosophy with the people who
invented it? "But what will you *do* there?" her mother asked in mock
horror. "It's tucked off nowhere, way out in the left-hand corner!"
Yvonne tried to reassure her that since her childhood friend, the
studious Freddy, was already enrolled at Seattle University, the two
of them could concoct some plot or other.

Theo couldn't help but smile; she'd been considered wild herself
all her life, and took some vicarious pleasure in her daughter's high-
spirited decision to shock the neighbors—this was 1950—with the
spectacle of a seventeen-year-old girl going off to school at the other
end of the country. That Freddy would watch over her was thought

a dubious blessing; he was already suspect in the neighborhood for his "swell-headed" bragging that he intended to study Russian and become a diplomat (what he hadn't announced was that he, too, was gay).

To the neighborhood's satisfaction, Yvonne lasted only two years at Seattle University (though Freddy graduated with honors). She did well academically—thanks to how bright she was, not to how diligently she applied herself. And she dutifully joined the prestigious Alpha Kappa Alpha black sorority. But then, as an antidote to that conventional social scene, she got in with an older black crowd that included Patti Bown (later well known as a pianist) and spent much of her time, as she had in high school, in the jazz clubs—and also in pursuing a love affair, the last she would have with a man. Moreover—and without really needing the money, but attracted to the thrills—she set up an inventive fence operation in which she sold (at a 50 percent commission) the booty some of her navy friends won while gambling aboard ship.

Yvonne enjoyed the edgy secrecy of moving in and out of disparate worlds, some of them clandestine, some of them proper. And that included the gay world. While still back in New Rochelle, she had managed to connect with a few very discreet lesbians in the surrounding towns, but when she set out to explore gay life in Seattle, she soon found that there was little to explore.

The West Coast certainly had its share of bars; although there were not more than thirty exclusively lesbian clubs in the whole country in late 1963, the West Coast had for several decades boasted a fair number of them—as well as the ubiquitous undercover agents and surprise police raids that were their invariable accompaniment. Mona's in San Francisco, which opened for business in 1936, was probably the best known of the early lesbian bars. Their number increased during and after World War II, with the If Club and the Star Room in Los Angeles becoming especially popular.[1]

But Seattle lagged far behind. Yvonne did locate a few places *rumored* to be gay, but she had scant success in meeting other lesbians or getting connected to a gay network. Not that she felt at all desperate; she was "having a ball" exploring a variety of worlds, and felt content in not committing to any of them.

During the summer vacation following her second year at Seattle, when she was back in her family's house in New Rochelle, Yvonne suddenly broke out in an acute case of acne. She had never had so much as a pimple before; now her face was a mass of bumps and

sores. Her mother took her to a well-known dermatologist, who promptly prescribed a series of X-rays—the then-touted experimental treatment. The X-rays literally burned the face, leaving patches of black skin that slowly peeled off. Yvonne felt so disfigured after the treatments that she decided not to return to Seattle, and indeed rarely left the house for a year. The experimental X-ray treatment for acne soon fell out of favor with dermatologists, but not before, in Yvonne's view, it had inflicted hidden internal damage that may well have contributed to the string of physical problems, and especially lupus, that would subsequently plague her.

Even before the X-ray treatments, she had seemed unusually susceptible to physical ailments. At twelve she had had a mild form of polio, which thereafter made her tire easily whenever she tried to play sports—though her tight, wiry body made her look like a natural athlete. Then at fourteen she had developed dysmenorrhea—painful cramps accompanying menstruation—later followed by endome-triosis, which predisposed her to vaginal cysts and tumors.

None of this had kept her from being her mother's daughter—a high-energy, can-do person who could party till dawn. But two or three days a month, when the cramping and medications got her down, Yvonne took to her bed; the only up side was that her physical prob-lems turned her into a lifelong reader. She was especially drawn to Faulkner, Nietzsche, Sartre, and Hesse. Ibsen's *A Doll's House* ex-cited her incipient feminism, and Orwell's *Down and Out in London and Paris* her wanderlust (though his descriptions of rat-infested pan-tries kept her from eating in restaurants for years).

When the acne finally receded, and Yvonne was willing to venture out of the house, she enrolled at New York University in Greenwich Village to complete her B.A. Billy, a gay male friend, took her on a tour of the Village clubs, and she quickly became a regular. She went occasionally to a few places on Eighth Street, including the famed Bon Soir, but soon developed a special fondness for Lenny's Hideaway and, somewhat later, the Grapevine, an interracial, upscale bar, just off Seventh Avenue, that had dancing and catered to both men and women. But there weren't many such places in the Village; the barriers of race, class, and gender that centrally characterized mainstream American culture in the fifties were also decidedly in place, though perhaps marginally less noticeable, in the gay subculture.

As Yvonne became increasingly comfortable with a lesbian iden-tity, she continued to travel—much more than most—between several worlds that straddled racial and class divides. She spent at least as

much time in the working-class bars and after-hours places of Harlem and Brooklyn as in the middle-class Greenwich Village clubs. A lesbian subculture seems to have developed earlier in Harlem than elsewhere, probably because blacks, knowing the pain of being treated as outsiders, had developed an attitude toward homosexuality relatively more tolerant than was characteristic of white heterosexual circles, with their unrelieved insistence on "sickness" and "degradation." Harlemites might ridicule stereotypic bulldaggers or drag queens, but in the twenties especially, bisexuality had a certain cachet in sophisticated circles, and in the world of show biz the rumored lesbianism of such favored entertainers as Bessie Smith, Ma Rainey, Alberta Hunter, and Ethel Waters tended to be ignored as irrelevant.[2]

Given this complex set of attitudes, heterosexual Harlem was sometimes willing to share nightclub and bar space with gays and lesbians. That included, in the 1920s, such well-known hangouts as Lulu Belle's, Connie's Inn, and the Clam House (which featured the 250-pound, tuxedo-clad singer Gladys Bentley belting out her raucous double-entendre lyrics), as well as the drag balls that attracted thousands to the huge arenas, like Rockland Palace, in which they were staged. Subsequently, Harlem clubs like Snooky's, the Purple Manor, and the Dug-out continued to mix straight and gay, thereby providing homosexuals with a proportionately greater number of gathering spots than were available in the more uptight downtown white world. When Yvonne arrived on the scene in the early fifties, these traditions, though diluted, were still intact. One of her favorite Harlem hangouts, the Wellsworth, on 126th Street and Seventh Avenue (just behind the Apollo Theater), was in fact two bars: a straight bar in front, and then behind it, with a separate side entrance, a black lesbian bar.

Harlem became a retreat from the endemic racism of the Village scene. Going into one of the few lesbian bars in the Village—the Seven Steps, Bagatelle, Swing Rendezvous, Pony Stable, Page Three, Laurel's (famed for its free Chinese food on Sunday afternoons)—meant essentially going into a white women's bar and finding herself ignored or treated like an oddity. That is, if in the first place she got by the Mafia thugs at the door, who often turned away, and sometimes insulted, anyone with black skin. The male bouncers were supposedly there to keep out straight men keen to convert a "lezzie," but it was also their job to keep out "undesirable" women.[3]

One night in the Bagatelle, Yvonne and her friends Tootsie and Debby were talking together at the bar when a white woman sitting nearby tried to flirt with them. When they ignored her, she went up

to the thug on the door and said the three women had been bothering her. He, in turn, told them that they would have to leave the club, but Yvonne and her friends were so outraged at the injustice that they refused. The thug then tried to evict them forcibly, a furious fight ensued, and Yvonne had to threaten him with a broken beer bottle before they could edge their way out of the place.

The tough, divey Swing Rendezvous, and the Seven Steps on Hudson Street, were more likely to admit black lesbians than was the upscale Bagatelle, which, with its tiny dance floor, was the most popular mid-fifties lesbian bar in the Village. But even in the Swing, the scene was essentially the same: a few black women in a sea of white faces. Nor did black lesbians necessarily form bonds of solidarity. The writer Audre Lorde, Yvonne's contemporary and later her friend, thought for a time that she was the *only* black lesbian living in the Village, and even after she met more black lesbians in the bars, they formed few friendships among themselves. In Lorde's words, "We recognized ourselves as exotic sister-outsiders who might gain little from banding together. Perhaps our strength might lay in our fewness, our rarity."

For Lorde, part of the trouble was the tendency of black lesbians, even more than white, to get into heavy butch/femme roles. As a "kiki" (or "Ky-Ky," as Lorde spells it)—that is, someone who refused to label herself in an either/or way—Lorde was considered unacceptably "AC/DC," a confused "bluff" (a combination of "butch" and "fluff"), unwilling or unable to find a suitably clearcut identity.

Yvonne was more comfortable than Lorde with the strict roles lesbian bar culture enforced, and herself leaned toward the butch side (her butch name was Vonne, short for Vaughan). As she put it years later, "I cross-dressed primarily to take on the power of the other gender; and also to make a clear statement to women what my preference was and a clear statement to men that I was not available to them." Yet she shared Lorde's misgivings, if not her vehemence, about the bar scene being a "reflect[ion of] all the deprecating attitudes toward women which we loathed in straight society. It was a rejection of these roles that had drawn us to 'the life' in the first place . . . we recognized oppression as oppression, no matter where it came from."

In the fifties and sixties, middle-class and upper-class lesbians relied less on the bars for a social life than working-class women did—just as they were less invested in butch/femme role dichotomies. Yvonne was again atypical in the way she socialized across class lines. She would sometimes be invited as a token black to an otherwise all-

white cocktail party of professional women, or to Fire Island, a summer playground that only wealthier lesbians could afford. And Yvonne would go, pleased to be part of so many different worlds. But she would deliberately dress down in sneakers and jeans, in those years decidedly déclassé, eschewing "respectable" Bermuda shorts.

Nor did she often date across racial lines. Only once in these years did she get seriously involved with a white woman, and then it was with someone who traveled almost entirely in the black lesbian world. Not that Yvonne was much interested in settling down with *anyone*; though intensely romantic, she was also intensely wary—a trait that often comes as second nature to those brought up in an alcoholic environment of erratic or excessive emotion that needs to be defended against. Yvonne would later describe herself as "frightened of intimacy," unable to handle closeness, afraid of being smothered —or abandoned. And she would herself increasingly use alcohol and drugs as a way of holding those fears at bay.

In 1956, following a protracted argument with her mother, Yvonne decided to get her own apartment in New Rochelle. After moving in, she supported herself by doing everything from babysitting to running numbers to driving factory workers back and forth to their jobs in Mamaroneck and Pelham. She was now in her mid-twenties, still hell-bent on catching every jazz set, on closing every club, on burning every candle at every end. The relentlessness of her partying naturally put a crimp in her studying, and it was not until 1959 that she was able to complete her B.A. at NYU.

CRAIG

In 1954, when fourteen-year-old Craig graduated from the Junior School, he went back to live with his still-struggling mother, Marion, in Chicago and enrolled as a freshman in Sullivan High School. That alone proved traumatic. The intimate, rural, all-boy atmosphere of the Junior School abruptly gave way to the urban anonymity of a big-city high school with twelve hundred students, male and female, mostly Jewish—a bewildering kaleidoscope of shifting faces. To compound Craig's feelings of dislocation, he had to contend with a new surrogate father, his mother having recently remarried.

Hank, an ex–Golden Gloves champion who worked in a print

shop, was "the sweetest guy in the world" when sober, but one of the nastiest when drunk, which was often. He and Craig's mother would get into shouting matches, but he interfered very little in Craig's own life. On the rare occasions when he tried to, Craig, though pint-sized, quickly put him right. One night after dinner, when Craig was about to leave the house, Hank abruptly said, "Where do you think you're going?" Craig said he was going out; Hank said he was not; Craig repeated that he was. Then Hank pointedly said, "When I was your age we used to go down to Diversey [a gay area in a then rough neighborhood] and beat up queers." Craig may have been surprised, but he wasn't intimidated. "You big, brave man," he said, glaring at Hank—and walked out of the house.

Hank *had* been on to something. Craig had been leaving home after dinner nearly every night for exactly the reason Hank had guessed: to cruise the gay areas. It had all begun, and quite accidentally, soon after he had come to live in his mother's apartment.

Craig had been interested in politics from an early age; at the Chicago Junior School he had avidly pored over the *Christian Science Monitor*, the only newspaper the boys had been allowed to read, and at thirteen he was subscribing to the *Democratic Digest*, a publication of the Democratic National Committee. For Craig, the daily newspaper was an absolute necessity—both to follow politics and to see how his beloved Cubs had done.

One night, after he had been living with his mother for about a month, he went out to Howard Street to get the evening paper. It was raining lightly; as Craig headed back home, a man suddenly started to walk next to him and then said something about how it was too wet out even for the ducks. Craig instinctively knew the guy was coming on to him, and he wanted him to, but he was scared—he guessed the man was at least twenty-three years old. Yet he gave him his home phone number and told him to call from three to six in the afternoon, when his mother would still be at work.

The man did, and Craig agreed to go for a ride in what turned out to be a yellow MG convertible. They drove out to the cornfields near Skokie, had sex in the car, and started to head home—only to discover that the car was stuck in the mud. They tried putting corn husks under the wheels, but to no effect, and the man had to walk to a gas station and hire mechanics to haul them out. "I'll never forget the look on their faces," Craig said years later, with a laugh—"a mixture of amazement and disgust."

But for Craig it was high adventure—the first time he had ever

had sex with someone older than himself. That is, give or take some furtive experiences at Comiskey Park, which to Craig, a fanatical Chicago Cubs fan, had become a kind of second home. He would let men pick him up in Comiskey and then, apparently fearless, would either give out a phone number or go directly with the pickup to one of the bathrooms in a deserted area of the stadium. From one of the men he learned the technique of avoiding detection while getting a blow job in a stall by standing in two shopping bags.

But it was from the man who owned the MG that Craig first heard the word "gay" and first learned that there were gay cruising areas all around Chicago—around Clark and Division streets, Bughouse Square, Wilson Avenue, Howard Street, Rush Street, the Clark Theater (in the top two balconies one could even have sex), department-store bathrooms (especially at Marshall Field's, Carson Pirie Scott, and Goldblatt's), and, in summertime, the gay beach at Oak Street.

There was even a coffee shop on the corner of Division and State, called Marx's, that was a hangout for gay high school kids. Craig, and the friends he soon made at Marx's, would sit in booths drinking Coca-Cola while eyeing the older guys walking by to cruise them. If the eyes connected, that could lead to renting a room at the Lawson YMCA or in one of the cheap hotels dotting the Loop, or to hours of driving around and parking in the older men's cars.

Craig loved the cruising and loved the sex, but even at that age would never go with anyone he didn't feel drawn to in other ways; he was always "hot to fall in love, to form an attachment." And to make himself look older—he usually claimed to be seventeen—he wore a leather jacket and engineer boots and chain-smoked cigarettes. But at least once, Craig badly miscalculated. One night on Howard Street he met Dave, a Loyola University student in his early twenties, and started to see him with some regularity in the afternoon, when Craig's mother was at work. Dave always wanted to fuck Craig, and Craig always said no. Finally one afternoon Dave grabbed and raped him, hurting him badly. But Craig couldn't scream for fear the neighbors would discover what was going on. He told Dave he would never see him again.

A few weeks later, when reading the *Chicago Daily News*, Craig came across Dave's picture along with an article describing how the police had come to his room after a thirteen-year-old had reported him, and had found pictures of young boys—at which point Dave had gone to the dresser, pulled out a gun, and shot himself in the

mouth, dying instantly. Craig was terrified that his mother would see the article; he had told her Dave's name and address and had made up some story—that Dave was the high school track coach, or some such—to explain his visits to the apartment. Craig cut the article out of the paper and when Marion asked why, he said, "I needed it for biology class."

Sometimes Craig walked the streets till one o'clock in the morning; when he got home his mother was usually waiting up for him, and furious. He'd make up long stories about losing track of the time while playing chess, or about the subway breaking down, or about being caught up in a bowling competition. Since he was usually out three nights a week, the stories wore a bit thin, but if Marion suspected anything, she kept her own counsel, probably out of the realization that Craig's will was too strong and he had been living by it for too long to brook interference now.

And if Hank had any plans to rein the boy in, those soon came to a halt. Afraid that Hank might physically hurt his mother during one of their shouting matches, Craig bought himself a knife, "just in case." Sure enough, one night he heard glass breaking and his mother screaming. Craig burst through the door brandishing the knife, yelling "I'll kill you!"—but was stopped by his mother grabbing hold of his wrist. But that was the end of the marriage; Marion asked Hank to leave.

Since Marion couldn't control Craig, she gave him the silent treatment when he did something that displeased her. At one point she didn't speak to him for months, and even Craig acknowledged that in that instance she had reason. It all began with one of his casual pickups. Frank, a dishwasher in his thirties and a gentle, sweet man, took Craig back to his tiny slum apartment one night, gave him a blow job, and then kindly offered to walk him to the subway. In the 1950s Chicago had a ten o'clock curfew for those under seventeen; Craig had always kept an eye peeled for the cops but had never had any run-ins with them.

This night was different. As Craig and Frank reached the corner of Clark and Schiller, two blocks from the subway station, three or four police cars suddenly roared up from different directions. They quickly separated Craig and Frank and questioned them individually on the sidewalk. The first thing they asked Craig was how old he was, and he said seventeen. Then they asked him for his mother's name and phone number and Craig—having been trained to tell the truth—gave both. Marion was allowed to take him back home, but that was hardly the end of it.

Both Craig and Frank had to stand trial. The prosecutor tried to coax Craig into testifying that Frank had given him money for sex but Craig resolutely refused to embellish the truth. Though the prosecutor was furious, he still managed to put Frank away for five years on the charge of committing "a crime against nature." He then tried to get Craig sent to a reformatory, but Marion cried and begged so piteously that the prosecutor relented; Craig was put on probation for two years on condition that he see a psychiatrist for six months.

Once again Craig's luck held. In the fifties, psychiatry was united behind the notion that homosexuality was diseased, pathological behavior that—this was supposed to be the good news—could be cured. In those years there were very few dissenters from that view, yet Craig, almost miraculously, found himself in treatment with one of them, Calvin Fentress. Instead of trying to change Craig's sexual orientation, Fentress told him about the ancient Greeks and their acceptance of same-gender love as natural; and he told the probation officer that Craig was dating girls and progressing well. Fentress tried telling Marion the same thing, but since she had been forced by the court to foot the psychiatric bills on her meager salary, she remained obdurately angry with Craig and for months subjected him to the silent treatment. As for Frank, Craig never saw him again, though many years later he thought he caught a glimpse of him washing dishes in a cafeteria.

Craig continued, of course, to cruise. Within a few months, still only fifteen and still too young to get into the bars, he met a man named Harry at the Oak Street Beach. Harry proved to be different in several critical ways. He was in his forties. He never seemed to want to do anything more with Craig than kiss. And he had an intriguing stack of magazines on his coffee table, including issues of *ONE* and *The Mattachine Review*. Craig didn't know either publication, and Harry explained that they were put out by an organization of homosexuals.

Craig had never heard of homosexuals organizing, let alone to promote their rights, and was instantly "thrilled" at the news. Harry told him where he could buy *ONE*—only a single newsstand in all of Chicago carried it—and also showed him a listing in *The Mattachine Review* of local chapters of the parent organization. To Craig's delight, there was a branch listed for Chicago, and the very next day, with typical assertiveness, he went down to the building on Dearborn Street to sign up. But when he got there, he could find no reference to a Mattachine Society on the directory, and he realized with a sinking

heart that the Chicago listing was a mailing address only—and one he could not write to, since the mail would come to his mother's apartment and he *was* still on probation.

But Craig made up his mind right then and there that he would save up his money and go to New York to live. He had heard for years that more queers lived in New York City than anyplace else on earth, and Harry told him that Mattachine had a large branch there. To help save money, he worked in the mail room of a Chicago law firm, took a summer job with Kaiser Aluminum as an office boy, walked to school every day to avoid the expense of carfare, and when anybody asked him what he wanted for Christmas or Easter, always said "cash." By the time he graduated from high school, Craig had saved nearly six hundred dollars.

But then Marion refused to let him move to New York. So Craig hit on a subterfuge. He had been studying ballet, in a desultory sort of way, since he was six years old and now announced that he intended to become a ballet dancer. Marion, who had apparently silently accepted by this point that Craig was gay, agreed to his career choice —but thought it could be best pursued in Boston. And so, in late summer of 1958, she went with Craig to enroll him in the Boston School of Ballet, and saw to it that he would live in a rooming house specializing in genteel old ladies.

Craig hated ballet school from the beginning, but solaced himself with exploring the gay scene in Boston. In the late fifties it was just as furtive and small-scale as Chicago's, but at least had the advantage of being unfamiliar. On the very day Marion left to go back to Chicago, Craig went out cruising on Commonwealth Avenue and the Boston Common—then notorious meeting spots, and dangerous ones (within weeks, Craig had to flee from a gang of toughs throwing rocks and screaming "Faggot!" at him). That first night, he met three different guys, gave each of them his phone number, and before long had discovered the few gay bars that then existed: the piss-elegant Napoleon Club and the two rougher bars, the Punch Bowl and Jacques.

But the drinking age in Boston was then twenty-one, and Craig had trouble getting into the bars, though he sometimes managed to ease his way in with a crowd. One way or another he quickly succeeded in meeting people, and one of his new friends soon got him a furnished apartment, springing him from the genteel boarding house. He also managed a mini-affair with a Native American who lived in Salem and had a morning radio show devoted to local news and obituaries.

None of this was enough to hold Craig's interest, and after a few months he decided to get out of Boston. He told his mother that if he was ever going to make it in ballet, he would have to go to New York to study. Reluctantly, she gave permission, and Craig packed his suitcase and took the next bus out. He arrived in New York not knowing a soul, but having somehow heard that the Thirty-fourth Street Sloane House YMCA was "simpatico." He immediately checked in there.

K A R L A

Karla was astonished when, years later, she found out that most of her classmates at the Bromley Institute had bitter memories of the place. There were reasons enough, as even Karla—who felt Bromley had saved her life—acknowledged. The school was not merely strict, but hawklike in its scrutiny of the girls' behavior. Only certain kinds of clothing, preeminently white blouses and skirts decidedly below the knee, were deemed appropriate for young ladies being "finished." If a girl was caught teasing her hair, or smoking, or playing Beatles records, she was likely to be expelled. When Richard Burton came to Broadway in *Hamlet*, the school forbade the girls to see it: "Richard Burton is a divorced man." Karla went anyway, and got away with it.

The curriculum was entirely prescribed, with no electives to allow for individual tastes (when one teacher overstepped the bounds and encouraged the girls to read Updike's *Rabbit, Run*, she was promptly fired). Chapel was mandatory twice a week (the school was Protestant, though most of the girls were Catholic or Jewish). All the girls were required to play sports, and even their diets were closely supervised. When the Good Humor ice cream truck came by Bromley's iron fence, the girls were refused permission to buy—not for nutritional reasons but rather, as headmistress Mrs. Moore explained, because the school was in a Hispanic area of Brooklyn and the man selling the Good Humor bars was undoubtedly slipping drugs into them. Karla wondered what drug you could buy for fifteen cents and decided Mrs. Moore meant aspirin.

None of these rigors and deprivations much bothered Karla. Though Bromley restricted her body, the school opened up her mind,

and she would always be passionately grateful to it for showing her how smart she was and for fostering her intellectual development. Thanks to small classes, every student at Bromley got close individual supervision—which Karla (if not many of the others) welcomed. Her English teacher told her she had talent as a writer, her French teacher praised her skill with languages; and her math teacher was so impressed with her gifts (her father Abraham was also a wiz at numbers) that Karla was sent to NYU to take an advanced course (she got a 98).

Bromley was intellectually nurturing not least because all the teachers were women (the only man at the school was the janitor), and a girl was *always* the smartest person in class and *always* editor-in-chief of the school newspaper. And the students, all of whom were white, got on well with each other. From Karla's perspective anyway, "there were no outcasts. . . . It didn't seem to me on looking back that anyone was particularly mean to anybody else. . . . There was no one who was ostracized for any reason, either because a kid was fat or a kid was unattractive. Everybody seemed to be friendly."

If that smacks of a rose-colored retrospective, it suggests that for Karla, anyway, Bromley was indeed "wonderful." And although she "still didn't have any words for what I was feeling," being at Bromley also gave her at least a rudimentary start at understanding her own sexuality. A lot of the girls had boys' nicknames for each other, sometimes those of well-known male actors. Only two of her classmates, Karla later learned, openly identified as lesbians, but labeled or not, there seems to have been a fair amount of homoerotic activity at Bromley, with necking and petting something of a commonplace.

Karla never developed any sense that such activity was "wrong." But two of the Bromley girls did overstep an ill-defined line. They were among the school's wealthy contingent; they lived in fancy houses and were driven to school in chauffeured cars. The two had been inseparable friends since elementary school, but by junior year at Bromley their behavior became notably more "eccentric"—to the point where even Karla felt confused and embarrassed by it. During lunch hour, when everyone else ate together at long tables, the two girls would sit ostentatiously apart, constantly touching, loudly calling each other "dearest" and "darling." They even appeared in ties now and then.

Finally, Headmistress Moore called the mother of one of the girls and pointedly asked whether her daughter came home for the night or spent it at the other girl's house. The mother's purported answer

—"None of your fucking business"—spread like gleeful wildfire throughout the school, giving the girls enormous pleasure. (Mrs. Moore was not well liked.) But the daring twosome's blatancy continued to make Karla nervous: "I felt sort of threatened by them because I felt they might endanger all of us, could cause the school to crack down on all of us." She learned later in life that both girls had married men—and had gone right on seeing each other and spending nights alone together. Perhaps, Karla mused, the relationship represented a special category of "upper-class lesbianism"—no labels, no apologies, no guilt, no remorse.

Bromley held periodic dances with Poly Prep, the boys' academy in Brooklyn, but few of the girls dated more than occasionally. Rhoda expressed some mild concern at Karla's apparent lack of interest in boys, but retreated when Karla pronounced them "boring"; that was still about the limit of her vocabulary. But by junior year at Bromley, Karla had discovered the locked case at the local library, and had discovered, too, that the librarian *would* allow her to read the books in it—though insistent on rattling her keys loudly to alert everyone in the room that another dirty-minded young girl had revealed herself.

About the first book Karla fell upon—it was a prototypical lesbian discovery—was Radclyffe Hall's *The Well of Loneliness*. But unlike so many other lesbians in these pre-liberation years, Karla did not feel a shock of recognition, nor was she filled with relief at the realization that other women like herself existed. She hadn't felt tortured enough for that, hadn't been guiltily hiding the desperate secret of her sexuality from herself and others. In this regard, the all-girl environment of Bromley had served her much as the all-boy environment of Chicago Junior School had served Craig Rodwell: Same-gender intimacy came to seem utterly natural to them. About all that Karla got from *The Well of Loneliness* was a newly depressing awareness that a lesbian lifestyle could be centrally characterized by confined options and negative consequences.

Again unlike so many lesbians in these years, Karla never read the lesbian pulp novels that began to appear in abundance in the fifties. Many of the books portrayed loneliness, alcoholism and suicide as the common lesbian lot. Some women found such desperation to be no more than an accurate reflection of their own unhappy lives, and took some solace in knowing that their misery was shared. But many other women have cited the pulps as having given them what limited empowerment they were able to find back then. For not all the novels were filled with wretched, self-hating "inverts." In Claire Morgan's

1952 novel, *The Price of Salt*, for example, the women are presented as complex, admirable figures insisting, against great odds, on their own worth and on making dignified lives for themselves.[4]

Karla seemed to have arrived at comparable self-esteem without benefit of the pulps. Her double distinction in the classroom and on the playing fields gave her, by the time of her graduation from Bromley, a settled self-confidence that she had previously lacked. She had a wall of trophies in athletics (in college she would become a semi-professional bowler), and in her senior year she won a coveted Regents Scholarship and graduated second in her class. It was quite a road for "Number 36" to have traveled.

The Regents Scholarship came in the nick of time. Up until the early sixties, Karla's father had been part-owner of the dunnage company he worked at, and he had made a fairly good living on the docks. His job status might have been blue-collar, but his income was middle-class. Karla never felt that she lacked for anything while growing up, though throughout high school she contributed what she could through baby-sitting and dog-walking jobs. But then, with the opening of the St. Lawrence Seaway, an alternate shipping route, Abraham's fortunes started to decline. He told Karla he would be unable to finance a college education for her.

He was ambivalent anyway about a girl getting too much book learning—he *did* manage to find the money to send his son, Paul, to college. But Karla was determined on more education. The Regents Scholarship, which paid well in those years, made that plausible. The money wasn't enough for her to go to her first choice, Vassar, where charges were too expensive for her means, but it proved just enough for Barnard. Besides, a cousin had gone there and had raved about it. So Barnard it was. Abraham pledged ten dollars a week, and the scholarship covered tuition. Not enough money was left over for a dormitory room, however. And it was not at all clear how Karla would eat.

F O S T E R

Shortly before the end of World War II, U.S. Steel was casting about to find new uses for the metal in the coming postwar period. Foster Gunnison, Sr., a superb salesman, managed to convince the company

that it could substitute steel for wood in his prefabricated houses, turn out models in the $2,800-to-$5,000 range, and thereby open up a huge new market, comparable to that for automobiles. Persuaded, U.S. Steel bought out Gunnison Homes for two million dollars, kept Foster Sr. on as its president, and also put him on the parent company's board of directors.[5]

By the early fifties, Foster Sr. had become convinced that U.S. Steel was making a botch of things; it might have been a giant company but its managers had no experience in the highly specialized housing field, and they seemed unwilling to rely on his. U.S. Steel, for its part, gradually became convinced that it had bought a white elephant; the company never built a single house with any steel in it, and soon discontinued Gunnison Homes, turning the plant into a warehouse. In 1950, before that final debacle, Foster Sr. decided to step down as president of Gunnison Homes (while remaining on the board of U.S. Steel) and to set up a prefab-house dealership in St. Petersburg, Florida, run by his son.

Foster Jr., now in his mid-twenties, had been floundering since his graduation from Columbia in 1949. Struggling to get a handle on a possible career, he decided to undergo a series of psychological, aptitude, and intelligence tests at the New York University and Columbia University counseling centers. The results were revealing, though somewhat disquieting. Foster's scores for general intelligence surpassed those of over 99 percent of twenty-six-year-olds, and on the verbal sections his performance was rated "truly outstanding." That alone had to be a comfort to someone who had barely survived his freshman year at Haverford.

But the rest of the news seemed to confirm what his father viewed as Junior's "maladjustment." The test results portrayed a somewhat formal, meticulous man, obsessive about detail work yet generally lacking in confidence. The report described him as "extremely sensitive, moody, unstable and rather immature," and ominously concluded, as well, that "he is not at present making a favorable sexual adjustment." The experts recommended a prolonged course of psychotherapy. Foster opted for Florida instead.

His father had bought up several blocks of land in north St. Petersburg, had had his prefabricated homes shipped down there from the plant in Indiana, had put them up, and had then sold houses and lots together, at 2 percent financing, for little more than six thousand dollars. Though Foster Sr. didn't himself move to Florida until 1953, about a year after his son, he handled most of the sales himself, leaving

Foster Jr. to take care of the dealership's internal business affairs. In all, some three dozen houses got built in a two-year period, with handsome profits for the father-son team. Foster Jr. accumulated enough capital, further parlayed through investments, to become financially independent.

But the work itself never captured his interest—though, as always, he did enjoy being behind the scenes in a structured situation that emphasized detail work. By the time Foster Sr. moved to Florida in 1953, following his marriage to his secretary (after a long-standing affair), Foster Jr. had decided he wanted to leave the firm to pursue an academic career. That hardly seemed a logical choice, given his mediocre undergraduate record, but, with the psychological testing results to bolster him, Foster felt that his previous under-par performance had been due to boredom with the subject matter of his courses. Of recent years he had begun to develop an interest in psychology, and as he did so, apathy toward academic study had given way to enthusiasm. Foster decided to enroll at Trinity College in Hartford, Connecticut, for a master's degree. His intention was to continue on to an eventual doctorate and to a life in academia.

But his reentry into the academic world was not easy. He found himself unable to concentrate for very long. His mind wandered when he read, and his interest wavered from subject to subject. No sooner had he enrolled at Trinity than he began to increase his involvement with barbershop quartets. No sooner had he started out in psychology than he began to take elective courses in philosophy.

By the mid-fifties he was spending more time with barbershoppers than with academics, and he began to doubt whether he was really cut out to be a student and scholar after all. But he did get confirmation and encouragement from various quarters. His professors gave him uniformly high grades, and as one of the college officials wrote Gunnison Sr., "Foster's record here speaks for itself. I think I need not tell you that few people achieve such excellence."

Moreover, one of the most touted young professors in the school went out of his way to praise Foster's abilities. Paul W. Kurtz, an assistant professor of philosophy at Trinity, had only gotten his own doctorate at Columbia in 1952, yet was already regarded as one of the guiding lights behind the emerging movement of humanism—and as an inspiring teacher as well. His sympathy for metaphysical speculation, at a time when logical positivism had taken over philosophy, appealed both to Foster's penchant for the "big questions" and to his pronounced psychological identification with the underdog. Though

Kurtz was very nearly the same age as Foster, he played a major role in arousing Foster's dormant academic abilities and interests. He might even be said to have become something of a surrogate father—except that this time, the father's interest seemed genuine. When Kurtz went to Venice in the summer of 1958 to attend the International Philosophical Congress, he took Foster with him and the two did some traveling together en route to the congress. Foster seemed at last to have found a congenial mentor and an academic home, and by 1958 he had formally enrolled as a student in both psychology and philosophy.

But the college dean had begun to suggest that he was being dilatory in completing his master's degree in psychology. Foster had chosen to make his thesis an evaluation of Adorno's study of the authoritarian personality, drawn to it, perhaps, as a way of better understanding the context of his own upbringing. But it was not until 1960, his sixth year in graduate school, that he was finally able to complete the thesis and earn his degree. The psychology faculty awarded him a grade of 97—the thesis apparently contained a genuinely original mathematical formula—but then reduced the grade to a 90 because of the inordinate amount of time he had taken.

With the master's in psychology behind him, Foster continued to pursue a second degree in philosophy with Paul Kurtz. But just as he was about to begin his thesis, Kurtz announced that he was leaving Trinity to teach elsewhere. He later encouraged Foster to join him in promoting the burgeoning humanist movement, but by then Foster felt too rooted in Hartford to leave. Besides, he may have been experiencing, on a level too deep to be fully conscious, a rejection that Kurtz had never intended; he may have been feeling that the surrogate father had turned out, after all, to be much like the original: willing to enlist Foster in his own projects, while controlling the terms of the relationship from a safe distance.

In 1961, the same year Kurtz left Trinity, Foster's own father died, succumbing at age sixty-five after a decade's struggle with heart trouble and diabetes. Foster's ever more difficult mother never remarried; a lifelong health fanatic, she concentrated her energies on a daily routine of walking and dieting. She announced her determination to live to be ninety—and did, by seven days. On Foster's infrequent visits to her at Gypsy Trail, she continued to subject him, between dollops of brewer's yeast and vitamin supplements, to her unpredictable, explosive mood swings.

In a farewell letter to Foster, Kurtz offered him some parting

advice: He would be "much better off," Kurtz wrote, if he "resituated" himself. "You have too much to offer, and you should have every opportunity to make the most of it." But for now this was not a message Foster could hear. After a brief spell of academic success, he lapsed back into his long-settled self-image as someone marginally gifted whose existence didn't much matter. He reverted to lessons he had learned as a youngster: *not* to call attention to himself, *not* to attempt distinction that was "clearly" beyond his grasp. As a child Foster had survived life with his demanding, domineering parents by becoming, on the surface, unobjectionably "nice." But beneath that accommodating surface lay dormant discontent that had not yet found an expressive channel. For a while longer, Foster would settle for working semi-anonymously in a non-profit environment free from demanding responsibilities. But by the mid-sixties, when in his forties, he would finally find a "cause" able to call out to the full his uncommon talent for nurturance and his tenacious dedication.

J   I   M

Jim could never bring himself to sleep with people in order to get parts. He thought of himself as a romantic: sex was "a big deal," a way to get to know someone with whom he planned to spend the rest of his life. Not that he didn't pick people up in bars for casual sex on occasion, or go to Everard, the gay Turkish baths; but even in those places he was searching for a boyfriend, for tenderness and connection. He didn't "do" a lot of sex, though not—as an eighteen-year-old, stereotypically pretty blond—for want of opportunities.

He was, in fact, constantly fending off passes—and not always in a way that (at least in retrospect) pleased him. He thinks he may have been too arrogant and haughty when rejecting a proposition— "How dare you!" indignantly written all over his face. It was not simply a matter of priggishness, though; Jim was also angry at being approached as merely another pretty boy (at eighteen he looked twelve), at his pursuers' consistently ignoring what he knew was his complexity and intelligence.

He blames himself most for having sometimes led people on. He was, he can now admit, "a fabulous cock-tease." Once he accepted a director's invitation to vacation in Puerto Rico, with the stipulation

that he would have his own bedroom; when Jim discovered, on arriving, that the two of them were sharing a bed, he made a huge stink about it, withdrawing into huffy chastity. "I shouldn't have gone in the first place," Jim now says. "I knew perfectly well what would happen if I did."

Paula Strasberg, the wife of Lee (head of the Actors Studio), and herself a respected coach, once said to Jim, "I don't care *how* you get the part. It's only when you get the part that you know if you can do any good work." Jim wasn't able to proceed on that advice, but he came to cherish nearly everything else he heard at the West Forty-sixth Street Actors Studio. In the early sixties, it was decidedly *the* place for theater people; every actor wanted to be accepted as a member of the hallowed Studio. In Jim's case, he won admission by a hair.

During the interview, Lee Strasberg told him peremptorily that he was underage, and then asked him who his two favorite actors were. Despite his mask of naïveté, Jim could be shrewdly calculating; he answered "Marilyn Monroe," knowing that she was close to the Strasbergs. Then he named Montgomery Clift, and said that whenever Clift performed "something unusual happened." (He omitted telling Strasberg that on first arriving in New York, he had found out Clift's address, gotten wildly drunk, and crooned "Monty, Monty" under his window; he had awakened the next day in Clift's guest room, but never got to meet him.) Jim added that he had first heard about the Actors Studio after asking one of the Phoenix Theater actresses he most admired where she had studied. Strasberg was apparently taken with all of Jim's answers, and decided not only to admit him to his own private classes held at Carnegie Hall, but to give him a full scholarship.

Jim ended up studying with Strasberg for nearly seven years. Where others found Strasberg self-aggrandizing and pretentious, Jim found him almost wholly admirable, something of a surrogate father. "Lee changed my life," Jim says simply. "I was a very smart kid, and a sensitive kid, but I was very much out of touch with my own feelings." Going to class became more important to him than anything else in his life, more important than holding down a job and eating, even more important than going for an audition. Strasberg sent him to other teachers besides himself: to Master Chang, a t'ai chi teacher on Canal Street, and to Sevilla Fort, a black dancer who taught Jim that he didn't have to wait until he could do something perfectly, or better than anyone else, before taking a chance; it was okay to do the best he could, so long as it *was* his best.

Jim briefly found "true love" in Strasberg's class—with Frank, a fellow student. They lived together for a while in a twenty-nine-dollar-a-month garden apartment on Forty-sixth Street (sublet from Richard Hepburn, the brother of Katharine Hepburn). When he and Frank broke up, two of Jim's heterosexual friends decided that he needed a girlfriend, and for a while Jim had an affair with the woman they introduced him to. But he never pretended to be straight, and in the world of the Actors Studio never had to. Homosexuality was commonplace among members of the Studio, though no one talked openly of it, or ever publicly declared—in the later style of gay liberation—his or her orientation. In the early sixties, to be a declared homosexual would have been like asking to be an unemployed actor.

The same attitude held even in the far-out reaches of the Living Theater, which Jim got connected with in 1962, a year after joining the Actors Studio. By then, the earlier distinction between Broadway and off-Broadway theater had blurred, and avant-garde work had started to move from off-Broadway to the coffeehouses, lofts, churches, cellars, and storefronts that Jerry Tallmer, drama critic of *The Village Voice*, had labeled in late 1960 "off-off-Broadway." In the world of the avant-garde—still fermenting in the early sixties, but soon to burst forth—Judith Malina and Julian Beck's Living Theater ("The Living" in the jargon of the cognoscenti) was considered by many the most radically innovative. It was self-consciously political, prided itself on its interracial company, combined communal living with theatrical experimentation in its Fourteenth Street space, and mounted a sweeping assault on mainstream American values.

Yet even at the Living Theater, homosexuality was more practiced than spoken of. By 1962 Jim was sharing an apartment with the Living Theater's stage manager and performing in its production of Auden and Isherwood's *The Dog Beneath the Skin*, but he almost never heard any open talk about the same-gender love and lust being played out all around them. Still, he valued his stint with the Living Theater. He had known few Jews or blacks while growing up in East Providence—blacks lived on South Main Street, not in his neighborhood, and Jews were rich people who owned big houses on Blackstone Boulevard; now he finally got intimate exposure to both, and took easily to both (indeed, in Jim's view, gay people have a sixth, sympathetic sense that draws them naturally, compassionately to other outsiders).

He was particularly drawn to Joe Chaikin, a member of the Living Theater who had made a strong impression in the company's path-

breaking play about junkies, *The Connection*. In 1963 Chaikin would form his own group, the Open Theater, with which Jim would get involved and which, in the minds of many, would come to epitomize the theatrical ferment of the decade. Jim credits Chaikin with actually saving his life at a point when he was feeling down about being gay. Chaikin simply took him to bed, cuddled and kissed him, made him feel good about himself.

Still, there was only one avant-garde theater in New York in the early sixties where it was thoroughly okay to be gay: the Caffè Cino, the earliest (1958) of all the off-off-Broadway experimental groups and a significant if rarely credited crucible for an emerging gay male sensibility. The Cino was the brainchild and alter ego of Joe Cino. Born in Little Italy, he had originally intended to become a ballet dancer, an unlikely aspiration for an Italian-American boy, but when he was in his twenties that passion had given way to a *somewhat* more seemly preoccupation with theater. (In the early-morning hours after the Caffè had closed its doors to paying customers, Joe Cino, stark naked and by then overweight, would perform solo dances under the stage lights in nostalgic tribute to his youthful dreams.)[6]

The Caffè Cino, at 31 Cornelia Street in Greenwich Village, functioned as a coffee shop cum performance space and was essentially an extension of Joe Cino's own apartment (he usually slept on a mattress in the back room). He packed the small Caffè with assorted *chotchkês*, glitter, and crystal, hung paintings by Kenny Burgess (a Cino waiter) on the walls, and constructed a tiny (twelve-foot) stage surrounded by tables and chairs that accommodated no more than fifty people.

A large espresso machine stood on a counter off to the side. It produced the countless pots of brew that, together with sandwiches and sodas, provided the Caffè's fare (and sustenance—it never got a dime in arts grants). The wall behind the espresso machine was covered with pictures of movie stars, opera divas, and unidentified beauties of both genders. Each evening Joe Cino, usually dressed in a trademark black cape, would start the performance with a flourish— "It's magic time!"—and would then retreat behind the espresso machine to serve up coffee and, now and then, to follow along (audibly) with the proceedings onstage.

A number of gay male theater artists who later became well-known—Lanford Wilson, Tom Eyen, Marshall Mason, Robert Patrick, Jean-Claude Van Italie, Paul Foster, William M. Hoffman, Tom O'Horgan, Neil Flanagan, H. M. Koutoukas, Doric Wilson, and Ron-

ald Tavel (not to mention nongay playwrights like John Guare and Sam Shepard)—worked at some early point in their careers at the Cino, as did a bevy of future stars, including Bernadette Peters, Harvey Keitel, and Al Pacino.

Joe Cino encouraged a kind of gay-hip atmosphere. Years before an emergent gay movement helped to legitimize such subjects, Cino's favorite injunction to gay male playwrights was "Get real, Mary!"— that is, "Let's bring the gay thing out into the open!" The result was a large number of plays with gay male themes or characters, including some—like Lanford Wilson's *The Madness of Lady Bright*, Tom Eyen's *Why Hanna's Skirt Won't Stay Down*, and Robert Dahdah's campy, if not overtly homosexual, production of *Dames at Sea*—that have achieved the status of classics. And the message that it was okay to be gay filtered out beyond the Cino circle itself. Arthur Bell, later a prominent gay activist and *Village Voice* columnist, recalled that for him and others, the Caffè "exemplified the freedom that was to come. . . . The Cino group made me want to assert my own gayness to the world."[7]

Jim Fouratt found his way to the Cino in the early sixties. He performed the role of a Mae West–like spider in *Fairies I Have Met*, a play based on the poems of Oscar Wilde (the playwright, Allen James, later committed suicide), and acted in several plays by Joe Bush, who in the fifties had written the first "outing" book, *Famous People Who Are Gay*. Ondine, born Robert Olivo and later a Warhol star, was part of the Cino while Jim was performing there, and much talked of as the possessor of the largest cock in North America. Intrigued, Jim accepted Ondine's invitation one day to view his prodigious organ in the bathroom. When they got there, the cock proved to be prodigious indeed, but all Ondine wanted to do with it was shoot it up with a hypodermic needle. Apparently he couldn't get off unless someone was watching.

The experience scared Jim. He was not yet twenty, and did not want to become part of the endemic drug-taking at the Cino. Indeed as the sixties wore on, Joe Cino, always drawn to intensity and ecstatic abandonment, himself became increasingly addicted to speed—and increasingly paranoid. When his lover, John Torrey, the Cino's electrician, was electrocuted while doing a lighting job in New England, a despondent Joe moved closer to the edge. On March 31, 1967, he carved up his own body with a kitchen knife. A hundred and twenty people gave blood at St. Vincent's Hospital in an effort to save him, but he died three days later, aged thirty-six. Friends and associates

tried to keep the Caffè Cino going, but it closed its doors for good in 1968.

Jim acted at the Cino during its heyday, and although he never became a central figure in its operations (or its mythology), he did a number of eye-catching turns—including a pathbreaking nude scene ("I was primarily worried about how my dick was going to look") in which he was sexually abused by, among others, Jesus, Mary, Dale Evans, and Roy Rogers, and which ended with him ecstatically fucking a TV set.

Robert Heide, one of the Cino playwrights, thought Jim was "incredibly pretty, something like the famous photo of himself that Truman Capote put on the back jacket of *Other Voices, Other Rooms*." And he also thought Jim was a good actor, a hypertheatrical, incandescent presence, with an almost "Marilyn Monroe aura about him." Heide was among the few who also recognized that Jim was "superintelligent," even if he himself wasn't admitting to it much, preferring the then current "Let's be cool" style.[8]

Jim and Bob Heide never had anything more than a brief flirtation, but did hang out together for a time. They shared much: the notion that theater was somehow going to save their lives; sardonic amusement at all the "straight" Actors Studio–Living Theater types who were somehow available for gay sex; and, too, some mutual friends—Jim Spicer, the Living Theater's general manager, who ran its Monday night "new playwrights" series at the Cherry Lane Theatre, and Ron Link, the stage manager and director with whom Jim shared an apartment for a time.

Hanging out in the Village in the early sixties meant a mix of bars and coffee shops. There were far fewer gay bars than in later years, and those that did exist were run by the Mafia and subject to frequent police raids. Jim, Bob Heide and their friends frequented (as did Yvonne Flowers) Lenny's Hideaway, a cellar bar on Tenth Street off Seventh Avenue South, as well as the popular gay dancing bar (about the only one in existence at the time) that adjoined the Cherry Lane Theatre on Commerce Street. Sometimes, too, they would go to the Old Colony, Mary's, and the gay and straight artists' hangout, San Remo, on MacDougal Street, which specialized more in drama than in sex (Jim Spicer's habit of draining black Russians and throwing the glass on the floor barely raised an eyebrow).

Coffee shops were also places to rendezvous. Mother Hubbard's in Sheridan Square was a special favorite. Open all night, it was famous for its apple pie and its generosity to actors. Owner-manager

Adele Speare (the gay crowd called her Mildred Pierce in tribute to her Joan Crawford–like looks and her Cadillac) offered a hamburger, apple pie, and coffee for ninety-five cents—or for nothing if you were one of the out-of-work actors she favored. Around the corner from Mother Hubbard's was Pam-Pam's, where another generous woman, Clara, let Bob Heide and Ron Link run up a $500 tab at one point. And across the street was Riker's, where a large gay crowd would go after the bars closed.

For those single-mindedly on the prowl for sex, there were the all-night Everard Baths, the balcony at the Regency Theater (which showed old movies) on Sixty-sixth Street, the men's rooms at assorted subway stops and at Rockefeller Center, the working-class Howard Baths in Newark, and the McBurney and Sloane House YMCAs (Stella Adler, with whom Heide was studying acting, would archly tell her classes, "Now, I don't want my boys running around the YMCAs!").

Alcohol was still the preferred drug in gay circles in the early sixties, but mescaline and LSD were finding advocates. One Living Theater actor specialized in mixing mescaline and apricot nectar, and Johnny Dodd, a waiter and co–lighting designer at the Cino (he died of AIDS in 1991) would throw periodic LSD parties in his apartment on Cornelia Street—the apartment from which in 1964 Freddie Herko, a dancer with the James Waring company, made a naked ballet leap out the sixth-story window to his death. When Bob Heide showed Andy Warhol the spot on the street where Herko had landed, Warhol nonchalantly said, "I wonder when Edie [Warhol's superstar, Edie Sedgwick] will commit suicide. I hope she lets us know so we can film it!"[9]

A favorite cure for drug excess was a visit to the Lemon Guru —Dr. Soltonoff, a chiropractor with offices on Houston Street who developed a devoted following that included Bob Dylan and Joe Louis. Soltonoff insisted that lemon juice in a glass of hot water three times a day, in combination with fasting, would cure just about anything. But should it not, there was the still-sanctified path of psychotherapy. Dr. Robert Akeret was a particular favorite with theater people. Working closely with Rollo May, Akeret developed his own special technique of "photoanalysis" in which he would analyze old family pictures in order to diagnose interfamily tensions and relationships.

Also much consulted was the gay psychoanalyst Dr. Karl Goldman, who had survived internment in a concentration camp during the war. Goldman's apartment on Waverly Place became a drop-in

salon; of an evening you could ring his bell and usually find a congenial group gathered in the living room. He sometimes cooked for the more "interesting" gay men he collected—including, occasionally, Jim Fouratt and Bob Heide—discoursing at length after dinner on existentialism or the meaning of paranoid psychosis. A genuine intellectual, Goldman was also tight and aloof, literally hunched over with tension and incapable of looking anyone directly in the eye. He could be archly patronizing, effectively using his wide-ranging knowledge to cow those who were younger or more impressionable (but really to establish his own right to exist). Goldman was later found handcuffed and dead in his bathtub, drowned by an ex-con he had been treating as a patient.

Lee Strasberg told Jim that his success in the theater would depend not on his abundant talent—which by itself could prove an obstacle —but on the extent of his ambition and his perseverance. Though Jim became addicted to neither drugs nor sex, he did become something of an excitement junkie, always wanting to be where the action was, and preferably at the center of it. His early years in New York coincided with the fading influence of one oppositional culture, the Beats, and the gradual emergence of a new one, with several strands—from hippie to New Left—that would coalesce by the middle of the decade around the issue of the Vietnam War. Jim, barely twenty, managed to meet some of the luminaries of the older protest movement and to participate in some of the earliest manifestations of the newest one.

In 1963, the IRS seized the Living Theater's Fourteenth Street space for failure to pay taxes, and rather than bow to pressure from the state, the company decamped for Europe. Saul Gottlieb, variously connected to the Living Theater as writer, director, and fund-raiser, and his lover, Dale Evans, who would later become a significant figure at the SDS publication New Left Notes, decided to drive cross-country to San Francisco; they invited Jim to go along with them.

Though the car broke down in Montana and they had to pull an elaborate airline scam to afford a flight the rest of the way, the trio did manage to arrive in San Francisco. Gottlieb had ties to the beatnik enclave there, and during their two-month stay Jim had dinner at Lawrence Ferlinghetti's house, and met everyone from the poet/playwright Michael McClure, to the poet John Wieners, to the avant-garde jazz musician Cecil Taylor, to then-beatnik Phyllis Diller (who had gotten her start at the Purple Onion, a beat hangout).

When he returned to New York, Jim soon found himself, almost inadvertently, involved in the incipient antiwar movement. In 1962 the radical Students for a Democratic Society (SDS) had issued its touchstone "Port Huron Statement," a searching critique of American life that indicted as well the country's colonialist posture on the world scene and its willingness to go to war in the name of countering a bogusly inflated Communist "threat." By 1963, moreover, the black civil-rights struggle was in high gear, with hundreds of demonstrations that year in dozens of cities. And after Lyndon Johnson's ascension to the presidency in late 1963, American involvement in Vietnam seemed poised on the verge of escalation.

Marketta Kimball, a fellow student at Actors Studio with whom Jim was preparing a scene for class presentation, asked him one day to meet her in Times Square before starting to rehearse. Jim agreed without giving the matter any thought. He arrived to find himself in the middle of one of the first demonstrations in New York against U.S. participation in the escalating Vietnam War. About sixty people had gathered, and all of them were arrested.

In the weeks before the case came up, Jim gathered a variety of letters, including one from Senator John Pastore of Rhode Island, testifying to his "good character." Nonetheless, he was found guilty, and given a suspended sentence. He felt "a little had" by Marketta, but the entire experience proved a milestone for him. Up to that point Jim's only real politics had been a kind of moral imperative, derived from his Catholic training, to "tell the truth." But now he had discovered—just as had Craig Rodwell, with his own brand of Christian Science truth-telling—that if you spoke truth, everything did *not* come out all right. He had been pulled off the street by FBI agents and branded explicitly a criminal and implicitly a traitor. That infuriated him—and would soon propel him into a radical activism that would push *stage* acting to the periphery.

R   A   Y

Gay hustling had been centered in the Times Square area for a long time. In 1948, the popular pulp *Salute* published an article entitled "Nightmare, USA" that lamented the "sad decline" of what, until the 1920s, had been the glamorous heart of New York's theater district.

Of late, the article contended, the Times Square area had become the scene of a well-entrenched, "horrifying" spectacle in which "dozens of twisted, money-mad kids, aged ten to eighteen, daily offer themselves to homosexuals." *Salute* insisted that "none of the lads is homosexual" ("possibly excepting a few of the older youths"); they were hustling out of dire necessity, disgusted at their "grisly profession, revolted at what they do."[10]

When Ray Rivera, eleven years old, scrawny but beautifully proportioned, with high, dramatic cheekbones and almond-shaped, languid eyes, arrived at "Forty-two" in 1962, he was decidedly one of the younger hustlers—but he was hardly heterosexual and hardly felt "disgusted." "Elated" was closer to the mark. When a man offered him ten dollars to have sex his very first night on the street, Ray was ecstatic: "Ten dollars?! Wow! Ten dollars of my own! Great! Let's go!" Needless to say, his grandmother, Viejita, didn't share his enthusiasm; when a neighbor reported spotting Ray on Forty-second Street, Viejita threatened him so violently—at that point he hadn't yet left her house for good—that the next day, after she had gone to work, he swallowed a whole bottle of her medication.

Someone called an ambulance, and Ray spent the next two months on a ward in Bellevue Hospital. Convinced that he was going to die, Viejita tried to take the cross that had belonged to her daughter (Ray's mother) from around his neck. When Ray fiercely held on to it, Viejita yelled, "But you're going to die!" "So I guess," Ray shot back, "I'm going to need it"—and refused to relinquish his grip.

As soon as he got out, he was back on Forty-second Street, more euphoric than ever at discovering that so many queens hung out and hustled there, determined this time to move out of Viejita's apartment for good. She tried to stop him by getting him recommitted to Bellevue, and from there sent to a foster home in Central Islip on Long Island. But after a few months Ray ran away, ran back to Forty-second and back to "Gary," an eighteen-year-old hustler he had fallen in love with. He and Gary took an apartment together on Seventy-third Street and Columbus Avenue and, against all the odds, stayed together for seven years, both of them hustling, both of them getting high on black beauties and bennies, both of them becoming well known and well connected in the Times Square world of queens, pimps, hustlers, and addicts.

Before long, Ray even had a new name. All the queens on the street renamed themselves; it was part of assuming a new life and a new identity. After Ray decided that he belonged among them, that

he had finally found his real family, one of the old-timers told him, "Well, there's no Sylvia. There's no Sylvia right around at this realm. If there is, we don't know about it. You'll be Sylvia. What's that other name you like?" "Lee," Sylvia answered.

So Ray became Sylvia Lee Rivera. And she was formally re-christened. The ritual took place in someone's apartment uptown, with fifty friends from the street in attendance, most of them Hispanic and black but with a sprinkling of white queens. Sylvia was decked out in a white gown, a preacher from one of the Pentecostal Hispanic churches performed the christening ceremony, and afterward every-one partied. "It was just like being reborn," Sylvia later remembered. "You knew you were going into a different life. And I remember the preacher saying when he put the water on my head, 'Don't forget: This is going to be a hard life.' "

Among those present for the rechristening was "Miss Marsha P. Johnson" (Malcolm Michaels, Jr.), one of the very first people Ray had met on the street. Marsha was a black queen some five years older than Sylvia, who had started out as a boy hustler and now mostly worked in "full face" makeup. In Sylvia's words, "Marsha plugged in the light for me." On the day Sylvia first spotted her, Marsha was panhandling on the corner of Forty-second Street and Sixth Avenue, still dressed in the waitress pants and white shirt she wore on her job in Childs' restaurant. Ray felt immediately drawn to her and went right up to Marsha and started talking.

Marsha explained that yes, she did work Forty-second Street, but right now was just trying to get some spare change so she could get herself a dinner over at Romeo's—a special deal: spaghetti and meatballs for ninety-nine cents. "Mind you," she told Sylvia, jiggling a pocketful of money, "I made out good on tips today at Childs', but you never can be too sure. Besides, I might get lucky standing here, and pick up a trick."

"What *is* this queen talking about?!" Sylvia thought to herself, simultaneously confused and mesmerized. "What's your name, chile?" Marsha demanded. "Ray," the not yet rechristened Sylvia said. "Oh Miss Ray, you so *young*! How old are you?" "Eleven and a half," Ray answered. "Chile, you should be home with your mama!" "Well, how old are you?" Ray shot back, even at eleven not easily silenced. "Oh honey, don't worry about it," said seventeen-year-old Marsha with a yawn. "They call me the old queen, I've been around for so long. Did you eat today, chile?"

When Ray said he wasn't hungry, Marsha briskly took him in

hand. "Come on, I'm going to buy you somethin' to eat. I made tips. I made a few dollars. We'll go sit down and eat at Romeo's." And down they went to Forty-second and Seventh, every queen and most of the boy hustlers on the way calling out greetings to "Miss Marsha." At Romeo's, too, everybody seemed to know her. "Hey Marsha girl, how ya doin'?" the cashier called out. "How ya doin', girl?" the straight counterman repeated. Marsha nodded regally and gave her commands: "The usual, the ninety-nine-cent special. We'll have two of those. And make sure the plate's clean. We don't want no greasy plates."

For much of the next decade, Sylvia and Marsha were there at the important events in each other's lives, and toward the end of that decade were together at many of the central events in the early days of the gay liberation movement. In the beginning, Marsha was a guide for Sylvia, showing her the ropes, counseling her to "show a happy face all the time, not to give a fuck about nothing, not to let nothing stop you." Later on, politically, it would be Sylvia who took the lead and in fact far outdistanced Marsha in energy and commitment, who, applying Marsha's early advice literally, "refuse[d] to let anything stop her, refuse[d] to take any shit from anybody."

But in the early sixties, Marsha played the big-sister role, teaching Sylvia how to apply face makeup skillfully (in those years full drag was only for special occasions, not for hustling); getting her a part-time job as a messenger for Childs' restaurant (Sylvia later won promotion to billing clerk and then, working in suit and tie and full face makeup, to the accounts payable department); showing her how to rap to potential clients; and instilling the rules of the street: "Don't mess with anyone's lover; don't rip off anyone's dope or money." And that went for wigs, too. When Luisa, a Spanish queen, grabbed Marsha's wig off her head one night, Marsha ran screaming after her, finally catching up with her in Bryant Park, where she read her the riot act.

And it was Marsha who tried to prevent Sylvia's first arrest. One night, Marsha was stationed on Eighth Avenue by the Blarney Stone (the boy hustlers tended to stay on Forty-second Street proper; the queens usually hustled around the corner on Eighth), when Sylvia came down the avenue on her way to see some friends on Forty-second. "Don't go down there, girl," Marsha warned. "They're going to arrest people tonight; I feel it in my bones. Stay up here with me." But Sylvia, just turned twelve, insisted she *had* to "see some people" and down she went to Forty-second.

Thirty years ago, as Sylvia remembers it, the Times Square scene

wasn't nearly as dangerous as it later became. "The street actually belonged to gay people back then. If anything jumped off, it jumped off with us knowing about it." To some extent that included police harassment. The paddy wagon would back up with such predictable regularity to Bickford's, in the middle of Forty-second Street, to take on a load of arrested queens ("Aw right, ladies, let's go!") that the event took on mixed overtones of boredom and mirth ("It was almost like something you look forward to"). The police would hold the queens overnight in the Tombs, near the Centre Street Courthouse, and then release them the next morning to return again to Times Square.

But the police were not *that* predictable. As Sylvia sauntered onto Forty-second that night, she saw a whole slew of hustlers and queens being crammed by the police into a narrow space in the middle of the street between one of the movie theaters and a hot dog stand; a few of the queens were busily tearing up their parole cards and sticking the pieces between the grates. Undaunted, Sylvia went right up to the crowd—and was promptly scooped up along with the rest into a waiting paddy wagon.

At the station, Sylvia told them she was sixteen and gave her name as "Robert Soya" ("I couldn't even spell it!"). Never having been arrested before, Sylvia found the whole thing vastly amusing. When the arraigning judge looked down on the crowd of some fifty queens and hustlers in front of him and said out loud to the assistant D.A., "The names you read are all male names, but I see quite a few females here," Sylvia burst out laughing, thinking the judge had made a deliberate joke.

He hadn't. "Oh, so you think that's funny?" the judge said, glaring at Sylvia. "Then I suppose you'll also think it's funny that I'm locking the whole lot of you up till Monday morning." That meant three days in the Brooklyn House of Detention, and the other queens were no more amused than the judge. They came down hard on Sylvia, and at the end of the three days, with all those "noisy and tacky queens on my case, I was glad to get out of there." Sylvia told Marsha that "the next time you tell me not to go anywhere, I will not go anywhere."

By this time, Sylvia and her eighteen-year-old-lover, Gary, had moved to the Aristo Hotel on Sixth Avenue in the Forties. For twenty-five dollars a week, they got a big room with private bath, and Sylvia, who had learned to cook as a child, hooked up a hot plate. It was "something like having a home," and their many friends from the

street used it as headquarters. To complete the sense of family, Sylvia would often go with Gary to visit his mother and father in Flushing ("his parents were very accommodating"), and would take in Gary's brother for a few days when he was out on a pass from reform school.

But when Viejita met Gary, the reception was quite different. Sylvia had been visiting Viejita regularly every few weeks, and had also been sending her money (though Viejita never spent it and later returned it all to Sylvia—by then a tidy sum—denouncing it as "blood money"). When Sylvia told her about Gary, Viejita at first refused to meet him, convinced that Gary had talked Sylvia into hustling. When Sylvia protested that Gary was "a nice boy and hadn't made me do nothing," Viejita yelled, "You can't love another man!" After she belatedly accepted that Sylvia could and did, Viejita shifted to a new complaint: that Gary was white. "Why can't you have a Spanish boy?" she would yell at Sylvia, and Sylvia would shout back, "Oh, sure, sure—so I can go kill myself like my mother did?" When Viejita finally agreed to come to dinner one night, she sat stony-faced through the meal.

Sylvia did love Gary—more than any other man she would ever meet—and felt he "really did help my mind; he was there when I really needed him." They would sometimes "beat the shit out of each other," but they also had a great sex life—"I remember one time it got so good that we bent the rods on the fucking bed, the metal bars." They began to turn tricks together, too—for more money, not pleasure. Stoned on black beauties, they were willing to perform almost any scene, if the price was right.

But whether with Gary or alone, Sylvia tried to keep an eye out for danger. "I didn't want no problems. I just wanted to turn a trick, make my money, and go on about my business." Nor did she ever have much trouble. Gifted with a voluble, forceful personality (even at age twelve), and the ability to make quick, shrewd judgments of people, Sylvia never went with a client or climbed into a car until she had a chance to size the person up for at least a couple of minutes.

But after she started to wear more drag, at about age fifteen, the odds got somewhat worse. People did pull guns on her several times and did try to rip her off, though she outsmarted them by keeping only twenty or so dollars in her purse and putting the rest into a slit she had made in the hem of her miniskirt. And when hustling as a woman rather than as a boy, she managed to get over on almost all of her johns. If a trick got suspicious and asked her right out if she was a man, Sylvia, pretending indignation, would say, "Oh, so you

think I'm a man, huh? So here, so go ahead and stick your hand in my crotch—c'mon, put it down here!—and tell me if I'm a man!" She'd be wearing a G-string that brought her balls up on her stomach and her dick halfway up her ass—"in the beginning it was painful" —and, to fool the client further, had sewn wig hair onto the G-string; to the touch, the wig hair was indistinguishable from pubic hair.

Almost everyone bought it. But one night when she was in drag she agreed to go home with an unusually young and attractive john. When they started to make out, Sylvia got turned on; the force of her erection popped the G-string, and her dick fell out. The john jumped out of bed, screaming "You fucking faggot!" at the top of his lungs, and started to hit her. One blow was so powerful it sent Sylvia flying across the room. She reached for her purse—friends had given her a gun to carry "just in case"—thinking the sight of it would slow the guy down. But when Sylvia pointed the gun at him, instead of backing off he lunged at her in a rage—and she fired. Not waiting to find out how badly he was wounded, she grabbed her clothes and ran.

That was not the end of it. Recovered, and determined on revenge, the man toured the Times Square area night after night, with two policemen in tow. When he finally spotted Sylvia, the cops arrested her. In the station, she got on the phone to Viejita, who came down to the precinct and did a tearful-grandmother bit, getting Sylvia released to her custody. On the advice of their Spanish lawyer, Sylvia washed off the makeup, cut her hair, enrolled in school, and on the day of the trial appeared in court as a model clean-cut teenage boy. "I ask you, your honor," Sylvia's lawyer intoned, "does this look like a street hustler or a transvestite?" The judge agreed it did not, and Sylvia beat the case.

P A R T
T H R E E

THE
EARLY
SIXTIES

Resistance to oppression takes on the confident form of political organizing only after a certain critical mass of collective awareness of oppression, and a determination to end it, has been reached. There are always isolated individuals who prefigure that awareness, who openly rebel before the oppressed community of which they are a part can offer them significant support and sustenance. These individuals—the Nat Turners of the world—are in some sense transhistorical: They have somehow never been fully socialized into the dominant ideology, into its prescriptions and limitations; they exist apart, a form of genius.

Resistance, of course, can take many forms short of open defiance. The day-to-day resistance of African-American slaves who deliberately broke their hoes, feigned illness, slowed their work pace, or ran away—and the development of vehicles, especially religion and music, to express their unique experience—may never have reached Nat Turner's level of dramatic visibility, but did nonetheless provide outlets for "refusal."

In the years before World War II, gay men and lesbians, too, developed subcultural forms of daily resistance—from Walt Whitman's encoded language of "adhesiveness," to the female "support networks" that emerged with the settlement-house movement, to distinctive forms of dress, body language, and "camp" argot. Now and then an individual voice would be raised publicly—Edward Carpenter's in England, Magnus Hirschfeld's in Germany—to argue for the

"naturalness" of homosexuality or to make an overt plea for greater public acceptance. In the United States, there is at least one documented instance of an individual in these years openly protesting homosexual oppression.

His name was Henry Gerber. He had emigrated to Chicago from Bavaria when he was twenty-one, and as an American soldier during World War I had returned to Germany. There he discovered Hirschfeld's homosexual-emancipation movement and decided to attempt a similar organization in Chicago. But Gerber's Society for Human Rights, founded in 1924, lasted less than a year. Although Chicago in the 1920s had a well-developed gay male subculture centered in "Tower-town," few came forward to join the Society. Gerber, as well as those who signed the Society's articles of incorporation, were arrested, and Gerber spent his life savings of two hundred dollars to cover their trial expenses. The "scandal" subsequently cost him his job with the post office. He then reenlisted, served several years on Governors Island in New York, and continued his sporadic, often lonely, protest.[1]

But if the United States lagged behind Weimar Germany or Edwardian England in the pre–World War II period, the experiences of gay men and lesbians during that war went a long way toward creating the needed critical mass of consciousness in this country that could eventuate in an organized political movement. During World War II many men and women who had grown up in rural areas or small towns and had regarded themselves as singular freaks, discovered in military service legions of others who shared their sexual orientation. The experiences and bonding that followed led many gay men and lesbians to decide, after the war, against returning to their hometowns and in favor of settling down in one of the subcultural enclaves that existed in the large cities, and particularly on the two coasts. Their presence helped to fuel a proliferation of gay and lesbian bars in the postwar period; several mid-sized cities like Richmond, Kansas City, and San José opened their very first ones. And the bars, in turn, became primary social institutions for gay men in general and for working-class lesbians, allowing for increased contact and cooperation.

And then, in 1950, the Mattachine Society (the name taken from a medieval secret fraternity) came into existence in Los Angeles. A small group of left-wing gay men (including Rudi Gernreich, later famous as a fashion designer), some of whom were self-described Communists, formed around the early leadership of Harry Hay. They

put together an elaborate, hush-hush skeleton organization that in its hierarchical, cell-like structure reflected the order of the Freemasons, and in its secrecy reflected the realities of a Cold War climate that had made deviance of any kind subject to swift repression.[2]

The Mattachine analysis of homosexuality was, at its inception, startlingly radical. This small group of some dozen men pioneered the notion—which from mid-1953 to 1969 fell out of favor in homophile circles, only to be picked up again by gay activists after 1969 —that gays were a legitimate minority living within a hostile mainstream culture. They further argued that most gays had internalized the society's negative judgment of them as "sick," that such "false consciousness" had to be challenged, and that political struggle was the best vehicle for doing so.[3]

Someone in Mattachine suggested that they needed a magazine to get their message out, and to create such a publication, a committee began meeting independently of Mattachine. In January 1953 it put out the first issue of ONE, a small monthly that would last until 1968 (with a brief revival in 1972). Several women were active in publishing ONE, especially, in the early years, Ann Carrl Reid and Joan Corbin, but Mattachine itself remained overwhelmingly male (and white).[4]

In 1955 a group of women, led by Del Martin and Phyllis Lyon, decided to launch Daughters of Bilitis (DOB), the first lesbian organization. DOB initially put heavy emphasis on meeting social needs —on ending the profound isolation and invisibility of lesbians—but it did gradually involve itself in education and law reform. Throughout the fifties, the Big Three—Mattachine, DOB, and ONE—maintained sometimes strained but essentially friendly relations, even though ONE periodically attacked Mattachine for being too conformist and assimilationist.

And indeed Mattachine had quickly shed its initial radicalism. Most of those who joined in the two years after its founding were far more conservative than the originators and by 1953 had wrested control of the organization from them. The newcomers were primarily interested in winning acceptance on the mainstream's own terms, not in challenging mainstream values; they regarded themselves as patriots and good Americans; and they preferred to rely on "experts" rather than on political organizing to plead their cause—having internalized the view of that era's prime experts, the psychiatrists, that their "condition" was pathological. Mattachine's original organizers had soon found themselves isolated; Harry Hay resigned and the conservative newcomers took over the organization.

C R A I G

By the time Craig Rodwell arrived in New York City in the late fifties, Mattachine had long since ceased to be a radical voice. Its dominant message to other gays had become an assimilationist one: Reform your own image so that it comports with respectable, middle-class sensibilities. But if Mattachine had become too conservative for its radical founders, it remained too radical for the vast majority of gays and lesbians, who had been cowed by the experts into a negative self-image, and were fearful that membership (even though pseudonyms were used) could threaten the loss of jobs, friends, and community status.

Only the most intrepid would consider joining Mattachine or DOB in these years. In 1960 Mattachine had only 230 members, and DOB had enrolled less than half that number.[5] But the spirited, mettlesome Craig Rodwell, though just eighteen when he arrived in New York from Boston in the summer of 1958, could hardly wait to join up—though he reluctantly accepted the fact that he would first have to find a place to live and get a job.

The Sloane House YMCA, on Thirty-fourth Street, provided a good, inexpensive start (along with a fair amount of action in the shower room), and Craig soon met someone there, Collin, with whom he became friendly. Like Craig, who had gotten a scholarship to the School of American Ballet, Collin was a dance student, hopeful of becoming a chorus boy on Broadway. Along with a friend of Craig's from Chicago, the teenagers took an apartment together—two tiny rooms—on Sixteenth Street and Seventh Avenue. It soon became a camping (in both senses) ground for the raft of street strays they began to meet; on some nights eight or nine people would be sleeping on every available inch of floor space.

Next came the problem of getting a job. All Craig had was a high school diploma and a few clerical skills. So he did what generations of the young have always done to survive in the big city: took a restaurant job. In a sense he was lucky; he was hired (even if only as a lowly salad boy) at Aldo's, the popular gay restaurant in Greenwich Village. His job was to stock up the two-tiered salad cart—local mythology insisted it had been donated by Christine Jorgensen—with

a big bowl of lettuce, assorted dressings, and smaller bowls of condiments such as olives, tomatoes, and watermelon rinds, and move from table to table, serving the mixture of choice.

As befitted the camp atmosphere, Craig would sing out on arrival at each table, "Roquefort, garlic, or gasoline?" but in fact he hated the job from the start. Stanley, the man who ran Aldo's, was clearly Mafia, and the line of division between the straight, homophobic bartending and managerial staff, and the gay waiters and salad boys, was sharp. Having grown up in an all-boy atmosphere where same-gender affection was part of the natural flow of everyday life, Craig, unlike so many gays in these years, hadn't internalized his full share of homophobia. The condescension of the staff, in combination with the self-deprecation of some of the waiters and the uppity airs of some of the customers, put him in a state of simmering rage.

One night he decided he'd had it—and also decided that he was going to leave in style. He went to the kitchen, got some packing straw from the melon crate, and substituted it for the lettuce on the salad cart. After the customer made his choice of dressing, Craig obligingly put it over the salad/straw and served it. This went on for nearly an hour, with Craig serving almost the entire restaurant before anyone complained—intimidated either by Craig or by lifetime gay training in swallowing abuse without complaint. It was finally Stanley who caught wind of something being wrong and confronted Craig. He, in turn, called Stanley a "Mafia pig"—and stormed out.

That meant job-hunting again. Fortunately, Craig had taken typing in high school and had gotten good at it. Even so, he had to tip the man doing the hiring before he could get a clerical job in a plastic-flower factory, where he mostly did shipping work and typed invoices. About the only good thing that could be said for the job—aside from the fact that it paid the rent—was that the factory was located off Union Square on Sixteenth Street, near Craig's apartment.

By that point, Craig had already made his first trip to the Mattachine Society of New York at 1133 Broadway. In the tiny third-floor office he found one person at work—the president, "Al de Dion" (almost everyone in those years used a pseudonym). De Dion was cordial and pleasant, but when he found out that Craig was only eighteen, informed him that he had to be twenty-one before he could officially join Mattachine. Craig had never anticipated such a barrier and was crushed. But de Dion cheered him up by saying he *could* subscribe to the newsletter, volunteer to help out in the office, and also attend Mattachine's West Side Discussion Group, which met

once a month in the basement room at Freedom House on Fortieth Street.

Attending his first meeting of the West Side Discussion Group soon after, Craig had mixed feelings of elation and dismay. He was thrilled to be in a room with several dozen people willing to attend a public meeting on the subject of homosexuality, but was alarmed to find that almost all of them were men over forty in business suits, and paying what to him was far too much deferential attention to the speaker of the evening—a stodgy psychiatric "expert" who pontificated at length about the entitlement of homosexuals to civil rights *even though* their sexual development might have been distorted by a "faulty" family configuration.

The more meetings Craig attended, the more his dismay grew. He discovered that New York Mattachine had decided to confine its operations to two areas, education and research, and had disclaimed political agitation as counterproductive. Yet as Craig got to know more and more of the individuals involved, he found many whom he liked personally and even a few who shared his view that Mattachine should become more activist and visible. "George Desmannes," editor of the newsletter, was among the people Craig grew fondest of—"a warm and wonderful" man who quickly and gratefully put Craig to work doing pasteup, editing, and production of the newsletter.

Craig turned out to be an ideal volunteer. Not only was he an enthusiast with seemingly limitless energy, but he could actually type on the massive old IBM which had defeated everyone else. Craig even insisted on justifying right-hand margins; he would spend days counting up the number of letters by which each line was too long or too short, assigning pluses and minuses, and then laboriously retyping copy. He loved doing it, and George loved having him do it. Over time, Craig got more and more involved on the editorial side and by 1961, when he reached twenty-one and became an official Mattachine member, he had pretty much taken over the newsletter—though, typically, he never cared about being listed as its editor and getting credit for his work.

As Craig became increasingly active, George advised him to use a pseudonym to avoid having the FBI come snooping around his apartment. Craig dismissed that as paranoia, but bowed to his fondness for George and let him put "Craig Phillips" among the other names on the masthead. But he felt awful about giving in to what he viewed as cowardice and for hiding what he was in fact proud of. So within a few months, he started using his real name, scandalizing the

many conservatives in Mattachine who lived in constant fear of police reprisals.

They were even more frightened when Craig and several others decided to organize a gay picket line in front of the draft board on Whitehall Street in protest against its policy of releasing information on sexual orientation to employers. The night Craig "casually" mentioned the plans, the two other volunteers working in the office at the time looked as if they "were both going to have heart attacks." "You can't do that!" one of them yelled, "Mattachine will lose its incorporation. Our charter forbids *any kind* of political activity—you'll ruin us if you do anything militant like that!"

Others later warned Craig that the last thing Mattachine wanted was press coverage, that publicity of any kind would lead not to additional recruits (as Craig claimed) but to the police shutting down the office. But they had no power to *forbid* Craig from acting in an individual capacity, and besides, they were a little intimidated by this seemingly fearless young dynamo. In the upshot, only half a dozen people joined Craig, and only one other (Renée Cafiero) was affiliated with Mattachine.

The small band included two young firebrands of the day, one of whom was straight. Jefferson Fuck Poland (he insisted the name was on his birth certificate) was the founder and head of the League for Sexual Freedom, and he brought along his girlfriend of the moment, who in turn brought along a baby. The other (who had helped Craig organize the event) was "Randy Wicker" (Charles Hayden), who had joined Mattachine on arriving in New York in 1961 but had found its tone so tepid that he had formed his own one-man organization, the Homosexual League of New York, and had been using it to achieve some breakthrough coverage on homosexuality in the previously indifferent radio and print media.

Randy's lover, Peter, and Renée Cafiero's lover, the children's-book writer Nancy Garden, brought the group up to seven (not counting the baby). They may have been brave, but they were also scared. In the early sixties, the climate of Cold War conformity had lifted, but countercultural protest and challenge did not yet rend the air. People simply did not picket draft boards—let alone a mere handful of people acting in defense of a despised sexual minority. There seemed a fair chance that they would be summarily arrested, carted off to jail, and possibly beaten.

What in fact happened was that they walked back and forth in front of the draft board, and tried to hand passersby a flyer they had

made up. But it was a rainy Saturday and only a few people were on the streets. The sergeant stationed in front of the building glared at them from time to time, but nobody else seemed to notice them much. It was something of an anticlimax, and yet they felt euphoric. They had done something different and daring, made a beginning. And they believed bigger and better actions would soon follow.

Craig was hardly all work and no play. In his early years in New York, his friends were mostly street queens, although—unlike Sylvia Rivera and her friends up on Forty-second Street—few of them hustled for a living; the only coinage in Craig's crowd was fantasy talk of meeting a rich sugar daddy. Their circle consisted of a rotating dozen or so late-teenagers, half of them black, with a smattering of Puerto Ricans and whites. In those years being a queen meant wearing eyeliner and mascara, and sometimes "doe eyes," with dark black lines on the top, and bottom lids filled in to a point. Anything more—that is, jewelry, teased hair, or drag—not only would have invited arrest, but would have meant debarment from many of the gay clubs. Even in modest mascara, Craig's friends were often either denied entrance or (as happened in the Club Fifty) marched straight into the bathroom to wash their faces.

Not that bars were their chief hangout. Craig and his friends might stop in on Sundays at the Wishbone on West Fifty-eighth Street to get free hot dogs and macaroni salad, but generally they were too poor to afford the inflated prices of gay clubs. And besides, in the early sixties, the outdoor scene was much more in vogue than the bars. The three most popular downtown places were Greenwich Avenue, Eighth Street, and Washington Square Park (the railing along MacDougal was known as the meat rack). On Greenwich Avenue on a given night, hundreds of gay men would sit on doorsteps or car hoods watching the promenaders move back and forth. An eye always had to be kept out, of course, for the cops. They never let anyone stay still for long; "Keep moving, faggot, keep moving," they would growl, poking their nightsticks into the men's ribs. At one point, the city cut down all the bushes in Washington Square Park and imposed a curfew in order to rid the area of "undesirables."

It was in Washington Square Park, when Craig was out cruising alone one night, that three plainclothes cops jumped him. Acting as if he were an escaped serial murderer, they screamed epithets, slapped him in handcuffs, and took him down to the old Sixth Precinct on Charles Street. Sitting in the squad room, surrounded by cops, the

teenage terror of Mattachine let them know that he was no ordinary frightened faggot. Furious at the way he'd been treated, he started to harangue the cops, demanding to know by what right they had dragged a citizen off the streets. Indignant at having a "pervert" talk back to them, the cops took Craig into a side room and beat the shit out of him. The next day, his roommate Collin got him out, but Craig then had to appear at FBI headquarters on Sixty-ninth Street with his draft card to prove he was properly registered.

When Craig and his friends went out together, it was not primarily to cruise but to have fun. Part of that fun was "going wrecking"— taunting straights. That was pretty easily accomplished; the mere sight of two men holding hands on the street was enough to produce instant apoplexy in most heterosexuals. But if any of them made the mistake of trying to rough the faggots up, they were in for a rude surprise; some of the doe-eyed sissies were in fact tough street kids who didn't let anybody mess with them. The powerfully built Johnny Italiano was notorious for his quick fists; a straight who came at Johnny rarely walked away under his own power.

Sometimes, daringly, Craig and his friends went "wrecking" outside the gay areas. On one romp (thirty years before Queer Nation supposedly invented such noisy escapades) they went to a live broadcast of *The Carol Burnett Show*. Arriving at the studio in full face makeup, they created a deliberate stir in the balcony and—to nobody's surprise—got thrown out. They were also fond of spending an entire evening riding the subways (bargain entertainment at a fifteen-cent fare). Poured into blue jeans or chino pants made deliberately too tight by endless soakings in hot water, singing in loud falsetto the saccharine popular tunes of the day, they would, when feeling particularly exuberant, form a chorus line, kick their legs in the air and, to the tune of "It's Howdy Doody Time," perform their own special lyric:

> *We are the Village queens,*
> *We always wear blue jeans,*
> *We wear our hair in curls,*
> *Because we think we're girls.*

Perhaps because they seemed fearless, or perhaps because people thought they were lunatics, they rarely got hassled. On the contrary, a few fascinated young guys would usually end up tagging along during the evening.

Craig's daring caught up with him one day at Riis Park, the beach in Queens that was popular with gays. A local ordinance banned "suggestive" bathing suits on the beach, but the police, using the ordinance as a means of harassment, enforced it only against gay men. The cops would appear on a Sunday or a major holiday and station themselves near the refreshment area on the boardwalk above the beach. When word spread that they were there, a gay man going up on the boardwalk for a hot dog or a trip to the bathroom would dutifully cover his bikini with a towel—often making a major camp production out of the compliance.

Craig decided one Sunday to shift from camp indirection to straight-out protest. Hearing that the cops had arrived, he marched up to the boardwalk—*without* a towel over his bikini—and simply walked past them. They were initially startled, then angry. The police were used to gay men humbly begging their pardon and meekly promising never, never, never to do that (whatever it was) again. They stopped Craig in his tracks and asked him what the hell he thought he was doing. Running, as always, against type, Craig returned anger with anger, berating the cops for antigay harassment.

They responded by dragging him off to a small police room behind the bathhouse and demanding his name and address, which he quickly provided; but to badger him further, they kept asking for the same information over and over. Tiring of the game, Craig finally refused to answer again. This was astounding impertinence, and the outraged cops proceeded to knock Craig around. Still, he refused to break his silence. The cops then loaded him into a van, took him to the local precinct in Queens, and locked him up. Around midnight they brought him, in handcuffs, down to Criminal Court at 100 Centre Street for arraignment.

By this time Craig had lost his shoes and shirt; he appeared before the night court judge dressed only in shorts. The judge took him into his chambers and asked sympathetic, fatherly questions. He told Craig that because he was under twenty-one he would have to appear in juvenile court in two weeks; there, the judge predicted, he would almost certainly be let off with a ten- or fifteen-dollar fine. Two gay men who had been sitting in on night court (then a popular diversion), and had heard the testimony about what this defiant gay boy had done, drove Craig back home in their car.

But the trial two weeks later did not go according to the judge's script. When Craig arrived, he learned that charges of resisting arrest and inciting a riot had been added to his bathing-suit violation. He

tried to argue his case before the presiding judge, insisting that he had not resisted arrest and could not have "incited a riot" since the police had taken him off almost immediately to their room behind the bathhouse. Then, his own volatility again getting the better of him, he heatedly told the judge that the police harassment of homosexuals at Riis Park was cowardly and indefensible.

Up to that point, the judge had been blank and uninterested. But with the mention of homosexuals, his face turned beet red, the realization having finally dawned that the teenager in front of him was one of "those" people. He banged down his gavel as Craig was in mid-sentence, and threw the book at him—which, since the judge had already dismissed the resisting-arrest and rioting charges, amounted to three days in jail or a twenty-five-dollar fine. Having been told two weeks earlier that the fine would be no more than fifteen dollars, Craig had brought exactly seventeen dollars with him. The judge banged down the gavel again and told the bailiff to take him away.

He landed in the Brooklyn House of Detention, where Sylvia Rivera, that same year of 1961, had suffered her own first incarceration. On arriving, Craig was brought into a large holding cell filled with both cops and prisoners. Suddenly a bruiser of a cop strode to the center of the room and said, "Awright, who's the one who's refusing to speak?" Before Craig could decide whether, against all experience, he should once more tell the truth, several of the other policemen pointed him out. Without another word, the burly cop strode over and hit Craig so hard on the side of his head that he landed up against the wall. Then the cop grabbed Craig's wallet and scattered the contents on the floor, yelling, "Pick them up, faggot. *Now!*" By then Craig was dripping blood and in tears. He picked up the stuff from the floor, answered when asked what his name was, and was locked up in the notorious "Queens' Tank."

Craig spent much of his three-day sentence teaching ballet to the thirty or forty street hustlers—doubtless some of them friends of Sylvia's—locked up with him. He was a huge hit. The queens loved learning the graceful movements, and were fascinated with Craig; it seemed unfathomable that a clean-cut, educated white boy was being treated the same way they were. Which for prisoners in the Queens' Tank, as Craig quickly learned, meant no commissary privileges, no movies, and no recreation beyond the walk from their cells to meals.

When released after his three-day stint, Craig, still traumatized, went directly across the street to a hamburger joint, gobbled up several

burgers in a row and then, too upset to be thinking clearly, left the luncheonette without paying his bill. When he realized what he'd done, he was terrified that "they" would somehow come after him again and throw him back in jail—so terrified that instead of returning to the luncheonette and paying, he simply ran in the opposite direction as fast as he could.

But if the jail experience had unnerved him, it had hardly made him contrite. He went back to his friends, back to Mattachine, back to cavorting on the subways and streets. And everywhere he went, his volatility went with him. One night in the gay Tic-Toc bar on Second Avenue, he threw a glass of wine at Farley Granger after the actor had patted his ass uninvited and made some "friendly" comment about its attractive contours; Craig took it as an insult comparable (he was also a proto-feminist) to the way straight men pawed women, and he had come to the conclusion that *nobody*, straight or gay, was entitled to put him down.

It was an attitude that deeply unnerved the man who in 1961 became Craig's lover. They first met at the popular outdoor cruising area along Central Park West in the Seventies and Eighties, immediately started to see each other on a regular basis, and soon decided that despite all their dissimilarities—the man was ten years older than Craig, had a prestigious job as an actuary, dressed in Brooks Brothers suits and had conservative political values to match—they were very much in love. The man's name was Harvey Milk.

He was a romantic, enveloping personality, and he swept Craig off his feet. As soon as Harvey got to work every morning, he would call Craig to wake him for ballet school, usually with a joke. Three or four nights a week Harvey would take him out—his treat—to assorted ethnic restaurants; Harvey loved the cultural mosaic of New York and was determined to experience at least its culinary aspects. Alternatively, he cooked Craig elegant meals in his own apartment, which was only eight blocks from Craig's. And he was quick with bouquets of flowers and gifts. Hearing that Craig, between classes, ate his sandwich-and-soda lunch on a rock in Central Park, Harvey presented him with a miniature porcelain vase, complete with paper flower, to put on the rock next to him while eating.

They had already been seeing each other when Craig got arrested at Riis Park. The episode frightened Harvey; he was afraid it might get in the papers and he might somehow be implicated. He had already been made nervous by Craig's activities at Mattachine, and his voluble insistence that *all* gay people had to stand up for themselves. When

Craig and his friend Collin hand-made some flyers for a meeting of the West Side Discussion Group and stuffed them in every mailbox in the neighborhood where two men or two women were listed as living together, Harvey was furious. He told Craig that the flyer would scare some people to death: they'd assume that the truth about them was known and their whole lives would be ruined. Craig shouted back that Harvey was simply afraid that his own cover might be blown. (Yet Craig was chastened by remembering that when he had done the same thing back in Chicago, everyone had assumed that two nelly hairdressers in the neighborhood had been responsible for the mailbox stuffings, and they had been evicted from their apartment.)

But when the relationship finally disintegrated, it was over sexual fidelity, not politics. Craig, twenty years old, found it impossible to be monogamous, whereas Harvey required monogamy as a *sine qua non*. One night when they were dining out at an Indian restaurant on Ninety-sixth Street and Broadway, Harvey—ordinarily full of playfulness—became very serious and told Craig there was something he had to discuss: He had gonorrhea. Since he hadn't been with anybody else, he held Craig responsible. Craig acknowledged that he had slept with other men, and promised that he would stop, but the relationship never really recovered. Harvey started calling every *other* morning, and then gradually, over the period of a few months, stopped calling altogether.

Craig was grief-stricken. Harvey had been the love of his life, and the loss drove him to despair. Without a satisfying job, much education, or a career, "the future now looked a total blank." He quit ballet school, stopped seeing his friends and going to Mattachine, and finally decided to kill himself. He had attempted suicide once before, in his early teens, after he and Frank had been arrested on the street and Frank sent to jail. Put on probation, frightened, and with no one to talk to, Craig had swallowed a handful of aspirins with a Coca-Cola, having read somewhere that the combination was lethal. He had gotten sick but survived.

This time, Craig planned more carefully. He gave notice to his landlord, to his roommate Collin, and to his employer (at the time, an advertising agency). He bought a bottle of Tuinals on the black market, waited for Collin to go out to the movies one night, and then wrote him a formal note with instructions to call his aunt so she could tell his mother.

Then he began to take the pills. He had gotten through about half the bottle when he remembered that he hadn't put the note on

the chair by the door so that Collin would see it first thing on arriving home. So he jumped off the couch and left the note on the chair. Then suddenly, before he could get back to the couch, he blacked out, hitting his head on the fireplace as he fell to the floor. The last thing he could remember was lying on the floor, desperately trying to reach the rest of the pills.

For some miraculous reason, Collin came back early from the movies. Finding Craig on the floor and thinking him dead, he dialed the police, the fire department, and an ambulance. The ambulance arrived first and took an unconscious Craig to Harlem Hospital, where he was given a shot of adrenaline and where he woke up strapped down to the bed. The first thing he saw when he opened his eyes was a cop, and he became instantly enraged, actually breaking loose from one of the straps. Then he passed out again, and when he next woke up, he was in the psychiatric ward at Bellevue.

They kept him there for a month, the worst month of his life. Each day began with the hospital's terrifying "morning lineup": All the patients on the floor had to stand in the corridor to hear a list read off of who was going to have electric-shock therapy that day. Craig's name was never called. Nor was he given psychotherapy. But he did get plenty of experimental drugs, which he quickly learned to put under his tongue and then, after the nurse had left, to spit out. The doctors asked Craig's father, whom he hadn't laid eyes on in years, to come down from Boston, and his mother to fly in from Chicago; when they arrived, the doctors told them that they would release Craig only if he were transferred to a private institution. Craig's father reluctantly agreed to foot the bill, and Craig was sent to the psychiatric ward at St. Luke's.

In Craig's words, "it was like going from Bed-Stuy to Park Avenue"—only two to a room, bedspreads, gourmet meals, television, and recreational therapy. To complete what felt like a restoration, Harvey came up to visit one day along with Collin; but Harvey proved uninterested in a reconciliation and it took another five years before even a distant friendship could develop.

Part of the agreed-upon deal in getting Craig out of Bellevue was that he be in psychiatric treatment for at least six months, starting while he was still in St. Luke's. From the first session, Craig adopted his silent strategy, and since the doctor never said a word either, there was no exchange between them at all. That is, until some time later, when Craig announced he was quitting and the doctor threatened to

notify the police. "You go right ahead," Craig said, and walked out. His bluff was never called.

After three weeks in St. Luke's, Craig was released to a relative's house in Pleasantville, New York, where he stayed for a few months and then returned to Manhattan. He got a new job, this time doing clerical work for Marine Transport Lines, and his life seemed on the mend. But then Marine Transport got a big contract with the navy, requiring security clearances for all employees. Since Craig's homosexuality was a matter of police record, he couldn't get a clearance and was let go. So he went back to live with his mother in Chicago and took a job at an enameling factory. After years of being on his own, he found close-quarters living with his mother intolerable and, on impulse, accepted an invitation from a sometime admirer to join him in California. As soon as Craig stepped off the bus in Los Angeles, he knew he'd made a mistake; within a month he decamped for New York.

Arriving in the city in January 1964, he immediately plunged back into political work. Mattachine had begun to shift somewhat away from its previous conservatism, and Craig was eager to do everything in his power to accelerate the process.

YVONNE

Yvonne Flowers sometimes went to the Village poetry cafés that had sprung up in the late fifties, and especially to the Gaslight on MacDougal Street, where Allen Ginsberg, her favorite poet, was known to give impromptu readings. (What she didn't know was that Ginsberg, in turn, idolized her other hero, Thelonious Monk.)[6]

To accommodate her penchant for nightlife, and her part-time job as an attendant in the psychiatric ward at St. Vincent's Hospital, Yvonne had arranged to take all of her classes in the late morning or early afternoon. She would sometimes arrive at NYU without having had any sleep at all, and still high from club crawling. After class, she would crash at home for a few hours and then rush to her four-to-midnight shift at St. Vincent's. There she could easily cop a "dexie" (Dexedrine, an amphetamine pill popular in the sixties) and rev herself up again. Though she worked as an attendant, her job was in fact not

very difficult and she was surrounded by buddies. In the early sixties, numbers of students, actors, and writers worked part-time at St. Vincent's and some of the people Yvonne partied with by night worked on the same floor with her by day. Other party friends appeared regularly in the emergency room, victims of drug overdoses and suicide attempts.

Drugs were not then kept under careful lock and key, nor guardedly counted out pill by pill, and Yvonne and her friends had fairly open access to the stockroom. Doriden (a hypnotic similar to that later popular favorite, Quaalude) was especially in vogue, and usually taken with wine. Dexamyl was also available. But as casual as Yvonne's attitude toward drugs was, she drew the line at anything experimental. In the early sixties, some research on LSD was being done at St. Vincent's, in conjunction with the U.S. Army; the LSD was given to psychiatric patients as an alternative to electric-shock treatment. Some of them flipped out and stayed out, so when the hospital employees were asked to serve as a control group, Yvonne firmly declined.

On weekends when she wasn't working or in class, Yvonne went to lesbian softball games—that defining institution of working-class lesbian life. These were the years in which lesbian softball teams and leagues (and to a lesser degree, the winter substitute, basketball) were all the rage. Yvonne didn't actually play—her assorted physical ailments made her tire too easily—but she enjoyed the scene. She loved cheering on the Montereys or the New York Aces, and loved the partying that followed the games (the teams were usually sponsored by bars). She especially liked watching the New York Aces' eighteen-year-old first basewoman in action; a fierce ball player who hooked her mitt onto her trousers "like the last little butch," she later became a celebrated newscaster (though not the sports commentator she had dreamed of becoming).

As an alternative to the bars, a number of black women specialized in throwing house parties. Yvonne herself gave one every few months, going in with friends who had a big loft on Second Street and Second Avenue. Dozens of people (mainly women) would pay a dollar each to get in to dance, drink, eat, and gamble, and Yvonne made a tidy profit. House parties were a venerable Harlem tradition, going back at least to the 1920s, when they were called rent parties. They were raucous, merry affairs that managed all at once to pay the landlord and keep the participants dancing till dawn.

Yvonne's friend Audre Lorde later contrasted on several levels

the parties black and white women gave. The latter never had enough food (they offered a little bowl of sour cream and onion dip rather than hearty cornbread or fried chicken wings and potato salad); they never had music that could be danced to, or hard liquor (they preferred "sophisticated" wine), or laughter. The subdued tone at white lesbian parties always put Lorde off: "Mostly, women sat around in little groups and talked quietly, the sound of moderation . . . thick and heavy as smoke in the air . . . I always thought parties were supposed to be fun."

Yvonne, too, much preferred black lesbian gatherings, but being a party animal, she didn't turn down many invitations of any kind. And neither finding God nor falling in love slowed Yvonne's pace. The spiritual revelation came first—swiftly and suddenly. She had always wanted to believe that there was a God who made the world, that somebody was in charge, and her search had included, for a time, attendance at Zen Buddhist gatherings. But for years she "couldn't get it." Then one day, walking along Ninth Street from the Lower East Side to the Village, talking to God as she frequently did, she said, "I want to believe. I really *want* to believe." And just like that, she did. She quite suddenly "understood," finally believed in her heart "that there was a creator and this world was not a joke, not an accident."

Talking about God was not a hip thing at that time in Yvonne's circles, so she kept her revelation to herself. Nor did she take her newfound conviction into the fold of the black church. She found the level of homophobia there too high—about equal to the level of hypocrisy. It was perfectly clear that the black church was filled with gays and lesbians, yet their presence was either denied or denounced. *That* kind of Christianity, Yvonne felt she could do without. She had found God, and would not contaminate His loving presence in her life with the prejudices of those who purported to speak in His name.

She felt something similar about black civil rights organizations. Part of the dissonance was temperamental: Yvonne was a loner, most comfortable when *not* attempting to involve herself with others. But whenever she did make a feint in the direction of joining up, she ran smack up against the endemic homophobia that characterized the black political movement in these years. The case of Bayard Rustin—the man who organized the 1963 March on Washington and had been a close associate of Martin Luther King, but was shunted to the background once it had been publicly revealed that he was gay—was merely the most famous example of how the religiously oriented civil

rights movement tried to distance itself from the "taint" of homo-sexuality.[7]

Yvonne thought of herself as inclined toward socialism, toward the vision of a classless society in which, as a black person, a woman, and a lesbian, she would no longer be excluded and forced to choose among her several identities. Much of her struggle during the sixties—juggling, not committing, observing—was at bottom an at-tempt to work out for herself the possibility of freeing all three of the identities she embodied, and to learn how, when they sometimes seemed to conflict, to establish appropriate priorities among them.

She did go to a fair number of rallies and meetings, including the 1963 March on Washington. Her stepfather had died just a week before the march, but Yvonne and her mother felt they *had* to be there. Saddened with grief, they barely talked during the trip, but they were both glad they had gone. "It made me *very* proud," Yvonne later said. "I *knew* it was a historic moment. And it gave me a lot of hope—it showed things *could* happen."

And although she continued to be wary about committing to organizational work, at parties she would frequently go around the room and collect money for a particular cause—for the Patrice Lu-mumba Collective, say, or for almost *anybody*'s defense fund. Among the groups she felt closest to was Women Strike for Peace, which began late in 1961 with a call for disarmament and a protest against the resumption of nuclear-bomb testing. Yvonne would, in a nearly anonymous way, without knowing anybody else involved, simply get on one of the WSP buses loading up in Union Square to go down to Washington, and add her body to the rally count.

Then, in 1963, came the death of one of her coworkers at St. Vincent's. He was a Haitian immigrant named Bernie, who had joined the army as the only way he could think of to save up enough money for medical school. He was among the first American soldiers killed in Vietnam, and when Yvonne saw his name listed on the TV nightly news she was enraged that such a sweet, gentle man had been wasted in so inexplicable a war. She vowed to enlist more actively in the antiwar movement that was beginning to gather strength, and went down to Washington for one of the earliest demonstrations.

It proved a frightening experience. Tear-gassed and chased by police, she tried to climb a lamppost to take photos and discovered she barely had the strength to shinny up. During subsequent winter demonstrations, she had trouble getting her hands and feet warm, no matter how stout her boots or heavy her gloves. Years later she realized

that these episodes marked the beginning of the physical problems that would eventually be diagnosed as lupus. But at the time, she simply put her puzzling symptoms out of her head, determined to continue living life at full tilt.

But full tilt was not the equivalent of full commitment—may, indeed, have been a substitute for it. There were only so many hours in the day, and Yvonne's devotion to partying left little time over to pursue her degree, to work steadily in a political movement, or to get deeply involved with another human being. Even when she found herself in love, she did her considerable best to sabotage the relationship, telling herself that she was too highly sexed ever to settle into monogamy.

She first saw Anne from a car window, saw a beautiful, pregnant black woman "strutting down the street." Who is *that*? Yvonne thought, never dreaming that within days she would be meeting her. Anne, it turned out, was the next-door neighbor of one of Yvonne's good friends. She had recently left her husband, was raising their son on her own, and would soon give birth to a daughter. She didn't see herself as lesbian, but decidedly did respond to Yvonne. It wasn't long before the two became lovers; soon after that, they decided to live together. And they would stay together for seven years.

But they were not easy years. Anne smoked a little pot and drank a little wine, but didn't consume nearly the amounts that Yvonne did—perhaps because she didn't have the same level of pain. Nor did Anne share Yvonne's passion for jazz and nightlife; she much preferred quiet domesticity. Yvonne might have, too—she deeply loved Anne—but her demons kept her on the go, kept her away from the apartment they had taken together in Brooklyn, away from the threatening closeness of the relationship, away from sharing herself in any consistent way.

Anne never fought with Yvonne about her late hours, her drugs, her affairs, her seeming preference for hearing jazz above anything else. She took Yvonne as she found her, knowing any alteration would have to come from within. But Yvonne, at least in retrospect, bitterly blames herself, and carries to this day considerable guilt and regret over what she insistently labels her "destructive" behavior. She *wanted* to do it differently, had clear values about what was the right way to live, and knew that she wasn't measuring up to her own view of what a relationship should be.

She felt certain that she wanted to live with Anne for the rest of her life and help raise Anne's two children, yet she couldn't get a grip

on her own fear of being "trapped," her panic at the prospect of being "captured and smothered, or rejected and abandoned." And so she persisted in staying out all night, in pretending she could handle her escalating drinking and drugging, in juggling several simultaneous affairs on the side. She hated her own dishonesty. She knew she was hurting herself and hurting Anne.

Finally, in 1963, when one of Yvonne's side affairs looked as if it was getting serious, Anne picked herself and her children up and left. Yvonne was crushed, but well aware that she had pushed Anne to the breaking point. She missed the two children desperately, and on top of that, she worried about the subsequent effect on them of being raised around so much pot and alcohol. (Years later, Anne's son did develop a drug problem.) Yvonne knew that she had repeated her own parents' pattern, had let the need to get high prevent her from being consistently present emotionally.

Later, Yvonne and Anne would try—unsuccessfully—to reconstitute their relationship. But in 1963, filled with regret, Yvonne got an apartment of her own in Brooklyn and decided to try and get her life in order. She was thirty-one years old, still unsettled in a career, still "ripping and running" through several worlds without getting much succor from any of them. Within a year she had made the decision to pursue occupational therapy as a career and to go back to school to get a master's degree.

THE
MID-SIXTIES

At the close of 1963, *The New York Times* published a lengthy article entitled "Growth of Overt Homosexuality in City Provokes Wide Concern." The title said it all: The "concern" was that of psychiatrists, religious leaders, and law-enforcement officials; the "growth" was in visibility, in the perception that homosexuals were emerging from "the shadows" (the *Times*'s term), with a small number of militants openly agitating for increased acceptance. Predictably, the *Times* gave over the bulk of its article to the dominant psychoanalytic view of the day, preeminently associated with the theories of Irving Bieber and Charles Socarides, that homosexuality was a pathological disorder. The article even allowed Socarides the closing quote: "The homosexual is ill, and anything that tends to hide that fact reduces his chances of seeking and obtaining treatment." The "good news," according to the article (and the psychoanalytic profession), was that through psychotherapy the homosexual could be cured.[1]

The *Times* piece, despite being weighted toward a traditional, negative view, was a marker in ending public silence. In various media, the years 1962 to 1965 saw a sharp increase in the amount of public discussion and representation of homosexuality. Lesbian pulp novels appeared in far greater numbers than previously; male pornography, thanks to a Supreme Court decision clearing physique magazines of obscenity charges, proliferated; both best-selling fiction (such as James Baldwin's *Another Country*) and popular films (*The L-Shaped Room, Li-*

lith, Darling) continued to emphasize negative images but, at least peripherally, began to offer some sympathetic portraits.

The new frankness about homosexuality was part and parcel of a much larger cultural upheaval. The conformity and dutiful deference to authority that had held sway during the fifties were giving way under the hammer blows of the black civil rights struggle, the escalating war in Vietnam, and the emerging ethos of a counterculture that mocked traditional pieties and valorized "doing your own thing." A rapid-fire succession of events from 1963 to 1965 marked a seismic shift in national consciousness. The number of civil rights demonstrations in 1963 alone reached 930; they were highlighted by "Bull" Connor turning his police dogs loose on demonstrators, the bombing of Birmingham's Sixteenth Street Baptist Church, which took the lives of four little black girls, and the massive civil rights march on Washington (in which Yvonne and her mother, Theo Flowers, participated). And the year closed with the assassination of President Kennedy.

During 1964, local insurgencies continued to spread. And riots in Harlem; the murder of civil rights workers Michael Schwerner, Andrew Goodman, and James Chaney; and the refusal of the Democratic National Convention to seat the Mississippi Freedom Democratic Party delegation further dramatized the national upheaval. When, in August of that year, President Johnson used a series of episodes in the Gulf of Tonkin to win a free hand from Congress to "take all necessary measures" for the protection of American forces in Vietnam, the stage was set for a greater upheaval still.

Then in rapid succession in 1965 came the dramatic civil rights march from Selma to Montgomery, the bombing of North Vietnam, the rioting in Watts, and the emergence of black nationalism as symbolized in the "black power" slogan. Compared to these large-scale events and the substantial number of people enrolling in one or another national protest, the budding homophile movement remained minuscule—even when adding to the earlier Mattachine, ONE, and Daughters of Bilitis organizations the prominent new (mostly West Coast) Council on Religion and the Homosexual, the Tavern Guild, and the Society for Individual Rights.

Yet the homophile movement did both reflect and further contribute to the general assault on traditional values and, with respect to homosexuals themselves, represented the first glimmers of a possible improvement in status. To a greater extent than is usually credited, the homophile movement in the early sixties did challenge the dom-

inant psychiatric view of homosexuality by arguing—contra Bieber and Socarides—that sexual orientation was inborn, was only *possibly* a disorder (the matter was much debated *within* homophile organizations), and in any case was *not* susceptible to "cure" and not deserving of the severe social and legal strictures imposed on it.

Resistance to oppression did not begin in 1969 at Stonewall. The West Coast had given birth both to Mattachine and the Daughters of Bilitis in the 1950s and, in the 1959 mayoral election in San Francisco, candidate Russ Wolden had made a political issue of homosexuality for the first time by accusing his opponent, the incumbent George Christopher, of making the Bay Area national headquarters for sexual deviates. All three dailies condemned Wolden for "stigmatizing" the city, and Christopher easily defeated him in the election.

In 1961, openly gay José Sarria, a charming, inventive drag performer at the venerable Black Cat bar, ran for city supervisor in San Francisco and polled more than three thousand votes—a decade before Jim Owles attempted a comparable run in New York. In 1964, police harassment of San Francisco's gay bars led to the formation of the Society for Individual Rights (SIR) which, thanks to its willingness to meet the social as well as political needs of gay men, had enrolled a thousand members by 1966, thus becoming the largest homophile organization in the country.

An important turning point for the movement in San Francisco came on New Year's Eve, 1964. A four-day conference between gay activists and progressive Protestant ministers in May of that year had led to the formation of the Council on Religion and the Homosexual. To spread word of the new organization and raise funds for it, a New Year's Eve dance had been announced at California Hall on Polk Street. The police had agreed to let the dance proceed on the stipulation that anyone appearing in drag be instantly whisked inside the hall, out of public view.

But on the night of the dance, five hundred gay men and lesbians arrived in their formal clothes to find that they had to walk through a gauntlet of police photographers. Thereafter, at roughly twenty-minute intervals, police inspectors entered California Hall on the pretext of needing to make a fire inspection or check the liquor license. When, after an hour or so, their right to enter the hall was challenged ("Where's your invitation?" one man demanded of the police), a scuffle ensued and arrests were made. The next day, the outraged ministers held a press conference to denounce the police—and the *San Francisco Chronicle* featured it on page one. When the case came to court, the

presiding judge threw out all charges against the gay defendants and lectured the police on their dereliction of duty.

In several senses the California Hall incident marked a turning point: Heterosexual ministers had spoken up not to denounce gays but to defend their humanity; the courts had sided with homosexuals; the police, previously behaving as if invested with a natural right to harass gays, had been reprimanded and curtailed; and gay activists had learned the precious lesson that open, organized defiance could yield positive results. Ted McIlvenna, the minister who had spearheaded the Council on Religion and the Homosexual, was perhaps justified in his later assertion—after nearly all the credit for gay liberation had gone to the 1969 Stonewallers and those who followed—that "the Harvey Milks and those people were Johnny-come-latelies."

In New York City, too, resistance was mounting. Randy Wicker, co-organizer with Craig Rodwell of the 1962 protest in front of the Whitehall Street draft board, had continued—as had Craig—to resist the frightened conservatism of New York Mattachine's leaders; Wicker also served as a media gadfly, calling public attention to the harassment and discrimination under which gays suffered. The old guard, both in Mattachine and the Daughters of Bilitis, was to retain control in New York for several more years, but in Washington, D.C., Franklin Kameny's leadership of the local Mattachine Society had led in the early sixties to a series of radically aggressive statements and actions that had all at once reflected the confrontational strategy of the black civil rights movement and heralded the rejection of apologetics that would subsequently typify the gay movement.

CRAIG, FOSTER

One day in June 1964, Craig Rodwell was sitting at the Mattachine reception desk in New York when a man in his late thirties, sporting a crew cut, bow tie, and cigar, with a broad smile and a prematurely spreading waistline, entered the office. Craig was immediately on guard, thinking this might well be one of those fakely affable government agents rumored to be poking into "subversive" organizations of all kinds. (Though proof was not available at the time, definitive evidence has since surfaced that agents from BOSS—the Bureau of Special Services—did indeed have homophile activities in New York

under surveillance as early as the 1950s. And in 1963, an agent covering Randy Wicker's speech "The Homosexual in Our Society," given at City College, revealed in his report to superiors that postal inspectors had also been "conducting an investigation" of Wicker's mail.)[2]

Craig, with a decided edge to his voice, asked the smiling man who stood above his desk just who he was and what he wanted. The man introduced himself as Foster Gunnison, Jr., said he lived in Hartford, Connecticut, had read about the existence of Mattachine in Donald Webster Cory's book, *The Homosexual in America*, and had come looking for more information. Craig was a quick study, his bullshit detector always on alert, and he decided Foster was telling the truth. He invited him to have a seat and the two men talked for some time.[3]

Foster explained that he had recently completed a second master's degree, this time in philosophy, at Trinity College; that he had known for some time that he was "not developing into a heterosexual"; and that he had read about New York Mattachine and had been thinking about doing some sort of organizational work—which, he told Craig, he thoroughly enjoyed and was rather good at.

Craig was delighted at the prospect of another volunteer, and especially one who seemed affable and prosperous. (Since Foster had not mentioned holding down a job, Craig had assumed, rightly, that he was financially independent.) Foster made it clear that he was unlikely to get much involved in New York Mattachine, other than in some distantly supportive way, since he did, after all, live in Connecticut. But he signed up for formal membership, took some Mattachine literature home with him, and agreed to Craig's suggestion that they stay in touch.

The activist seed had been planted. Foster had taken a crucial first step in aligning himself with the homophile movement (as it was increasingly calling itself)[4]—a step surprising for a man who had all his life behaved dutifully. The successful completion of his second master's degree had given Foster a new burst of confidence. He had earned the degree in half the time he had taken to complete his first master's, and had done so with real distinction: his thesis on "Soft Determinism, Responsibility and the Idea of Control" was highly praised, and he compiled an outstanding academic record.

All of which did wonders for Foster's self-esteem, and for a time he contemplated going on for a doctorate. Yet ultimately he would decide against a life in academia. Enough self-doubt remained to make

him wonder whether his gifts would really prove competitive in the university world, and besides, he felt no particular affinity for either research or teaching. What he *had* always been drawn to was organizational work, preferably in a behind-the-scenes capacity, and once he had discovered the homophile movement, his involvement quickly accelerated.

The Mattachine Society was no longer national in scope. As a result of internal divisions that included charges of malfeasance and competitive bickering between the San Francisco and the New York chapters (New York having become the largest by 1960), Mattachine had dissolved as a national organization in March 1961, leaving local chapters to chart their own course. That had led, in short order, to a duplication of effort and a decrease in effectiveness. So in late 1962, Franklin Kameny, the guiding (and militant) spirit of the Mattachine Society of Washington, had suggested that East Coast homophile groups form at least some loose affiliation.

Accordingly, four organizations—New York DOB and the former Mattachine chapters of New York, Washington, and Philadelphia (the latter having renamed itself the Janus Society after the national organization disintegrated)—met in Philadelphia in January 1963 and formed the East Coast Homophile Organizations (ECHO). Craig Rodwell became an ECHO member soon after, and over the next two years he and others in the movement who were inclined toward greater militancy got to know each other and began to plan strategy for securing more aggressive homophile leadership.[5]

"Militancy" in these early years of the homophile movement was not synonymous with across-the-board defiance. Even Frank Kameny himself—though more responsible than any other individual for the newly aggressive tone in the movement—put decided boundaries on protest. He insisted that "you are not going to cure the effects of the impact upon the homosexual of society's prejudices by leading the homosexual into a rejection of society's values." He felt nonconforming students, especially, needed to be kept in line by older, wiser heads. As an individual, Kameny sympathized with nonconformity of all kinds, but he felt certain (about almost everything, Kameny felt *certain*) that homosexuals would "never gain acceptance by assuming the appearance of unacceptability."[6]

Foster Gunnison read about ECHO in the literature he had brought home with him from New York Mattachine, and began to go to their meetings. There he met, among others, Jack Nichols ("Warren D. Adkins"), a friend and ally of Kameny's, and Richard Inman,

who had started Mattachine of Florida, an ECHO affiliate. Foster and Inman were both prodigious letter writers, and the two men started a lengthy correspondence, which Foster later credited with having helped him sharpen his understanding of the homophile movement and the role he might play in it. When the correspondence began, late in 1965, Foster was still feeling (as he wrote Inman) "brand new to, and not a little overwhelmed by, this movement." Within six months, he was gratefully writing Inman that "anything I am able to do eventually to assist the movement will owe a good deal of credit to you."[7]

Foster recognized that Inman was a difficult man, a "lone wolf" who chafed against organizational restraints (he would later describe Inman as "halfway between a drifter and a taxi driver"). But Foster also came to see him as "an unsung hero of the movement," an outspoken, one-man crusade in Florida, and he felt indebted to Inman for helping him to clarify a number of his own views. When Foster, for example, expressed concern to Inman over proliferating antidraft and anti–Vietnam War demonstrations that seemed to him "badly lacking in rational justification" and in danger of giving protest of all sorts "a bad name," Inman wrote back that for homosexuals to affiliate with other groups or issues was "a VERY dangerous course." Homophile goals, he insisted, should never be "contaminated" with the agenda of any other movement—be it pro-black or anti-war.

He also buttressed Foster's sense that the breakup of Mattachine as a national organization in 1961 had been a lamentable mistake and that a new, unifying central body was urgently needed. Not that either man was keen about resuscitating Mattachine itself. Foster had started to come down frequently from Hartford to attend Mattachine meetings in New York, but what he saw and heard left him with mixed feelings. "I might just as well visit a brickyard," he wrote Inman after one Mattachine meeting. "The room can be full of fifty people and no one seems to know you or anyone else or anything that's going on."

Foster was heartened to hear various people at the ECHO meetings speak of the need to form a new national coalition. But he was less pleased that much of the interest seemed to center on some sort of informal federation. That would not, in Foster's view, be adequate; he instinctively leaned toward a more centralized organization that could encourage the development of a powerful, militant movement. He believed (presciently) that the movement *would* gain in militancy ("someday this movement is going to break out into the open and hit

the headlines"), would push with "reasonable aggressiveness" the view that homosexuality was "a fully acceptable and rewarding way of life."

His emphasis *was* on "reasonable." If Foster wanted to get the homophile house in order, he wanted it to be a house cleansed of "fringe elements." He deplored the possibility that the movement might get identified with "beatniks and other professional non-conformists"; their presence would prevent homosexuals from establishing a "decent" reputation and "gaining acceptance." He was therefore "strictly against" an "open door policy": in Foster's view, any emerging national organization would have to "keep as tight a rein as possible" over admissions, selecting its membership with an eye to "a certain degree of reasonable conformity."

He also believed that a new organization should take its cue from the successful West Coast group, SIR, and provide its members with social outlets (which some Mattachine old-timers frowned on); but at the same time he wanted to keep social activities to a modest level. Foster worried that too much emphasis on in-group activities might encourage the further development of the kind of gay subculture he disapproved: "affected mannerisms, special shops for the Homo tastes and styles, various other group interests and ways of life." He did not believe that homosexuals and heterosexuals were identical, but did feel "reluctant to see ourselves committing ourselves to differences that have not been thoroughly established as valid and as good. I believe that a subculture will always be readier prey for discrimination and pogroms than an integrated variation in behavior."

None of which meant that Foster blamed homosexuals themselves for aspects of a life-style he disapproved of, or for their current lack of acceptance. He did see much in homosexual life that he found "maladaptive," but he believed "any unhappiness or difficulties" were "principally due to the destructive consequences of prejudice." On the other hand, he questioned neither psychotherapeutic claims (since disproved) of successful "conversion" from gay to straight, nor even the advisability of some individuals' undergoing such "therapy." He believed that homosexuality was not always "ego-syntonic with the basic personality pattern"—just as he also believed that "a repressed homo seeking compulsive hetero adjustment might do better to come to terms with his H instincts." Individuals, according to Foster's libertarian philosophy, had the right to make those decisions for themselves, had the right to opt out of a life-style that gave so little pleasure and so much pain.

Yet Foster was firm in his belief that homosexuality was not an

illness—and in those years, when the psychoanalytic equation of homosexuality with pathology was all but universally accepted, his view automatically put him in the avant-garde. In speculating about etiology, moreover, Foster daringly (for those years) suggested that "there was no reason to believe the causes [of homosexuality] are any different from heterosexuality." In both instances, he argued, "the drives behind sexual orientation are very profound and quite the opposite of simple matters of choice." Which did not mean to him, in turn, that orientation was simply a product of biological factors. On that question, he threw up his hands—as even the best informed have continued to do since.

Foster, like most people, was imprisoned by the assumptions of his time. Unlike most, he had managed to transcend at least some of them.

After Craig returned to New York from Los Angeles in January 1964, he plunged deeper than ever into movement work. And on several fronts. To try to draw younger (and, Craig assumed, more militant) people into Mattachine, he started Mattachine Young Adults. To advertise their meetings, Craig took out "Bulletin Board" ads in *The Village Voice*, and that involved a running battle with the paper, the *Voice* objecting, at various points, to the use of the words "homophile" and "homosexual" in the ads. After much arguing, Craig ultimately got the okay for both—but it would take a full-scale Gay Liberation Front action in 1969 before the *Voice* would sanction the use of the word "gay."

To further attract recruits for Mattachine Young Adults, Craig organized two-person (one male, one female whenever possible) leafleting teams in the Village. Expecting some hostile reactions, the teams developed strategy for forestalling actual physical attack: "If someone calls you a fag or a dyke, don't respond to them verbally. Be dignified. Don't get on their level. That will only encourage them to do something further, possibly worse. And it will put you in a state of mind where you can't really think about what's going on. Try to stay calm and centered."

The tactics worked most of the time. And as often as not, the teams got a positive response. On one snowy night when Craig was leafleting at the Sheridan Square subway entrance, a woman who had taken a flyer and read it came back and told Craig she didn't know anything about homosexuals, but their cause had to be good if he was willing to stand outside in such terrible weather.

He was willing to do a lot more. One of his ideas, which came to him in a fit of anger and which he never pushed, was that every time there was a gay-bashing, gays should announce that they were going to randomly beat up a straight. Something else he wanted to do—twenty-five years before the controversy over "outing"—was to place an ad announcing that all gay people would have five years to come out, and then on January 1, 1970, the name of every gay person would be published.

In Craig's mind visibility *was* the key to ending oppression, and he kept searching for ways to swell the ranks of the openly gay. To that end, he willingly appeared in the public media, doing a number of radio shows with his cohort Randy Wicker, who had already proven himself something of a genius in media manipulation. Wicker could be arch and self-aggrandizing, which grated on Craig, but he was grateful to find somebody who shared his belief that Mattachine should act as if it were a movement, not a hospital ward; and in tribute, Craig entitled a column of political tidbits that he gathered for the Mattachine newsletter "The Wicker Basket."

When *The Alan Burke Show*—a Saturday night TV talk show that for a time rivaled David Susskind's in popularity—called Mattachine for "a homosexual" to interview, Craig volunteered to go. By that time, he had become well aware that the media were primarily interested in sensationalistic "entertainment," and he did his considerable best to forestall such exploitation. When he was told to appear a full hour before airtime to be made up for the Burke show, Craig got a straight actress friend of his who knew all about stage makeup to come with him. She stood over him while the makeup man went to work, and made sure that nothing more than a little powder and cheek coloring was used.

Craig also dressed for the occasion, donning a rare tie and jacket, looking for all the world like Joe College. And when he got the usual hostile questions from the audience about "sickness" and "child molestation," he fielded them expertly. One macho young man stood up in the audience to describe the "sick" experience he had had when staying overnight at a YMCA—how "a coupla homo-sexuals tried to come on to me, they're *always* tryin' to come on to me." Craig waited a beat, and then said quietly, "You flatter yourself." The audience broke up.

Craig's efforts to bring more young people into Mattachine, and in general to swell its membership rolls, paid off handsomely. The person actually in charge of the membership committee in 1964 was

Alfred Sawahata, a Japanese-American architect who was one of Craig's favorite people at Mattachine. Sawahata taught Craig how to color-code the membership list in order to tell at a glance who needed to renew his or her dues, and how to send out discreet reminders to mail them in.

Craig went several steps further. He printed up a membership form urging people to join Mattachine, and then aggressively distributed it throughout the Village. And to create the impression that Mattachine was awash in activity, he also made sure that the newsletter came out on time. Thanks largely to these efforts, Mattachine's monthly meeting at Freedom House was, by 1965, often playing to full houses, and the rolls showed some three hundred paid-up members. By mid-1966, the number had gone to five hundred.

Craig personally recruited some of the people who would shortly become prominent in the struggle to steer New York Mattachine into more militant waters. Through Mattachine Young Adults he brought in Renée Cafiero, Bobby Gonzalez, and Michael Belser. And through a love affair, he brought in Dick Leitsch, who would become the dominant figure in Mattachine for the next half-dozen years.[8]

Craig and Dick met in a doorway while both were cruising Greenwich Avenue one night, and they started to see each other fairly often. Leitsch was working at the time in the paint department at Gimbel's department store, and had never attended a Mattachine meeting. But it quickly became apparent to him that Mattachine was Craig's passion and that if he wanted to see more of Craig he would have to start going to meetings, since that was where Craig seemed to spend all his spare time.

Leitsch soon became interested in the proceedings and from the first, he (like Craig) eschewed the use of a pseudonym. And he soon began to think of himself and Craig as lovers—though Craig never did. Craig enjoyed sex with Leitsch, but rejected his possessive attempts to control his every breath. Growing up with an alcoholic mother, and a father who worked long hours, Leitsch from an early age had felt "in charge." He was an articulate, persuasive man, and could be an exceedingly charming one. But when he wasn't getting his way, he could become explosively dictatorial.

One night when the two men were sitting at a restaurant counter having coffee, Craig said he didn't want Dick to come back with him to his apartment on Horatio Street; he felt like being alone that night. Leitsch, without a word, threw his coffee cup to the floor with such violence that the owner of the restaurant came running—and Craig,

frightened, beat a hasty retreat out the back door. But ten minutes after he got home, the doorbell rang downstairs. Knowing it was Leitsch, Craig ignored the ring. Then he heard Leitsch screaming out his name in the street. Again he ignored it. But somehow Leitsch got into the building and tried to break down Craig's door. Terrified, Craig was about to go down the fire escape, when he heard a neighbor (who knew both men) calming Leitsch down, and ultimately persuading him to leave.

Craig's affair with Leitsch, not surprisingly, lasted less than a year. But by then Leitsch was thoroughly hooked on Mattachine and he and Craig, despite residual anger at each other, became staunch political allies. In 1964–1965, New York Mattachine was still controlled by the conservatives. They believed in gradualism and quietism, in modifying *gay* comportment so that it would better coincide with middle-class notions of proper behavior, in concentrating on education, in allying with and relying on whatever sympathetic experts they could find in straight religious, legal, and psychiatric circles.

Where the conservatives emphasized the need for the homosexual to adjust to society, the militants, taking their cue from the black civil rights struggle, insisted that society had to do the adjusting, had to stop belittling and persecuting gay people. Frank Kameny summed up the militant view succinctly in a speech he gave to New York Mattachine in July 1964. Assailing the unproven assumptions and sloppy research that lay behind the psychoanalytic view of homosexuality as a disorder, Kameny threw out this challenge to the conservatives: "The entire movement is going to stand or fall upon the question of whether homosexuality is a sickness, and upon our taking a firm stand on it."

Kameny's speech helped to shift the views of Julian Hodges, another man Craig had gotten interested in Mattachine. Hodges was from a prominent North Carolina family (a close relative, Luther Hodges, was Kennedy's secretary of commerce), and after he joined New York Mattachine in 1964 he, like Leitsch, had quickly assumed a leading role in the organization. Craig, Hodges, Leitsch, and sometimes Randy Wicker took to having dinner together after Mattachine meetings to talk about how they could wrest control of the organization from the conservatives. They finally decided to run an opposing slate in the upcoming May 1965 election, with Julian Hodges standing for president against the conservatives' candidate, David Goldberger (who headed Mattachine's West Side Discussion Group).

Mattachine elections were formal and secret. Ballots went out in

the mail, within a doubly sealed return envelope. Then, at the annual meeting, the ballots were opened in front of the entire membership present. In the May 1965 election, Leitsch and Hodges were entrusted with the responsibility of bringing to the annual meeting all the ballots that had been received in the mail.

Leitsch later confessed to Craig that he and Hodges had steamed open the envelopes the night before the meeting and changed some of the ballots to make sure that Hodges would be declared the winner. As indeed he was, by a three-to-two margin. Not realizing that the election may have been stolen from them, the conservatives left Mattachine in droves immediately afterward. And they took the West Side Discussion Group, which they had long controlled, with them. But despite, or—in a national climate that was increasingly confrontational—perhaps because of those conservative defections, the membership roles of New York Mattachine continued to climb toward five hundred. "See what action does?" Leitsch wrote exultantly to Frank Kameny.[9]

New York Mattachine now joined Washington Mattachine, led by Kameny, in the militant column. Yet Leitsch and Kameny, two strong-willed, ambitious, authoritarian men, were soon at odds. Leitsch complained that Washington Mattachine was out "to dominate," presenting itself as "the conscience of the movement." In Leitsch's view, the Kameny group was in fact "a thorn in the side of the Eastern organizations," given to excommunicating individuals and groups not abiding by its own "puritanical" standards. After Kameny "chastised" the Philadelphia Janus Society and its leader, Clark Polak (known to be as testy and egocentric as most of the other East Coast leaders), for including "titillating" pictures in its magazine, DRUM, and helped to get Janus kicked out of ECHO, Leitsch scornfully pointed out that DRUM had a circulation of ten thousand whereas Washington Mattachine's Eastern Mattachine Review had a mere 2,500 readers.[10]

Not that Leitsch had much use for Polak, DRUM, Janus—or, for that matter, ECHO. When some of his associates in the movement sent him glowing reports of an ECHO conference in the fall of 1965, Leitsch sent enthusiastic congratulations even as he was expressing to other correspondents his disdain ("ECHO is a trifle silly . . . and possibly ridiculous"), and simultaneously attempting to undercut ECHO by forming a separate alliance with the New York chapter of Daughters of Bilitis. "ECHO no longer provides our two organizations," Leitsch wrote a DOB officer, "with a real means of coopera-

tion," and he suggested dates for a get-together "to explore means and methods of working together."[11]

After he succeeded Hodges as president of Mattachine New York in November 1965, Leitsch seemed to take every criticism of MSNY as a personal affront, and to take every opportunity to vilify other movement leaders and groups. He roundly denounced Polak, Inman, Shirley Willer of DOB and Dorr Legg of Los Angeles's ONE as "obstructionists," and ascribed their motives to jealousy of MSNY's prominence and accomplishments; they were, in Leitsch's view, hankering to "get in on the headlines."[12]

What *was* unequivocally true was that Leitsch and Hodges had embarked on an aggressive series of actions and could point to an impressive set of working relationships with New York City officials. Among other moves, Leitsch had kept after the State Liquor Authority to clarify its policies regarding gay bars and, when its replies proved evasive, had denounced the SLA chairman for his "uncooperative and . . . non-committal" response. Leitsch had also held the *Suffolk County News* to point when it continued to print the names, occupations, and addresses of men arrested in police sweeps of the gay Fire Island resorts, excoriating the paper for conducting "a witch-hunt" that encouraged blackmail, crimes of violence, and police harassment.[13]

And when the New York mayoral election in 1965 was won by John Lindsay, a liberal Republican thought to be more of a genuine reformer than his Democratic predecessors, Leitsch was quick to hail his victory as marking "hope for New York City to become a free and open society in which the rights of minority groups and the rights of those who are different will be protected and respected." Yet when Lindsay, a few months later, authorized a "cleanup" of Times Square and Greenwich Village, Leitsch was equally quick to protest the infringement on civil liberties. That led to a meeting between Lindsay, Leitsch, and others which later culminated in the mayor ordering the police to end all efforts to entrap homosexuals.[14]

In San Francisco, too, the successful fight against an attempted police crackdown on the bars in 1964–1965 slowly swelled homophile ranks. Matters culminated in 1966 with three major events: the appearance of Democratic party powerhouses John Burton and Willie Brown at SIR meetings to appeal for gay votes; a series of demonstrations in several California cities (and elsewhere as well) to protest the exclusion of homosexuals from the armed forces; and a battle between gays and the police in San Francisco that lasted for three

nights following a police attempt to raid Compton's Cafeteria, a gay hangout at Turk and Taylor streets.[15]

Within ECHO, the strategy of picketing produced a considerable uproar, and Craig became centrally involved in the issue. Inspired by the direct-action tactics that black college students and Freedom Riders had employed in their confrontations with segregated facilities, Craig was eager to take a comparable stand against the institutional structures that perpetuated gay oppression. Through his involvement with ECHO, he got to know Frank Kameny, Barbara Gittings, Kay "Tobin" (Lahusen), and other militants well; at Kameny's suggestion, they had started to meet together in 1964 to talk about organizing a series of public demonstrations. (At Craig's first encounter with Barbara and Kay, he watched them carefully, lovingly, set up tape recorders and microphones for an ECHO conference, and was moved to tears—moved at the absence of the kind of egotistical, aggressive power-tripping he had been witnessing in New York Mattachine.)

The group decided that to protest the exclusion of homosexuals from federal employment and the armed services, it would picket in front of the Pentagon, the Civil Service Commission, the State Department, and—to culminate the series—the White House. Kameny, based in Washington, did most of the legwork in getting permits and picket signs readied (and the American flags that by law had to be carried at all demonstrations). Most of the troops, a hard core of twenty to forty people, came down from New York and Philadelphia, with smaller contingents from Boston and Washington. They were joined for the climactic White House demonstration by Foster Gunnison, Jr., from Hartford.

At Kameny's insistence, a strict dress code was enforced on all participants. "If we want to be employed by the Federal Government," Kameny intoned, "we have to look employable to the Federal Government." Craig protested that the focus on federal employment was Kameny's own hobbyhorse (Kameny had been fired from government work in the late fifties when it was discovered that he had been arrested in 1956 on the catch-all charge of "lewd and indecent acts"), and was *not* the sole or even primary purpose of the demonstrations. But Kameny and his allies replied that whatever the purpose, it was important to look ordinary, to get bystanders to hear the message rather than be prematurely turned off by appearances.[16]

Refusing at first to yield, Craig stubbornly insisted that "the only thing we have in common with heterosexuals is what we do in bed"

(a radical notion indeed in 1965), and he grumbled about the need to let people make their own personal statements, and about not wanting to look like a church group on a Sunday picnic. But—for the time being—he finally decided to defer to Kameny's activist record and to his authority (though he disliked the iron way Kameny wielded it). Craig joined the other men in dutifully donning suit and tie. The women wore dresses.

Dick Leitsch shared Craig's contempt for Kameny's dress code —but went beyond it to descry the demonstrations in their entirety as tactically ill-conceived. *Numbers* were what mattered, Leitsch insisted. "The difference between us," he wrote Kameny, "is that I believe we must impress authority and the power-structure with our strength; you seem to believe we must impress Everyman with our decency. (Whatever that is.)" Far better, in Leitsch's view, to mobilize two hundred people in casual, neat clothing than fifty suited and dressed to look like super-respectable citizens. Government officials *might* respond to the presence of significant numbers of demonstrators, but would remain indifferent to being picketed by a small group of "quality" folks—especially since the picketing would be focused not on one site but, consecutively, on three or four.[17]

But Kameny, who prided himself on being "practical," continued to insist that "clean-scrubbed demonstrations will get us ahead . . . FAR, FAR faster than court cases. . . . [T]he man in a suit is STILL the overwhelming norm in this country." "Hundreds of beatnik types in front of the Civil Service Commission," he wrote Leitsch, would be not only a tactical mistake but a misrepresentation of the homosexual community. "Grubbiness has never, to my knowledge," he huffily asserted, "been a stereotype of a homosexual. Do our pickets *your* way, and it will soon become so."[18]

Kameny had his way. Marching quietly in single file, carrying their signs (SEXUAL PREFERENCE IS IRRELEVANT TO FEDERAL EMPLOYMENT; CIVIL SERVICE COMMISSION IS UN-AMERICAN), wearing their "Equality for Homosexuals" buttons, kept in constant motion by the police, his intrepid group of demonstrators—no gay protest had ever been seen in the nation's capital, and precious few anywhere else— carried out their picketing without serious incident. The final demonstration, in front of the White House in April 1965, was to Craig the most thrilling. More than seventy marchers participated, and more media showed up than previously (though the biggest press notice came from the sensationalistic rag *Confidential*, which in its October 1965 issue ran an article under the heading "Homos on the March").

Craig thought it was "the most wonderful day of my life," and sitting afterward in a coffee shop with Kameny, Jack Nichols, and a few others, he felt too excited to eat. As people shared their sadness that the whole series of demonstrations had now wound down, with no plans for anything further, Craig suddenly had a brainstorm. "It doesn't *have* to be over!" he fairly shouted. "I couldn't bear for it to be over!" And then he presented his idea: to demonstrate every Fourth of July in front of Independence Hall in Philadelphia—"create like a gay holiday. We can call it the Annual Reminder—the Reminder that a group of Americans still don't have their basic rights to life, liberty and the pursuit of happiness."

Everybody was instantly entranced (though Kameny seemed a little annoyed that someone else had seized the initiative), and enthusiasm proved so high that the first Annual Reminder, sponsored by the New York, Washington, and Philadelphia Mattachine societies, took place that very July, only three months after Craig had come up with the idea. Thirty-nine people (including several from Midwest Mattachine) picketed in front of Independence Hall from three-thirty to five P.M., and the demonstration got mentioned on the local TV news and on the front page of *The Philadelphia Inquirer*. Kameny had taken pains to notify the appropriate authorities in advance, and he was pleased that police behavior was "proper and cordial" and the demonstrators "dignified and orderly."[19]

For the next five years, an indefatigable band of thirty to a hundred people, always including Craig, Frank Kameny, Barbara Gittings, and Kay Tobin, would appear with their placards and buttons (BILL OF RIGHTS FOR HOMOSEXUALS; 15,000,000 HOMOSEXUAL AMERICANS ASK FOR EQUALITY, OPPORTUNITY, DIGNITY) in front of Independence Hall, earnestly asserting what then seemed the far distant and possibly utopian demand for "gay rights." As Barbara Gittings later recalled, those who participated in the Annual Reminders would "smile and smile," would hand out leaflets to anyone who passed by (though many refused to take them), and would try to swallow their own discomfort at "not knowing what the consequences would be," whether their names would be printed in the paper and their jobs lost, or whether they might even be arrested.

By the time of the Second Annual Reminder, in 1966, the event had attracted enough attention to warrant the presence of agents from the Bureau of Special Services. Their reports dutifully quoted from Craig's advertisement for the picket ("this annual demonstration is held to call to the attention of the American people discriminatory

laws and regulations by the government directed against its homo-sexual citizens"), as if uncovering a monstrous conspiracy against the Constitution. Following the event, moreover, BOSS agents also sat in on New York Mattachine meetings, and earnestly reported the momentous news that a guest speaker had "spent 30 years handling Immigration and Deportation cases," and that a doctoral candidate in psychology had requested volunteers to fill out a questionnaire.

More ominously, three men dressed in dark business suits knocked on the door of Craig's apartment one night and then barged in, flashing FBI badges. They said they were looking for Michael Levy (a man Craig had recently had a brief affair with), who was wanted for passing bad checks. Then they searched the apartment—Craig was too stunned to ask to see a warrant—and left. But that was not the end of it. One of the agents continued to call Craig every few months for years, blandly asking him each time "if everything was okay." Then, in 1970, the same agent relayed a suggestion from his boss, John Caufield (as head of White House security, Caufield would later testify at the Watergate hearings), that Craig attend Gay Lib-eration Front meetings and report back to them what had taken place. Craig turned the offer down.

Instead of sating Craig's appetite for activism, the successful launching of the Annual Reminder further stimulated it. He, Leitsch, and Leitsch's current lover, John Timmons, decided to combine forces for an action they dubbed "the sip-in." The point was to challenge the State Liquor Authority regulation that prohibited bars and restaurants from selling drinks to homosexuals, on penalty of having their licenses revoked. Leitsch sent out press releases and telegrams announcing their impending defiance of the regulation.[20]

On April 21, 1966, the trio, dressed immaculately in suits and ties ("the picture of a Madison Avenue executive," the *Voice* later reported), rendezvoused as planned and found reporters from *The New York Times*, *The Village Voice*, and the *New York Post* waiting for them—which promised greater media coverage than had attended any previous movement event. Activists and reporters moved off together to the Ukrainian-American Village Bar on St. Mark's Place, which had long had a hand-lettered sign above the bar reading, "If you are gay, please stay away." But the bar must have gotten wind of the pending invasion: When the group arrived there, they found the place locked.

They decided to shift the action to the Howard Johnson's on

Sixth Avenue and Eighth Street (which had a famously cruisy men's room in the basement, even if the restaurant supposedly didn't sell drinks to faggots). Sitting down in a booth, the trio called over the manager and handed him their pre-prepared statement: "We, the undersigned, are homosexuals. We believe that a place of public accommodation has an obligation to serve an orderly person, and that we are entitled to service as long as we are orderly. We therefore ask to be served on your premises. Should you refuse to serve us, we will be obligated to file a complaint against you with the State Liquor Authority."

"How do I know you're homosexuals?" the manager genially responded—and then, to the trio's astonishment, broke out laughing. "Why shouldn't they be served a drink?" he asked the reporters. "They look like perfect gentlemen to me. I drink. Who knows if I'm a homosexual or not?" He then went on to declare that he had problems, too, what with two children and three grandchildren, and whose business was it anyway what a person's sex life happened to be. He ordered the waiter to "bring the boys a drink"—and the reporters, too. Clearly Howard Johnson's was not going to play the part assigned it in the activist drama.

So on they went to the Waikiki, a bar on Sixth Avenue between Ninth and Tenth streets. Once again, the manager foiled the protest. "I serve anybody," he said, "so long as he doesn't annoy anybody." And once more drinks appeared for all hands. By now John Timmons was feeling a little woozy from the liquor, but the trio, still trailed by the expectant reporters, decided to press on. They next entered Julius' on West Tenth Street, confidently telling the reporters that they *would* be denied service there: Though long a gay hangout, Julius' had recently been the scene of several plainclothes-police entrapments, and Craig had himself been thrown out of there for wearing an "Equality for Homosexuals" button.

When they entered Julius', several gay men were having drinks at the bar. "We are homosexuals and we would like a drink," Dick Leitsch said to the bartender. "I don't know what you're trying to prove," the bartender answered. "You can't serve us if we are homosexuals?" Leitsch asked hopefully. "No," came the long-desired answer. John Timmons sighed contentedly. "Another bourbon and water and I would have been under the table."

The point had been made, the action completed. New York Mattachine immediately announced that it was filing a complaint with the State Liquor Authority against Julius' for unconstitutionally dis-

criminating against homosexuals in violation of the First and Fourteenth amendments. And it announced further that it would pay any
legal expenses Julius' incurred.

But it was unclear for some time longer whether a victory could
be claimed. The State Liquor Authority quickly announced that it
would take no action against bars that refused service to homosexuals.
And there the matter might have ended, the Mattachine action
thwarted, had it not been for William H. Booth, the black chairman
of the Commission on Human Rights. Booth responded to the SLA
statement by saying publicly that the Human Rights Commission had
jurisdiction over discrimination based on sex, and he *would* try to put
an end to SLA policy on serving homosexuals if a complaint against
Julius was filed with his office. Mattachine immediately complied.

By then, several newspapers had run editorials against the SLA's
discriminatory policies, and a committee of prominent heterosexuals,
including the Episcopal bishop of New York, had formed in support
of Commissioner Booth's position. Still, the case had to go to court,
and it wasn't until the following year that the state's Appellate Division
ruled that serving a homosexual was not (as the SLA had previously
held) the equivalent of running "a disorderly house" and that a bar's
license could be revoked only if "substantial evidence" of indecent
behavior had been demonstrated.

The ruling was well worth having, but it hardly put an end to
police harassment of gay bars or to the police practice of sending out
comely young cops, carefully attired in up-to-date chinos and tennis
shoes, to entrap gay men on the street. Given Commissioner Booth's
stance in the Julius case, Dick Leitsch turned to him for help against
entrapment. Booth discussed the issue with Chief Inspector Sanford
D. Garelick, who assured him that the police department gave no
official encouragement to entrapment, and solemnly promised to investigate any such incidents that came to his attention.

Needless to say, none did. Instead, Mattachine continued to get
calls from desperate gay men who had been arrested for "soliciting"
a police officer. Mattachine kept a list of those few lawyers willing to
handle such "distasteful" cases, but the field had pretty much become
the monopoly of two of them, Gertrude Gottlieb ("Dirty Gertie," to
the boys) and Enid Gerling. As the mythology of the day had it, even
before family or friends had heard the news, Gottlieb and Gerling
would appear at the police station, apparently tipped off by the
cops—for a piece of the standard two-thousand-dollar action, of
course.

This double-dealing game of collusion and blackmail enraged Craig, and he helped to persuade Mattachine's officers to remove the two women's names from the referral list. Enid Gerling was not one to take that lying down. She came storming into the Mattachine office, her voice already at full volume, screaming that they couldn't do this to her, that they would rue the day they had crossed her path, that she would have the place closed down if her name wasn't put back on the referral list *at once*. But Mattachine held its ground. And Gerling never followed through on her threats.[21]

But police entrapment and bar raids continued. Indeed, in 1966, "liberal" Mayor John Lindsay (who would subsequently put an end to entrapment) endorsed a sweeping police campaign to rid both Times Square and Washington Square Park of "undesirables." On the night the police poured from their vans into Times Square, Sylvia Rivera was standing at her usual spot on Ninth Avenue and Forty-fourth Street, trying to turn just one more trick before calling it a night— but ended in jail instead.

K A R L A

During Karla's first week as a Barnard freshman in 1964, she heard about the two women who had been expelled the previous year. A male student at Columbia (directly across the street from Barnard) had peered into the women's dormitory room with a pair of binoculars and seen them making love. The Peeping Tom was allowed to stay and, by some, was praised; the women were kicked out. Hearing the story, Karla "realized for the first time that there was something wrong with being a lesbian," and decided she "had better cover up."

She started dating a young man from Yale whom she had met at one of the freshman dances. He was from Louisiana and had never seen a Jew. Karla tried a joke to relieve his astonishment, saying something about how Jews nowadays clipped off the infant's horns at birth. But he took the statement at face value and solemnly replied that he "hadn't known that." The relationship was never romantic and never sexual; yet it persisted throughout Karla's undergraduate years. The two would see each other every few weeks, talk superficially about events of the day, peck each other on the lips—and make

another date. Karla is convinced, in retrospect, that her Yalie was gay and that they were using each other as cover.

But Karla soon had a steady female date as well, and that relationship quickly became sexual. Not that *they* ever talked about it, either. The woman, an undergraduate at City College, had a boyfriend on the side and treated her relationship with Karla in the spirit of the rising counterculture: something she did because it felt good—no guilt, no attachments. But Karla was looking for some other kind of connection, though she had trouble defining it even to herself. It had something to do with wanting to find out more about herself by meeting women who already shared her emotional space, including its confusions.

In a subculture that could not yet claim many social or institutional structures, let alone a political voice, bars were among the few places where lesbians felt they could congregate and be themselves in relative safety. This was especially true for working-class women, who, much more than their middle-class and upper-class sisters, were given to strict "butch" and "femme" role divisions. Karla's family background was a mix of working-class status and middle-class income, and her own high educational level had un-classed her still further.

In appearance, too, Karla failed to fit neatly into either of the dichotomous butch-femme roles that the lesbian bar world encouraged in these years. She was athletic and compact in build, but her self-presentation was "muddied" (in the eyes of the bar world) by long hair and dangling earrings. All at once strong and feminine (even glamorous), Karla invited instant disapproval from those who insisted on a choice between one or the other. But Karla refused to choose. She regarded strict role divisions as destructive mimicry of rigid heterosexual norms; in her view, they narrowed and pigeonholed the wide actual range of human impulses and identifications.[22]

Not surprisingly, then, the first time Karla walked into the Sea Colony, a popular lesbian bar during the mid-sixties, her immediate reaction was that she didn't belong there. The smoke and noise confused her; she felt upset watching women consume alcohol as if it were soda pop, and annoyed at the alternatively demure or belligerent patrons. She didn't meet any women who went to college (or who admitted they did), and in fact had trouble meeting anybody at all. Her self-presentation was apparently experienced as threatening; she evoked distrust without meaning or wanting to. When asked—which always happened quickly—whether she was butch or femme, Karla

wouldn't know what to say, and the other woman would soon walk away. If these women were lesbians, Karla thought, then maybe she wasn't. Far from giving Karla the feeling that she had come home at last, the Sea Colony made her think that she might have made a terrible mistake. She went back not more than three or four times during her entire undergraduate life.

Even if she had not found the bar scene uncongenial, Karla would have had little time for it. She was kept busy simply trying to make ends meet. Through a ruse, she managed to live illegally in one of the Barnard dorms. Since she had no meal card, she would simply pick up a plate and join the cafeteria line, pretending she was going back for seconds on the main course (which was allowed). Almost every night of the week she baby-sat, for $1.25 an hour *and*—this was more urgent than the money—permission to raid the refrigerator. When she and friends compared notes on clients, it wasn't about whether the child was difficult or easy but about how much and what kind of food the family had.

She picked up other kinds of work as well. During the summers, she would hold down both day and evening jobs—everything from camp counseling, to sales work in a department store, to punching and cataloging material for a Columbia professor's encyclopedia-in-progress. During the school year she was able to use her two years of Latin and five of French at Bromley to get a job at the Barnard language laboratory; it paid well (four dollars an hour) and allowed her time, in between signing out tapes and explaining how the machines worked, to get some studying done.

It was about the only time she did have for schoolwork, and as a result she got mostly B's. She gave some thought to a premed major, but realized she would never be able to afford medical school; besides, she turned off to the profession after experiencing firsthand—one of her part-time jobs was as an operating-room clerk—its routine malpractices. Karla's main interest continued to be languages. She was especially drawn to French and Russian, and ended up majoring in French.

She had as little time for a social life as for studying. In her junior year she moved into a seventy-five-dollar-a-month apartment at 107th Street and Broadway, which she shared with several roommates; they became her main social outlet. They ate spaghetti together every night (managing to find a powdered sauce that cost nine cents a serving), and her roommates introduced Karla first to pot and then to a variety of other drugs. Being poor, they tried smoking anything they heard

produced a high, including peppers and banana skins, and inhaling the gas from Reddi-Wip cans (which did work). Karla believes that taking drugs "really did expand my mind and loosened me up in many ways."

But becoming more countercultural did not immediately make her more political. Nothing in her background predisposed her to activism. She describes her parents as "slightly to the right of Archie Bunker"; they had no politics but plenty of prejudices, especially about Christians and blacks. Nene, they insisted, was different from other blacks, and they treated her like one of the family. As for Nene, she understandably never spoke of the black civil rights struggle around the Jays, and simply said that she "accepted people as people." (She had left when Karla was twelve and no longer needed her, going to work as a nurse's aide in the Brooklyn Eye and Ear Hospital.) And Karla's years at the Bromley Institute, with its unbroken expanse of privileged white faces, did nothing to raise her consciousness about injustice.

Yet she did think of herself as a liberal, and ascribes that mostly to Nene, whose presence, not preachments, in her life had kept her from growing up with clearcut notions about race or gender. It never occurred to Karla as a child that her lighter skin color made her different from Nene in any significant way; the closeness and identification were complete. As to gender, when she and Nene were rooting for Pee Wee Reese at Ebbets Field, Nene never hinted that Karla couldn't duplicate his feats or that the game of baseball was reserved for boys.

Like almost everyone else at Barnard, Karla was against the war in Vietnam and for the civil rights movement. But as late as her senior year in 1968, she had not joined any of the proliferating marches or protests in support of those positions. And then came the upheaval at Columbia University in April of her senior year, an event that would change Karla irrevocably, moving her from abstract sympathy to emotional identification with the outsiders of the world.

There were two key issues during the Columbia disruptions. The first was the university's pending construction of a gym in a park used by Harlem residents—the latest of a long series of encroachments by Columbia that, with little or no concern for the wishes and well-being of poor tenants, had forced them out. The second issue concerned the university's affiliation with the Institute for Defense Analyses (IDA), an affiliation symbolic of academia's widespread involvement with government-sponsored weapons research (at Columbia the re-

search focused on antisubmarine warfare), and on complicity with what was aptly being called the military-industrial complex. In 1968 more than two thirds of university research funds came from agencies of the federal government connected with defense matters, and about a quarter of the two hundred largest industrial corporations in the country had university officials on their boards of directors.[23]

Columbia's insensitivity to its black neighbors seemed to many on the left of a piece with its willingness to create instruments of death for use against Asians. But when student representatives tried to open up a dialogue with the Columbia administration, they were swiftly rebuffed—and on top of that, had to listen to faculty mandarins like Jacques Barzun smugly reprimand them for operating on the false assumption that the university did or should function as a democracy, for having failed to "earn" a voice in policy deliberations—and for being "mere transients," ill equipped and ill prepared to participate in the higher councils of higher education.

The student radicals thought otherwise, and on April 23, 1968, a group of them seized a building on the Columbia campus and issued a set of demands denouncing the planned gym and the university's complicity with weapons research. In the following days, more buildings were occupied. Live-in "communes" and round-the-clock speak-outs were set up within them, and Columbia found itself faced with a full-scale insurrection. Karla went in and out of the buildings all week long, astounded by the audacity of her fellow students, electrified by their compelling arguments. Talking to the radicals, hearing for the first time the dismaying details of Columbia's callousness toward its black neighbors and of America's brutality toward the Vietnamese, changed her life. "I had just never had time before to think about it all," she later said, "but now I felt the injustice in a very personal and deep way."

She was also present when, in the early morning hours of April 30, the Columbia administration called in the police. She witnessed the cops dragging students out of the buildings and—though most of them offered only passive resistance—beating them indiscriminately. She also watched, terrified, as mounted police charged through the campus, striking out at any student in their path and, before the rampage was over, injuring more than two hundred. That barbarous police attack brought the faculty (though not, of course, its Jacques Barzuns) over to the side of the students, and the next day a campus-wide strike shut the university down.

Karla's education had taken a giant leap forward. She had been

radicalized in several directions at once. The viciousness of entrenched authority—whether embodied in university administrators or in uniformed police—was no longer a rhetorical abstraction; nor were bleeding protesters any longer a distant image on some front page or television screen. She had now seen it all for herself.

And what she had also seen—and this was perhaps the least expected and therefore the most revelatory—was that many of the radical male students fully matched their antagonists in strident, strutting machismo. "I was appalled by the behavior of the men," Karla later said. "I could see that left-wing men were not any different." They, like their right-wing brothers, felt that women were made to be auxiliaries, secondary backups for their own frontline heroics. During the building takeover, some of them had actually told Karla and other female students to take off for the local stores to buy food supplies. They even had a little rap about it, about how everyone who wanted to help the revolution should do the job they were best qualified to do. The men didn't know how to make coffee and the women did, so the women should do it—for the "greater cause"—and should do it cheerfully.

Karla thought all that was self-justifying crap—even if she didn't say so at the moment. But she did think it. And that alone, as she would soon discover, put her straight on the road to feminism. The family trait of stubbornness was about to find a new channel.

R   A   Y

On the day Sylvia went to jail at Rikers Island, she weighed a strapping 140 pounds. When she came out two and a half months later, she was down to 115. It wasn't jail food, bad though that was, that caused the drop. It was heroin.

Sylvia was turned on in jail by a "nice queen" named Penny—"pure peer pressure" is how Sylvia later described it. When Penny asked her one day, "Do you shoot drugs?" Sylvia answered with her customary bravado: "Well, of course I do. I love them." It was easy to get dope in jail. True to her word, Penny came up with both heroin and a needle. Afterward, Sylvia was as sick as a dog for three days. It was the start of a habit that would grip her for five years.

She had a huge tolerance for heroin. When everyone else was nodding out, kissing their toes, Sylvia would be wide awake and more than a little annoyed that she hadn't gotten off. So one night (this was later, after she got out of jail) when their connection warned Sylvia and her friends that the dope they had just bought was super-strong, Sylvia ignored him and shot up a full dose. She went out like a light and woke up in a snowbank on the street. Her friends had dragged her down three flights, afraid she was dead. But she came out of it, and within seconds was cursing them out for "fucking up my coat" by dumping her in the snowbank.

Due to the police crackdown in 1966, the cellblock in the Rikers Island prison reserved for gay-related "crimes" was filled to overflowing. Most of the queens welcomed the separate unit as a refuge from rape and harassment and as a place where, with a little ingenuity, they could recreate some semblance of their life on the outside. They saved pats of butter from meals to use as grease for sex, and they used Kool-Aid to dye the dreary blue prison garb more becoming shades. To prepare for the Christmas party, they pieced together outfits, converting work clothes into dresses and using bars of soap to press them. It was even rumored that a few of the queens got themselves rearrested in order to take part in the Christmas party.[24]

Yet conditions were harsh on the block. While other prisoners on Rikers were allowed to shower every day, the queens got to shower once a week, even during the steamy summer months. They were also denied library privileges, could receive visits only from family members, not from friends, were offered no prison jobs (like working in the bakery or the kitchen) to break the monotony of the day, and indeed were let out of their cells only for twenty minutes every evening to wash up.

Sylvia made at least one good friend while in jail, a beautiful black queen named Bambi Lamour. On their way to breakfast one morning, Bambi looked over disdainfully at the newly arrived Sylvia and demanded, "Who are you, bitch? Since when did they let dykes in the block?" Sylvia knew it was her cue to be haughty. "I'm no dyke, bitch," she sniffed back. "I'm more boy than you. But *you* can call me Sylvia." That did it. They became fast friends on the spot and for the next few months gloried in their reputation as "crazy, abnormal bitches." They'd walk down the corridor snapping their fingers and calling out "Taxi! Taxi! Take us to Forty-second and Ninth. We got to make us some money!" Or they'd refuse to sit with

anyone else at meals, once upending a table and dragging it into a corner for privacy. "Nobody ever fucked with us," Sylvia recalls with satisfaction.

Soon after she got out of jail, Sylvia teamed up with a straight hooker named Kim as her hustling partner. They figured—correctly, it turned out—that they could make more money that way, play into a greater range of fantasies, open up more opportunities to steal. One standard variation went this way:

> CUSTOMER (*approaching Kim and Sylvia on the corner*): Are you two dykes?
> KIM: Yeah. (*pointing to Sylvia*) That's my butch over there. You want to party?
> CUSTOMER: How much is standard?
> SYLVIA: If you ain't spending enough money, we ain't going. You want to have a freebie trip, or you want to have a good trip?

Usually, the customer would opt for the "good trip." Once they had him back in the hotel room, Sylvia—who had started to take hormone shots—would pop off her bra and jiggle her breasts for the customer to play with. But she always kept her G-string on, and the customer at a safe distance. In another variation, Kim and Sylvia would take turns sucking on each other's breasts or feeling each other up on the bed. That usually drove the customer crazy—at which point Sylvia would announce that it was "time for him to pop his nut." According to the game plan, Kim would then screw him while Sylvia rifled his wallet. Sylvia would snap her fingers—"Time's up!"—to signal that she had secured the guy's money; they would then quickly end the scene.

They made a lot of money, enough to finance Sylvia's heroin habit—at one point she was shooting up two hundred dollars' worth a day—as well as the white fox coat she took to hustling in. And enough money to pay for her hormone treatments as well. She had started the treatments thinking she wanted to have a sex-change operation, and had trooped along with her friends to a doctor on the Lower East Side—that is, until she started to get a discharge from her right breast, and discovered that she was being given monkey hormones. She then shifted to a Dr. Stern on Fifth Avenue, who, "if you let him play with you for a little while, he'd give you anything for free." (Craig Rodwell also had his experiences with Dr. Stern

when sent to him, under suspicion of having gonorrhea, by Harvey Milk. Stern told Craig to "lie down on the examination table, take out your penis and get it hard." Stern then discreetly left the room, returning to masturbate Craig while explaining that he needed the semen to test for gonorrhea. Afterward, he invited Craig into his office and showed him a photo album filled with attractive male models, every now and then exclaiming, "Oh, this one is from Chicago, too." Craig never got a bill.)

Initially, Sylvia liked what Dr. Stern's hormones did to her body, reducing facial hair and making her more curvaceous. But she soon decided to stop the injections. "I came to the conclusion," she later recalled, "that I don't want to be a woman. I just want to be me. I want to be Sylvia Rivera. I like pretending. I like to have the role. I like to dress up and pretend, and let the world think about what I am. Is he, or isn't he? That's what I enjoy. I don't want to be a woman. Why? That means I can't fuck nobody up the ass. Two holes? No, no, no. That ain't going to get it. No, no, no."

She did love drag, though. But like so many others in the life, she disliked the actual term. As one of her friends, Ivan Valentin (who later headlined the "Leading Ladies of New York" show), explained, "A drag or transvestite is somebody who always dresses as a woman. A female impersonator is somebody who claims to actually *be* a woman. I'm just a man who likes to dress up." Sylvia felt more or less the same way (less, in her hormone-taking phase). In part, Ivan and Sylvia were accepting the inescapable: they tended to look like boys or butch dykes even when dressed in full drag. (Many of Sylvia's customers would have disagreed, perhaps to avoid the realization that their cocks were getting hard in reaction to a boy.) In any case, neither Sylvia nor Ivan was interested in having cosmetic surgery to burnish the illusion.[25]

And that helps to explain why Sylvia never attempted to work as a performer, though by the mid-sixties there were many more such opportunities opening up in New York than had recently been the case. In an earlier era, the drag performer Julian Eltinge had been so hugely popular that he had had a Broadway theater named after him, and in the forties and fifties Phil Black's drag shows in Harlem, Frankie Quinn's in midtown Manhattan, and Dazee Dee's in Brooklyn—reputedly the classiest of them all—were major events.[26]

It was still possible in the 1950s for T. C. Jones to bring in a crowd for his Broadway revue, *Mask and Gown* (and to do his impersonations of Bette Davis and Tallulah in Leonard Sillman's *New Faces*

of 1956). But the great drag star Minette recalls that by the late fifties only two drag clubs existed in New York City—fewer than in some small Southern cities (though those were subject to sudden closings and arrests). The opening of the 82 Club on East Fourth Street, which became something of a tourist attraction in the sixties, helped to spark a revival, and by the end of that decade, drag had been featured in several off-off-Broadway productions (including H. M. Koutoukas's *Medea in the Laundromat* at Caffè Cino).[27]

By the early seventies, drag had very nearly gone mainstream, with Jackie Curtis, Candy Darling, and Holly Woodlawn all becoming Warhol-made celebrities, though the *term* "drag" continued to be variously regarded. Individual definitions ranged from "dress-up artist" and "performer" to, in Holly Woodlawn's case, a simple "fabulous." ("It's not a man or a woman, it's *fabulous*. When men's fashions start to be more fabulous, I'll use *them* to dress up.") Holly further insisted, contradicting Ivan Valentin, that a "true" drag was not someone who "always dresses as a woman," but rather someone who "only gets it on for the stage." Since prostitution might be regarded as a form of dramatic presentation, Sylvia would have qualified under Holly Woodlawn's definition, as she surely did under Holly's more encompassing "fabulous."[28]

But Sylvia didn't care much about definitions, which was precisely why she would emerge as a radical figure. She disliked any attempt to categorize her random, sometimes contradictory impulses, to make them seem more uniform and predictable than they were. That was precisely why she decided against a sex change. She didn't want to be cast in *any* one mold. Her own description of her cross-dressing best captures the spontaneity at its core: "I like to pull some shit out of the closet, throw on some female attire, a blouse or whatever—not complete drag—paint on a little makeup—and hit the streets."

Sylvia's grandmother did not share her enthusiasm for drag. One night on Ninth Avenue, a queen who lived in Viejita's building yelled over to Sylvia that her grandmother wasn't feeling well and wanted to see her. "Oh sure," Sylvia yelled back, "she pulls that one on me all the time." But she hailed a cab immediately, though stoned and in drag—and though it was two o'clock in the morning. The first thing Viejita said when she opened the door was "Oh my God, you look just like your mother!" "Well, who am I supposed to look like?" Sylvia shot back.

The visit went downhill from there. Viejita told Sylvia that she

had to change. "Change what?" Sylvia answered, as if mystified (while wondering, in her stoned state, if Viejita was encouraging her to go back on hormones). "You have to get *married*!" Viejita shouted. "Married? Married? I *am* married—you met Gary. And I ain't gettin' married again." Another ten minutes of shouting at each other and Sylvia slammed the door behind her and took a cab back to Times Square.

But Viejita wasn't finished with her. One night in the "Hostro" (as the Hispanic prostitutes called the Times Square area), Sylvia was talking on the street with one of her steady customers ("a good trick —fifty dollars just to give him a lousy blow job!") and getting ready to clinch the deal when a woman behind her shouted, "Don't you know that's a man?" Sylvia, in an instant rage, whirled around ready to pop what she assumed was a competing hooker in the face—and came flat up against Viejita. "That's a man! That's my grandson!" Viejita repeated, screaming at the potential customer. When Sylvia tried to calm her down, Viejita accused her (falsely) of no longer sending money home and (accurately) of rarely coming to see her. By this time, the potential customer had fled into the night, never to return.

The running battle with Viejita went on for years, but six months after their confrontation in Times Square, Sylvia was able to use drag to save herself from a much larger battlefront. Approaching the ripe old age of eighteen, and with the country, in 1967, exploding in militant resistance to the escalating war in Vietnam, Sylvia abruptly got notice to report to the local draft board in Jersey City (where she was living at the time).

She made an instant decision: She was not, under any circumstances, going to war. She considered herself a patriotic American, and swore that if anybody ever tried to invade this country, she would pick up a gun—"and I know how to use a gun, honey"—and "blow them away off the continent." But she was "*not* going over there to fight for something that I don't know really what we're going for." The only question was how to get out of it.

Sylvia made up her mind to appear at the draft board in full drag: high heels, miniskirt, long red nails, the works. But she nervously wondered if that would do it; she had heard rumors that even queens had been drafted, to do clerical work. When she arrived at the draft board on the scheduled morning, in full regalia, she was directed to a desk at which sat two sergeants, one male, one female. The female sergeant assumed the new arrival was in her jurisdiction: "Women

who are enlisting," she said, smiling and pointing, "go to *that* side of the room."

"But I'm one of the boys," Sylvia said. "My name is Ray. Ray Rivera."

Now it was the turn of the male sergeant. Gruffly, unsmilingly, he repeated—whether because of nearsightedness or incomprehension—that Sylvia should join the ladies on *that* side of the room. And next thing Sylvia knew, she was on a bus with a bunch of women headed for the induction center in Newark. "All of these bitches got no nails and short cropped hair. They looked butcher than I do at my best." Halfway into the trip, Sylvia noticed one of the tougher-looking women giving her the eye. Sylvia wheeled on her indignantly. "I am *not* a woman!" she yelled. "I *happen* to be one of the boys!"

At the induction center they took Sylvia straight to the psychiatrist's office.

"What's your name?" the psychiatrist asked.

"Which one, darling?"

"Your male Christian name."

"Oh. That's Ray José Christian Rivera. Alias Miss Sylvia Lee Rivera."

"Is there a problem with your sexuality?"

"Is there? I don't know," said Sylvia, arching her eyebrows in feigned innocence. "I know I like men. I know I like to wear dresses. But I don't know what any *problem* is."

The psychiatrist frowned, so Sylvia knew she was on the right track and plunged ahead. "I got papers here from when I was in the hospital. A doctor signed them. The papers state that I am a homosexual. Is that what you mean by a 'problem'?"

Without another word, the psychiatrist stamped "HOMOSEXUAL" in three-inch-high red letters on Sylvia's induction notice, then told her that she could go home.

Knowing she had gotten off, Sylvia giddily opted for one last bit of grandstanding camp. "I ain't got no money to go home," she announced with maximum petulance. "You all brought me here, now you all got to get me home. Somebody's *got to take me home!*"

And damned if they didn't drive her all the way back to Jersey City.

J   I   M

Jim Fouratt was finding his own ways to resist the draft—to resist what he had come to view as entrenched and irresponsible American power. After his first, almost inadvertent antiwar demonstration in Times Square in 1964, he rapidly became politicized. A crucial turning point for him was getting to know Abbie Hoffman in 1966. As an offshoot of his involvement in the black civil rights struggle, Hoffman had come to New York to open Liberty House—a store devoted to selling handmade goods produced in Mississippi—on the Lower East Side. Impressed with Jim's work in helping to organize New York's first "be-in"—a gathering and display of the countercultural hippie tribes at the Sheep Meadow in Central Park—Abbie sought him out.[29]

Jim's guess is that Abbie was also drawn to him as that intriguing Other, the blond, blue-eyed and—Jim encouraging the notion—purportedly upper-class WASP. Whatever the source of the initial attraction, the two men became increasingly involved in political work together and between 1967 and 1969, Jim became one of the most prominent figures in the "Yippie!" wing of the movement. ("Yippie" was the name given to politicized hippies.) Abbie defined the Yippie group with his characteristically stylish blend of humor and high purpose: The Yippies, he wrote, represented a "blending of pot and politics into a political grass leaves movement—a cross-fertilization of the hippie and New Left philosophies." The group's aim—though in true Yippie fashion it would have disavowed so linear a goal and the planning and leadership implied—was to "tie together as much of the underground as was willing into some gigantic national get-together" whose purpose would be to develop "a model for an alternate society."[30]

Jim grew to love Abbie "in a way that one loves a comrade," even though he felt early on that Abbie, and even more, his fellow Yippie leader, Jerry Rubin, were deeply, almost reflexively homophobic—which Abbie himself acknowledged late in life. Jim remained indifferent to Rubin, dismissing him as a manipulative careerist, but emotionally, he invested heavily in Abbie—and would end up feeling that Abbie had misused and betrayed him. There were

early signs, signs that for the most part Jim chose to ignore. On a television program he and Abbie did in the spring of 1967, Abbie declared, with a big grin, "I'm not a hippie. Hippies are fags. Sorry about that. I don't think they know how to love." Jim said nothing, either during the show or after (though he would later, on the Susskind show, come out publicly), preferring to chalk up Abbie's remarks to his fondness for playing the macho, gay-bashing street hood in public, even though he seemed comfortable in private with people he knew to be gay.[31]

But the trouble with this theory was that in private Abbie *wasn't* always comfortable. In 1968, when Jim was living with his then lover, Howie Weinstein, in a loft on Bond Street, Abbie would frequently drop by. But he would look through Howie as if he weren't there and sometimes, right in front of him, make some clunky remark about a woman he wanted to fix Jim up with. Afterward, Howie would be angry and would berate Jim for not having spoken up. "But what was there to say?" Jim would lamely respond, "You're here. This is our house. You sleep in this bed with me. Everybody knows that. What is there to say?" "But he can't even *look* at me!" Howie would howl, "How can you trust a man like that?"

For several years Jim buried his own doubts about Abbie. He closely identified with the values Abbie espoused, and preferred to believe that the espousal and the practice were essentially one, give or take the usual human discrepancies. Jim had found a political home and didn't want to lose it, a prominent identity and didn't want to jeopardize it. He was so immersed for a time in the Yippie cause that he actually called himself Jimmy Digger in tribute to the parent group in California, the Diggers, whose philosophy had centrally inspired the Yippies.

The Diggers took their name from the seventeenth-century English revolutionaries who denounced private property and heralded the reign of love. The Californians regarded all forms of authority (and especially that of the state) as illegitimate, felt a romantic solidarity with the underclasses, denied the morality of a money economy, distributed surplus goods free for the asking, and were devoted to spontaneous forms of expression, pleasure, and resistance. They were more serious-minded and theoretically coherent than the Yippies, who popularized the Digger views and won, with their bowdlerized version, far more publicity than the parent group ever had or wanted.

With his keen analytic intelligence and philosophical seriousness, Jim probably felt more closely identified with the Diggers than did

any of the other Yippie leaders. His androgynous look, his flowing blond hair and delicate features, belied the intense, committed person within. Jim *looked* the part of a boundaryless hippie more than most of those who claimed the label, but if one was foolish enough to equate that look with a limp, passive personality, one was in for a rude shock.

For—except with Abbie—Jim rarely pulled his punches or hesitated about speaking his mind. And rather than behaving like a docile follower, he was quick to initiate a line of action. He had been impressed in San Francisco with Chester Anderson's "Communications Company," which periodically published leaflets to disseminate news of interest to the hip left community. When Jim's friend Howard Smith, a *Village Voice* writer, offered him a Gestetner duplicating machine that the *Voice* was discarding, Jim suddenly had the means to start a comparable operation in New York. He single-handedly wrote and distributed a street newspaper which, in homage to the San Francisco operation, he called *The Communications Company*. And on his travels in and out of various worlds, Jim was always careful to bring along copies of his paper to distribute.

The preeminent gathering place of the influential avant-garde in the late sixties was Max's Kansas City—or simply "Max's," to those in the know—the favorite late-night hangout for Andy Warhol and friends (and those who wanted to be). Warhol himself often occupied the corner table in the back room, the silent puppeteer, expertly working the strings, delighting in the manipulated dance—a fake Zen master who rationalized his indifference to other people's pain as a "necessary" offshoot of his artistic self-absorption. Jim first met Warhol in 1965, and found him charming, if maddeningly passive-aggressive; he also saw clearly that Warhol was a control freak who goaded people to perform for him while rejecting all responsibility for the behavior he had elicited.

Jim's friend from Caffè Cino days, Bob Heide, could personally testify to Warhol's ice-cold exploitations. Though he had given Warhol the idea (at a time when Warhol was lamenting his artistic bankruptcy) of changing around the colors and doing repetitions on his Campbell's Soup and Marilyn Monroe series, Warhol neither credited him nor subsequently showed him a tinge of gratitude. To the contrary, he mistreated him. Warhol filmed Heide's play *The Bed*, but when the film's financial backer tried to get it shown, Warhol hid it and denied its existence, and then later spliced a sequence from it into his movie *Chelsea Girls*—without crediting Heide's play as the source.[32]

Much as he sometimes found Warhol repellent, Jim was willing

to put up with him. He enjoyed being part of whatever the red-hot scene of the moment was—especially if he could juggle it with several other scenes bidding for attention—and that meant hanging out in Max's. Warhol's holding court there was not a compelling reason for staying away, and Jim made a point of ending nearly every evening by dropping into Max's. He distributed the latest edition of *The Communications Company*, picked up information for the next one, and congratulated himself on being in the scene without being in Warhol's orbit.

Like Yvonne Flowers, Jim loved the simultaneous life, loved a multiplicity of actions—perhaps not least because he could never quite find the *one* channel that could maximally focus his gifts, could not stay quiet long enough to allow that channel to emerge. At the same time that he was doing a turn at personal journalism, he was continuing his acting classes with Lee Strasberg and periodically landing a part in a play. In 1967 he acted in *The Peace Creeps*, performed in the theater above the trendy nightclub Arthur's, with James Earl Jones and a shy, promising newcomer named Al Pacino (Jim thought Pacino's chief talent onstage was an ability to get believably angry).

Next came a Broadway production, *The Freaking Out of Stephanie Blake*, with Jean Arthur—a play about hippies that became legendary for its three months of previews and its failure ever to open. Jean Arthur was a notoriously difficult person to work with, a demanding perfectionist who had previously walked out on *St. Joan of the Stockyards*. But Jim developed enormous respect for her hard work and her magical abilities (though he was considerably less enamored of her lesbian lover/nurse, an ex-marine who always hovered threateningly at Jean's side). After changing directors three times, Jean walked off the stage during a preview performance of *Stephanie Blake* in the middle of her one scene with Jim, leaving him the nightmarish job of having to ad-lib until the curtain finally came down. She never returned to the play, and the producers closed it.

Soon after, Jim hooked up with Joe Chaikin's experimental group, the Open Theater. Distrustful of the theater's traditional reliance on words, Chaikin had begun to use intense physical exercises to explore nonverbal forms of communication; his brilliant production of *The Serpent* in the late sixties would make the Open Theater the most admired of all the experimental companies. But by then, Jim, typically, had already left—this time sparking off to do an electric "up-to-the-minute" column for a Hearst publication called *Eye*. Since it

had a three-month lead time, Jim would make up events and then, with his friends, see to it that they came true in time for the column to appear.

His most consistent (though never singular) commitment in the mid-to-late sixties remained with Abbie Hoffman and the Yippies, and he played a central role in several of the "spontaneous" actions that all at once imaginatively protested the inequities and deformities of American life and the escalating war in Vietnam, "blew the minds" of the Yippies' straight-shooting comrades on the left, and made the Yippies media celebrities and countercultural heroes.

In June 1967 Jim, wearing purple pants, accompanied Abbie (in his now *de rigueur* beads and bell-bottoms) to the SDS "Drawing Board" conference in Michigan. The gathering had been called mostly to redefine the New Left's relationship to an emergent "black power" movement that advised whites henceforth to work in their own communities. The New York Yippies were joined in Michigan by a delegation from the San Francisco Diggers, led by Emmett Grogan, and together they managed to wreak havoc with the "rational discourse" favored by SDS.

After Tom Hayden had finished his evaluation of white organizing efforts in the black ghetto of Newark, the Digger contingent disrupted the meeting with assorted shouts and antics. Emmett Grogan told the crowd (in Grogan's recollection) "about the importance of anonymity to persons who seriously attempted to effect relevant changes in any social order," and he made fun of the fondness of Abbie Hoffman and others for the limelight. When Abbie countered that Grogan would end up on the cover of *Time* magazine, Grogan vehemently denied it, and to punctuate his point kicked over a Formica table, punched and slapped people, yelled that they were all "fags," that they didn't have "the balls to go mad" or to make a real revolution, that they would "piss in their pants" if violence ever erupted. Then he read aloud Gary Snyder's poem "Day of Judgment upon Us."[33]

The Diggers, the Yippies, and some SDSers then proceeded to get stoned (Jim was known in Yippie circles as comparatively abstemious), and talk till dawn about the need for the New Left to understand that a revolution in consciousness had to precede, or at the least accompany, any hoped-for revolution in social arrangements. According to one printed account—which Jim decries as apocryphal—he tried to make the countercultural point concrete by abruptly kissing the square-rigger SDS leader, Bob Ross, full on the

lips. When the stunned Ross purportedly recoiled, Jim is said to have explained that he had always been powerfully attracted to Jewish men.[34]

Back in New York, Jim and Abbie led a series of daringly theatrical actions that employed the symbols of authority in order to discredit them. In a Flower Power demonstration, perhaps the very first dramatization of ecological concerns, they set off soot bombs at Con Edison headquarters and, to the accompaniment of a rock band playing from a nearby flatbed truck, planted a tree in front of the popular disco the Electric Circus, as a way of protesting the city's lack of greenery. But their most imaginative and best-publicized action took place at the New York Stock Exchange.

The original idea for the action had been Jim's, but Abbie, as was his disconcerting way, soon claimed it for his own. Alerting the media in advance, a group of eighteen Yippies simply joined the line of tourists and thus made their way into the gallery overlooking the trading floor. They then started throwing wads of dollar bills down onto the floor below. The ticker tape stopped; the brokers stared up at the balcony in disbelief; and then a number of them rushed to scoop up the dollar bills, as the Yippies rapturously applauded—until the guards collared and ejected them. (In 1989, apparently unaware of the earlier precedent, members of ACT UP threw thousands of fake hundred-dollar bills onto the floor of the Stock Exchange.) Back out in front of the Exchange, the Yippies, for the further edification of the gathered reporters, burned a final bundle of bills in symbolic disdain for the material life.

The Wall Street action was widely covered in the media—with the usual discrepancies. Some of the accounts had the Yippies tossing Monopoly money, others twenty-dollar bills, and still others ripped-up singles. "It was the perfect mythical event," Abbie later gloated, and he took special delight in the CBS report, which alone among the networks accurately reported his insistence that he was really Cardinal Spellman and had tossed at least a thousand dollars in small bills onto the trading floor.[35]

Jim's growing prominence as a result of his Yippie activities did not go unnoticed by the FBI. Deciding to gather additional information on him, the Bureau sent two FBI agents to his parents' home in Rhode Island. Not finding his mother in, they went to the Newport restaurant where Jim's stepfather worked as a chef and told him that Jim was wanted for a bank robbery. His stepfather begged the FBI agents not to bother Jim's mother; she had recently been hospitalized

after a breakdown and was still in fragile shape. The agents promised to leave her alone, and promptly returned to her house. This time she was in, and the agents convinced the trembling woman that she could best protect her son by turning over everything that related to him—pictures, letters, whatever. Which she did.

Jim was furious when he heard about the cruel intimidation. Except for an occasional telephone call or postcard, he hadn't been in regular contact with his parents for some time. They knew nothing about his political life except that he was against the war in Vietnam—which they supported, as they supported all official acts of the government. The FBI visit put an end to their innocence. Hearing from Jim that he had never been involved in a bank robbery, and from her husband that the FBI had promised *not* to bother her, Jim's mother wrung her hands in guilty remorse over having coop-erated with the agents. Jim quieted her down, but the FBI's casual disregard for the defenseless woman's well-being got emotionally linked in his mind with the fate of defenseless Vietnamese peasants. It further hardened his determination to resist the impervious, cold-hearted men in Washington.

But his next major action, on March 22, 1968, ended in disaster. The Yippies decided to stage a "celebration of the spring equinox" in the heart of the working world's bustle: Grand Central Station. The demonstration drew a large crowd of some six thousand, and soon veered from benign antics to heated confrontation. Several people— possibly provocateurs, possibly members of the anarchist East Village group Up Against the Wall Motherfuckers, who believed in confron-tational tactics—scrambled on top of the information booth in the center of the huge main hall, started chanting "Burn, baby, burn!" and tore the hands off the booth's clock. Then two cherry bombs went off, and a large contingent of police charged the crowd, flailing about with their nightsticks, clubbing those already fallen. They rammed a *Village Voice* reporter headfirst into a glass door and beat Abbie (who had come dressed as an American Indian) into uncon-sciousness. He nonetheless hailed the event for putting Yippies "on the map."[36]

Jim was not nearly so sanguine. Having helped to announce the event on WBAI and organize it through handouts of his paper, *The Communications Company*, he felt personally responsible for the debacle. And he was deeply shaken by it as a possible harbinger of what might happen that summer at the planned "Festival of Life" demonstration during the Democratic National Convention in Chicago. Jim's politics

did not encompass violence, revolutionary or otherwise. His activism, as he saw it, derived from moral imperatives and was concerned above all with the transformation of consciousness—and he even defined his work in avant-garde theater as further feeding into that "revolution in feeling." He was now worried that there would be another explosive confrontation at the Democratic convention and that it would put everything he valued in jeopardy.

Abbie reassured him that the Yippie presence in Chicago would focus (as the posters promised) on "Lights–Theater–Magic–Free Music," thereby abetting precisely the cultural renovation Jim had been working for. But Abbie's giddy talk to the press about slipping LSD into the water supply, fucking openly in the parks, and releasing greased pigs on the convention floor, struck Jim as irresponsible and heightened his anxiety. As the time for the convention drew near, he became increasingly convinced that confrontation, not celebration, would be the end result. During Yippie planning sessions, he openly predicted a "bloodbath" and insisted that if people were going to have to fight in the streets then they damn well ought to be told what was coming so they could prepare for it—instead of being encouraged to believe, as official Yippie releases had it, that some wondrously benign love-in was afoot.

Abbie later claimed that the Grand Central Station Massacre had "let the whole world know there would be blood on the streets of Chicago" and that anyone who came there knew full well in advance "that they were risking their life." It is certainly true that others besides Jim—if not Abbie himself—gave ample warning that events in the Windy City could take a violent turn. Abe Peck, editor of the underground publication *Seed*, had written, for example, "If you're coming to Chicago, be sure to wear some armor in your hair." And those warnings were ultimately heard. No more than a couple of thousand young people showed up for the Festival of Life.[37]

Abbie did finally arrange for medical and legal assistance at the planned Lincoln Park and Grant Park gathering sites, but he apparently continued to believe—such was his optimistic nature—in a peaceful outcome. If so, he hadn't reckoned on Richard J. Daley, Chicago's mayor. Many months before the Democratic delegates were due to arrive, Daley talked as if a berserk cadre of "hoodlums and Communists" was determined on a bloody takeover of the city, and he darkly hinted at assassination plots against the leading presidential candidates. To meet this wildly exaggerated threat, Daley armed his police to the teeth and set the city's nerves on edge with his doomsday

rhetoric. When, just a few months before the Democrats were due to convene, Robert F. Kennedy was gunned down, the apocalyptic mood deepened.

Daley proved a self-fulfilling prophet. For the better part of a week, the police, with little or no provocation, literally assaulted antiwar demonstrators and yippies alike, spilling so much blood, and bashing onlookers, reporters, and "freaks" so indiscriminately, that TV images of their rampaging brutality produced national revulsion. A number of convention delegates expressed open horror at the police riot, but the convention nonetheless proceeded to vote down a peace plank and to nominate Hubert Humphrey, closely identified with the Vietnam War, as the Democratic presidential candidate.

As much as Jim deplored on all counts the outcome at Chicago, he recognized, with some satisfaction, that hordes of "mere" liberals had been driven leftward and that the heightened polarization of the country held out the eventual promise of its rejuvenation.

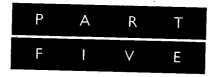

P A R T

F I V E

THE
LATE
SIXTIES

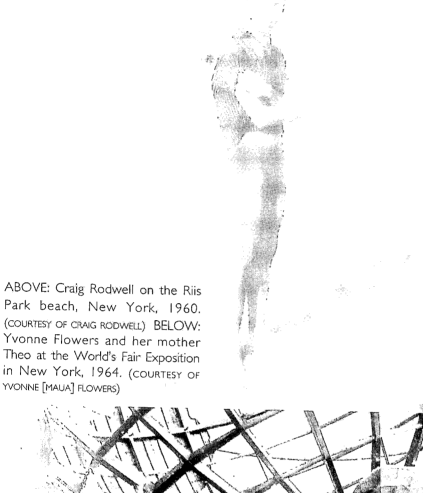

ABOVE: Craig Rodwell on the Riis Park beach, New York, 1960. (COURTESY OF CRAIG RODWELL) BELOW: Yvonne Flowers and her mother Theo at the World's Fair Exposition in New York, 1964. (COURTESY OF YVONNE [MAUA] FLOWERS)

Police raid on the Artists' Exotic Carnival and Ball at the Manhattan Center, Halloween, 1962. (UPI/BETTMANN NEWSPHOTOS)

RIGHT: Foster Gunnison, Jr., 1958. (COURTESY OF FOSTER GUNNISON, JR.) BELOW: ECHO Convention, 1965. Kneeling at far left: Julian Hodges next to Dick Leitsch. Standing: second from left, Clark Polak; third from left, Bill Beardemphl; fourth from left, Shirley Willer; fifth from left, Jack Nichols; second from right, Franklin Kameny (I.G.I.C. COLLECTION, NEW YORK PUBLIC LIBRARY)

ABOVE: Picketing for gay rights in front of the White House, May 21, 1965. Franklin Kameny is second in line. (UPI/BETTMAN NEWSPHOTOS) LEFT: Sylvia Ray Rivera and two unidentified drag queens, 1969-70. (GAY FLAMES #5; I.G.I.C. COLLECTION, NEW YORK PUBLIC LIBRARY) OPPOSITE: Jim Fouratt, in the mid-sixties. (COURTESY OF JIM FOURATT)

ABOVE: Gay Activists Alliance
meeting in the Firehouse, 1970.
(I.G.I.C. COLLECTION, NEW YORK PUBLIC
LIBRARY) CENTER: The Firehouse,
home of the Gay Activists Alliance.
(UPI/BETTMANN NEWSPHOTOS) BELOW
AND OPPOSITE PAGE: Various
zaps by the Gay Activists
Alliance in New York City.
(UPI/BETTMANN NEWSPHOTOS)

ABOVE: Karla Jay and friends, Los Angeles, 1970. BELOW: The Stonewall Inn on Christopher Street, post-riots and vacant. (PHOTO BY GEORGE DESANTIS, "GAY FREEDOM 1970," QQ MAGAZINE)

Gay Liberation Front poster. (PHOTO BY PETER HUJAR)

ABOVE: Craig Rodwell negotiating with the police before the first gay pride march. (PHOTO BY GEORGE DESANTIS, "GAY FREEDOM 1970," QQ MAGAZINE) BELOW AND RIGHT: The first gay pride march, Sixth Avenue, New York City, 1970. (THE NEW YORK TIMES)

Conclusion of the first gay pride march, the Sheep Meadow in Central Park, New York, 1970. (UPI/BETTMANN NEWSPHOTOS)

ABOVE: Sylvia Rivera and Bebe Scarpi at the GLF Bellevue demonstration, Fall 1970. BELOW: Yvonne (Maua) Flowers at a political meeting in 1988 at the Lesbian and Gay Community Services Center in New York City. The black glove on her right hand was being worn prior to her first surgery for Lupus. (COURTESY OF YVONNE [MAUA] FLOWERS)

ABOVE, LEFT: Foster Gunnison, Jr.,
1991. (COURTESY OF THE HARTFORD
COURANT; PHOTO BY PAULA BRONSTEIN)
ABOVE, RIGHT: Karla Jay, 1992.
(PHOTO BY YEMAYA KAURI-ALETO)
BELOW: Craig Rodwell in front of
the Oscar Wilde Memorial Bookshop,
1992.

Gay pride march, New York City, 1991. Left to right: Ivan Valentin, unidentified, Sylvia Ray Rivera, Jim Fouratt, Marsha P. Johnson. (PHOTO BY JOE CAPUTO)

Y V O N N E

Yvonne felt that being single was a temporary state. As she put it, "I was always falling in love and there was always somebody ready to fall in love, too. And there were always women ready for sex." In retrospect she thinks of herself as having been "compulsively romantic" in the mid-sixties, "always having two or three affairs going on at the same time. . . . I was used to the insanity. Good old dyke drama."

Her intense interactions were almost entirely with other black women; over the years she became involved with only three or four women who were white. She found black women more political ("If she doesn't have any politics I'm not even interested in her"), more mature emotionally, and with greater "energy for living, for dancing, for life, for people. . . . There are so many things about me they understand, where it comes from, what it's about, so I can cut across a whole lot of stuff."[1]

After Anne left her in 1963, Yvonne still came into Manhattan often from Brooklyn; she had a passion for museums and galleries, for staring transfixed at buildings and bridges ("My eyes were hungry")—and, of course, she came to hang out in the gay clubs and to hear her beloved jazz. She heard "every musician who was anybody who passed through New York"—including, at the Five Spot, one of the last appearances by Coleman Hawkins and one of the first by Ornette Coleman. For a week, jazz aficionados showed up for every one of Ornette Coleman's sets, but true to the supercool style of the

clubs would only allow as how "this dude with the plastic horn, you'd have to say, it ain't bad."

Following a midnight set, Yvonne would take off, say, for a dance given by the M.C. Social Club in the Bronx or at the Audubon Ballroom in Manhattan; and, when that party ended at three A.M. or so, would go on to an all-women's after-hours place like Snooky's, and dance, eat, and drink till daybreak. But she found more time for studying than she had when younger, and it took her no more than the usual two years to get her O.T. (occupational therapy) graduate certificate from NYU, in 1966.

But it was a close call. In her last term before graduating, Yvonne developed a huge fibroid tumor and several gynecological cysts, and had to have major surgery. Unable to attend classes for the final weeks of the semester, she nonetheless managed, with the help of classmates and friends, to complete her assignments and graduate in June.

She went straight to work at Hillside Psychiatric Hospital. She had done some of her undergraduate field work there (indeed, she had worked in psychiatric facilities, off and on, since she was eighteen), and the hospital administrators, impressed with her abilities and experience, had offered her a staff job in occupational therapy as soon as she graduated.

Hillside specialized in young adults and drug abusers—meaning, in those years, mostly acidheads and potheads. Yvonne, of course—along with others on the staff—herself qualified in both categories. When she became a supervisor a few years later, she would often, come three o'clock on a Friday afternoon, push the furniture in her office to one side, put on some music, turn the lights down low, get the booze out of the filing-cabinet drawer—and party. From that point on in the weekend, Yvonne was off and running. Her hangovers would be so intense by Monday that she made sure not to schedule anything before one o'clock. (She made up the time by working late one night a week.)

Yet her work performance remained superior, and before long she was promoted to director of vocational rehabilitation. In addition—remarkably, given the fact that undiagnosed lupus was already sapping her energy—she managed to find time, between work and partying, for participation in a variety of political actions. Those ranged from occasional antiwar protests to demonstrations for community control in the Ocean Hill–Brownsville school district to joining a lie-in at the Downstate Medical Center building site to protest the lack of black construction workers.

The 1968 Ocean Hill–Brownsville controversy particularly engaged her. The conflict was essentially between poor black parents
and the mostly white, Jewish teachers who taught their children.
Claiming that the teachers were doing a lousy job of it, the parents
fought for control of the school board. But the conflict took on broader
dimensions still: It seemed to pit the social vision of decentralization
and "participatory democracy" against those who believed in centralized authority and the transmission of knowledge and services *down*
to the client. Citywide battle lines were drawn accordingly.

Yvonne's sympathies were with the black parents, and she took
vigorous part in the assorted marches and meetings that attempted to
rally support for them. But as the strike dragged interminably on,
Yvonne's activism gradually weakened. Resisting any consistent, prolonged organizational affiliation had become something of a pattern
with her. And she had some good reasons for resisting (along with
some unexamined private ones). Above all, she was reluctant to deal
with the endemic homophobia of the left, and felt she could not pass
as straight even if she had wanted to participate in that kind of subterfuge. She had heard that there were *some* out lesbians working with
the Black Panthers—but had also heard that the brothers had been
giving them a hard time. But if she steered clear of any sustained
organizational ties, she made it a point of honor to turn the lights up
at a party—often to indignant shouts—in order to pass the hat for
this group or that action.

Hers was a sharply compartmentalized life, with few overlaps in
her professional-partying-political activities. The closest she came to
bridging the divisions, to bringing the different parts of her life together, happened almost against her will. "Ellen," a white, heterosexual woman with whom Yvonne worked, inherited a good deal of
money from her parents (a well-known actress and a famous playwright), bought a house with it in Rowe, Massachusetts, and kept
inviting Yvonne to come up for a weekend.

Yvonne resisted. She didn't want to spend time "with these
straight white people," and especially not with Ellen's husband, a
Vietnam War vet with decidedly unpredictable moods. Finally Ellen
walked into Yvonne's office one day, threw the keys to the house on
her desk, and said, "Look: This is a *nice* house. I love this house and
I love you, and I want you to enjoy it. So you take whoever you want
and you go up there."

It proved to be a nice house indeed—spacious, set on a lake, with
a sun deck, a large front porch, and a huge kitchen that invited free-

flowing, intimate talk. It also had a backyard filled with wildflowers in the spring, and a creek with beaver dams. Yvonne loved the house and the setting immediately, and over the years would come to think of Rowe, Massachusetts, as a cherished second home. But on her first visit, she took along Audre Lorde's ten-year-old daughter, as well as her then lover Yolanda's three-year-old child—as a kind of protection during this incursion into foreign territory.

After the initial few visits, Yvonne would go up to Rowe with various combinations of people, including even Ellen and her husband. She loved to walk in the woods, to have her own sense of solitude comfortably confirmed by the serene surroundings, and she eventually grew to love the place so much that she bought a formal share in it. The house had a piano, which Yvonne constantly played, reliving the childhood days when her mother's musicality and her own would, more or less harmoniously, blend. In Rowe, Yvonne would play, as she later put it, "this very weird music—now it would be called New Age music, but at that time it was just the music I heard in my head."

Yvonne and her friends brought their city drugs with them— including LSD. They were enchanted with the effects of seeming to see the fish at the bottom of the lake or the trees literally dancing in the breeze. But once, unexpectedly, Yvonne had a terrible trip, and it so frightened her that she thereafter swore off LSD. Ellen, on the other hand, became so entranced with her mystical experiences that in the early seventies she left on a pilgrimage to India and ultimately ended up in Oregon with Rajneesh, to whom she reportedly gave all her money.

But for the five to six years before the household in Rowe broke up, Yvonne was able to find there a needed respite from her frantic, disjunctive life in the city. The comfort of the place, in combination with the solidity of her professional life, provided ballast for a life otherwise unbalanced by late hours, too much booze and too many drugs, and a frantic sexual pace that kept any sustained emotional connection at arm's length. The balance would hold well into the seventies, and then, in a simultaneous double blow, she would lose both the house and her job.

By then she had gained a reputation at Hillside for being not only a skillful occupational therapist and supervisor, but a superb grant writer. Influenced by her own political activism in behalf of community control in Brownsville, she decided to write a grant for outpatient drug treatment that, through the device of advisory boards, would involve the local community in Queens Village in the decision-

making process. She wrote the grant proposal with two male psychologists on the Hillside staff with whom she had worked earlier, and ended up liking it so much that when the National Institute of Mental Health funded it, she decided to direct the program herself.

That meant leaving her post as director of vocational rehabilitation and, though she didn't realize it at the time, putting herself in a position where she could be fired. As it turned out, the two psychologists were more interested in the funding than in the project. After Yvonne had been heading the program for nine months, and enjoying it enormously, she was called into the office of her immediate boss, the director of activities therapy, and told that she was being let go. The news took her utterly by surprise, and it was years before she could piece together what had happened. Even then, she managed only an incomplete, unsatisfying version.

The project had received funding for a full four years, and the two psychologists apparently decided that they wanted to control the funds for their own purposes, which only peripherally included the outpatient drug program. One of the woman volunteers in the program was also involved in the move to get Yvonne fired; she wanted to direct the activities-therapy program herself, and since (as Yvonne later discovered) her uncle was on the Hillside board of directors, she had the needed clout behind her ambition.

The sense of personal betrayal was the most painful part of the firing. Yvonne had gone to school at NYU with the activities director, and considered him a close friend. Her intuition had told her that he was a closeted gay, but Yvonne, figuring that it was none of her business, had never attempted an alliance on those grounds. Nor did she think that in turning on her, he was projecting outward his own unacknowledged self-hatred. More likely, she believed, he had become seriously addicted and needed to secure his own job by doing the unquestioned bidding of the higher-ups at Hillside.

As is usually the case with black lesbians, Yvonne found it difficult to tell which of the "isms"—racism, heterosexism, sexism—was most operative against her at Hillside. Though she *was* the only black person in the activities-therapy department at Hillside, she had experienced little overt racism there, and had been given regular promotions and salary increases. Because Yvonne was too scrupulous to assign blame without solid proof, and was further hamstrung by the fact that concrete evidence is always difficult to obtain in discrimination cases of any kind, the suit she finally did bring against the hospital was dismissed for lack of specificity. Yvonne was left with a

festering sense of failure—she was unable to convert unease into righteous anger—coupled with the debilitating feeling that people she had
trusted had turned on her for no apparent reason.

What she did have to fall back on was a substantial severance
payment. That allowed her not to work for a year, and the respite,
in turn, had two decidedly positive results. The day before the firing,
Theo, Yvonne's widowed mother, who had been living with her,
became ill (terminally, as it turned out), and not having to go to work
every day gave Yvonne the precious opportunity to spend the last
three months of her mother's life entirely by her side. Theo, too ill
to get around much, would often watch television from her bed,
exclaiming in disbelief at this or that retrograde or racist development.
A born optimist, she had actually believed the whole issue of race
was going to be resolved in her lifetime. Yvonne would shake her
head in amazement at her mother's rosy expectations, never having
believed herself in anything more than the necessity for ongoing struggle. Today, she "thanks God that Mother isn't alive to see the backwardness that's going on here now."

The severance from Hillside also led to a career change. It began
with Yvonne being invited to give guest lectures at this or that college
and ended with the staff at CUNY's York campus being so impressed
with her presentation that she was offered a permanent faculty appointment. Becoming a teacher was about the last thing Yvonne—
who had never even liked school, much as she had always loved
learning—had dreamed of. Yet it would open up a new and satisfying
world to her.

F O S T E R

At age forty-one, Foster Gunnison was, along with Frank Kameny,
the oldest delegate to the homophile planning conference. In all, some
forty people (only eight of them women) from fourteen organizations
gathered at the State Hotel in Kansas City, Missouri, from February
18 to 21, 1966, to discuss whether and how cooperation between local
homophile groups could be increased.[2]

New York Mattachine was not among them. Dick Leitsch had
acidly expressed the hope that the gathering would accomplish something "besides the breast-beating, navel-contemplating and smugness

that characterized ECHO meetings"—but had then refused to pay expenses for MSNY members whose presence might have helped to make that hope a reality.

The militants associated with Kameny and Gittings came to Kansas City hoping to win approval for the formation of a national organization, and one with an activist philosophy. But it rapidly became clear that they would have to settle for an arrangement considerably short of that.

At the very first session of the conference, spokespeople for each organization gave brief descriptions of their group's activities, staking out, with pardonable pride, what they took to be their special accomplishments. Phyllis Lyon emphasized the importance of the Daughters of Bilitis in providing a place for women in what was a predominantly male homophile movement; Bill Beardemphl emphasized the success San Francisco's SIR had had in inducing homosexuals to become politically involved by first offering them an array of social activities; Chuck Thompson outlined the essential educational and research programs at ONE, Inc., of Los Angeles; Mark Forrester underscored the unique mission of San Francisco's Council on Religion and the Homosexual in acting as a bridge between homosexuals and heterosexuals; Robert Walker talked of Mattachine–San Francisco's work in counseling individuals; Guy Strait pitched his own crusade to persuade the homosexual that "salvation lay within himself and not in society's acceptance of him," while Kameny, oppositely, spoke of the importance of getting people to see that "all the problems of the homosexuals are questions of [social] prejudice and discrimination."

It was clear from the initial presentations that any movement toward merger would likely fall victim to entrenched local devotions. Indeed, only four of the fourteen organizations had authorized their representatives to commit to policies or programs that the conference might recommend; and it sometimes proved necessary, before a given matter could be brought to a vote, to state explicitly that it would be "in principle only" and would carry no mandate for action. Under that formula, such noncontroversial goals as "the right of homosexuals to equality of opportunity" could be affirmed—but not specific programs designed to make that goal a reality.

Indeed, it even proved difficult getting consensus for a resolution that declared homosexuality irrelevant for security clearance and employment by the government. When Clark Polak pressed for a statement that homosexuality "must be considered as neither a sickness, disturbance [nor] neurosis," some delegates thought the matter best

left to "experts" in mental health and some wanted to go *beyond* the resolution to argue that "a more definite assertion of the nonpathological nature of homosexuality should be made." In the upshot the Polak resolution failed to carry, but the conference did issue a statement that "objective research projects undertaken thus far have indicated that findings of homosexual undesirability are based on opinion, value judgments or emotional reaction rather than on scientific evidence or fact."

When it came time for the conference to turn its attention to the possible creation of a national homophile organization, it voted, not surprisingly, "against considering the item." Yet the militants did win support in Kansas City for the establishment of a national legal fund, for a nationwide day of protest in May against the military's policy of excluding homosexuals, for a "cooperative exchange of ideas and information among homophile groups," and for another conference to be held in August in San Francisco—all of which gave the militants considerable grounds for optimism. They felt hopeful that in San Francisco five months hence, a national organization with real powers could be established.

Foster played a backseat role at the convention. Sensitive to the fact that he was still "a complete novice" in the movement, and modest by temperament, he kept out of the more heated debates. But he was eager to learn more and to meet people, and on all three nights of the conference he hosted a "hospitality suite" that went from eleven P.M. to four A.M. He had already met several movement leaders at ECHO conferences and during the 1965 White House demonstration, and came away from Kansas City admiring Frank Kameny, Barbara Gittings, and Kay Tobin all the more. ("My mind runs in the same track with Kameny's," Foster wrote; "we both instinctively lean toward formalisms.") Of those homophile movers and shakers whom he now met for the first time, he expansively decided that he "liked most everyone."

Yet within that ecumenical embrace, he allowed for some gradations. He was especially taken with twenty-two-year-old Bill Kelley of Chicago's Mattachine Midwest, who served as recording secretary of the convention, awarding him the highest Gunnison virtues: "tactful, sincere, solid reasoning, good detail man." And at first, he found a few of the more celebrated movement figures less than endearing. He thought Don Slater, the head of L.A.'s Tangents, "wispy, waspy" and temperamental; was intimidated by "butch" Shirley Willer, the president of New York DOB; considered Clark Polak, the leader of

Philadelphia's Janus Society, "brash and brassy"; and thought Guy Strait, editor of the *Citizens' News*, his "temperamental opposite"—"a rank individualist opposed to anything that smacks of discipline, order or authority . . . a living symbol of all that is wrong with the movement."

But basically Foster was thrilled with being in the thick of things and felt inspired by the presence of so many dedicated people. If a few of them had rubbed him the wrong way, and if the conference had not talked as much as he would have liked about concrete actions and the need to create a new national structure, he nonetheless came home from Kansas City convinced that "the importance of the movement and the happiness to millions of suffering persons that it will bring in the long run easily overshadows the pains of growing." Resolving to devote himself to the homophile cause, he immediately began to disengage from some of his organizational work with barbershop quartets.

And he began to put some of his thoughts to paper. Within a few weeks after returning from Kansas City, and apparently influenced by the militants there, he wrote a compelling essay for *The Homosexual Citizen* (Washington Mattachine's monthly) entitled "The Agony of the Mask." In it, Foster—the least self-promoting of men —made a strong plea for ending secrecy and openly avowing one's homosexuality. It was the only way, Foster argued, that gay people could "help repair the damage done to them by others"—a phrasing that reflected the militant view that an oppressive society, and not bad genes or character, had produced whatever disabling aspects were present in the homosexual life-style.

Yet Foster's cautionary side remained. He was not advocating, he hastened to make clear in the article, any form of "disconcerting melodrama," any belligerent "exhibitionism." His goal was social acceptance, not social upheaval; he wanted the homosexual to gain entry into mainstream institutional life, not, as later radicals would, to press for revamping the institutions themselves along more egalitarian lines. Indeed, Foster argued against secrecy precisely in order to win "institutional support," convinced that the emergence of a legion of well-behaved, well-dressed homosexuals would contradict the view that all gay people were "far-out types and professional nonconformists." Once that stereotype was contradicted, Foster believed, experts and institutions of "caliber" would rally to the homosexual's support.[3]

This was a complex appeal, not simply a call to conformity. Foster personally found "far-out types" distasteful, but in calling on homo-

sexuals who did not fit "the storybook caricatures" to publicly declare themselves, he was working on a track somewhat parallel to that of the psychologist Evelyn Hooker. Starting in the late fifties, Hooker had published several pathbreaking articles—which Foster had read —that used a nonclinical sample of gay men (previous studies had been drawn from patient and prison populations) to demonstrate that the psychological profile of the "healthy" gay men in her study differed in no essential way from her control group of heterosexual men.

In other words, Hooker had shown that at least *some* homosexuals existed who were not "maladjusted" or unhappy with their lives, and did not fit the dominant psychiatric view that equated their "condition" with pathology. Though Foster had thought Hooker's work "hardly immune to criticism," he, like her, was trying to increase the pool of publicly visible homosexuals whose lives were similar to those of other middle-class Americans (and thus could be validated as "normal")—even if, unlike Hooker, he was personally uncomfortable with any nonconforming behavior *other* than homosexuality.

At the "Ten Days in August" conference, which convened in San Francisco in the summer of 1966, Foster got a chance to share his views with a wider audience, having been chosen as one of five speakers scheduled to give major addresses. And he spoke to a crowd double the size of that attending the Kansas City gathering some five months before—though it had fewer than a dozen women among some eighty delegates. Indeed, the San Francisco conference proved to be the largest homophile gathering ever held in the United States, and its offerings ranged from a panel discussion of law reform (with an impressive roster that included California state legislators Willie Brown and John L. Burton), to a theatrical presentation, "Gay 90's Night," to a picnic that one gay paper claimed more than six hundred people attended.[4]

The increase in numbers produced the usual corollary: heightened tension. This was a gathering worth fighting over. There was contention, even before the convention opened, about which organizations should be accredited and how many votes should be delegated to each. And the convention itself produced such a proliferation of resolutions—and of arguments for and against them—that many delegates felt more numbed than enlightened. Perhaps because one of his own resolutions was voted down, and he was unable to get the floor as often as he wanted (which was often), Guy Strait—a flamboyant San Franciscan whose penchant for youthful partners got him in periodic trouble with the law—later wrote that "never before in

the history of mankind has so much time been wasted by so few people in order that they may hear their own voices."

The disgruntled also included two of the West Coast's legendary activists, Harry Hay and Dorr Legg. Hay was the convener of that small group of gay men who had founded the Mattachine Society in 1950, but now, in 1966, his interest had veered to his newest creation, the Circle of Loving Companions, a group meant to function according to Whitmanesque principles of comradely love. The Circle did occasionally broaden out to include a few friends, but it was usually made up solely of Hay and his lover, John Burnside. The two attended the San Francisco conference as representatives of the Circle, and Hay came away from it more confirmed than ever in the splendor of his chosen isolation: No one else was evolved enough to share his vision—"conservative" Easterners, with their attraction to assimilation, least of all.[5]

Dorr Legg arrived at the conference already bruised. In the spring of 1965, the ONE, Inc. mini-empire over which he presided with an acerbic voice and iron hand, had come apart. Don Slater, a disaffected board member of ONE, simply packed up the organization's thousand-volume library one weekend and hauled it to his own quarters. "The Heist," as it became known, produced years of litigation and decades of ill feeling. Long rumored to have ice water in his veins, Dorr Legg frostily impaled almost everyone who took a prominent role at the San Francisco gathering—and especially the militants.

Legg used *ONE Confidential*, the newsletter he edited under the pseudonym "Marvin Cutler," to skewer the keynote speakers one by one. Frank Kameny, described as "somewhat fanatic and doctrinaire," had given, according to Legg, a typically "belligerent, militant paper." The speech by William Beardemphl, president of SIR, was said to contain "so many inaccuracies" as to be very nearly worthless. Shirley Willer, recently elected national president of the Daughters of Bilitis, was chastised for "a booming delivery that took some listeners aback"—a putdown that went a long way toward corroborating the central contention in Willer's speech that DOB should be wary of participating in homophile coalitions, since they were dominated by gay men patronizingly insensitive to their lesbian sisters.[6]

Not that Legg, for one, was any more sensitive to his gay male brethren. He characterized Clark Polak, president of Philadelphia's Janus Society and the fourth keynote speaker, as an "arrogant and insufferable boor," whose "conduct throughout the entire Conference . . . alienated most of the delegates." Polak had indeed spoken strong

words, accusing some of the leaders in the movement of failing to "rid themselves of their own anti-homosexual sentiments" and of caring only for the welfare of the "good" homosexual—attitudes Polak had labeled "Aunt Maryism."

Of the five keynoters, only Foster escaped Dorr Legg's bitter tongue. This was the more surprising because Foster had all his life been terrified of public speaking and was a despised Easterner—and Legg had announced that "the loudest noises and most extreme behavior seem to be coming from the East Coast" (a view directly counter to Harry Hay's that the East Coast was more conservative than the West). Legg did not regard Foster's arguments in favor of a national organization as "conclusive," but did feel that "in the main" Foster had argued his case "reasonably" well—and for Dorr Legg, that was remarkably high praise.

Foster deserved it. His speech cogently argued that the homophile movement had reached a point where only a national organization could advance it to the next stage. In the name of gaining greater prestige, security, publicity, and stability, he pressed the case for ending the confused duplication of disparate local efforts. "When homosexuality finally hits No. 1 topic of the day—and I think the day may be approaching fast," Foster argued, "it would be well to be prepared. . . . If we don't define ourselves—they will. If we don't state our aims—they will."[7]

Foster went on in his speech to reiterate the view that homosexuals had to abandon secrecy—or accept the fact that their image would continue to be constructed with data taken from psychiatric patients alone. But in a spasm of conservatism that drew him away from militants like Kameny, he did call for continued reliance on well-placed, sympathetic "experts"—on the physicians, judges, legislators, clergy, et al., who Foster confidently felt, despite the experience of recent decades, would rally to the homosexuals' side once a more "substantial" image had been presented.

Foster also recoiled in his speech from any suggestion that he was advocating "flamboyant" direct action. "It won't be necessary," he predicted, "to trot down to city square, climb up on the statue of General Sheridan, and wave a banner"; such behavior, "violating the law," would not do anything "constructive" to effect change. And yet in nearly the same breath—convulsing back again to a position *beyond* anything that Kameny and other militants had suggested—Foster proceeded to champion "public displays of affection." This, he felt, could "demonstrate to the public, as in no other manner, the futility

of its laws and perhaps its attitude." It could further demonstrate, he argued—perhaps with his own situation in mind—"that there is more to homosexuality than sex."

Somehow Foster felt that this could be done without crossing the line to "exhibitionism" and without becoming "intentionally provocative." All that he was advocating, he insisted, "was physical expression of genuine affection under prevailing ethical norms and accepted rules of propriety and good taste that govern heterosexual behavior." But the "accepted norms" of the mid-sixties could never tolerate *any* open expression of gay affection. And for Foster to hold out hope that it would, reflected an innocent, unwarranted faith in the American way.

When it came time for the conference to set up a national organization, the final product was closer to Shirley Willer's blueprint for a loosely structured federation—what Foster called "a sort of U.N.-type forum for ideas"—than to the more centralized organization he and others had argued for. Named the North American Conference of Homophile Organizations (NACHO), the new grouping was bound by an Articles of Confederation, as it were, not a Constitution. Even so, a number of prominent lesbians, led by Del Martin (the cofounder of DOB), were wary of it and insisted on the primary importance of maintaining DOB's autonomy. Martin and others had begun to shift their energies into the emerging women's movement. They distrusted the ability or willingness of their gay male associates to understand feminism, let alone the special needs and perspectives of lesbians.[8]

Though NACHO had not been given the extensive powers Foster thought necessary, he felt optimistic about the organization's future and left the conference full of high spirits. He had had "a great time" and had been delighted at being appointed chairman of the Credentials Committee—even though one disgruntled young delegate had told him that he exemplified the "pompous, midaged, overweight men" who held leadership positions in the movement. Foster good-naturedly acknowledged the need of each generation to cannibalize the preceding one and, on his return to Hartford following the conference, contentedly applied himself to his new duties. It would be essentially his responsibility to decide who should or should not attend the next NACHO conference, to be held in Washington, D.C., in August 1967.[9]

The month after returning home from San Francisco, Foster decided to try psychoanalysis. As part and parcel of his excitement at linking·up to the homophile movement, his juices had apparently

started to flow again and he wanted to see if he couldn't do something about his now entrenched pattern of celibacy. The therapist told him that treatment would require four visits a week (at twenty-five dollars per visit) for three years, and Foster nonchalantly embarked on it. But he "kept falling asleep on the couch," and after less than a year, he "gave it up as a bum deal."[10]

In the postconference period, he also turned to writing. Utilizing his academic skills, he embarked on an extended essay, "An Introduction to the Homophile Movement." Over the following year, the essay would turn into a thirty-seven-page pamphlet, which Foster published at his own expense in time to distribute at the 1967 Washington conference. Dorr Legg (under his pseudonym, Marvin Cutler) had ten years earlier published *Homosexuals Today—1956*, a comprehensive guide to the contemporary movement; but that was no longer up-to-date and, besides, it lacked the comprehensive historical overview that Foster attempted.[11]

In the first line of his preface to the pamphlet, Foster announced that "homosexuals are getting themselves organized to challenge a society that rejects them," and he went boldly on to describe the goals of the new movement as "not rehabilitation, not cure, not acceptance of homosexuals as persons in distinction from their acts, nor restriction of their acts to a special privacy." Rather, flatly rejecting such "fatuous" aims and "false distinctions," Foster characterized the emergent homophile movement as "a struggle for equal rights and, eventually, equal social status."[12]

As always with Foster, one vigorous step forward was followed by a cautious step backward. Having sounded a militant note in the opening section of his booklet, he went on to urge homosexuals— even as he acknowledged that they were rightfully angry at organized religion and the psychiatric profession for reinforcing oppressive views—*not* to abandon the hope of a beneficial rapprochement with both. In Foster's view, "many homosexuals who have associated themselves with the movement . . . if not always in actual need of psychiatric treatment could nonetheless benefit extensively from it, as they could from religious counselling."

Moving on in the pamphlet to a historical discussion, Foster drew a portrait of pre-nineteenth-century efforts at homosexual solidarity as "highly secretive and cult-like" and characterized the common purpose of these early groups as "debauchery" and their few clandestine publications as "pornographic." These early attempts were not, in Foster's view, constructive, did not appeal to homosexuals on a "high

enough plane." He looked far more favorably on late-nineteenth-century and early-twentieth-century efforts, reserving special praise for Magnus Hirschfeld's Scientific Humanitarian Committee in Weimar Germany and Edward Carpenter's intellectual circle in England. Gone was the old secrecy, he exulted, and gone, too, the unfortunate previous concentration on "orgies, pornography, magic and ritual." The new groups aimed to create a unified movement with well-defined grievances and strategies for reform (in other words, a movement in Foster's own image).

When he turned in the pamphlet to the United States, Foster showed surprising awareness of some early attempts to organize that remain poorly documented even to this day: Henry Gerber's short-lived Society for Human Rights, in Chicago in the 1920s; the Veterans Benevolent Association, which formed after World War II in New York City; and two possibly apocryphal groups, the Sons of Hamidy and the Legion of the Damned, whose existence Foster accepted at face value, as have most historians since. When his chronology came to the Daughters of Bilitis and the Mattachine Society of the 1950s, Foster gave generous credit to both for their pioneering efforts, but lamented how much time they had wasted on trying to figure out the *why* of homosexuality—what its origins were in the individual.[13]

He applauded the recent shift of energy into promoting social reforms and challenging long-standing discriminatory practices. The old emphasis on "How did we get here?" was giving way to the new: "Here we are, let's take it from there." Understandably, Foster reserved his fullest enthusiasm for the contemporary movement in which he was himself active; he welcomed the emerging sense of homosexuality "as in no way inferior to its counterpart" and the growing expectation "that society will eventually come around to a similar view."

Foster was particularly proud of the determination of those (including himself) who, in gathering to plan for the 1967 Washington conference, decided that homophile organizations would be judged as qualified to participate only if they agreed to the central aim of establishing the homosexual in society as "a first class human being and a first class citizen." He was proud, too, of his call for "concrete action programs," with new initiatives for "injecting our views into the planning of sex education programs" and for a large scale fund-raising effort to finance a national legal defense fund.[14]

But as he himself realized, not everyone agreed that the organization should be strengthened. Mattachine New York continued to

stand entirely aloof, with Dick Leitsch privately characterizing "the so-called 'homophile movement' [as] . . . too often an albatross around the necks of those who are trying to be effective in the cause for which we are all supposedly working." Leitsch was determined to avoid the rest of the movement "as much as possible. . . . If this means MSNY is isolationist, so be it. I believe it is better to be alone and effective than to be part of an ineffective crowd."[15]

To get a clearer sense of the divisions within the homophile movement, Foster went out to the West Coast during the summer of 1967 and had a round of talks with representatives of various groups. He concluded that there was a decided regional difference of opinion. Many on the West Coast preferred to put their energies and limited resources into a new regional network; and they tended to be *somewhat* less single-mindedly certain than were many Easterners that their way was the *only* way and that anyone disagreeing was either stupid or evil. The Western leaders were therefore inclined, for the time being anyway, to hold a national organization "to a consultative rather than a legislative level" and to confine it largely "to communications problems and projects."

Stopping off in Chicago to see Bill Kelley of Mattachine Midwest, Foster listened to the puzzlement of the "in-between" region. "What's all the controversy about?" Kelley asked. "Why all the in-fighting? Why all the legalistic technicalities?"—especially since most of the participating organizations had made it clear that no vote would be binding on them. Foster basically agreed with Kelley; he was eager to get beyond regional fears and jealousies and to set up a national organization with real teeth in it. But, a conciliator by nature, he was prepared to advise patience. "We all know," he wrote in summarizing his trip, "that cooperation amongst homophilers is going to come very hard. It's going to take time. The nationals may really be serving little more purpose at present than 'group therapy' "—a channel for venting "hostile feelings, fears, [and] individualistic . . . personalities." Besides, Foster felt, "it is perfectly natural that cooperation should be sought first in one's 'neighborhood' before taking on the country as a whole."

The 1967 homophile conference met in Washington, D.C., in mid-August and received decidedly mixed reviews. The new West Coast publication, *The Advocate*, hailed the conference as "the most productive and beneficial" of the meetings thus far, and quoted the pioneering activist Jim Kepner, among others, as pleased with the impressive presence of delegates from seventeen organizations and

the improved communication that developed between East and West Coast groups.[16]

But that was putting the best face on matters. New York Mattachine had again refused to participate; indeed, Leitsch had begun to toy with the idea of forming a "meaningful" national association of his own. On the West Coast, Dorr Legg had persuaded ONE to boycott the convention (Don Slater's rival L.A. group, Tangents, did attend) out of the growing conviction that the "eastern generals" were intent on a legislative body aimed at displacing the valuable variety of Western organizations, with their diverse aims and memberships.[17]

At the root of the problem was Foster's Credentials Committee. The Westerners and Midwesterners were on the whole committed to the principle of inclusiveness and objected strenuously to Foster's "extremely meticulous nosing" (in Jim Kepner's words) into every aspect of an applicant group's structure, purpose, and membership— especially since Foster himself had no real organizational affiliation, other than his own one-person creation, the Institute of Social Ethics. Dorr Legg, among others, fumed over Foster making final judgments about which organization was or was not a legitimate part of the movement, when he himself was an unaffiliated Johnny-come-lately.

Jim Kepner was the only Westerner to remain on the Credentials Committee in the face of Foster's meddlesome ways. He thought it was important for *someone* to fight a rearguard action in favor of a diverse movement ("I favored, as many Westerners did, a conference open to anyone willing to attend") against Foster's tendency to homogenize it into respectable conformity. But even Kepner—who liked Foster personally—joined the angry protest when it was discovered that Foster, in consultation with Kameny, had peremptorily barred the critic Leslie Fiedler (an avowed heterosexual who nonetheless had wanted to "observe" the proceedings, for a possible essay). "I didn't have any idea who the hell he was," Foster confessed, "I thought he was a bum off the streets." The mistake led to a volatile general discussion of the Credential Committee's policies, and only a timely, public apology from Foster averted a vote of censure.

Fiedler was ultimately admitted to the conference, but the performance of the Credentials Committee continued to be excoriated in postconference discussions. One of the committee's own members angrily denounced its "power-hungry" ways, insisting that some organizations with what he termed little or no evidence of actual existence—such as Pursuit and Symposium (Los Angeles) or the So-

ciety Advocating Mutual Equality (Rock Island, Illinois)—had been given voting privileges, while more substantial groups (like Craig Rodwell's HYMN*) had been turned away. In the past year, the dissident committee member charged, "the movement has created an *establishment*," and in protest he resigned.[18]

In arguing against admitting the "motley hordes," Foster had been especially concerned about unaffiliated "leftwingers" who might (as one of the articles later written on the conference put it) "jeopardize the social acceptance necessary to put into constructive action the expressions of the group's needs." In 1967, few such left-wing radicals were present at the national planning conference, but by the following year, at the gathering in Chicago, Foster's annoyance at what he called "infiltrators" would increase—and at the 1969 conference in Kansas City would become pronounced.[19]

Foster also opposed the view that "prejudice against homosexuality is but one manifestation of an unhealthy attitude on the part of society toward sex in general, and that this attitude must be attacked in its totality before homosexuals can hope to improve their status." Foster called such a view "speculative" and, "from a public relations standpoint, risky." Similarly, he argued against the notion that "anything goes so long as no one else is being 'harmed,' " characterizing that attitude as "an implied rejection of the authority of convention." Such doctrines, he wrote, "have not yet received official sanction by the homophile movement," and he expressed the personal hope that "they will not."[20]

Though later a defender of the women's movement, Foster also had trouble dealing with emerging feminism. He felt in 1967 that homophile and feminist concerns should be kept separate (though within two years he *would* be able to recognize their linkage), and he saw the small group of women who had affiliated with the national planning conference as "becoming very defensive," and some of them downright "disruptive." The "problem," like that of left-wing "infiltration," would grow over the next few years, exacerbated by the— yes—"defensive" attitude of gay men like Foster.

As the activist lesbian leader Del Martin put it in specifically singling out Foster's Credentials Committee for condemnation, it was (she wrote) "a debating society, an exercise in self-aggrandizement of self-proclaimed leaders of an unrepresented minority." Del Martin did not advocate that lesbians withdraw entirely from participation in the

* About which more on p. 164.

homophile movement—"for there are many worthy mutual endeavors demanding and deserving the support of female homosexuals." But she did insist that "consuming and costly" participation should be limited to areas where there is "some semblance of cooperation, or at least some hope thereof"—and she did not see any such semblance in the national conference.[21]

But there were too few women connected with it, and too few of that limited number who thought of themselves as what would soon be called feminists, for the dominant divisions within the planning conference to take on a specifically male-female cast—just as the contentiousness during the 1967 convention cannot be ascribed to a falling-out between men sympathetic to New Left views and men to the right of them. In fact, few of the men active in the conference had—or would ever have—strong connections to Left protest movements of the day (though some did derive inspiration from those movements). Such divisions as developed seem to have been contests more for turf than for principles—though principles were assuredly involved. On both sides of a given dispute, politically centrist men— marginalized only because of their deviant sexuality, not because they were in any other sense radical—battled over which individuals, ideas, and organizations would control a movement which was itself something of a Robert's Rules replica of mainstream political groupings (just as the very idea of battling for turf was very much a mainstream male phenomenon).

The battle was comparatively muted and polite in 1967. It focused on what kind of national organization should be attempted, what degree of unity was both desirable and feasible. Not much had yet been done among affiliates to explicate, let alone resolve, existing ideological differences between local and regional homophile organizations. Nor had much been accomplished by way of joint participation in public projects designed to improve the lot of homosexuals. Of the nationally conceived activities that *had* won sanction at the two previous conventions in 1966, few had actually materialized. Only the idea of a national legal defense fund had seen any significant implementation, and even that was still in a preliminary, formative stage.

What was needed at the 1967 national convention, in Foster's view, was the adoption of at least a rudimentary constitution and statement of purpose, as well as some sort of governing council to make decisions between conventions. But Foster understood that "the extreme fear on the part of the [local] organizations to a national structuring, and jealousy of their own individual sovereignty" required

that the convention proceed with "extreme caution" lest the fragile coalition be rent asunder.[22]

What came out of the convention was a good deal less than Foster had envisioned, and more caution than even he had thought necessary. The statement of purpose on which the convention finally agreed was vague enough to put it beyond dispute: The delegates merely pledged themselves to "the improvement of the status of the homosexual." To further that end, "intergroup projects and cooperation" were "encouraged," but lest that be taken as a mandate, the national conference was specifically described as merely "consultative in nature and function." At least the organization's future life had been assured: the delegates did vote that the planning conference be regarded as "a duly constituted continuing body." They even proved willing to hold out the "ultimate goal of establishing a legitimate homophile movement on a national scale."[23]

C R A I G

Craig wanted Mattachine to get out of its fifth-floor office, which was only open in the evenings, and into a location more accessible to the gay community. He thought a storefront office would be just the thing—especially if it could double as a bookstore and thereby help to augment the lack of available movement materials. The San Francisco homophile organization, SIR, put out an attractive monthly magazine called *Vector*, but *The Mattachine Review* had trailed off, and two versions of *ONE* magazine competed uncertainly in the aftermath of the punishing 1965 internecine struggle in the Los Angeles movement. Craig felt strongly that if Mattachine would open a storefront-cum-bookstore in New York, it could all at once do a public service, increase awareness of the organization's existence, and help pay the rent.

He persuaded Dick Leitsch to look at possible sites with him, and they found a place on Hudson Street that seemed ideal. Leitsch expressed interest and said he would take the matter up with the Mattachine board. But in retrospect, Craig doubts that he ever did. Leitsch had never been really enthusiastic about moving Mattachine out into the community, and he soon reported back to Craig that the board's decision had been negative.

Craig was furious at what he took to be Mattachine's endemic fear of risk-taking. The conservatives had supposedly been routed in the 1965 election, and Leitsch had himself recently led a successful protest against discriminatory practices by the New York Civil Service Commission. But Craig had increasingly come to distrust the quality of Leitsch's militancy, and to fear that he had become an accommodationist in order to maintain his control over New York Mattachine's councils. Besides, Craig had become uneasy over renewed rumors that Leitsch was involved in financial impropriety. Back in 1965—and as a direct result of Craig's suspicions and prodding—Mattachine treasurer Jack Weeden had discovered that Leitsch and Hodges had used a $5,000 gift to Mattachine to cover their own expenses, including a house rental on Fire Island. Hodges had been forced to resign from the presidency, but Leitsch had been given a second chance. Within a year, rumors of impropriety were again circulating—though it wouldn't be for another two or three years that Leitsch would be discovered diverting Mattachine funds to a secret bank account in Albany.

In April 1966, Craig decided that the time had come to resign from Mattachine and to pursue on his own the idea of opening a bookstore. But how to raise the needed money? Casting around for ideas, he hit on the notion of working summers at Fire Island Pines as a way of accumulating capital. The Pines was a relatively recent gay community, which had developed as an alternative for upscale homosexuals disenchanted with the "plebeian" atmosphere of Cherry Grove, the gay Fire Island community that dated back to the 1920s. Following a disastrous fire in the Pines, Yetta Cohen and her partner, John Whyte—both grandes dames—had built the Boatel, which sat at the Pines's harborside dock and served as a focal point for the new community.

In joining the Boatel staff in the summer of 1966, Craig knew in advance that the job would not be easy. He had heard the rumors of Mafia control and the tales of John Whyte's demanding ways (Whyte was secretly known as the Queen of Romania, or Snow—as in "Snow Whyte"). He worked his staff long hours, treated them like subjects, and played them off against each other to ensure maximum competition for his favor—just as Mr. Kilburn had back when Craig was at the Chicago Junior School. Whyte was especially fond of his "gold whale" ceremony, the Pines version of being knighted. Whyte would gather the Boatel staff to watch him award a particularly trustworthy employee with a gold pendant in the shape of a whale—which Whyte

would himself place around the honoree's presumably grateful neck. Most of the staff regarded the whale as a brand and would thereafter refrain from saying or doing anything around the honoree that they were unwilling to have reported immediately to Whyte.

Each staff member was given one day off a week, and a half-hour every afternoon to go to the beach. Those breaks aside, they worked away steadily at making beds, cleaning toilets, ensuring that each room met Whyte's standards of spotlessness. "John thought he was running the Plaza" is how Craig later put it; "he would personally inspect each room." And with good reason, since rates were (for the mid-sixties) high: about $70 a weekend for a small double without private bath, and $175 for two rooms facing the ocean. The staff was housed in a long barrackslike structure referred to as Steerage.

The occupants of the Boatel rooms were almost all gay, but an occasional straight couple, devotees of the magnificent Pines beach, would arrive for a few days at a time. (The actress Monique van Vooren was a weekend regular; all Craig can recall is an "overpowering trail of perfume wherever she went.") Occasionally a high-priced female prostitute would take a room in the Boatel to service the heterosexual men from the yachts tied up in the basin. Since the "yacht people" paid high fees for dockside rights, John Whyte instructed the staff to ignore their antics.

The staff was also told to treat the police as honored guests—to give them free meals and drinks—just in case the Mafia go-betweens hadn't made their payments on time. These were the years in which gay people, even in their secluded vacation resorts, survived on sufferance. Plainclothesmen would come over from the Long Island town of Sayville, across the bay from Fire Island, and conduct spot raids at the Meat Rack (then located in front of the co-op apartments on the beach) or entrap unsuspecting singles along the cruisy boardwalks.

The cops would take the arrested men to the telephone pole that used to sit in the middle of the Pines dock and chain them together to the pole. Then the cops would return to the Meat Rack and boardwalks for another series of arrests, and repeat the process until they had some thirty to forty men chained at the dock. By now it would be two or three A.M. A special police launch would take the men over to Long Island, where a kind of kangaroo court, held in the back of a drugstore, would collect steep fines and then release the arrested men with thirty-day suspended sentences. Terrified, none of the men dared report what was in fact organized theft.

When Craig saw what was going on, he was livid. One night he

tried to find a hacksaw to free the chained men from the pole while the cops were temporarily away from the dock, but he couldn't get any of the other employees to join him. He himself had to participate directly in another of the more humiliating rites that characterized the supposedly carefree Fire Island atmosphere of those years.

On Saturday nights, when the dance floor was packed with people, Boatel employees had to take turns sitting on top of a huge ladder, ten rungs high, and be ready to shine a flashlight as rudely as possible into the eyes of anyone engaging in "illegal" behavior. That was defined as two men even *facing* each other; actually dancing together was beyond the pale. All male eyes on the dance floor were supposed to be aimed exclusively at the occasional female—somebody's lesbian friend or one of the straight women from the yachts—who had been persuaded to participate. Sometimes there would be four or five circles of men on the dance floor, all facing the sole woman in the middle.

Craig only had to do ladder duty occasionally, to relieve another staffer, but even so, he had to psych himself up for it—had to keep reminding himself "that it was worth putting up with anything for the sake of the future bookstore." Some of the bolder dancers would push against the ladder, or even shake it, and Craig had to restrain himself from egging them on. He learned that marijuana was a big help in cooling himself out, and by the second summer, 1967, he had learned about "little greenies," amphetamine tablets that did wonders to replenish exhausted energy.

Hard work and humiliations aside, the two summers at Fire Island accomplished what Craig had intended. With free room and board, he had no expenses except cigarettes, and he managed to bank a fair portion of the $125 he made each week. By the fall of 1967, he had saved a little more than a thousand dollars and felt ready to make his move. The cheapest storefront he could find in the Village, at 291 Mercer Street, went for $115 a month. He also had to plunk down two months' security—which meant a third of his nest egg was gone before he could start buying stock. But he did quickly come up with a name: the Oscar Wilde Memorial Bookshop. He wanted the store named after someone who was readily identifiable as a homosexual, and Wilde seemed the most obvious candidate. (A few years later, Craig felt some regret at not having named the store after "a more militant and upfront" figure, but being "a rather sentimental person," he decided to stick with the original name.)[24]

As the day of the opening approached, and with a thousand things still undone, Craig asked his mother to fly in from Chicago to help

out with last-minute preparations. He met Marion at the airport on Thanksgiving Day, 1967, and took her straight to his shop. They stayed up all night finishing the dozen bookshelves (with about twenty-five titles total), then opened up on schedule the next day for business, serving free coffee and cookies to all comers.

In those years a "gay" bookstore had meant only one thing: pornography. But Craig had a straitlaced, proper side, and he had decided early on that the Oscar Wilde Memorial Bookshop would carry only "the better titles" and no pornography of any kind. Though hardly a puritan sexually, he regarded the sex magazines as exploitative—"a ten-dollar price on something that makes sex look dirty and furtive." He was determined to have a store where gay people did not feel manipulated or used. There was no ADULT READING sign in the window, and no peep show in the back room. And the ad Craig later took out in *The Village Voice* was headlined GAY IS GOOD.

Craig was determined to carry that message to his customers. True activist that he was, he viewed the Oscar Wilde shop as a vehicle for promoting a more positive view of homosexuality. And toward that goal, he invited none other than Foster Gunnison to sit in the bookstore on opening day and autograph copies of his recently completed booklet, "An Introduction to the Homophile Movement." "There Foster sat," Craig later recalled, "in his bow tie and his crew cut and his cigar. To look at Foster physically, he'd be the last person in the world you'd think would write that booklet."

Along with books and pamphlets, the shop carried buttons and cards relating to the homophile movement, and it had a community bulletin board that listed announcements of interest. Moreover, as Craig put it in his first press release, the bookshop "will also act as a clearing house for individuals and organizations supporting homosexual law reform in New York State." He also used Oscar Wilde as the storefront headquarters for a new group he now started: the Homophile Youth Movement. (He then added "in Neighborhoods" to the name, so that the acronym could be HYMN instead of the sexist HYM.) In the first issue of the group's *The New York Hymnal*, Craig wrote a blazing article denouncing Mafia control of gay bars. During the bookshop's first year of existence, it served as a counseling agency for more than a thousand young homosexual men and women, "helping them to gain a sense of identity and pride as young homosexuals."[25]

The Oscar Wilde shop was a pioneering enterprise, and customers were happily startled to find a "real" bookstore devoted solely to gay and lesbian titles. Craig's earlier lover Harvey Milk dropped by fre-

quently, his fascination marking (in Craig's estimate) "the beginnings of an interest on Harvey's part in the movement." Indeed, when Milk moved to San Francisco soon after, he told Craig that he intended to open a similar bookstore as a way of getting involved in community work. He settled for a camera store instead, but it did serve the same function as a community center.

Jim Fouratt also came by the bookstore often. He and Craig would stand in the crowded little store arguing each other to a standstill about political strategy. Jim was contemptuous of the Annual Reminders as misguided efforts to win acceptance from a mainstream America that was itself in desperate need of renovation, and he thought of Craig and other "earnest" reformers as "not real radicals"—not, like the Yippies, involved in any fundamental challenge to a sick society. But he admired Craig, even while discounting him, aware that he was someone who "always tried to tell the truth." Years later, Jim would come to have much more respect for the courage of those who, like Craig and Foster, had stood with their "Equality for Homosexuals" signs, unprotected, outside those symbolic citadels of American power, the White House and Independence Hall.

Though Craig put in seventy-hour weeks and for the first eighteen months ran the store entirely himself, the verdict on Oscar Wilde was not unanimously favorable. Those who missed porn on the shelves denounced Craig as an antisex puritan. And lesbian customers complained from the beginning that the store was too heavily weighted toward gay male titles. Karla Jay would occasionally drop in and was among those who felt uncomfortable there. It wasn't so much Craig himself that she objected to, but some of the other men; more intent on browsing for pickups than for books, they would give her nasty looks, as if to say "What are *you* doing in *our* store?"

Craig stiff-armed the pro-pornography crowd, but tried to be responsive to lesbian discontent. He felt that his Christian Science upbringing, which had included the teaching that God is a Father-Mother, had made him nonsexist, and he wanted to create a better balance in his store between gay male and lesbian titles. The problem was that he had no respect for what he called the "trashy" lesbian pulp novels of the day, and those aside, he felt the pickings were slim.

But he did increase his stock of lesbian titles as much as he felt he could, and Karla was able to find *The Ladder* there ("which I would have been afraid of subscribing to on my own"), as well as two books she would always cherish: Violette Leduc's *La Bâtarde* and Jane Rule's *Desert of the Heart*. To further signal his concern, Craig hired two

lesbian architects to remodel the store in 1969. But even by then, no more than 30 percent of the titles in Oscar Wilde were lesbian-oriented, and it was only later, with the expansion of lesbian publishing, that he achieved the parity he had always wanted.

The straight reaction to Oscar Wilde ranged from oblivious to venomous. The *New York Post* columnist Harriet Van Horne, listing aspects of the New Permissiveness that disgusted her, included—along with see-through dresses, topless dancers, and "skin-flicks"—the Oscar Wilde Memorial Bookshop (little dreaming or, apparently, caring that Craig shared her antipathy to porn).[26] But Van Horne was politeness itself compared to the anonymous harassment that plagued Craig from the day he opened the doors. Phone threats were a constant, with the most frequent callers insisting that they would burn the store down or carve Craig up. At first the threats frightened him, and, ever the activist, he would try to reason with the callers. But—perhaps to preserve his own sanity—he soon decided that venting on the phone was itself enough to sate the callers' anger. Still, it was hard not to feel unnerved when arriving at the shop in the morning to find swastikas or "Kill Fags" scrawled on the outside.

Besides, the landlord was hardly cordial. He had asked Craig, when they were drawing up a lease, what the store was going to be, and Craig had simply said it would be a bookshop—the Oscar Wilde Memorial Bookshop. The landlord allowed as how he had heard of Oscar Wilde, said nothing beyond that—and did sign the lease. Then came opening day, with the sign in the front of the store announcing BOOKSHOP OF THE HOMOPHILE MOVEMENT, and the sign in the window reading GAY IS GOOD. Livid, the landlord threatened Craig with eviction. Craig consulted a lawyer, and learned that his lease was airtight. But the lawyer warned him never to be late with the rent and never to pay less than the full amount—never, in other words, to give the landlord an out. It was a timely warning since Craig, always more interested in helping the movement than in fattening his bank account, usually lived close to the edge.

Some years later, in 1973, when Craig decided to relocate, his old landlord came by the new store to wish Craig well and to tell him that he had "learned a lot." He had always thought gay people were a "sick bunch," he told Craig, but over the years he had seen all the "nice people" who came into the store, and had been impressed with how "well behaved" they were. Craig was not one to downplay differentness or to encourage polite behavior, but he thanked the landlord for his good wishes—and went back to plotting the revolution.

1969

As the sixties came to a close, the United States was a notably different country from what it had been a mere decade before. The image of the fifties as a period *merely* of conformity and consensus has probably been overdrawn; after all, there was *Mad* magazine, rock and roll, the Beats, and that much imitated, sloe-eyed soul of alienation, James Dean. But compared with what came after, the fifties were decidedly a time of quiescence. The Bomb did indeed cause foreboding, and the Cold War a tangible sense of pending disaster. But left-wing agitation no longer marked the national scene, and the country remained secure in its self-image as the repository of Rectitude in a world beset by (Communist) Evil.

By the close of the sixties, that smugness had come undone. Within a six-month period from late 1967 to early 1968, the maverick Eugene McCarthy announced for the presidency; the Tet offensive in Vietnam blew apart the claims of an inevitable American victory; the police in Orangeburg, South Carolina, fired on black demonstrators, killing three and wounding dozens; Martin Luther King, Jr., was assassinated, and enraged black Americans rioted in dozens of cities; college students across the country took over campus buildings to protest war-related research; and the assassination of Robert Kennedy seemed to many to spell the end of hope for peaceful domestic reform.

When the police rioted at the Democratic National Convention that summer in Chicago, the drift toward militancy became a

stampede. By the fall of 1968, there were at least a third again as many SDS chapters as before the convention; black students took over administration buildings at Cornell while boldly brandishing their rifles in front of the television cameras; the Black Panthers and the Oakland police had a shoot-out; a contingent of feminists invaded the hitherto sacrosanct Miss America pageant; and incidents of arson and bombings became commonplace.

This fevered escalation gave heart to those on the left who believed that confrontation was a necessary precursor to substantive change: Out of polarization, the argument went, would come realignment; out of realignment, shifts in power—and out of widespread disruption, the first seedlings of a new and better world. The forces of repression, exemplified by the state, seemed in this scenario, to play their part to perfection. The Justice Department, as if on cue, duly indicted the "Chicago 8" on conspiracy charges. And then, in Berkeley, California, in May 1969, the whole repressive might of state power seemed epitomized when the police sealed off People's Park, bulldozed its gardens, and, in a major confrontation with protesters, wounded some hundred people.

Governor Ronald Reagan promptly sent in the National Guard —and growing legions of the young promptly decided that all the rules were off, their allegiance to established institutions severed, the cement of loyalty dissolved. By early 1969, circulation figures for the counterculture press shot upward; the readership of the weekly *Berkeley Barb* rose from a mere five thousand four years earlier to nearly 100,000, while New York's *East Village Other* soared to 65,000. And a Yankelovich poll found that 20 percent of American college students identified more with Che Guevara than with presidential candidates Nixon and Humphrey.[1]

Arbitrary authority, in all areas of national life, was now decidedly under siege. (Indeed, not only in the United States: Rebellions were spreading throughout Western Europe as well.) The Black Panthers demanded "Power to the People," and the students in SDS insisted on "participatory democracy," the right of those affected by a decision to set its parameters. Over and over, the question was being raised: "Who makes the rules—and by what right?"

In this confrontational context of anger and defiance, the assimilationist civil rights goals of NACHO, the national homophile planning conference, and NACHO's characteristic tactic of petitioning for the redress of grievances, seemed old-fashioned—just as their long-standing insistence that homosexuals *were* an oppressed minority and

had legitimate grievances suddenly seemed in harmony with the newly widespread resistance to traditional authority. Most younger gays and lesbians who sympathized with the New Left's broad agenda for ending inequality at home and interventionism abroad, joined not NACHO—which struck them as hopelessly bourgeois—but Students for a Democratic Society, or one of several organizations enlisted in the struggle for black empowerment.

But that is not the whole story, either. A fair percentage of the radical young who were gay or lesbian had not yet come to terms with their own sexuality. Some of them steered clear of NACHO not—or not simply—because of its centrist political views, but because they felt unready and threatened in the one area where NACHO did take a radical stance: namely, in its insistence that homosexuality was neither abnormal nor unnatural. Here was irony aplenty. The members of NACHO, centrist in all else, were raising one radical standard under which the nonconforming young did not dare to rally.

Leo Laurence, a reporter for radio station KGO in San Francisco, covered the confrontations between antiwar demonstrators and the police at the 1968 Chicago Democratic Convention, and the experience changed his life. A thirty-six-year-old gay man who had previously toed the polite homophile line, Laurence now decided that gays, too, needed to adopt a militant posture. He began to write articles for the *Berkeley Barb* and for SIR's *Vector*, calling for an alliance with Black Panthers and antiwar radicals. After he became editor of *Vector*, Laurence denounced the guilty, apologetic style that he felt was favored by "timid" homophile leaders—whom he characterized as "a bunch of middle-class, uptight, bitchy old queens"—and called for the same "proud" affirmation that characterized other radical groups.[2]

Laurence and his lover, Gale Whittington, posed together bare-chested for a picture accompanying a *Berkeley Barb* article in which Whittington openly proclaimed his homosexuality, saying it was time for gays to declare themselves. When, as a result, he lost his job as an accounting clerk with the States Steamship Company, he, Laurence, and a half-dozen other gay men demonstrated, in early April 1969, in front of the company's offices in San Francisco's financial district. They carried signs reading FREEDOM FOR HOMOS NOW and LET GAYS LIVE, Laurence wore a button proclaiming "Gay Is Good," and he and Whittington told reporters that they were beginning a "vigorous and public" progay campaign that was being opposed by the gay world's own "square" establishment. "They are scared," Laurence

asserted. But, as he soon found out, not *that* scared. In May, Laurence was fired from *Vector* and kicked out of SIR—perhaps for his belligerence as much as his militance.

A similar scenario developed within the Daughters of Bilitis. When Rita Laporte and Barbara Grier tried to convert the organization and its publication, *The Ladder*, to a feminist perspective, urging DOB to leave NACHO and join forces instead with heterosexual feminists, a serious split developed among lesbian activists. The ensuing fight for control would end, by 1970, in both the demise of *The Ladder* and the dissolution of DOB's national structure.[3]

New York City was also astir. The Student Homophile League at Columbia had come into being in 1967 on a campus where, only two years before, the famous classicist Gilbert Highet had canceled a lecture in protest over a representative of New York Mattachine having been allowed to speak in Ferris Booth Hall. The foundation of the League led to a deluge of outraged letters, but the handful of courageous students who signed up as members proceeded with their work of education and counseling. (They also formed a largely figurehead alumni committee, headed by Foster Gunnison, Jr.) By the fall of 1967 several other New York campuses had followed Columbia's example and had formed Student Homophile League chapters (Rita Mae Brown was a member of the New York University group).

In 1968, the Columbia Student Homophile League initiated a notable assault on the psychiatric establishment. When the medical school staffed a panel discussion on homosexuality with a group of "experts" known (except for the Kinsey Institute's Paul Gebhard) to regard it as a pathological adjustment, SHL representatives invaded the meeting and publicly demanded that in the future the discussion of homosexuality be placed "in its proper setting as a sociological problem of deeply entrenched prejudice and discrimination against a minority group."[4] That very evening, the Columbia campus exploded in student protests over U.S. incursions overseas and the university's incursions against its black neighbors—and many members of the Student Homophile League joined in the occupation of campus buildings that accompanied the protests.

K A R L A

Karla had gone to a few NOW meetings, but had quickly decided they weren't for her; she found the organization too oriented toward winning legislative changes, and overall too tame, too focused on asking to be "let in." Working to achieve equality in an unjust society was pointless to Karla. She also disliked the then common notion that feminism should take a backseat to the "main" struggles against capitalism, racism, and imperialism. She saw that argument as a convenient one for men, as a long-standing rationale for deferring women's liberation by insisting that its time had not *yet* come, while arguing that it would *automatically* come once the "larger" struggle had been won.

Karla had less trouble pulling away from the male left than some women did, for the simple reason that she had never been closely identified with it. For her, the upheaval at Columbia University had been the starting point, not the culmination, of struggle. And during the Columbia fracas, she had been appalled at the macho behavior of the left-wing male students. Unlike some radical feminists, Karla became convinced early on that male-supremacist behavior was not simply the result of men being the agents of an oppressive capitalist system, and would not automatically disappear with the destruction of that system. She was in favor of changing the country's economic structure, but was skeptical that such change alone would liberate women—or, for that matter, free blacks either.

These views drew Karla to Redstockings, a radical feminist group founded by Ellen Willis and Shulamith Firestone in February 1969. Her membership in the group, in turn, further clarified her views. Without being rigidly Marxist, the Redstockings selectively employed Marxist analysis, and particularly in insisting that women's behavior resulted from the material circumstances in which they found themselves; they married, for example, not because they had been conditioned to believe they should (as many feminists argued) but because they consciously realized that women's low-paying, alienating work made the single life too difficult.[5]

Karla was not among the original organizers of Redstockings, but did join the group within a few months of its founding. By then, the

dominant faction (and one had to be part of a faction to feel fully alive in the late sixties) had decided to downplay activism in favor of establishing and participating in consciousness-raising groups. In Marxist style, Redstockings created those groups along the lines of semi-independent cells. Each group was assigned a single letter of the alphabet as a name, and each sent a single delegate to the meetings of a central committee. Karla was often chosen as her group's representative, and she also went out often on speaking engagements to explain to other women how they could form their own consciousness-raising groups.

Unlike some other feminist groups—for example, the celibacy-advocating Boston-based Cell 16—the dominant faction in Redstockings did not denounce heterosexuality as an institution that perpetuated male dominance; women, they argued, should confront, not abandon men. The charismatic Rita Mae Brown was among those who felt that Redstockings was not merely pro-heterosexual, but downright heterosexist. When she decided to come out as a lesbian to her consciousness-raising group (not the one Karla was in), she found maximum discomfort and minimal support—and left Redstockings soon after.

Rita Mae Brown was at first alone in her daring. Karla had picked up early, in her own group, the same hesitant, uncomfortable reaction to any hint of lesbianism, but for a while she chose to be silent about it. She had finally found women with whom she felt comfortable personally and politically—more comfortable, certainly, than she had felt with the butch/femme women she met in the lesbian bars. They had insisted, because of her flowered dresses and long hair, that she was a femme, but she had resented the attempt to lock her into a role that constricted the actual range of her impulses. Knowing her own aggressive strength, she hated being stereotyped on the basis of outer appearances alone.

She felt differently typecast, but typecast nonetheless, on the few occasions when she went to a Daughters of Bilitis meeting. She looked much younger than her actual age—hitchhiking at the age of twenty-three, she was mistaken for a fifteen-year-old runaway and arrested—and the conservative women in DOB reacted to her in terror. She tried to convince them that she was not jailbait, but they kept nervously insisting that DOB was not in the business of bringing out teenage girls. Angry and disgruntled, Karla would afterwards refer to them as "the Daughters of Bursitis."

By comparison with being pigeonholed as a femme and fled from

as a juvenile, Karla felt herself well treated—respected as a many-faceted adult—in Redstockings. And the group's reluctance to discuss lesbianism did not especially faze her because she was not, in 1969, at all eager to label herself a lesbian. While an undergraduate at Barnard, both she and her steady girlfriend from CUNY thought of themselves as bisexuals. Though that particular relationship ended at about the time Karla graduated, and though it was followed by a series of casual affairs with women, she had several prolonged affairs with men during the same period.

Her boyfriends ranged from an upstairs neighbor, to a Swiss body builder (who also self-identified as bisexual), to a countercultural printer. What she liked about these men was not their conversation —"I didn't like men's patriarchal heads," she later said—but their ability to give her physical pleasure. The men she chose seemed turned on by her aggressiveness, and she got them to do what *she* wanted to do sexually. Which didn't mean that she always controlled the relationships and got to end them whenever they stopped working for her. Her most satisfying lover, the printer, walked out abruptly on her after finding her in bed one day with a woman.

Karla was juggling several kinds of lives simultaneously—much like Jim and Yvonne. Along with her bisexual affairs and her political involvement with Redstockings, she was taking graduate courses in comparative literature at night and holding down a full-time job during the day. Her first choice for graduate school had been U.C. Berkeley, where her high board scores, offsetting her B average, had won her a scholarship. But she felt unable to accept it. She had so little money that it seemed less risky to stay in familiar New York, get a daytime job, and work on her doctorate at night. She decided on New York University, though the school didn't make it easy for her: two of her male friends, with lower grades and board scores, got scholarships there, but she was turned down.

The first summer following graduation from Barnard, Karla found a temporary job—thanks to her excellent French—with the prestigious literary agent Georges Borchardt. Impressed with her work, Borchardt, at the end of the summer, got her a full-time, ninety-five-dollar-a-week position as an assistant editor with the David McKay Corporation. Kennett and Eleanor Rawson, the owners of the McKay publishing house, were in the process of editing David Reuben's *Everything You Ever Wanted To Know About Sex but Were Afraid to Ask*—a book that would become a runaway best-seller.

Asked if she wanted to have a look at the manuscript, Karla was

horrified to find it filled with racist and homophobic remarks—like the question-and-answer colloquy in which the query "How could the Mayor's daughter get VD?" was answered by "Sleeping with a guy who slept with a black prostitute." Karla brought the material to the Rawsons' attention, and found them sympathetic to her complaints. But in the end they were unable to persuade Reuben to remove most of the offending remarks.

Soon after starting work with McKay, Karla was riding her bike one day when several teenagers appeared out of nowhere. She tried to speed away but they grabbed her, threw her down a nearby flight of cellar stairs, and ran off with her bike. When she got up, she was unable to straighten out her leg and the pain was excruciating. X-rays revealed that her back was broken in three places. When the doctor saw the plates, he was incredulous and asked Karla how she had managed to get to his office. Who had carried her in? When she said she had walked in by herself, the doctor gasped, "Impossible!" He wanted to put her in a hospital, but she refused to go, so she was given a steel brace and put in traction in her own apartment.

Her roommate and friends took care of her. The doctor had told her that she would *probably* be able to walk again but would never be able to straighten her leg. With typical spunk, Karla set out to prove him wrong. Among the friends ministering to her were the novelist Joel Lieber (later a suicide) and his wife, Sylvia, who lived around the corner. The couple was involved with Zen Buddhism and gradually got Karla interested too.

She started doing meditation in which she visualized herself whole and well, and every day she would try to straighten out her leg a little more, painful though the exercise was. She also became a vegetarian. She had already been leaning in that direction because of the war in Vietnam: "I considered myself a pacifist," she said later. "I was really into Gandhi. I didn't approve of killing and I didn't want other people killing in my place. And that included killing a cow for me. I haven't eaten red meat since 1968."

She had to wear a corsetlike brace for about a year, and limped badly for several more years after that. But her leg did gradually straighten, and later X-rays revealed that her back had regenerated. She had to give up bowling, because the jerking motion was inadvisable, but apart from that had no residual problems of any kind. Did meditation and vegetarianism do the trick? Karla doesn't pretend to know, saying simply, "I have no explanation." But once well, she vowed never again to feel so defenseless, and took up judo. That, in

turn, helped her quickly lose the fifty pounds she had gained from lying around in bed.

And, limp and all, she also returned to politics. In September 1969, she took part in the second feminist protest at the Miss America contest in Atlantic City. (The first protest, a year earlier, had involved day-long picketing and guerrilla-theater skits but not—as the massive coverage claimed—bra-burning.⁶) At the second demonstration, Karla and the other feminists passed out roses on the boardwalk and told each woman they gave one to that *she* was the real Miss America.

Karla was beginning to notice strange things about her telephone. If she hung up and then quickly lifted the receiver again to make a second call, there was a little space before she could get a dial tone. And then came the time when she picked the phone back up and heard one man asking another, "What do you think she meant by that?" Karla had previously assumed that her phone was being tapped, but the actual discovery still proved a shock.

It later turned out that the New York City "Red Squad" was not only listening in on the conversations of various women in Redstock-ings, but had planted someone at meetings—in much the way the FBI had long had socialists and Communists under surveillance and was currently doing its best to subvert the black civil rights struggle. Karla later became one of the plaintiffs in the famed *Handschu* case against the Red Squad, which dragged on for years; in the process she saw full reports of the Redstockings' central committee meetings, complete down to descriptions of objects in the room. Though Karla was one of only seven or eight women who sat on that committee, they were never able to find out who the plant was.

The day finally came in Karla's consciousness-raising group when Micela Griffo—who had been brought out sexually by Rita Mae Brown, and who would be active in the Gay Liberation Front just a short while later—finally spoke openly of her lesbianism. Some of the straight women in the group, especially Alix Kates Shulman, were supportive, and Karla felt encouraged to speak out herself. She still disliked labels, but since she *was* sleeping with women she felt the responsibility of sharing the burden of whatever negative conse-quences might follow.

But what she discovered was that "there were quite a number of lesbians in quite a number of closets in Redstockings," and instead of opprobrium she got "a whole new supply of lovers"—though, in many cases, not very good ones. As a "gesture of solidarity" with their

lesbian sisters, some straight women had started to take on the lesbian label and to do some experimenting in bed. These "political lesbians," as they were known, tended to be lousy sex partners. Despite themselves, they brought their homophobic leftist baggage with them to bed, and were likely to find their sexual experiences with women disappointing. "They were really boring in bed," Karla said later. "It was like eating matzoh." It didn't take her long to decide that if any more straight women wanted to experiment sexually, they could do it with somebody else. Then, if they decided they liked lesbianism, Karla would be there.

JIM

Jim Fouratt regarded Abbie Hoffman as his brother. They had been through a lot together—from the action on the floor of the stock exchange to the confrontation at the Democratic convention in Chicago. And in 1969 they managed to bring the David Susskind television show to a dead stop by unveiling a live duck that promptly shat all over the stage. (Jim had already stunned Susskind by appearing dressed all in white; an apparition, complete with flowing blond hair, that seemed a miraculous reincarnation of Jesus Christ himself.)

Through all the high jinks and the serious politicking, Jim had swallowed his doubts about Abbie—about his self-celebration, his drug-taking, his (in Jim's view) "irresponsible" tendency to lead people into more trouble than they had bargained for. But an incident finally occurred that crystallized Jim's doubts and led to a definitive break between the two men. In order to do his political work—to notify and mobilize people for actions through his fly sheet, *The Communications Company*—Jim had long relied on his trusty Gestetner duplicating machine. One night he returned to his apartment to find the machine gone, apparently stolen. His suspicion immediately focused on Abbie, because of the disagreements the two had recently had over the 1968 Chicago confrontations and Abbie's dismissive comment that Jim "didn't really understand politics."

Jim went straight over to Abbie's place and confronted him. Abbie didn't even bother to deny the theft. Instead he acted as if the Gestetner was legitimately his by right of his superior understanding of the requirements of political organizing. Deeply wounded—"I

would have died for Abbie"—Jim gave up the contest in despair, reluctantly concluding that he could never again trust Abbie, could never believe in his ability to put loyalty to a friend above the presumed exigencies of politics.

Ever the moralist, Jim decided there was a lesson to be learned: "not to endow people with what I want them to be, but to try to see them as they are so that I'm not set up to be disappointed or destroyed." But like anyone with a good heart and a large capacity for trust, Jim would have to learn that lesson over and over. Fortunately, he never learned it for long—fortunately, because an optimistic sense of the "goodness" of human nature is always the essential fuel for activism.

But for the moment, hurt and confused, Jim retreated from the movement. He went out to San Francisco for three months with his lover, Howie, and took up weaving—the hippie alternative to confrontational politics. But weaving turned out not to be "it" after all —"I was bored out of my mind"—and early in 1969 Jim was back in New York, where he dabbled for a time in that other hippie alternative, drugs. Give or take an occasional puff, Jim had previously avoided drugs, but now he started going regularly to the Sutton Place office of "Dr. Feelgood" (John Bishop). There, assorted celebrities crowded the waiting room for their "vitamin" shots ("Amphetamines? Well, of course not!" Dr. Feelgood would reassure those patients determined to be gullible). But after overdosing one day—and being peremptorily put out on the street by Dr. Feelgood—Jim at first cut down on and then kicked the shots.

Within a few months, Jim landed a paying job in the music world. Music had always been an important ingredient in his life, and his contacts with musicians had proliferated over the years. One day his friend Al Kooper, who had started the group Blood, Sweat & Tears, asked him if he was interested in a job with CBS as a staff producer. Jim grabbed it. Not only had his life lost its political focus, but his bills had mounted, and the notion of steady, well-paying work seemed the perfect simultaneous cure for ennui and indebtedness.

CBS hired Jim as the "house freak" with its corporate eyes wide open. Its recent "hip" ad campaign—"The Man Can't Bust Our Music"—had backfired. *Rolling Stone* had made fun of CBS's sudden countercultural conversion, and the underground press had reacted indignantly to what it branded a slick, commercial exploitation of the reality of police brutality. Jim Fouratt was hired to repair all that damage, to serve as liaison among the music executives, the cutting-

edge artists CBS represented—Joplin, Chicago, Santana—and the radical communities from which they had emerged.[7]

Jim took to his job with gusto and proved a superlative liaison (the personal dividends included a weeklong affair with Jim Morrison). Before long, he had worked himself up to be an assistant to CBS president Clive Davis, who was not then known to be gay. And he had also discovered an unexpected knack for writing advertising copy. Developing a whole new campaign of his own around the slogan "Know Who Your Friends Are," he featured countercultural images of long-haired hippies, blacks, and Native Americans. And he deflected any negative reaction from the underground press for this latest appropriation of its imagery by persuading CBS to invest hefty advertising sums in left-wing and hippie publications. The infusion of revenue helped to keep the underground newspaper consortium, Liberation News Service, alive, and it gave Jim enormous satisfaction to know that he was making a significant political contribution through his job.

But if criticism from the underground press was defused, the response from elsewhere was inflamed. An FBI memo sent from San Francisco to Washington in January 1969 assailed CBS's infusion of money into left-wing publications as "giving active aid and comfort to enemies of the United States," and "suggested that the FBI should use its contacts to persuade" CBS to stop. Within three months, that wish had come to pass: CBS withdrew all advertising from the underground press. Jim blamed the turnabout on the avalanche of negative mail, apparently orchestrated by right-wing groups, that had poured into the network. At the least, the mail confirmed a shift in policy that conservative CBS bigwigs Frank Stanton and William S. Paley, who had their own cherished network of ties to D.C. bigwigs and the CIA, had already determined on. Whatever the reasons, CBS ceased to place ads in any but mainstream publications, even as they cynically began a new campaign—which Jim opposed and argued against—featuring the proclamation that "the Revolutionaries" were on the CBS label.[8]

S T O N E W A L L

Craig Rodwell—like Leo Laurence in San Francisco—wanted militant activism to be the touchstone of New York's homophile movement. He was thoroughly fed up with Dick Leitsch's controlling influence over Mattachine, for if Leitsch had once been a militant, he was now, in Craig's view, interested solely in the advancement of Leitsch. He had become a mere politician, concerned more with protecting and inflating his own role as the broker between gays and the city administration than with empowering gays themselves, through confrontational action, to build a proud, assertive movement.[9]

Craig was also fed up with the gay bar scene in New York—with Mafia control over the only public space most gays could claim, with the contempt shown the gay clientele, with the speakeasy, clandestine atmosphere, the watered, overpriced drinks, the police payoffs and raids. His anger was compounded by tales he heard from his friend Dawn Hampton, a torch singer who, between engagements, worked the hatcheck at a Greenwich Village gay bar called the Stonewall Inn. Because Dawn was straight, the Mafia men who ran Stonewall talked freely in front of her—talked about their hatred for the "faggot scumbags" who made their fortunes.

Indeed, the Stonewall Inn, at 53 Christopher Street, epitomized for Craig everything that was wrong with the bar scene. When a hepatitis epidemic broke out among gay men early in 1969, Craig printed an angry article in his newsletter, New York Hymnal, blaming the epidemic on the unsterile drinking glasses at the Stonewall Inn. And he was probably right. Stonewall had no running water behind the bar; a returned glass was simply run through one of two stagnant vats of water kept underneath the bar, refilled, and then served to the next customer. By the end of an evening the water was murky and multicolored.[10]

Craig also thought Stonewall was a haven for "chicken hawks" —adult males who coveted underage boys. Jim Fouratt shared that view. He characterized Stonewall as "a real dive, an awful, sleazy place set up by the Mob for hustlers, chickens to be bought by older people." But this was, at most, a partial view. One segment of Stonewall's varied clientele did consist of street queens who hustled; but

even for that contingent, Stonewall was primarily a social, not a business place. Some sixteen- and seventeen-year-olds did frequent Stonewall, and were admitted with the friendly complicity of somebody at the door (the drinking age was then eighteen)—but not for purposes of prostitution. As in any club, of course, the occasional cash transaction undoubtedly took place.

Figuring prominently in Craig and Jim's scenario is the figure of Ed Murphy, one of the bouncer-doormen at the Stonewall Inn, whom they accuse of purveying drugs and young flesh there. The indictment, though overdrawn, has some substance. Murphy did deal drugs, did lech after teenagers, did make "introductions" (for which he accepted "tips"), and was involved in corruption, simultaneously taking payoffs from the Mafia and the New York Police Department. (That is, until the police badly beat him up one night, and he stopped informing for them.)[11]

Sascha L., who in 1969 briefly worked the door at Stonewall alongside Murphy, began by thinking of him as a father figure— posing as a cop, Murphy had once rescued Sascha from an angry john wanting more than Sascha had been willing to give—but finally decided that Murphy was a run-of-the-mill crook. Sascha was eyewitness one night to an underage boy named Tommy turning over to Murphy, in the Stonewall basement, a bag of wallets stolen during the evening.[12]

But Murphy and the Stonewall Inn had many defenders. Murphy had been employed in gay bars and after-hours places since 1946 and in the course of that long career had made—along with detractors and enemies—some staunch friends. (Indeed, in later years the Christopher Street Heritage of Pride Committee would canonize Murphy as an originating saint of the gay movement.) And as for the Stonewall Inn, it had, in the course of its two-and-a-half-year existence, become the most popular gay bar in Greenwich Village. Many saw it as an oasis, a safe retreat from the harassment of everyday life, a place less susceptible to police raids than other gay bars and one that drew a magical mix of patrons ranging from tweedy East Siders to street queens. It was also the only gay male bar in New York where dancing was permitted.[13]

Sylvia Rivera was among the staunchest defenders of Stonewall, and of its omnipresent bouncer Ed Murphy. When down on their luck, which was often, Sylvia and her street-queen friends always knew they could turn to Murphy for a handout. Some of them called him Papa Murphy, and Sylvia's friend Ivan Valentin seems to have been his special favorite. "To me," Ivan says, "Ed Murphy never did

anything wrong." Murphy had a soft spot in general for Hispanics like Ivan, and also for blacks; indeed, later gay bar owners who employed Murphy would worry that he would "turn the club black" and—since racism has always been alive and well in the gay world —frighten off the white clientele.[14]

But though Sylvia and her friends enjoyed going to Stonewall, their bars of choice were in fact Washington Square, on Broadway and Third Street and, to a lesser extent, the Gold Bug and the Tenth of Always (an after-after-hours place that catered to all possible variations of illicit life and stayed open so late it converted by nine A.M. into a regular working-class bar). The Washington Square was owned by the Joe Gallo family, which also controlled Tony Pastor's and the Purple Onion (whereas the Genovese family operated Stonewall, Tele-Star, the Tenth of Always, the Bon Soir on Eighth Street, and—run by Anna Genovese—the Eighty-Two Club in the East Village, which featured drag shows for an audience largely composed of straight tourists). Washington Square was Sylvia's special favorite. It *opened* at three in the morning and catered primarily (rather than incidentally, as was the case with Stonewall) to transvestites; the more upscale ones would arrive in limos with their wealthy johns and spend the evening ostentatiously drinking champagne. But others, like Sylvia, went there for relaxing nightcaps and gossip after a hard evening of hustling on the streets.[15]

The Mob usually provided only a limited amount of money to Family members interested in opening a club; it thereafter became the individual's responsibility to turn a profit. That meant, among other things, not investing too heavily in liquor. When Washington Square first opened, the Mafia members who ran the place lost twelve cases of liquor and fifty cases of beer during the first police raid. Thereafter, only a few bottles were kept in the club and the rest of the liquor was stored in a nearby car; when the bartender was about to run out, someone would go around the corner to the parked car, put a few bottles under his arm, and return to the club. (Other bars had different strategies, such as keeping the liquor hidden behind a panel in the wall.) By thus preventing the police from confiscating large amounts of liquor during any one of their commonplace raids, it was possible—and also commonplace—to open up again for business the next day.[16]

The Stonewall Inn had, in its varied incarnations during the fifties, been a straight restaurant and a straight nightclub. In 1966 it was taken over by three Mafia figures who had grown up together on

Mulberry Street in Little Italy: "Mario" (the best-liked of the three), Zucchi, who also dealt in firecrackers, and "Fat Tony" Lauria, who weighed in at 420 pounds. Together they put up $3,500 to reopen the Stonewall as a gay club; Fat Tony put up $2,000, which made him the controlling partner, but Mario served as Stonewall's manager and ran the place on a day-to-day basis.[17]

Tony Lauria was the best-connected of the three. He had gotten a B.A. at Xavier, had married and divorced, and lived at 136 Waverly Place, a Mob-owned apartment building. It was home to a host of related Mafia figures involved in assorted rackets: vending machines, carting companies, and sanitation. Tony's two uncles and his father also lived in the building; the latter (whose other son was a stockbroker) was high up in Mob circles and sat on the board of the Bank of Commerce on Delancey Street, a bank that laundered a fair share of Mafia money. Lauria Senior did not approve of his wayward son's penchant for hanging around street mobsters and getting involved in the "fag bar" scene.[18]

Fat Tony lived from 1966 to 1971 with Chuck Shaheen, an openly gay man in his mid-twenties of Italian descent. The relationship was secretarial, not erotic. Shaheen acted as a man Friday, serving at different times as everything from a Stonewall bartender to the trusted go-between who "picked up the banks"—the accumulated cash—at the bar several times a night and carried the money home to his boss. According to Shaheen, Tony developed a heavy methamphetamine habit, shooting the crystal several times a day into his veins. Under the drug's influence, Tony lost about two hundred pounds, stayed up all night at clubs (at Stonewall, his favorite hangout, he would embarrass his partners by insistently doing parlor tricks, like twirling cigarettes in the air), and began, for the first time in his life, to go to bed with men—though, to Shaheen's relief, not with him. Tony's father stopped speaking to him altogether and Shaheen had to carry messages between them. Increasingly shunned, Tony, so the rumor mill had it, was later killed by the Family.[19]

Tony and his partners, Mario and Zucchi, had opened Stonewall as a private "bottle club." That was a common ruse for getting around the lack of a liquor license; bottles would be labeled with fictitious names and the bar would then—contrary to a law forbidding bottle clubs from selling drinks—proceed to do a cash business just like any other bar. The three partners spent less than a thousand dollars in fixing up the club's interior. They settled for a third-rate sound system, hired a local electrician and his assistant to build a bar and raise

the dance-floor stage, and got their jukebox and cigarette machines—
had to get them—from the local don, Matty "the Horse" Iannello.[20]

As the man who controlled the district in which Stonewall was
located, Iannello was automatically entitled to a cut in the operation.
Shaheen never once saw Iannello in Stonewall, nor did he ever meet
him, but Matty the Horse got his percentage like clockwork. The
Stonewall partners also had to pay off the notoriously corrupt Sixth
Precinct. A patrolman would stop by Stonewall once a week to pick
up the envelopes filled with cash—including those for the captains
and desk sergeants, who never collected their payoffs in person. The
total cash dispensed to the police each week came to about two thousand dollars.[21]

Despite the assorted payoffs, Stonewall turned a huge weekly
profit for its owners. With rent at only three hundred dollars a month,
and with the take (all in cash) typically running to five thousand dollars
on a Friday night and sixty-five hundred on a Saturday, Stonewall
quickly became a money machine. Some of the profit was made
through side gigs for which Stonewall as a place was merely the
occasion. In Shaheen's words, "all kinds of mobsters used to come
in. There were all kinds of deals going on. All kinds of hot merchan-
dise. They would deal the stuff out of the trunks of cars parked in
front of the bar. You could buy all kinds of things at Stonewall."
Shaheen recalls vividly the time a Cuban couple was swindled out of
a clay plate with multicarat diamonds hidden under the glaze; they
had taken the plate with them when fleeing Castro. Fat Tony had a
ring made from one of the bigger (five-carat) stones and, when he later
fell on hard times, had Shaheen negotiate its sale to Cartier.

Some of the Mob members who worked gay clubs were themselves gay—and terrified of being found out. "Big Bobby," who was
on the door at Tony Pastor's, a Mafia-run place at Sixth Avenue and
MacDougal Street, almost blew his cover when he became indiscreet
about his passion for a Chinese drag queen named Tony Lee (who,
though going lamentably to fat, was famed for her ballerina act). The
Stonewall Inn seems to have had more than the usual number of gay
mobsters. "Petey," who hung out at Stonewall as a kind of free-lance,
circulating bouncer, had a thick Italian street accent, acted "dumb,"
and favored black shirts and ties; he was the very picture of a Mafia
mobster—except for his habit of falling for patrons and coworkers.

He took a shine to Sascha L., but they would have sex only when
Petey was drunk, and no mention could be made of it afterward.
Some of the other mobsters would take Sascha aside and question

him—Sascha was openly gay—about whether Petey "didn't seem a little funny." Sascha would dutifully answer no, and as a reward—and perhaps, too, because his presence made Petey nervous—Petey got Sascha a better-paying job at Washington Square.[22]

Petey turned his attentions to a drag queen named Désirée, apparently figuring that if he were caught, getting a blow job from a drag queen would be far more forgivable than giving a blow job to a stocky male doorman. Besides, Désirée was Italian. A beautiful boy with shoulder-length hair and huge amber eyes, she had a figure so stunningly "feminine" that she passed as a woman—as a gorgeous woman—in broad daylight.

But even the beautiful Désirée was outclassed by blond Harlow. (Petey had developed a huge lech for Harlow, too, but he couldn't get near her.) Harlow rarely came to Stonewall, preferring a tonier, straight uptown scene, but when she did, her chic black dresses and real jewelry set the standard for aspiring queens on the Washington Square–Stonewall circuit. Harlow never had the luck to catch Andy Warhol's eye, and so never achieved the widespread notoriety of Holly Woodlawn, Jackie Curtis, and Candy Darling, who made it into Warhol's movies and were thereby elevated into mainstream New York stardom. But Harlow—at least according to drag-queen mythology—later achieved her own kind of stardom, purportedly marrying a congressman, getting a sex-change operation at his expense, and buying (again courtesy of the congressman) a club in Philadelphia.

As for Désirée, she and Petey eventually ran off together to live outside of New York as a heterosexual couple. But—again according to the rumor mill—theirs was not a storybook ending: Petey subsequently turned "bad" and, in a fit of jealousy, shot and killed Désirée.

Most of the employees at Stonewall, and some of the customers, did drugs, primarily "uppers." Desbutal—a mix of Desoxyn and Nembutal—was a great favorite (though later banned by the FDA), and the bar was also known as a good place to buy acid. The chief supplier was Maggie Jiggs, a famous queen who worked the main bar at Stonewall, along with her partner, Tommy Long. (Tommy kept a toy duck on the bar that quacked whenever someone left a tip.) They were a well-known team with a big following. Maggie, blonde, chubby, and loud, knew everybody's business and would think nothing of yelling out in the middle of the crowded bar, "Hey, girl, I hear you got a whole new plate of false teeth from that fabulous dentist you been fucking!" But Maggie loved people, had good drugs, was always surrounded by gorgeous men, and arranged wonderful three-

ways, so her outspokenness, and even her occasional thievery, were usually forgiven.

Maggie and Tommy were stationed behind the main bar, one of two bars in the Stonewall. But before you could get to it, you had to pass muster at the door (a ritual some of the customers welcomed as a relief from the lax security that characterized most gay bars). That usually meant inspection, through a peephole in the heavy front door by Ed Murphy, "Bobby Shades," or muscular Frank Esselourne. "Blond Frankie," as he was known, was gay, but in those years not advertising it, and was famous for being able to spot straights or undercover cops with a single glance.[23]

If you got the okay at the door—and for underage street kids that was always problematic—you moved a few steps to a table, usually covered by members of what one wag called the Junior Achievement Mafia team. That could mean, on different nights, Zucchi; Mario; Ernie Sgroi, who always wore a suit and tie and whose father had started the famed Bon Soir on Eighth Street; "Vito," who was on salary directly from Fat Tony, was hugely proud of his personal collection of S.S. uniforms and Nazi flags, and made bombs on the side; or "Tony the Sniff" Verra, who had a legendary nose for no-goods and kept a baseball bat behind the door to deal with them. At the table, you had to plunk down three dollars (one dollar on weekdays), for which you got two tickets that could be exchanged for two watered-down drinks. (According to Chuck Shaheen, *all* drinks were watered, even those carrying the fanciest labels.) You then signed your name in a book kept to prove, should the question arise in court, that Stonewall was indeed a private "bottle club." People rarely signed their real names. "Judy Garland," "Donald Duck," and "Elizabeth Taylor" were the popular favorites.[24]

Once inside Stonewall, you took a step down and straight in front of you was the main bar where Maggie held court. Behind the bar some pulsating gel lights went on and off—later exaggeratedly claimed by some to be the precursor of the innovative light shows at the Sanctuary and other gay discos that followed. On weekends, a scantily clad go-go boy with a pin spot on him danced in a gilded cage on top of the bar. Straight ahead, beyond the bar, was a spacious dancing area, at one point in the bar's history lit only with black lights. That in itself became a subject for camp, because the queens, with Murine in their eyes, all looked as if they had white streaks running down their faces. Should the police (known as Lily Law, Alice Blue Gown—Alice for short—or Betty Badge) or a suspected plainclothes-

man unexpectedly arrive, white bulbs instantly came on in the dance area, signaling everyone to stop dancing or touching.[25]

The queens rarely hung out at the main bar. There was another, smaller room off to one side, with a stone wishing well in the middle, its own jukebox and service bar, and booths. That became headquarters for the more flamboyant contingent in Stonewall's melting pot of customers. There were the "scare drag queens" like Tommy Lanigan-Schmidt, Birdie Rivera, and Martin Boyce—"boys who looked like girls but who you knew were boys." And there were the "flame" (not drag) queens who wore eye makeup and teased hair, but essentially dressed in male clothes—if an effeminate version with fluffy sweaters and Tom Jones shirts.

Only a few favored full-time transvestites, like Tiffany, Spanola Jerry, a hairdresser from Sheepshead Bay, and Tammy Novak, who performed at the Eighty-Two Club, were allowed to enter Stonewall in drag (Tammy sometimes transgressed by dressing as a boy). Not even "Tish" (Joe Tish) would be admitted, though he had been a well-known drag performer since the early fifties, when he had worked at the Moroccan Village on Eighth Street, and though in the late sixties he had a long-running show at the Crazy Horse, a nearby café on Bleecker Street. Tish *was* admitted into some uptown straight clubs in full drag; there, as he sniffily put it, his "artistry" was recognized.[26]

Some of the younger queens were homeless and more or less camped out in the small park directly opposite the Stonewall bar. Bob Kohler, a gay man in his early forties who lived nearby, became something of a protector. (Kohler would later be prominent in the Gay Liberation Front, but had long since developed empathy for outsiders: In the early sixties, his talent agency on West Fifty-seventh Street represented a number of black artists no one else would take on.) Kohler would give the young queens clothing and change, or sometimes pay for a room in a local fleabag hotel; and when out walking his dog, he would often sit on a park bench with them and listen to their troubles and dreams. He was able to hear their pain even as he chuckled at their antics. Once, when he went down to bail out Sylvia Rivera's good friend, Marsha P. Johnson, he heard Judge Bruce Wright ask Marsha what the "P" was for. "Pay it no mind," Marsha snapped back; Judge Wright broke up laughing and told Kohler to "get her out of here."[27]

Yet for all their wit and style, Kohler never glamorized street queens as heroic deviants pushing against rigid gender categories, self-

conscious pioneers of a boundary-free existence. He knew too much about the misery of their lives. He knew a drugged-out queen who fell asleep on a rooftop and lay in the sun so long that she ended up near death with a third-degree burn. He knew "cross-eyed Cynthia," killed when she was pushed out of a window of the St. George Hotel in Brooklyn—and another "Sylvia," who jumped off its roof. He knew Dusty, "ugly as sin, never out of drag, very funny, big mouth," who made the mistake of calling the wrong person "nigger" and was stabbed to death. And he knew several queens who had themselves stabbed a recalcitrant customer—or a competitive sister.

The queens considered Stonewall and Washington Square the most congenial downtown bars. If they passed muster at the Stonewall door, they could buy or cajole drinks, exchange cosmetics and the favored Tabu or Ambush perfume, admire or deplore somebody's latest Kanecalon wig, make fun of six-foot transsexual Lynn's size-12 women's shoes (while admiring her fishnet stockings and miniskirts and giggling over her tales of servicing the firemen around the corner at their Tenth Street station), move constantly in and out of the ladies room (where they deplored the fact that a single red light bulb made the application of makeup difficult), and dance in a feverish sweat till closing time at four A.M.

The jukebox on the dance floor played a variety of songs, even an occasional "Smoke Gets in Your Eyes" to appease the romantics. The Motown label was still top of the heap in the summer of 1969; three of the five hit singles for the week of June 28—by Marvin Gaye, Junior Walker, and the Temptations—carried its imprint. On the pop side, the Stonewall jukebox played the love theme from the movie version of *Romeo and Juliet* over and over, the record's saccharine periodically cut by the Beatles' "Get Back" or Elvis Presley's "In the Ghetto." And all the new dances—the Boston Jerk, the Monkey, the Spider—were tried out with relish. If the crowd was in a particularly campy mood (and the management was feeling loose enough), ten or fifteen dancers would line up to learn the latest ritual steps, beginning with a shouted "Hit it, girls!"[28]

The chino-and-penny-loafer crowd pretty much stayed near the main bar, fraternizing with the queens mostly on the dance floor, if at all. ("Two queens can't bump pussy," one of them explained. "And I don't care how beefy and brawny the pussy is. And certainly not for a relationship.") The age range at Stonewall was mostly late teens to early thirties; the over-thirty-five crowd hung out at Julius', and

the leather crowd (then in its infancy) at Keller's. There could also be seen at Stonewall just a sprinkling of the new kind of gay man beginning to emerge: the hippie, long-haired, bell-bottomed, laid-back, and likely to have "weird," radical views.

Very few women ever appeared in Stonewall. Sascha L. flatly declares that he can't remember *any*, except for the occasional "fag hag" (like Blond Frankie's straight friend Lucille, who lived with the doorman at One-Two-Three and hung out at Stonewall), or "one or two dykes who looked almost like boys." But Chuck Shaheen, who spent much more time at Stonewall, remembers—while acknowledging that the bar was "98 percent male"—a few more lesbian customers than Sascha does, and, of those, a number who were decidedly femme. One of the lesbians who did go to Stonewall "a few times," tagging along with some of her gay male friends, recalls that she "felt like a visitor." It wasn't as if the male patrons went out of their way to make her feel uncomfortable, but rather that the territory was theirs, not hers: "There didn't seem to be hostility, but there didn't seem to be camaraderie."[29]

SYLVIA, JIM, CRAIG

Sylvia Rivera had been invited to Marsha P. Johnson's birthday party on the night of June 27, but she decided not to go. It wasn't that she was mad at Marsha; she simply felt strung out. She had been working as an accounting clerk in a Jersey City chain-store warehouse, keeping tally sheets of what the truckers took out—a good job with a good boss who let her wear makeup whenever she felt like it. But it was an eleven-to-seven shift, Sundays through Thursdays, all-night stints that kept her away from her friends on the street and decidedly short of the cash she had made from hustling.

Yes, she wanted to clean up her act and start leading a "normal" life. But she hadn't counted on missing the money so much, or on her drug habit persisting—and sixty-seven dollars a week in take-home pay just wasn't doing it. So she and her lover, Gary, decided to piece out their income with a side gig—passing bad checks—and on June 27, a Friday, they had just gotten back from papering Washington, D.C. The first news they heard on returning was about Judy

Garland's funeral that very day, how twenty thousand people had waited up to four hours in the blistering heat to view her body at Frank E. Campbell's funeral home on Madison Avenue and Eighty-first Street. The news sent a melodramatic shiver up Sylvia's spine, and she decided to become "completely hysterical." "It's the end of an era," she tearfully announced. "The greatest singer, the greatest actress of my childhood is no more. Never again 'Over the Rainbow' "—here Sylvia sobbed loudly—"no one left to look up to."

No, she was not going to Marsha's party. She would stay home, light her consoling religious candles (Viejita had taught her *that* much), and say a few prayers for Judy. But then the phone rang and her buddy Tammy Novak—who sounded more stoned than usual—*insisted* that Sylvia and Gary join her later that night at Stonewall. Sylvia hesitated. If she was going out at all—"Was it all right to dance with the martyred Judy not cold in her grave?"—she would go to Washington Square. She had never been crazy about Stonewall, she reminded Tammy: Men in makeup were tolerated there, but not exactly cherished. And if she was going to go out, she wanted to *vent*—to be just as outrageous, as grief-stricken, as makeup would allow. But Tammy absolutely *refused* to take no for an answer and so Sylvia, moaning theatrically, gave in. She popped a black beauty and she and Gary headed downtown.

Jim's job at CBS required long hours, and he often got back to his apartment (after a stopover at Max's Kansas City) in the early morning. On the night of June 27 he had worked in the office until midnight, had gone for a nightcap at Max's, and about one A.M. had headed back to his apartment in the Village. Passing by the Stonewall Inn —a bar he despised, insistent it was a haven for marauding chicken hawks—Jim noticed a cluster of cops in front of the bar, looking as if they were about to enter. He shrugged it off as just another routine raid, and even found himself hoping that *this* time (Stonewall had been raided just two weeks before) the police would succeed in closing the joint.

But as Jim got closer, he could see that a small group of onlookers had gathered. That was somewhat surprising, since the first sign of a raid usually led to an immediate scattering; typically, gays fled rather than loitered, and fled as quietly and as quickly as possible, grateful not to be implicated at the scene of the "crime." Jim spotted Craig Rodwell at the top of the row of steps leading up to a brownstone

adjacent to the Stonewall Inn. Craig looked agitated, expectant. Something was decidedly in the air.

Craig had taken up his position only moments before. Like Jim, he had been on his way home—from playing cards at a friend's—and had stumbled on the gathering crowd in front of the Stonewall. He was with Fred Sargeant, his current lover, and the two of them had scrambled up the brownstone steps to get a better view. The crowd was decidedly small, but what was riveting was its strangely quiet, expectant air, as if awaiting the next development. Just then, the police pushed open the front door of the Stonewall and marched in. Craig looked at his watch: It was one-twenty A.M.

Sylvia was feeling *very* little pain. The black beauty had hopped her up and the scotch had smoothed her out. Her lover, Gary, had come along; Tammy, Bambi, and Ivan were there; and rumor had it that Marsha Johnson, disgusted at all the no-shows for her birthday, was also headed downtown to Stonewall, determined to party *somewhere*. It looked like a good night. Sylvia expansively decided she did like Stonewall after all, and was just saying that to Tammy, who looked as if she was about to keel over—"that chile [Tammy was seventeen, Sylvia eighteen] could not control her intake"—when the cops came barreling through the front door. (The white warning lights had earlier started flashing on the dance floor, but Sylvia and her friends had been oblivious.)

The next thing she knew, the cops, with their usual arrogance, were stomping through, ordering the patrons to line up and get their IDs ready for examination. "Oh my God!" Sylvia shouted at Gary, "I didn't bring my ID!" Before she could panic, Gary reached in his pocket and produced her card; he had brought it along. "Praise be to Saint Barbara!" Sylvia shrieked, snatching the precious ID. If the raid went according to the usual pattern, the only people who would be arrested would be those without IDs, those dressed in the clothes of the opposite gender, and some or all of the employees. Everyone else would be let go with a few shoves and a few contemptuous words. The bar would soon reopen and they would all be back dancing. It was annoying to have one's Friday night screwed up, but hardly unprecedented.

Sylvia tried to take it in stride; she'd been through lots worse, and with her ID in hand and nothing more than face makeup on, she knew the hassling would be minimal. But she was pissed; the good

high she had was gone, and her nerve ends felt as raw as when she had been crying over Judy earlier in the evening. She wished she'd gone to the Washington Square, a place she preferred anyway. She was sick of being treated like scum; "I was just not in the mood" was how she later put it. "It had got to the point where I didn't want to be bothered anymore." When one of the cops grabbed the ID out of her hand and asked her with a smirk if she was a boy or a girl, she almost swung at him, but Gary grabbed her hand in time. The cop gave her a shove toward the door, and told her to get the hell out.

Not all of the two hundred or so people who were inside Stonewall fared that well. Chico, a forty-five-year-old patron who looked sixty, was arrested for not having an ID proving he was over 18. Another patron, asked for "some kind of ID, like a birth certificate," said to the cop, "I don't happen to carry mine around with me. Do you have yours, Officer?"; the cop arrested him. Eighteen-year-old Joey Dey had been dancing for a while with a guy in a suit, but had decided he wasn't interested and had tried to get away; the man had insisted they go on dancing and then, just as the police came through the door, pulled out a badge and told him he was under arrest.[30]

Harry Beard, one of the dance-floor waiters, had been coming off a ten-day amphetamine run and was crashed out in one of the side-room booths when the police arrived. He knew that the only way to avoid arrest was to pretend he was a customer, so he grabbed a drink off the bar, crossed his legs provocatively, and tried to act unconcerned. Fortunately for him, he had gone into one of the new unisex shops that very day and was wearing a soft pink blouse with ruffles around the wrist and down the front. One of the cops looked at him quizzically and said, "I know you. You work here." Harry was on welfare at the time, so, adopting his nelliest tone, he thrust his welfare card at the cop and replied, "Work here? Oh, don't be silly! I'm just a poor girl on welfare. Here's my welfare card. Besides, I wouldn't work in a toilet like this!" The cop looked skeptical but told Harry he could leave.[31]

The Stonewall management had always been tipped off by the police before a raid took place—this happened, on average, once a month—and the raid itself was usually staged early enough in the evening to produce minimal commotion and allow for a quick re-opening. Indeed, sometimes the "raid" consisted of little more than the police striding arrogantly through the bar and then leaving, with no arrests made. Given the size of the weekly payoff, the police had an understandable stake in keeping the golden calf alive.

But this raid was different. It was carried out by eight detectives from the First Division (only one of them in uniform), and the Sixth Precinct had been asked to participate only at the last possible second. Moreover, the raid had occurred at one-twenty A.M.—the height of the merriment—and with no advance warning to the Stonewall management. (Chuck Shaheen recalls some vague tip-off that a raid *might* happen, but since the early-evening hours had passed without incident, the management had dismissed the tip as inaccurate.)[32]

There have been an abundance of theories as to why the Sixth Precinct failed on this occasion to alert Stonewall's owners. One centers on the possibility that a payment had not been made on time or made at all. Another suggests that the extent of Stonewall's profits had recently become known to the police, and the Sixth Precinct brass had decided, as a prelude to its demand for a larger cut, to flex a little muscle. Yet a third explanation points to the possibility that the new commanding officer at the precinct was out of sympathy with payoffs, or hadn't yet learned how profitable they could be.

But evidence has surfaced to suggest that the machinations of the Sixth Precinct were in fact incidental to the raid. Ryder Fitzgerald, a sometime carpenter who had helped remodel the Stonewall interior and whose friends Willis and Elf (a straight hippie couple) lived rent-free in the apartment above the Stonewall in exchange for performing caretaker chores, was privy the day after the raid to a revealing conversation. Ernie, one of Stonewall's Mafia team, stormed around Willis and Elf's apartment, cursing out (in Ryder's presence) the Sixth Precinct for having failed to provide warning in time. And in the course of his tirade, Ernie revealed that the raid had been inspired by federal agents. The Bureau of Alcohol, Tobacco and Firearms (BATF) had apparently discovered that the liquor bottles used at Stonewall had no federal stamps on them—which meant they had been hijacked or bootlegged straight out of the distillery. Putting Stonewall under surveillance, BATF had then discovered the bar's corrupt alliance with the Sixth Precinct. Thus when the feds decided to launch a raid on Stonewall, they deliberately kept the local police in the dark until the unavoidable last minute.[33]

When the raid, contrary to expectations, did get going, the previous systems put in place by the Mafia owners stood them in good stead. The strong front door bought needed time until the white lights had a chance to do their warning work: Patrons instantly stopped dancing and touching; and the bartenders quickly took the money

from the cigar boxes that served as cash registers, jumped from behind the bar, and mingled inconspicuously with the customers. Maggie Jiggs, already known for her "two for the bar, one for myself" approach to cash, disappeared into the crowd with a cigar box full of money; when a cop asked to see the contents, Maggie said it contained her tips as a "cigarette girl," and they let her go. When questioned by her employers later, Maggie claimed that the cop had taken the box *and* the money. She got away with the lie.[34]

The standard Mafia policy of putting gay employees on the door so they could take the heat while everyone else got their act together, also paid off for the owners. Eddie Murphy managed to get out ("Of course," his detractors add, "he was on the police payroll"), but Blond Frankie was arrested. There was already a warrant outstanding for Frankie's arrest (purportedly for homicide; he was known for "acting first and not bothering to think even later"). Realizing that this was no ordinary raid, that this time an arrest might not merely mean detention for a few hours at Centre Street, followed by a quick release, Frankie was determined not to be taken in. Owners Zucchi and Mario, through a back door connected to the office, were soon safely out on the street in front of the Stonewall. So, too, were almost all of the bar's customers, released after their IDs had been checked and their attire deemed "appropriate" to their gender—a process accompanied, as in Sylvia's case, by derisive, ugly police banter.[35]

As for "Fat Tony," at the time the raid took place he had still not left his apartment on Waverly Place, a few blocks from the Stonewall. Under the spell of methamphetamine, he had already spent three hours combing and recombing his beard and agitatedly changing from one outfit to another, acting for all the world like one of those "demented queens" he vilified. He and Chuck Shaheen could see the commotion from their apartment window, but only after an emergency call from Zucchi could Tony be persuaded to leave the apartment for the bar.[36]

Some of the campier patrons, emerging one by one from the Stonewall to find an unexpected crowd, took the opportunity to strike instant poses, starlet style, while the onlookers whistled and shouted their applause-meter ratings. But when a paddy wagon pulled up, the mood turned more somber. And it turned sullen when the police officers started to emerge from Stonewall with prisoners in tow and moved with them toward the waiting van. Jim Fouratt at the back of the crowd, Sylvia standing with Gary near the small park across the

street from Stonewall, and Craig perched on top of the brownstone stairs near the front of the crowd—all sensed something unusual in the air, all felt a kind of tensed expectancy.

The police (two of whom were women) were oblivious to it initially. Everything up to that point had gone so routinely that they expected to see the crowd quickly disperse. Instead, a few people started to boo; others pressed against the waiting van, while the cops standing near it yelled angrily for the crowd to move back. According to Sylvia, "You could feel the electricity going through people. You could actually feel it. People were getting really, really pissed and uptight." A guy in a dark red T-shirt danced in and out of the crowd, shouting "Nobody's gonna fuck with me!" and "Ain't gonna take this shit!"[37]

As the cops started loading their prisoners into the van—among them, Blond Frankie, the doorman—more people joined in the shouting. Sylvia spotted Tammy Novak among the three queens lined up for the paddy wagon, and along with others in the crowd started yelling "Tammy! Tammy!," Sylvia's shriek rising above the rest. But Tammy apparently didn't hear, and Sylvia guessed that she was too stoned to know what was going on. Yet when a cop shoved Tammy and told her to "keep moving! keep moving!," poking her with his club, Tammy told him to stop pushing and when he didn't, she started swinging. From that point on, so much happened so quickly as to seem simultaneous.[38]

Jim Fouratt insists that *the* explosive moment came when "a dyke dressed in men's clothing," who had been visiting a male employee inside the bar, started to act up as the cops moved her toward the paddy wagon. According to Jim, "the queens were acting like queens, throwing their change and giving lots of attitude and lip. But the dyke had to be more butch than the queens. So when the police moved her into the wagon, she got out the other side and started to rock it."

Harry Beard, the Stonewall waiter who had been inside the bar, partly corroborates Jim's account, though differing on the moment of explosion. According to Beard, the cops had arrested the cross-dressed lesbian inside the bar for not wearing the requisite (as mandated by a New York statute) three pieces of clothing "appropriate to one's gender." As they led her out of the bar, so Beard's version goes, she complained that the handcuffs they had put on her were too tight; in response, one of the cops slapped her in the head with his nightstick. Seeing the cops hit her, people standing immediately outside the door started throwing coins at the police.[39]

But Craig Rodwell and a number of other eyewitnesses sharply contest the view that the arrest of a lesbian was *the* precipitating incident, or even that a lesbian had been present in the bar. And they skeptically ask why, if she did exist, she has never stepped forward to claim the credit; to the answer that she may long since have died, they sardonically reply, "And she never told another soul? And if she did, why haven't *they* stepped forward to claim credit for her?" As if all that isn't muddle enough, those eyewitnesses who deny the lesbian claimant, themselves divide over whether to give the palm to a queen—Tammy Novak being the leading candidate—or to one of the many ordinary gay male patrons of the bar. Craig Rodwell's view probably comes as close as we are likely to get to the truth: "A number of incidents were happening simultaneously. There was no one thing that happened or one person, there was just . . . a flash of group— of mass—anger."[40]

As the police, amid a growing crowd and mounting anger, continued to load prisoners into the van, Martin Boyce, an eighteen-year-old scare drag queen, saw a leg in nylons and sporting a high heel shoot out of the back of the paddy wagon into the chest of a cop, throwing him backward. Another queen then opened the door on the side of the wagon and jumped out. The cops chased and caught her, but Blond Frankie quickly managed to engineer another escape from the van; several queens successfully made their way out with him and were swallowed up in the crowd. Tammy Novak was one of them; she ran all the way to Joe Tish's apartment, where she holed up throughout the weekend. The police handcuffed subsequent prisoners to the inside of the van, and succeeded in driving away from the scene to book them at the precinct house. Deputy Inspector Seymour Pine, the ranking officer, nervously told the departing police to "just drop them off at the Sixth Precinct and hurry back."[41]

From this point on, the mêlée broke out in several directions and swiftly mounted in intensity. The crowd, now in full cry, started screaming epithets at the police—"Pigs!" "Faggot cops!" Sylvia and Craig enthusiastically joined in, Sylvia shouting her lungs out, Craig letting go with a full-throated "Gay power!" One young gay Puerto Rican went fearlessly up to a policeman and yelled in his face, "What you got against faggots? We don't do you nuthin'!" Another teenager started kicking at a cop, frequently missing as the cop held him at arm's length. One queen mashed an officer with her heel, knocked him down, grabbed his handcuff keys, freed herself, and passed the keys to another queen behind her.[42]

By now, the crowd had swelled to a mob, and people were picking up and throwing whatever loose objects came to hand—coins, bottles, cans, bricks from a nearby construction site. Someone even picked up dog shit from the street and threw it in the cops' direction. As the fever mounted, Zucchi was overheard nervously asking Mario what the hell the crowd was upset about: the Mafia or the police? The *police*, Mario reassured him. Zucchi gave a big grin of relief and decided to vent some stored-up anger of his own: He egged on bystanders in their effort to rip up a damaged fire hydrant and he persuaded a young kid named Timmy to throw the wire-mesh garbage can nearby. Timmy was not much bigger than the can (and had just come out the week before), but he gave it his all—the can went sailing into the plate-glass window (painted black and reinforced from behind by plywood) that stretched across the front of the Stonewall.[43]

Stunned and frightened by the crowd's unexpected fury, the police, at the order of Deputy Inspector Pine, retreated inside the bar. Pine had been accustomed to two or three cops being able to handle with ease any number of cowering gays, but here the crowd wasn't cowering; it had routed eight cops and made them run for cover. As Pine later said, "I had been in combat situations, [but] there was never any time that I felt more scared than then." With the cops holed up inside Stonewall, the crowd was now in control of the street, and it bellowed in triumph and pent-up rage.[44]

Craig dashed to a nearby phone booth. Ever conscious of the need for publicity—for visibility—and realizing that a critical moment had arrived, he called all three daily papers, the *Times*, the *Post*, and the *News*, and alerted them that "a major news story was breaking." Then he ran to his apartment a few blocks away to get his camera.

Jim Fouratt also dashed to the phones—to call his straight radical-left friends, to tell them "people were fighting the cops—it was just like Newark!" He urged them to rush down and lend their support (just as he had long done for *their* causes). Then he went into the nearby Ninth Circle and Julius', to try to get the patrons to come out into the street. But none of them would. Nor did any of his straight radical friends show up. It taught Jim a bitter lesson about how low on the scale of priorities his erstwhile comrades ranked "faggot" concerns.

Gary tried to persuade Sylvia to go home with him to get a change of clothes. "Are you nuts?" she yelled. "I'm not missing a minute of this—it's the *revolution*!" So Gary left to get clothes for both of them. Blond Frankie, meanwhile—perhaps taking his cue from Zucchi—

uprooted a loose parking meter and offered it for use as a battering ram against the Stonewall's door. At nearly the same moment somebody started squirting lighter fluid through the shattered glass window on the bar's façade, tossing in matches after it. Inspector Pine later referred to this as "throwing Molotov cocktails into the place," but the only reality *that* described was the inflamed state of Pine's nerves.[45]

Still, the danger was very real, and the police were badly frightened. The shock to self-esteem had been stunning enough; now came an actual threat to physical safety. Dodging flying glass and missiles, Patrolman Gil Weisman, the one cop in uniform, was hit near the eye with a shard, and blood spurted out. With that, the fear turned abruptly to fury. Three of the cops, led by Pine, ran out the front door, which had crashed in from the battering, and started screaming threats at the crowd, thinking to cow it. But instead a rain of coins and bottles came down, and a beer can glanced off Deputy Inspector Charles Smyth's head. Pine lunged into the crowd, grabbed somebody around the waist, pulled him back into the doorway, and then dragged him by the hair, inside.[46]

Ironically, the prisoner was the well-known—and heterosexual—folk singer Dave Van Ronk. Earlier that night Van Ronk had been in and out of the Lion's Head, a bar a few doors down from Stonewall that catered to a noisy, macho journalist crowd scornful of the "faggots" down the block. Once the riot got going, the Lion's Head locked its doors; the management didn't want faggots moaning and bleeding over the paying customers. As soon as Pine got Van Ronk back into the Stonewall, he angrily accused him of throwing dangerous objects—a cue to Patrolman Weisman to shout that Van Ronk was the one who had cut his eye, and then to start punching the singer hard while several other cops held him down. When Van Ronk looked as if he was going to pass out, the police handcuffed him, and Pine snapped, "All right, we book him for assault."[47]

The cops then found a fire hose, wedged it into a crack in the door, and directed the spray out at the crowd, thinking that would certainly scatter it. But the stream was weak and the crowd howled derisively, while inside the cops started slipping on the wet floor. A reporter from *The Village Voice*, Howard Smith, had retreated inside the bar when the police did; he later wrote that by that point in the evening "the sound filtering in [didn't] suggest dancing faggots any more; it sound[ed] like a powerful rage bent on vendetta." By now the Stonewall's front door was hanging wide open, the plywood brace behind the windows was splintered, and it seemed only a matter of

minutes before the howling mob would break in and wreak its vengeance. One cop armed himself with Tony the Sniff's baseball bat; the
others drew their guns, and Pine stationed several officers on either
side of the corridor leading to the front door. One of them growled,
"We'll shoot the first motherfucker that comes through the door."[48]

At that moment, an arm reached in through the shattered window, squirted more lighter fluid into the room, and then threw in
another lit match. This time the match caught, and there was a whoosh
of flame. Standing only ten feet away, Pine aimed his gun at the
receding arm and (he later said) was preparing to shoot when he heard
the sound of sirens coming down Christopher Street. At two-fifty-
five A.M. Pine had sent out emergency signal 10-41—a call for help
to the fearsome Tactical Patrol Force—and relief was now rounding
the corner.[49]

The TPF was a highly trained, crack riot-control unit that had
been set up to respond to the proliferation of protests against the
Vietnam War. Wearing helmets with visors, carrying assorted weapons, including billy clubs and tear gas, its two dozen members all
seemed massively proportioned. They were a formidable sight as,
linked arm in arm, they came up Christopher Street in a wedge formation that resembled (by design) a Roman legion. In their path, the
rioters slowly retreated, but—contrary to police expectations—did
not break and run. Craig, for one, knelt down in the middle of the
street with the camera he'd retrieved from his apartment and, determined to capture the moment, snapped photo after photo of the on-
coming TPF minions.[50]

As the troopers bore down on him, he scampered up and joined
the hundreds of others who scattered to avoid the billy clubs but then
raced around the block, doubled back behind the troopers, and pelted
them with debris. When the cops realized that a considerable crowd
had simply re-formed to their rear, they flailed out angrily at anyone
who came within striking distance. But the protesters would not be
cowed. The pattern repeated itself several times: The TPF would
disperse the jeering mob only to have it re-form behind them, yelling
taunts, tossing bottles and bricks, setting fires in trash cans. When
the police whirled around to reverse direction at one point, they found
themselves face to face with their worst nightmare: a chorus line of
mocking queens, their arms clasped around each other, kicking their
heels in the air Rockettes-style and singing at the tops of their sardonic
voices:

"We are the Stonewall girls
We wear our hair in curls
We wear no underwear
We show our pubic hair . . .
We wear our dungarees
Above our nelly knees!"

It was a deliciously witty, contemptuous counterpoint to the TPF's brute force, a tactic that transformed an otherwise traditionally macho eye-for-an-eye combat and that provided at least the glimpse of a different and revelatory kind of consciousness. Perhaps that was exactly the moment Sylvia had in mind when she later said, "Something lifted off my shoulders."[51]

But the tactic incited the TPF to yet further violence. As they were badly beating up on one effeminate-looking boy, a portion of the angry crowd surged in, snatched the boy away, and prevented the cops from reclaiming him. Elsewhere, a cop grabbed "a wild Puerto Rican queen" and lifted his arm as if to club him. Instead of cowering, the queen yelled, "How'd you like a big Spanish dick up your little Irish ass?" The nonplussed cop hesitated just long enough to give the queen time to run off into the crowd.[52]

The cops themselves hardly escaped scot-free. Somebody managed to drop a concrete block on one parked police car; nobody was injured, but the cops inside were shaken up. At another point, a gold-braided police officer being driven around to survey the action got a sack of wet garbage thrown at him through the open window of his car; a direct hit was scored, and soggy coffee grounds dripped down the officer's face as he tried to maintain a stoic expression. Still later, as some hundred people were being chased down Waverly Place by two cops, someone in the crowd suddenly realized the unequal odds and started yelling, "There are only two of 'em! Catch 'em! Rip their clothes off! Fuck 'em!" As the crowd took up the cry, the two officers fled.

Before the police finally succeeded in clearing the streets—for that evening only, it would turn out—a considerable amount of blood had been shed. Among the undetermined number of people injured was Sylvia's friend Ivan Valentin; hit in the knee by a policeman's billy club, he had ten stitches taken at St. Vincent's Hospital. A teenager named Lenny had his hand slammed in a car door and lost two fingers. Four big cops beat up a young queen so badly—there is

evidence that the cops singled out "feminine boys"—that she bled simultaneously from her mouth, nose, and ears. Craig and Sylvia both escaped injury (as did Jim, who had hung back on the fringe of the crowd), but so much blood splattered over Sylvia's blouse that at one point she had to go down to the piers and change into the clean clothes Gary had brought back for her.[53]

Four police officers were also hurt. Most of them sustained minor abrasions from kicks and bites, but Officer Scheu, after being hit with a rolled-up newspaper, had fallen to the cement sidewalk and broken his wrist. When Craig heard that news, he couldn't resist chuckling over what he called the "symbolic justice" of the injury. Thirteen people (including Dave Van Ronk) were booked at the Sixth Precinct, seven of them Stonewall employees, on charges ranging from harassment to resisting arrest to disorderly conduct. At three-thirty-five A.M., signal 10-41 was canceled and an uneasy calm settled over the area. It was not to last.[54]

Word of the confrontation spread through the gay grapevine all day Saturday. Moreover, all three of the dailies wrote about the riot (the *News* put the story on page one), and local television and radio reported it as well. The extensive coverage brought out the crowds, just as Craig had predicted (and had worked to achieve). All day Saturday, curious knots of people gathered outside the bar to gape at the damage and warily celebrate the implausible fact that, for once, cops, not gays, had been routed.

The police had left the Stonewall a shambles. Jukeboxes, mirrors, and cigarette machines lay smashed; phones were ripped out; toilets were plugged up and overflowing; and shards of glass and debris littered the floors. (According to at least one account, moreover, the police had simply pocketed all the money from the jukeboxes, cigarette machines, cash register, and safe.) On the boarded-up front window that faced the street, anonymous protesters had scrawled signs and slogans—THEY INVADED OUR RIGHTS, THERE IS ALL COLLEGE BOYS AND GIRLS IN HERE, LEGALIZE GAY BARS, SUPPORT GAY POWER—and newly emboldened same-gender couples were seen holding hands as they anxiously conferred about the meaning of these uncommon new assertions.[55]

True to her determination not to miss *anything*, Sylvia hadn't slept all night. Even after the crowd had dispersed and gone home, she kept walking the streets, setting garbage cans on fire, venting her pent-up anger, the black beauty still working in her, further feeding

her agitation. Later she put it this way: "I wanted to do every destructive thing I could think of to get back at those who had hurt us over the years. Letting loose, fighting back, was the only way to get across to straight society and the cops that we weren't going to take their fucking bullshit any more."

Craig finally got to sleep at six A.M., but was up again within a few hours. Like Sylvia, he could hardly contain his excitement, but channeled it according to his own temperament—by jump-starting organizational work. What was needed, Craig quickly decided, was a leaflet, some crystallizing statement of what had happened and why, complete with a set of demands for the future. And to distribute it, he hit upon the idea of two-person teams, one man and one woman on each, just like those he had earlier organized at Mattachine. He hoped to have the leaflet and the teams in place by nightfall. But events overtook him.

Something like a carnival, an outsized block party, had gotten going by early evening in front of the Stonewall. While older, conservative chinos-and-sweater gays watched warily, and some disapprovingly, from the sidelines, "stars" from the previous night's confrontation reappeared to pose campily for photographs; handholding and kissing became endemic; cheerleaders led the crowd in shouts of "Gay power"; and chorus lines repeatedly belted out refrains of "We are the girls from Stonewall."

But the cops, including Tactical Patrol Force units, were out in force, were not amused at the antics, and seemed grim-facedly determined not to have a repeat of Friday night's humiliation. The TPF lined up across the street from the Stonewall, visors in place, batons and shields at the ready. When the fearless chorus line of queens insisted on yet another refrain, kicking their heels high in the air, as if in direct defiance, the TPF moved forward, ferociously pushing their nightsticks into the ribs of anyone who didn't jump immediately out of their path.

But the crowd had grown too large to be easily cowed or controlled. Thousands of people were by now spilling over the sidewalks, including an indeterminate but sizable number of curious straights and a sprinkling of street people gleefully poised to join any kind of developing rampage. When the TPF tried to sweep people away from the front of the Stonewall, the crowd simply repeated the previous night's strategy of temporarily retreating down a side street and then doubling back on the police. In Craig's part of the crowd, the idea took hold of blocking off Christopher Street, preventing any vehicular

traffic from coming through. When an occasional car did try to bull-doze its way in, the crowd quickly surrounded it, rocking it back and forth so vigorously that the occupants soon proved more than happy to be allowed to retreat.

Craig was enjoying this all hugely until a taxicab edged around the corner from Greenwich Avenue. As the crowd gave the cab a vigorous rocking, and a frenzied queen jumped on top of it and started beating on the hood, Craig caught a glimpse inside and saw two terrified passengers and a driver who looked as if he was having a heart attack. Sylvia came on that same scene and gleefully cheered the queen on. But Craig realized that the cab held innocent people, not fag-hating cops, and he worked with others to free it from the crowd's grip so it could back out.

From that point on, and in several parts of the crowd simulta-neously, all hell broke loose. Sylvia's friend Marsha P. Johnson climbed to the top of a lamppost and dropped a bag with something heavy in it on a squad car parked directly below, shattering its wind-shield. Craig was only six feet away and saw the cops jump out of the car, grab some luckless soul who happened to be close at hand, and beat him badly. On nearby Gay Street, three or four cars filled with a wedding party were stopped in their tracks for a while; some-body in the crowd shouted, "We have the right to marry, too!" The unintimidated and decidedly unamused passengers screamed back, angrily threatening to call the police. That produced some laughter ("The police are already here!") and more shouts, until finally the wedding party was allowed to proceed.[56]

From the park side of Sheridan Square, a barrage of bottles and bricks—seemingly hundreds of them, apparently aimed at the police lines—rained down across the square, injuring several onlookers but no officers. Jim had returned to the Stonewall scene in the early evening; when the bottle-throwing started, he raced to the area in the back where it seemed to be coming from, and—using his experience from previous street actions—tried to persuade the bottle-tossers that they were playing a dangerous game, threatening the lives of the protesters more than those of the police.

They didn't seem to care. Jim identified them as "straight an-archist types, Weathermen types," determined "to be really butch about their anger" (unlike those "frightened sissies"), to foment as large-scale and gory a riot as possible. He thought they were possibly "crazies"—or police provocateurs—and he realized it would be inef-fective simply to say, "Stop doing this!" So, as he tells it, he tried to

temper their behavior by appealing to their macho instincts, suggesting that it would be *even* braver of them to throw their bottles from the front of the line; that way, if the police, taunted by the flying glass, charged the crowd, they could bear the brunt of the attack themselves. The argument didn't wash; the bottle-throwing continued.

If Jim didn't want people actually getting hurt, he did want to feed the riot. Still smoldering from the failure of his straight friends to show up the previous night (some of his closeted left-wing gay friends, particularly the crowd at Liberation News Service, had also done nothing in response to his calls), he wanted this gay riot "to be as good as any riot" his straight onetime comrades had ever put together or participated in. And to that end, he carried with him the tools of the guerrilla trade: marbles (to throw under the contingent of mounted police that had by now arrived) and pins (to stick into the horses' flanks).

But the cops needed no additional provocation; they had been determined from the beginning to quell the demonstration, and at whatever cost in bashed heads and shattered bones. Twice the police broke ranks and charged into the crowd, flailing wildly with their nightsticks; at least two men were clubbed to the ground. The sporadic skirmishing went on until four A.M., when the police finally withdrew their units from the area. The next day, *The New York Times* insisted that Saturday night was "less violent" than Friday (even while describing the crowd as "angrier"). Sylvia, too, considered the first night "the worst." But a number of others, including Craig, thought the second night was the more violent one; that it marked "a public assertion of real anger by gay people that was just electric."[57]

When he got back to his apartment early Sunday morning, his anger and excitement still bubbling, Craig sat down and composed a one-page flyer. Speaking in the name of the Homophile Youth Movement (HYMN) that he had founded, Craig headlined the flyer GET THE MAFIA AND THE COPS OUT OF GAY BARS—a rallying cry that would have chilled Zucchi (who had earlier been reassured by co-owner Mario that the gays *only* had it in for the cops). Craig went on in the flyer to predict that the events of the previous two nights "will go down in history"; to accuse the police of colluding with the Mafia to prevent gay businesspeople from opening "decent gay bars with a healthy social atmosphere (as opposed to the hell-hole atmosphere of places typified by the Stonewall)"; to call on gay people to boycott places like the Stonewall ("The only way . . . we can get criminal elements out of the gay bars is simply to make it unprofitable for

them"); and to urge them to "write to Mayor Lindsay demanding a thorough investigation and effective action to correct this intolerable situation."[58]

Using his own money, Craig printed up thousands of the flyers and then set about organizing his two-person teams. He had them out on the streets leafleting passersby by midday on Sunday. They weren't alone. After the second night of rioting, it had become clear to many that a major upheaval, a kind of seismic shift, was at hand, and brisk activity was developing in several quarters.

But not all gays were pleased about the eruption at Stonewall. Those satisfied by, or at least habituated to, the status quo preferred to minimize or dismiss what was happening. Many wealthier gays, sunning at Fire Island or in the Hamptons for the weekend, either heard about the rioting and ignored it (as one of them later put it: "No one [at Fire Island Pines] mentioned Stonewall"), or caught up with the news belatedly. When they did, they tended to characterize the events at Stonewall as "regrettable," as the demented carryings-on of "stoned, tacky queens"—precisely those elements in the gay world from whom they had long since dissociated themselves. Coming back into the city on Sunday night, the beach set might have hastened off to see the nude stage show *Oh, Calcutta!* or the film *Midnight Cowboy* (in which Jon Voight played a Forty-second Street hustler)—titillated by such mainstream daring, while oblivious or scornful of the real-life counterparts being acted out before their averted eyes.[59]

Indeed some older gays, and not just the wealthy ones, even sided with the police, praising them for the "restraint" they had shown in not employing more violence against the protesters. As one of the leaders of the West Side Discussion Group reportedly said, "How can we expect the police to allow us to congregate? Let's face it, we're criminals. You can't allow criminals to congregate." Others applauded what they called the "long-overdue" closing of what for years had been an unsightly "sleaze joint." There have even been tales that some of the customers at Julius', the bar down the street from Stonewall that had long been favored by older gays ("the good girls from the fifties," as one queen put it), actually held three of the rioters for the police.[60]

Along with Craig's teams, there were others on the streets of the Village that Sunday who had been galvanized into action and were trying to organize demonstrations or meetings. Left-wing radicals like Jim Fouratt, thrilled with the *lack* of leadership in evidence during the two nights of rioting, saw the chance for a new kind of egalitarian

gay organization to emerge. He hoped it would incorporate ideas about gender parity and "rotating leadership" from the bourgeoning feminist movement and build, as well, on the long-standing struggle of the black movement against racism. At the same time, Jim and his fellow gay radicals were not interested in being subsumed any longer under anyone else's banner. They had long fought for every worthy cause other than their own, and—as the events at Stonewall had proven— without any hope of reciprocity. They felt it was time to refocus their energies on themselves.

The Mattachine Society had still another view. With its head--quarters right down the street from the Stonewall Inn, Mattachine was in 1969 pretty much the creature of Dick Leitsch, who had con-siderable sympathy for New Left causes but none for challenges to his leadership. Randy Wicker, himself a pioneer activist and lately a critic of Leitsch, now joined forces with him to pronounce the events at Stonewall "horrible." Wicker's earlier activism had been fueled by the notion that gays were "jes' folks"—just like straights except for their sexual orientation—and the sight (in his words) "of screaming queens forming chorus lines and kicking went against everything that I wanted people to think about homosexuals . . . that we were a bunch of drag queens in the Village acting disorderly and tacky and cheap." On Sunday those wandering by Stonewall saw a new sign on its boarded-up façade, this one printed in neat block letters:[61]

> WE HOMOSEXUALS PLEAD WITH
> OUR PEOPLE TO PLEASE HELP
> MAINTAIN PEACEFUL AND QUIET
> CONDUCT ON THE STREETS OF
> THE VILLAGE—MATTACHINE

The streets that Sunday evening stayed comparatively quiet, dominated by what one observer called a "tense watchfulness." Knots of the curious continued to congregate in front of Stonewall, and some of the primping and posing of the previous two nights was still in evidence. By Sunday, Karla Jay had heard about the riots, and she tried to get Redstockings to issue some sort of sympathetic statement. But just as Jim had failed to rally his left-wing male friends, so Karla was unable to get any gesture of support from straight radical fem-inists.

She went down to the Village herself for a quick look at the riot scene. But she didn't linger. She had learned during the Columbia

upheaval that uninvolved bystanders could be routinely arrested and, headed for a career in academia, she didn't want that on her record. She would wait to see where the riots would lead. She had never been taken with the bar crowd, gay or lesbian, and this unsavory bunch seemed to have inadvertently *stumbled* into rebellion. She wanted to save herself for the *big* arrest, for the *real* revolution. She was sure that was coming, but not at all sure the Stonewall riots represented its imminent arrival.

The police on Sunday night seemed spoiling for trouble. "Start something, faggot, just start something," one cop repeated over and over. "I'd like to break your ass wide open." (A brave young man purportedly yelled, "What a Freudian comment, officer!"—and then scampered to safety.) Two other cops, cruising in a police car, kept yelling obscenities at passersby, trying to start a fight, and a third, standing on the corner of Christopher Street and Waverly Place, kept swinging his nightstick and making nasty remarks about "faggots."

At one A.M. the TPF made a largely uncontested sweep of the area and the crowds melted away. Allen Ginsberg strolled by, flashed the peace sign and, after seeing "Gay Power!" scratched on the front of the Stonewall, expressed satisfaction to a *Village Voice* reporter: "We're one of the largest minorities in the country—10 percent, you know. It's about time we did something to assert ourselves."[62]

By Sunday some of the wreckage inside the bar had been cleaned up, and employees had been stationed out on the street to coax patrons back in: "We're honest businessmen here. We're American-born boys. We run a legitimate joint here. There ain't nuttin' bein' done wrong in dis place. Everybody come and see." Never having been inside the Stonewall, Ginsberg went in and briefly joined the handful of dancers. After emerging, he described the patrons as "beautiful—they've lost that wounded look that fags all had 10 years ago." Deputy Inspector Pine later echoed Ginsberg: "For those of us in public morals, things were completely changed . . . suddenly they were not submissive anymore."[63]

In part because of rain, Monday and Tuesday nights continued quiet, with only occasional, random confrontations; the most notable probably came when a queen stuck a lit firecracker under a strutting, wisecracking cop, the impact causing him to land on what the queen called his "moneymaker." But Wednesday evening saw a return to something like the large-scale protest of the previous weekend. Perhaps as a result of the appearance that day of two front-page *Village Voice* articles about the initial rioting, a crowd of some thousand people

gathered in the area. Trash baskets were again set on fire, and bottles and beer cans were tossed in the direction of the cops (sometimes hitting protesters instead); the action was accompanied by militant shouts of "Pig motherfuckers!" "Fag rapists!" and "Gestapo!" The TPF wielded their nightsticks indiscriminately, openly beat people up, left them bleeding on the street, and carted off four to jail on the usual charge of "harassment."[64]

That proved the last of the Stonewall riots, but when it came time only two days later for the fifth annual picket of Independence Hall, the repercussions could be clearly measured. As the originator of the Annual Reminder, Craig was again centrally involved in organizing it. But when he placed ads in The Village Voice to drum up interest, he got, along with some fifty recruits (half of whom were women, including two who brought along their young children), a series of ugly, threatening phone calls. The callers warned Craig that the bus he had rented to go to Philadelphia would be followed and capsized, and its occupants beaten to a pulp.

Sure enough, when the participants gathered at eight A.M. on July 4 to board the bus in front of Craig's bookstore on Mercer Street, a convertible with four "white rednecks in it brandishing baseball bats" pulled up and parked across the street. The four men simply sat there, glaring at the group in front of Craig's shop, apparently waiting for them to set off. But Craig was a step ahead of them. After he had gotten three or four of the threatening calls, he had contacted the police and had somehow convinced them to put an officer on the bus with them up to the Holland Tunnel. Then, on the other side of the tunnel, Craig managed to arrange for a New Jersey state trooper to board the bus and accompany it halfway down to Philadelphia.

The men in the convertible never followed the bus beyond Craig's bookstore. This was not, in Craig's view, because the sight of a policeman frightened them off, but because the presence of women and children took them by surprise; they had expected to see "just faggots," and as well-indoctrinated macho men felt they had to desist from a physical attack on "innocents." In any case, the bus arrived in Philadelphia without incident.

The demonstration in front of Independence Hall began in much the way it had in previous years: the group of some seventy-five people—men in suits and ties, women in dresses, despite the ninety-five-degree heat—walked silently in a circle, radiating respectability, eschewing any outward sign of anger. (Craig even kept his temper when a mean-looking man on the sidelines hissed "Suck!" in his face

every time he passed by.) But the events at Stonewall had had their effect. After a half hour of marching quietly in single file, two of the women suddenly broke ranks and started to walk together, holding hands. Seeing them, Craig thought elatedly, "O-oh—that's *wonderful!*"

But Frank Kameny, the Washington, D.C., leader who had long considered himself to be in charge of the demonstration, had a quite different reaction. Back in 1966 Kameny hadn't hesitated in pulling a man from the line who had dared to appear without a jacket and wearing sneakers, and Kameny was not about to tolerate this latest infraction of his rule that the demonstration be "lawful, orderly, dignified." His face puffy with indignation and yelling, "None of that! None of that!" Kameny came up behind the two women and angrily broke their hands apart.[65]

Craig instantly hit the ceiling. When Kameny went over to talk to the two reporters who had turned up for the event (one from a Philadelphia paper and one from Reuters), Craig barged up to them and blurted out, "I've got a few things to say!" And what he said—in his own description, "ranting and raving"—was that the events in New York the previous week had shown that the current gay leadership was bankrupt, that gays were entitled to do whatever straights did in public—yes, wearing cool clothes in the heat, and, if they felt like it, holding hands too.

Kameny was furious at this unprecedented challenge to his authority, and, on different grounds, the veteran activists Barbara Gittings and Kay Tobin chided Craig for calling so much "personal attention" to himself. But, as had not been the case in previous years, many of those who had come down on the bus from New York were young people personally recruited by Craig at his bookstore. Some of them were students at NYU and, being much younger than Kameny or Gittings, had no prior movement affiliation (and no respect for what the homophile movement had accomplished). They had been energized by Stonewall, were impatient for further direct confrontation with oppressive traditions and habits—and vigorously applauded Craig's initiative.

All the way back on the bus, they argued with their recalcitrant elders for a new impetus, a new departure that would embody the defiant spirit of Stonewall. As the contention continued, it became clear to Craig that this would be the final Reminder—that a new day had dawned, which required different tactics, a different format. Yet it saddened him to think that a common enterprise of five years standing would pass from the scene without any immediate replacement

in sight. And then it came to him. Why shouldn't there be an immediate replacement? Didn't the events at Stonewall themselves require commemoration? Maybe the Annual Reminder simply ought to be moved to New York—but, unlike the Reminder, be designed not as a silent plea for rights but as an overt demand for them. Craig thought of a name right then and there: Christopher Street Liberation Day.

That same July Fourth evening, New York Mattachine called a public meeting at St. John's Church on Waverly Place, designed to derail precisely the kind of rumored plans for new demonstrations and organizations that Craig had in mind. Dick Leitsch, described by one reporter as wearing a "staid brown suit" and looking like "a dependable fortyish Cartier salesclerk," told the packed crowd of two hundred (mostly male, mostly young) that it was indeed important to protest police brutality, but it was also important to remember that "the gay world must retain the favor of the Establishment, especially those who make and change the laws." Acceptance, Leitsch cautioned, "would come slowly by educating the straight community with grace and good humor and—"[66]

Leitsch was interrupted by an angry young man who stood up and yelled, "We don't want acceptance, goddamn it! We want respect!"—and he was seconded by shouts from others. Leitsch's loyal lieutenant at Mattachine, Madolin Cervantes (who was heterosexual) took the mike to call for a candlelight vigil, saying, "We should be firm, but just as amicable and sweet as—" She, too, was interrupted—this time by Jim Fouratt, who had been sitting agitatedly in the audience and had held his peace up to that point.

"*Sweet?*" Jim hollered, "Sweet! *Bullshit!* There's the stereotype homo again . . . soft, weak, sensitive! . . . That's the role society has been forcing these queens to play. . . . We have got to radicalize. . . . Be proud of what you are. . . . And if it takes riots or even guns to show them what we are, well, that's the only language that the pigs understand!"

His impassioned speech led to a wild burst of applause. Leitsch tried to reply, but Jim shouted him down: "All the oppressed have got to unite! . . . Not one straight radical group showed up at Stonewall! If it'd been a black demonstration they'd have been there. . . . We've got to work together with *all* the New Left!" By then a dozen people were on their feet, shouting encouragement. Leitsch tried to regain control of the meeting, but to no avail. "This meeting is over!"

Jim yelled, and invited all those who shared his views to follow him over to Alternate University, a loft space on Fourteenth Street and Sixth Avenue that was home to a variety of radical enterprises. (It was known to the cognoscenti as "Alternate U.") By Jim's recollection, some thirty-five or forty people followed him out of St. John's. In the reconstituted meeting at Alternate U., they began to talk about forming a new activist gay organization—talk that would soon culminate in the Gay Liberation Front.

As for "Fat Tony" Lauria, he was quick to see the handwriting on the wall. He and his partners, Mario and Zucchi, decided that with the Knapp Commission currently investigating corruption within the police department, and with Stonewall now notorious, the bar could never again operate profitably. Fat Tony soon sold the Stonewall lease to Nicky de Martino, the owner of the Tenth of Always, and had the satisfaction of watching him fail quickly—even though, with the help of Ed Murphy, de Martino got some street queens to parade around in front of Stonewall with balloons for a week or two.[67]

POST- STONEWALL: 1969–70

CRAIG, JIM

Jim and Craig were not the only ones with new ideas. True, in the immediate aftermath of Stonewall, *Time* magazine went right on referring to homosexuality as "a serious and sometimes crippling maladjustment" and to the homosexual subculture as "without question shallow and unstable." And U.S. attorney Thomas Foran (who had prosecuted the Chicago Seven) gravely announced that "We've lost our kids to the freaking fag revolution."[1]

But homosexuals themselves, in a rush of suddenly released energy, and in unprecedented numbers, were newly determined to challenge those hoary stereotypes. Two days after Craig returned from the Annual Reminder, a meeting was called at the Electric Circus, the popular (and straight) night spot on Eighth Street in Greenwich Village. "If you are tired of raids, Mafia control, and checks at the front door," the flyer advertising the meeting read, "join us for a beautiful evening on Sunday night, July 6th."[2]

The organizers asked Randy Wicker to speak at the meeting in his capacity as a "premature" gay militant. Bounding to the mike in an American flag shirt and striped blue-and-white bell-bottoms, he looked for all the world like the gay equivalent of a militant Yippie. But what he said to the packed crowd of long-haired, mustachioed, hip young men and blue-jeaned, tie-dyed young women, was in a far different vein. He told them that he was appalled at what had happened at Stonewall, that "rocks through windows don't open doors,"

that the way to find public acceptance was not to "behave disorderly" in the streets.

But he had barely begun his windup when a heterosexual customer—apparently realizing for the first time that the Electric Circus had inexplicably been overrun by queers—began swinging wildly at anyone within reach, yelling "Faggots! Goddamn faggots!" He was subdued long enough for Wicker to say a few more words and for Dick Leitsch to get up and ask for donations from homosexuals to help replant the trees recently uprooted in a Queens public park by vigilantes trying to discourage gay cruising there. But fighting soon erupted again, and the meeting—along with the experiment in gay-straight nightlife integration—was adjourned.[3]

Dick Leitsch had no intention of ceding the foreground either to straight rowdies or to gay lefties. He blamed Craig above all others (as perhaps only an ex-lover can) for the rioting at Stonewall, and yet he wanted to harness the youthful energies of the emergent gay radicals to Mattachine's own cart. When a twenty-eight-year-old New Left gay man named Michael Brown came to see him one day, Leitsch hit upon what he felt was the ideal plan. Brown was one of those numerous radicals who were gay but had remained in the closet while working in left-wing organizations. Once a staff member in Hubert Humphrey's 1968 presidential campaign, Brown now considered himself countercultural and socialist in sympathies.[4]

He told Leitsch that the events at Stonewall had opened up the opportunity for an alliance between gays, blacks, and antiwar activists that could work to restructure American society. Leitsch told him that such expectations were unrealistic, that the maintenance of good relations—as pioneered and exemplified by Mattachine—between the homosexual community and the powers-that-be had to take priority above all other considerations. As an individual, Leitsch argued, he might feel sympathy for, say, the Black Panthers, but any overt association with them could "endanger the liaisons we have made with civil-rights organizations who disagree" with the Panthers' philosophy. In the privacy of a letter, Leitsch was blunter still: "Panthers . . . are none of our damned business, as homosexuals."[5]

But as a compromise to accommodate the young gay radicals, Leitsch set up the Mattachine Action Committee and offered Michael Brown the job of heading it. Brown warily accepted, and for a brief period did try to work within the Mattachine traces. He brought in some of his activist friends, including "Stephen Donaldson" (Bob Martin) and Martha Shelley (née Altman; she had legally changed her

last name to Shelley, the nickname her first lover had given her because of the romantic poetry she wrote). Donaldson had been one of the founders in 1967 of the Student Homophile League at Columbia University and was currently involved in organizing a youth caucus bent on radicalizing NACHO—Foster Gunnison's chief base of operations—at its forthcoming August meeting.[6]

Martha Shelley had had an affair with Donaldson, had already, at age twenty-six, been president for a brief period (she decided she wasn't good at organizational work) of New York Daughters of Bilitis, and on the second night of rioting at Stonewall had stumbled on the uproar while giving two women from Boston DOB a tour of the Village. Shelley had also taken part in the antiwar protests at the 1968 Democratic National Convention in Chicago, had represented DOB at NACHO conferences, and had just come back from participating in the Annual Reminder in Philadelphia on July 4 (where the injunction to wear a skirt and be "ladylike" had seemed to her annoying and absurd).[7]

The Mattachine Action Committee sponsored two open meetings to discuss the implications of the Stonewall riots. The first, on July 9 at Freedom House at 20 West Fortieth Street, where Mattachine held its monthly lecture series, was attended by some 125 people (as well as by two police informers). Leitsch chaired the meeting, made a few introductory remarks acknowledging "the importance" of the riots, and then opened up the floor for general discussion. It proved much too tame for Brown and his friends, focusing as it did on future plans for a silent vigil in Washington Square Park—*with* the permission of the proper authorities.[8]

In the interim before the second meeting, Brown, Shelley, Jim Fouratt, and others posted notices for a demonstration in support of the Black Panther party members currently jailed in the Women's House of Detention (the huge stone prison in the heart of the West Village). Leitsch had been insistent that Mattachine *not* be associated with any action that might prove offensive to the authorities, so in order to be able to list a sponsor for the demonstration, Brown and his friends came up—in what Jim remembers as "a spontaneous eruption"—with the name Gay Liberation Front, as a way of paying homage to the liberation struggles in Algeria and Vietnam.[9]

At the Mattachine Action Committee's second meeting, Leitsch spoke against the planned rally at the Women's House of Detention, arguing instead for his own earlier suggestion of a silent vigil in Washington Square to protest continuing police harassment. Still keyed up

from his earlier confrontation with Leitsch at the Mattachine gathering of June 29, Jim was in no mood for further counsels of moderation. He again jumped to his feet, heatedly insisted that gays ought to stop asking and start demanding, and challenged Leitsch to "get with the revolution." But Leitsch was unmoved, and young radicals like Jim, Michael Brown, and Martha Shelley realized that it was time to give up on Mattachine and put their energies into the nascent Gay Liberation Front.[10]

Leitsch's concern with continuing police harassment may have been narrowly conceived, but was nonetheless warranted. In the aftermath of the Stonewall riots, the police had instituted a widespread, sometimes savage crackdown. Sascha L., who had once worked briefly at Stonewall and was now on the door at the Washington Square bar, remembers walking by the Tele-Star bar about a week after the riots and telling Ed Murphy, who had gone to work there, about rumors of a pending series of raids. Murphy told him not to worry; those rumors were always in the air (perhaps secretly confident that if they had any real substance, his police buddies would tip him off in advance).[11]

Sascha shrugged and went off to work at Washington Square— not failing, on his way inside the bar, to smile coquettishly at the handsome Con Edison workers who had been digging up the street all week. (On one recent hot day, he had even jokingly plopped on the lap of another employee seated in a chair out front, and nervily waved to the Con Ed boys.)

Early that same evening, with no more than a dozen customers on the premises, Sascha spotted some forty men dressed in suits and ties coming down Third Street toward the Washington Square bar. He dashed back inside to warn the others; they barely had time to pick up the liquor and throw it into the yard behind the bar when the federal agents marched in. Brisk and businesslike, the feds used a bullhorn to tell the customers that they would all be let go, that no one would be harmed, that they were interested only in arresting employees of the bar. They then read a list of the employees' names and brandished photographs—taken, Sascha later learned, by those cute "Con Edison" boys working in the street.

A queen named Michelle saved Sascha by hugging him close and yelling at the cops, "No one—*no one!*—is going to separate me and my husband! My husband *has* to come with me!" When a cop asked Sascha his name, he gave a false one, and since he had quickly disposed of his trademark cap and eyeglasses, he got through the gauntlet

without being recognized as the campy employee who had waved seductively at the Con Edison crew. Sascha hid out for the weekend and then on Monday decided to turn himself in, figuring he had to be able to work and couldn't spend his life hiding. Enid Gerling, the well-paid specialist in "springing" entrapped gay men, took Sascha's case.

When he arrived in court, he ran smack into Ed Murphy, who was covered with cuts and welts; he had bandages all over his face, his arm was fractured, and he seemed barely able to walk. It turned out Murphy had refused to let the cops into Tele-Star and they had beaten him up badly—at the instigation, Sascha later heard, of Deputy Inspector Seymour Pine, the same officer who had led the raid against Stonewall. In jail, Murphy was subsequently (so he later told Sascha) raped by a black man—again, perhaps, at the behest of the police, who had heard that he "liked niggers" and that he hung out with and protected black teenagers. When Murphy was released, he forswore (again, according to Sascha) any further cooperation with the police, and never again gave them tips or did their bidding.[12]

YVONNE, KARLA

Yvonne had been upstate at the country house she shared in Rowe, Massachusetts, when the events at Stonewall began to unfold, and it was two days before she had any news of the rioting. Her initial reaction was a mix of exhilaration and fear. "Uh-oh," she thought, "here comes the Gestapo, beating people up. And winning. Being able to just crush people . . ." Her style, as always, was to stay aloof, to warily reconnoiter just a little longer—not primarily out of fear of the police, but from uncertainty about whether and where, in the ranks of the protesters, a hard-drinking black lesbian would find a genuine welcome.

Karla had been initially disdainful of the "little penny-ante thing" going on at Stonewall; to her it was just another all-male squabble with the prize nothing more than the right to lead an unhampered bar life—a life she scorned. But then she got wind of the effort afoot to form a Gay Liberation Front—men *and* women working together to produce broad social change. Now that *did* interest her. When she heard that a series of open meetings were scheduled for late July at

Alternate U.—with which she was already familiar from her radical-feminist work—she decided to attend.

What she found were a number of suddenly visible young gays and lesbians who, like herself, had had experience in prior radical struggles. Martha Shelley, Jim Fouratt, and Michael Brown had marched for black rights and against the Vietnam War; Susan "Silverwoman" had been active in various feminist groups; Lois Hart had been involved with Timothy Leary and was a follower of the mystic Meher Baba; Ron Ballard was an avowed Marxist, John O'Brien a sometime member of the Young Socialist Alliance, and Pete Wilson an adherent of the League for Sexual Freedom. Though they had come out for all these causes, few of these radical gays had revealed their sexuality to their co-activists.[13]

Jim Fouratt, it is true, had made his way in the political left without ever explicitly *denying* that he was a gay man. But he had never explicitly affirmed it, either; and so the possibility could be ignored or disbelieved. And Jim, if anything, had gained his left-wing credentials *less* anonymously than most radical young gays, who had often made a point of dating the opposite gender and had steered carefully clear of tipping their actual sexual preference. They had had little choice—that is, if they wanted to join forces with others who shared their passionate concern for social change. The straight men who dominated the antiwar and black civil rights struggles had persistently condescended to heterosexual women, treating them essentially as bed partners or coffee-makers. Gay men and lesbians had been beyond the pale.

When these young gay and lesbian radicals now flocked to join the Gay Liberation Front, they brought with them a rich set of insights from their prior involvements: from the black civil rights movement came an awareness of the inequities of American life; from the women's movement, consciousness of sexism and the profoundly important idea that the personal is the political, that one's experience *mattered*; from the antiwar struggle, the revelation that the government operated as a bulwark of conformity and privilege; from the countercultural revolution, the injunction to reject all received authority, to "do it now, to be what you want to be." They had learned much in making everybody else's revolution; now they would apply that learning to making their own.

Karla responded to the Gay Liberation Front with immediate enthusiasm. The message articulated in the first issue of *Come Out!*, the GLF paper, that "we are going to transform the society at large

through the open realization of our own consciousness," was something she had learned in her Redstockings group—but this time around, the message was devoid of any overtones of homophobia. Consciousness-raising was, from nearly the beginning, a central feature of GLF, and Karla, familiar with the process, joined with Lois Hart and others in explaining—for not everyone in GLF had been a left-wing activist—that the process of self-realization that would emerge from speaking freely and honestly to other gays in the protected atmosphere of a consciousness-raising session would ramify outward, that speaking truth would end by cleansing and reconstituting the society at large.

Karla felt "like the religious fanatic who constantly searches for just the 'right' spiritual base—and is astounded to actually find it." Redstockings had come close, but GLF seemed to have the same devotion to substantive social change, and without any attendant nervousness over lesbianism. The women who turned up for the early GLF meetings—only some half dozen in a sea of fifty men—were no more into butch or femme self-presentations (which Karla deplored) than had been the women in Redstockings; but Karla had never been a separatist, had never felt the need for women to struggle apart from men—and in GLF radical women and men seemed determined on struggling *together*.

GLF appealed to Karla's millenarian side. She could be hardheadedly practical, but she was also strongly committed to the notion that the corrupt world should—and *could*—be cleansed. She shared with GLF the optimism essential for sustained political work: the bedrock, magical belief that if one took an action, consequences, *good* consequences, would follow, and the conditions of life would be transformed.

Karla felt she had finally come home, and she plunged into GLF with all of her formidable energy.

FOSTER, CRAIG, JIM

As GLF plunged ebulliently ahead in the early summer of 1969, Foster Gunnison was toiling away at the yeoman work of preparing for the August 1969 national conference. If GLF's natural habitat was heady abstraction, Foster was never happier than when dealing with

the minutia of organizational work. As head of the Credentials Committee, he had a thousand matters to attend to and he fluttered over them with chipper, efficient enthusiasm. "It's one hell of a job running this operation," he wrote Bill Kelley of Mattachine Midwest. "I enjoy it . . . [but] hate to think of what it will be when we get up to 100 or 150 organizations (which of course we all nonetheless want)."[14]

In the wake of the Stonewall riots, it was clear that the conference could not proceed with business as usual. For a time, it was not entirely clear that it could proceed at all. The previous year's meeting in Chicago had not gone well. Some progress could be claimed for the 1968 convention: the name North American Conference of Homophile Organizations (NACHO), frequently used informally, had been officially adopted as a replacement for North American Planning Conference; an executive committee had been created to carry out business between conventions; a Homosexual Bill of Rights had been passed and—in a resolution proposed by Kameny and Gittings—the motto "Gay is good" had been adopted as NACHO's official slogan in an effort "to replace a wishy-washy negativism toward homosexuality with a firm no-nonsense positivism."[15]

These were genuine accomplishments, yet the close of the 1968 conference had seen a torrent of complaint: DOB (too "hidebound" in the view of Shirley Willer, its ex-president, to agree to demonstrations and the like) announced that it was pulling out of NACHO for good; Bill Beardemphl and Larry Littlejohn from San Francisco's SIR (the country's largest homophile organization) had grumbled that "no action program had been discussed" and had implied that their further participation was in doubt; others had complained about the protracted speechifying, the continuing rigidity of Foster's Credentials Committee in screening applicant organizations, the scant progress in creating genuine unity, and the continuing absence of Mattachine New York. "We must be doing something wrong," Arthur Warner, an ally of Dick Leitsch's, had groused, "if SIR, the largest organization, was unhappy and Mattachine New York, the second largest, was not even present."[16]

In March 1969, William Wynne ("Marc Jeffers"), the NACHO chair (and founding member of Kansas City's Phoenix Society), felt it necessary to assert in his interim report that "NACHO is not dead but very much alive and kicking." But no funds were available to cover travel expenses, and at the last minute, the meeting place had to be shifted from Houston to Kansas City because the Promethean

Society, the small homophile group in Houston, had been unable to make the needed arrangements.[17]

Some forty delegates—all of them white and only half a dozen women—representing some twenty homophile groups gathered at the Bellerive Hotel in Kansas City from August 23 through August 31. Each organization had an equal number of votes (five), despite the fact that some of them—including Foster's own Institute of Social Ethics—were essentially one-person organizations. This alone led to anger and conflict—to charges that a small number of "Kamenyites" were unfairly perpetuating their control over NACHO.[18]

But far more pronounced conflict came from what Foster and others would call GLF "infiltration." Initially, the dispute centered on Stephen Donaldson. He had earlier helped to form within NACHO a "Young Turks" group, which had been active in the 1967 and 1968 conferences. Foster had gotten to know and like Donaldson during those two prior conferences, even while being "continually irritated with him," and even though he acknowledged that Donaldson's general reputation for being "devious" and "manipulative" was well deserved.[19]

Donaldson chaired the NACHO "Committee on Youth," which at its meeting of August 28—right at the midpoint of the conference—unanimously adopted "A Radical Manifesto." The twelve-point document closely reflected the views of the GLF chapters proliferating across the country. It linked the homophile struggle to that of other minorities, declaring support for "the black, the feminist, the Spanish-American, the Indian, the hippie, the young, the student, the worker, and other victims of oppression and prejudice." It identified the "enemy" as "an implacable, repressive governmental system," along with "much of organized religion, business and medicine," and declared that these negative forces would never be moved by appeals to reason and justice, "but only by power and force." The manifesto further insisted that homosexuals develop a life-style and aesthetic that were independent of and made no reference to, heterosexual mores. And it specifically rejected "the insane war in Vietnam," refusing all complicity with it and opposing any attempt by the gay movement to work for security clearances for homosexuals—which had been a long-standing homophile project.[20]

In both tone and content, the manifesto represented a significant departure from NACHO's earlier posture. The Stonewall riots had indeed sparked a new mood. Yet they had not—as GLF radicals

sometimes insisted—invented either gay pride or gay protest. Part of what outraged homophile old-timers like Foster Gunnison about GLF *was* its political platform; but antagonism also resulted from the seeming presumption of the militant young that nothing significant or worthy had preceded their own efforts.

As a man of scholarly instincts, Foster knew (and had so written in his pamphlet, "An Introduction to the Homophile Movement") that the homosexual liberation movement had roots deep in the nineteenth century—in the pioneering publications of the German scholar Karl Heinrich Ulrichs and the German-Hungarian writer Karoly Maria Kertbeny—and had continued in the early twentieth, with Magnus Hirschfeld's Scientific Humanitarian Committee in Berlin. Not even militant rhetoric and confrontational tactics were entirely new; Frank Kameny, among others, had been spitting bullets for half a dozen years.

East Coast parochialism further fanned the generational flames. It had been on the West Coast, after all, that the Mattachine Society had been formed, and where—for more than a decade before Stonewall—a score of publications, organizations, legal challenges, and militant actions had taken place. (And, beginning with the mid-sixties, Chicago and a few other midwestern cities had seen comparable developments.)

But if the Stonewall riots did not *begin* the gay revolution (as East Coasters, younger gays, and the national media have been wont to claim), it remains true that those riots became a symbolic event of international importance—a symbol of such potency as to serve, ever since 1969, as a motivating force and rallying cry. There was enough glory for both coasts, the hinterland, and several generations—though not many could see it in 1969.

But if Foster was outraged at the radical agenda and attitude, he was also soft-hearted. He could not bear to reject young Donaldson (who, among other things, had interrupted Foster's decades-old celibacy when the two shared a room at a NACHO conference). As dislike of Donaldson's arrogance mounted, Foster continued to plead his case with detractors like Barbara Gittings, characterizing him as "a sort of diamond in the rough" despite his "tendencies toward arbitrariness and manipulation." Indeed, after the 1969 conference elected Foster treasurer of NACHO, leading him to decline to continue as chair of the Credentials Committee, he successfully pushed Donaldson for the job—even while declaring that "it would crush me

if Steve used his committee to promote the radical views that he holds."[21]

In the postconference period, Foster did try to remain scrupulously fair about those "radical views"; it was his nature to be fair. At one point he even suggested that GLF "could be an asset" to the older homophile movement, could inject it with "heavy doses of militancy" that might profitably "shake things up a bit . . . maybe substitute a demonstration or two, or even an occasional riot, in place of paper resolutions and positions on this or that." In the months following the NACHO conference, Foster even traveled down from his home in Hartford to sit in on several GLF meetings in New York City in order to form a firsthand opinion of the group.[22]

But that was Foster stretching to the outer limit of his open-mindedness—and the stretch soon slackened. Too much, temperamentally and philosophically, weighed against his ability to accommodate himself to the GLF agenda. Once his feelings against GLF solidified, he summed up his objections in three parts: "rudeness in personal behavior; resentment against authority and systematic procedure"; and involvement with other minority groups and their "alien issues." The most dangerous of the three, Foster felt, was the feeling that "if the homosexual is going to make any progress he must ally his groups with every other minority group in the country" (or rather, every minority group "with a strong leftist bent"), and the corollary view that if the homosexual is to make any progress, "the entire existing social/political/economic establishment must be overthrown—possibly with force."[23]

But it was not a matter of the homophile veterans simply wanting to confine their goals to civil rights and being unable to conceive of any strategy other than apologetics or earnest appeals for acceptance. In the month before the NACHO convention, for example, Foster had drawn up a proposed set of "aims and purposes" for the organization that did include "the firm establishment in society of the homosexual as a first class citizen," but went considerably beyond civil rights in asserting that "the unqualified acceptance by society of homosexuality as a wholly natural personal trait, and a highly valued expression of human love" was "the chief over-all long-range aim of the movement."[24]

Moreover, Foster opposed the notion that heterosexuality was somehow the norm "by which all other relationships must be judged." He urged homosexuals "to expose themselves for what they are, and

to refrain from withdrawing from heterosexual society"—to aim instead at the "free and open public expression of homosexual affections." And in the name of these goals, Foster declared himself in favor of "radical-militant tactics," including confrontations, street demonstrations, "blatant and open hard-hitting assaults on social institutions practicing or fomenting discrimination," and even welcomed, "where called for," riots and violence.[25]

Foster's antagonism was to "disorderly" procedures and "alien" (nonhomophile) goals. The dangers (as he saw them) of anarchistic methods and "extraneous" involvement in other causes were made manifest at the November 1–2, 1969, meeting of ERCHO, the Eastern Regional Conference of Homophile Organizations. ERCHO was one of three regional divisions of NACHO, and far more active than the two others, the Midwest and Far West conferences. Craig Rodwell and Jim Fouratt were both centrally involved with what happened at the November ERCHO meeting, and although Foster would soon work closely and affectionately with Craig, he would never forgive Jim Fouratt for *his* behavior at the conference.[26]

Craig had some hope of utilizing ERCHO as the conduit for the planned Christopher Street Liberation Day March in June, on which he had already been working. At the same time, he was deeply sympathetic with GLF's championing of other minority causes (and would himself soon march in a Black Panther demonstration), and he happily stocked GLF flyers in his bookstore. Yet his sympathy was ambivalent. When he went to GLF meetings he felt "thrilled at the energy level, at the numbers of women present, and at the obvious dignity and pride at being lesbians and gay men—something which hadn't ever been seen before."

Yet he never developed any strong allegiance to GLF. The lengthy discussions, in which everyone was encouraged to vent at length, turned him off—especially since the sought-for consensus often proved elusive and the meetings failed to produce the kind of clear-cut decisions Craig temperamentally required. Besides, the "rhetorical stuff" bored him, especially the "dialectical arguments," the private "terminology and language" spouted by committed socialists like John Lauritsen and John O'Brien (who with a few others soon withdrew into the Red Butterfly, a gay Marxist study group). Craig, in turn, despite his passion and his extraordinary record for radicalism within Mattachine, tended to be viewed in GLF as that most unhip of creatures—a Midwestern Christian Scientist, the essential square.[27]

Due to attend the November 1969 ERCHO conference as head

of his own organization, HYMN, Craig obligingly made it possible for half a dozen staunch GLF partisans (including Lois Hart and Jim Fouratt) to attend as well. Craig and Jim had put their heads together and found a loophole in the ERCHO procedural rules that allowed any member organization to bring representatives of other organizations as guests. On behalf of HYMN, Craig forthwith invited the GLFers, furnishing them with HYMN badges for accreditation.

The November ERCHO conference took place in the immediate aftermath of the October 15 Moratorium, when millions of Americans had stopped business as usual to register their disapproval of American policy in Vietnam, and just before the gigantic November 15 Mobilization would convene in Washington, D.C., to protest the war's continuation. It was an apocalyptic time. President Nixon had been secretly and mercilessly bombing the neutral country of Cambodia for more than six months, Vice President Agnew had been denouncing the "effete snobs" and "small cadres of professional protesters" who had refused to hail the massacre of hundreds of thousands as a triumph for democracy, and in early December, the Chicago police would invade Black Panther headquarters and kill its state chairman, Fred Hampton, in his bed.

The student left had recently divided into antagonistic splinter groups, and the 1969 SDS national convention would be its last. Several of the new factions employed revolutionary rhetoric and talked increasingly of armed struggle, and the Weatherman faction had, just three weeks before the ERCHO convention, embarked on its Days of Rage action in Chicago, smashing through the streets of the Loop and the Gold Coast and confronting the police, who shot six, beat dozens and arrested 250. Less than five months later, a Weatherman cell in Greenwich Village would blow itself sky-high in its Tenth Street townhouse bomb factory.

It was in this riven, overheated national climate that the ERCHO convention opened on November 1, 1969. The GLF contingent was in no mood for moderation, convinced more than ever that to compromise with evil was to collaborate with it. On their side, many of the older homophile delegates were more inclined than ever to view anything other than moderation as destructive extremism. The confrontation between the two began when some of the conference participants decided to question the legitimacy of the GLF accreditation, and to pose a few pointed questions to their delegation. Did they regard themselves as revolutionaries? Were they prepared to work for their ideas within the frame of parliamentary procedures? Did they

consider themselves Good Americans, or were they bent on destroying the country's basic institutions? Jim Fouratt, experienced in politics and trained as an actor, took on the role of chief spokesperson for the group. He characterized the questions as "too insulting" to merit a direct response, and substituted instead a forceful argument in behalf of the GLF agenda. His antagonists promptly dubbed him "Goldilocks," yet to his critics' surprise—and Jim's—his remarks generated considerable applause.[28]

Indeed, Jim and the other GLFers managed to dominate the ERCHO convention to an unexpected degree. They did so with the help of Student Homophile League delegates from Columbia, Cornell, and NYU, and a scattering of radicals (like Martha Shelley of DOB) who were serving as representatives from older homophile organizations. Together they convened a "radical caucus," drew up a set of resolutions calling, among other things, for support of the Black Panthers, the striking West Coast grape pickers, and the Chicago Eight (one of whom was Abbie Hoffman), then under indictment for conspiracy. Debate on those resolutions took up so much convention time that Arthur Warner of New York Mattachine, one of many outraged old-guarders, accused the GLF delegates of foisting "by questionable parliamentary tactics" a platform involving matters "not even remotely pertinent to the homophile movement."

Warner focused his anger as much on Craig as on Jim, characterizing Craig as the owner of a bookstore which "already serves as general field headquarters for every revolutionary gay in the New York area," and denouncing his proposal for a demonstration on the last Sunday in June to commemorate the Stonewall riots as itself "revolutionary," as little more than a call for *new* riots. Yet Warner and the other delegates from New York Mattachine found themselves in a minority in their opposition to the commemorative march; and to their horror, several other resolutions presented by Jim and his friends (including a call to homosexuals to participate in protests against the Vietnam War, and a denial of the right of educational, religious, and governmental institutions to "define and limit sexuality") found, in diluted form, some favor with the convention—leading a majority of the delegates to dissociate themselves from the resolutions.[29]

Foster was if anything even more horrified than Arthur Warner at the "unbelievable crudeness, rudeness, and vulgarity" of the GLF delegates. A few days after the convention, he wrote Bill Kelley, the

NACHO activist in Chicago, that the ERCHO meeting had been a "disaster"; it had been "invaded," he wrote, by "radical, revolutionary, anarchistic (& I think communist) GLF." He thought Lois Hart "was the most insidious of the lot" ("an intellectual shyster if I ever saw one"), but he also condemned as a "brawl" ("Wild. Chaotic. Awful") Jim Fouratt's "up in your face" confrontation with Madolin Cervantes (during which Jim had yelled that she, a heterosexual MSNY delegate, was not qualified to comment in any way on homosexuality).[30]

Jim acknowledges that he and the other GLFers were so strident that the old-timers felt as if they had been literally assaulted. He and his friends had no patience with counsels of moderation and no appreciation for the work previously done, against great odds, to bring the gay movement to its current level of visibility. "We wanted to *end* the homophile movement" is how Jim later put it. "We wanted *them* to join *us* in making a gay revolution." And he adds, with retrospective compassion, that "we were a nightmare to them. They were committed to being nice, acceptable status quo Americans, and we were not; we had no interest at all in being acceptable."

Bill Kelley, himself sympathetic to at least part of the GLF agenda, apparently admonished Foster for his vehemence against the young radicals. In reply, Foster reassured Kelley that he was not "a 'reactionary.' . . . I fear you may suspect I'm something of a fascist. NO—I'm just as liberal as you are on most of these social issues. A few (like the Vietnam war) I am 'on the fence' about (i.e. undecided). But I do object strongly to injection of these other issues (eg. Black Panthers . . . grape pickers . . . and so on into our homophile cause —especially when I know that they are being injected less for a sincere belief in them than for an attempt to overthrow the establishment & the government lock-stock-&-barrel, as well as for ulterior purposes such as anarchy & communism. But even without these ulterior motives I still object to involving us in external issues. We have *enough* problems just finding agreement among ourselves on strictly homosexual issues."[31]

In claiming to "know" that the motives of Jim and the other GLFers were "insincere," Foster was substituting personal distrust for proof—even though Jim would have agreed with Foster's contention that he and his friends were intent on doing away with current institutional arrangements and their established inequities. But Foster, too, felt misunderstood. He insisted that he was not the knee-jerk reactionary GLF claimed he was, and he tried to salvage his middle-

of-the-road credentials by drawing a distinction between militancy, which he said he favored, and "subversion," which he declared he would "forever oppose." He had been "thrilled," he asserted, with the Stonewall "uprising," but that didn't mean he felt the social order was so rotted with inequities that it deserved the wholesale attack GLF and other "revolutionary" groups had launched on it.[32]

After attending a few GLF meetings at the Church of the Holy Apostles in New York City, Foster was honest enough to admit that GLF members were *not* united behind a single revolutionary program. This discovery, he subsequently wrote in a report on GLF to various homophile leaders, was "a pleasant surprise"—but not pleasant enough to negate his fears.[33]

He continued to disapprove of GLF's lack of structure, continued to conspiratorially suspect that behind the loose leadership arrangements lay "a cohesive manipulating force," a subversive, not merely militant, direction. And (like Craig) he found the free-flowing discussion during the GLF meetings "chaotic," an obstacle to making unified decisions. So if Foster had discovered "some normal people" in GLF whose presence held out "some faint hope for the group as a worthy addition to ERCHO or NACHO," on the whole he thought the odds were stacked against such a positive outcome. For one thing, he had heard ERCHO denounced during GLF meetings as "a meaningless, non-existent, non-entity . . . where people got together and did nothing." For another, he simply saw what in his mind were too many "Marxian theorists, assorted crackpots and obvious headcases."[34]

Foster's "report" somehow got leaked to GLF, and he got two blistering letters from Bob Kohler (a GLF mainstay, and the friend and protector of Sylvia Rivera and other street queens). In reply, Foster retreated somewhat, claiming that his hostility had really been aimed at the "shocking" behavior of the GLF contingent at the recent ERCHO conference. He insisted to Kohler that he and other homophile leaders did feel sympathy for many of the causes GLF championed ("though I may not be actively involved in them"), but didn't like "being told what causes I am going to support," and felt strongly, moreover, that the homophile movement needed to focus exclusively on homophile issues. (Which was precisely the ground on which a significant number of members would themselves defect from GLF a few months later in order to found the Gay Activists Alliance, an organization devoted solely to achieving gay rights.)[35] Bending over

backwards to be (or to appear) fair, Foster concluded his letter to Kohler by "urging that there is no one right road to heaven—let a hundred flowers bloom. . . . Only time will tell" whether the ERCHO or the GLF strategy was the more valuable.

Unlike most of his adversaries, Foster could indeed be open-minded on many subjects. But in fact he had long since concluded that the emergence of GLF would prove destructive to the moderate homophile organizations to which he had devoted his energies. And in the months following the 1969 ERCHO conference, signs began to proliferate that the homophile movement was indeed succumbing to a combination of attack from without and discontent within. Arthur Warner, for one, continued to wage his longstanding war against Frank Kameny's leadership in NACHO and ERCHO. Foster characterized Warner's attacks as a "personal vendetta," but a serious disagreement about how to change the law did underlie the antipathy. Kameny wanted to bring discrimination suits at every level and to pursue them all with utmost vigor, whereas Warner argued that "bad cases make bad law"—insisting that *his* legal committee had to pass on the viability of all pending suits. Though Kameny, especially in the heat of argument, outstripped Warner in abrasive omniscience, Warner's outsized tantrums were legendary.[36]

Warner, in the past, had often denounced ERCHO for "wallowing" in "sterile mediocrity," but now he found others echoing that view—if not for his reasons. A number of ERCHO delegates had, after all, supported the GLF resolutions presented at the recent convention (albeit in modified form), and homophile activists like Scoop Phillips of Kansas City raised their voices in the postconvention period to insist that NACHO "does need some radicalization" and that it was "better to die swiftly in the quicksand than starve to death in the bush."

But attrition was in fact to be NACHO and ERCHO's fate. And as the homophile movement began to fall apart, Foster's own health declined in tandem. It started with a series of episodes in which his heart pounded and his body spasmed; then one night he felt suddenly short of breath, started to tremble, and went to the Hartford hospital, convinced he was having a heart attack. But the doctors' verdict was "cumulative nervous tension." They put Foster on medication and advised him to reduce stress in his life.

That was easier said than done. Foster felt his "heart was breaking." Here were these "wild-eyed kids" in GLF thinking "they are

going to take over America and the world," when in fact, Foster was convinced, they "will trigger a right-wing reaction in this country that will sink all of our ships together."[37]

On December 21, 1969, nineteen people gathered in writer Arthur Bell's Greenwich Village apartment to put the finishing touches on the constitution for a new organization, the Gay Activists Alliance. Dissent from GLF's philosophy and tactics had been present almost from that group's inception, but now, with the birth of GAA, it took on institutional form. In the constitution GAA drew up that day, it declared itself "completely and solely dedicated"—unlike GLF, with its concern for minority oppression of all kinds—to securing basic rights for homosexuals. To achieve those rights, GAA would prove entirely willing to take to the streets and employ militant, confrontational tactics, but would do so in order to win acceptance for gays within the country's institutional structure—not to topple or transform that structure, as was GLF's intent.[38]

Jim Fouratt thought GAA mistaken in its one-issue politics, Karla Jay denounced it as "a cop-out—as much too interested in mainstream establishment stuff," and Craig Rodwell saw the organization—at least in comparison with GLF—as "rather conservative." But Foster Gunnison, not surprisingly, thought better of GAA than he had of GLF. And as GAA grew in strength over the next two years, he expressed pleasure that it (and not GLF) was "top dog"; in Foster's view GAA had "earned its position—and well deserves it." The new organization, after all, did share the older homophile view, which Foster exemplified, that gay groups must focus on gay rights to the exclusion of all else, and must conduct their affairs in orderly, Robert's-Rules fashion. But that is not to say that the reformers of GAA merely continued the policies of the homophile movement, elbowing to the sidelines, to their mutual relief, the "dangerous" radicals of GLF.[39]

GAA was much more assertive than NACHO or ERCHO had been in affirming the validity (and health) of the gay life-style, even as it denied that homosexuals were, except for the little matter of sexual orientation, carbon-copy heterosexuals. Where the homophile movement had stressed the importance of gays acting "responsibly" in order to win mainstream acceptance, GAA emphasized building pride in subcultural *difference* and organizing a political bloc to *demand* equal rights.[40]

The demands were imaginatively packaged in the form of "zaps"—lightning-quick confrontations with offending institutions,

organizations or individuals. Mayor Lindsay got his at a Metropolitan Museum of Art reception; dressed in appropriate dinner jackets, GAA members joined the reception line to greet the mayor and when he extended his hand, grasped—and held—it long enough to insistently ask, "What are you going to do about civil rights for homosexuals, Mr. Mayor?" Within the year, GAA had, among other actions, infiltrated the *Dick Cavett Show*; carried off a series of disruptions at the various branch offices of Household Finance for refusing loans to known homosexuals; demonstrated at the county clerk's office to demand the right to marry; and traveled to Long Island, Hartford, and Albany to protest gay-bashing and employment discrimination and to lobby for a statewide gay-rights bill.[41]

A little more than a year after its inception, GAA decided to lease an abandoned firehouse in the SoHo district of Manhattan, south of Greenwich Village. The Firehouse quickly became the political and cultural headquarters for the gay movement in New York, its spacious quarters a beehive of assorted activities. On Saturday nights, the large meeting hall would be converted into a dance floor and the packed revels (an average crowd of fifteen hundred per dance) become a cherished alternative to the bar scene, drawing the apolitical as well as the committed, and attracting both men and women (though men were always in a decided majority).

Y V O N N E

Yvonne Flowers was among the many venturing down to the Firehouse who had never previously belonged to a liberationist organization (though she had participated in any number of black and left-oriented demonstrations). For her, the experience proved both confirmatory and surprising. The absence of black faces confirmed her earlier sense that the gay movement had not succeeded in drawing—or perhaps had not even tried to draw—people of color. Yet at the same time, she was surprised to see at least a scattering of blacks present.

The numbers were small, yet marked some advance over the homophile movement. With the exception of "Ernestine Eppinger," who had participated in the Washington, D.C., picketing during the mid-sixties, no black person had played a prominent role in Matta-

chine, DOB, NACHO, or ERCHO, though many white members of those groups had been sympathetic to the black civil rights struggle, and Frank Kameny, for one, had always credited it with centrally shaping his own ideas. Ernestine Eppinger herself believed that "the homophile movement [was] more open to Negroes than, say, a lot of churches," but she acknowledged that few blacks had felt comfortable enough actually to join. Once, in the early sixties, Yvonne had gone with another black woman to a DOB meeting on Manhattan's Lower East Side, and had been repelled by it. The white women reacted to the black women's presence first with shock, then with a supercilious casualness that was at least as offensive. Yvonne never returned; "I can't be here," she decided, "with all these white girls."[42]

With the advent of GLF and GAA, the gay world became *some- what* more integrated (sexually, gay men had long crossed racial and class lines). Even so, gay blacks within the movement felt sufficiently at odds with it—perceiving their needs to be distinct enough, their perspectives ignored enough—to form their own Third World Caucus. Of course, in the feminist movement in these years as well, women of color were few and the issue of racism was muted. Yvonne Flowers was hardly alone in the late sixties or early seventies in feeling caught between the endemic sexism and homophobia of the black struggle and the pervasive racism in the feminist and gay ones.[43]

Yvonne found just enough black faces to keep her coming back to the Firehouse with some frequency. Before long, she and a few other black lesbians, including Luvinia Pinson (whom she had known before) and Donna Allegra, were getting together every Sunday as the Black Lesbian Caucus. "There were never enough people to really get a structure," Yvonne recalls, "to have officers or dues, but it was good in that we could at least talk to each other without being in a bar scene, and talk about racism within the gay community." None of them, it turned out, felt comfortable being in the Firehouse—which they called "a white boy's playhouse"—and since few of the women showed up on a regular basis, the group soon stopped meeting. Still, they *had* formed a loose network and within a year, they would again try to form an organization.

S Y L V I A

Given how fully Sylvia had involved herself in the Stonewall riots, she was by comparison detached in the months following. The reasons were mostly circumstantial, the result of living and working in New Jersey. Cut off from her usual contacts, she had heard nothing about the sudden emergence of GLF, or the subsequent formation of GAA. Bumping into Marsha P. Johnson on the street one day, she listened in amazement to Marsha's excited talk of the GLF meetings she had started to attend. Then, soon after, Sylvia spotted a copy of *Gay Power* on a newsstand (the biweekly had started publishing on September 15, 1969, about six weeks before *Gay* and GLF's *Come Out!* also hit the stands), and realized something really *had* happened following the riots, and that she had to find out exactly what.

Sylvia and another queen, Josie, both of them in full face makeup, descended on a GAA meeting. Sylvia was given some static at the door, but managed to get inside, where she and Josie decided to sit in the back of the meeting on the unlikely chance they would be inconspicuous. Looking around the room, Sylvia "didn't see a queen in there," and she and Josie started talking loudly in Spanish about how this didn't seem like exactly the place for them. A head turned around in the row directly in front: "I understand some of what you girls are saying, because I'm Italian." "Ooh my," thought Sylvia to herself, "I do think this chile is one of ours." She was. Her name was Bebe Scarpi, she was an undergraduate at Queens College (which she denied choosing for its name), and she assured Sylvia and Josie that they *were* in the right place, that "the sisters were welcome." Bebe was to become a fast friend of Sylvia's (and later, as a transvestite, would sit on the first board of the National Gay Task Force).[44]

But Bebe wasn't entirely right about "the sisters being welcome." They were and they weren't, depending on whom you asked and which night you asked them. Arthur Bell, one of the founders of GAA, observed that "the general membership is frightened of Sylvia and thinks she's a troublemaker. They're frightened by street people." A Hispanic street queen's transgressive being produced automatic alarm: Sylvia was from the wrong ethnic group, from the wrong side of the tracks, wearing the wrong clothes—managing single-handedly

and simultaneously to embody several frightening, overlapping categories of Otherness. By her mere presence, she was likely to trespass
against *some* encoded middle-class white script, and could count on
being constantly patronized when not being summarily excluded. If
someone was not shunning her darker skin or sniggering at her passionate, fractured English, they were deploring her rude anarchism
as inimical to order or denouncing her sashaying ways as offensive to
womanhood. Sylvia's ability to represent herself in unconventional
form had enabled her to have a life, but it had also made her a haunting
affront to those inhabiting standardized shapes.[45]

In the years ahead, Sylvia would often feel rejected and only
occasionally welcome. But she stuck it out. Taking immediately to
confrontational politics, she jumped into "actions" full blast, feeling
hurt when the chino set tried to shunt her to the sidelines, but rarely
feeling discouraged. *No one*, she quickly decided, was going to prevent
her from fighting for her own cause.

And just like Yvonne Flowers, Sylvia found enough friends and
allies to keep her coming back, at least for a few years. In GAA Arthur
Evans could always be counted on to defend her ("many times Arthur
and me sat down and talked heart-to-heart"), and in both GLF and
GAA she met some lesbians (like Kay Tobin and Judy Rathill) who
accepted and respected her. Never known for being tactful, Sylvia
told Judy Rathill on their first meeting, "You look like one of those
tough old dykes I used to hang out with up at the Hilltop in Harlem."
Judy laughed, assured her that she was "not a dyke, but a woman,"
and opened up her apartment to Sylvia and her friends whenever they
had no other place to stay. Sylvia affectionately remembers how she
and Judy "raised each other's consciousness."

But the angry denunciation of Sylvia by GAA's Jean O'Leary
(subsequently cochair of the National Gay Task Force) for "parody-
ing" womanhood was more typical of how movement women responded to her. Later, at the 1973 Gay Pride Rally, O'Leary would
attempt to keep Sylvia from speaking, and the angry public confrontation that resulted would lead Sylvia, as an aftermath, to attempt
suicide and to drop out of the movement. And many years after that,
O'Leary would express deep regret at her attitude: "Looking back, I
find this so embarrassing because my views have changed so much
since then. I would never pick on a transvestite now."[46]

O'Leary's denunciation of Sylvia was atypically heated. A more
standard exchange between Sylvia and a GLF woman went (according
to Sylvia) something like this:

WOMAN: Why do you like to wear women's clothing?

SYLVIA: Because I feel very comfortable. Do you like wearing pants?

WOMAN: Yeah.

SYLVIA: Well, I like wearing a skirt. What can I tell you? I
   like to feel flowing. You like to be confined. That's your
   problem.

Karla Jay was one of the GLF women who liked Sylvia personally. But even Karla felt ambivalent about her. She, Sylvia, and Marsha often had fun together; they would be part of a group that piled
into a car after a GLF meeting to go "liberate" an all–gay male or all-
lesbian bar. And in transit, Sylvia and Marsha would feel Karla up
in the backseat; it wasn't sexual—it was comparative shopping. They
would feel themselves up at the same time, judging how they measured
up against "the real thing." Karla remembers that after Marsha had
felt her breasts one time, she distractedly lamented, "I've worked
really hard and all's I got is lemons; she's got watermelons."

Despite the fun they had together, Karla would tell Sylvia and
Marsha that their jewelry, makeup, and tight clothes were exactly
what women were trying to get rid of; she resented the way they were
"copying and flaunting some of the worst aspects of female oppression." Besides, Karla would say, "you are *not* really women, you are
biological men and can reclaim that privilege at any time. *We* are
females forever." Sylvia, more than Marsha, would sometimes get
offended, and Sylvia offended was not some trifle. "She was as tough
as nails," Karla remembers, "I could see her getting a crew cut and
going out and joining the marines."

In GLF, Bob Kohler often made a pitch for the queens: "These
people started the riot, they're starving, *do* something for them!" That
would usually be greeted by more boos than applause—heavy role-
playing, whether by effeminate queens or by bulldykes, was viewed
by many as a residue of the bad old days of trying to win acceptance
from heterosexuals by mimicking their dichotomous role-playing. But
the influential Lois Hart strongly supported Kohler's position, and
indeed urged him to try to get more queens to attend the GLF meetings. Kohler at various times brought along Li'l Orphan Annie (red
curls and big eyes), Lola Montez, Hormona, Boom-Boom Santiago,
Black Bambi, Nova, and a host of other queens. But only a few had
Sylvia's commitment and staying power—were willing, as Kohler
puts it, to "tough it through."[47]

Kohler was a member of the Aquarius Cell, the GLF affinity group that organized the dances. He put Sylvia on door duty, where she would sit, usually stoned on speed and brandishing a large butcher knife, fiercely collecting and guarding the money. "Fierce" became the operative word in describing Sylvia. She would throw herself into every meeting, party, or action with such passion that those who insisted on remaining her detractors had to shift their vocabularies: She was no longer Sylvia, the flighty, unreliable queen, but rather Sylvia, the fierce harridan, ready to run any risk and run through any obstacle in order to achieve her frequently shrieked goal of FREEDOM.

Jim Fouratt was one of Sylvia's defenders. In his view, "her instincts were always correct." Even when she was screwed up on drugs or booze and being abrasively loud, Sylvia had, to Jim's mind, a gut-level understanding of oppression and a willingness to speak her mind that more than made up for her "incorrect" vocabulary, her brazen, bullhorn voice, her inability to shut up. Jim, in general, saw himself as favoring "a revolution that transformed not only society, but roles," and he could witheringly enunciate a position not far from Jean O'Leary's: "Men dressing up as women to play out roles that men have created to entice and seduce men, has nothing to do with being female." Yet he felt he understood Sylvia's need for "narcissistic visibility," for flamboyantly asserting, over and over, a right to exist that she herself had trouble accepting.

Jim was especially impressed with the way Sylvia handled her critics. When attacked by a GLF woman for "showing off" or for "denying her male privilege by pretending to be a woman," Sylvia would only rarely attack back, would not (like some of the other GLF queens) try stridently to put the woman down as "a jealous bitch." Instead, Sylvia would try to explain that she was simply being "Sylvia," a man with a penis who liked to dress up as a woman—it was as untheoretical as that.

When attacked by a GAA man—who, in trying to liberate himself from traditional ridicule about being a surrogate woman, could be impatiently moralistic about cross-dressing "stereotypes"—Sylvia would attack back; she would remind him how tough you had to be to survive as a street queen, how you had to fight, cheat, and steal to get from one day to the next. Most impressive of all to Jim was that Sylvia never stole from or physically attacked anyone within the movement; she treated people in GAA and GLF as comrades, exempt from the treacheries of the street. Jim may have been romanticizing what

he chose to call Sylvia's "lumpen morality," but if so, not by much. Like so many others in the movement, Sylvia felt she had found a home. And she would defend it with ferocious loyalty.

Jim was himself strongly committed to a movement that welcomed diversity. He had long identified with countercultural hippies and Third World revolutionaries, and he believed passionately in the need for multi-issue—not simply gay—politics. He also had an impressive track record of putting his beliefs into practice, of "making revolution in our lifetime" (as the New Left liked to put it). And so, during 1969–1970, he went to live for a time in the GLF Seventeenth Street commune—three white and two black men—out of which came a collective that traveled around the country trying to organize Gay Liberation Fronts.[48]

Their first stop was Minnesota, where one of their group, Richard, invited them to stay on his family farm. Having grown up there, Richard knew how to handle a gun and he offered to teach the others. To heighten the experience, they got high on LSD before trooping off to the nearby woods to shoot at cans and trees and bull's-eyes. The acid didn't fully kick in until they had returned to the farm, where Richard's mother had prepared a huge meal for them. As Jim, a vegetarian, later described it, "there was all this red meat which she had cooked for us. And I'm tripping my brains out and I'm seeing this meat looming on the table and talking to me and crying. And also we're trying not to let his parents know that we're gay, and not to let his parents know that we're on acid. And I'm taking this meat, putting it into my mouth, chewing it a little bit, taking a napkin and surreptitiously spitting into it, and holding it under the table while in my hand the meat is crying out."

Following that epiphany, the group went south for another. The two black men in their commune had lived (just like Sylvia, whom they knew) as transvestite hookers, and (again like Sylvia) were not afraid to speak their minds to whites, not afraid to express their anger at *and* their attraction to the oppressor. A great deal of consciousness-raising—always an emblematic activity for GLFers—got done on that trip south; and also a fair amount of organizational work. "A correct

idea," Jim believed, "catches the imagination of people everywhere," and "even in a small town in Alabama, we would find people who wanted what we had. And it wasn't about one supergroup in New York leading everybody else; it was about forming a network together, dealing with the needs of the local communities."

In late 1969, Jim also helped organize the first Venceremos Brigade, a group of some two hundred volunteers who went to Cuba by way of Mexico—in open defiance of a State Department ban on travel to Cuba—to cut sugar cane in support of Castro's revolution. Jim fully intended to go with the Brigade and, expecting to be in Cuba for two months, went ahead and sublet his apartment. But then he was told that he had not been accepted. Why? Because it was felt that his chief purpose in going to Cuba would be to organize gays and lesbians there, and that would not sit well with the revolutionary comrades. Furious that straight radicals were once again refusing to take his own cause (and his nature) seriously, Jim tried arguing against the decision. He pointed out that he didn't speak Spanish and added, with acid sarcasm, that it would be exceedingly difficult to organize Cuban gays on the basis of blow jobs alone. But the decision held.

Bitter at being rejected, and with no apartment to return to, Jim took his savings (and his sublet money), bought himself a VW van, and drove down to Texas to visit his friend Kit Carson, a screenwriter, and to attend a gay liberation conference in Austin. On the way back, he ran into some serious trouble. Dressed in black leather pants, a cowboy hat, and a brightly colored shirt, and with his long blond hair flowing loosely down his back, he was "a rather startling sight." So, at least, thought the police officers who stopped him. It seemed his license plates were out of date, and he had failed to get a new sticker. But that was the least of it: After searching his van, the police charged him with possession of heroin and dynamite.

Neither was in the van, but a hefty collection of New Left, Black Panther, and gay liberation literature was—and Jim was arrested and put in the Dallas County jail. He managed to get a call out to Kit Carson, who arranged for a lawyer and worked to get Jim released on bail. It took three months. In the interim, Jim sent a letter to his friend Howard Smith, the *Village Voice* columnist, asking him to raise some money for him, and Smith put a notice in the *Voice* announcing the Jim Fouratt Defense Fund.

The three-month wait was hellish. On first arriving in the Dallas jail, Jim was paraded in front of the holding tanks while a loudspeaker blared, "Who wants her? Who wants her?" He was then given a

uniform and put in an overcrowded cell. Remarkably, he was not raped. As he remembers it—though his actor's attraction to dramatic emphasis sometimes heightens that memory—he had read enough books about jail to come up with a successful strategy for avoiding rape. When another prisoner threatened him with a knife, Jim, though "scared to death," grabbed the man's wrist—and the cell broke up with laughter: The "pussy" had proven himself. But just to be sure, Jim later found a protector. Not a "husband," but a friend—"a huge, tough, redneck hippie," arrested for drug smuggling, who took Jim under his wing when he found out he was in jail for political reasons.

Possibly the worst moment came with the arrival of another gay man, a porn-theater projectionist in his forties. He acted—so Jim saw it—"flamboyantly, as if arriving in heaven," and, with no complaint on his part, "proceeded to get fucked by anybody who wanted to fuck him." Jim felt he should reach out to the man, "felt a comradeship on some level, even though really disgusted by his behavior"; but he didn't know how to do it without blowing his own cover. In the end he did nothing, preferring to believe that the man "was having a great time."

Kit Carson's lawyer finally got the charges against Jim reduced to possession of marijuana—though Jim rarely smoked pot and swears none was in the car. To pay the legal fees and have money to eventually get back to New York, Jim intended to sell his car. But he emerged from jail to discover that—in accordance with Texas law, which allowed the property of a drug dealer to be auctioned off—his car had been sold for fifty dollars to a police officer's wife. And there was nothing he could do about it; if he had gotten the car on credit, instead of paying cash for it, he could have relied on the finance company to contest the seizure.

Out on bail, Jim was restricted to the Fort Worth area and, as he tells it, an interlude of surreal luxury followed. Jim Meeker, a friend of Carson's and a well-known art patron, took him under his wing. He stayed at Meeker's Fort Worth mansion and did his bit as "the interesting hippie kid from New York" to entertain the likes of Kris Kristofferson and Samantha Eggar at dinner parties; as Jim put it years later, "it was more like my Warhol than my gay liberation phase."

After Jim went back into court, he was allowed to shift his residence to Dallas, where he lived with June Josie, a friend of Meeker's. She was "a Tennessee Williams lady," complete with flaming red hair, five Cadillac convertibles (to match her changing outfits), and a dead

gay husband who had been killed by her father when he found him in bed with another man—all of which appealed hugely to Jim's penchant for dramatic amplitude. For further amplitude still, he helped form the Dallas Purple Star Tribe collective, headquartered in Gene Leggett's house. Leggett was a pompous, charming Methodist minister who had left his wife and three children and founded a mission for homosexuals, drug addicts, and the homeless. Through him, Jim managed to get connected as well to the Dallas Theater Center, for which he quickly developed a New York actor's predictable disdain.[49]

Put on four years' probation at a third court hearing and finally allowed to leave Texas, Jim was in short order rearrested on his way to a New Left meeting. His probation officer, it turned out, had sent word ahead of his "gay liberationist" activities and, since homosexuality was against the law in Texas, he was picked up by marshals and once again remanded to jail. All that was bad enough—he was soon released again—but what was worse, what he could *not* shake and what bothered him infinitely more than his assorted jail stays, were the rumors he began to hear that he was himself a federal agent.

Those rumors pursued him for the next twenty years, and have persisted down to the present day. From the outside, Jim's glamorous life (or rather, his multiple lives)—his travels, his expensive wardrobe, his fancy friends—invited both envious speculation and, among political purists, considerable disapproval. How did a self-declared radical become personal assistant to Clive Davis, president of CBS? What was a Yippie leader doing consorting with the likes of Andy Warhol? How could someone who never seemed to have much money or, until the CBS job, any visible means of support, manage to fly off, at the drop of a hat, for mysterious meetings in distant parts?

If Jim had not been so articulate and opinionated for so long, had not so persistently engaged during political meetings in "disruptive shenanigans" (as one GAA member put it), had not sometimes acted holier(more Left)-than-thou (jumping over the subway turnstile, he once mocked an activist friend for paying his token, for "playing the capitalist game")—had he not done and been all these things, Jim might have made fewer enemies and created less resentment. But his detractors were—and remain—legion, and they proved determined to believe the worst about him.

In Jim's view, the rumors of his FBI/CIA connections arose when they did—in the period immediately following the November 1969 ERCHO meeting—because he had deeply offended many of the old-

line homophile leaders there. Several of them had noisily speculated about his being a provocateur of one kind or another; in Jim's scenario, Foster Gunnison became so convinced that he was a Communist, that he actually reported Jim to the FBI—which Foster, however, denies.

It was generally accepted in both GLF and GAA that one or several undercover agents *had* infiltrated the organizations. And those suspicions were well founded. The FBI had been attending gay political meetings in New York since the heyday of Mattachine, and would continue to cover movement events right through the seventies ("Wendy Wonderful," for example, was drummed out of the feminist *RAT* collective in 1970 for being an agent—though Karla, for one, was never convinced of Wendy's guilt). The FBI didn't always get their facts right: Initially they rendered "gay" as "gaye," and "Alternate U." as "Ultimate You"; they defined the Transvestites as "a militant group of women," and characterized the GLF Marxist study group, Red Butterfly, as prototypically anarchist (they "do not recognize authority of any kind"). But usually the FBI got it right, and no wonder, since the Bureau could rely (as one of its agent reports puts it) on "highly placed, sensitive source[s]" serving as informers from within the gay movement. Those sources have never been identified.[50]

Jim thinks it's possible that the FBI might itself have deliberately planted the false rumor that he was one of them in order to destroy his credibility within the New Left—just as it had done earlier in the case of the Communist party leader Bill Albertson. Years before, the FBI had floated the false rumor that Albertson was one of its agents; he had been expelled from the party—and broken in spirit. Only after his premature death was it revealed that the FBI had wholly invented the purported evidence of Albertson's connection to them.[51]

Jim wanted more immediate vindication and, as the rumors mounted, he finally demanded a formal hearing at GAA, where an ex-lover, Marty Robinson, had, in Jim's view, been leading the effort to discredit him. Jim relished the prospect of rising dramatically to his own defense, and at the GAA gathering he did eloquently represent himself, telling the assembled group how, as an actor and a hippie, he had learned to live resourcefully, with little money, and how angry and deeply hurt he was at the false accusation that he was a paid FBI informant. The proceeding may have been exhilarating theater, but Jim also found it "incredibly painful." In the upshot, the GAA meeting did exonerate him of all charges. That was a sweet victory indeed, but as it turned out, an incomplete one. Not even a

formal vote in GAA proved capable of laying the rumors permanently to rest.

KARLA

In January 1970, the feminist staff members of the countercultural paper *RAT*, dissatified with the lack of space devoted to women's issues, physically seized the Fourteenth Street premises and sent out a call to other feminists to join them. Karla Jay was one of those who responded. She had remained a committed feminist after leaving Red-stockings, and had recently begun to write. To her multiple other activities, she now added attendance at *RAT* editorial meetings and writing up movement-oriented material for publication in it.

One of her major efforts was a participant-observer piece about the March 1970 occupation of the *Ladies' Home Journal*. To Karla, that action was "the most successful ever done in the early women's movement"—though not many other feminists agreed with her esti-mate.

The move against the *Journal* resulted from months of planning by women from various New York liberation groups (including Red-stockings). On the day of the action, between a hundred and two hundred women invaded the *Journal* and "liberated" the office of its editor-in-chief, John Mack Carter. They denounced a magazine pur-portedly for women that was run and written by men and that catered to consumerism; instead of selling detergent, as Karla put it in her subsequent *RAT* article, "the magazine should in fact be telling their consumers how detergents pollute water." The protestors also pointed out that the few women who did work for the *Journal* were underpaid and that black women were notable by their absence. They then read Carter a set of demands that included his own resignation in favor of a woman editor.

When the reading was over, Carter, known to be imperious, said flatly, "I will not negotiate under siege!" Karla yelled, "You have no choice!" But Carter thought he did, and the stalemated sit-in went on for a number of hours. Tempers began to fray and at one point Karla, thinking Shulamith Firestone was about to lunge at Carter and want-ing to save her from injury or jail, grabbed Firestone's arm and re-strained her. Carter finally deigned to negotiate with the women's

demands, but announced that he would do so not with the group as a whole, but with a delegation—to be no larger than twelve.

The offer produced considerable dissension among the women, some of whom were fearful that it was a divisive tactic designed to appeal to some of the more prominent, career-minded among them. After another lengthy stalemate, a delegation was chosen and did meet with Carter—but emerged with only a single demand met: The *Journal* agreed to put up ten thousand dollars for a separate issue of the magazine devoted solely to the women's movement; the issue would be written collectively by the protestors themselves (though with Carter maintaining final editorial control). The women were ultimately able to use the bulk of the money to support feminist work—providing bail money, for example, for women in prison—but the compromise was angrily denounced both at the time, and later in print, by some of the protesters.

Karla was herself at first inclined to view the result as "elitist." As she wrote in *RAT*, "What good had we done? Aside from the publicity, which might awaken Middle Amerika [a spelling commonplace among 1970 radicals] to its hypocrisy and lies, we had succeeded only in getting Vassar girls higher paying jobs in publishing." But on reconsideration, Karla decided the action had succeeded in several important ways. Five of the largest—and in the past, squabbling—women's groups had managed to work together with reasonable harmony. The number of women participating in the action had sent "a firm warning" to the media to mend their ways in reporting on women's lives. And finally, the protesters had gotten an issue of the *Journal* all to themselves, and that promised to reach large numbers of women across the country with the message of liberation.

Other feminists thought the negatives outweighed—some thought *far* outweighed—the positives. The special "women's-liberation issue" of the *Journal*, they argued, would probably prove a commercial bonanza for its male owners. (The "issue" became a centerfold insert and appeared a year later.) And what of all the other demands which had been shunted to the side? The same issue of *RAT* that carried Karla's description of the protest carried a second article (by "Verna Tomasson") lamenting that nothing had been done about the just call for child-care facilities, for more black employees, for a training program to enable secretaries to move into editorial work, for an end to insulting ads, and for an increase in wages. "Somewhere in the night," Tomasson wrote, "the action came down with a severe case of anemia." It may have produced some effective publicity, but

measured by the standards of a *radical* action—"one which effects changes in the existing structure"—it had in Tomasson's view proven a failure.[52]

SYLVIA, JIM, KARLA

Sylvia was worried about her sisters. Worrying about something other than survival was one of the wondrous new luxuries attendant on the birth of GLF and GAA. Suddenly new possibilities and expectations were in the air. People began to dream about something other than getting from one day to the next with a minimum of discomfort. Sylvia's new dream was to have a place that underage street queens could call home.

At first she thought that place might be the new gay organizations themselves: "I thought that night in 1969 was going to be our unity for the rest of our lives." But as Sylvia and everyone else in GLF and GAA soon learned, the diversity of gay and lesbian life would require multiple, sometimes conflicting, expression, just as the traditional dominance of educated, middle-class white men would require constant challenge.

It did not seem, initially, that diversity had to generate disagreement, or disagreement, in turn, division. Many besides Sylvia harbored a vision of unbroken, harmonious solidarity, a determined linking of arms to march into a mistily tender-hearted future. And in the hope of containing differences, GLF had from the first organized around affinity cells, encouraging people, in accord with good anarchist tradition, to congregate around work of mutual interest. It had also opted for one large weekly meeting every Sunday night, run without the formal structure of permanent leaders or parliamentary procedures. Anyone who wanted to could attend and vote, though consensus was considered the ideal—and achievable—form of reaching resolution.

It wasn't long before the Sunday night meetings became forums of excited antagonism—revolutionaries advocated armed struggle, socialists called for an end to capitalism, moderates defended the reliability of American institutions and the basic decency of American life. Debates often became protracted, resolution difficult, bedlam the

norm. Some of the men, newly alive to the possibility that although gay they could reclaim their male prerogatives, did what their socialization had trained them to do—interrupt, monopolize discussion, insist on the correctness of their own views, belittle and denounce those who disagreed. And some of the women, true to *their* socialization, deferred to male authority and kept a low profile. But certainly not all of the women.

Rita Mae Brown, for one, had worked hard to raise consciousness within the feminist movement about lesbianism; in GLF, she, Lois Hart, Martha Shelley, and others encouraged lesbians to form feminist consciousness-raising groups—not solely to resist "male chauvinism," but also to end personal feelings of alienation. Lois Hart argued that the women in GLF were better off than heterosexual women "on the outside" because many gay men in the organization *did* believe in feminist principles of gender parity and did applaud all-women consciousness-raising groups that would further encourage independence and equality. "We are in a really tough situation," Hart wrote. "We want to be able to call each other brother and sister, yet we are still in some ways in the roles of oppressor and oppressed. Women are going to feel anger and men will feel fear and resentment."[53]

Many of those feelings surfaced over the issue of separate women's dances. GLF women, including Karla, had worked hard (even chopping ice and sweeping floors) to make the GLF dances at Alternate U. a success. But they grew to resent the "pack 'em in" attitude of the GLF men. Outnumbered by at least five to one, the women had trouble even finding each other at the overwhelmingly male dances, which to them seemed increasingly to resemble nothing so much as a standard gay male bar, overcrowded and dimly lit, with human contact "limited to groping and dryfucking."[54]

Deciding that they wanted a space of their own for dances, the GLF women (never more than ten to twenty percent of the organization) demanded that one of the large rooms at Alternate U. be declared off-limits to men and that a portion of the GLF treasury be set aside to finance separate women's dances. Some of the GLF men denounced the plan as divisive, others denied that there was a male-female problem significant enough to require so "drastic" a solution, and still others instantly supported the women's demands. After a great deal of discussion, which was the GLF way, funds for the separate dances were somewhat reluctantly voted.

The GLF women wanted a social space that would not only be

free of male domination, but would also serve as an alternative to the lesbian bars then in existence. The famous Sea Colony having closed in 1968, there were only two lesbian bars in Manhattan in 1970: Kooky's, on West Fourteenth Street, and Gianni's, on West Nineteenth; both served watered-down, overpriced drinks in an atmosphere less than congenial. Kooky's was named after the fearsome woman who was herself always on the premises. A heterosexual, and purportedly an ex-prostitute, Kooky had dyed, lacquered blond hair and was given to wearing pink crinoline dresses. Karla has described Kooky as looking "more like a poorly put-together transvestite than a woman."[55]

And she ran her bar like a tyrannical man, ordering the lesbian patrons around as if they were scum, beneath contempt. She would think nothing of coming up to a woman sitting at the bar, grabbing her glass, and shoving it up to her mouth. "Drink up, drink up," she would growl in her Brooklynese accent. "This ain't a church, y'know. You wanna spend all your time talkin', go to a church and talk in the pew." Then Kooky would turn to the bartender and bark, "She's buying another drink." The women were afraid of her, sensing her violence, guessing at her Mafia connections. The occasional patron who resisted Kooky's commands could be sure that Kooky would take the lit cigarette always dangling from her mouth, put it right under the woman's chin, and then signal the two bouncers to throw her out.[56]

When Karla and some other GLF women tried to leaflet Kooky's one night with announcements of the forthcoming lesbian dance at Alternate U., Kooky had her male bouncers toss them outside into the snow. It was clear Kooky would not look kindly on the prospect of business being taken away by "some goddamned liberation group." The women then tried leafleting near the bar, but when Kooky saw the flyers in some of her customers' hands, she sent her bouncers outside to threaten retaliation.

Karla and the other GLF women were understandably on edge when the night of the first lesbian dance, April 3, 1970, arrived. Would Kooky try something to disrupt the evening? Would enough women show up to justify all the planning effort? The answer on both counts proved to be a decided yes. A number of straight women showed up in response to a plea from their lesbian friends for support (though one woman Karla phoned—a woman who came out a year later—accused Karla of trying to force her into lesbianism). Even without

straight sympathizers, the dance was mobbed and was declared by all hands a huge success; from then on, it became a regular event. But at three A.M., as a group of GLF women, including Karla, were cleaning up, the expected trouble finally arrived.

According to Karla, several large men wearing unholstered guns in their belts suddenly appeared in the Alternate U. doorway. They claimed to be police and said they were investigating charges that liquor was being sold without a license (the dance had adopted the legal ruse of requesting a "donation" at the door). The women were pretty sure at a glance that these men were not cops, but just in case, some of them ran in panic to flush their drugs down the toilet or to stash them under a couch.

It wasn't long before the goons started to push some of the women around; at that, Karla and a friend of hers ran out the back exit. Having expected trouble, they had earlier gotten the black lesbian lawyer Flo Kennedy (who was also a friend of Yvonne's) to promise to stay by her phone, and they now ran to a booth a block away—and directly in front of Kooky's—to call her. Kennedy advised them to notify the police (that is, the real police) and the media immediately, which they did. But just as Karla hung up from making the last call, two drunken men reeled out of Kooky's, where they had apparently wandered inadvertently and been thrown out. Furious, and seeing the two women in the phone booth, they started harassing them, calling them "pussy suckers" and threatening to kill them. Karla insisted she had not been in Kooky's, as the men claimed. "So then what the fuck are you doing here?" one of the men demanded. Thinking fast, Karla said, "Fixing the phone. We're from the phone company"—and to make her point, she ripped out the receiver. "See. It's broken." Grumbling, the men staggered off.

When the two women got back to Alternate U., the police and press had arrived and the goons had fled. The GLF women felt certain that Kooky had sent them, but couldn't prove it, even though the police confirmed that the men had not been officers. As for Kooky (and many of the other bar owners as well), she continued to denounce and harass the gay liberationists—that is, until it eventually became clear that the GLF dances, despite their ongoing success, did not present any significant threat to her own bar business.

Karla shared the view that gay male sexism was an impediment to gender equality and cooperation within GLF. And she thought Jim

Fouratt was among the occasional offenders—though hardly the worst. On the whole she liked and admired Jim. And she was fascinated by the disparity between the way he looked and the way he sometimes sounded. (And fascinated, too, by the same pair of tight black leather pants that he seemed always to wear; she secretly wondered how—or if—he washed them.) In looks Jim seemed androgynous, ethereal, fragile—yet as soon as he opened his mouth he became one more powerfully assured male.

Karla and some of the other GLF women complained about the aggressive way Jim and other GLF men simply stood up, interrupted, and talked whenever they felt like it. Jim took the complaints to heart. Priding himself on having a feminist consciousness, he didn't want his own aggressive behavior to become part of the problem. And so he *tried* to modulate his tone and monitor his interruptions, realizing that among other things, he had to learn the difference between standing up at a GLF meeting and shouting, "Let the women speak!" and simply saying nothing, letting a space develop in which women *could* speak—and without his patronizing intervention in their behalf.

But though gender issues were real in GLF, Jim and Karla shared the view that the organization was honest in its determination to confront sexism *and* racism, that the consciousness-raising groups which were a GLF feature provided the mechanism for doing so, and that to dilute GLF's strength through separatism would be to weaken one of the few organizations willing to challenge the basic sexist and racist assumptions of American life. For both of them, unity was the key, keeping all disparate elements under one political umbrella.

But on the issue of allying with other oppressed minorities, Karla was more ambivalent than Jim, and though she believed a revolution was coming, she recoiled from any glib talk of armed struggle. She agreed completely with Jim that GAA was misguided in its emphasis on single-issue politics, but she also felt strongly that groups like the Panthers, whom Jim tended to champion uncritically, were uncertain allies. She deeply sympathized with the Panthers' militancy but worried about their blatant chauvinism; they may have been the "vanguard," but they were "incredible pigs about women." She thought the group's politics had to be supported, but resisted the wholehearted embrace endorsed by Jim and others. And she resisted, too, the call to get behind Fidel's revolution in Cuba, to excuse Cuban homophobia by citing their Catholic heritage—since politically, after all, they were "way ahead of the rest of us." Karla wasn't buying it. She refused to

dissolve her conflicted feelings about the Panthers or the Cubans into *self*-denying apologetics.

As a Hispanic, Sylvia strongly identified with those righteous revolutionaries of the Third World, the Black Panthers and their Hispanic counterpart, the Young Lords. She marched occasionally with both groups, though often in a stoned-out state, and later, in 1971, she would attend the People's Revolutionary Convention, and would count her five-minute meeting with Panther leader Huey Newton among the highlights of her life. Though Sylvia concluded that GAA wasn't "radical enough," she never left the organization, and her friend Bebe Scarpi always made sure that Sylvia's dues were paid up. But her primary allegiance, like Karla's and Jim's, came to center on GLF.

And it was primarily to GLF that she turned for help when her dream of creating a refuge for underage street queens began to stir. Sylvia was still only nineteen herself, yet she had begun to worry about "the youngsters," the kids who started to hustle on the streets, as she had, at age ten or eleven and, within a few years, were dead from a stabbing or an overdose or were locked into dead-end lives. She wanted to somehow set up a place where these young queens not only could find emotional comfort but could maybe even learn enough skills to start another kind of life.

The first person she talked all this over with was her old street-hustling buddy, Marsha P. Johnson. Marsha always had a problem staying focused in conversation; she would wander, start off talking about one thing and end up miles away; people said that drugs had ruined her mind, that she was a permanent space cadet. But when Sylvia started talking to her about "getting a place" for the young sisters, Marsha's mind concentrated wonderfully. She was instantly excited, eager to help. Sylvia had decided that she would make Marsha president of any group they formed, but Marsha, wisely, wouldn't hear of it. "You stay on one thought when you speak," she told Sylvia. "I go off in all directions. You'll be president. I'll be vice president."

They quickly hit on a name for their as-yet-nonexistent group: Street Transvestites Actual Revolutionaries (STAR), then changed "Actual" to "Action." Their first home was the back of a trailer truck seemingly abandoned in a Greenwich Village outdoor parking area; it was primitive, but a step up from sleeping in doorways, and Sylvia and Marsha were quickly able to gather together some two dozen young street transvestites. The ground rule in the trailer was that nobody *had* to go out and hustle her body, but that when they did,

they had to kick back a percentage to help keep "STAR House" going. Marsha and Sylvia took it upon themselves to hustle on a regular basis and to return to the truck each morning with breakfast food for everybody.

Rounding Christopher Street on the way back to the trailer at daybreak one morning, their arms loaded with groceries, Sylvia and Marsha stopped dead in their tracks. The trailer was moving! Apparently somebody had reclaimed it and was driving it off—not realizing that some twenty queens were asleep inside. As Sylvia and Marsha watched, dumbstruck, the young queens, apparently awakened by the start-up noise, started to jump out of the back of the truck. But was anyone still inside? "We're standing there like two *yentas*," Sylvia later recalled. "I mean, we're talking about two crazy women: 'Oh, my God, the kids, the kids! Oh Lord Jesus, please don't take the children!' Two crazy women, hysterical. And in full drag." As it turned out, only one queen was still in the van. Stoned out on downers, she woke up several days later—on her way to California.

It was time for a new plan. Bubbles Rose Marie, one of the queens who had lived in the truck, airily suggested that she go talk to her "friend" Michael Umbers, a well-known Mafia figure in the Village. (The following year Umbers opened the gay after-hours club Christopher's End on the ground floor of the Christopher Street Hotel; still later, he employed Dick Leitsch as a bartender.) "He's got a building on Second Street," Bubbles added casually. Sylvia and Marsha looked at each other and shrugged, as if to say, "Why not let the crazy bitch do it? If anything goes wrong, they'll kill *her*." For a small amount of money up front, and a firm deadline on payments, Umbers let Bubbles have the building at 213 East Second Street. And why not? It was standing empty, little more than a shell.

Elated, Sylvia and Marsha sent all the queens out to panhandle and to "hustle their asses off" to raise the needed money, while they, Bambi Lamour (whom Sylvia had first met in jail at Rikers) and Andorra ("a heavyset, high-yaller black queen") set about making the building livable. There was no electricity or plumbing, and not even the boiler worked; there they sat, "four queens that don't know shit about nothing, we're looking at the tools, we're looking at each other. We just started taking things apart, putting them back together, and the next thing we knew, the motherfucker was working!" Grateful that they hadn't blown each other sky-high, they celebrated by shooting up.

People in both GLF and GAA had promised Sylvia that they

would come by and help fix up STAR House. And she had gotten some of the gay teachers in GAA to swear they would turn the top floor of the building into a kind of school, teaching some of the illiterate young runaways how to read and write. But in fact few showed up, and only Bob Kohler of GLF came by with any regularity, helping them to paint, clean up the yard, and get some primitive plumbing installed. When Sylvia decided to throw a benefit dance for STAR House at Alternate U., GLF did front her enough money to buy beer and setups. But when she went to GAA and asked that she be allowed to rent their stereo equipment, she was turned down. Arthur Bell and a few others spoke out in favor of the rental, but the dominant view was that "when we started GAA, we hadn't a thing either. . . . We're not in the rental business."[57]

The experience further embittered Sylvia toward GAA, but the benefit dance did come off in style. Sylvia and what she called her "STAR House Kids" decorated the hall with flashing Christmas bulbs and necklaces of spangled reflectors; and the costumes were extravagant—Bob Kohler appeared in a white T-shirt covered with thousands of beads and with an Indian sash draped across one hip. But Sylvia herself was not a pretty sight. Not having slept or washed for days, she settled for a simple outfit of pants and blouse and, giving off a decided odor and a lot of attitude, sat resolutely at the door collecting money. Shortly after midnight she stopped the gyrating dancers and gave a little speech: "This dance is for the people of the streets who are part of our gay community. Let's give them a better chance than I had when I came out. I don't know if any of you ever lived on the streets. Many transvestites who make up STAR do. We are asking you for money tonight. Winter is coming and we need money for clothes and rent. Please dig into your pockets and help STAR. . . ." Then some of the queens surprised Sylvia by presenting her with a huge bouquet of red roses. She wept buckets.[58]

The dance did bring in a fair amount of money, and STAR House seemed to have gotten a foothold. Sylvia started to cook big dinners at night, sternly telling "the children" that they "don't have to live off that candy shit." And before everyone went out in the evening, she "worked with the saints." Devoted from childhood to Santería, and convinced that St. Barbara was the patron saint of gay Hispanics, Sylvia set up an altar, complete with incense and candles, around which everyone would gather and "pay tribute" before they left the house.

Nobody was forced to participate, but Sylvia made it clear that

they would be better protected on the streets if they showed a little respect for the saints, and especially for St. Michael. To him, her prayer would be, "I know we're doing wrong, but we gotta survive, so please help us." And she believed he did: "We *were* watched over—though Marsha came close to getting killed by tricks a number of times, and I looked down the barrel of many a gun and would say, 'Shoot me. You'll be doin' me a favor. I won't have to pay no rent.' But my saints protected me."

Then one day on Christopher Street, Sylvia found Mike Umbers blocking her path. He glowered at her and said he hadn't gotten rent money for three months and wanted the nine hundred bucks *now*. Sylvia raced home and confronted Bubbles, who had been handling the payments. Bubbles mumbled something about the cost of repairs, and Sylvia was about to light into her when Umbers himself showed up. He told Bubbles that unless he got his money, she was as good as dead. At that, Sylvia changed sides. If anything happened to Bubbles, she screamed at Umbers, she would go to the police and tell them she had heard Umbers threaten her.

"For chrissake," she yelled, "it's only money! Don't kill somebody over it! The bitch fucked up. Fine. So kick her ass. But don't kill her. You can take her outside right now and I won't stop you. Or make the bitch get out on the corner." "That bitch can't make no money," Umbers grunted. "That bitch is fat." "Well," Sylvia shot back, "if you kill her, I'll be the first one to speak up." Umbers told Sylvia she'd always been "a fucking bitch" and left.

The next thing Sylvia knew, Bubbles had skipped town ("like she always does when she gets in hot water"). Sylvia decided to make a last-ditch appeal to GAA for a loan, but her request was turned down on the grounds that it would be a dangerous precedent for GAA to get into the business of lending money. But if Sylvia wanted to, they added, she could leave a box at the front table soliciting donations. Desperate, Sylvia left the box, but the donations amounted to only a few dollars. She wasn't close to paying off what she owed Umbers.

And there were other problems. Bambi and Andorra had taken to beating each other up when they got high, and though they were soon kissing again, the dream of sisterhood was getting a little frayed. Then Marsha had a serious attack of "nerves." Her fifth husband, Candy, who was heavily into drugs, got his head blown off right on Second Street and First Avenue when he made the mistake of trying to rob a plainclothesman. Sylvia went with Marsha to the funeral in New Jersey, but no sooner had they gotten back than Marsha's beloved

dog died. Marsha said she "couldn't hardly stand it," two deaths in a row, and she had to consult a doctor for her "bad nerves."[59]

Before things could get back on an even keel at STAR House, Mike Umbers evicted them. Apparently deciding against violence, he simply called the city marshals and had Sylvia and her brood put out on the street for nonpayment of rent. Knowing that they were "in no position to mess with Umbers," Sylvia threw in the towel. But before she and her "kids" left STAR House, they destroyed all the work they had put into the place and threw the refrigerator out the back window. "That's the type of people we are: You fuck us over, we fuck you over right back."

FOSTER, JIM, SYLVIA

Foster was by temperament an optimist. In the early months of 1970, as ERCHO and NACHO faltered and the future of the old homophile movement seemed in doubt, Foster preferred to emphasize its ongoing activities and potential staying power. Yet simultaneously, this complex man was able, in some moods, not only to accept that the homophile movement might have had its day, but even to urge his old comrades to jettison the past and "get with it." And Foster was impressively capable of following his own advice: Even as he worked hard to preserve the older homophile organizations, he joined hands with Craig Rodwell and others in the new gay liberation movement to prepare for the Stonewall commemorative march, scheduled for June 27, 1970.[60]

There was reason to believe that ERCHO and NACHO might survive into the new era. Some of NACHO's committees continued to show vitality, even if most of their work was being done by lone individuals. Louis Crompton, a professor of English at the University of Nebraska, kept the Religious Committee going largely through his own diligence, and in late December 1969 single-handedly produced a survey of religious attitudes toward homosexuality. And both Arthur Warner, head of NACHO's Legal Committee, and Frank Kameny, guiding force behind the effort to change federal policies toward homosexuals, continued to produce significant bodies of work.[61]

Foster himself kept up a steady bombardment of exhortatory memos and letters, quick to encourage and praise any signs of life in

the old organizations. He rushed to congratulate a NACHO member for starting a newsletter early in 1970 (it lasted for exactly two issues), rejoiced when the NACHO clearinghouse for publications seemed back in regular operation (it quickly became irregular again), and continued to put an enormous amount of time and energy into drawing up agendas and sending out "bulletins" in preparation for the forth-coming NACHO convention (as it would turn out, the last). Even as he worked at maximum pitch, Foster sensed, as he wrote NACHO chair Bill Wynne, that "we may be fighting a losing battle even under the best of circumstances."[62]

ERCHO was the first of the two organizations to disintegrate. It had never really recovered from the disruptive 1969 convention, voting soon afterward to "suspend" itself for a year—"a curious move," Foster had written at the time, "akin to shooting yourself in the head before the next guy does it for you." All that he could think to say in defense of the suspension was that it probably "prevented a take-over by the extremists" and sped the day when "the homophile cause can be resurrected as a sane and rational movement."[63]

For a few months in early 1970, Forster refused to accept that ERCHO was no more. He feared (along with losing his own ballast) that the East would "be in the same boat with the Midwest and the Far West—with no effective regional conference," and for a time he struggled "with all my heart to try and save our ERCHO." He even rebuked Steve Donaldson for describing the organization as "defunct," admonishing him to remember that "the proper way to refer to the ERCHO at present is to say that 'most of the ERCHO administrative machinery has been suspended for a period of one year.' "[64]

But the ERCHO game was decidedly up, and Foster soon faced that fact. He of course couldn't resist, in a few postmortems, putting most of the blame ("75%") squarely on GLF, on what he called "the insurgency of leftist and communist oriented new radical elements." But he didn't let the older homophile leadership entirely off the hook. He chastised Frank Kameny and others for "lack of will" in putting the radicals down and, even more, blamed the corrosive jealousies that had developed among some of the old-timers themselves—above all, the long-standing, venomous rivalry between Kameny and Arthur Warner of New York Mattachine (for which Foster mostly blamed Warner's "indiscretions" of speech, even while acknowledging that Kameny could be "curt and abrasive").[65]

But NACHO seemed a much more viable and necessary orga-nization, and Foster still hoped that hard work might save it. He

described himself as "incurably an optimist, so I'll be the last to drop out or throw in the sponge." And in that spirit, he sent off a mound of proposals to various correspondents in the spring of 1970 outlining the direction that he felt the upcoming NACHO conference in San Francisco should take. He advocated doing *less* in terms of setting up committees and projects that in the past had ended up undone or half done, and concentrating instead on doing a few things well. He urged that communications—"not good throughout the movement"—be improved, starting with a functioning newsletter, and that most business matters be kept off the floor of the convention and delegated to a separate, representative body.[66]

He felt strongly that NACHO's integrity as an organization could be preserved only if the new gay liberation groups which had proliferated over the past year were kept from "inundating" the convention. Foster regarded himself "as militant in the movement as anyone you will find," but rejected what he called "a fawning and demeaning effort to suck ass with every other minority cause." He insisted that the left-wing slogans of GLF—"Power to the People!" and so on— were the essence not of liberation but of doctrinaire conformity. "Indeed," he wrote, "I have encountered few more rigid examples of conformity—in dress, thought, and action, than in some of these professional non-conformists."[67]

Foster's vehemence reflected his long-standing views, but also some very recent experience. In late April 1970, he witnessed a rally for the Black Panthers—and the police reaction to it—at Yale University. During 1968–1969, the police had raided Panther offices across the nation thirty-one times, culminating in the slaying of Chicago leader Fred Hampton; the New Haven rally was in support of the jailed "Panther Twenty-one." Foster, in his conscientious way, had gone to Yale as part of his continuing education. And he got one. The tear gas and pepper gas used by the police to break up a demonstration were so thick that he had to vacate his eighth-floor hotel room for several hours.

Later that same evening, he went to a meeting called by all the New York political groups to plan campus strikes in protest against the continued bombing of Cambodia. Foster managed to last an hour, even though it was only a matter of minutes before "inquisitive eyes" began staring at his three-piece Brooks Brothers suit. A student finally came up to him and asked him point-blank to leave—apparently on the suspicion that he was an FBI agent. Foster quickly obliged. Writing about the episode soon after to NACHO chair Bill Wynne, he

played it deadpan: "I don't think these people trust me." This was Foster's version of playfulness, which never failed to startle people who preferred to see him as a one-dimensional, pontificating heavy.[68]

While in New Haven, Foster did not get to hear the speech Jim Fouratt gave at the Panther rally. If he had, it might have softened Foster's attitude toward his old antagonist. Though still a staunch supporter of the Panthers, Jim had decided that the time had come to publicly criticize their negative, patronizing view of homosexuality. "The homosexual sisters and brothers who are in this crowd," Jim told the New Haven rally, "have a complaint to make." He went on to say that the very oppression that had made so many gay people identify with the Panthers was being reproduced within the Panther movement. He called upon "every radical here today to Off the word faggot," and also "to Off the sexism which pervades this place and to begin to deal" with their hostility to "the homosexual brothers and sisters." It took considerable courage for Jim to stand up before a crowd uncritically adoring of the Panthers and bring it a message that few were yet ready to hear.[69]

Jim's own attitude had undergone considerable evolution. When Eldridge Cleaver had published his best-selling *Soul on Ice* in 1968, in which he had expressed the view that "homosexuality is a sickness, just as are baby-rape or wanting to be head of General Motors,"[70] Jim had defended Cleaver, and by implication all heterosexual left-wing men who casually disparaged "faggots." The term "faggot," Jim tried artfully to explain, had emerged from prison jargon, where it had been a metaphor for "any castrated male made impotent by society."

As he himself later said, he would "rue the day" that he leaped to Cleaver's defense, pretending to a knowledge of ghetto language he didn't have and letting his enthusiasm for the black struggle blot out the realities of black homophobia. In the two years after the publication of *Soul on Ice*, the Panthers' unwillingness to open any kind of dialogue with GLF had produced some raucous debates within GLF between those wanting to commit money to the Panthers' bail fund and those enraged at the Panthers' knee-jerk homophobia. Jim always argued for giving the bail money, but over those two years he also came to conclude that the Panthers had to be publicly confronted on their homophobia. And it was at the New Haven rally on May 1, 1970, that he chose to issue his challenge to them.[71]

It was one of "the greatest thrills" of Jim's life when Huey Newton, a short time later, published a statement in the *Black Panther* that admonished militant blacks to face up to their "insecurities" about

homosexuality and expressed the view that "we should try to unite with them in revolutionary fashion," welcoming them to all future conferences and rallies. In accordance with Huey Newton's advice, the Panthers soon after extended an invitation to GLF to send a delegation to the Revolutionary People's Constitutional Convention at Temple University in Philadelphia. Not only was Jim Fouratt part of that delegation, but so was Sylvia Rivera.[72]

The Philadelphia convention—which drew upwards of ten thousand people—had been called to draft a new constitution, one that would "represent all oppressed people." Each participating group was to have its own workshop, from which would issue statements of needed rights. But the only workshop the female delegates were allowed to have was one controlled by committed Panther women—with the result that most of the female delegates, and almost all of the two dozen lesbians present, angrily bolted the convention.[73]

But for Sylvia, it was "a great moving moment to be there." When she first got off the bus and saw that she was surrounded by straights, she "panicked," sure that she wouldn't be accepted. She resolved—"completely stoned out" and carrying a knife—that "if anybody fucks with me, I'm going to cut their dick off or cut their throat." But everything came miraculously right for her when she ran into Huey Newton himself coming down a corridor and he said that he remembered meeting her ("Yeah—you're the queen from New York") at one of the earlier Panther demonstrations she'd been at. Sylvia's soaring spirits came back to earth only after she returned to New York and an angry Marsha P. Johnson accused her of having stolen STAR funds to make the trip to Philadelphia. Well yes, Sylvia acknowledged, she *had* "borrowed" the money—"and why the fuck not? I wanted to see Huey, and I'll pay the money back!" And she did—by putting in a few more hours each week hustling on the street.

Unlike the women, the gay men did get to present their statement to the convention, and consequently had a more positive reaction to the proceedings. "The Statement of the Male Homosexual Workshop" was greeted with some snickering, but it also got some applause. If it was clear that the Panthers had not been converted overnight to a more positive view of homosexuality, Jim and most of the other GLF men felt that it was only a matter of time before additional Panther leaders—probably David Hilliard and Erika Huggins—followed Huey's lead in advocating a stronger alliance with gay liberation.[74] But Jim remained uncomfortable with Panther attitudes, and his ambivalence was captured in a single incident during the convention.

He had on a sterling silver bracelet that was not only very beautiful, but had been given to him by someone he had deeply cared about. At one point during the convention, while sitting outside on the grass talking to some of the Panthers and trying to explain why gay liberation was a legitimate movement, Jim heard one of the Panther women ask if she could try his bracelet on. "Of course," he said, nervously sensing some potential unpleasantness.

After she had worn the bracelet for a while, the woman, looking him straight in the eye, abruptly asked, "Can I have this?" Jim felt "caught in my white guilt. I knew that I didn't want to give it to her and I knew it would be inappropriate to say no." Wanting to be a "good gay," he resolved his ambivalence with an offhanded "sure." Later he berated himself both for having been taken in by "a revolutionary con" *and* for not being "truly egoless and nonmaterial." Jim was not so liberated that—like most gay people at most times—he was ever at a loss in finding multiple ways to berate himself.

As the 1970 NACHO conference approached, Foster's excitement mounted. He chose to see the preregistration figures (some twenty organizations and nearly a hundred individuals) as "amazing" proof that NACHO had a viable future. But as it turned out, the conference proved more a nightmare than a triumph for him. The very first motion from the floor after the convention had been called to order was in support of the Black Panther party. It narrowly squeaked by in an initial ballot and then was sustained when a later motion to reconsider was soundly defeated. Capitalizing on that victory, the Radical Caucus, claiming to speak in the name of "the entire West Coast," next objected to the conference's "restrictive membership policy" (Foster had sweated over the elaborate formula for long hours) and successfully pushed through the principle of one person, one vote.[75]

A second humiliation soon followed. The delegates decided to hold another NACHO convention in 1971 and proceeded to elect a Conference Committee to prepare for it. Foster was one of sixteen people nominated, but he got the third-lowest number of votes and failed to be elected. On the other hand, Dick Leitsch—who was attending a NACHO convention for the first time (outflanked by the rising tide of Gay Power, he had become interested in NACHO as a possible countervailing force)—*was* elected to the committee. And when the 1971 convention failed to come off, Foster would directly blame Leitsch's "erratic, unreliable" behavior, rightly seeing that

Leitsch, at bottom, was "anti-NACHO"—or rather, "anti-anything that he's not top dog in."[76]

Not only did NACHO never again hold a convention, but by 1972 the organization would cease to exist. The times had changed. Radical young lesbians and gays were in the saddle; they generally considered the older homophile generation irrelevant, and their accomplishments nil. Yet homophile accomplishments had been real, however necessary it may have been for a newly assertive generation to scorn them in order to establish its own hegemony. When Bill Wynne, chair of the 1970 NACHO convention, rose to address the delegates, he gave a succinct valedictory accounting of those accomplishments.

Wynne began by acknowledging that the goals NACHO had originally set at its founding in 1966 may have been "mostly grandiose and naive," and that the proliferating committees set up to accomplish those goals in the years since had mostly been nonfunctional. But nonetheless "some things of a positive nature," as Wynne put it, *had* been done and deserved enumeration. Above all, communication had been opened up between individuals and groups previously isolated from each other. That, in turn, had served to stimulate local organizing, even as it had clarified the fact that "our problems" were not merely local but national in scope. And NACHO gatherings over the years had helped to develop confidence among those attending them that a national gay response could become a reality. "Develop[ing] confidence"—that was probably the subsuming accomplishment. In Wynne's words, the homophile movement had "given courage to people to open up the whole subject."[77]

Fortunately for Foster's peace of mind, he had already, by the time of NACHO's final convention in 1970, become deeply involved in several new projects that would amply fill the vacuum in his life. Earlier on, in Foster's hometown of Hartford, Connecticut, Canon Clinton R. Jones of Christ Church Cathedral had started a counseling group for gays that by mid-1968 had helped give birth to an activist organization called the Kalos Society. Foster had been involved with Kalos from the beginning, though in early 1970 it still had only fifteen or twenty members and in Foster's view hadn't really " 'gelled' yet." But he had hopes it might eventually become "a high-powered organization for New England." It never did; but it lasted well into the seventies and left behind a news bulletin, *The Griffin*, later transformed into *Metroline*, a regional gay publication that in 1993 continues to publish.[78]

Through his own one-man organization, the Institute of Social Ethics, Foster also started work in 1970 on some elaborate publishing ventures. In order to "promote and facilitate communication," he planned to put out a "comprehensive directory of organizations, publications, events, and projects associated with the homophile movement." Initially, he entitled the pending publication *Homophile Organizations of the World*, but later chose the shorter *The Directory*. Setting to work with his usual enthusiasm and zeal, Foster tossed off memos, mailed out press releases, gathered far-flung data. After nearly a decade of work, he would ultimately abandon the project, convinced that the emergence by then of the New York City–based *Gayellow Pages*, with its national coverage, had made *The Directory* redundant. But over the years he gathered a remarkable body of material, creating an archive that is today an indispensable resource on the homophile movement.[79]

Foster was also, by 1970, deeply involved in helping Craig Rodwell plan a commemorative celebration of the first anniversary of the Stonewall riots. Long since convinced that "the main problem holding us back from where we want to get to is that of secrecy or fear, and the failure of homosexuals to get out of the closet," Foster hoped that Craig's Christopher Street Liberation Day Committee might prove an ideal vehicle for encouraging greater openness and broader movement participation.[80]

S Y L V I A

Carol Greitzer of the New York City Council represented a district that included Greenwich Village and its large gay and lesbian population. Yet in the past Greitzer had more than once worked against the needs of that constituency. In 1964 she had joined Councilman Ed Koch in calling for more plainclothesmen to control the "perverts" in Washington Square Park and, in 1966, had urged that the Village be included in Operation New Broom, a police campaign to get rid of "undesirables." Nor did Greitzer's attitude seem to change after the emergence of gay liberation; when GAA leaders Jim Owles and Marty Robinson asked her in 1970 to support a fair-employment-practices bill, she tartly replied that it wasn't a proper area for legislation. GAA decided it was time to increase the pressure on Greitzer

and started circulating a petition that demanded she introduce a City Council bill barring antigay discrimination and repealing existing sodomy laws.[81]

Sylvia Rivera had previously taken part in several GAA "zaps," including one against Mayor John V. Lindsay for refusing to speak out on gay rights, but somehow the petition drive caught her fancy and she decided to give it her full, formidable energy. Since she was still working Forty-second Street on a part-time basis, Sylvia decided to do her petition work right there. She parked herself in the middle of Forty-second between Seventh and Eighth Avenues and, dressed in partial drag, her auburn hair flying, raucously called out to passersby, "Sign this petition! Please sign this petition to help change the laws against homosexuals!" Some people did stop and sign. Others moved nervously on, eyes straight ahead. A few asked questions in a friendly way, but wouldn't sign. And a few others shouted slurs about "faggots."[82]

Sylvia's street-hustling friends stood around and gaped with amazement at the sister's audacity ("This be the butchest thing you ever done, girl!"), and several warned her that she was asking for trouble. But for several nights in a row Sylvia managed to gather her signatures with no interference. Then, at about seven-thirty on the night of April 15, she suddenly saw a crowd of people running toward her. She was startled and frightened—until someone explained that the Tactical Patrol Force had just broken up an antiwar demonstration in nearby Bryant Park. And right behind the fleeing crowd, of course, came a number of TPF police dressed in full riot gear.

"Move on," one of them yelled at Sylvia, "and make it snappy." Sylvia held her ground. "I'm only getting signatures to stop the discrimination against homosexuals," she said. "You have to move," the cop repeated. "Well, I'm not moving," said Sylvia, a little surprised and more than a little alarmed at her own firmness. "I got my constitutional rights, just like everybody else. I got the right to stand here and petition to change the laws just like anybody else."

"Not without an American flag, you don't," the cop said, surprisingly patient. "You can't set up a stand without an American flag—that's the law." Sylvia still wouldn't budge. "Now don't give me that," she said, her voice rising. "Number one, I'm not out here preaching the gospel like Rosy down the street. I been to jail with Rosy many a time because you don't let her preach even though she *has* the American flag." By now a police cruiser had pulled up behind Sylvia and she started to feel "a little shaky," afraid they would beat

her up. Instead they arrested her on charges of "disorderly conduct" and "incitement to riot," threw her into the cruiser, and took her to the Fourteenth Precinct station.

Now she was worried she might lose her job at the A & P warehouse in Jersey if she didn't show up for the start of her eleven P.M. shift. She wanted to call her boss, but a Legal Aid lawyer told her she would have to plead guilty before they'd let her use the phone. Sylvia refused: "I'm not pleading guilty to nothing! I'm not pleading guilty to a charge that's unjust!" The lawyer finally got her out on fifty dollars bail. Fortunately she had just been paid from her warehouse job and was able to put up the money.

By now it was midnight. She called her sympathetic boss, who told her it was too late to bother to come to work, so she decided to head back up to Forty-second Street and try for a few more signatures—"and I wasn't even high on black beauties." This time nobody bothered her, and later she went to her friend Josie's apartment to sleep. The next evening she and Josie went down to the GAA meeting in the Village, and the reporter Arthur Bell overheard her tearfully telling someone about her escapade the previous night. Knowing a good story when he heard one, Bell took Sylvia and Josie back to his own apartment to get the full account. Soon after, he published it as an article in *Gay Power*, and Sylvia was made as a movement celebrity. Thereafter, as she puts it, "I could just snap my fingers and everyone would come running." A couple of people in GAA wanted to nominate her for office, but Sylvia said she "couldn't be bothered"—she wanted to "argue with the hierarchy, not be the hierarchy."[83]

But she did have to go back to court. Again accompanied by Josie (who died the following year of a drug overdose), Sylvia arrived at 100 Centre Street in a lavender pantsuit she had sewn herself; it had wide bell-bottoms and a tunic top, and across the blouse she had embroidered "GAA." She didn't have a lawyer and was scared to death, but when she pushed open the door into the courtroom, she let out a gasp. Dozens of gay men and lesbians from both GAA and GLF filled the seats, and they jumped to their feet and started to applaud as soon as Sylvia appeared. The case dragged on over a four-month period, and was eventually thrown out of court when the arresting officer failed to show up. In all likelihood, his superiors had told him not to, since the incident had already gotten more publicity than they wanted. But Sylvia, in a twist of illogic, prefers to believe that the no-show cop was the same one—"a Jewish cop, very good-

looking, from Ocean Avenue in Brooklyn"—who she later discovered had signed her petition.[84]

Sylvia was part of the thirty-five-person gay activist delegation that went to the May 13 meeting of the Village Independent Democrats in order to confront Greitzer with the accumulated petition signatures. Jim Owles stood up at the meeting and declared it an outrage that homosexuals could not petition their own representative for a redress of grievances. Greitzer tried to get the VID chairman to explain that she had a bad cold and couldn't talk, but he insisted that she state her views. So she reluctantly took the microphone and said that the state attorney general was the person to introduce gay rights legislation, that she wouldn't be able to get such a measure through the City Council. And then she bumblingly added that she had no room to store the petitions in her desk.[85]

Owles asked her at least to make a public statement declaring herself on the side of gay rights—just as she had made statements in favor of women's rights and black rights. Greitzer responded obliquely, suggesting that the activists gather documentation for their claims of job discrimination. Asked point-blank by Marty Robinson if she would cosponsor an antidiscrimination bill, Greitzer said yes —in a tone Arthur Bell later described as one of "exasperated defeat." She also agreed in the end to accept the petitions—though when a GAA member later asked her to affix her own signature, Greitzer purportedly answered, "I really don't have your problem," and walked away.

Sylvia claims—though the incident is not reported in any of the other existing accounts—that at some point in the proceedings, she lost patience with Greitzer, rolled up the petitions she had herself collected and "bopped Greitzer upside the head" with them, yelling "Well, you're going to take them now, bitch!" A few weeks later, again according to Sylvia, she spotted Greitzer walking with two men on Forty-second Street, rushed up to her, called her "a fucking whore," and screamed, "Whatsa matter? You don't make enough money in the City Council, you have to come up here and steal the money from your queens, huh? You fuckin' bitch!" Greitzer, as Sylvia tells it, looked terrified, told one of the men to get the car and, pointing at Sylvia, said to the other man, "That's the one. The mean one. Because he's out." "You betcha life, bitch!" Sylvia purportedly shouted at Greitzer as she got in the car, "Don't forget—the name is Ray Sylvia Rivera, honey. And I will bop you upside your head again!"[86]

Y V O N N E

Yvonne and her black lesbian friends decided to try again. Their earlier attempts to meet together on a regular basis had dissolved after a few months, and they thought that might have been because they had held their meetings at the Firehouse, headquarters of the overwhelmingly white GAA. So this time around they started meeting in the gym of a church, a space gotten for them by one of their own group, a minister. A few Hispanic women joined them, and occasionally an Asian woman would show up as well.

By early 1970, the feeling was well advanced that it was necessary for like-categorized people to meet apart from others (however dissimilar the individuals thus categorized might turn out to be). The "Black Power" concept had by then weakened integrationist civil rights organizations, and within the gay movement not only were women of color separating themselves from white women, but also the feeling that lesbians should meet separately from gay men had become common.

Many men in GLF supported the women's movement, and some of them gave it a good deal more than lip service. Still, they had been socialized as men and despite good intentions and vigorous efforts at self-examination in consciousness-raising groups, many proved unable to rid themselves of the assumption that their male insights were superior, their male leadership essential, their male issues paramount. Nor did the lesbians in GLF feel any greater understanding from their straight sisters in the women's movement. Lesbians were tolerated rather than welcomed even in most of the radical feminist groups, and had frequently felt misunderstood and patronized.[87]

And so GLF lesbians inaugurated a Women's Caucus, which met every Wednesday night and, in April of 1970, held the first all-women's dance. Though Karla Jay continued to feel some uneasiness that the separation of women from men might sap the overall strength of the gay movement, she helped to organize the lesbian GLF action that marked the opening session of the second Congress to Unite Women on May 1, 1970. While three hundred women were sitting quietly in the auditorium waiting for the Congress to come to order, the lights suddenly went out. When they came back on, thirty or so

women wearing LAVENDER MENACE T-shirts had taken over the stage. They held the convention floor for two hours, trying to explain to their straight sisters what it was like to be lesbian in a heterosexist culture, and succeeded in getting a set of pro-lesbian resolutions passed.

Dramatic as that action was (and huge fun for those who planned and executed it), lesbianism hardly swept the feminist field. Betty Friedan, for one, was furious at the "Lavender Menace" action and continued to do her considerable best to keep lesbians from holding office in NOW's New York chapter. Running into Karla at a meeting more than a decade later, Friedan *still* seemed to be fuming over what had happened in 1970. Pointing an angry finger at Karla, she hissed, "*You* caused me a lot of trouble." Karla told her to lighten up, that that had been a long time ago.[88]

The separation of women from men in gay organizations was paralleled by the separation of women of color from white women in the feminist movement. Indeed, with a few exceptions, most black women had never participated in the women's movement, dismissing it as irrelevant to their primary needs and preferring to put their energies into black causes—a situation that was not to change significantly until the 1980s. But in Yvonne's case, the black movement had proven no solution either. Whenever she had joined a black-oriented march, demonstration, or sit-in, she had come away angry and disappointed at the black male's macho insistence on running the show and on relegating women to an "appropriately" subordinate role.

Yvonne *was* black *and* lesbian, but the black movement recoiled from both her strength and her sexuality, while the white gay movement had an incomplete understanding of issues relating to her color (and gay men, of issues relating to gender). She rejected the bifurcations that her committed membership in either movement would have demanded of her; sanity—wholeness—seemed to dictate that she confine her allegiance to those who would accept all aspects of her being: namely, her own black lesbian sisters.

Despite the abortive effort to form an organization at the Firehouse, and then a second brief attempt at cohesion that also failed to survive, the black lesbian women were determined on a third try. Most of those who attended the new round of meetings came in couples (including Yvonne, who brought Yolanda, a black–Puerto Rican woman she had been seeing a lot of). As they had in their previous attempts, the women opted for an unstructured organization based on the principle of rotating leadership and devoted to grass-roots in-

itiatives. They named the new group The Black Lesbian Counseling Collective.

But despite the name, the women were not in agreement about the group's purpose. Many of them were looking for a support group and a social alternative to the bars. But a minority, Yvonne among them, wanted to do "more outreach, more direct service to other lesbians, more political stuff." The division was between those who felt they had to get *themselves* together before they could do work in the world, and those, like Yvonne, who felt that doing work in the world was *how* people got themselves together.

Establishing a stable core of members also became a problem. The number present at each meeting varied widely. Sometimes only three or four people would show up; sometimes there would be forty. The Reverend Delores Berry, the minister who had earlier found church space for the group, was herself soon reassigned to Washington, D.C. Some of the Hispanic sisters, moreover, seemed restive in a setting dominated by black women (and indeed would later form the separate organization Las Buenas Amigas). And finally, what Yvonne calls "intrigue and seduction" also began to take a toll. Even in so self-selected and marginal an enterprise, struggles for control developed—bids to be powerful *somewhere*. Romantic infatuations, moreover, began to wreak havoc with the stability of the couples involved—people "started messing with each other's friends and whatnot."

Yvonne herself began to resent the special aura that, in the broader community of black lesbians, had begun to settle over the writers and artists among them. To her mind, there should be no special status among equals, no elite group that was somehow considered better than everyone else. She would argue angrily that lesbians were inventing "a new class"—a phenomenon she considered absurd, since they were already "on the bottom rung—as women, as people of color, and as lesbians." To elevate a few women in their midst, to suggest that those few were worthy of special privilege or had a special place, seemed to Yvonne a contradiction of the group's egalitarian, grass-roots orientation.

And she put special blame for this development on some of the artists themselves. She felt they "were there on an ego trip"; they would do a reading from their work, enjoy the attention and adulation—but then not come back on any regular basis, "were not really committed to the women there or to the organization." Yvonne herself wrote poetry now and then, good poetry:

. . . Now you can't always tell a black goddess
by how she looks.
She may laugh too loud or
stand in the middle of a silence
like my Grandma at the kitchen table
mixing cornmeal and egg.
But you can't always tell a black goddess
by what she cooks.
She may not,
or burns it,
or cooks only your flesh. . . .[89]

And a few years later, she would join the black lesbian Jamima Collective, started by Georgia Brooks. But Yvonne was determined not to let her literary efforts overshadow her political ones. And she did feel that a choice between them was necessary: "Was I going to write or was I going to do?" She made a fierce resolution that henceforth she would write maybe one piece a year, and for the rest of the time, "would live my politics rather than write about them."

Her chief work, Yvonne decided, was "to empower black lesbians to come out and to organize." A few years hence, when her long-standing physical problems had finally been diagnosed as lupus, she added health issues to her political agenda. She wanted to share with others what that disease—what any serious illness—can do to a woman's sense of herself. "So this is the work," she concluded. "I'd rather do that than write a *piece* about the poor women who are suffering from lupus. Or my personal suffering with lupus."

The third effort to form a black and Hispanic lesbian organization, beset by tensions, also failed to sustain itself. But many of the women had not only made contact, but had formed lasting bonds with each other. From those bonds, Salsa Soul Sisters would soon emerge. And this fourth time around, the glue would hold. Though Salsa Soul, too, would go through many transformations and some disaffection, it continues down to the present day; it is now called African Ancestral Lesbians United for Societal Change. And Yvonne, the last of the original founders, is still consistently active in its councils.

CRAIG, FOSTER, JIM, SYLVIA, KARLA, YVONNE

The first thing Craig did, after the final ERCHO convention in November 1969 gave its blessing to the formation of a Christopher Street Liberation Day Committee, was to diplomatically send out notices to all of ERCHO's constituent groups that such a committee had indeed come into existence. The niceties performed, Craig then had to find people to do the actual work. He began by notifying all the New York gay groups of the committee's formation and—making clear (more niceties) that the planned celebration was not owned by any one organization—asked that they send representatives.

GAA delayed until some six weeks before the celebration, and Mattachine was overtly negative until the last minute, when DOB also decided to join in. But GLF responded immediately, and from that group Brenda Howard, Marty Nixon, and Michael Brown became mainstays. To fill out the committee, Craig buttonholed some of his regular customers at the Oscar Wilde Bookshop, and managed to bag Judy Miller, recently arrived in New York from Denver, and a pair of lovers, Jack Waluska and Steve Gerrie. All three turned out to be hard workers, and stayed the course.

Foster Gunnison was part of the organizing committee from the beginning. He and Craig were in some ways at opposite ends of the political spectrum—"conservative" and "radical," in common usage. Yet those ends do meet ideologically in conservatives and radicals who identify as "libertarians" ("anarchists" is the preferred term on the left); what they share is a distrust of authority, a distrust that on the right (Foster) focuses primarily on the state, and on the left (Craig) becomes a more encompassing rejection of all established pieties handed down by church, state, law, and family.

The two men came from sharply different class backgrounds, yet took to each other as human beings, recognizing, beneath their contrasting styles, the same basic warmth and decency—which both were too modest to acknowledge about themselves. Craig was fascinated by the anomalous Foster, the only dedicated gay activist he had ever met who smoked cigars, wore three-piece Brooks Brothers suits, sported a crew cut, and spoke in an accent vaguely redolent of some upper-crust private school—"the house dick," Craig used to call him.

Foster was well aware that in both appearance and opinion he "stood out like a sore thumb" in the countercultural sixties, and that made him grateful for Craig's recognition that beneath the starchy exterior, Foster was in fact "a puppy." He, in turn, thought Craig was "a swell fellow," honest, reliable, and, by Foster's lights, also something of an anomaly—the hardworking, no-nonsense type, willing day after day to do laborious detail work, that Foster thought did not exist among the radical young. Craig was now thirty, considerably older than most of the new activists, and not closely identified either with GLF or GAA—but he was still a "kid" to forty-five-year-old Foster.[90]

Foster sometimes lamented Craig's "dislike of structure," his individualistic insistence on "doing his own thing," and his determination that the CSLDC (Christopher Street Liberation Day Committee) be a grass-roots project uncontaminated by any connection to commercial interests (such as gay bars) and uncorrupted by prior organizational loyalties (Foster confessed to harboring some hope that ERCHO could be rebuilt on CSLDC's activities). But despite these minor disagreements and annoyances—inevitable in any ongoing, close-quarters organizational work—Foster fully credited Craig with being the heartbeat of the committee: He was "like a guru," Foster later said, "everything revolved around him, and yet he was very unassuming. It was almost like a spirit sitting in the room."[91]

In February 1970, the small group of eight or so people began to meet monthly in Craig's apartment on Bleecker Street; in April, as deadlines approached, they met weekly. Foster came down faithfully from Hartford for every meeting, serving as the group's official treasurer and helping Marty Nixon keep track of assorted financial transactions. The group had hoped to add a two-day block festival in Greenwich Village to the planned march, but that fell by the wayside when they discovered that city ordinances required the posting of a million dollars worth of bonds to "protect against damage." By April 1970, the committee had firmly focused on a "march for freedom" through midtown Manhattan up to Central Park, where "a variety of activities and events, planned or spontaneous," would follow in Sheep Meadow. In its bulletins and press releases, the committee continuously announced its hope that other gay and lesbian organizations across the land would sponsor comparable efforts in their own localities.[92]

The first anniversary of the onset of the Stonewall riots would have fallen on June 27, 1970, but the committee decided to hold the

celebration on Sunday, June 28. They believed that more people would be free to participate on a Sunday and that it would be easier to obtain permits and in general to cut through red tape. To raise operating funds for the planned event, the committee tried various strategies. Foster sent out notices to "All East Coast Homophile Organizations" asking for $10 donations, and he also sent an "appeal" to individuals, along with a rather peremptory pitch: "I have often thought," Foster wrote, "that the least a homosexual can do—if he doesn't want to get involved in public demonstrations or action-oriented programs—is to contribute cash to enable programs to be conducted by others on his behalf. Will you agree with that?" Not much resulted from either effort. Two months before the scheduled march, seven organizations had sent in a measly total of a hundred dollars—and Dick Leitsch, speaking for the New York Mattachine Society, had declared himself against the notion of a march entirely.[93]

But in 1970 it took only about a thousand dollars to put on the Christopher Street Liberation Day March, and Craig brought in additional money by asking his bookstore customers for donations. (He also found a twenty-dollar bill on the street and, deciding that "God has sent it for the march," added it to the treasury.) It helped, in making ends meet, that Michael Sabanosh, a graphic designer, did all of CSLDC's announcements, posters, and buttons free of charge, and that Marty Nixon, who had a job with the Arthritis Foundation, stayed late after work to surreptitiously grind out thousands of pages of CSLDC material on the Foundation's photocopy machine.[94]

In the spring of 1970, Karla was thrown so hard to the mat during a judo match that she broke several ribs. Stoic about physical pain, she hobbled along for a week. But then, when she was on her way to a GLF meeting one night, the pain grew so severe that her friend Alan Sample finally persuaded her to go to nearby St. Vincent's Hospital in Greenwich Village. The doctors there were convinced that she had been battered and they called in the police. Feeling mischievous, Karla gave Alan—who had long blond hair and looked like Greta Garbo—a glance as if to say, "What if I tell them you did it? Wouldn't that be a hoot, the idea of *you* beating up *me*?" Knowing Karla's penchant for practical jokes, Alan gave her a beseeching look back, as if to say "Don't do this to me!" So Karla bit her lip in restraint, and the police let them go.

It was clear she wouldn't be able to work for a while, which was no great blow to her. She hated the new job she had taken at Collier's

Encyclopedia: "It was very right-wing. We all hated it there. It was like the Gestapo. They had dress rules and I was in constant battles with them to wear pants." Besides, her boss had seen her picture in the paper as part of the *Ladies' Home Journal* action, and Karla was sure the reaction would be "So *that's* what she does with her day off—she seizes magazines." She thought maybe she ought to quit before being fired.

The urge was part and parcel of her growing ambivalence about graduate school. She had made some good gay male and lesbian friends at NYU, including Rita Mae Brown and Alan Sample, and she enjoyed reading for her courses. But she had been increasingly treated in class as The Feminist, and being mechanically turned to ("And what does Karla, The Feminist, think?") had angered her. She had told the professors to try finding out what some of the other women in class felt, but they had gone right on patronizing her as their token revolutionary.

Karla decided the time had come for a break from a hateful job and a conflicted academic career. It seemed an ideal time to take disability and to go sit in California for a while. She waited until early June so that she could participate in a big antiwar march. And then she headed out to the West Coast.

Jim Fouratt's lover in 1970 was Peter Hujar, who had been one of Richard Avedon's prize pupils and was in his own right already a well-known fashion photographer. Jim thought Hujar was "the most handsome man I had ever seen in my life; he looked exactly like Gary Cooper." But Hujar was notoriously difficult, too—which was perhaps understandable for a man whose mother had twice tried to kill him after discovering that he was gay.

Hujar was interested in Jim's political activities but, after going along to a few GLF meetings, had decided he wasn't *that* interested. Still, he wanted to do "something." About a month before the Christopher Street March was due to take place, Jim came up with a "something" that caught Hujar's fancy: take a photograph of a group of gay liberationists running joyously through the streets, fists clenched on high, à la the Paris Commune, that could be used as a poster to advertise the coming march.

Hujar took to the idea immediately. But bringing it to fruition proved difficult. Jim set up a telephone chain call asking all GLF members willing to be photographed to show up for the shoot at the designated time, day, and street (a semi-deserted area in the West

Twenties). The response was less than overwhelming. Appearing on the poster would be tantamount to publicly coming out, and in 1970 that was still a terrifying prospect for most people. Many of the phone messages went unanswered, and many others called back to stammer invented regrets or to express real fears.

Ultimately, some fifteen people showed up to be photographed. Hujar had them run back and forth, back and forth, down the deserted street, shouting and laughing in triumph. Dressed in the pseudo-shabby workers' drag then fashionable, they looked as if they had been recently liberated from the Bastille—and had somehow emerged singing.

In the final poster, the fifteen marchers crowd the center, and it only gradually becomes clear that the sidewalks behind them are empty; these ebullient troops seem to have no backup forces. What also becomes apparent is the nearly equal number of women and men—though in GLF itself the women were far outnumbered. That ratio seemed proud confirmation to some that the women were more willing to put up than the men were to shut up.[95]

Some of the participants had nervously hoped that the photo would take its place in the revolutionary pantheon alongside Black Panther posters and those from the 1968 French student uprising. They had expected to see it on every wall of every building—a rallying cry to come out and march in the Liberation Day Parade. But the poster was a good deal less omnipresent than that. Its real visibility came only later, when it was widely and continuously displayed on the walls of movement organizations, bookstores, and offices. Still, enough people saw it at the time to give those who had participated some strange turns. Being recognized from the poster meant being subjected to strained, worried looks from friends and even strangers, looks that seemed to say "You realize, of course, that your life is finished."

That could make the participants momentarily catch their breath, fear suddenly surging back. And they had to quickly remind themselves that their lives felt much more like they were just beginning.

The night before the march, GLF held an open house at the Washington Square Methodist Church on West Fourth Street in the Village; they offered food, housing information, literature, and around-the-clock talk. At the Church of the Holy Apostles, at Twenty-eighth Street and Ninth Avenue, a comparable set of events for women

featured a bring-your-own communal supper, a "dance–party–rap session," and the promise that for the entire weekend, "there will always be sisters around with literature or time to talk. Women with no place to go or no spirit to get there can crash at the church."[96]

And over at Alternate U., a two-person team from the Quaker Project on Community Conflict was giving a crash course on crowd control to a hundred hastily gathered marshals. Many of them were still feeling skittish about having decided to march, to say nothing of taking on the responsibility of a marshal's role. As one of them later put it, "I decided I would march, but I left little clauses in my mind. . . . If I didn't feel good, I wouldn't go. If there was any violence, I would drop out. . . . If the march was going to include too many effeminate men or butch women, I would drop out. . . ."[97]

The Quaker team warned the marshals about what everybody already knew: No one had any idea how many people would show up in the morning or how much violence to expect. Nor could anyone predict whether the cops would contain or abet hostility among the spectators toward the marchers. "Be prepared for anything," the Quakers warned. Then, for several hours, they helped the novice marshals simulate pugnacious situations of all sorts. "Cocksucker!" one man was told to shout angrily at another as he lunged toward him, while the others were shown how to surround and "smother" the two combatants.[98]

Karla had arrived in Los Angeles some three weeks before the scheduled march and, though ostensibly resting, had quickly gotten involved with the local GLF. She found the same divisions that had characterized the New York group: The women and men had begun to tangle and some of the more radical men, like Sandy Blixton, were at odds strategically with moderates like Morris Kight. But the worst of the antagonisms were put on (temporary) hold in order to plan the first Christopher Street West Parade.

As it was, arrangements were begun belatedly; the request for a parade permit was submitted just four days before the deadline—and then the Police Commission insisted on security bonds totaling a million and a quarter dollars. Police Chief Ed Davis said publicly that giving the marchers a permit would be like "discommoding the citizens by permitting a parade of thieves and burglars"; he further predicted that should such a march take place, it would be mobbed by hard hats. The ACLU brought suit on behalf of Christopher Street West

—and in a photo finish, the presiding judge ruled, just hours before the march was due to begin, that the amount of money demanded in bonds was unprecedented and therefore excessive.

In New York, Sunday, June 28, dawned cloudless and cool—"An omen, an omen! *She*'s on our side!"' was the nervous chorus in a thousand apartments across the city. Craig had barely slept, and Foster, arriving the night before from Hartford, had been up late talking with friends and reviewing his chronometer calculations for measuring crowd size.

Sylvia was itching to get going; after facing the random violence of the streets for most of her life, she viewed a daytime march up Sixth Avenue, surrounded by friends, as a piece of cake. One of her street-queen buddies announced she would be wearing her hair in a bun—"suffragette-serious"—out of respect for the solemnity of the occasion, and would do her best not to "pluck people's nerves."

Jim, uncharacteristically, had recently taken something of a backseat; in the last weeks, as GAA had rapidly accelerated its involvement in the march, leafleting the Village, hosting a big dance at NYU, he had grown concerned that the GAA "reformers" would somehow dull the cutting edge. Jim would march, of course, but would stay close to the GLF banner.

As for Yvonne, so long on the organizational sidelines, she thought she just *might* join the march; she set her alarm, anyway, putting off a final decision until the morning.

Craig anxiously paced his apartment early Sunday. Half a dozen meetings over the preceding months with the Sixth Precinct had—just as in Los Angeles—failed to win a permit, and though the promise of one had finally been made, the permit had *still* not arrived. He was determined to go ahead regardless, especially since a second permit, to congregate in Central Park's Sheep Meadow after the march, *had* been obtained (though, again, only after half a dozen meetings). Just as Craig was about to give up and leave his apartment, the Sixth Precinct permit was delivered.

He raced up to the assembly point, on Washington Place between Sixth and Seventh Avenues. The police were already there—lots of them. They had set up sawhorses for crowd control, and dozens of cops lined the march perimeter. Most of them looked indifferent, even bored, as if this were just another parade, water off a duck's back. No more than a handful of cops seemed openly hostile, and even they,

unwilling to acknowledge that such a gathering was *worth* their anger, opted for the snickering, offhanded joke. All of which was expected. The one real surprise was when a couple of the cops accepted leaflets being passed out—and when one or two were seen actually reading them.

The march wasn't scheduled to kick off until two P.M., but by late morning the marshals, with their orange armbands, were already in place, and knots of people had begun to mill around. It was impossible to tell how many had come to gape and how many to march, and Craig, now joined by Foster, nervously agreed that "not that many were going to end up marching"; Craig thought *maybe* a thousand. Had they overestimated political awareness in the community? Were people too frightened to show up—or too lazy to get out of bed on Sunday? By one P.M., an hour before the official starting time, there were still only enough apparent marchers to spread out for about two thirds of a block.

Craig held down any feelings of disappointment, reminding himself that he had successfully argued for making the march a reasonably long one, from the Village up Sixth Avenue into Central Park, on the assumption that many of the older or less committed gays and lesbians would be afraid to start out with the marchers, but might later yield to impulse and fall in somewhere along the line. He cheered up still more when balloons and signs began to appear. BETTER BLATANT THAN LATENT made him laugh out loud.

At two-ten, the march was still being held in place; some of the organizers apparently felt that a short delay might help to swell the ranks with latecomers. But the day had grown considerably warmer, and as people anxiously waited for the kickoff signal, with marchers and onlookers eyeing each other warily, with members of the news media dashing in and out of the crowd in search of the still-more-flamboyant queen, the still-angrier militant, and with marshals warning people to remove their glasses and loose jewelry "just in case," discomfort steadily grew. Word of an incident that had happened the previous night snaked its way insidiously through the crowd: At one A.M. five young gay men had been set upon in the Village by a group of toughs and beaten up; a cruising police car had finally rescued them, but at the station house the gay men had been urged to walk away from the incident and warned that if they pressed charges they would in all likelihood themselves be found guilty of "disorderly conduct."

By the time the kickoff came, at about two-fifteen, everyone, as

Foster put it, was "scared to death." As they fell in under their organizational banners—the GAAers notably resplendent in blue T-
shirts with gold lambda crests, the GLFers crowded under a banner
adorned with same-sex symbols—they shouted encouragement at each
other, hugged their neighbors fiercely, raised clenched fists in the air,
and spread their fingers wide in the V sign—for many, less a gesture
of absolute defiance than a cover for embarrassment, an antidote for
fear.

Confined to the far left lane of Sixth Avenue, they hoisted their
signs high (HOMOSEXUAL IS NOT A FOUR–LETTER WORD; SAPPHO WAS A
RIGHT–ON WOMAN), shouted their transgressive slogans—"Two, four,
six, eight / Gay is just as good as straight"; "Ho-ho-homosexual / The
ruling class is ineffectual." And right up front, leading the cheers all
along the sixty-block route, was Sylvia. "Gimme a G!" she screamed
over and over. "Gimme an A . . . a Y . . . a P . . . an O . . . a W
. . . an E . . . an R . . . Whadda we want? *Gay Power!* When do we
want it? *Now!*"

The kickoff in Los Angeles was just as fervent, a splash of color and
sound down Hollywood Boulevard that had all the panache of what
one reporter called "a political Mardi Gras." Some thirty organizations
were represented, with GLF/LA and Troy Perry's Metropolitan Community Church among the largest. GLF members took turns por-
traying Jesus tied to a cross, being continuously prodded by a cop—
with a nearby sign reading KILLED BY LAPD and listing the names of
four homosexuals purportedly beaten to death by the L.A. police.

Transsexual Connie Vaughan, over six feet tall, rode proudly in
an open convertible, and underground gay porn stars from Pat Rocco's
films rode in other cars. Lesbian separatists did an intermittent group
can-can. Banners and signs (some of which had caused controversy
within the organizing committee) declared that FUCKING IS BETTER
THAN KILLING and advocated MAKE LOVE, NOT BABIES. And a pickup
truck exhibited an eight-foot-tall plaster-of-Paris Vaseline jar with
"Gay Petroleum Jelly" on the label and an accompanying sign declaring AIN'T NOTHIN' NO GOOD WITHOUT THE GREASE. New Yorker
Karla Jay found it all "*so* Hollywood!"

Karla had donned a lavender T-shirt for the march; she laughed
out loud at her sartorial modesty when she ran into two male gender-
fuck friends, Mother Boats and Jefferson Fuck Poland: Jeff was wearing a woman's bikini bottom, long hair—and nothing else. As in New
York, a lot of closeted gays and lesbians watched from the sidewalk,

but unlike New York, L.A. seems to have had a fair number of hecklers. Though the L.A. newspapers reported a relatively noncommittal crowd—without outbursts of either violence or spontaneous applause—veteran activist Jim Kepner heard a lot more cheers than that, and Karla ran into a fair amount of hostility. Whenever she tried to rest—her ribs still bothering her—people would gather around and shout nasty remarks. And at several different points, she saw bystanders angrily throwing things at the marchers.

Yvonne had awakened late with a hangover and had taken additional hours to make up her mind. It was nearly two when she finally got disgusted with her own ambivalence, jumped in her car, and headed in from Brooklyn to the Village. By the time she got to Washington Place a half hour later, the marchers had already set off. Now determined to take part, Yvonne hurried uptown to find and join them. Just as she rounded the corner approaching Macy's department store at Thirty-fourth Street, there they were—placards and banners waving bravely in the sun, voices raised on high.

She fell into the march—was *pulled* in by the sounds and sights, like so many others who had initially watched from the sidewalks, nervously calculating the risks. The exhilaration of the moment overwhelmed most calculations, just as Craig had hoped. Joining in was a major turning point for Yvonne: "It was clear to me from then on that it could no longer be just about partying. I had to save and protect myself by committing to my own liberation. It was like work time. . . ."

Foster, running back and forth through the line of marchers with his chronometer, sampling the numbers, realized with a thrill that the size of the march had more than doubled, that at least two thousand people were now taking part. Though later estimates would go as high as five thousand to ten thousand, the two FBI agents present at the march sent a teletype to J. Edgar Hoover that agreed with Foster's count: "approximately two thousand individuals." That made it twice the size of the four or five other Stonewall commemorative marches that came off across the country. Chicago managed to put fewer than a hundred people on the streets, while Los Angeles, with twelve hundred marchers, had the second-biggest turnout. By the following year, there were public celebrations in London and Paris.[99]

The marshals, fearing hostility from the onlookers and prodded by the cops, had kept the march moving at a rapid clip. But little overt anger was seen along the route. Many of those watching from the sidelines seemed to be gay; sometimes silently, and sometimes

noisily, they urged the marchers on. "You're doing it for us" seemed to be their message, even as they themselves ricocheted between exhilaration and fear.

Aside from a few predictable SODOM AND GOMORRAH signs, and a Black Panther newspaper hawker shouting, "Get the Panther paper and stop all this foolishness!" the reaction of the spectators ranged from frozen to benign to overtly encouraging. The only persistent pests were tourists snapping photographs. They would rush up—"Oh look, Jane, that lesbian is eating *an ice cream cone!*"—and stick a camera in the startled lesbian's face, determined to immortalize the sight of one of the depraved licking away like the innocent child she wasn't.

It took only a little more than an hour to reach Central Park. Foster, forty-five years old and overweight, staggered in, huffing and puffing, but elated. Craig was so excited he could hardly stop smiling—at the size of the crowd, the good feeling and courage everywhere manifest. Karla, in L.A., let out a whoop when she crossed the finish line, her back killing her, her spirit soaring. Sylvia arrived yelling, Yvonne in exhausted tears. Jim, too, had tears pouring down his face as he stood on a rise in the ground and looked back at the line of people stretching some fifteen blocks into the distance: "I saw what we had done. It was remarkable. There we were in all of our diversity."

They were all, in their own ways, euphoric, just as, in their own ways, they had all somehow come through, had managed to arrive at this unimaginable coming together, this testimony to a difficult past surmounted and a potentially better future in view.

E P I L O G U E : 1 9 9 3

YVONNE FLOWERS continues to teach occupational therapy at York College, CUNY. During the seventies she was politically active with a wide variety of groups, including Black Women for Wages for Housework, the National Black Feminist Organization, and the Center for Women's Development at Medgar Evers College. She also founded "Sweet Sensations," a group that organized erotic "Tupperware parties as a means for increasing women's right to sexuality." In the mid-seventies, she got a second master's degree and, as part of an ongoing process of reclaiming her African-American heritage, changed her first name to Maua ("Flowers" in Swahili). She has long since given up drugs and alcohol, but is still afflicted with lupus.

JIM FOURATT has never ceased to be a political activist, of recent years dividing his time between New York City and Los Angeles. He was a founding board member of the Lesbian and Gay Community Services Center in New York and of Wipe Out AIDS (now known as H.E.A.L.), as well as a cofounder of ACT UP. In addition, he has been a contributing editor of SPIN magazine and writes a cultural column, "Ear Candy," syndicated in the gay press. He is currently (1993) working as the director of national publicity for Rhino Records.

FOSTER GUNNISON remained active in the CSLDC through 1973, but by the mid-seventies had phased himself out of the gay liberation movement—except for his archival work, which continues to this day.

Thereafter, he spent a decade cofounding several conservative political organizations in Connecticut, wrote for business magazines, and did research for the *National Conservative Digest*. In recent years he has taken growing offense (as a devoted cigar smoker) at what he calls "the neo-prohibitionary" antismoking crusade, and has helped to found a national smokers' liberation movement, which occupies most of his time today.

KARLA JAY spent the early seventies doing movement work and wandering between New York and California. She preferred the latter, but could never find any literary work there; so she lived on food stamps, hung out at Venice Beach, and wrote. She finally got a teaching assistantship in the French department at NYU (Bronx campus) and returned East for good. She began teaching English at Pace University in 1974, completed her doctorate in Comparative Literature in 1984 and then rose to the rank of full professor at Pace. She has published a number of books, including (with Allen Young) the pathbreaking *Out of the Closets*, and is currently the editor of NYU Press's series *The Cutting Edge: Lesbian Life and Literature*.

SYLVIA RIVERA quit the gay movement in 1973. Her departure was precipitated by the bruising struggle on Gay Pride Day that year over her right to speak; the more encompassing reason was the general lack of visibility and acceptance in the movement of transvestites. But in honor of her own past, she has continued to march in the yearly Christopher Street Liberation Day Parade, missing only twice in twenty years. After a close friend died from an overdose, Sylvia decided to kick drugs (but not alcohol) cold turkey. Some ten years ago, she moved to Tarrytown, New York, where she has held a variety of jobs in food services.

CRAIG RODWELL is still the proprietor of the Oscar Wilde Memorial Bookshop in Greenwich Village, and still maintains deep respect for the teachings of Mary Baker Eddy. He has begun an autobiographical and theoretical work based on his experiences in the gay movement. Of recent years he has been particularly concerned with the lack of outreach and services for gay and lesbian youth.

N O T E S

(Pages 3–40)

GROWING UP

1. The description in the following pages of Foster Gunnison, Sr.'s career and marriage is drawn from material in the Gunnison Papers, kindly made available to me by Foster Gunnison, Jr. The following items have been of particular importance: Foster Gunnison, Sr., to William Adams Delano, Dec. 14, 1954; *St. Petersburg* (Florida) *Independent*, Oct. 20, 1961 (Gunnison obit); "A Keystone for a Nickel," *Forbes*, April 15, 1940; *The Prefabricated House, #*1: "A Movement Emerges," *Architectural Forum*, Dec. 1942; "Where Is Prefabrication?" *Fortune*, April 1946; "The Viceroys," *Life*, Nov. 11, 1946. Three towns in the United States—in Colorado, Utah, and Mississippi—carry the name Gunnison. For more information on the Gunnison family, see Russ Gammon, "Who Was John Gunnison?" *The Gunnison Country Times*, Dec. 28, 1988; George W. Gunnison, *A Genealogy of the Descendants of Hugh Gunnison . . . 1610–1876* (George A. Foxcroft, 1880); Foster N. Gunnison and Herbert Foster Gunnison, eds., *An Autobiography of the Reverend Nathaniel Gunnison* (Herbert Foster Gunnison, publisher, 1910); and Dwayne Vandenbusche, *The Gunnison Country* (B & B Printers, 1980).
2. The following letters in the Gunnison Papers have been the sources for reconstructing Foster Gunnison, Jr.'s college career: Gunnison Sr. to Gunnison Jr., Feb. 8, 21, 1945, Oct. 29, 1946; Thomas C. Gibb (Acting Dean) to Gunnison Sr., Feb. 6, 1945; Gunnison Jr. to Gunnison Sr., Feb. 1945; Evans to Gunnison Sr., June 14, 1945.

YOUNG ADULTHOOD

1. John D'Emilio, *Sexual Politics, Sexual Communities* (University of Chicago Press, 1983), pp. 98–99; Lillian Faderman, *Odd Girls and Twilight Lovers* (Columbia University Press, 1991), pp. 107–108, 127, 164–66.

2. For the information in this and the following paragraph: Eric Garber, "A Spectacle in Color: The Lesbian and Gay Subculture of Jazz Age Harlem," in Martin Duberman, Martha Vicinus, and George Chauncey, Jr., *Hidden From History: Reclaiming the Gay and Lesbian Past* (NAL, 1989; Meridian, 1990), pp. 318–31; and Lillian Faderman, *Odd Girls*, pp. 72–79.

3. The following description of lesbian life in the fifties and sixties draws especially on: Audre Lorde, *Zami: A New Spelling of My Name* (The Crossing Press, 1982), pp. 177–78 ("our rarity," the quotation in the next paragraph), 220–21, 224; "Audre Lorde & Maua Adele Ajanaku [Yvonne Flowers]: An Interview," in Andrea Weiss and Greta Schiller, *Before Stonewall: The Making of a Gay and Lesbian Community* (Naiad Press, 1988), pp. 54–55; Lillian Faderman, *Odd Girls*, chapter 7 (for "bluff," see p. 168).

4. For appreciations, however qualified, of lesbian pulp fiction, see Fran Koski and Maida Tilchen, "Some Pulp Sappho," in Karla Jay and Allen Young, eds., *Lavender Culture* (Jove/HBJ, 1978), pp. 262–74; Kate Brandt, "The Lifelines Still Hold," *Visibilities*, Jan.–Feb. 1991; Roberta Yusba, "Strange Sister: Literature of the Lurid," *Windy City Times*, June 22, 1989; and Diane Hamer, " 'I am a Woman': Ann Bannon and the Writing of Lesbian Identity in the 1950s," in Mark Lilly, ed., *Lesbian and Gay Writing: An Anthology of Critical Essays* (Temple University Press, 1990), pp. 47–75.

    For Claire Morgan, see Barbara Grier, *The Lesbian in Literature*, 3rd ed. (Naiad Press, 1981). Grier awards *The Price of Salt* an A***, which she gives only to "those few titles that stand out above all the rest and must properly belong in any collection of Lesbian literature." Bonnie Zimmerman's comprehensive study of lesbian fiction from 1969 to 1989, *The Safe Sea of Women* (Beacon, 1990), has a chapter dealing with pre-1969 work. There, Zimmerman agrees that most of the pulp fiction of the fifties contained "dreary portrayals of self-hating 'inverts' " (p. xi). But she singles out *The Price of Salt*, along with Jane Rule's *Desert of the Heart* (1964), as "sensitive and dignified . . . freed from stereotypes . . . [and containing characters] who make choices . . ." (p. 10) and who project "a positive and empowering image of lesbians" (p. xi).

5. This section draws on the following material in the Gunnison Papers, as well as on my interviews with Foster Gunnison, Jr.: press release by U.S. Steel, May 2, 1944; a "Confidential Report" on Gunnison Junior's test scores; Robert M. Vogel to Gunnison Sr., Oct. 29, 1954 ("such excellence"), Gunnison Jr. to Langhorn, May 23, 1960 (mathematical formula).

6. Little has been written about Joe Cino and his theater, but two articles do contain much useful detail: Michael Feingold, "Caffè Cino, 20 Years After Magic Time," *The Village Voice*, May 14, 1985; and Robert Heide, "Magic Time at the Caffè Cino," *New York Native*, May 6–19, 1985.

7. Arthur Bell, "The Sixties," in *The Christopher Street Reader*, eds. Michael Denneny, Charles Ortleb, and Thomas Steele (Coward-McCann, 1983), p. 28.

8. Much of the information and all of the quotes in this section come from my three interviews with Heide in 1990 and 1991.

    Heide had become connected with the Caffè Cino when Joe Cino offered him encouragement, and a home, after the critics had brutalized Heide's 1961 play, *West of the Moon*, one of the very first gay-themed plays ever done in New

York. (It had been preceded by Edward Albee's *The Zoo Story*, but the sexuality of the characters in that play was far more disguised than in Heide's; during the late fifties and early sixties, Albee and Heide were . . . good friends.)

Heide subsequently had two gay-themed plays produced at the Cino: *The Bed* (with sets and lights by Ron Link, and directed by Robert Dahdah), which ran for 150 performances in 1965; and *Moon*, which opened in 1967 and was performed widely in the late sixties. But in 1967, even so avant-garde a figure as Ellen Stewart, whose Café La Mama was an offshoot of Caffè Cino, was not cordial—though she later did provide a refuge for gay plays and playwrights (including Harvey Fierstein). In 1967, she told Heide, after seeing *The Bed*, that he should stop writing plays about homosexuals.

9. Interviews with Heide, 1990 and 1991. John Dodd had a distinguished later career in lighting; see Michael Smith's obituary in *The Village Voice*, Aug. 6, 1991. The Warhol quote is from Victor Bockris, *The Life and Death of Andy Warhol* (Bantam, 1990), p. 157.

10. The *Salute* article is reprinted in Martin Duberman, *About Time: Exploring the Gay Past*, 2nd ed. (Meridian, 1991), pp. 163–68. For the scene in the mid-sixties, see James Miller, "The Detective," *Life*, Dec. 3, 1965. Though the information and quotations in this section come almost entirely from my series of interviews with Sylvia Rivera in 1990 and 1991, I am indebted to Steven Watson's 1979 interview with her (tapes courtesy Watson) for some of the material relating to the Rivera-Johnson relationship.

THE EARLY SIXTIES

1. I am indebted to Jim Kepner (Kepner to Duberman, April 29, 1992) for some of the details in this paragraph. For more on Gerber, see Jonathan Katz, *Gay American History* (Meridian, 1992), and Jonathan Ned Katz, *Gay/Lesbian Almanac* (Harper & Row, 1983). Gerber's essay, "In Defense of Homosexuality," written under the pseudonym "Parisex," is reprinted in Martin Duberman, *About Time*, 2nd ed. (Meridian, 1991), pp. 145–48.

   For more detail on the other subjects in these introductory pages, see: on the World War II experience, Allan Bérubé, *Coming Out Under Fire: The History of Gay Men and Women in World War Two* (Plume, 1991); on the founding of Mattachine, John D'Emilio, *Sexual Politics, Sexual Communities: The Making of a Homosexual Minority in the United States, 1940–1970* (University of Chicago Press, 1983), pp. 57–74, and Stuart Timmons, *The Trouble with Harry Hay* (Alyson, 1990), pp. 139–72; on the origins and early years of DOB, D'Emilio, *Sexual Politics*, pp. 101–107.

2. I am grateful to Jim Kepner (Kepner to Duberman, April 29, 1992) for the analogy to Freemasons (which is more accurate than the Communist-party analogy often made).

3. According to Jim Kepner (Kepner to Duberman, April 29, 1992), *ONE*, which was led until 1960 (when Kepner left) by Kepner, Dorr Legg, and Don Slater, continued to adhere to the notion that gays were a legitimate minority. Another West Coast group, SIR, organized in 1964, took up that same view "in practical

ways," though the "minority" theory was "stridently opposed by [Franklin] Kameny & most Eastern leaders." As to the reference in the next paragraph to *ONE*, Kepner has pointed out that philosophically the magazine stood in much the same relation to Mattachine as the NAACP did to the Urban League: "Mattachine and DOB leaders accepted that comparison, regarding *ONE* & the NAACP as too pushy or strident."

4. Jim Kepner, *Our Movement Before Stonewall* (International Gay and Lesbian Archives [IGLA], 1989).

5. Hal Call, one of the conservative leaders of Mattachine San Francisco, inflated that city's membership rolls by soliciting small donations in bars and making the donors "members"; he then got them to sign over proxies to him, which he used to maintain control of the organization. According to Kepner, *ONE* magazine had twelve hundred subscribers by 1960, about four hundred of them classified as "members" because they gave donations beyond the magazine's subscription price. By the mid-sixties, *ONE* was averaging 2,300 copies sold per issue, far outdistancing *Mattachine Review* or *The Ladder*. ONE also began to expand organizationally, setting up chapters in other cities. Today ONE of Long Beach, now an independent group, is larger than the parent organization, which is today called ONE Incorporated (Kepner to Duberman, April 29, 1992).

6. For this section, the following sources were especially useful: Barry Miles, *Ginsberg: A Biography* (Simon and Schuster, 1989), pp. 252–53 (Monk); Eric Garber, "A Spectacle in Color: The Lesbian and Gay Subculture of Jazz Age Harlem," in Duberman, et al., *Hidden from History*, pp. 318–31 (Harlem rent parties); Ira L. Jeffries, "Strange Fruit of the Purple Manor," *NYQ*, Feb. 23, 1992 (house parties); Audre Lorde, *Zami*, pp. 217–18 (food).

7. George Chauncey, Jr., and Lisa Kennedy, "Time on Two Crosses: An Interview with Bayard Rustin," *The Village Voice*, June 30, 1987.

THE MID-SIXTIES

1. For this section, the following sources (along with my interviews with Foster Gunnison, Jr.) have been central: *The New York Times*, Dec. 17, 1963, reprinted in its entirety in Duberman, *About Time*, 2nd ed. (Meridian, 1991), pp. 238–42. (For my own public quarrels with Bieber and Socarides, see Duberman, *Cures: A Gay Man's Odyssey* (Plume, 1992), pp. 64–66, 267–69; D'Emilio, *Sexual Politics*, especially, chapter 8 (1962–65 growth), pp. 150–160 (Kameny; Wicker), pp. 190–92 (SIR); Todd Gitlin, *The Sixties: Years of Hope, Days of Rage* (Bantam, 1987), p. 129 (Connor); Beth Hughes, "San Francisco's Own Stonewall," *San Francisco Sunday Examiner and Chronicle*, June 4, 1989 (Wolden; McIlvenna).

2. For examples of surveillance by government agents of homophile activities, see this book, *passim. Observation Post* (CCNY campus paper), Oct. 16, 1963 (for Wicker speech).

3. Cory's pioneering book, published in 1951, pleaded for an end to persecution and described gays as a legitimate minority group; it became something of a bible for the homophile movement. "Donald Webster Cory" was in fact a pseudonym for Edward Sagarin, who later became a professor of sociology and whose views

shifted so decisively over the years that he ended up as a defender of the psy-chiatric model of homosexuality as sickness, an antagonist to any kind of gay militancy, and a purported convert to heterosexuality.

4. Kameny to Hodges, March 15, 1964, International Gay Information Center Papers (henceforth IGIC Papers), NYPL: "the word *homophile* is coming into increasing currency." "Homophile" was preferred to "homosexual" because it deemphasized the stereotypical association of homosexuality with sex. (Toby Marotta, *The Politics of Homosexuality* [Houghton Mifflin, 1981], pp. 11–12.)

5. By 1965 New York Mattachine had become disaffected from ECHO, its presi-dent, Dick Leitsch, furious at (among other things) never having been reimbursed for the cost of transcribing the 1965 ECHO conference proceedings. In trying to coax the transcripts out of Leitsch (to no avail), Foster personally pledged a hundred dollars toward a total cost of some three hundred dollars. But by then Leitsch was saying that "ECHO is almost a dirty word around here," and when ERCHO (the Eastern Regional Conference, an offshoot of The North American Conference of Homopile Organizations, known as NACHO) failed in 1968 to pass resolutions of thanks to MSNY for its accomplishments (having thanked just about every other group), Leitsch was made angrier still. (Gunnison to Leitsch, Jan. 22, 26, 1967 [misdated 1968]; Leitsch to Gunnison, Jan. 23, Feb. 6, 1968—all in IGIC Papers, NYPL.)

6. Kameny to Leitsch, July 12 (students), 17, 1965. IGIC Papers, NYPL.

7. Inman to Robert Q. Achzehner, June 8, 1967; Gunnison to Inman, March 22, 1966—both in Gunnison Papers; see also D'Emilio, *Sexual Politics*, pp. 123, 152, 161–62. Inman initially called the Florida group The Atheneum Society. He "abolished" Florida Mattachine in early 1967.

The account that follows of Foster's initial involvement with the homophile movement, and his friendship with Inman, derives (in combination with my own interviews with Gunnison) from material in the Gunnison Papers, especially the following: Gunnison to Inman, Oct. 11, 19, Nov. 18, Dec. 21, 1965; March 9, 22, April 5, 1966; *Viewpoint* (Florida Mattachine), March, April, 1966; Inman to Kameny, Dec. 21, 1965; Inman to Clark Polak, April 7, 1966.

As an example of Inman's outspokenness, he was quite capable of admon-ishing his fellow militant Frank Kameny—whom he enormously admired ("no one in the Homophile Movement has so much influenced my own thinking as you")—that "when pinned down, you either lash out at those who disagree, or you attempt to totally subjugate those who do agree" (Inman to Kameny, Dec. 21, 1965). Nichols and Inman, like Kameny, were, in the context of the homophile movement, militants; in the context of our own day, that militancy seems cir-cumscribed. As late as 1965, for example, Jack Nichols was writing *against* those who were demanding civil liberties for homosexuals—and "who are unbalanced enough to have demonstrations—before the question of sickness had been laid to rest. . . . [The] experts can tell us whether or not we are sick. Let them decide. . . ." ("Warren Adkins" [Jack Nichols] to Dick Leitsch, April 1, 1965. IGIC Papers, NYPL.) Richard Inman, for his part, helped in 1965 to organize, in conjunction with the South Florida Psychiatric Society, a program of free coun-seling for teenagers who "want to get out of the gay life." (Elver A. Barker to Adkins and Inman, May 23, 1966. IGIC Papers, NYPL.)

8. Leitsch himself credits Craig with bringing him into Mattachine (interview with Leitsch in the gay paper *Equal Time*, Oct. 12–26, 1990).

   For the following account of developments within the New York and San Francisco homophile movements, I have relied heavily on the extensive Leitsch correspondence in the IGIC Papers, NYPL; see also D'Emilio, *Sexual Politics*, pp. 163–64, 168–73, 185–86; Beth Hughes, "San Francisco's Own Stonewall" *San Francisco Sunday Examiner and Chronicle*, June 4, 1989; Stuart Timmons, *The Trouble with Harry Hay* (Alyson, 1990), pp. 214–20 (L.A. rift).

9. Leitsch to Kameny, "Sunday" (July 1965). IGIC Papers, NYPL.

10. Leitsch to Robert S. Walker (treasurer, Council on Religion and the Homosexual), Jan. 6, 1965; Leitsch to Elver Barker, May 27, 1966 (IGIC Papers, NYPL); Kepner to Duberman, April 29, 1992. Whereas much of the male pornography of the mid-sixties was on the order of muscular, toga-clad, ill-at-ease "Roman soldiers," the models in *DRUM* were more straightforwardly erotic.

11. Inman to Leitsch, Oct. 2, 1965; Bill Beardemphl to Leitsch, Oct. 11, 1965; Leitsch to Rev. Henry Wiesbauer, Oct. 21, 1965; Leitsch to Kameny, July 25, 1965 ("silly"); Leitsch to Emma Van Cott (DOB "cooperation")—all in IGIC Papers, NYPL.

12. No doubt they [the other leaders] "mean well," Leitsch acidly wrote one supporter, but "so, undoubtedly, did Adolf Hitler . . . their effectiveness is eliminated by massive egos" (meant in contrast, apparently, to Leitsch's own). He quoted with satisfaction Craig's characterization of Polak as "the homosexual's Adam Clayton Powell," scorned Shirley Willer's "constant reactionary tactics," and described his opponents within MSNY and the breakaway West Side Discussion Group as a bunch of "old aunties." (Leitsch to Elver Barker, aka Karl B. Harding, May 27, 1966. [Barker was the effective, modest leader of Denver Mattachine]; Leitsch to *CLEARING HOUSE Newsletter*, Nov. 3, 1967; Robert Hinton to Inman, March 7, 1966; Leitsch to Polak, March 23, 1965 ["old aunties"]; Polak to Leitsch, June 4, 1965—all in IGIC Papers, NYPL. The following year, Leitsch insisted that *Playboy* separate MSNY clearly from Polak's Janus Society. (Leitsch to Carol Rubel, Oct. 23, 1967.)

13. Leitsch to Elver Barker, May 27, 1966; Leitsch to Donald S. Hostetter (SLA chairman), July 6, 1965; Leitsch to the editor, *Suffolk County News*, Nov. 8, 1965; Leitsch to Henry diSuvero (New York Civil Liberties Union), Sept. 12, 1966; Leitsch to Sanford D. Garelik (chief inspector, N.Y. Police Dept.), Oct. 11, 1966—all in IGIC Papers, NYPL.

14. Leitsch to John V. Lindsay, May 13, 1966; Leitsch to Evander Smith, May 13, 1966. IGIC Papers, NYPL.

15. Kepner to Duberman, April 29, 1992; Beth Hughes, "San Francisco's Own Stonewall." *San Francisco Sunday Examiner and Chronicle*, June 4, 1989. Kepner's letter includes information on several small-scale demonstrations in regard to inclusion in the armed forces; he opposed the demonstrations, "feeling that it was time for us to join the growing peace movement instead of asking for a fair share of the killing—even though I wasn't a committed dove." Mattachine in San Francisco had by this time pretty much become a front for the varied commercial operations of longtime activist Hal Call, including an "adult" bookstore that served as an entryway to a sex club where porn films, many of them

(Pages I I I–I I7)

also made by Call, were shown. In Los Angeles, a bitter battle for internal control of ONE, Inc., had resulted by April 1965 in two separate organizations, both claiming to be the true church, with the insurgents' magazine, *Tangents*, quickly outstripping the earlier *ONE* magazine. In both cities, the older homophile organizations were being bypassed by newer, more militant groups: the Southern California Council on Religion and the Homosexual, and PRIDE, whose newsletter had evolved, by September 1967, into *The Advocate*. As for Daughters of Bilitis, it remained, on *both* coasts, wedded to polite quietism. The most vocal dissenter from that policy was Barbara Gittings, who had become editor of *The Ladder* in late 1962, and who, along with her lover, Kay "Tobin" (Lahusen), became active allies of Kameny's in ECHO.

16. *Viewpoint* (Florida Mattachine), June 1966. Richard Inman, too, had been arrested—twice in 1954—for "simply being in a gay bar"; both times he put up a $250 bond and was not prosecuted (Inman to Hodges, March 12, 1965. IGIC Papers, NYPL). For the account of the 1965 demonstrations and, subsequently, of the 1965–1968 Reminders, the following (along with my interviews) were most important: the Mattachine Society Papers in IGIC Papers, NYPL; Vito Russo interview with Barbara Gittings, Channel L (TV, NYC), Feb. 27, 1983 (tape courtesy of Russo); advertisement for Second Annual Reminder, courtesy Rodwell; Bureau of Special Services agents' reports, May 25 (twice), Aug. 17, 1966 (courtesy Scherker Estate). An agent was also present when Craig helped to organize a demonstration in front of the United Nations in response to press reports that the Cuban government had put homosexuals in labor camps. The agent reported placards that read, among others, SEX IN ANY FORM IS GOOD, and SEX IS A FUNDAMENTAL HUMAN RIGHT, and he added that he had overheard several bystanders say that the demonstration was "a disgrace" (agent's report, dated April 18, 1965 [courtesy Scherker Estate]).

17. Leitsch to Kameny, "Sunday" (July 1965). IGIC Papers, NYPL.

18. Kameny to Leitsch, July 12, 1965. IGIC Papers, NYPL.

19. *The Insider* (Mattachine Society, Washington, D.C.), July 1965. As a sample of Kameny's advance planning: Kameny to Colbert (Pennsylvania Department of Forests and Waters), June 11, 1966; Kameny to Rodwell, June 20, 1966. IGIC Papers, NYPL.

20. The account of the sip-in that follows derives from *New York Post*, April 17, 1966; *Village Voice*, May 5, 1966; *New York Times*, May 5, June 5, 1966; and Leitsch to Sheila Paine, April 29, 1966, Leitsch to Evander Smith, May 13, 1966, both in IGIC Papers, NYPL.

21. For a particularly graphic account of entrapment, see Andrew Velez, "Looking Back in Anger," *NYQ*, Nov. 3, 1991. Sascha L., who briefly worked the door at Stonewall (see p. 182), describes Gerling in those years as "looking like a drag queen—pumps and wigs." She was admired, even beloved, Sascha L. says, for cursing out the cops (and occasionally even the judge) in open court for having entrapped and arrested homosexuals. "Don't you have a girlfriend?" she would bellow. "Don't you want to get laid or something? Why are you bothering these people?" The secret to Gerling's success in getting so many gay men sprung from jail was, according to Sascha L., not simply payoffs, but her willingness—"she used to be very hot"—to put out for several of the judges. She would postpone

a case if the "right" judge—i.e., one she had slept with—wasn't sitting. (Interview with Sascha L., Aug. 26, 1991.) Chuck Shaheen (interview, Nov. 20, 1991) also heard rumors that Gerling slept with some of the judges, and adds that she was also used by the Mafia as a lawyer.

Like many gay men of my generation, I carried Enid Gerling's phone number with me when I went out for a night's cruising. And like many others, too, I (though never arrested) came to regard her as something of a heroine for having gotten so many gay men out of jail. I said as much in the speech I gave dedicating Stonewall Place in 1989—and was promptly set right by Craig Rodwell (see Duberman, *About Time*, pp. 424–27). As recently as 1990, Gerling was employed as defense counsel for fourteen men arrested on drug charges in the West Village gay bar, the Ninth Circle (*Outweek*, Oct. 24, 1990). For a one-sided whitewashing of Gerling, making her into a selfless patron saint of liberation, see *NYQ*, Feb. 16, 1992.

22. A substantial debate has opened up as to whether butch-femme categorization in the lesbian world of the forties and fifties *was* role-playing, and if so to what degree. The debate has been further enkindled by what has become known in the nineties as "the return of butch-femme." For an introduction to the large literature relating to both the historical and contemporary debate, see especially Joan Nestle, *The Persistent Desire: A Femme-Butch Reader* (Alyson, 1992); Madeline Davis and Elizabeth Kennedy, *Boots of Leather, Slippers of Gold* (Routledge, 1993); the Karen Kahn interview with Nestle, "Constructing the Lesbian Self," *Sojourner*, June 1992; and Lillian Faderman, "The Return of Butch and Femme: A Phenomenon in Lesbian Sexuality of the 1980s and 1990s," *Journal of the History of Sexuality*, vol. 2, no. 4 (1992), pp. 578–96.

23. The material on the Columbia strike is mostly taken from my essay, "On Misunderstanding Student Rebels," *The Atlantic Monthly*, November 1968 (reprinted in Duberman, *The Uncompleted Past* [Random House, 1969], pp. 309–31). But a large literature exists on the strike; see, for example, Ronald Fraser, *1968* (Pantheon, 1988).

24. Most of the details on life at Rikers are from my interview with Gregory Terry, August 29, 1990. Terry was also in the queens' cellblock in 1966, having been given a four-month sentence for "solicitation of a police officer." Two years later, the same plainclothesman, not recognizing Terry, tried to entrap him again. Terry simply walked up to him and said, "Excuse me, *Officer*, do you have the time?" In 1974, by then employed as an investigator for the Legal Aid Society, Terry had the satisfaction of returning to Rikers to work on cases involving prisoners' rights.

25. Interview with Ivan Valentin, July 5, 1991. Later, Ivan helped to win a major legal decision. In 1975, a moribund Connecticut state law barring female impersonators was resurrected to close Ivan's "Leading Ladies of New York" show. He took his case to the University of Connecticut School of Law, and the matter ended in more permissive legislation. (The story is told in Eric Gordon, "An Imitation of Images," *The Hartford Advocate*, Oct. 27, 1976, Feb. 9, 1977.)

26. Interview with Joe Tish, Nov. 15, 1991. Both Tish, in his late sixties, and Frankie Quinn, in his late seventies, continue to do drag shows—mostly at senior-citizen centers.

(Pages 126–146)

27. Steven Watson interview with Minette, 1979 (transcript courtesy Watson); Robert Heide, "Drag Queens," *Other Stages*, vol. 2, no. 16 (April 17–30, 1980).
28. Steven Watson interview with Holly Woodlawn, n.d. (transcript courtesy Watson). See also Holly Woodlawn's *A Low Life in High Heels* (St. Martin's, 1991).
29. Free [Abbie Hoffman], *Revolution for the Hell of It* (Dial, 1968), p. 29.
30. Hoffman, *Revolution*, p. 102.
31. The TV clip is from the PBS show *Making Sense of the Sixties* (tape courtesy Marty Jezer, to whom I'm also grateful for letting me see the page proofs of his book, *Abbie Hoffman: American Rebel* (Rutgers University Press, 1992).
    In *Do It!* (Ballantine, 1970, p. 129), Jerry Rubin wrote: "Look at the criminal record of a political activist. It reads like the record of a sex deviant—public nuisance, loitering, disorderly conduct, trespassing, disturbing the peace."
32. Interviews with Robert Heide, 1990 and 1991.
33. Hoffman, *Revolution*, pp. 33–37; Jezer, *Hoffman*, 109–110; Emmett Grogan, *Ringolevio: A Life Played for Keeps* (Little, Brown, 1972), pp. 399–401.
34. The account is in Todd Gitlin, *The Sixties: Years of Hope, Days of Rage* (Bantam, 1987), p. 231. The fabrication, in Jim's mind, is the more egregious in a book that—except for this trivializing incident—entirely lacks any treatment of gay oppression or liberation.
35. Hoffman, *Revolution*, pp. 32–33.
36. This account is largely drawn from my interviews with Fouratt, but the "on the map" quote is from Hoffman, *Revolution* p. 91.
37. Hoffman, *Revolution*, pp. 91–92; Jezer, *Hoffman*, 146, 149–50.

THE LATE SIXTIES

1. As quoted (in both paragraphs) in Clare Coss, "Single Lesbians Speak Out," *Lesbians at Midlife: The Creative Transition*, Barbara Sang, Joyce Warshow, and Adrienne J. Smith, eds. (Spinsters Book Company: 1991), pp. 137–38.
2. The following account of the Kansas City conference, and the events surrounding it, largely derives from the IGIC Papers, NYPL, and two privately held manuscript collections: the Gunnison Papers and the William B. Kelley Papers. The two private collections are storehouses of previously unresearched material on the homophile movements, and I am indebted to both Gunnison and Kelley for giving me access.
    The essential items used for describing the first planning conference are as follows: Gunnison to Leitsch, Jan. 22, 1967 (formalisms); William Kelley to Leitsch, Feb. 26, 1966; Leitsch to Kelley, Feb. 28, 1966—all in IGIC Papers, NYPL; "Persons in Attendance," Feb. 18–21, 1966, Gunnison Papers, gives a complete roster of individuals and organizations; William B. Kelley, "Minutes of the National Planning Conference of Homophile Organizations, Kansas City, Mo.," 21 typed pages, Kelley Papers. Kelley was recording secretary for the conference. The full "Statement of Purposes," drawn up by Clark Polak, is in the Gunnison Papers; it includes the resolution about "objective research." For Gunnison's reactions to individuals: Gunnison to Inman, March 9, 22, Sept. 18,

1966, Gunnison Papers. For his retreat from barbershop work: Gunnison to Inman, Oct. 11, 1965, Gunnison Papers.

3. *The Homosexual Citizen*, April 1966. Foster repeated his argument on the importance of "upgrading our image" in *Mattachine Midwest Newsletter*, vol. II, no. 1 (January 1966).

4. "Ten Days in August" was actually three consecutive conferences rolled into one: the Fourth National Convention of the DOB; the Consultation on Theology and the Homosexual; and, from August 25 to August 27, the National Planning Conference of Homophile Organizations (a name Del Martin had suggested during the Kansas City meeting). The roster at San Francisco, compiled by Gunnison, is in his papers. Most of the leaders present in Kansas City returned for the San Francisco conference (but not Nichols, Gittings, Grier, Inman or Tobin); and Dorr Legg, Harry Hay, and Jim Kepner were present for the first time. For the range of events: *Viewpoint* (Florida Mattachine), October 1966, and *Citizens' News*, vol. V, no. 10 (October 1966).

    The account of the San Francisco conference that follows, is again drawn largely from materials in the Gunnison and Kelley manuscript collections. For the argument over accreditation: Dorr Legg to Kelley, March 16, 1966, and Clarence A. Colwell to "Dear Friends," Aug. 5, 1966, both in Kelley Papers. For the proliferation of resolutions: William B. Kelley, "Preliminary Summary of Substantive Actions Approved by the National Planning Conference of Homophile Organizations . . ." Kelley Papers. For Strait's remark: *Citizens' News*, vol. V, no. 10 (October 1966). Another negative assessment ("National Conference Made Few Advances") is in *The ARC News* (Sacramento), vol. 1, no. 8 (Sept. 1966).

5. Stuart Timmons, *The Trouble with Harry Hay* (Alyson, 1990), pp. 214, 223.

6. *ONE Confidential*, vol. XI, no. 9 (September 1966). Polak's remarks, which follow in the next paragraph, are excerpted in *Citizens' News*, vol. V, no. 10 (October 1966).

7. The quotes in this and the following two paragraphs are from the typescript of Foster Gunnison, Jr., "Three Concrete Steps to Further the Homophile Movement," Gunnison Papers.

8. Del Martin, "The Lesbian's Majority Status," *The Ladder*, June 1967. The name "NACHO" was not formally adopted until the 1968 convention.

9. Jerome Stevens to Richard Inman, Sept. 12, 1966, Gunnison Papers. Gunnison had been appointed by the Rev. Clay Colwell, who was "Moderator" of the August 1966 conference. Colwell, a heterosexual, was chosen to preside because he was "independent" of the organizations involved and could be "trusted" (Gunnison to Duberman, Dec. 22, 1991)—less a shrewd calculation, perhaps, than a measure of homosexual self-distrust. Gunnison thought Colwell "the best non-homo homo that ever was," and adduced as proof that when Colwell had been " 'groped' at the Saturday evening SIR dance," he "didn't do anything about it. That's the acid test of dedication as far as I am concerned" (Gunnison to Inman, Sept. 18, 1966, Gunnison Papers). When Colwell resigned in 1967 due to ill health, he was replaced by another heterosexual, Robert W. Cromey, of St. Aidan's Episcopal Church in San Francisco (Inman to Colwell, Sept. 5, 1966, and May 25, 1967; Inman to Cromey, June 24, 1967—all in Gunnison Papers).

(Pages 154–155)

One of Foster's most enjoyable times during the convention was the evening he took Doris Hanson and Virginia Bruce out to San Francisco's famed nightclub Finocchio's, to see the female-impersonator floor show. Hanson, a close friend of Barbara Gittings, "took a crush" on him (that is, according to Foster) and "was in a most unlesbianlike frame of mind whenever I was around." Virginia Bruce was a well-known transsexual who wrote and lectured on the subject. Foster "admired her. She's really no kook," he wrote Inman, "quite sincere, a real tough problem she has to deal with, and a wry sense of humor." (Gunnison to Inman, Sept. 18, 1966—Gunnison Papers.) A few years later, Foster was asked to escort a transsexual named Charlayne to a meeting in New York of the West Side Discussion Group, and though he found her "kind of cute," he added (in a letter to Barbara Gittings, Jan. 12, 1970—Gunnison Papers), "Why can't people just stay with what God gave them? I didn't know whether to offer her a cigar on the train, or what to do."

10. Gunnison to Inman, Sept. 18, 1966, Gunnison Papers; attached note to Duberman describes the course of the therapy.

11. Marvin Cutler, *Homosexuals Today—1956: A Handbook of Organizations and Publications* (ONE, Inc., 1956). "Warren D. Adkins" (Jack Nichols) published a brief (seven-page) "The Homophile Movement: A Historical Perspective," in *The Homosexual Citizen* (Washington Mattachine's monthly), April 1967.

12. The quotations in this and the following paragraphs are all from Foster Gunnison, Jr., "An Introduction to the Homophile Movement" (The Institute of Social Ethics, Sept. 1967), Gunnison Papers.

Foster's bolder side can also be seen in two other pieces he wrote in 1966–1967. In an extended review of Ronald Atkinson's *Sexual Morality* in *The Homosexual Citizen* (December 1966), he chastised Atkinson for failing to demolish the psychoanalytic view of homosexuality as "illness"; argued that homosexuality was "an unchosen condition, resistant to change"; and even made an oblique case for homosexual marriage. In another piece for *The Homosexual Citizen* ("The Hidden Bias: The Homophile Movement and Law Reform," March 1967), Foster argued against a pending British bill that would place the age of consent for heterosexuals at sixteen, but for homosexuals at twenty-one, as a double standard that would compromise the effort to win acceptance "under the same rules that apply to everyone else."

13. For more on the Society for Human Rights and the Veterans Benevolent Association, see Jonathan Katz, *Gay American History* (2nd ed., Meridian, 1992), and (for the Society) Jonathan Ned Katz, *Gay/Lesbian Almanac* (Harper & Row, 1983).

According to Jim Kepner, whose encyclopedic knowledge is unparalleled, the Sons of Hamidy was "a *projected* organization in 1942–44, starting in Rhinelander, Wisc. . . . My Rhinelander pen pal, Wally Jordan, wrote to me & others that SOH had previous incarnations in the 1880's & 1930's, each time falling victim to 'bitch fights.' He said the organization was led by important people like 'Senators and Generals,' but there is no evidence for these earlier incarnations. . . . Years later, he wrote me that SOH, like the Legion of the Damned, was simply a wish of his—LOD being his camp term for a few gay servicemen he met at bars in Cooledge & Holbrook, AZ. . . . It was never an organization. I

wrote the original of the account of SOH which appeared in [Dorr] Legg's *Homosexuals Today, 1956*—but Dorr, with no personal knowledge of SOH, altered what I wrote to make it seem that SOH had real existence." (Kepner to Duberman, April 29, 1992.)

14. Jim Skaggs, "Committee on Unity Reports," *Vector*, March 1968.
15. The quotes in this and the following two paragraphs are from Leitsch to Elver Barker, May 27, 1966, IGIC Papers, NYPL; Kepner to Duberman, April 29, 1992; Gunnison, "REPORT—July 20, 1967," Gunnison Papers; and Kelley and Roland Keith to "Members of the Conference" [NACHO San Francisco, Aug. 25–27, 1966], Kelley Papers.
16. *The Advocate*, vol. 1, no. 1 (September 1967). Stephen Donaldson also referred to "a miraculous spirit of good will" at the Washington conference, though he acknowledged as well a certain amount of "acidity" (Donaldson, "The Fine Art of Compromise," Kelley Papers). Gunnison's official tally of accredited organizations came to twenty-eight (from twelve cities), but not all those accredited actually sent delegates (Gunnison, "ACCREDITED ORGANIZATIONS—June 22, 1967." Gunnison Papers).
17. Arthur Warner ("Austen Wade") to Leitsch, July 26, 1967; Leitsch to Warner, Aug. 1, 1967; Leitsch to Homophile Clearinghouse, Feb. 7, 1968; Leitsch to Randy Wicker, Feb. 20, 1968—all in IGIC Papers, NYPL; Kepner to Duberman, April 29, 1992. Leitsch leaned at one point toward forming an association with new homophile groups in Cincinnati and Phoenix, at another toward forming a statewide Mattachine Society of New York. What he was aiming for, he wrote his loyal lieutenant, Arthur Warner, was to ensure that participants be "carefully screened and selected to sift out social clubs, profiteers, vanity groups and the like." By 1970, Leitsch was trying to enlist the wealthy gay businessman Jack Campbell in his ongoing efforts to form an "affiliation of like-minded groups who can work together in harmony." He assured Campbell that the groups would be handpicked, and would avoid the "fighting and jockeying for power, and . . . back-stabbing"—"Some of us are too mature and too serious for that crap"—characteristic of other regional and national associations (Leitsch to Campbell, March 2, 1970, IGIC Papers, NYPL).
18. Typed minutes of the Aug. 16–18, 1967, NACHO conference, Kelley Papers; Kelley was not the secretary—he had been ill and unable to attend. Jerome Stevens, "A Model Program?" n.d., Gunnison Papers. Jim Kepner has listed some of the other groups denied admission: "Vancouver's ASK because they got an application in late (months before the conference); the National League for Social Understanding because they dabbled in occultism (which would bring us all into disrepute); the National Legal Defense Fund because it was initially a conference committee, later separately incorporated . . . etc" (Kepner to Duberman, April 29, 1992).
19. Virginia O. Roak, "Report on the Third North American Homophile Conference 17–19 August 1967," *The Ladder*, January 1968.
20. Gunnison, "An Introduction to the Homophile Movement," Gunnison Papers.
21. Del Martin, "The Lesbian's Majority Status," *The Ladder*, June 1967; Gunnison to Donn Teal, n.d., Kelley Papers. According to Jim Kepner, Martin "did make

a loud withdrawal later, insisting that lesbians had little to gain in the homophile movement" (Kepner to Duberman, April 29, 1992).

22. Gunnison to Jim Skaggs (SIR chair), Nov. 5, 1967. Kelley Papers.
23. Typed minutes of the Aug. 16–18, 1967, NACHO Conference, Kelley Papers. A "Unity Committee" was also established, with seven members each from the Eastern, Western, and Midwestern regions (Craig Rodwell was one of the Eastern representatives). The committee was empowered "to study the question of stronger national cooperation and influence through a possible federation of all interested homophile organizations." It functioned, sporadically and inefficiently, over the next two years. ("Committee on Unity Reports," n.d. IGIC Papers, NYPL.)
24. The "militant-sentimental" quote is from *The Gay Crusaders*, Kay Tobin and Randy Wicker, eds. (Paperback Library, 1972), p. 66.
25. The press release and ads are courtesy of Rodwell. Some of the meeting notes, and a statement of purpose, are in the IGIC Papers, NYPL. Craig's sensitivity to sexism was apparent in 1966 when he became vice president of MSNY. The nominating committee (of which Craig was a member) had originally presented Renée Cafiero for the post. But when a conservative opposition slate developed, it was thought unwise to present a ticket of three women and two men, and so Cafiero withdrew in favor of Craig. He told her at the time that he would later resign the position and recommend her appointment—and he did so, effective January 1, 1967 (Rodwell to Board of Directors, MSNY, Dec. 7, 1966. IGIC Papers, NYPL).
26. Harriet Van Horne, "Enough of All This," *New York Post*, April 9, 1969.

1969

1. Gitlin, *The Sixties* (Bantam, 1987), pp. 343–44. See Gitlin, *passim*, for more details on all of the developments and incidents described in this section.
2. For Laurence and Whittington: D'Emilio, *Sexual Politics*, pp. 230–31; *San Francisco Chronicle*, April 10, 1969. For comparable confrontations in L.A., especially around the police action in Wilmington against a bar called PATCH II, see John Hammond's interview with Morris Kight, "A Quarter Century of Liberation—Plus," *New York Native*, Feb. 18, 1991; and Jim Kepner, *Our Movement Before Stonewall* (IGLA, 1989), p. 14. Kepner reports that when patrons of PATCH II protested against being fag-bashed, the police response was "We aren't interested in protecting cocksuckers!" In response, Lee Glaze and forty other gay men (including Troy Perry) protested in front of the Harbor Police Station.
3. D'Emilio, *Sexual Politics*, pp. 229–30; interviews with Gunnison. (A curious sidelight: Rita Laporte had grown up with Foster Gunnison at Gypsy Trail; the two had lost track of each other as adults until they met again years later at a NACHO national planning conference.) Laporte was later a suicide.
4. This account of the league and its action against the Columbia Medical School panel is from D'Emilio, *Sexual Politics*, pp. 209–210, 216; and Robert A. Martin ("Stephen Donaldson"), "Student Homophile League: Founder's

Retrospect," *Gay Books Bulletin*, no. 9, Spring/Summer 1983, pp. 30–33.

5. Alice Echols, *Daring to Be Bad: Radical Feminism in America, 1967–1975* (University of Minnesota Press, 1989), p. 60. I have relied heavily on Echols, along with my interviews with Jay, for the discussion of radical feminism and the Red-stockings.

6. Echols, *Daring to Be Bad*, pp. 92–96.

7. Interviews with Fouratt; also, Abe Peck, *Uncovering the Sixties: The Life and Times of the Underground Press* (Pantheon, 1985), pp. 169–70.

8. Peck, *Uncovering the Sixties*, pp. 176–77.

9. Randy Wicker was also fed up with Leitsch's leadership. He accused Leitsch of "spending the major part of your time writing a book [never completed] & entertaining your new lover," and withdrew from any further financial support of MSNY (Wicker to Leitsch, Feb. 11, 1968. IGIC Papers, NYPL). In response, Leitsch asked, "When, and if, I leave who else will you find who will work night and day, live and sleep Mattachine, and put up with all of the shit one has to take around here?" (Leitsch to Wicker, Feb. 20, 1969. IGIC Papers, NYPL.)

10. Interview with Chuck Shaheen, Nov. 20, 1991. Nor did Stonewall even have an ice machine; the staff used to buy huge quantities, several times a night, from Smiler's Deli.

11. Shaheen (interview, Nov. 20, 1991) confirms that Murphy was "very involved with the procurement of young boys" (though *not* at Stonewall), and that, as part of his job as bouncer and doorman, he would be told to beat up certain people. Tommy Lanigan-Schmidt (interview May 2, 1992) remembers seeing a young Puerto Rican, regarded as one of Murphy's lovers, being whisked off the sidewalk into a waiting car and never being seen again; the rumor was that he had cheated on Murphy or stolen from him. Yet Shaheen liked Murphy, and thought of him as a "perfect gentleman." And Lanigan-Schmidt talked compassionately of how the need to survive drove Murphy to reprehensible behavior.

   Bob Kohler (who at the time owned a talent agency and hung out at Stonewall) confirms that Murphy "was a police informer" (interview with Kohler, Aug. 20, 1990). In an interview given on the tenth anniversary of the Stonewall riot, Murphy additionally identified himself as having until recently (1979) been "an undercover agent, specializing in gay bars and corruption, for the New York State Select Committee on Crime" (Harold Pickett, "I Like to Call It an Uprising," *Gay Community News*, June 23, 1979). Bebe Scarpi confirms that Murphy "set people up to be mugged and robbed" (phone interview with Scarpi, Aug. 22, 1990). For the police beating later administered to Murphy, see p. 219.

12. Interview with Sascha L., August 26, 1991. Sascha is currently (1992) the doorman at a popular gay bar in Greenwich Village.

13. Chris Davis interview with Murphy, n.d. (1987?), tape courtesy Davis. My Nov. 15, 1991 interview with Joe Tish (the drag performer) and my Nov. 20, 1991 interview with Chuck Shaheen, confirm Murphy's saint/sinner reputation. Murphy died, aged sixty-three, on Feb. 28, 1989, and New York City's Heritage of Pride designated him the honorary grand marshal for the twentieth-anniversary march that June. The printed 1989 Heritage program led off with "A Tribute to the 'Mayor of Christopher Street.' " Later in life, Murphy did do outstanding charitable work on behalf of the retarded.

(Pages 183–187)

Among the many positive comments on the Stonewall are Dick Kanon's "It was the best place we ever had" (*New York Post*, July 8, 1969); and Thomas Lanigan-Schmidt's "Here the consciousness of knowing you 'belonged' nestled into that warm feeling of finally being *HOME.* . . . We loved the Stonewall." ("Mother Stonewall and the Golden Rats," courtesy Lanigan-Schmidt.)

14. Interview with Ivan Valentin, July 5, 1991; interview with Sascha L., Aug. 26, 1991. It should be added, however, that Ivan, too, has been described as having been sometimes involved in "shady dealings."

15. Interviews with Sascha L. (Aug. 26, 1991) and Shaheen (Nov. 20, 1991). Shaheen and Sascha disagree in part on the ownership of some of the bars. I have accepted Shaheen on the Stonewall (Sascha has it owned by the Gambino family) because he knew its operations intimately; and I have accepted Sascha on Washington Square (Shaheen has both it and the Gold Bug owned by the Gambino family) because he knew the operations of those two establishments far better than Shaheen did.

    Tommy Lanigan-Schmidt (interview May 2, 1992) went frequently to the Tenth of Always and said that so many young kids hung out there (partly because of Murphy's presence), that from his own perspective as a Catholic kid from New Jersey, it had the air of nothing so much as "a surreal Catholic Youth dance."

16. Interviews with Sascha L. (Aug. 26, 1991) and Shaheen (Nov. 20, 1991).

17. Interview with Chuck Shaheen, Nov. 20, 1991. Some details, though irregularly reliable, about the Stonewall Inn's history prior to its incarnation as a gay bar, can be found in Larry Boxx, "Remembering Stonewall," *Bay Area Reporter*, June 22, 1989 (also printed, with some slight variations, in *Long Beach/Stonewall 20—1989*), and Mark Haile, "The Truth about Stonewall," *BLK*, June 1989.

18. Interview with Shaheen, Nov. 20, 1991.

19. The details in this and the next four paragraphs are from my interview with Shaheen, Nov. 20, 1991. Before he met Tony, Shaheen had worked in the coat-check room at the One-Two-Three, an after-hours club on University Place between Thirteenth and Fourteenth Streets.

20. Interview with Ryder Fitzgerald (assistant to "T.L.R.," the electrician), May 5, 1992.

21. Not every police precinct in New York was corrupt. It was part of Mafia lore never to open a gay club on the East Side above Fifty-ninth Street, because the police there couldn't be bought. And when Fat Tony, disregarding that advice, later opened an East Side gay club, it lasted exactly one night; the police not only raided and closed the place but, atypically, arrested everyone on the premises.

22. The information in this and the next four paragraphs is from my interview with Sascha L., Aug. 26, 1991. Many of the Mafia figures described in this section are still alive, and wherever that is the case, Sascha L. and Chuck Shaheen have asked me—for their protection and mine—to use pseudonyms.

23. Frank Esselourne, "Doorman Remembers," *Gay Community News*, June 23, 1979. "Bobby Shades" also slept with men, and dated Chuck Shaheen at one point (interview, Nov. 20, 1991).

24. Interview with Ryder Fitzgerald, May 5, 1992 (Ernie and Vito); *New York Sunday*

News, June 29, 1969 (Verra); Shaheen interview, Nov. 20, 1991. According to Shaheen, it was Ernie, somewhat older than the others, who dealt with Matty the Horse. In regard to the watered drinks, Shaheen puts it this way: "We didn't throw the bottles away. We reused those bottles all the time. We kept *a* real bottle of Dewar's and *a* real bottle of Smirnoff—for special customers."

25. Interviews with Tommy Lanigan-Schmidt, May 2, 1992, and Martin Boyce, May 19, 1992; Scherker interview with Danny Garvin, Dec. 15, 1988 (courtesy Scherker Estate). Lanigan-Schmidt added that the police cars, which then had one large light on top of the hood, were known as "bubble-gum machines." According to Shaheen (interview Nov. 20, 1991), there was bad blood between Fat Tony and the owners of the Sanctuary; when they took him on a tour of the about-to-open Sanctuary, Tony had Shaheen accompany him with firebombs strapped to his body. He distributed them strategically during the tour, but they failed to detonate.

26. Interview with Joe Tish, Nov. 15, 1991. Tiffany, who had silicon breast implants, lived for a while with Fat Tony and Chuck Shaheen. She once tried suicide and had to be taken out by ambulance; Tony's father "went through the roof" (Shaheen interview, Nov. 20, 1991).

27. The material in this and the following paragraph comes from an interview with Kohler, August 20, 1990.

28. Will Hermes, "Summer '69: Sweet Stone(wall) Soul Music," *Windy City Times*, June 22, 1989. Tommy Lanigan-Schmidt, at the time a dirt-poor street queen (in 1992, a well-known artist), described in our interview of May 2 the various hurdles he had to get over during a given night at Stonewall: getting admitted at the door; hurrying by the coat check to avoid paying the twenty-five-cent charge; evading the waiters' constant pressure to buy drinks. Many of the queens had a set routine for not having to buy drinks they couldn't afford: They would find discarded cans of beer, or glasses, and hold them; a beer can was preferable, because then you could go into the bathroom and fill it up halfway with water so that when one of the meaner waiters ("one of the vicious queens looking to throw his power around") checked the weight of the can, it would feel half full; "Then they'd leave you alone and wouldn't throw you out." Those with no money at all would sit along the wall, try to fade into the crowd, and when they saw one of the waiters bearing down on them, would quickly get up and dance.

29. Interviews with Sascha L. (Aug. 26, 1991) and Shaheen (Nov. 20, 1991). Bebe Scarpi (phone interview, Aug. 22, 1990) also confirms that "a few lesbians did go to Stonewall." The quote about "territory" is from an unidentified lesbian, one of the many "testimonies" about Stonewall recorded by Michael Scherker at the Lesbian and Gay Community Services Center on May 13, 1989 (tape courtesy Scherker Estate).

30. Testimony of Jerry [?] and an unidentified man on "Stonewall Reunion" tape made by Scherker at the Lesbian and Gay Community Services Center on June 13, 1989; Scherker with Joseph Dey, June 6, 1989 (tapes courtesy Scherker Estate).

31. Scherker interview with Harry Beard, Aug. 3, 1988; see also the reminiscences

of Beard, Gene Huss, and Don Knapp in Mike Long, "The Night the Girls Said No!" *San Francisco Sentinel*, June 22, 1989.

32. Howard Smith, "Full Moon over Stonewall," *The Village Voice*, July 3, 1969 (First Division); interview with Chuck Shaheen, Nov. 20, 1991; Scherker interview with Beard, Aug. 3, 1988; the time is established by the Sixth Precinct police records, obtained by Michael Scherker (courtesy Scherker Estate).

33. Interview with Ryder Fitzgerald, May 5, 1992. Fitzgerald also heard Ernie swear that he would reopen Stonewall the very next night as an expression of "displeasure" with the local police; in his determination, he borrowed stools and glasses from other bars to replace what the police had smashed.

34. Chris Davis interview with Ed Murphy, 1987 [?], tape courtesy Davis; interview with Sascha L., August 26, 1991.

35. Interview with Ryder Fitzgerald, May 5, 1992. Frankie later died in a bomb "accident."

36. Interview with Shaheen, Nov. 20, 1991.

37. "Queen Power: Fags Against Police in Stonewall Bust," *RAT*, July 1969 (for guy in T-shirt); *New York Times*, June 29, 1969; Lucian Truscott IV, "Gay Power Comes to Sheridan Square," *The Village Voice*, July 3, 1969.

38. Bebe Scarpi (phone interview, Aug. 22, 1990) confirms Sylvia's description: "Tammy hit the cop and was so stoned she didn't know what she was doing—or didn't care."

39. Though Harry Beard seems in general to be a reliable witness with a precise memory, there are some small discrepancies between his interview version (with Michael Scherker, Aug. 3, 1988; tape courtesy Scherker Estate) and his printed version (Mike Long, "The Night the Girls Said No!" *San Francisco Sentinel*, June 22, 1989). In the printed version, for example, Beard says the cop "slapped her upside the head with something—I can't recall if it was a blackjack or a nightstick or what it was"; in the interview version he describes the cop as "hitting her over the head with his billy club."

   Section 887 (7) of the New York State Criminal Code was the one traditionally invoked by the police against transvestites. The law was supposedly ignored on Halloween, though the police department handbook specified that even then, someone dressed in costume had to be wearing a certain number of garments "appropriate" to their sex. Mattachine received a number of reports of people being arrested on Halloween (Leitsch to Chief Inspector Garelik, Oct. 11, 1966—IGIC Papers, NYPL).

40. Bob Kohler (interview Aug. 20, 1990) is another who denies the involvement of a lesbian, but Kohler does add that Tony Lightfoot, "a lesbian who people thought was a drag queen," used to hang out with the queens in the small park opposite the Stonewall bar.

   Of the printed sources that give the credit to a lesbian, see *Gay Community News*, June 23, 1979; *Windy City Times*, June 22, 1989; *BLK*, June 1989; and the *San Francisco Sentinel*, June 22, 1989. But these offer no concrete evidence and seem to be merely repeating the assertions by Howard Smith and Lucian Truscott IV in their firsthand accounts in *The Village Voice*, July 3, 1969 (Truscott: "A dyke . . . put up a struggle—from car to door to car again"). But the Truscott

article, especially, is hardly incontrovertible: It contains a number of disputed points and is in places markedly homophobic in tone. Moreover, except for Truscott's and Smith's, no contemporary newspaper accounts of the riot mention the involvement of a woman (*New York Times*, June 28, 1969; *New York Post*, June 28, July 6, *Sunday News*, June 29, 1969). The eyewitness account in *RAT* (July 1969) specifically credits "one guy" (not a lesbian *or* a queen) for precipitating a scuffle by refusing to be put into the paddy wagon.

Of the accounts that specifically credit a queen with initiating the riot, the most important are unprinted sources: Chris Davis's interview with Ed Murphy (1988?, tape courtesy Davis); my interview with Sascha L. (Aug. 26, 1991) and the testimonies of Robert "Birdie" Rivera and Deputy Inspector Seymour Pine, recorded for David Isay's 1989 NPR show *Remembering Stonewall*.

In his interview with Chris Davis (1988?, tape courtesy Davis), Murphy claimed that he stepped between the cop and the queen being pushed and said to the cop, "Why don't you leave us alone. Didn't you do enough fucking damage, asshole?" But there is no corroboration for Murphy's claim, and other accounts (for example, Ivan Valentin, interview July 5, 1991) have him quickly leaving the scene.

At least two people credit Sylvia herself with provoking the riot: Jeremiah Newton (*New York Native*, June 25, 1990) has her throwing an empty gin bottle that smashed in front of the Stonewall door; and Ivan Valentin (interview, July 5, 1991) insists that Sylvia actually jumped a cop and thereby "started the Gay Liberation movement." But I've found no corroboration for either account and Sylvia herself, with a keener regard for the historical record, denies the accuracy of both versions. She does remember "throwing bricks and rocks and things" *after* the mêlée began, but takes no credit for initiating the confrontation.

41. Interviews with Joe Tish, Nov. 15, 1991, and Martin Boyce, May 19, 1992; Rivera and Pine testimonies on Isay's show *Remembering Stonewall*. The Pine quote is from Howard Smith, "Full Moon," *Village Voice*, July 3, 1969. Seymour Pine had been assigned in 1968 as deputy inspector in charge of enforcing public morals (that is, enforcing all laws relating to vice, gambling, prostitution, narcotics, and homosexuality) in the police department's First Division, which ran from Thirty-eighth Street in Manhattan to the Battery. According to Sascha L., Pine "worked both ways . . . he used to have his friend pick up money [from gay bars] in a patrol car" (interview, Aug. 26, 1991).

Once again, there are confusions and contradictions in the evidence. For example, in Blond Frankie's printed account (Frank Esselourne, "Doorman Remembers," *Gay Community News*, June 23, 1979), he credits only himself with engineering the escape from the van, and has the arrested queens *following* him out.

42. Scherker interview with "D.D.," Dec. 24, 1988 (Puerto Rican), and Robert Rivera, June 10, 1989 (mashed cop); Isay show, *Remembering Stonewall*.

43. Interviews with Shaheen, Nov. 20, 1991 (Zucchi) and Sascha L., Aug. 26, 1991 (dog shit); Scherker interviews, courtesy Scherker Estate, with "D.D.," Dec. 24, 1988 (dog shit), and Beard, Aug. 3, 1988 (overheard Zucchi); my phone interview with Marty Robinson, Oct. 10, 1990 (Timmy).

(Pages 198–206)

44. Frank Esselourne, "Doorman Remembers"; Pine's testimony on Isay show, *Remembering Stonewall*.

45. Mike Long, "The Night the Girls Said No!"; Pine testimony on Isay show, *Remembering Stonewall*. Martin Boyce (interview May 19, 1992) credits "the demented" "Miss New Orleans" and two other queens with tearing up the parking meter.

46. Howard Smith, "Full Moon over the Stonewall"; *Sunday News*, June 29, 1991; *New York Times*, June 28, 1969.

47. Phone interviews with Jim Slaven (*sous-chef* at the Lion's Head), Sept. 3, 1990, and Nick Browne (bartender at the Lion's Head), Sept. 12, 1990; Smith, "Full Moon over the Stonewall."

48. Smith, "Full Moon over the Stonewall."

49. Smith, "Full Moon over the Stonewall"; police records, June 28, 1969 (time; signal; courtesy Scherker Estate).

50. Police records (courtesy Scherker Estate) give the names of the TPF squad members. They came from three different precincts, the Fourth, Fifth, and Tenth. Sad to report, none of Craig Rodwell's photos came out.

51. Marty Robinson, "I Remember Stonewall," *San Francisco Examiner*, June 4, 1989; Maida Tilchen, "Mythologizing Stonewall," *Gay Community News*, June 23, 1979.

52. The incidents described in this and the following paragraph are from Dick Leitsch, "Police Raid on New York Club Sets Off First Gay Riot," *The Advocate*, Sept. 1969, p. 3. According to Ryder Fitzgerald (interview, May 5, 1992), Blond Frankie told him that he had himself smashed the windshield of a police car.

53. Interview with Ivan Valentin, July 5, 1991; Scherker interview with Rivera, June 10, 1989 (Lenny); "Stonewall Reunion" tape made by Scherker at Gay and Lesbian Community Center, June 13, 1989 ("feminine boys").

54. *New York Times*, July 29, 1969. The injuries are detailed in the police records, June 28, 1969 (courtesy Scherker Estate).

55. Interview with Ryder Fitzgerald, May 5, 1992; Truscott, "Gay Power"; Donn Teal, *The Gay Militants* (Stein & Day, 1971), p. 20; Leitsch, "Police Raid," *The Advocate*, Sept. 1969 (pocketed money).

56. Scherker interview with Lorenzo Rodriguez, June 3, 1989 (tape courtesy Scherker Estate).

57. *New York Times*, June 30, 1969. Truscott, in his *Voice* article (July 3, 1969), agreed with the *Times*'s view.

58. Copy of the HYMN flyer courtesy Rodwell.

59. Mel Horne, "20 Years of Changing Clothes," *Gay Community News*, June 23, 1979; Scherker interviews with "D.D.," Dec. 24, 1988 (courtesy Scherker Estate).

60. Scherker interview with Wicker, Aug. 8, 1988; John Wilben to Scherker, July 4, 1989 (sleaze joint—courtesy Scherker Estate); interviews with Thomas Lanigan-Schmidt, May 2, 1992 ("good girls"; Julius') and Martin Boyce, May 19, 1992 (Julius'); Rex Wockner, "It Was a Hot Night in June," *Gay Community News*, May 22–24, 1988 (Julius'). Wockner also claims (without citing sources) that some members of Mattachine "fingered people out to the police." This same view of Stonewall continued to be expounded in the early seventies by the Los Angeles Homosexual Information Center—Don Slater's renamed Tangents

group ("Tangents" was found to be legally reserved by a Nevada company). HIC called the Stonewall uprising "a defensive reaction by a group of jaded, role-playing bar queens who had rejected society . . . emotionally immature, self-ashamed patrons of a gay club . . ." (HIC *Newsletter* no. 21, January 1972, courtesy Scherker Estate).

61. Scherker interview with Wicker, Aug 8, 1988. As a sample of Leitsch's sometime sympathy with the New Left: Leitsch to Mayor Richard Daley, Sept. 5, 1968 (expressing his "horror" at the use of police force during the Chicago Democratic Convention). Leitsch also expressed pleasure at MSNY beginning to draw "a much younger, 'hipper' crowd" (Leitsch to Paul Speier, Feb. 5, 1969), and displeasure at the Annual Reminder's conservative dress code: "We encompass drag queens, leather queens, and many, many groovy men and women whose wardrobe consists of bell-bottoms, vests and miles of gilt chains"; Leitsch had therefore demanded that MSNY's name be dropped from the list of sponsors of the Reminder (Leitsch to Barbara Gittings, June 24, 1969; also Leitsch to James K. Mazurek, Nov. 18, 1967). All four letters are in IGIC Papers, NYPL.

   The tape of Isay's *Remembering Stonewall* has Wicker heatedly arguing against mob tactics that "violated everything we thought of as responsible behavior."

62. Robert Amsel, "Back to Our Future? A Walk on the Wild Side of Stonewall," *The Advocate*, Sept. 15, 1987; Teal, *Gay Militants*, p. 27; Truscott, "Gay Power" (quotation).

63. Truscott, "Gay Power"; Isay show, *Remembering Stonewall* (Pine's comment); phone interview with Nick Browne (at the time a bartender at the nearby Lion's Head), Sept. 12, 1990.

64. Ronnie Di Brienza, "Stonewall Incident," *The East Village Other*, July 1969 (shouts, beatings—though *EVO* erroneously states that July 2 was a Monday, it was a Wednesday); *New York Times*, July 3, 1969 (typically, the *Times* underestimated the crowd at about five hundred people).

65. The quotation ("lawful") is from a packet of material relating to the 1969 Annual Reminder in IGIC Papers, NYPL. It also contains instructions regarding dress that stress the need for a "conservative appearance," and authorizes a three-person committee to "rule off the line those not meeting standards."

66. The quotations from and description of the St. John's meeting are from Tom Burke, "The New Homosexual," *Esquire*, December 1969.

67. Interview with Chuck Shaheen, Nov. 20, 1991. De Martino did make some money by converting the space above the Stonewall into additional apartments. Tommy Lanigan-Schmidt put the Stonewall's closing in heroic terms: "Stonewall died giving birth!" (interview, May 2, 1992). Soon after the closing, Blond Frankie became the doorman at Dr. Feelgood's, the new Mafia-controlled gay bar in the Hotel Earle. But Dr. Feelgood's never caught on (interview with Ryder Fitzgerald, May 5, 1992).

POST-STONEWALL: 1969–70

1. *Time*, Oct 31, 1969; Jim Kepner, *Our Movement Since Stonewall* (IGLA, 1992), p. 2 (Foran).

(Pages 215–219)

2. The quotes in this and the following paragraph are from "Pampered Perverts," Lige Clarke and Jack Nichols's "Homosexual Citizen" column in *Screw*, July 25, 1969; and their article "N.Y. Gays: Will the Spark Dim?" *The Advocate*, Sept. 1969.

3. "Pampered Perverts," *Screw*, July 25, 1969; Madolin Cervantes (MSNY) to David Bird (*N.Y. Times*), July 13, 1969 (IGIC Papers, NYPL); Scherker interview with Wicker, Aug. 8, 1988 (courtesy Scherker Estate). The Queens vigilante incident is described fully in John Gabree, "Homosexuals Harassed in New York," *Guardian*, July 12, 1969. The tree-cutting had come about after ordinary harassment techniques had failed and, as Gabree put it, "had every Freudian in New York chuckling over his morning paper." The Mattachine announcement that it was starting a fund to replace the trees—a cost the Parks Department estimated at $15,000—had led left-leaning gays to mutter about so humble-spirited a response.

4. Toby Marotta, *The Politics of Homosexuality* (Houghton Mifflin, 1981), p. 77.

5. Leitsch to Philip Parris, Sept. 22, 1966 (expressing sympathy for Stokely Carmichael's views but rejecting any association with the Panthers); Leitsch to William Wynne, Feb. 4, 1970 ("none of our damned business"). Both letters are in IGIC Papers, NYPL.

6. Donaldson and Leitsch had recently been at loggerheads. Leitsch accused Donaldson of a gratuitous "personal attack" in the *Clearing House Newsletter* (vol. 1., no. 7); Donaldson accused Leitsch of threatening to walk out of a meeting simply because he (Donaldson) was supposed to say a few words; and the two squabbled angrily over whether the Columbia student homophile group should be allowed to use the name "Mattachine," Donaldson accusing Leitsch of "snobbery" and Leitsch attacking the Columbia group as "apologists" because its members used pseudonyms. (Leitsch to *Clearing House Newsletter*, Sept. 12, Nov. 3, 1967; Donaldson to Herman Slater, March 9, 1968; Leitsch to Gunnison, Oct. 8, 1968; Leitsch to Neil Donovan, Jan 24, 1969—all in IGIC Papers, NYPL).

7. Marotta, *Politics of Homosexuality*, pp. 78–79; Scherker interview with Shelley, June 5, 1989 (tape courtesy Scherker Estate).

8. Two Special Services police reports, dated July 9, 10, 1969 (courtesy Scherker Estate).

9. Marotta, *Politics of Homosexuality*, pp. 78–79.

10. Marotta, *Politics of Homosexuality*, p. 79; Michael Bronski, "Stonewall Stories, Part I," *Gay Community News*, June 11–17, 1989.

11. Interview with Sascha L., Aug. 26, 1991.

12. Interview with Sascha L., Aug. 26, 1991. According to Sascha, the payoffs also stopped—at least for a while—after the Stonewall riots. A number of cops (including, about a year later, Seymour Pine) were transferred.

    The police sweep through the Village gay bars that night was general; at about the same time Tele-Star was raided, Stonewall, too, was hit. Martin Boyce (interview, May 19, 1992) was among the seven or eight people sitting one afternoon, about a week after the riots, at the Stonewall bar (which had not yet closed, but had little business) when the police marched through; it was, as Boyce remembers it, "just a show of muscle; no arrests were made."

    It was a raid more than six months later that would fan the most indignation, and temporarily take on some of the symbolic importance of the Stonewall riots.

(Pages 220–222)

The Snake Pit was an after-hours basement bar on the corner of West Tenth Street, operated, like so many others, without a liquor license. When the police (again led by Seymour Pine) raided it at five one morning, they atypically arrested, along with the employees, all 167 patrons, on charges of "disorderly conduct." Among those patrons was an Argentine national named Diego Vinales, who had never before gone to a gay bar in New York. Brought with the others to the Charles Street police station, Vinales panicked. Terrified that his parents would be notified and that he would be deported, he made a desperate effort to escape by jumping from the second-floor window. He impaled himself on six fourteen-inch iron spikes on the fence directly below, and had to endure agonizing delays while rescue workers, using blowtorches, tried to extricate him. When they finally succeeded, he was rushed into surgery with one piece of the fence still piercing his body. Vinales survived, but barely. Craig was among the many thousands who joined a vigil at the hospital and then marched to the Charles Street police station to protest the Snake Pit raid. The fullest account of the whole affair is in Arthur Bell, *Dancing the Gay Lib Blues: A Year in the Homosexual Liberation Movement* (Simon and Schuster, 1971), pp. 39–49. The *Daily News* put the incident on its front page (March 9, 1970). "Any way you look at it—that boy was PUSHED!!" read a Gay Activists Alliance flyer announcing the protest march (the flyer is included in the Special Services police report of the Vinales incident, dated March 9, 1970, courtesy Scherker Estate).

13. Marotta, *Politics of Homosexuality*, pp. 80–91.
14. Gunnison to Kelley, May 11, 1968, Kelley Papers.
15. Douglas Sanders (the only Canadian delegate), 10 typed pages of Minutes plus Appendices for the August 1968 Chicago NACHO Conference, Kelley Papers. The Homosexual Bill of Rights had been proposed by SIR; in essence, it called for an end to all forms of harassment and discrimination. Beardemphl of SIR had suggested the name "American Conference of Homosexual Organizations" (IGIC Papers, Box 5, NYPL).
16. Fourteen of the twenty-three accredited organizations sent a total of twenty-three delegates to Chicago; and some eighty-five additional people participated as accredited "observers." Of the six organizations turned down by Foster's Credentials Committee on assorted grounds of late fees or recent formation, all six were admitted to the conference by vote of the delegates—a direct slap at Foster, who defended his criteria as "tough—yes, even rigid," but applied with "absolute fairness" (Gunnison to Cromey, May 17, 1968; also Gunnison to Southern California Council on Religion and the Homosexual, June 7, 1968, Gunnison Papers). Shirley Willer on DOB is in Eric Marcus, *Making History* (HarperCollins, 1992), p. 129. On the issue of Mattachine New York's participation, Foster wrote Bill Kelley, soon after the close of the conference, that he was "working with MSNY to bring them into the NACHO, with some success thus far. HOWEVER— my belief is that no organization is God Almighty, and we should not go down on bended knee. . . . And that goes for SIR or any of the others. We are all in this together, and no one organization is going to be the 'hero of the movement' . . ." (Gunnison to Kelley, Nov. 12, 1968, Kelley Papers). In an exchange of letters during 1967–1968, Leitsch vented his anger at the lack of appreciation for MSNY's accomplishments under his leadership, and Foster diplomatically en-

(Page 223)

couraged him not to be "concerned about what anyone else in the movement
thinks"—even as he warned Leitsch that "there is a tendency to resent MSNY's
being kept out of the general movement," and urged him to join NACHO
(Gunnison to Leitsch, Jan. 22, 1967, and Jan. 26, Feb. 9, Oct. 7, 1968; Leitsch
to Gunnison, Jan. 23, Feb. 6, 14, Oct. 8, 1968—all in IGIC Papers, NYPL).
Privately, Leitsch was writing that "Foster Gunnison himself is responsible for
much of the hostility to . . . [the Credentials] Committee . . . his rules, by-laws,
whatever they were called, [were] much too authoritarian and exclusionary," and
urging that he be replaced with Leitsch's recent ally Jack Campbell, of Cleveland
Mattachine (Leitsch to William Wynne, June 5, 1970, IGIC Papers, NYPL).
Wynne had been encouraging Leitsch to take over NACHO, writing that he was
tired of NACHO being in the grip for so long of those "who do not really
represent anyone except themselves" (Wynne to Leitsch, n.d. [1970], IGIC Papers, NYPL).

17. Eight Credentials Committee "Bulletins," March 12, 1969–June 24, 1969, Gunnison Papers; "Marc Jeffers," "Chairman's Interim Report," March 1969; "Jeffers"
to Robert Cromey, June 14, 1969 (travel); "Jeffers," "To All NACHO Organizations," n.d., Houston. (The Promethean Society soon reorganized as the Texas
Homophile Educational Movement: THEM—all in the Kelley Papers.)

18. "Report of the Committee on Credentials," July 24, 1969, and "Post-Conference
Report of the Committee on Credentials," Dec. 10, 1969, Gunnison Papers.
"Austin Wade" (Arthur Warner) and Madolin Cervantes, "Report to the Board
of MSNY Delegates to ERCHO," n.d., Gunnison Papers. Dick Leitsch had
been prepared, this time around, to attend the NACHO conference, but MSNY
had refused to vote expense money for him and other potential delegates on the
grounds that "the Gay Power movement is on and we're shoveling out dollars
like kindling for mimeograph paper." Leitsch had been of two minds about going
anyway, and professed not to be disappointed (Leitsch to "Frank," Aug. 19,
1969, IGIC Papers, NYPL).

    The Council on Equality for Homosexuals was an organization Gunnison
put together with a few members of the West Side Discussion Group; it included David Goldberger, "Sandy Penn," and Barbara Silverglate. ("A little
discussion group we had going in New York for a couple of years" was Gunnison's
own description during our interviews.) Part of CEH's history is in Credentials
Committee "Bulletin #5," May 31, 1969 (Gunnison Papers). Arthur Warner and
Madolin Cervantes were among those who attacked CEH as having "no plausible
reason for its existence"—other than to garner voting privileges at the NACHO
and ERCHO conventions and thereby help to perpetuate the control of the
"Kamenyites" (Warner and Cervantes, "Report to the Board of MSNY Delegates
to ERCHO." Gunnison Papers).

19. Donaldson to "Young Turks," March 20, 1968; Gunnison to Jeffers, Nov. 13,
1969, to Donaldson, Nov. 22, 1969, and to Kameny, Nov. 22, 1969—all in
Kelley Papers.

20. "A Radical Manifesto," dated August 28, 1969 (Kelley Papers), is signed by
Scoop Phillips, chair of the 1969 NACHO Arrangements Committee and a
Kansas City activist, as well as by Stephen Donaldson. One accompanying doc-
ument suggests that the age limit for membership on the Youth Committee be

(Pages 225–226)

set at twenty-five, and another set forth a "Bill of Rights" for homosexual studentson college campuses—both in Kelley Papers.

21. Gunnison to Kelley, Sept. 15, 1969; Gunnison to Jeffers, Nov. 13, 1969; Gunnison to Gittings, Nov. 15, 1969; Gunnison to Kameny, Nov. 22, 1969; Gunnison to William Wynne, Dec. 27, 1969—all in Kelley Papers.

22. Gunnison, "Subject: Gay Liberation Front," Nov. 12, 1969, Kelley Papers.

23. Gunnison to Robert Kohler, Dec. 21, 1969 ("rudeness," etc.); Gunnison to Jeffers, Nov. 13, 1969 (most dangerous), Kelley Papers.

24. Gunnison, "Proposed Set of Constitutional Aims and Purposes for NACHO," July 24, 1969, Gunnison Papers.

25. Gunnison, "Proposed Set of Constitutional Aims and Purposes for NACHO," July 24, 1969; Gunnison to Teal, n.d. (tactics)—both in Gunnison Papers. Foster once rebuked Kameny for being "a bit conservative" about confrontational tactics (Gunnison to Kameny, June 4, 1970, Kelley Papers).

26. ERCHO was not an independently formed regional association, as had been the case with its regional predecessor ECHO, which it replaced; rather, it was an offshoot of NACHO.

27. Rodwell insists to this day that nothing in Mary Baker Eddy's writings can be construed as homophobic. Indeed, he insists that Eddy discounted "male" and "female" as discrete categories, arguing that all human beings contain aspects of both. He further points out that in some of her writings Eddy attacks the institution of marriage. But Rodwell is well aware that the Christian Science *church* is today "one of the most homophobic institutions in the world." There is a long-standing split and constant tug of war between the comparatively liberal publishing society, which puts out the *Christian Science Monitor*, and the conservative board of directors, which runs the church.

Beginning in the late seventies, Rodwell helped to organize an action designed to awaken the church to the plight of its gay and lesbian members. He and others distributed a pamphlet they had written, "Gay People in Christian Science?" asking the board of directors to "re-examine their thought on the subject of human sexuality . . . and to take whatever loving and practical steps are necessary to rectify the present wrongs being done to Gay people in the name of Christian Science." Rodwell and his friends mailed out fifteen thousand copies of the pamphlet and then decided to attend the annual meeting of the church in Boston in June, 1980. Christine Madsen, then a reporter for the *Monitor* but later fired for being a lesbian, helped the group with logistical details. Dressed conservatively in suits and dresses, they stacked their pamphlets on card tables near the Mother Church Center—and put a decorative pot of geraniums on each table. But a unit from the Boston Police Department soon appeared, accompanied by the head of security for the Mother Church, and told them that if they failed to take the tables down at once, they would be arrested "for improper activity on public property." The group caucused for a vote; Rodwell voted to go to jail, but a large majority voted against him. They took down the tables and then distributed the pamphlets by hand. The next day, some of their group stood up during the church service to offer silent protest against their treatment; later, outside, they displayed signs to the same effect. But from that day to this (1993), the

(Pages 228–230)

board of directors has refused to reconsider its negative attitude toward gays and lesbians.

Rodwell no longer participates in Christian Science services, but does retain "great respect" for Mary Baker Eddy. To an outsider, this allegiance is somewhat perplexing. Toby Marotta, in *The Politics of Homosexuality*, p. 66n., suggests that in its emphasis on "the dignity of all things human and the importance of making things true by believing them so," Christian Science doctrine "inspired Rodwell to work at encouraging homosexuals to think of themselves positively." Perhaps so, but what still needs explaining is why the neo-Platonic insistence in Mary Baker Eddy's writings on the "unreality" of the material world, and the importance of transcending it, did not cause Rodwell (as it did so many other Christian Scientists) to steer clear of any political engagement with that evanescent world. Nor does it explain why Eddy's denigration of the body failed to restrain Rodwell from insisting on his right to bodily pleasure—unorthodox pleasure, no less.

28. Wade and Cervantes, "Report to the Board," Kelley Papers.
29. Austin Wade (Arthur Warner) and Madolin Cervantes, "Report to the Board of MSNY Delegates to ERCHO," n.d. (Nov. 1969); Gunnison to Robert Angell, Nov. 10, 1969 (dissociation); Gunnison to Gittings, Nov. 15, 1969—all in Kelley Papers. The resolutions passed by the conference are summarized and paraphrased in Gunnison to Robert Angell, Nov. 15, 1969; along with the two cited, they included a demand for control over one's own body as an "inalienable right" and a call to defend the "freedom from political & social persecution" of "all minority peoples."
30. Gunnison to Gittings, Jan. 12, 1970 (Lois Hart), Gunnison to Kelley, Nov. 5, 1969, both in Kelley Papers. Arthur Warner insisted that Fouratt had "physically assaulted" Cervantes ("Report to the Board of MSNY Delegates to ERCHO," co-authored with Cervantes, n.d. [Nov. 1969]); but in his interviews with me Fouratt has categorically denied that.
31. Kelley questionnaire response, Nov. 7, 1969, Gunnison to Kelley, Nov. 15, 1969—both in Kelley Papers.
32. Gunnison to Kelley, Jan. 21, 1970, Kelley Papers; Gunnison to Donn Teal, n.d., Gunnison Papers ("thrilled").
33. Gunnison, "Subject: Gay Liberation Front," Nov. 12, 1969, Kelley Papers. By the following summer, after attending many more GLF meetings in New York (and going to a few of their dances), he found even more "exceptions" and had his "fingers crossed" that GLF would "manage to straighten itself out and head off in constructive directions" (Gunnison to William Wynne, July 25, 1970, Kelley Papers).
34. Gunnison, "Subject: Gay Liberation Front," Nov. 12, 1969, Kelley Papers.
35. The quotes in this and the next paragraph are from Gunnison to Kohler, Dec. 21, 1969, Kelley Papers. To Barbara Gittings, too, Foster wrote (Nov. 15, 1969, Kelley Papers), "I do sympathize with them [other social causes] and I am always ready to put the first nickel in the pot for them." But as regards Kohler himself, Foster characterized him to Gittings as "a mealy-mouthed, sad-eyed, con man from way back." Still later, after attending more GLF meetings, Foster once went so far as to say that "there is every possibility that GLF will evolve as a reasonable organization . . . " (Gunnison to Kameny, June 4, 1970, Kelley Papers).

(Pages 231–236)

36. Kepner to Duberman, April 29, 1992 ("bad cases"); "Austin Wade" (Arthur Warner) and Madolin Cervantes, "Report to the Board of the MSNY Delegates to ERCHO," and Gunnison to Warner, Nov. 22, 1969—both in Kelley Papers. Foster wrote Kameny that those who opposed him were "nitwits" (Gunnison to Kameny, Nov. 22, 1969, Kelley Papers), and further evidence of Foster's devotion to Kameny is in Gunnison, "General Bulletin" (on Kameny's election to the Executive Board of the D.C. affiliate of the ACLU), Dec. 10, 1969, Kelley Papers. Yet Foster did acknowledge to Warner that Kameny was at times willful and intractable (Gunnison to Warner, June 5, 1970, Kelley Papers).

37. Phillips to Gunnison, Jan. 27, 1970; Gunnison to Bobbi Simpson/Sandy Penn, Nov. 21, Dec. 20, 1969; Gunnison to William Kelley, Jan. 21, 1970—all in Kelley Papers.

38. Bell, *Dancing the Gay Lib Blues*, pp. 20–24; Dennis Altman, *Homosexual: Oppression and Liberation* (Dutton, 1971), pp. 110–116.

39. Gunnison to Kelley, April 9, 1971, Gunnison to Wynne, July 25, 1970—all in Kelley Papers.

40. Marotta, *Politics of Homosexuality*, chapter 6, pp. 134–61.

41. Arnie Kantrowitz, *Under the Rainbow: Growing Up Gay* (Morrow, 1977), pp. 147, 179–80; Kantrowitz to Duberman, May 11, 1992.

42. An interview with "Ernestine Eppinger," conducted by Barbara Gittings and Kay Tobin is in *The Ladder*, June 1966, pp. 4–11. Jim Kepner sums up the role of blacks in the homophile movement this way: "There were usually one or two Blacks, two or three Latins and a very occasional Chinese, around ONE, DOB, Mattachine, and later groups such as Pride and SIR, but, except for Tony Reyes, who, as Don Slater's lover, then and now, was an incorporator of ONE, & long a silent vote on the Board of Trustees, they took no leadership positions." (Kepner, "Blacks & Women in the Early Gay Movement," 24-page typescript, courtesy Kepner.)

43. Joel Hall, "Growing Up Black and Gay," in Len Richmond and Gary Noguera, *The Gay Liberation Book* (Ramparts Press, 1973), pp. 51–56; the manifesto "Third World Gay Revolution (New York City)," is reprinted in Karla Jay & Allen Young, eds., *Out of the Closets: Voices of Gay Liberation* (NYU Press, 2nd ed., 1992), pp. 363–67; Alice Echols, *Daring to Be Bad: Radical Feminism in America, 1967–1975* (University of Minnesota Press, 1989), especially chapter 5. See also the discussion of blacks and gays in Altman, *Homosexual*, pp. 179–94, and Teal, *Gay Militants*, pp. 169–78; and for blacks and feminism, see bell hooks, *Ain't I a Woman: Black Women and Feminism* (South End Press, 1981).

44. Scarpi would also become active, in 1973, in planning the fourth Christopher Street Liberation Day—and would get into a tangle with Foster Gunnison, who was then in the process of disengaging from CSLDC (Scarpi to Gunnison, Jan. 15, April 30, 1973; Gunnison to Scarpi, Jan. 26, 1973; John Paul Hudson to Gunnison, April 12, 1973—all in Gunnison Papers).

45. Arthur Bell Papers, Box 94, IGIC Papers, NYPL.

46. I have written about the 1973 confrontation in *Cures* (Plume, 1992), pp. 278–79 (where—before Sylvia corrected me—I spelled her name "Silvia"). The confrontation was also captured on film; Vito Russo (who was emcee at the 1973

(Pages 237–248)

rally) screened it for me shortly before his death. In our interviews, nearly twenty years later, Sylvia was still full of bitterness at Jean O'Leary and at all the other "ingrates" in the movement who despised queens and refused to acknowledge their contribution during and after the Stonewall riots. O'Leary's recantation is in Eric Marcus, *Making History* (HarperCollins, 1992), p. 257.

47. Interview with Kohler, Aug. 20, 1990.

48. See Allen Young, "GLF Memories," *Gay Community News*, June 23, 1979, for the inspirational role Fouratt played in his own coming out. Young, who in late 1969 was a closeted member of the Liberation News Service, also came to live in the Seventeenth Street commune.

49. Leggett is the anonymous author of the moving "Father Knows Best," in Richmond and Noguera, *The Gay Liberation Book*, pp. 165–68. Leggett died of AIDS.

50. The relevant FBI documents, though heavily censored, are now available (I owe special thanks to Duncan Osborne for alerting me to that fact). But since many of the 4,500 pages of documents that I received have been inked out (on the absurd, continuing grounds of "national security"), research into their contents remains sharply limited. For the paragraph above, the relevant materials are SA to SAC, New York, 100-167120-19 through 100-167120-22 (12/10 & 16/69; 1/9 & 13/70); 100-167120-39 (5/22/70: "highly placed"); SA to SAC, Chicago, 100-49116-6 and 100-49116-7 (April 19, July 7, 1970); SAC Albany to Director (Hoover), 100-464380-1 (March 10, 1971 [Transvestites and Red Butterfly]; "gaye" is in April 30, 1970 to Director (100-459225-X). For the FBI and early Mattachine, see Stuart Timmons, *The Trouble with Harry Hay* (Alyson, 1990), pp. 131–32. The information on "Wendy Wonderful" is from an interview with Karla Jay, Aug. 17, 1992.

51. Along with Jim, a man named Lars Larson also came under suspicion in GAA (conversation with Arnie Kantrowitz, Jan. 3, 1992)—though, as in Jim's case, there was never a shred of evidence.

52. *RAT*, v. 3, no. 3, April 4–18, 1970. For the disappointment and anger expressed by other feminists over the results of the action, see Echols, *Daring to Be Bad*, pp. 195–97; and see footnotes 297 and 298 (p. 341) for "Verna Tomasson" probably being a pseudonym and for Karla grabbing Firestone (as well as testimony to the effect that her doing so may have been unnecessary).

53. Echols, *Daring to Be Bad*, p. 213 (Brown); Lois Hart, "Some News and a Whole Lot of Opinion," *Come Out!* (Times Change Press, 1970), pp. 29–32. For more detail, see Marotta, *Politics of Homosexuality*, chapter 9, "Radicalesbians," pp. 229–55. The debate over the lesbian–gay male relationship is well summarized in Rita Mae Brown, "Take a Lesbian to Lunch," and in Gay Liberation Front Women (New York City), "Lesbians and the Ultimate Liberation of Women." Both essays are reprinted in Jay and Young, *Out of the Closets*, pp. 185–95, 201–203.

54. Radicalesbians (New York City), "Leaving the Gay Men Behind," reprinted in Jay and Young, *Out of the Closets*, pp. 290–95.

55. Interviews with Karla Jay; Jay, "The First Lesbian Dance," *Gay Community News*, June 23, 1979. All the material in the next few paragraphs describing the dance comes from these two sources.

(Pages 248–256)

56. GAA held a demonstration one night in front of Kooky's to protest the bar's abusive treatment of its own lesbian customers, and their chant was "Kooky's gonna crumble" (Kantrowitz to Duberman, May 11, 1992).

57. Bell, *Dancing the Gay Lib Blues*, pp. 145–46. Sylvia's memory of being turned down is corroborated by the minutes of the GAA general meeting on Nov. 12, 1970 (in IGIC Papers, NYPL). On at least one later occasion, however, GAA did allow STAR to borrow its sound system (minutes, Jan. 14, 1971).

58. Bell, *Dancing the Gay Lib Blues*, pp. 157–58.

59. Interview with Bob Kohler, Aug. 20, 1990; "Rapping with a Street Transvestite Revolutionary: An Interview with Marcia [*sic*] Johnson," reprinted in Jay and Young, *Out of the Closets*, pp. 112–119. On July 6, 1992, Marsha P. Johnson was found floating in the Hudson River, her body badly decomposed; foul play has not been ruled out (*New York Newsday*, July 20, 1992; *New York Native*, July 20, 1992).

60. For example, Gunnison to Martin, April 29, 1970, Kelley Papers.

61. Crompton, "Report of the Religious Committee," December 1969; Kameny, "Workshop on the Federal Government"; Gunnison to Warner, Feb. 20, May 7, 1970; Warner to Kelley, Nov. 2, 1970—all in Kelley Papers.

62. Gunnison to Peters, Jan. 5, 1970 (newsletter); Gunnison to All Homophile Organizations, Feb. 15, 1970 (clearinghouse); Gunnison to members of ERCHO Executive Committee, Feb. 9, 1970 (a sample of his lengthy agenda suggestions); Gunnison to Wynne, Jan. 20, 1970 (losing battle)—all in Kelley Papers.

63. Gunnison letter to *Playboy* (in response to a piece by Stephen Donaldson in the May issue), Aug. 1970, p. 46. A letter responding to Gunnison denounced him for his "intoleration and prudishness" (Ralph Hall, *Playboy*, Dec. 1970).

64. Gunnison to Scoop Phillips, Feb. 11, 1970; Gunnison to Martin, April 29, 1970; Gunnison to Russell Nile, Feb. 21, 1970—all in Kelley Papers. ERCHO did manage to sponsor a meeting in Philadelphia in Nov. 1969, and its executive committee did meet several times in 1970, but by late 1971 Gunnison was himself describing the organization as "moribund" (Gunnison to Canon Clinton R. Jones, Nov. 5, 1971, Gunnison Papers). In his final financial report, Gunnison listed a closing surplus of $88.96 (1971 ERCHO financial report, dated Dec. 31, 1971, Gunnison Papers).

65. Gunnison to Jerome Stevens, March 30, 1970 (lack of will); Gunnison to Kameny, June 4, 1970; Gunnison to Leitsch, Feb. 21, 1970 (Warner); Gunnison to Warner, June 5, 1970—all in Kelley Papers.

   At the August 1970 NACHO convention, the Warner/Kameny feud continued unabated. Kameny sent a statement entitled "Austin's Aberration," dated August 28, 1970 (Gunnison Papers), to all the delegates; in it he characterized Warner as having "a well-developed delusional system which is quite impervious to facts," and charged him with contriving "vast, but totally non-existent conspiracies."

   Warner's primary loyalty was to Dick Leitsch, and his dislike of Kameny may have been in part a reflection of Leitsch's dislike. And Leitsch's anger at Kameny had, if anything, increased over the years. Six months before the 1970 NACHO convention, Leitsch wrote its chair, Bill Wynne, that Kameny "and his massive ego are a menace to the movement (and the prime cause the movement

(Page 257)

is in such disarray). . . . [Kameny's] roles in NACHO and ERCHO are well-known as divisive. His power plays have shocked and amused all of us. His egocentricity has aroused the sympathy of those of us who are soft-hearted, and the anger of those who are not . . ." (Leitsch to Wynne, Feb. 11, 1970, IGIC Papers, NYPL).

Within the year, Gunnison would draw closer to Warner and somewhat away from Kameny. He still "love[d] Kameny and the old crew . . . as much as ever, believe in them just as much as ever, but am no longer so intimately involved with them. On the other hand I've been able to get much closer to Arthur—he still pisses me off with his tirades—but . . . has begun to take a slightly dim view of MSNY [Mattachine Society New York]. . . . He CAN be objec-tive . . ." (Gunnison to Kelley, April 9, 1971; also Gunnison to Warner, Oct. 13, 1970, Kelley Papers).

66. A useful starting point in salvaging NACHO, Foster thought, might be a change of name. "North American Conference of Homophile Organizations" seemed a little grand, and somehow stodgy; maybe GPU—"Gay Power United"—would sound the right "punchy," contemporary ring. But no sooner had he thought of a new name than he doubted that a change would be a good idea: There was already too much "instability and lack of continuity" in the movement (Gunnison to Jerome Stevens, March 30, 1970 [sponge]; Garrison to Compton, April 10, 1970; Gunnison to Wynne, July 25, 1970 [GPU]—all in Kelley Papers).

67. The quotations in this and the following two paragraphs are from Gunnison to Stevens, March 30, 1970; Gunnison to Wynne, July 25, 1970; Gunnison to Crompton, April 10, 1970; Gunnison, "Bulletins" for March 19, April 10, 1970—all in Kelley Papers. The new gay liberation groups should, in Foster's view, attend the NACHO conference as observers for one or two conferences before being made voting members. And "revolutionary elements" should be kept, if possible, from attending at all; but if admitted, should be contained through a procedural rule that forbade the presentation of any resolution "not directly connected with the homophile cause."

On the central question of whether NACHO should aim at becoming a bridge organization that would link the homophile movement with gay liberation, Foster felt ambivalent. After all, he wrote one of the young militants, NACHO and GLF are "two different groups employing two different philosophies and two different methodologies," and it might be impossible, and even unwise, to try and tether them to a single organization. Yet Foster also believed that the two groups had "the same end in view"—namely, the homophile cause—and he kept open the outside hope that they could combine forces. He made no effort to conceal his own ideological commitment: "I am a gung-ho rightwinger and damn well proud of it, but I struggle against heavy odds to keep an open mind." Sample letters that sum up Gunnison's views are Gunnison to Bob Martin, April 27, 1970; Gunnison to Jim Chesebrough, Aug. 14, 1970 (two philosophies); Gunnison to Jerome Stevens, May 4, 1970; Gunnison to Wynne, July 25, 1970—all in Kelley Papers.

In a letter to Louis Crompton, Gunnison described the GLF–homophile conflict as "the age-old Apollonian vs. Dionysian tug of war," but even in that broad context he continued to indict "the arrogant attitude of some of the older

groups each of whom thinks it owns the movement lock, stock and barrell [*sic*], and are [*sic*] contemptuous and resentful of the newer groups coming along." But beyond the sin of "arrogance," Gunnison also indicted himself and other homophile leaders for having mistakenly devoted so much time at annual conferences to business matters. He felt they had failed to heed "a prime rule of organization management that you keep all business off the floor except where absolutely necessary, and you devote your conferences to programs and activities that will be of interest to all attending" (Gunnison to Compton, April 10, 1970, Kelley Papers).

68. Gunnison to Martin, April 27, 1970; Gunnison to Wynne, May 4, 1970, Kelley Papers. Frank Kameny, among others, would scold Foster for the inappropriate way he substituted "frivolity" for "sobriety." But Foster was "addicted in my belief that life is not one big funeral procession," and went right on signing the occasional letter, "Swish-cerely, 'Kid Basket' Gunnison" (Gunnison to Warner, Nov. 22, 1969, Kelley Papers).

69. As quoted in Marotta, *Politics of Homosexuality*, p. 128.

70. Eldridge Cleaver, *Soul on Ice* (McGraw-Hill, 1968), p. 110.

71. Teal, *Gay Militants*, pp. 167–68; John Murphy, *Homosexual Liberation: A Personal View* (Praeger, 1971), p. 80.

72. Huey Newton, "A Letter from Huey to the Revolutionary Brothers and Sisters About the Women's Liberation and Gay Liberation Movements," *Black Panther*, August 21, 1970. The FBI was also in attendance: Philadelphia to Director, Sept. 5, 1970, 100-65673-12.

73. Echols, *Daring to Be Bad*, pp. 222–23.

74. *Gay Flames*, Sept. 11, 1970; the "Statement" is in Teal, *Gay Militants*, pp. 176–77. During the People's Convention, members of the gay caucus picketed two gay bars for their racist policies (Jim Kepner, *Our Movement Since Stonewall*, L.A. International Gay and Lesbian Archives, 1992, p. 2).

75. Wynne to Leitsch, April 5, 1970 (IGIC Papers, NYPL). Gunnison, "Post-Conference Report of the Committtee on Credentials," Nov. 8, 1970; Gunnison's "Treasure Display"—both in Gunnison Papers.
    Minutes of the 1970 convention, signed by Madeline Davis (Kelley Papers). Foster put particular blame for the success of the radicals on the representatives of the revolutionary Socialist Workers Party, accusing them of having "infiltrated" the convention. SWP, in fact, *was* committed to the strategy of infiltration (see Marotta, *Politics of Homosexuality*, pp. 269n., 317), though Jim Kepner, for one, "saw no evidence of SWP presence at the last NACHO conference" (Kepner to Duberman, April 29, 1992).

76. Minutes of the 1970 Convention, signed by Madeline Davis; Gunnison to William Kelley, April 9, 1971 (Leitsch)—both in Kelley Papers. The top vote-getter in the balloting for Conference Committee members was a newcomer, Metropolitan Community Church founder Troy Perry. Foster thought Perry "may become the next great leader of the movement nationwide," though he had heard "mixed reports about him as a person" (Gunnison to Jerome Stevens, March 30, 1970). Jim Kepner of ONE, Inc. (LA), and Sandy Blixton of Homosexuals Intransigent (NYC) were the two candidates who got fewer votes than Gunnison. Of the nine elected to the committee, Frank Kameny got the smallest number of votes.

(Pages 261–266)

Leitsch to Jack Campbell, March 2, 1970. IGIC Papers, NYPL. According to Jim Kepner (Kepner to Duberman, April 29, 1992), "Legg, Leitsch & a few other real conservatives schemed to take over NACHO. . . . That plan included holding the next meeting in New York—but scuttlebutt was that Leitsch merely meant to bury NACHO."

77. William Wynne, "Chairman's Report," August 1970, Gunnison Papers. In the second part of his report, in which he presented his ideas for restructuring NACHO, Wynne adopted many of the suggestions (reshaping committees, keeping business matters off the convention floor, etc.) that Gunnison had earlier sent him (Gunnison to Wynne, July 25, 1970, Gunnison Papers).

78. Gunnison, "Treasury Notes" (1970); Gunnison, "Community Bulletin #5," May 31, 1969; Gunnison to Frank Morgan, Jan. 21, 1970; Gunnison to Bob Martin, April 29, 1970—all in Kelley Papers.

79. The many announcements, bulletins, and press releases relating to The Directory are in the Gunnison Papers.

80. Gunnison to Bob Martin, April 29, 1970, Kelley Papers.

81. Teal, Gay Militants, pp. 131–32. Koch later denied, in a letter to Dick Leitsch of New York Mattachine, that he had "ever taken the position that homosexuals are creating any special problem in the MacDougal Street area." His concern, he insisted, was with "the increase in violence," which he ascribed to "the increase in the number of young persons flowing into the area .. . who have little or no regard for the community or its residents. . . . What we have is not a homosexual problem but a community problem" (Koch to Leitsch, May 5, 1967, IGIC Papers, NYPL).

82. Bell, Dancing the Gay Lib Blues, p. 62.

83. Bell reprinted the article in his book Dancing the Gay Lib Blues, pp. 60–64. The quotes in this paragraph are from my interviews with Sylvia. Later, Bell and Sylvia together interviewed Chris Thompson, a black male transvestite; the interview is printed in Gay Flames, Nov. 14, 1970.

84. The account of Sylvia's courtroom appearances is drawn in part from my interviews with her, in part from the minutes of GAA general meetings (May 21, 28, June 4, 18, July 2, 9, Sept. 3, 1970) in the Papers of Arthur Bell, Box 93, IGIC Papers, NYPL. By the time of her second appearance in court, Sylvia was represented by Harold Wiener, a lawyer who had volunteered his services. During the drawn-out trial, Sylvia was arrested on a separate charge of "female impersonation," and GAA put up the required fifty-dollar bond (GAA minutes, July 30, 1970).

85. The fullest account of this episode is in Bell, Dancing the Gay Lib Blues, pp. 69–73, from which the quotes in this and the next paragraph are taken.

86. Arnie Kantrowitz, an officer in GAA, was also present at the May 13 confrontation with Greitzer; in his recall "Sylvia raised a thick envelope of petitions (too thick to roll up) and threatened Greitzer. I don't believe she actually hit her with them" (Kantrowitz to Duberman, May 11, 1992).

87. For sample GLF feminist analyses, see "Gay Revolution and Sex Roles" (Chicago), in Jay and Young, Out of the Closets, pp. 252–59; Marotta, Politics of Homosexuality, chapter 9; and Echols, Daring to Be Bad, chapters 4 and 5.

(Pages 267–272)

88. Most of the organizing for the "Lavender Menace" action took place in the apartment of Sydney Abbott and Barbara Love, and among the women prominent in it were Micela Griffo (who pulled the fuse box), March Hoffman, Rita Mae Brown, and Ellen Bedoz [Shumsky]. According to Karla, they couldn't figure out what to call themselves, and at first settled on "Lavender Herring" (in response to the dismissive term Susan Brownmiller had used). But the woman responsible for producing the T-shirts misspelled "herring," and to avoid another error they switched to "Lavender Menace." An account of the congress action is also in Echols, *Daring to Be Bad*, pp. 214–16.

89. Yvonne A. Flowers, "Black Goddesses," in The Jamima Collective, *Jamima from the Heart* (1977).

90. Gunnison to Kameny, June 4, 1970, Kelley Papers.

91. Gunnison to Duberman, Jan. 15, 1992. The "guru" quote is from my interviews with Gunnison.

92. Gunnison, "Christopher Street Liberation Day Umbrella Committee . . . Bulletin No. Two—4/10/70," Gunnison Papers.

93. Gunnison, "Two Appeals for Donations—April 10, 1970"; press release, April 28, 1970—both in Gunnison Papers. Gunnison to Kameny, June 4, 1970 (Leitsch), Kelley Papers. Gunnison accused Leitsch of "panicking" as "MSNY's influence in the New York area is ebbing away," and of "a desperate effort to maintain his dominance" by trying to forge an alliance with GLF, by "making Madolin Cervantes a scapegoat for MSNY's past conservatism and pointing to her (and I assume probably Austen [Arthur Warner] as well) as the reason for MSNY's stodginess." Foster offered, in confirmation, that "at the last Christopher St. meeting . . . Bob Kohler astounded all of us by standing up for Leitsch and challenging some negative reports about MSNY's role in bucking the Christopher St. event." Also: Harry L. Phillips, "Meeting of Homophile Leaders in New York" (1970), Gunnison Papers. When "Michael Kotis" became president of MSNY in April, 1970, he was able to persuade the organization's board to participate in the CSLDC and on June 10, 1970 mailed Foster a ten-dollar check—which, ironically, was lost in the mail (Kotis to Gunnison, July 22, 1970, IGIC Papers, NYPL).

94. For the second march in June 1971, another fund-raising strategy proved far more successful. CSDLC (in which both Craig and Foster remained active) arranged with New York University authorities in the immediate aftermath of the first march to put on a series of four gay dances in Weinstein Hall. The first dances drew crowds of up to a thousand; their success was due to an imaginative combination of live bands, twenty-five-cent beer (which Craig and Michael Brown picked up from a wholesaler on Fourteenth Street), side exhibits of photographs and crafts, and "talking areas" for relaxation.

But then, in the summer of 1970, NYU authorities banned any further gay dances in Weinstein Hall. That led to a four-day sit-in in the Weinstein basement in which both Sylvia Rivera and Jim Fouratt took part. Sylvia was by then living on the streets again, having quit her warehouse job; when told of the sit-in, she parked her suitcase and boxes at Craig's bookstore and joined the fifty or so demonstrators. While many of them, including Jim Fouratt, came and went during the four days, Sylvia (and some two dozen others) stayed in the Weinstein

(Pages 274–275)

basement nearly the entire time. Sylvia did her laundry, held consciousness-raising sessions with NYU students, denounced GAA for staying clear of the action, and loudly protested against any suggestion of compromise.

The only time Sylvia left the building was to go to a GAA meeting to ask for support—at least from individuals if not from the organization. That led to a few GAA members showing up at Weinstein. In response to the subsequent series of protests against NYU, the GAA Executive Committee concluded that "since GAA is politically oriented and the demonstrations were called by 'street people,' who are only a small segment of the gay community, it was suggested that members participate as individuals without the organization's commitment in future related actions" (Arthur Bell Papers, and Box 15 of the GAA Papers, both in IGIC, NYPL).

After the NYU administration called in the police, who cleared out Weinstein, injuring several people, an enraged Sylvia at first obstinately refused to leave and had to be carried out; she then led a protest in the streets surrounding the building. Bob Kohler (interview, Aug. 20, 1990) says that Sylvia "was nuts on drugs and almost got us killed," by which he meant, he went on to explain, that when the cops leveled their guns at the demonstrators and gave them ten seconds to leave the building, Sylvia tried to lead them in a cheer, screaming, "Give me a G. . . . Give me an A. . . . Give me a Y. . . . Whadda we have? . . . GAY!" Jim Fouratt, on the other hand, credits Sylvia with being a restraining force when (according to Jim) "a transsexual from Los Angeles" joined the sit-in and brought some firebombs with her. Determined to out-radical everyone else, she then proceeded to plant the firebombs in the building. Jim tried to tell her that burning down the building was not a solution and that the essence of gay consciousness was a determination "not to hurt anyone." He pointed to Sylvia as an example of someone who was loud and angry, and was always willing to "push the boundaries," but did not talk irresponsibly of picking up a gun in order to prove her commitment to the revolution. But that didn't persuade the transsexual either, and finally, according to Jim, he had to follow her and remove every one of the firebombs from the baskets in which she had placed them.

The police action led to a series of protests against NYU and its homophobic policies, with undercover agents present at least once (SSD to Chief Inspector, Oct. 6, 1970, S.S.D. #665-M). The fullest accounts of the Weinstein incident are in *Gay Flames*, no. 5; John Murray, *Homosexual Liberation* (Praeger, 1971), pp. 119–23; Bell, *Dancing the Gay Lib Blues*, pp. 110–119 (which is especially full on Sylvia's role); Teal, *Gay Militants*, pp. 202–209; and the Arthur Bell Papers in IGIC Papers, NYPL, which contain several drafts of his stories on the events at Weinstein.
95. The poster is on the cover of this book.
96. *RAT*, June 26–July 10, 1970.
97. Murphy, *Homosexual Liberation*, p. 96.
98. The descriptions in this and the following pages about the New York and Los Angeles marches rely on material from my interviews and on Teal, *Gay Militants*, p. 322 (Quakers), 324 (beating), 328 (Panther); Jim Kepner, *Our Movement Before Stonewall* (IGLA, 1989) and *Our Movement Since Stonewall* (IGLA, 1992); Kepner to Duberman, April 29, May 26, 1992; Martin Boyce (interview May 19, 1992) for "suffragette"; Kantrowitz, *Under the Rainbow*, pp. 151–56; Murphy, *Homosexual*

(Page 279)

Liberation, pp. 98–99 (cops reading); *Los Angeles Free Press*, July 3, 1970, and *Hollywood Citizens News*, June 29, 1970.

99. Teletype to Director, June 28, 1970, 100-459225-2. Foster himself, probably for publicity purposes, later inflated the figure to five thousand (Gunnison, CSLDC, "National Bulletin 11-08-70," Gunnison Papers. *Windy City Times*, June 23, 1988 (Chicago); *Gay Times*, June 1989 (London); *Mec* magazine, April 1988 (Paris).

INDEX

NEW HANOVER PUBLIC LIBRARY

3 4200 00304 1858

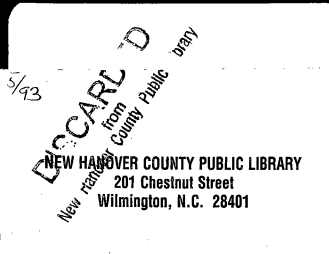
5/93

DISCARD
from
New Hanover County Public Library

NEW HANOVER COUNTY PUBLIC LIBRARY
201 Chestnut Street
Wilmington, N.C. 28401

GAYLORD
S